MW01629783

Systeme Lefaucheaux

CONTINUING THE STUDY OF PINFIRE CARTRIDGE ARMS

1802

the 200th anniversary of Casimir Lefaucheaux' birth

2002

Systeme Lefaucheux

Continuing the Study of Pinfire Cartridge Arms Including Their Role in the American Civil War

Chris C. Curtis

Armslore Press

2002

Library of Congress Catalog Card Number 98-73946

ISBN 1-882824-19-9

A fine collector arms volume from

division of Graphic Publishers
Post Office Box 10787
Santa Ana, California 92711-0787 USA
1-800-4-YOUR BOOK

Washington, D.C., 2002

The Company of Military Historians, through its Reviewing Board, takes pride in sponsoring *Systeme Lefaucheaux* as a most useful reference in American Military History.

Joseph M. Thatcher
President

Reviewing Board

Edwin M. Gewirz
Paul Lederer

Official:

David M. Sullivan
Administrator

This volume is dedicated to the memory of

Gene P. Smith

Author, Collector, Mentor, Friend

"Thanks, Geno, for helping me make a mark within the firearms collecting fraternity."

Also lost to the collecting world in general, and to the
study of pinfire arms in particular, during the preparation
of this volume were good friends F.W. "Bill" Hulbert,
Jim Lowther, and Jan Smith. Their contributions to the
original work were of great value. They too will be missed.

<h1 style="text-align:center">FOREWORD</h1>

BY NORM FLAYDERMAN

How times have changed! And to think that these fascinating arms have been under our very noses, unappreciated and misunderstood, all the time. It is ironic that firearms utilizing the pinfire ignition system, which were made in so many interesting models and variations, were so long and blatantly neglected in the literature of antique firearms. While many popular weapons have been studied and exhaustively debated, often to the point of tedium and redundancy, this equally deserving, fascinating group of antique arms has suffered unduly from the lack of factual data. The major obstacle has been the absence of a comprehensive reference... not merely to identify and categorize various types and models, but to understand their contribution to arms history. *Systeme Lefaucheux*, a definitive study, bridges that gap and represents a milestone in the literature of this hobby.

Commonly termed merely "pinfires" in the jargon of the antique gun world, these firearms have undeniably been the least studied of all various forms of nineteenth century guns. At long last, they have been extricated from a totally unwarranted stigma, one which had detracted from their deserved recognition and elevated stature in the hierarchy of firearms collecting. That inattention was attributable to the collecting generations of the immediate post-World War Two era, when the field of antique arms collecting in America was in its relative infancy, only beginning to experience the wide popular appeal it enjoys today. Pinfire arms were then not one hundred years of age, and the system itself was thought to be almost exclusively of European manufacture and usage, an unjustified anathema to the American collector in those earlier years of collecting. The association of pinfires to American history was completely unreported and unrecognized. Thus the system had the proverbial three strikes against it as far as American arms collectors were then concerned... and the much smaller European collector market generally looked askance because of the late era of manufacture.

But the tables have turned! Once given but passing mention in arms or cartridge literature, pinfires have reached collecting maturity. The passage of time and the attainment of venerable antiquity, along with an influx of later generations of collectors, have seen evolutionary changes in collecting patterns. Much of the credit, however, is due to the pioneering work in 1983 of Chris Curtis and Gene Smith for their groundbreaking treatise *The Pinfire System*. That work, with but a limited printing, introduced the collecting world to this "long seen but little heard" system, a few types so commonplace as to have been taken for granted. In their day, they were highly popular throughout Europe and many South American countries for sporting, military and personal protection weapons. However, the system received but scant attention in America, except for the Civil War years, where it was imported and issued in substantial quantities. That significant fact had been generally overlooked by most arms historians and latter-day collectors.

Systeme Lefaucheux is not merely an enlarged, re-titled, second edition of that 1983 work. Rather, it is a completely re-edited, tremendously expanded study with significant new material and illustrations. The earlier work, certainly a milepost in arms literature, represented the first attention ever paid to this shamefully neglected field of study. In that earlier edition the authors indicated that it was, for all practical purposes, merely a primer for the subject. However, it did generate heightened interest in pinfire arms. Much to

Curtis' credit, he did not yield to complacency with publication of that edition. Rather, it served as an incentive for his continuing extensive study of the weapons. It merely takes a glance at the Table of Contents and a brief leafing through this work to realize the author has credibly demonstrated that pinfire arms were worthy of his intensive, long-enduring study, as well as the deliberate attention and critical recognition by arms historians and the world of collecting.

The broad scope of this treatise is impressive. To those unfamiliar with pinfires, it will undoubtedly be revealing to learn of and see the exceptionally wide, intriguing range of firearms that utilize the novel ignition system; many of those weapons are unique only to this method. The guns range from the most commonplace pocket revolvers, many of which were used through to the beginning of the twentieth century, to large military handguns, officially adopted by various governments, to some truly startling types considered among the most intriguing rarities in the field of "firearms curiosa." The era in which pinfires were made was one prone to experimentation with systems for multi-fire weapons, to which pinfires proved highly adaptive.

The influence of this well researched, comprehensive work in the field of collecting will continue to be felt in these coming years, as it assumes a conspicuous position as the cornerstone for understanding these distinctive firearms. Chris Curtis and this book have made a major contribution to the lore of antique and historic weaponry.

Norm Flayderman
Fort Lauderdale, Florida

- Staff Arms Consultant to Springfield Armory Museum by appointment U.S. Army Corps of Ordnance

- Arms Consultant to the Marine Corps Historical Center, Washington, D.C., by U.S. Marine Corps appointment

- Member, Board of Overseers of U.S.S. *Constitution* Museum, Navy Yard, Boston

- Fellow of the Company of Military Historians

PREFACE

"The pinfire system is such a complex subject that the authors consider this work to be only an introduction."

The above lines are taken from the preface to the original 1983 edition of this work, titled *The Pinfire System*. Little could the authors have suspected then just how prophetic time would prove their words to be.

At that time, *The Pinfire System* was the only major work on pinfire arms and ammunition to have been written in English, and likewise the only *book* on the subject to have been published in any language. As a result of its publication collectors, dealers, and historians from around the world—many previously unknown to the authors—made contact, and the body of knowledge about pinfire arms quickly began to grow. At the same time demand for the book made copies virtually unobtainable, and prices on the secondary market soared to three or four times the original issue price, a demand that holds steady today.

The Pinfire System reached "out-of-print" status quickly. But the decision was made not to do another printing as the authors realized that only a completely new, revised and expanded book would do the subject justice.

Systeme Lefaucheux—Continuing the Study of Pinfire Cartridge Arms is the result of that effort. It combines the original book's research material that has survived the scrutiny of time with new material gathered over the last two decades, into a fresh presentation centered around the use of pinfire arms in the American Civil War. Many photographs from the original edition have again been used, although in some cases the firearms themselves now reside in different collections. Many of these guns are simply too scarce or too important to have been excluded from this volume merely on the basis of that earlier exposure.

The last several decades have proven to be the "Golden Age" of firearms interest, research, and collecting. This author's wish is to make a small contribution to the sum of that knowledge, by elevating the long-neglected pinfire ignition system to its rightful place in the history of firearms development.

So this book, too, is just a beginning. It is my sincere hope that the collectors and researchers of tomorrow will desire—and be allowed the freedom—to carry forward the torch.

Chris C. Curtis
Jefferson City, Tennessee

Acknowledgments

No work of this kind can ever be an individual effort. Thanks and recognition are due the many persons who assisted by contributing their time and knowledge, especially the many collectors who allowed the firearms in their collections to be studied and photographed. A special expression of gratitude is due Richard McMillan for making his photography talents available even at the most inconvenient times. Thanks also are due the many other photographers who contributed their work, both to the original volume and to this book.

The author also is grateful to

* William A. Albaugh III, *Rappahannock, Virginia*

D.J. Baker, *Cambridge, England*

John Peter Beckendorf, *Los Angeles, California*

H.L. Blackmore, *The Armouries, H.M. Tower of London, England*

Tom Bowen, *Romoland, California*

Robert E. Brooker, Jr., *Manchester by the Sea, Massachusetts*

Juan-Luis Calvo Pascual, *Barcelona, Spain*

Charles E. Carder, *Delphos, Ohio*

Ellen Coty Catabia, *Springfield, Massachusetts*

Donald Chaput, *Curator Emeritus of History, Natural History Museum, Los Angeles, California*

Larry T. Compeau, *Grand Blanc, Michigan*

John Delph, *Ponte Vedra Beach, Florida*

William B. Edwards, *Afton, Virginia*

Chris Elmers, *Senior Assistant Keeper, Museum of London, England*

Carol A. Fitting, *Hartford Public Library, Connecticut*

Norm Flayderman, *Fort Lauderdale, Florida*

* H. Gordon Frost, *El Paso, Texas*

Les Gensen, *Curator of Collections, Museum of the Confederacy, Richmond, Virginia*

Bill Gillespie, *Fort Collins, Colorado*

Annie B. Haygood, *Scientific Research, Patent & Trademarks Office, Arlington, Virginia*

Eugene Heer, *Director, Swiss Institute of Arms and Armour, Grandson, Switzerland*

Horst Held, *Midlothian, Texas*

George A. Hoyem, *Tacoma, Washington*

E.W.C. Houser, D.D.S., *Anaheim, California*

* F.W. "Bill" Hulbert, *Grants Pass, Oregon*

Leigh Hunt, *Glendale, California*

Ph. Joris, *Assistant Curator, Museé d'Armes de Liege, Belgium*

David Kenedrew, *North Yorkshire, England*

Don Kramer, *Camino, California*

Gérard Lautissier, *Montreuil, France*

* Herschel C. Logan, *Santa Ana, California*

Don Loughery, *Mission Viejo, California*

Robert W. Lowe, *Gun Collector Activities, National Rifle Association, Washington, DC*

* James Lowther, *Golden, Colorado*

John T. Luckey, *Richardson, Texas*

Pedro Calleja Manzanares, *Ingeniero Director, Fabrica de Armas, Oviedo, Spain*

James H. Marsh, *Newport, Michigan*

Y. Masson, *Directeur, Manufacture Nationale d'Armes de St. Etienne, France*

John Mullen, *Berne, New York*

Michael P. Musick, *Navy and Old Army Branch, Military Archives Division, National Archives, Washington, DC*

Herb Peck, Jr., *Nashville, Tennessee*

Archie Piacentini, *Santa Barbara, California*

Jose Claveria Prenafeta, *Servicio Historico Militar, Madrid, Spain*

Frank Rietta, *Montrose, California*

Ron Ruble, *San Diego, California*

Frank Russell, *Fort Lauderdale, Florida*

* Jacques Salzedo, *Studio City, California*

R. Servaos, *Le Conservateur, Museé d'Armes de St. Etienne, France*

Charles R. Suydam, *Azusa, California*

Catherine Turney, *Pasadena, California*

Ulysses Watson, *Scientific Research, Patent & Trademarks Office, Arlington, Virginia*

* *Deceased*

Last, but certainly not least, my thanks to Lisa Heaney for monitoring my vocabulary, spelling, and grammar, for listening to the roughly-constructed drafts, and for the use of the Heaney family cabin whose solitude provided the means necessary for completing this work.

Chris C. Curtis
Jefferson City, Tennessee
January 2002

CONTENTS

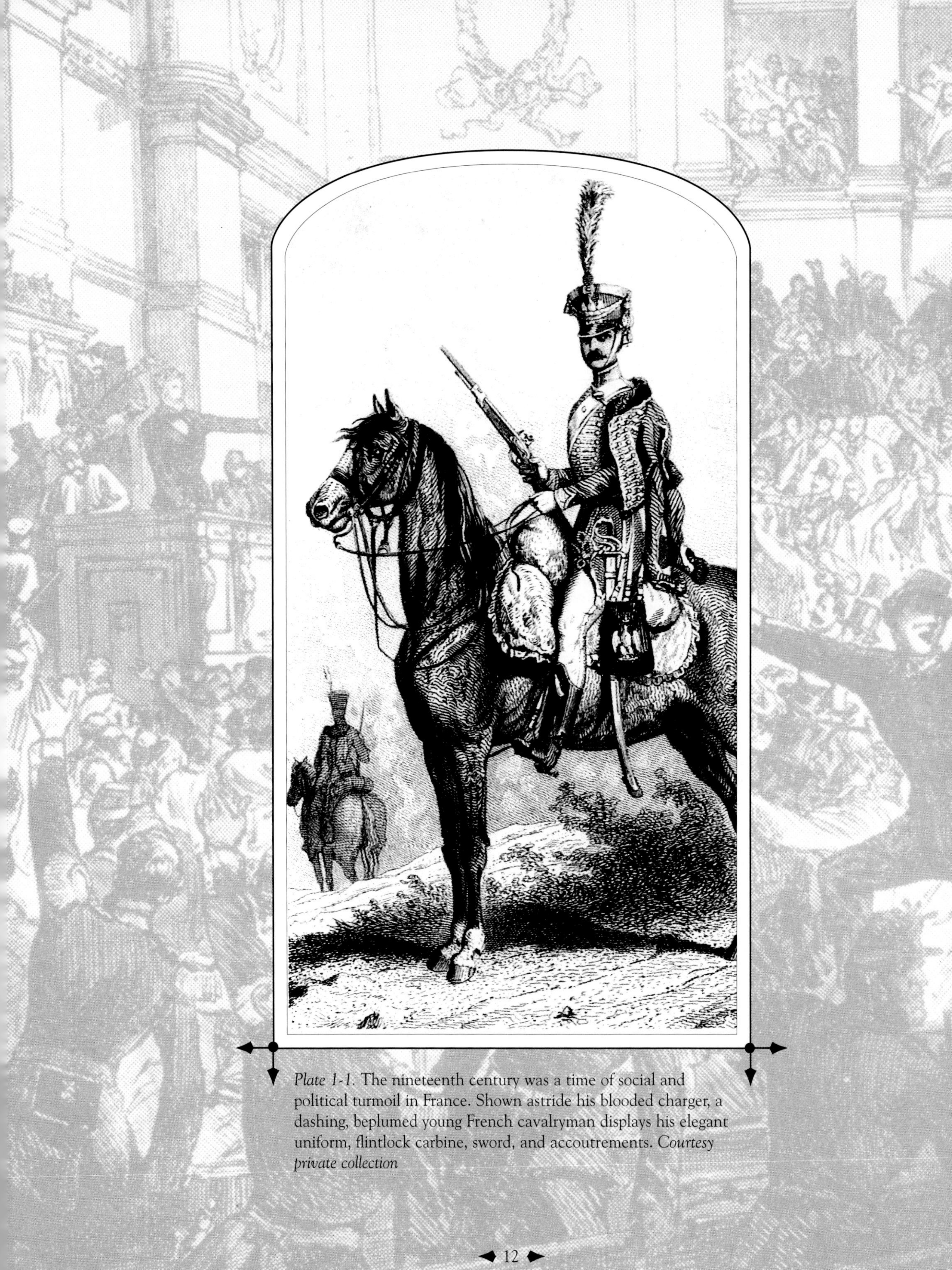

Plate 1-1. The nineteenth century was a time of social and political turmoil in France. Shown astride his blooded charger, a dashing, beplumed young French cavalryman displays his elegant uniform, flintlock carbine, sword, and accoutrements. *Courtesy private collection*

Casimir Lefaucheux:
Father of the Pinfire System

The faded and yellowed birth certificate reads, "Born yesterday at six o'clock in the morning seven Pluviose in the tenth year of the French Republic...."

So begins the official record of the life of Casimir Lefaucheux, originator of the pinfire system of firearms ignition.[1] He arrived in the world early on the morning of Wednesday, January 27, 1802 at the home of his parents, Marie Cornu and Pierre Lefaucheux, a local merchant. Their house was located in the village of Bonnetable, in the Sarthe district of northwestern France. The Lefaucheuxs had been married ten years.

Young Casimir Lefaucheux' early interest in and aptitude for firearms and other things mechanical led to the decision to break with tradition and not apprentice him to his father in the mercantile trade. Rather, records show that Casimir was apprenticed into the gun trade, first in Sarthe and later in Paris. In 1814, at the age of twelve, Casimir began his apprenticeship in the shops of the great Parisian gunmaker, Pauly. There his exposure to the Pauly patent breechloader, the first firearm to use a completely self-contained cartridge, sparked an early interest that was to shape his inventive career over the following four decades.

Pauly's remarkable invention had been awarded French patent number 843, on September 29, 1812. It appeared only seven years after Englishman Alexander Forsyth's invention of fulminate ignition,

and nearly sixty years before a cartridge firearm was patented in America by the Colt's Patent Fire Arms Manufacturing Company of Hartford, Connecticut. The cartridge used in Pauly's rifles and shotguns was constructed of a brass cap having a one-eighth-inch thick cup on one side and a screw protruding from the other side, with a smaller hole bored completely through the cup and screw. The screw was threaded into a previously paste-sealed cardboard tube that contained black powder, and shot or ball. The diameter of the cap was larger than the tube, thus forming a cartridge that was rimmed for better extraction. The cup in the brass cap was packed with a priming compound which, through the smaller hole, ignited the main charge much in the manner of today's centerfire cartridges. Pauly's pistols used a rimmed, all-brass cartridge that was reloadable and utilized the same method of ignition (*see Plate 1-4*).

Pauly, originally a Swiss, was known variously during his career by the given names of Samuel Johannes, Samuel John, and Jean Samuel. In 1832 he began manufacturing his breechloaders at #4 rue des Trois Freres in Paris. Pauly rifles and shotguns had breechblocks which resemble in function those of the later U.S. Model 1873 Springfield

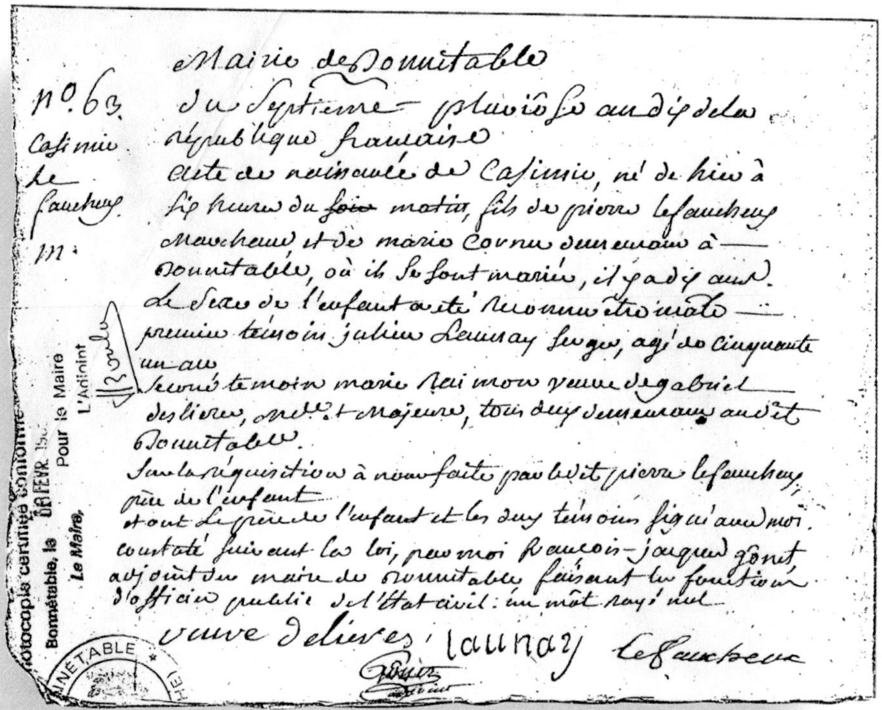

Plate 1-2. Reproduction of the original manuscript birth certificate of Casimir Lefaucheux, firearms inventor *par excellence*, born on January 27, 1802 "in the tenth year of the French Republic…." *Chris C. Curtis collection*

trapdoor rifle; his pistols had barrels that tipped down to expose the chamber. In less than two years, Pauly's guns were receiving accolades from the men of science of that day. In an attempt to expand the market for his guns, around 1814 *Monsieur* Pauly sailed on an extended trip to England, leaving his Parisian business in the hands of Henri Roux. Roux continued manufacturing the Pauly breechloaders in the master's absence.

One drawback to Pauly's cartridge design was the fragility of the exposed fulminate charge, which tended to return to powder form when the cartridge was tapped or jarred. Henri Roux devised a method of enclosing the fulminate in thin paper. It hardly constituted a significant improvement, however, as it afforded little extra protection.

In 1822 ownership of the Pauly business was transferred to Eugene Pichereau, who over the next few years experimented with improvements on Pauly's gun design. Pichereau produced a small quantity of weapons on the Pauly principle, but which utilized the new percussion cap and nipple to set off the main charge of the cartridge. Mounted on the pivoting breech, the cap and nipple made for a less complicated cartridge and constituted a minor change for the better.

In 1827 Casimir Lefaucheux succeeded Pichereau as manager, and then purchased the establishment from him. In addition to the business itself, the purchase included all patent rights and improvements to the Pauly system that had been awarded to Roux and Pichereau, the firm's last two owners. Though Lefaucheux continued to manufacture arms of Pauly's designs, he also spent much time experimenting with his own new ideas. Due to the management changes of the rue des Trois Freres establishment, Pauly guns manufactured thereafter are variously marked "*Pauly et Cie*", or with the names "*Roux*", "*Pichereau*", or "*Lefaucheux.*"

Now the owner of a respected business, on October 30th, 1827 Casimir Lefaucheux married

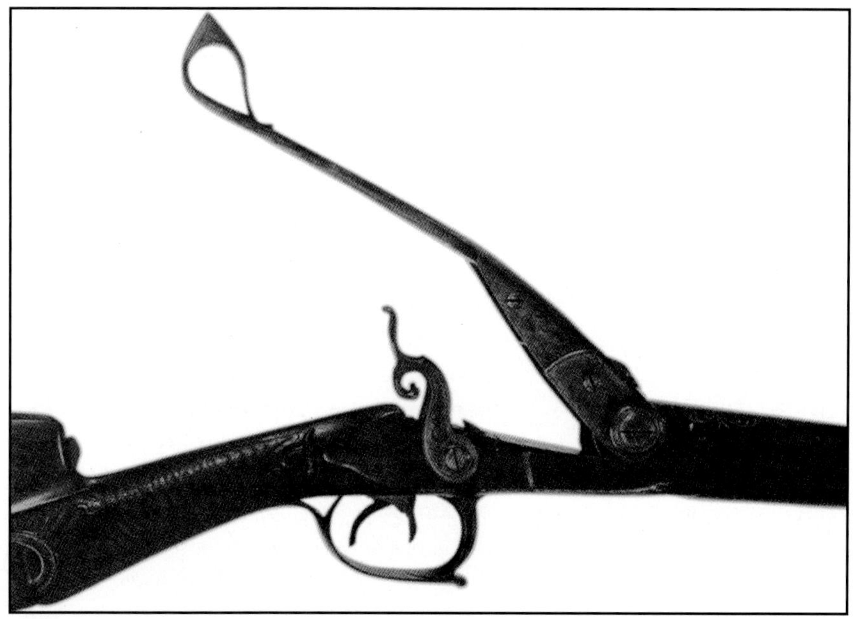

Plate 1-3. A gracefully designed Pauly patented breechloading rifle, shown with the loading breech open to accept its unique, self-contained pasteboard cartridge. *Courtesy private collection*

Françoise Constance Faivre, the daughter of a prominent local family. While it could not necessarily be considered a marriage of convenience, the union further enhanced Lefaucheux' standing in the Parisian business community.

Plate 1-4. Pauly metallic cartridges. At bottom left is the base for a Pauly shot cartridge; above it, a Pauly pistol cartridge. Both are Model 1812. Right: A Pauly Model 1816 cartridge, having a percussion nipple in its base. *Courtesy George Hoyem; George Hoyem photograph*

That same year continued to be an extremely important one in his life when at age twenty-five, during his first year in business, Casimir Lefaucheux was presented with an "honorable mention" award at the Paris Exposition for six high-quality double rifles, three of which were constructed utilizing the Pauly system.

During January of 1828 Lefaucheux submitted the first of his many applications to the French patent office, which was rejected on the basis of unacceptable design and precision. He resubmitted a more detailed version, and was granted patent number 3590 on May 10th of that year. The design was that of a Pauly-inspired breechloading longarm that utilized an external primer consisting of a capsule of fulminate. Two years later, Casimir Lefaucheux presented a rifle and a blunderbuss built on this design to the Commission of Vincennes, for testing and possible adoption by the military. That attempt to interest the military establishment was unsuccessful, and Lefaucheux returned to improving and refining his design.

There is no evidence to indicate that Casimir Lefaucheux was unduly concerned when the Pauly patent (which he owned) expired, or when Clement Pottet was granted French patent number 3930 on March 3, 1829, for a cartridge based on Pauly's principle. (Pottet's cartridge called for a percussion cap placed manually on a nipple in the position of the recess of the Pauly cartridge, and employed Pauly's design of a screw-in cap on a cardboard tube.) No doubt Lefaucheux also was aware of other French patents being granted at that time, such as Robert's patent number 8061 of April 27, 1831 for a type of self-contained cartridge, and LePage and Perrin's patent number 5468 of July 13, 1832 for another cartridge design employing an external percussion cap.

During this period Casimir Lefaucheux continued striving to correct the shortcomings of the Pauly gun, primarily those of the fragile primer and the lack of a gas seal (the latter problem would plague him for years). Then, on January 28, 1833 he was granted French patent number 5525 (*see Plate 1-5, top figures 1 through 5*), which claimed "a new mechanism to properly fasten the barrel to the [shot]gun with a pivot *á la* Pauly"; that is, an attempt to provide a better gas seal through the use of a T-shaped locking device. This new shotgun was designed to use a modified Pauly cartridge, hence the "*á la* Pauly", and was the basic design of the pivoting action that Lefaucheux was to retain throughout his production of shotguns. At the time the patent was issued, Lefaucheux' business location was listed as 5 rue Jean Jacques Rousseau.

Two months after his gas seal patent was awarded, on March 13, 1833, Casimir Lefaucheux was issued the first of five certificates of addition[2] to patent number 5525 (*see Plate 1-5, bottom figures 1 through 7*). This was for a forward-sliding barrel design which still utilized a Pauly-type cartridge. However, the new drawings have the barrels recessed into the standing breech, thus forming a better gas seal and a stronger action. A portion of this patent description reads,

The advantage to be received from guns that can be loaded from the breech made me work to perfect the many ways by which it can be done; up until now they all had for principle to break the action of the gun to

introduce the cartridge.

This new improvement for which I today ask an additional patent has for a goal to avoid this breaking open so as to not change the natural direction of the gun.

It consists in having the butt-end along the length of the line of the barrel, when ready to load, so as to pull it away the necessary length and then put it closer again.

To achieve that goal, at the end of the barrel I managed a strong flange (a), that rests against a similar flange (b), belonging to the butt-end of the gun. Furthermore, the barrel is lengthened by a quantity (a) to penetrate into a corresponding cavity (a'), made inside the butt-end. And so, when the latter is put close to the end of the barrel, nothing inside can be seen of this adjusting as picture 1 shows.

Although this particular design was never put into mass-production by Lefaucheux, it later was adopted and manufactured by Bastin of Paris (patent number 16042 of February 22, 1856), as well as by such notables as Francotte of Liége, Harvey of London, and others. The Bastin design was an improvement over Lefaucheux' in that the gun had a lever which moved the barrels forward and back, and locked them to the breechblock. Lefaucheux' patent drawings show the barrels being moved forward by hand and locking with a T-lever when in the closed position. This difference between the designs made Bastin's gun practical, though not overly successful, and it saw limited production.[3]

Lefaucheux' patent number 5525 shows that a cap and nipple were still being employed to ignite the cartridge. While the text of the patent does not state how ignition was conducted from cap to main powder charge inside the Pauly-type cartridge, it may be speculated that the cartridge had an opening in its side that aligned with the nipple. That being the case, the cartridge would need an aligning appendage protruding from the base of the shell; the simplest way to accomplish that would be to insert a pin in the side of the base and provide a

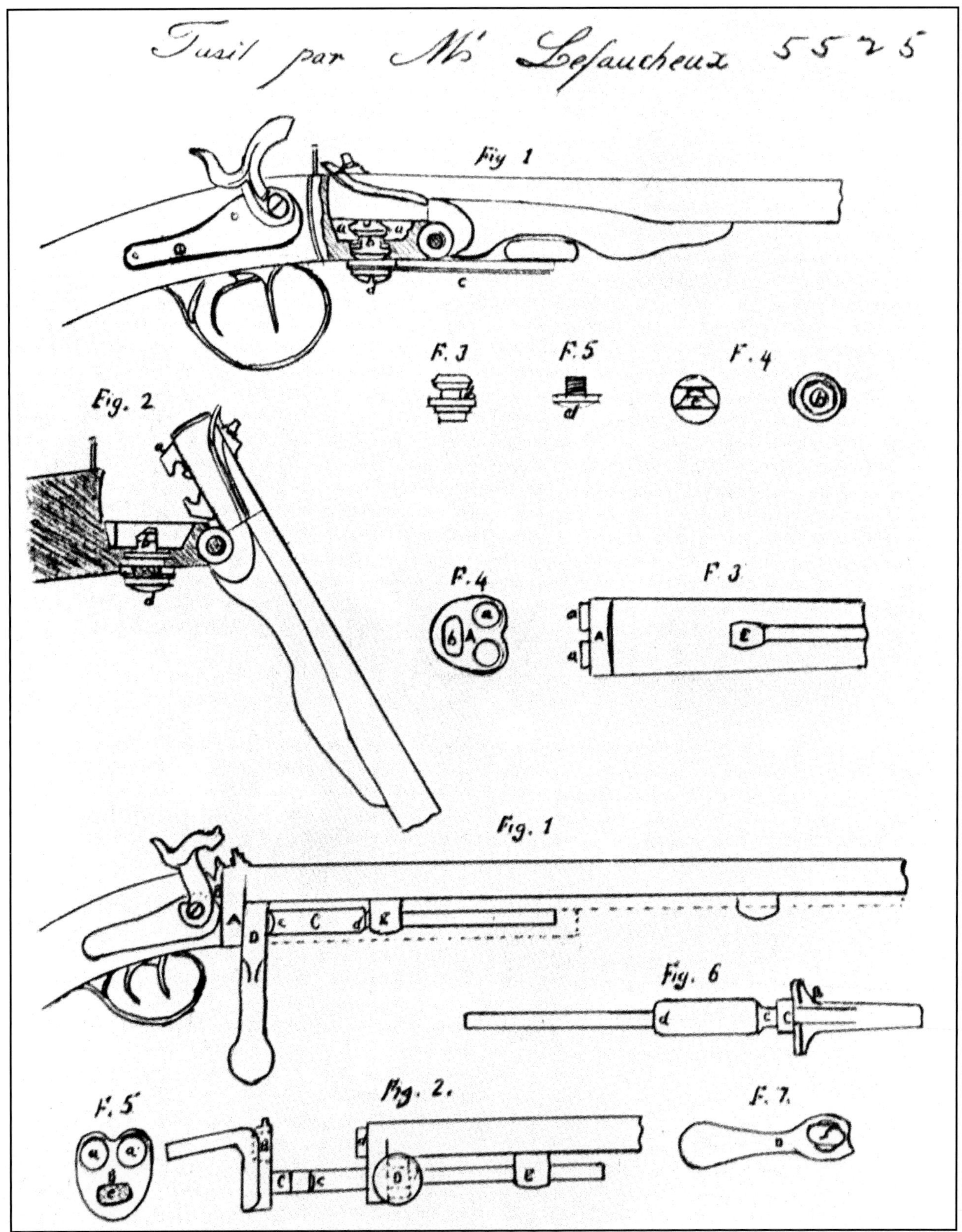

Plate 1-5. Drawings from French patent number 5525 of January 28, 1833, for Casimir Lefaucheux' improvements to the Pauly system of gas seals for shotguns. *Chris C. Curtis collection*

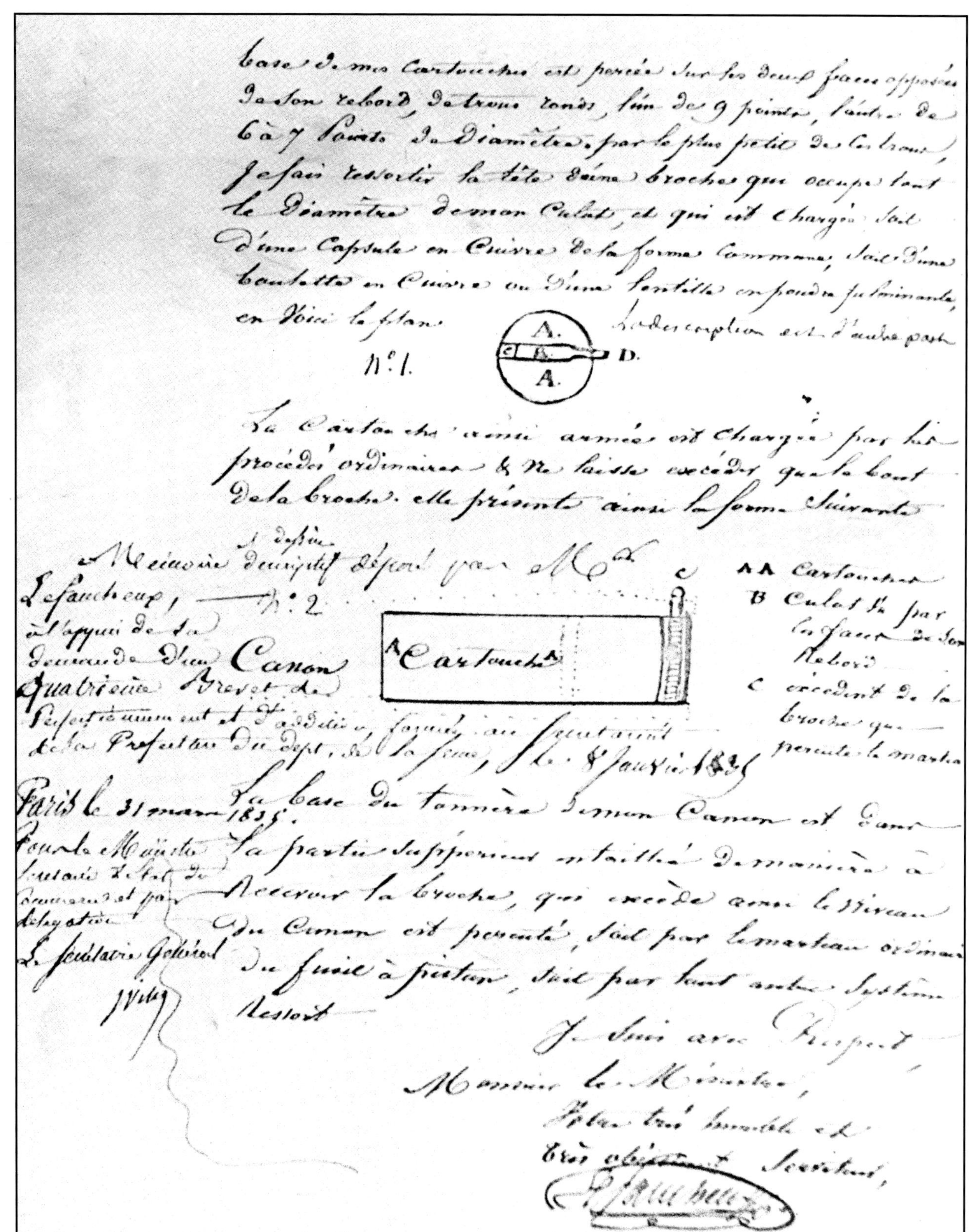

Plate 1-6. Casimir Lefaucheux' handwritten application for the fourth certificate of addition to his 1833 patent number 5525. Note his ornate signature at bottom. *Courtesy D.J. Baker*

slot for the pin in the breech of the barrel.

Continued improvements were incorporated into patent number 5525, with additions on October 29th and November 22nd of 1834; the latter addition locates Lefaucheux at a new Paris address, 10 rue de la Bourse. But it is the fourth addition to this patent, granted on March 31, 1835, that most concerns the arms historians and collectors of today, since the actual date of the invention of the pinfire cartridge has long been a source of confusion. As long ago as 1881 English gun author W.W. Greener had properly given the nod to Casimir Lefaucheux as inventor of the pinfire system. But Greener also erroneously attributed the date of invention as 1836, a mistake accepted and repeated by succeeding generations of authors and collectors. Others attributed the invention of the pinfire to Houllier of Paris. These mistakes are easily understood, inasmuch as Lefaucheux' fourth patent addition is easily missed, and it furthermore is not listed in any cartridge digest published during the last one hundred and sixty-five years.

Plate 1-6 illustrates Lefaucheux' original hand-written application for the fourth addition to patent number 5525, along with his own crude drawings of the first pinfire cartridge. Below the drawing of the cartridge is the date of submission, January 8, 1835, and at the left of the page is the date the patent addition was granted, March 31, 1835. The latter date concurs with the French *Catalogue des Brevets* in the collections of the U.S. Foreign Patents Office; it is repeated in subsequent patents such as number 4839 of October 2, 1849, in which Lefaucheux describes his invention as, "…using the pinfire cartridge invented by me in 1835." The above documents should once and for all settle the controversy, and at last give full credit to none other than Casimir Lefaucheux as the inventor of the pinfire cartridge system, in 1835.

The base of the cartridge illustrated in the fourth additon to patent number 5525 is crimped around the cardboard tube, and it looks very much like a modern shotgun shell. Lefaucheux originally had conceived a bottle-neck pin for this cartridge to ensure a better gas seal and to prevent acciden-

tal dislodging of the pin. The percussion cap was placed on the pin from the outside of the cartridge and the breech wall was used as an anvil. This fourth patent addition of 1835 states,

> *The lower part of my cartridge is bored on the two opposite sides of its edge with round holes, which diameter is nine points for one, and six to seven for the other. Through the smallest of these holes I pass the head of a pin which fills all the diameter of my metal end and which is loaded either with a copper percussion cap of the usual shape, a copper pellet or a fulminated-powder lens.*
>
> *The cartridge thus armed is loaded the usual way and lets extend only the very end of the pin. It offers the following shape:*

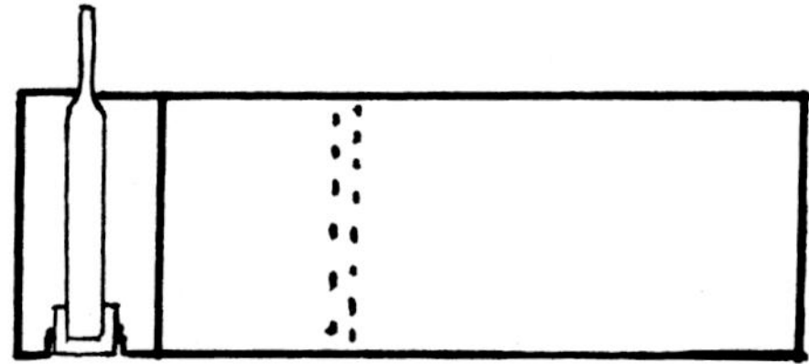

> *The base of the breech of the barrel is slit in its upper part so as to receive the pin which thus exceeds the level of the barrel and is struck by the usual hammer of piston type or any other spring system.*

Yet another improvement to the original design of the shotgun cartridge, the addition of a rim to the base, was made at a subsequent date in an effort to provide a still-better gas seal at the breech. Later, the rim was enlarged for easier extraction of the spent shell. Because of the low breech pressure in handguns, and the easy adaptation of an extractor, no rim was required for handgun cartridges.

A fifth and final addition to patent number 5525 was granted on June 27, 1835, and although Lefaucheux continued to deluge the patent office with new ideas for various minor refinements, Lefaucheux' gun was by then the basic pinfire shotgun known to collectors today.

Casimir Lefaucheux was by then recognized as

Plate 1-7. Drawings from the second certificate of addition (November 22, 1849) to French patent number 8955 of October 2, 1849, for improvements to breechloading shotguns. *Chris C. Curtis collection*

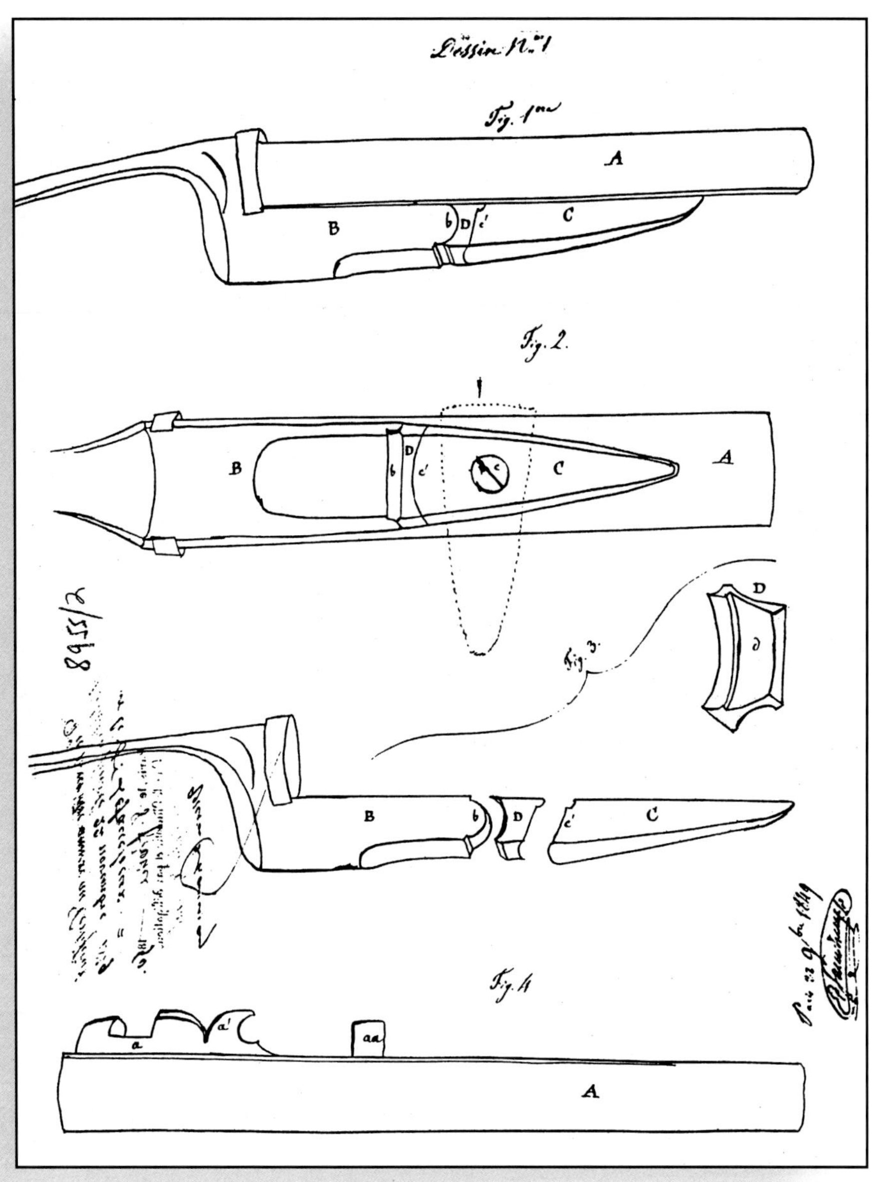

an innovative inventor within the arms community. Yet he was not altogether financially successful, due largely to the limited manufacturing capabilities of his armsmaking establishment. So in 1832, 1834, and 1835, he entered into a series of contracts with several other gunmakers of Paris and the surrounding areas. These contracts essentially were "agreements of partial cessation", which limited Lefaucheux' complete control of his patents and improvements and allowed others to manufacture arms based on his designs. Under those agreements Lefaucheux would receive a fee for each arm produced by another maker; the arms were to be numbered by the maker, but marked "Lefaucheux." The names of some of those makers would become well-known in the succeeding years of pinfire arms manufacture: Pirlot, Francotte, LePage, Devisme, and Blanchard, to name but a few. Lefaucheux, however, retained the exclusive right to manufacture arms based on his designs for the military.

The royalties received from the licensing agreements rendered Casimir Lefaucheux more financially independent, and eased the monetary burdens of his growing family, which now numbered four children. To continue on his course toward success in business, Lefaucheux entered into an expanded advertising campaign which included a portfolio complete with glowing accolades from his clients. He also displayed a selection of his wares at the 1834 Paris Exposition. That same year he relocated his business into a better area of Paris, to 10 rue de la Bourse, while still retaining the former location at 8 rue Sartines.

that, nor his previous failure in 1830 to interest the government in his design, however, were to deter Casimir Lefaucheux from making another attempt. Thus he submitted for testing an 18mm caliber breechloading pinfire blunderbuss intended for cavalry use. The new arm measured 890mm in overall length, with a barrel 510mm long, and had a triggerguard which swiveled to the side to unlock and open the breech. The final test trials held at the firing range at the Champs-Élysées were well-attended by representatives of the military establishment, including the Duke of Nemours, aides de camp of the King and the S.A.R., the commanding officer of the 2nd Lancers, and the inspector general of the cavalry.

But an idea too far ahead of its time is often as

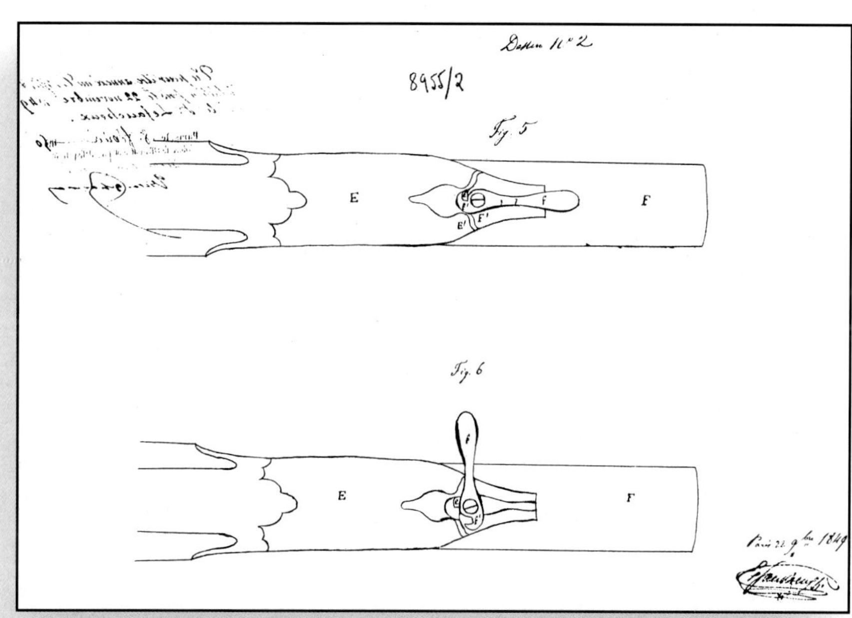

Plate 1-8. Additional drawings from the second certificate of addition to French patent number 8955. *Chris C. Curtis collection*

Henceforth the latter facility would be used for storage and supply purposes.

During 1835 the business climate in France was unfavorable toward private enterprise making guns for the military, as the French government considered the realm of arms development and manufacture to be exclusively its own. Neither

ineffective as one that has outlived its usefulness, and such seemed to be the case with Lefaucheux' revolutionary new weapon. While it received outstanding reviews from some quarters, his blunderbuss was never adopted. The new, rapid-firing arm with its special ammunition presented problems not only with its manufacture and logistics, but also threatened to alter drastically the infantry and cavalry tactics then firmly entrenched within the French military establishment.

Perhaps disappointed by this second rebuff from the military establishment, in December of 1835 Casimir Lefaucheux opted to sell his arms-making business for the sum of 25,000 *francs* to *Monsieur* C. Jube, an employee of the Ministry of Public Instruction. The transaction included all profits to be realized from Lefaucheux' existing patents, and the profits from all agreements signed earlier with other gunmakers, with the exception of his 1835 contract with LePage. Lefaucheux' name was to remain with the business, in exchange for a contract of non-competition which excluded him and his family from the manufacture of firearms for a period of twelve years.

Not yet thirty-six years of age, Casimir Lefaucheux and his family retired to Sarthe, the place of his birth. His keen inventive mind was never long at rest, however. Now Lefaucheux turned his efforts in the direction of farm machinery, patenting a horse-drawn tractor in addition to a cider press.

At about that same time, Alfred Krupp of Essen, Germany began developing a new process of forging gun barrels that was to play a significant role in the future of pinfire shotguns. Krupp's new process was cast steel, and although it was very slowly adopted, cast steel offered major improvements over the damascus barrels and cast iron frames used during the earlier periods of gunmaking. Steel, a low carbon iron alloy, is strong yet malleable, and when properly produced is far superior to iron in every way. As early as 384 B.C., Aristotle had described its use in fabricating the sword blades of the Near East and India. But the formula for making steel became lost until it was rediscovered by an English clockmaker, Benjamin Huntsman of Sheffield, in the mid-eighteenth century.[4] Key to the seemingly-simple process for making cast steel was the exclusion of air, which produces carbon, from the melting metal by enclosing it in an earthenware cupel, or crucible. The method coined the name "crucible steel", which later was called "cast steel" or "liquid steel"

by Krupp. Those names are found marked on barrels made in Essen for export to England.

So far as the gunmakers of Huntsman's era knew, however, cast steel did not exist, as Huntsman and his successors held the steel-making formula secret for some seventy years. Content with making springs, stamping dies, and mill rolls, they did nothing to advance the technology of weapons manufacture. Yet that situation changed in 1811, when Friedrich Krupp established a cast steel works in Essen. Oddly, it met with only very limited success. However, on Friedrich Krupp's death in 1826 his son Alfred became head of the firm, and within ten years the Krupp works was producing gun barrels in significant quantities.[5]

Gun barrels fabricated in Germany from cast steel were marked "*Guss Stahl*" well into the twentieth century, while guns made in France and Belgium were marked "*Acier Fondu*" until the end of the 1890s. As early as the 1870s the term "Cast Steel" was no longer being used in the United States, however.

The pinfire ignition system found its detractors, being harshly criticized most notably by British sportsmen and writers who claimed that the pinfire shotgun was inferior in every way to the percussion weapon. The three most common complaints were of flaws inherent in the pinfire design: failure of the breech to create a gas-tight seal; no provision for cartridge ejection; and the lack of an arrangement for rapid dismounting of the barrels from the stock and locks for cleaning, repair, or storage.

Such criticism inspired an almost continuous flow of patents for improving the pinfire system, not only on the part of Casimir Lefaucheux, but also by a number of other makers who had adopted the "Lefaucheux" cartridge.

A debt of thanks is owed those reluctant Englishmen, as their failure to embrace the pinfire system early-on resulted in subsequent improvements which ensured its continual use throughout Europe well into the twentieth century.

Casimir Lefaucheux' French patent number 8955 of October 2, 1849, and its additions, were to

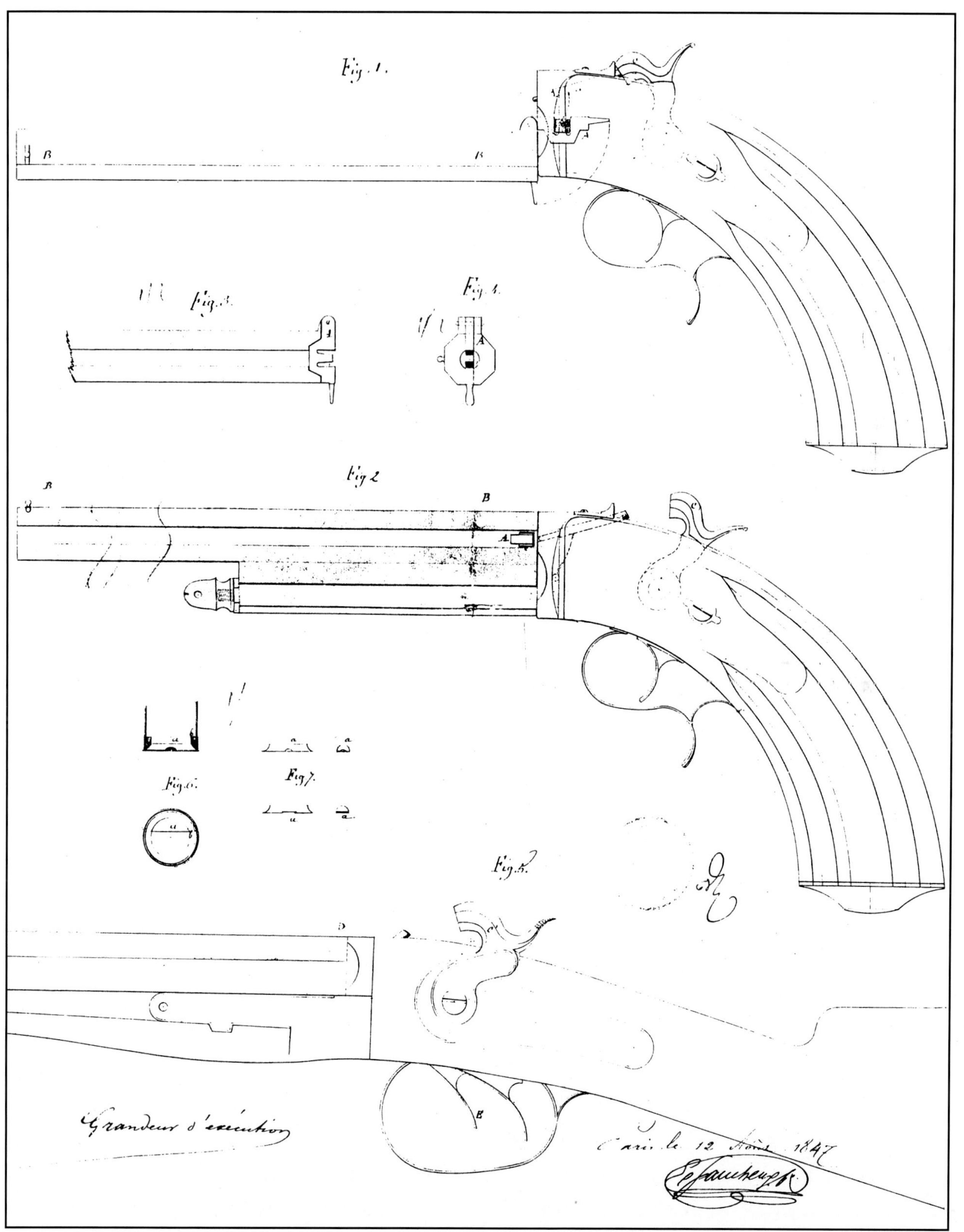

Plate 1-9. Drawings from the third certificate of addition to patent number 8955, showing Casimir Lefaucheux' early experiments with the centerfire cartridge system, here to a single-shot pistol and a breechloading longarm. *Chris C. Curtis collection*

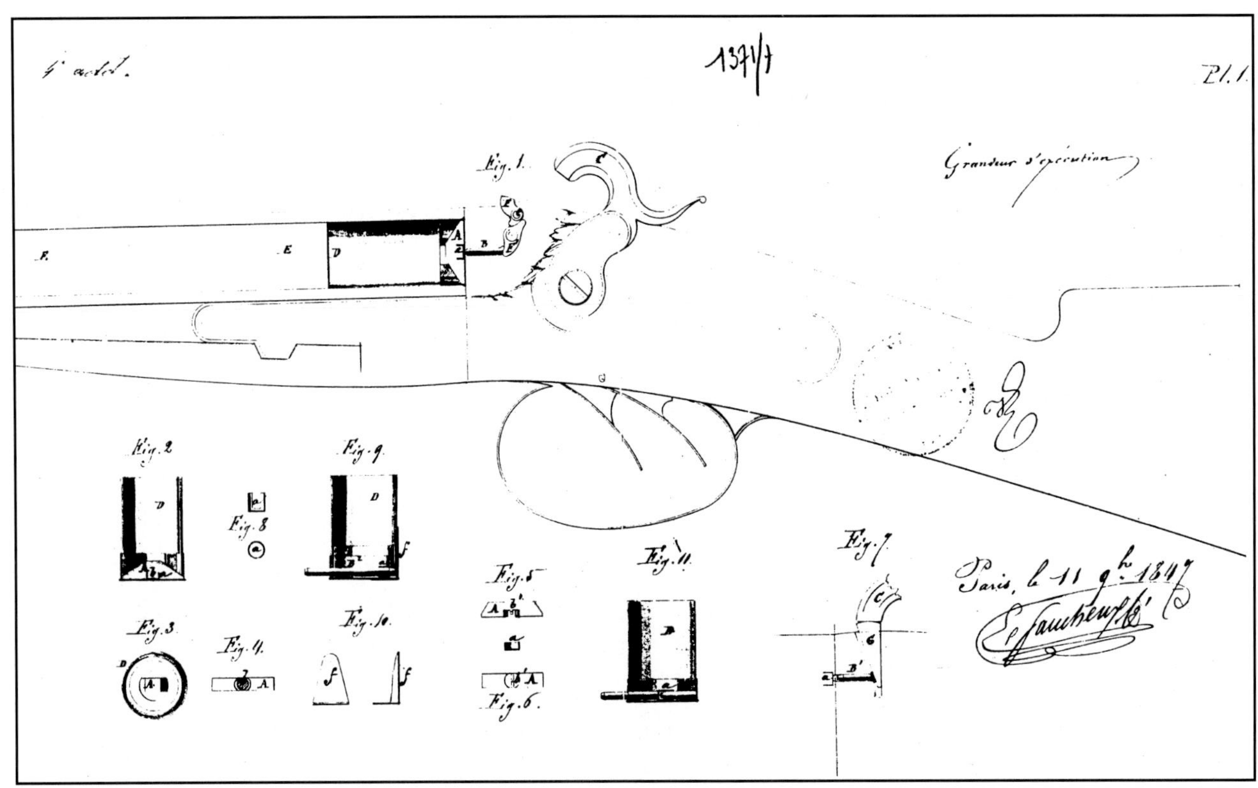

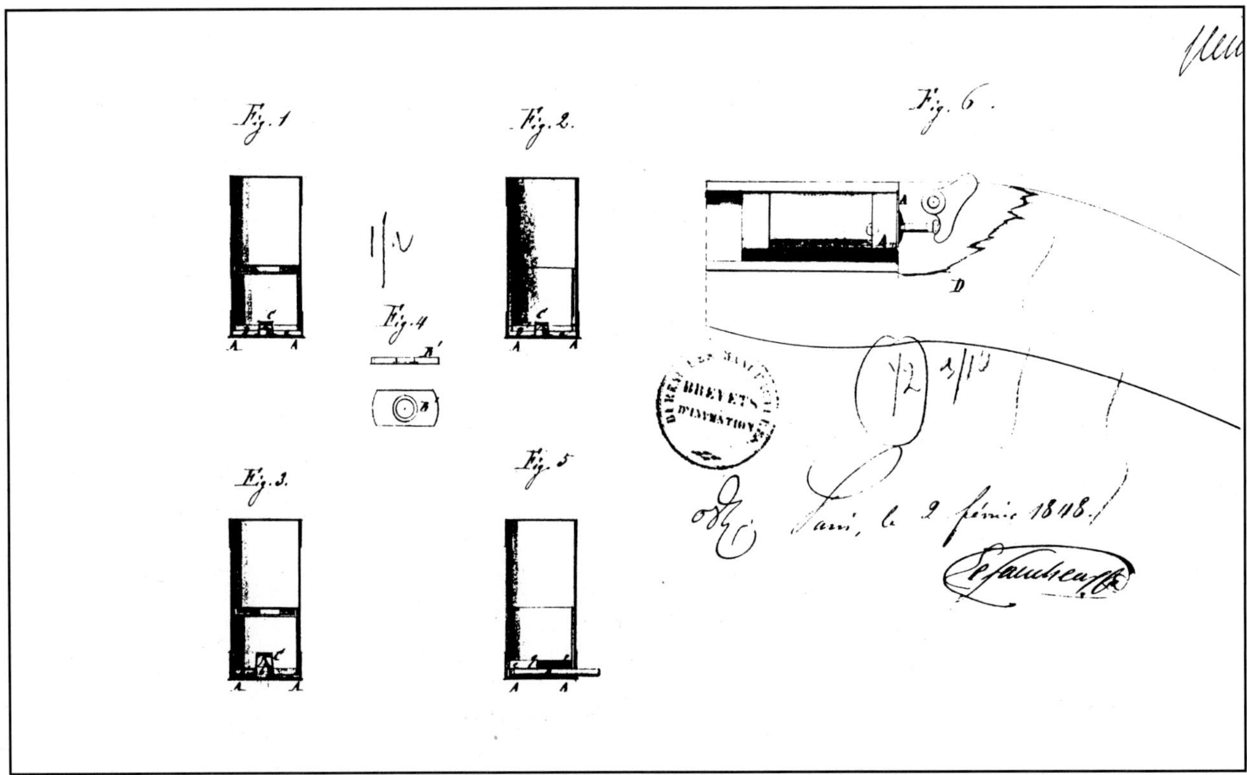

Plates 1-10, 1-11, and 1-12 (this and opposite page). Drawings from the third certificate of addition to patent number 8955, showing Casimir Lefaucheux' early experiments with the centerfire cartridge system, here to a breechloading longarm. *Chris C. Curtis collection*

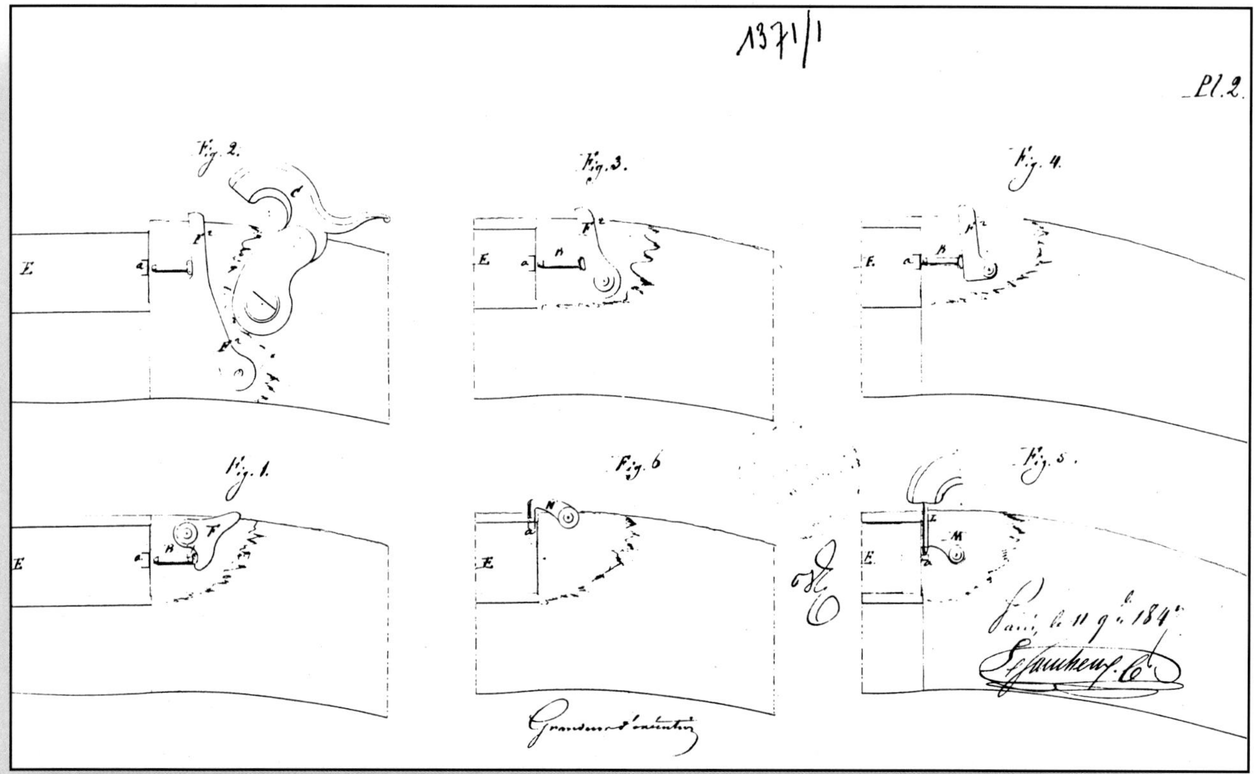

be among his last attempts to correct the flaws inherent in his breechloading pinfire shotgun. This patent and its second addition (November 22, 1849) afforded improvements for quickly and easily dismantling the gun, and for the addition of wood to the forestock for protection of the hand from heat caused by firing (*see Plates 1-5 and 1-6*). Lefaucheux' final patent addition, on July 26, 1850, was for the design of an all-metal cartridge.

While Lefaucheux' 1835 breechloading pinfire shotgun, like Pauly's breechloader of 1812, was almost totally ignored in Britain, their designs spawned scores of related inventions in France. There, many patents were issued for breechloading guns utilizing a "chimney" (the French term for a percussion nipple), either separate or as part of a cartridge. Then, in 1846, after expiration of Lefaucheux' patent the previous year, Houllier of Paris was granted a patent for a solid metal pinfire cartridge having a small rim. Houllier's patent, number 1936, was an obvious improvement over Lefaucheux' original design, although oddly it retained the bottleneck pin of the earlier design which by then Lefaucheux had discarded in favor of a straight pin. Perhaps Houllier, in striving for a better gas seal, had ignored the loading factor and simply copied Lefaucheux' patent for his purpose. Dozens of other patents were applied for and issued in France over the next decade, as inventors continued in their efforts to improve the pinfire cartridge.

During the years of his self-exile and "retirement" from the armsmaking business, Casimir Lefaucheux' ideas concerning firearms began moving in the direction of handguns. Following his invention of the pinfire system, Lefaucheux' interests and efforts after 1835 appeared to be concerned mainly with the development of longarms and with the improvement and correction of the flaws inherent in his basic design. However, closely following the 1845 expiration of his patent,

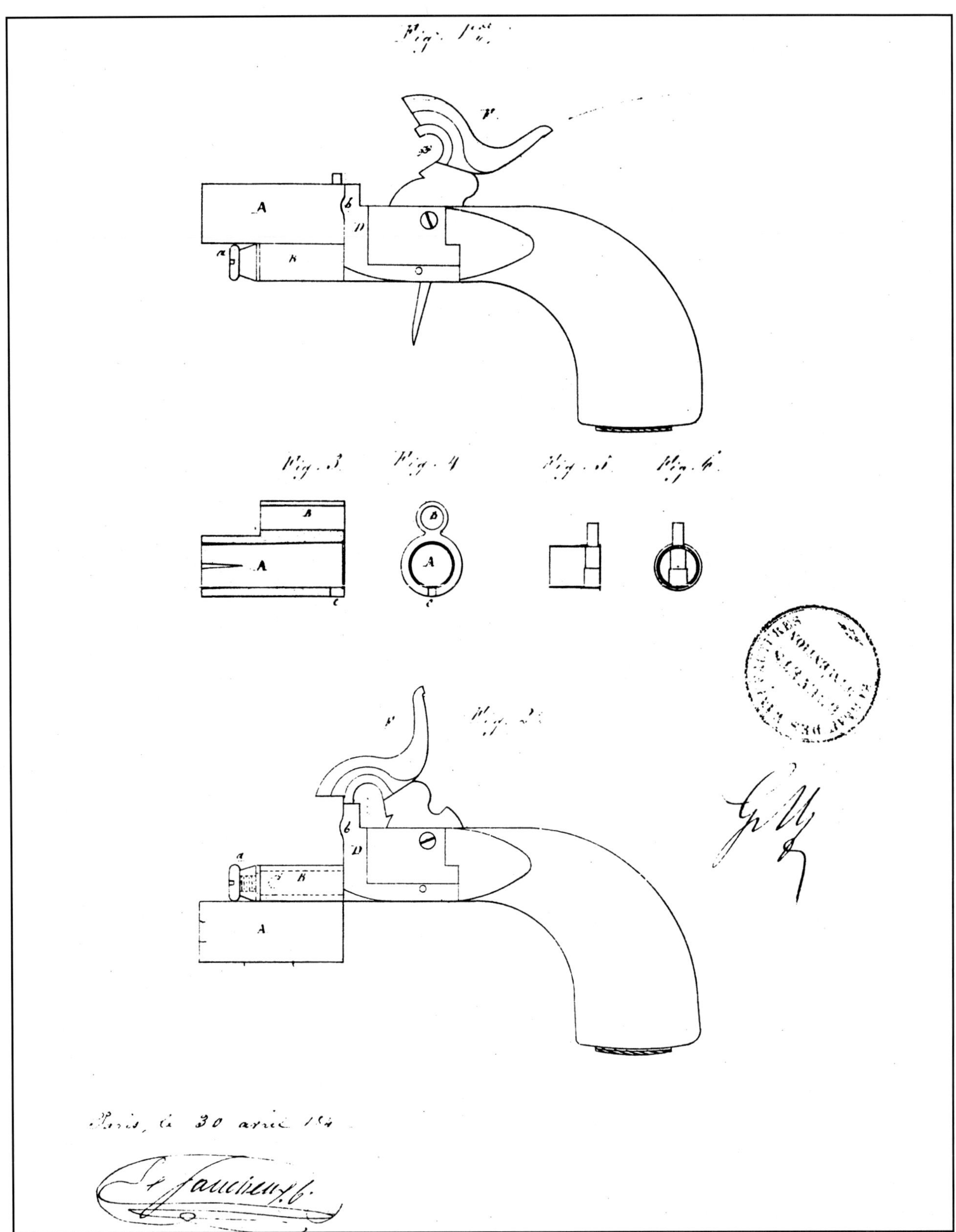

Plate 1-13. Drawings from the first certificate of addition to Casimir Lefaucheaux' French patent number 1371 of May 2, 1845, for pistols using the pinfire cartridge.
Chris C. Curtis collection

Lefaucheux submitted a new patent application that within its original text and additions constituted his first and only foray into the field of pinfire handgun design and manufacture.

By 1847 he not only had returned to Paris brimming with new concepts and this new patent, but Lefaucheux had resumed control and ownership of his former business at 10 rue de la Bourse. French patent number 1371 was granted on May 2, 1845, and received additions on February 7th, May 25th, and July 7th of 1846, on April 12th, 1847, and on February 2, 1848. Patent number 1371 is a remarkable document, totaling forty-nine pages of hand-rendered drawings and handwritten descriptions, and covering in detail a myriad of

ignition system as early as April of 1847 (*see Plates 1-9 through 1-12*, from the third certificate of additions to his 1845 patent number 1371). Possibly Lefaucheux was attempting to advance beyond flaws in his original inventions, that had been brought to the attention of the firearms world by contemporary critics. Yet no examples of centerfire arms or ammunition that can be credited directly to Casimir Lefaucheux are known to the authors, and it is doubtful that he ever seriously attempted the manufacture of such designs. In fact, even after Casimir Lefaucheux' death and his son Eugene's assumption of the gunmaking operations, those ideas were largely ignored in favor of the tried-and-proven pinfire system until nearly a

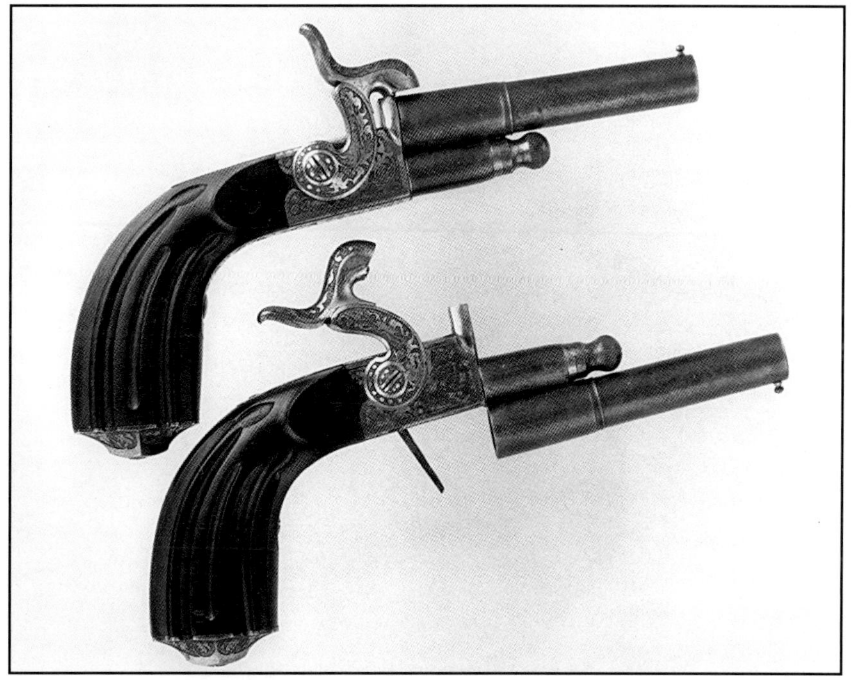

Plate 1-14. A matched pair of 12mm caliber, single-shot pinfire pistols manufactured by Casimir Lefaucheux after his designs contained in patent number 1371, and subsequent certificates of addition; right sides. *Chris C. Curtis collection; Richard McMillan photograph*

subjects ranging from single-shot pistols and pepperboxes to improvements to shotguns and the design of firing mechanisms. It even introduced Lefaucheux' revolutionary ideas about centerfire cartridges and firearms!

It is significant to note here that Casimir Lefaucheux was experimenting with the centerfire

quarter-of-a-century later. By 1871 a new government contract was being sought, and that year the Lefaucheux firm was forced into the centerfire arena by overwhelming competition.

Plate 1-13 illustrates the design for a single-shot pistol, which is from the first certificate of addition to patent number 1371. A single screw

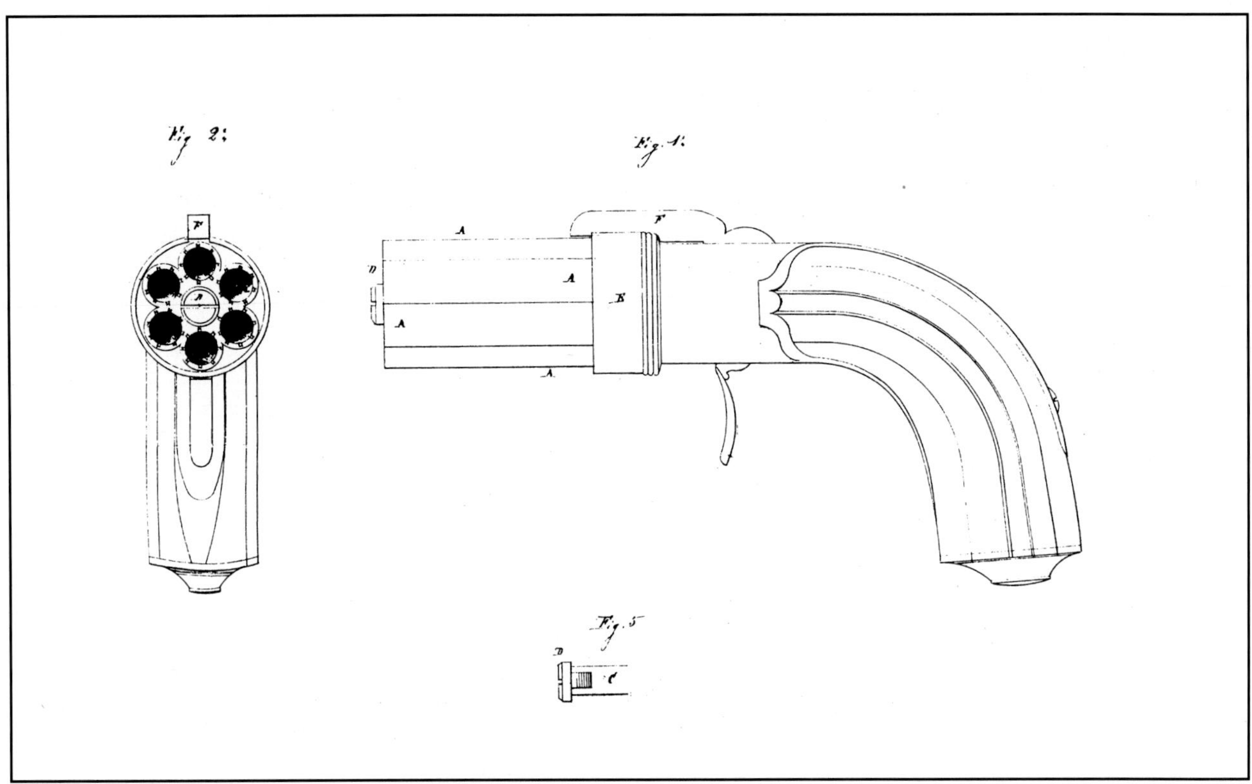

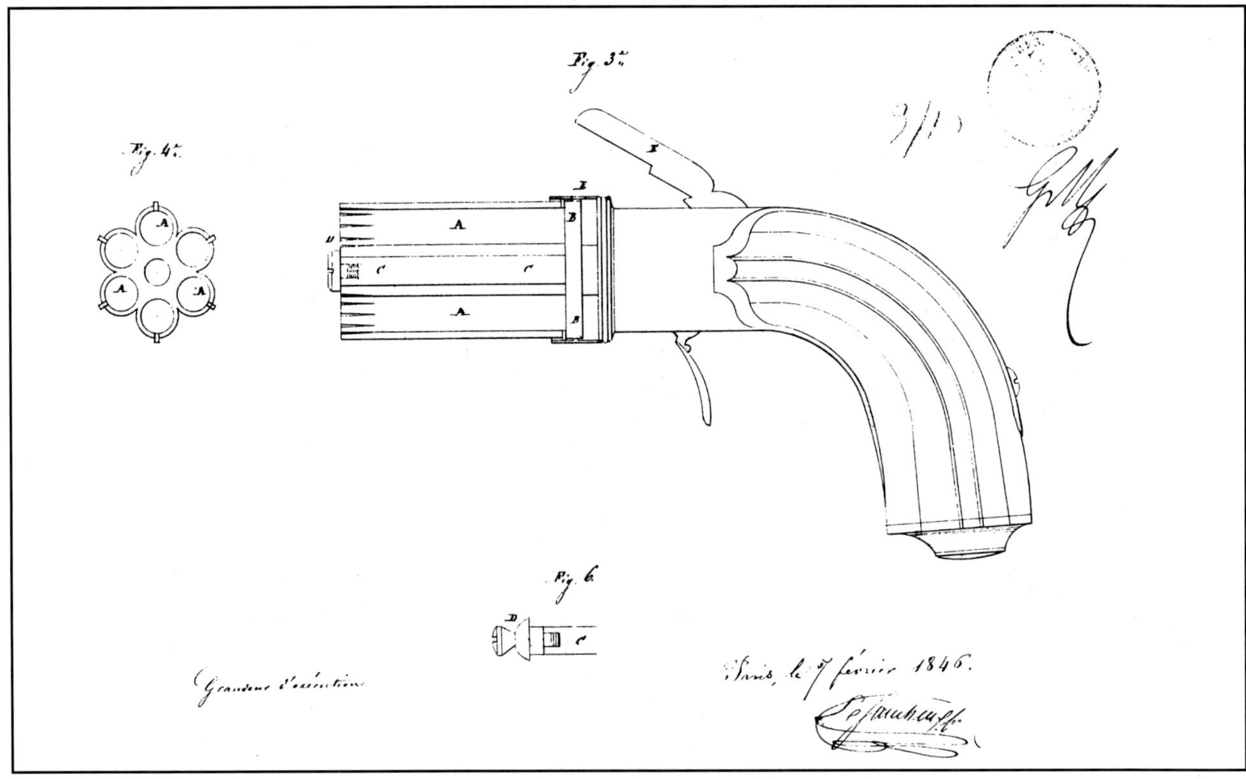

Plates 1-15 and 1-16. Drawings from the first certificate of addition to patent number 1371, for a six-shot, double-action pinfire pepperbox pistol. *Chris C. Curtis collection*

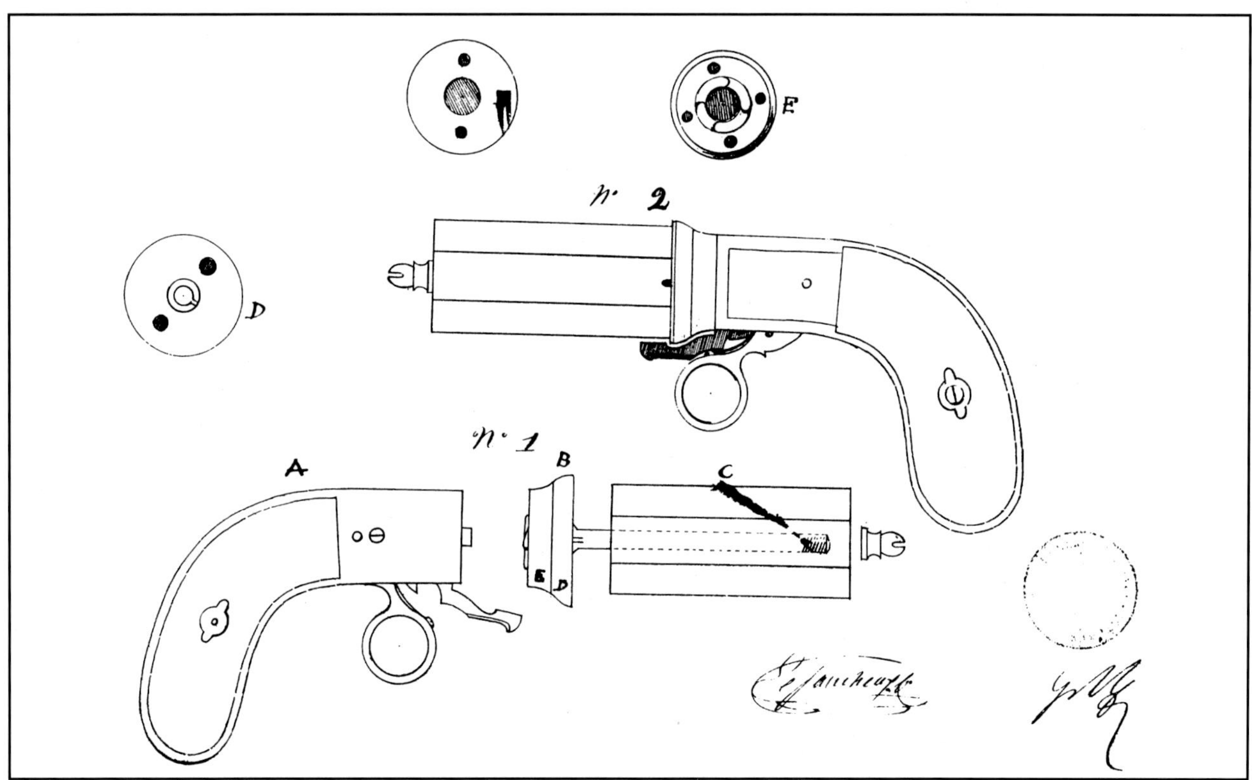

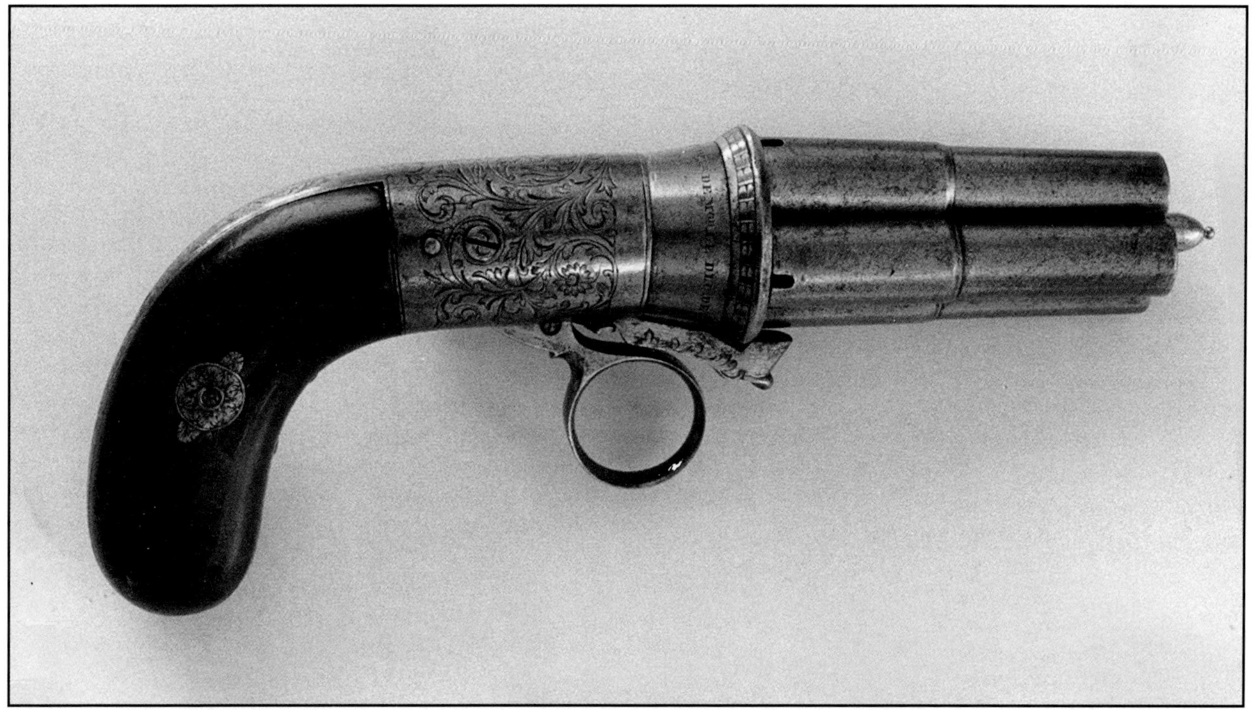

Plates 1-17 and 1-18. Drawings from the second certificate of addition to patent number 1371, for a ring-trigger, underhammer, double-action pinfire pepperbox pistol similar in design to the Belgian Mariette, and a four-shot, ring-trigger, underhammer double-action pinfire pepperbox pistol nearly identical to the example shown in the patent drawings illustrated above. *Courtesy F.W. Hulbert; F.W. Hulbert photograph*

holds the barrel assembly in place against the frame, creating a friction lock. To load, one simply manually twists the barrel 180-degrees so that a pinfire cartridge can be inserted into it. While of admirably simple design and construction, repeated firing of the weapon would have the potential to loosen the screw, which would constantly have to be checked and re-tightened by hand to maintain an adequate gas seal.

Plate 1-14 illustrates a pair of 12mm caliber pinfire single-shot pistols manufactured according to designs on the first certificate of addition to Casimir Lefaucheux' 1845 patent. These pistols, each serial numbered "367", are beautifully engraved and marked *"Lefaucheux a Paris"* on their barrels. The pair was found cased together beneath the false bottom of a period lap writing desk.

Plates 1-15 and 1-16 reproduce pages from the same 1846 certificate of addition to patent number 1371. They illustrate a six-shot, double-action pepperbox pistol similar in style to the Allen & Thurber percussion pepperboxes which were appearing in the American market at about the same time. Here, a folding trigger is introduced for the first time on a Lefaucheux gun. It would be used on many pinfire pepperboxes and revolvers manufactured by dozens of armsmakers and in a variety of countries over the decades to follow. An interesting feature of this design is the transfer bar located over the pin slot openings in the barrel group. The hammer strikes the bar a downward blow, which in turn strikes the cartridge pin. The barrel group is secured to the frame by a single bolt in the central arbor. No examples of this arm have been located by the authors for actual study.

Plate 1-17 illustrates a drawing from the second certificate of addition to patent number 1371. Also a double-action pepperbox, it features a ring trigger that cocks and releases the underhammer, which directly strikes the cartridge pin from below. This bag-grip, underhammer pepperbox is similar in design to the Belgian Mariette pistol.

Plate 1-18 illustrates an example of a four-shot, 12mm caliber pepperbox virtually identical to the patent drawing above. It is marked *"Inventor Lefaucheux Patent Gunmaker in Ordinary to*

Monsignor The Duke of Nemours." The second son of King Louis Philippe, the duke's full name was Louis Charles Philippe Raphael d'Orléans, *duc de Nemours* (1814-1896).

Plates 1-19 and 1-20 illustrate a slightly later, four-shot, 12mm caliber pinfire pepperbox which nevertheless still predates the London Exhibition of 1851. While its style of grip differs from the previous example, mechanically it is the same. Loading is accomplished by removing the rifled barrel group that is retained by a slotted thumbscrew at the muzzle; the arbor then is used as a cartridge extractor. The barrel group revolves counter-clockwise at a point halfway between its rear face and the trigger; it is held stationary by a key that fits into a corresponding slot. The pistol is eight inches long overall, with a four-inch, four-chambered barrel group designed to fire a brass-base paper pinfire pistol cartridge. The chamber is slightly larger than the actual bore, creating a ridge at the chamber's forward end which prevents the paper cartridge tube from following the projectile down the bore when the arm is fired. Separation of the tube body from the metal base happened frequently with early pinfire cartridges, representing a major design flaw. While an annoyance with a single-shot pistol, it could prevent the successful operation of a revolving gun when the paper tube moved forward between the face of the cylinder and the barrel and thus prevented further rotation of the cylinder. Although differing slightly from the patent drawing, this pepperbox is nearly identical to the example shown in the July 5th, 1851 issue of *The Illustrated London News*, with the exception that the *News'* pistol has five barrels instead of four. Also evident from the *News* illustration (*see Plate 1-21*) is that Lefaucheux was still using the paper tube cartridge, even though Houllier had patented a successful one-piece metallic cartridge in 1846, and Lefaucheux himself had patented an all-metal shotgun shell in 1850.

The pepperbox pistol illustrated in *Plates 1-19 and 1-20* is undoubtedly the type that was taken to England by Casimir Lefaucheux as part of his display at the 1851 London Exhibition. It is marked internally on the breechplate, *"Lefaucheux Brevete*

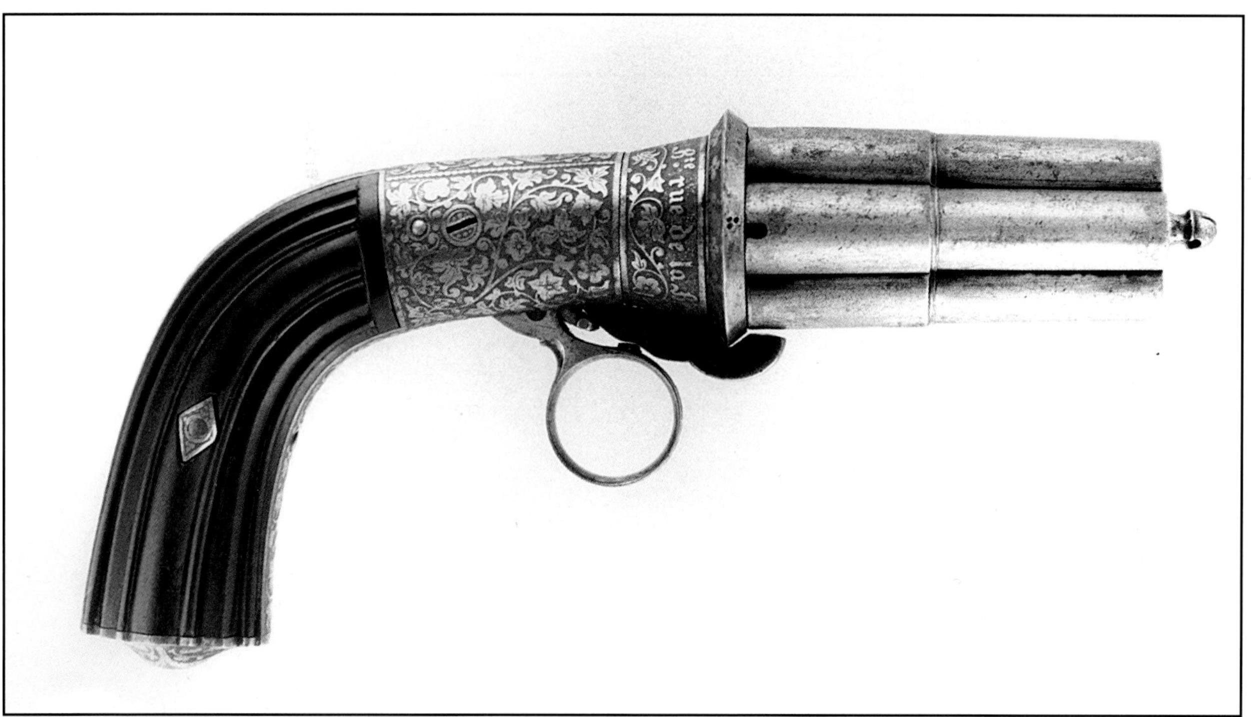

Plate 1-19. A later four-shot, ring-trigger, under-hammer double-action pinfire pepperbox pistol in 12mm caliber; right side. Note that the barrel group arbor doubles as an extractor. *Chris C. Curtis collection; Richard McMillan photograph*

Plate 1-20. Detail view of breech area of the pepperbox pistol pictured in *Plate 1-19*, showing etched "Lefaucheux" name and profuse coverage of etched decoration. Note openings for pinfire cartridge pins along cylinder periphery. *Chris C. Curtis collection; Richard McMillan photograph*

Inv 37." Externally the pistol's frame is acid-etched with the Lefaucheux name and business address, *"rue de la Bourse 10 a Paris Ivion Lefaucheux Bte."* The firm moved from the above early address to a new and larger location in Paris at 37 rue Vivienne, sometime between January and July of 1850. The catalogue for the 1851 London Exhibition notes the new address, and lists Casimir Lefaucheux as an "inventor and manufacturer of rifles, fowling pieces and pistols on his new principle."

Lefaucheux was not the only exhibitor to show pinfire weapons in London: A. Claudin of Paris, among others, had fine pinfire arms on display. Although the Lefaucheux guns were lauded for their workmanship by *The Illustrated London News*, the newspaper saved its highest praise for the Colt percussion revolver (a .44 caliber Dra-

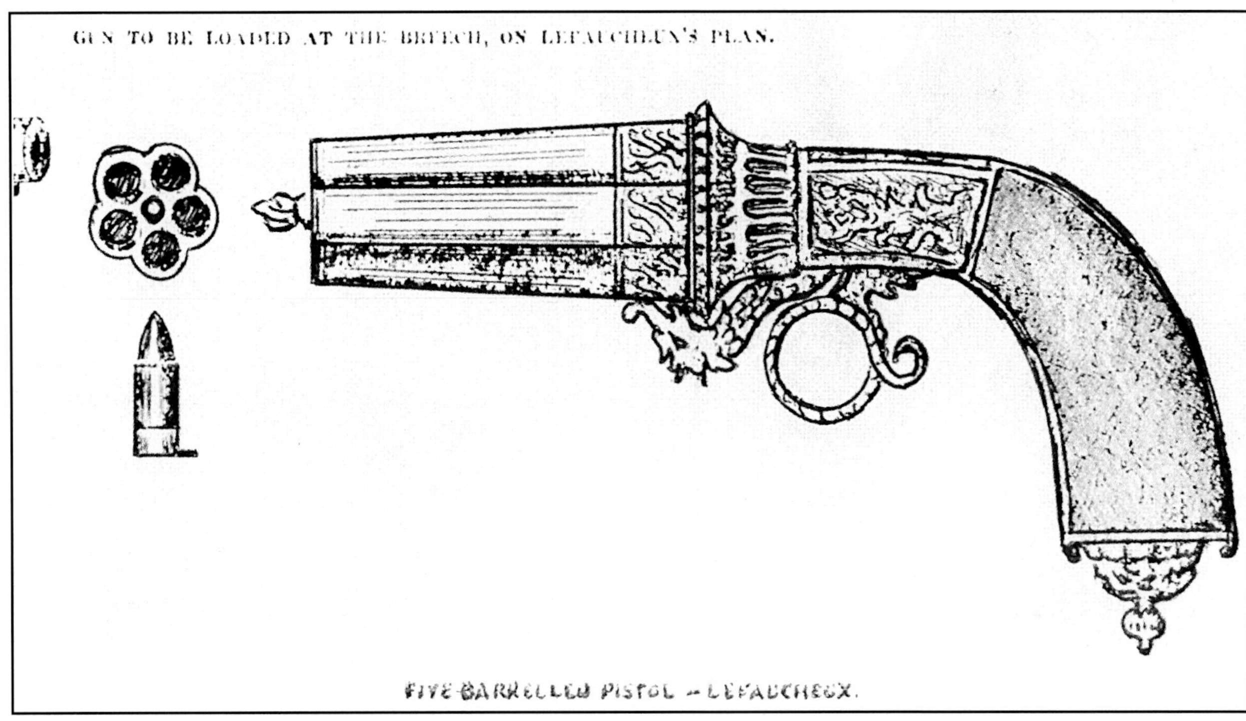

Plate 1-21. An illustration of Casimir Lefaucheux' ornate pinfire pepperbox pistol, reproduced from the July 5, 1851 issue of *The Illustrated London News.* Note also the drawing of an early paper-and-brass pinfire pistol cartridge. *Chris C. Curtis collection*

goon model was pictured), an arm "so terribly efficient in its operations as to leave all former inventions of the kind far in the background."

Despite the praise heaped on his American competition, the London Exhibition of 1851 was a professional triumph for Casimir Lefaucheux. He was awarded a Medal of Honor for his display, No. 1308, which was the first step toward universal recognition and acceptance of the pinfire system throughout the world.

Unfortunately, Casimir Lefaucheux did not live long enough to reap the full rewards of his inventive genius and pioneering work, which altered the evolutionary course of firearms development. He died in Paris on August 11, 1852 at the age of fifty, less than a year after the close of the London Exhibition.

All Lefaucheux arms made during the era of Casimir's reign—single-shot pistols, pepperboxes, and shotguns—were of the highest Old World quality and craftsmanship. But they were not manufactured in sufficient numbers nor over a lengthy enough period to achieve commercial success during their inventor's lifetime. Few examples survive, and today any such Lefaucheux arm constitutes a prized addition to a collection of early cartridge firearms (*see Plate 1-22*).

Casimir Lefaucheux left behind a legacy of high-quality firearms, many undeveloped ideas and patents, and an operating arms manufacturing facility in Paris, in addition to the esteemed and well-deserved Lefaucheux reputation. Those factors continued to impact and advance the design and fabrication of cartridge firearms well into the second half of the nineteenth century. They were destined to be soon merged with the master's greatest legacy: his son, Eugene Gabriel Lefaucheux.

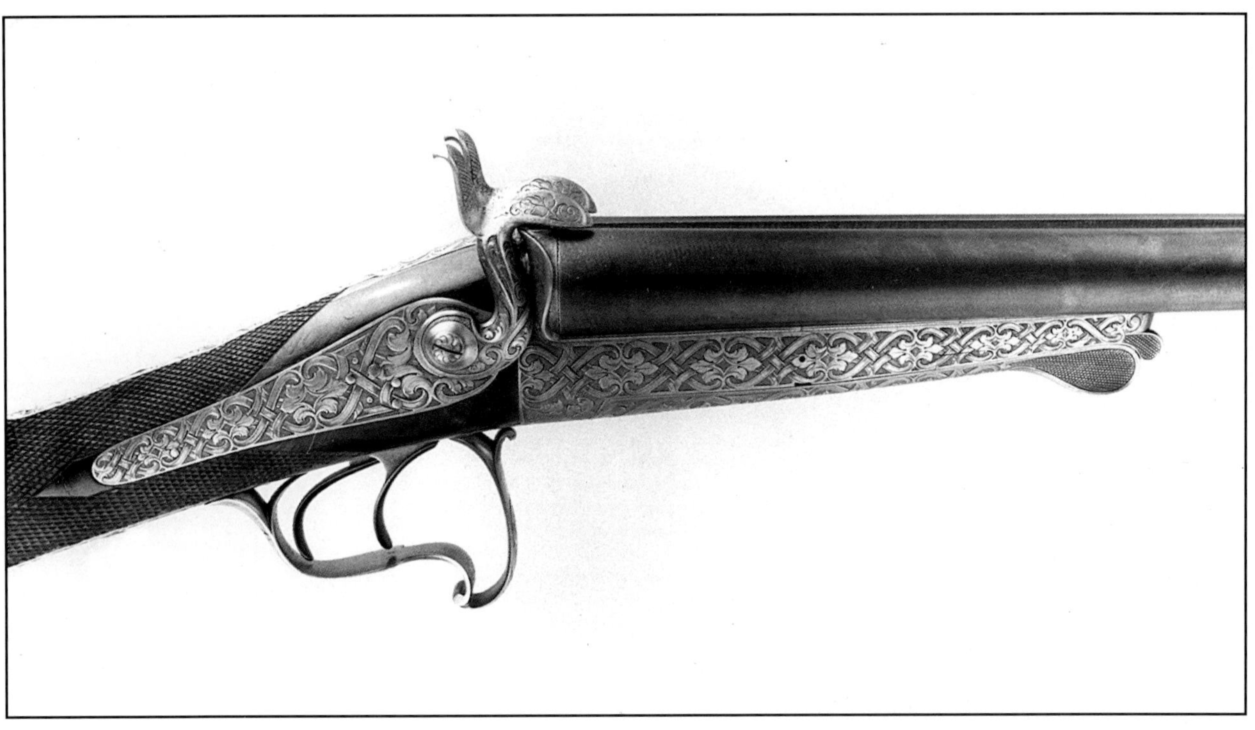

Plate 1-22. A 16 gauge, double-barrel Lefaucheux pinfire shotgun, beautifully engraved and stocked, and cased with full accoutrements. Barrels are marked *"Lefaucheux…."* The late *"37 rue Vivienne"* address is gold-embossed inside the case lid. *Chris C. Curtis collection; Richard McMillan photograph*

Chapter notes.

1. In the autumn of 1793, with French revolutionary ardor at its peak, the National Convention decreed the creation of a new calendar, the chronology and nomenclature of which would more closely correspond to the spirit and ideas of that "modern" time than to the old Gregorian calendar until then in use. In line with such other de-Christianizing developments as the conversion of some churches into "temples of reason", the names of days, months, and other intervals of time were to be separated from religious association and replaced by titles denoting the "natural" order of those things dear to Republican principles. Thus, days of the week were given names such as "Plow" and "Spinach"; holidays were renamed "Labor" and "Opinion." The new calendar system was to go into effect retroactively from September 22, 1792, which celebrated the true autumnal equinox and the creation of the French Republic. Monthly periods also were renamed, and "Pluviose", the "Month of Rain", encompassed January 20th through February 18th.

2. Unlike American and British patent laws, French regulations provided for the alteration or improvement to an existing patent without the formality of having to submit a separate new patent application. This was called a "certificate of addition", and served to amend the original patent during the duration of its legal term.

3. D.J. Baker, co-author with I.M. Crudgington of *The British Shotgun Volume I 1850-1870*, still hunts with shotguns using pinfire ammunition that he loads himself. Baker's Bastin action gun, retailed by Masu of London, he found to be the most awkward of his breechloaders. The ejection system, a recess in the hammers designed to catch the cartridge pins and thus hold them stationary while the barrels move forward, often tore the metal cartridge head off, leaving the cardboard tube stuck in the breech. (*Letter, D.J. Baker to Gene P. Smith*)

4. "Crucible Cast Steel", *Encyclopedia Britannica*, 1956.

5. William Manchester, *The Arms of Krupp 1587-1968* (Boston, MA and Toronto, ON: Little, Brown, 1968), pp. 39-40, 45-46.

Plate 2-1. A typical hunter from the 1830s era, armed with his trusty flintlock rifle. Eugene Lefaucheux' birth, in 1832, heralded the arrival of a new age of firearms technology. *Courtesy private collection*

Eugene Lefaucheux:
Heir to the Pinfire System

ugene Gabriel Lefaucheux was born on Friday the fourteenth of September, 1832, the fourth child of seven born to Casimir and Françoise Constance Lefaucheux. Typical of that day, young Eugene was one of only four of the family's children who survived into adulthood.

Casimir Lefaucheux died in August 1852, shortly before his only surviving son's twentieth birthday. But young Eugene had the great benefit of having apprenticed with his father from a very early age, and by now he was thoroughly versed in the history, design techniques, and manufacture of arms built on the principle of the pinfire ignition system invented by the elder Lefaucheux. During his years of training Eugene had been continually exposed to the inner workings of firearms manufacture as a profit-making business. Fortunately, Eugene Lefaucheux inherited not only his father's business and patents, but Casimir's keen mind, inventive genius, and varied interests in all things mechanical, as well.[1]

The young man's intent was to make his business not merely survive, but to prosper. Thus Eugene wisely traveled to Liége, and there formally apprenticed himself to his chosen profession. He had two objectives: to familiarize himself with the modern manufacturing techniques in practice within the impressive Belgian arms trade, and at the same time to study the art of negotiation between the well-established local firms such as Pirlot, Collette, Ancion *et Cie*, Dandoy, and Francotte. During Eugene's absence his mother continued to operate the shop at 37 rue de Vivienne. In July of 1853 Said Pasha, the governor of Egypt, purchased three carbines and a highly decorated pair of pistols from Mme. Lefaucheux, which were later displayed at the International Exposition of Paris, in 1855. She even submitted a patent application, and was awarded patent number 17391 on September 14, 1853, for a gun mechanism which automatically ejected spent cartridges. When Eugene came of legal age he assumed control of the family gunmaking operation, later to be assisted by Jean-Pierre Lafiteau, husband of Eugene's older sister, Constance Casimiere. In 1859 the elder Mme. Lefaucheaux retired to the Paris suburbs, where she passed away in 1863.

By late 1853 Eugene had returned to Paris brimming with new ideas, but with insufficient capital to realize them. History relates that he then convinced his future father-in-law, *Monsieur* Bigot, founder of a large local financial establishment, the Havas Agency, to advance him the necessary funds. That goal accomplished, Eugene immediately set out to expand, remodel, and modernize the Lefaucheux family's 37 rue de Vivienne arms manufacturing facility.

Now Eugene Lefaucheux' course for the future

was firmly set. He openly embraced the most modern manufacturing methods then being inspired by and implemented as a result of the European Industrial Revolution. While during his father's generation all fine arms had been made almost entirely by hand, with few gunmaking machines utilized (or even available), Eugene not only introduced mechanization and trained his workers in its use and benefits, but he designed and adapted other machines to perform specific functions to fit his needs. Small vertical machine types, some on wheels, were adapted to drilling and shaping; horizontal machines were made to cut rough cylinder blanks; rotary cutters and finishing machines did their work. While such precision machinery had to be adjusted and maintained by a few skilled workers, the large part of the work force might consist of unskilled young men who knew nothing of the gunmaker's art before entering the employ of Lefaucheux. Eugene's primary aim was not the exact interchangeability of parts, which was soon to become the world-accepted standard of both government armories and civilian arms factories such as Samuel Colt's in America; rather, Lefaucheux' goals were the speed, ease, and lower costs realized from mass manufacturing. The assembly and finishing workshop located on the second floor of the Lefaucheux factory was staffed by many skilled engravers, woodworkers, and cabinetmakers, all of whom were most capable artisans. By 1860 this staff of about 500 skilled workers and as many as 400 additional common laborers, was producing 150 or more finished revolvers during an average ten-hour work day. As needed, Lefaucheux could place into the commercial market some 3,500 to 4,000 such arms per month, and in that manner he had been able to fill orders totaling 40,000 arms in less than a year.

By seeking and utilizing these new methods of manufacture, by 1865 Eugene Lefaucheux had created a business unique of its kind, not only in Paris but throughout all of France. The Lefaucheux name was known worldwide.

Yet, as early as 1853 Eugene Lefaucheux had known that vision, enterprise, and even significant financial backing were not enough to ensure his success. What was needed was the proper product at the right time, and he had just the firearm in mind.

No records survive to tell us to what degree Lefaucheux had participated in the London Exhibition of 1851, but it is safe to assume that he did attend at some time during the five-month duration of the exhibition. There, Samuel Colt's large military-type "Dragoon" revolver was admired by the attending public and exhibitors alike. Gunmakers and sportsmen knew the advantages of the breechloading shotgun, yet oddly enough not a single armsmaker or government representative attending the London Exhibition recognized the potential of the pinfire cartridge for use in military arms.

Because in one place or another the European continent had been almost continuously at war for decades, most of the individual governments of Europe were keenly aware of the need for new and advanced types of firearms. Why none saw the possibilities of the pinfire system is a mystery to arms historians. Even the normally far-sighted Colonel Colt, who exhibited a varied display of small arms at the exhibition, did not forsee the potential for the use of the metallic cartridge in a military handgun.

During his year in Liége, Eugene Lefaucheux had been most impressed with the Belgian-made copies of the Colt Model 1849 Pocket and Model 1851 Belt revolvers being produced there. Doubtless his exposure to the London Exhibition, combined with his later studies of and experiments with various firearms types, had created the new idea of adapting the pinfire cartridge to a military revolver. As heavy-frame, large-caliber percussion revolvers were then becoming popular in military circles, and possessing the ammunition to make a metallic cartridge military revolver a reality, Lefaucheux proceeded to design a revolver that would be one of the most widely-used military sidearms in Europe for the next several decades.

The project was completed sufficiently to apply for French patent rights on April 15, 1854, and the fifteen-year protection of his French patent was officially granted on June 10, 1854 as patent number 19380.[2] The intent of the original patent was to protect the *idea* of a breechloading revolver more than to illustrate one of his own, specific designs. In the text of patent number 19380 Lefaucheux described the various mechanical functions of a revolver chambered for the "Lefaucheux" cartridge, by furthering the idea of his father's patent number 1371 of 1845. The latter described a cartridge handgun with a revolving barrel group (pepperbox). What follows is an English translation of Eugene's French patent application:

The name of Lefaucheux is attached to several ingenious arrangements or important betterments brought to the making of firearms.

In 1846, my now deceased father devised, among other things, a particular mechanism allowing the loading of pistols and multi-barreled rifles without having to take them to pieces, and proposed to apply to it [the mechanism] a particular cartridge carrying its bullet, its powder and its fulminant percussion-cap. Since then, this type of multifiring fire-arm has been perfected by several people and one seems to definitely adopt this single barreled system but at multiple loads, whose handling leaves nevertheless a lot to be desired from the loading point of view since one must always load from the opening of the cylinder with powder, wads, separate bullets and percussion-caps.

This inconvenience is probably redeemed by other qualities, but, if, while keeping the latter one could remove the inconvenience, there is no doubt that such an improvement would be important in terms of manufacturing, and commercially speaking.

I have obtained this result. I have obtained it through simple and safe methods....

I propose therefore to load multiple discharge fire-arms that function by rotating with

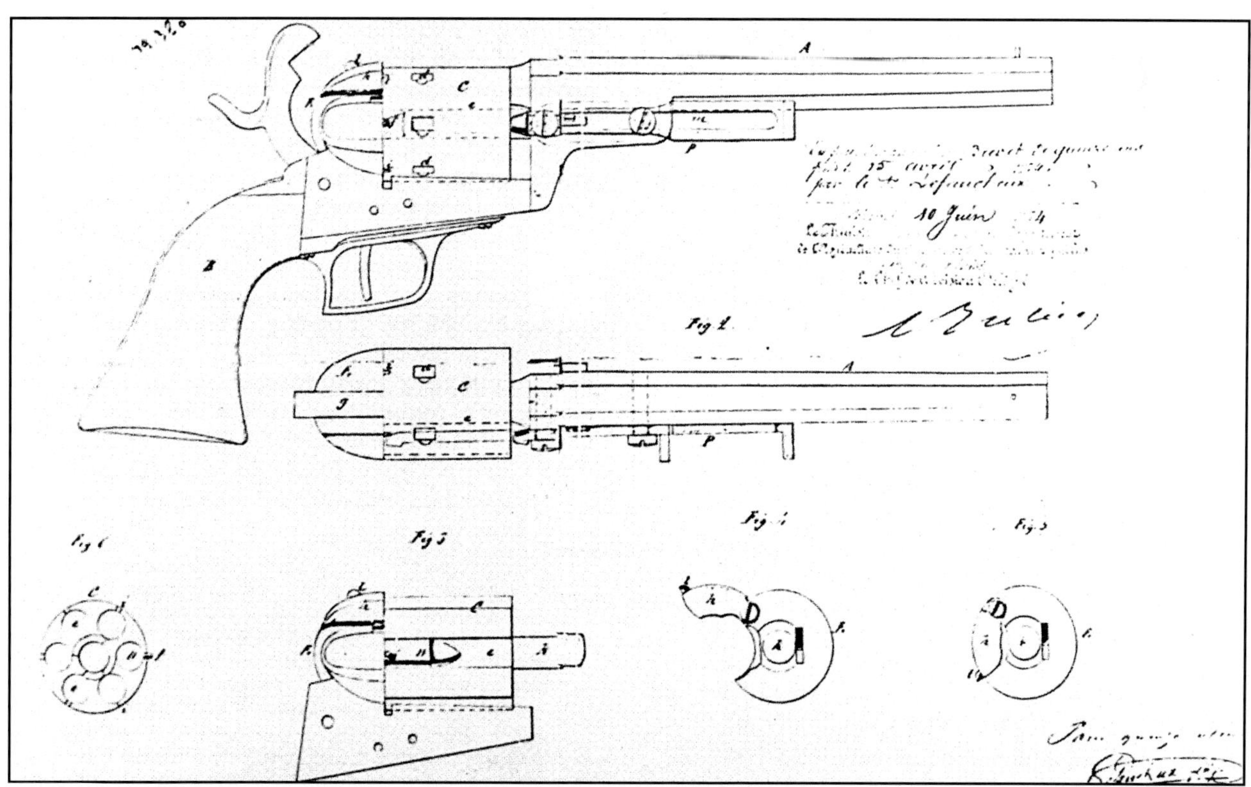

Plate 2-2. Drawings from Eugene Lefaucheux' French patent number 19380, of June 10, 1854, for converting percussion arms to the pinfire cartridge system. Note ejector rod on side of the barrel lug. *Chris C. Curtis collection*

complete cartridges, Lefaucheux cartridges, by operating successfully for each discharge, without having to use a ramrod.

This arrangment goes with the use of a fixed breech and an additional mechanism, to extract the metallic cartridge if there were difficulties to get it out after discharge.

To give a visual idea of these improvments I am adding to this memoire *a drawing which represents them applied to a six-shot pistol with a lone fixed barrel and a mobile cylinder, without nipple for percussion cap or ramrod.*

While the Colt name is never mentioned, the patent drawing (*see Plate 2-2*) clearly shows the familiar Colt Model 1851 Navy percussion revolver having the Lefaucheux-patented modifications present. All design improvements described are illustrated, including the side-mounted ejector rod. This first ejector rod was a flat metal piece sliding on two screws in the center of a channel. The revolver illustrated in the patent drawing never was manufactured, as Eugene Lefaucheux had already designed a newer model to be constructed as a cartridge revolver, rather than an existing model being converted to one. However, the patent sucessfully prevented Lefaucheux' competitors from converting percussion revolvers to fire pinfire cartridges during the time he was adding the final details to the revolver he intended to manufacture.

Just twelve days after the registration of his French patent, the new revolver's patent drawings and descriptions were registered in England. There, the configuration of the now-familiar Lefaucheux Model 1854 revolver was illustrated. For it, Lefaucheux secured protection in England under patent number 955 of April 27, 1854, sealed June 27, 1854. This patent, which expired in 1861, was granted to John Henry Johnson, a British

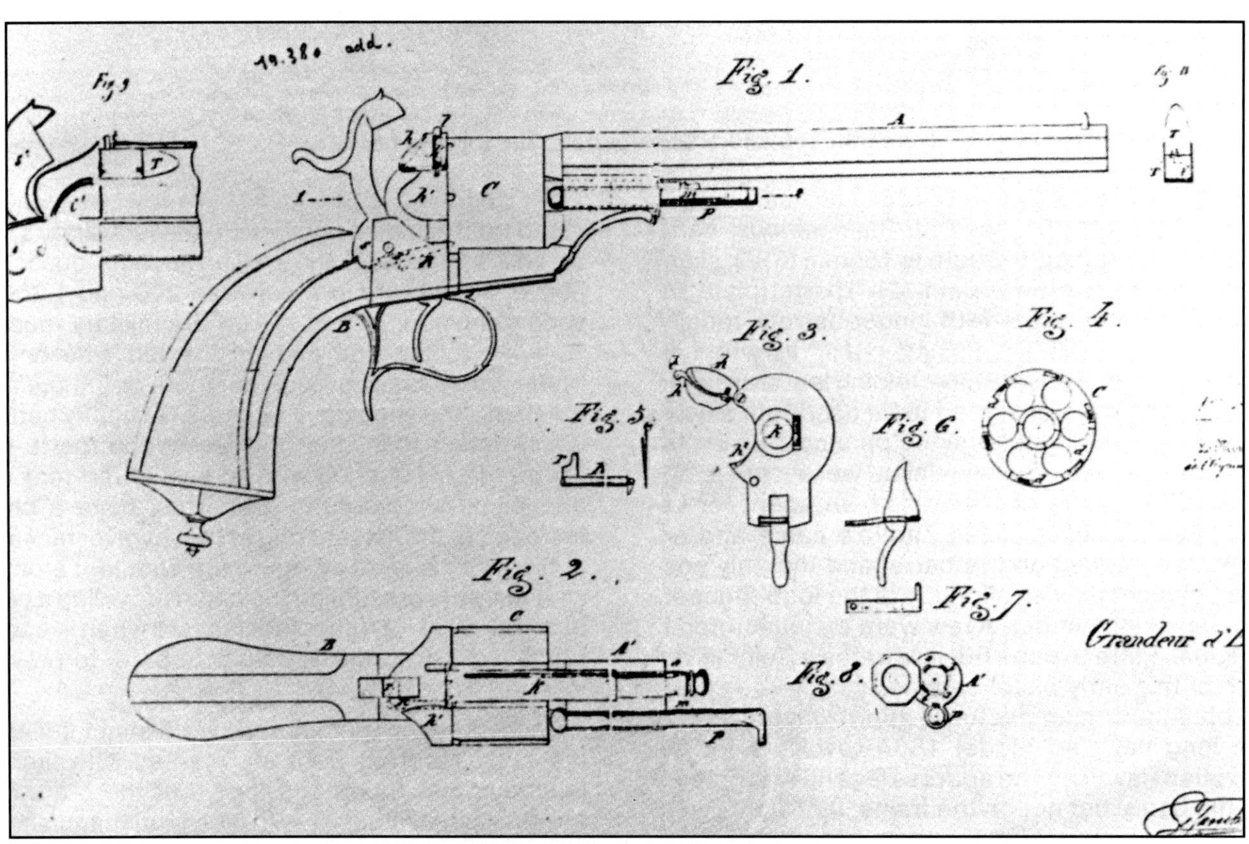

Plate 2-3. Drawings from first certificate of addition to patent number 19380, for the Model 1854 revolver. Note bored-through cylinder and side loading gate. *Chris C. Curtis collection*

patent agent acting on behalf of Eugene Lefaucheux. Johnson also registered British patents for several other continental inventors; most notable among them are A.E. Jarre's number 2002, of 1871, and P. Mauser's number 922, of 1878.

It was English patent number 955 that discouraged American firearms inventor Rollin White from seeking protection under British law a year later. It is most interesting to speculate on the transformation in the development of American cartridge guns that would have taken place, had Lefaucheux patented his new revolver in the United States at the same time he did in France and England. The stranglehold on the American manufacture of all rear-loading, bored-through cylinder, metallic cartridge revolvers would have been controlled by Eugene Lefaucheux, rather than by Smith & Wesson, who for that purpose employed the Rollin White patent protection from 1855 to 1869. White's U.S. patent number 12649 was dated April 3, 1855; he reached an agreement with Daniel B. Wesson and Horace Smith on November 17, 1856, and production by Smith & Wesson of a cartridge revolver began very late in 1857. By that time, Lefaucheux had not only produced a significant number of his Model 1854 revolvers for the civilian market, but examples of his new arm had been tested and adopted by the French Navy and were even briefly considered by the U.S. Ordnance Department.

The design of Lefaucheux' ejector rod was much improved in the 1854 British patent, being round with a small blade spring built into the shaft to prevent the rod from accidently sliding back into a cylinder chamber and blocking rotation. The rod was housed in an opening milled for it in the frame forward of the cylinder.

Eugene Lefaucheux was granted a certificate of additition to patent number 19380 on November 9, 1854. It was here that he first illustrated, in France, the Model 1854 revolver (*see Plate 2-3*). The integral leaf spring in the ejector rod was described again, as were several mechanical improvements involving internal springs. Another valuable improvement added, which is subsequently found on the majority of all conventionally-loaded pinfire revolvers, was the addition of a simple spring lock on the cartridge loading gate to hold it securely closed.

By the application of his father's pinfire cartridge to a rotating, bored-through cylinder revolver, Eugene Lefaucheux created a completely new genre of hand firearms. The hinged loading gate and movable rod to eject spent cartridges added to the overall advantage enjoyed by this revolver over those of the cap-and-ball percussion type. Its rapidity of loading, the ability to remove unfired cartridges without damaging them, and the general reliability and accuracy of the arm, all placed into the hands of the firearms novice a weapon that could be used effectively though he might lack experience with such a weapon. Certainly the same was not the case with existing revolver designs, most notably the Colt and Adams.

Given the aforementioned advantages, the

Plate 2-4. Detail view of right side of the frame of a Model 1854 revolver, showing logo stamping and serial number. *Chris C. Curtis collection; Gene P. Smith photograph*

popularity, use, and numbers of the new Lefaucheux arm spread rapidly and before long it enjoyed a global reputation. With his so-called "Model 1854" revolver Eugene Lefaucheux had successfully designed and produced the most advanced handgun in the world.

Lefaucheux manufactured the Model 1854 revolver for both civilian and open-market military

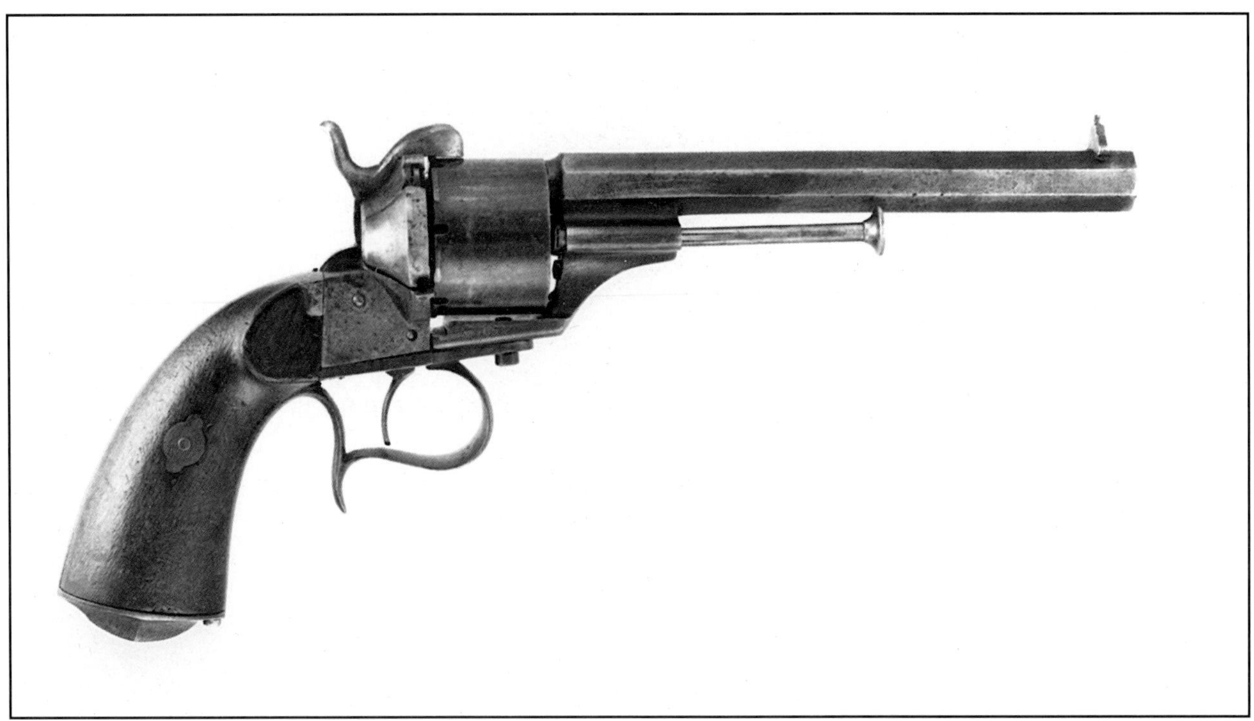

Plate 2-5. An early Lefaucheux Model 1854 pinfire revolver, serial number "1071." Note close similarity to patent drawings shown in *Plate 2-3. Chris C. Curtis collection; Richard McMillan photograph*

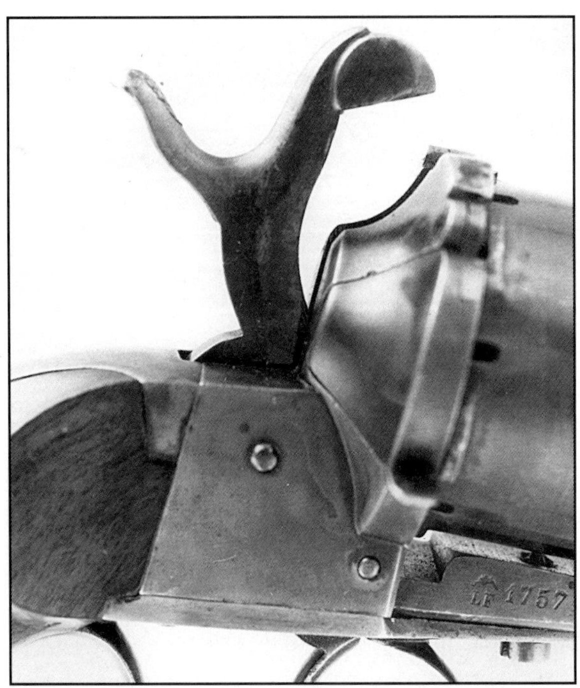

Plate 2-6. Detail view of right side recoil shield area of a revolver like the one pictured in *Plate 2-5*, showing early-style hammer and loading gate. *Chris C. Curtis collection; Richard McMillan photograph*

sales. The legend "*IVon E. Lefaucheux Bvte S.G.D.G. a Paris*" was applied to the top of the barrel, and the same wording often appears in an oval, usually located on the left side of the frame above the triggerguard. On some examples both markings are present; on others, either one or the other was used. On the right side of the frame, also above the triggerguard, the initials "*LF*" along with a small representation of a tip-down pistol open at the breech precede the serial number (*see Plate 2-4*); such markings are consistently present on all Model 1854 revolvers manufactured by Lefaucheux in France. It is interesting to note that on the Model 1854, the first firearm designed and manufactured entirely by Eugene, he was careful to add his first initial to the barrel legend, thus distinguishing his products from those made earlier by his father who had used only the Lefaucheux name.

Plate 2-7. A later-production Lefaucheux Model 1854 pinfire revolver, serial number "1757." Note part-round, part-octagonal barrel. *Chris C. Curtis collection; Richard McMillan photograph*

Eugene continued the practice throughout his gun-making career and, like the Model 1854, all other arms manufactured by him bear the initial "*E*" pre-ceding the name. Other makers licensed by Lefau-cheux, as well as those merely acknowledging his patents, also used the "*E*" in their barrel markings.

Plate 2-5 illustrates an early example of the Lefaucheux Model 1854 revolver. Note how close-ly the lines and contours of this piece match those of the patent drawing shown as *Plate 2-3*; the more graceful curve of the frame ahead of the trigger-guard is apparent, as is the full-length octagonal barrel. At the bottom of *Plate 2-3* the drawing marked "Figure 2" shows a top view of the revolver, and its scalloped loading gate and stand-ing breech are evident (*see Plate 2-6*). This difficult manufacturing practice was discontinued early on, after just over 2,000 such examples had been

Plate 2-8. Detail view of right side recoil shield area of a later-production revolver, showing new styles of hammer and loading gate. *Chris C. Curtis collection; Richard McMillan photograph*

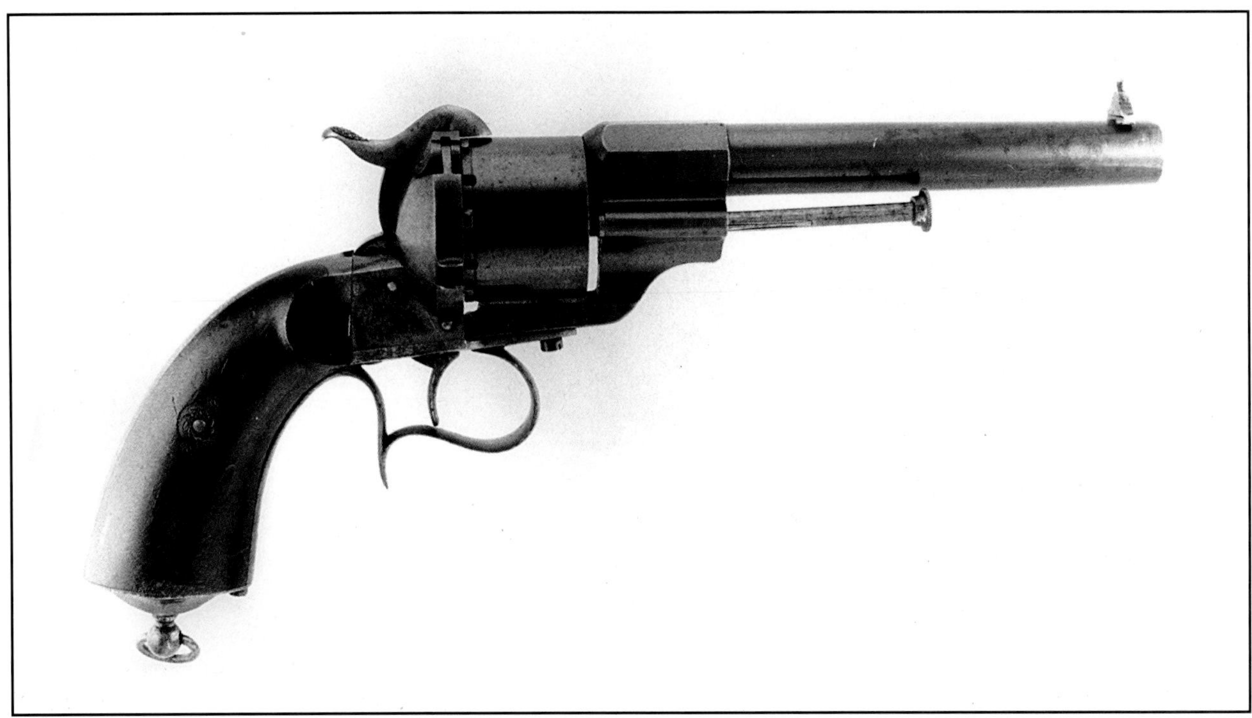

Plate 2-9. A standard Lefaucheux Model 1854 pinfire revolver in 12mm caliber, serial number "32770." Note spur on triggerguard; this type is known as the "Cavalry Model." *Chris C. Curtis collection; Richard McMillan photograph*

made. The revolver pictured in *Plate 2-5* bears the serial number "1071." While the full-octagon barrel was discontinued at about serial number 1100, as will be seen as we proceed further into our study of the pinfire system, there are variations and exceptions to each rule, and examples bearing higher serial numbers have been noted having full-length octagonal barrels.

Plate 2-7 illustrates an example of a Model 1854 revolver from later manufacture. The graceful lines of the frame, the contoured loading gate and standing breech, and the early-style hammer are still evident; the revolver has standard Lefaucheux markings, and bears serial number "1757." Also in evidence is a new-style barrel that has an octagonal section ahead of the cylinder and is round for the remainder of its length. Although it may appear to have been more difficult to machine and finish, the new barrel actually was less costly to manufacture, saved a bit of weight, and is seen on all Model 1854 revolvers from this serial range on but for a few exceptions as previously mentioned.

The early-style hammer, rarely seen after serial number 5000, also was gradually replaced by one that was easier to produce. *Plate 2-8* illustrates this new-style hammer, along with a new-style loading gate (the early, contoured loading gate is rarely encountered after serial number 2000). At about that same time a sturdier frame also was introduced. From approximately serial number 2000 on, the Lefaucheux Model 1854 revolver remained basically unchanged through the end of its production. Thus, the later style is the type most frequently encountered.

Plate 2-9 illustrates a Model 1854 revolver that is standard in all respects. Its barrel is 6 1/8 inches (155mm) long, and bears serial number "32770"; it is chambered for the standard 12mm (.472 inch) cartridge. (A very few Model 1854 revolvers were chambered in 9mm caliber, but

Plate 2-10. A Lefaucheux civilian Model 1854 pinfire revolver in 12mm caliber, serial number "111070." Note oval triggerguard; this type is known as the "Navy Model." *Chris C. Curtis collection; Richard McMillan photograph*

they are extremely scarce.)

Lefaucheux manufactured two basic, yet distinct, styles of the Model 1854 revolver. Both are marked with the Lefaucheux logo and address line, yet certain features allow one to easily distinguish between the two. The first, commonly known as the "Cavalry Model", is the standard style as shown in *Plate 2-9*. Among its identifying features are a projecting finger spur at the rear of the triggerguard, and a buttcap having a multi-contoured surface that lends an ornate and graceful appearance to the arm. The second type, usually referred to as the "Navy Model", is illustrated in *Plate 2-10*. It has an oval triggerguard and a slightly rounded, oval-shape buttcap. Both styles have military-style lanyard rings mounted on their buttcaps. "Cavalry" revolvers were not issued to and used solely by mounted units, nor were the "Navy"

revolvers issued to and used only by naval personnel. Rather, the terms are those given the respective types by collectors today.

Many variations are to be found within the Lefaucheux Cavalry and Navy style Model 1854 revolvers. Most differences occur in barrel length, but also will be seen in markings and frame contours. Occasionally an example will not have an ejector rod, but nearly all of these variations represent relatively limited production military contract specifications for various foreign governments. All known military types are illustrated and described in the following chapter.

Like Colt, and later Winchester, Lefaucheux would manufacture almost anything given a customer's special order, and, of course, the additional money that such custom work demanded. Certainly one of the more interesting variant Model 1854 revolvers examined for this study is shown in *Plate 2-11*. It has a 16-inch (406.4mm) barrel and is fitted with a detachable metal skeleton shoulder stock. Very few of this variation were made, and all have low serial numbers (below

1700). Strangely, all examples observed exhibit later production-style barrels, frames, and hammers, leading to the conclusion that these long-barrel "revolver-carbines" were numbered in a separate serial range outside of the regular Model 1854 production run. Within this variation barrel lengths have been noted from 13⅝ inches (346mm) up to the 16 inches (406.4mm), but all have folding leaf rear sights and are .472 (12mm) caliber. One example is housed in a French style (recessed) casing complete with loading and cleaning tools. Both the revolver's barrel and the inside lid of its case are marked with the legend, *"Zaoue of Marseilles"*, who was a retail sales agent for Lefaucheux. The only Lefaucheux marking on the pistol is the company's logo preceding the serial number.

These revolver-carbines are quite rare and

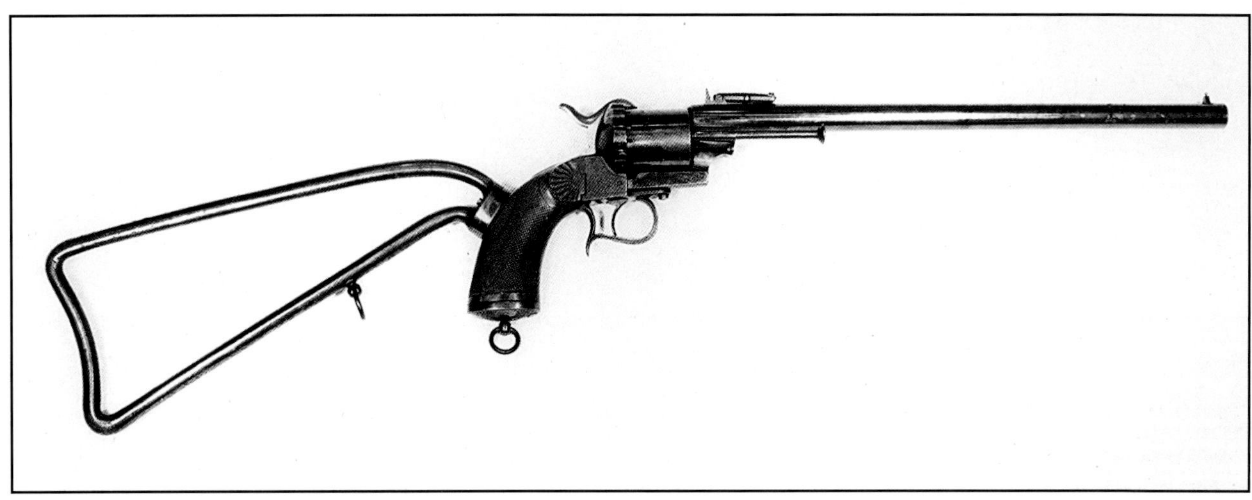

Plate 2-11 (above). A Lefaucheux Model 1854 pinfire "pistol-carbine" revolver fitted with scarce 16-inch barrel and detachable skeleton shoulder stock, serial number "1700." Note rear leaf sight. *Courtesy Museé d'Armes de Liége; Francis E. Niffle photograph*

Plate 2-12 (below). A Lefaucheux Model 1854, single-action pinfire revolving rifle in 12mm caliber. *Courtesy James Lowther; John Calcany photograph*

desirable today, as are the Lefaucheux revolving rifles manufactured on Eugene's same 1854 patent design. *Plate 2-12* illustrates a single-action revolving rifle in .472 (12mm) caliber. It is marked on top of the barrel, "*E. Lefaucheux Bvt a Paris.*" The underside of the barrel is fitted with a sling swivel, as is the buttstock. Note how closely the frame and cylinder of this rifle match those of the standard Model 1854 revolver. The rear sight is a groove cut into the top of the hammer, as on the pistol.

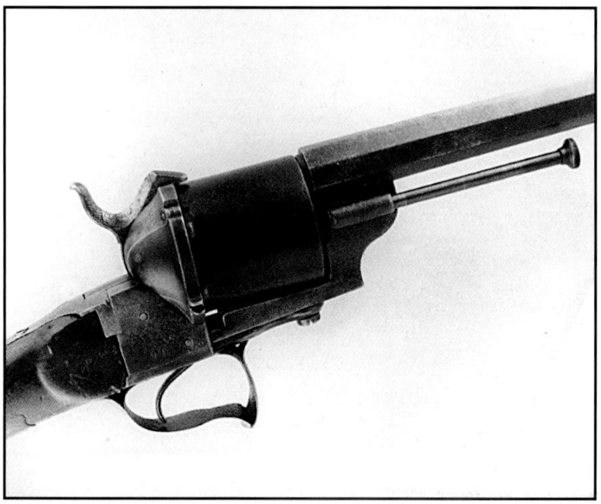

Plate 2-13. Detail view of another Lefaucheux Model 1854, single-action pinfire revolving rifle, serial number "158." 15mm caliber; large-size frame and cylinder; 24½-inch barrel. *Chris C. Curtis collection; Richard McMillan photograph*

Another example of a Lefaucheux revolving rifle is shown in *Plate 2-13.* This particular example was chambered for the huge 15mm (.59) caliber pinfire cartridge, and its frame and cylinder are correspondingly larger than the preceding piece, although it is only 42½ inches in overall length. The 24½-inch long barrel is marked "*E. Lefaucheux a Paris*" along with a short, crudely-etched inscription indicating Spanish ownership at one time; the frame has the familiar Lefaucheux logo preceding the serial number, "158." Revolving rifles chambered for this cartridge are considered very rare among today's collectors.

Early in the production of the Model 1854 revolver, Lefaucheux briefly experimented with the concept of a larger, "Dragoon"-size revolver based on the Navy-style 12mm caliber guns previously discussed. The single specimen available for this study was of typical Lefaucheux quality, well made and finished; its serial number is in the 3800 range, and the arm bears full Lefaucheux markings. While the overall length of the larger revolver is approximately 35mm to 40mm longer than the standard Model 1854, its weight is well over double, at a hefty 2300 grams. With such a significant increase in both size and weight, it seems reasonable that the idea behind the larger revolver would have been to chamber it for a longer, larger caliber round such as the 15mm pinfire cartridge. Curiously, however, it is 12mm caliber, the same as most standard Model 1854 revolvers. Recalling the accolades showered on Samuel Colt's .44 caliber percussion Dragoon model revolver at the 1851 London Exhibition, perhaps Eugene Lefaucheux was considering the addition of a "Dragoon" model to his expanding line of firearms. As with the large Colt, the additional size and weight would allow for a much larger powder charge and bullet to be used safely. Despite its advantages, Lefaucheux apparently abandoned the idea of a Dragoon revolver early-on, as today surviving examples are very rare.

Eugene Lefaucheux, like his father before him, used the French patent laws and their certificates of addition framework to his fullest benefit. Neither father nor son ever illustrated or described just a single idea or product, but instead utilized the medium to present several related ideas together. In addition to his many improvements to firearms components, Eugene also illustrated his improvements to the design of a centerfire cartridge, following his father's initial efforts of more than a decade earlier. Also shown in Eugene's second certificate of addition to patent number 19380, of May 12, 1855 (*see Plate 2-14*), is Lefaucheux' first venture into a double-action mechanism for a military-type revolver. A final addition was granted in April of 1860, the design of which reverted back to the single-action mechanism of the basic Model 1854 revolver, but with improvements to the cylinder that allowed it to swing laterally out of the frame for loading and cartridge ejection (*see Plate 2-15*).

Another French patent, number 29055, was granted to Lefaucheux on September 5, 1856 (*see Plate 2-16*). This patent drawing illustrates several improvements to firearms, but perhaps its most significant features are the interchangeable percussion and pinfire cartridge cylinders. The hammer on the revolver illustrated was designed to strike either the pins protruding from the cartridge cylinder or the capped vertical nipples of the percussion cylinder; thus the more traditional percussion system could be used if pinfire cartridges were unavailable. *Plate 2-17* illustrates a fine example of Lefaucheux' dual-ignition revolver, although the gun shown is of slightly later design.

With his original 1854 patent (number 19380) covering the method of converting percussion revolvers to fire pinfire metallic cartridges, and with the first addition to that patent covering the basic design for a pinfire cartridge revolver (the Model 1854), Eugene Lefaucheux now had adequately protected his ideas for a revolver to fire self-contained metallic ammunition. The later 1856 patent (number 29055) provided a workable combination of both the percussion and pinfire systems.

Lefaucheux' efforts did not go unnoticed. Again following in his father's footsteps, he was recognized by the world arms community as a firearms designer, innovator, and inventor of true merit. In 1855, at the age of twenty-two, he was awarded a medal of honor at the prestigious International Arms Exhibition held in Paris, for his refinements to the pinfire ignition system. Now firmly established, Eugene's reputation was additionally elevated when the French Navy chose the Lefaucheux Model 1854 revolver for testing and final adoption, which came in October of 1857. In addition to the small royalty received from the manufacture of each pistol for the Navy, under his agreement with the French government Lefaucheux retained the right to manufacture and sell his

revolver in both the civilian and open-market foreign military areas.

Despite the obvious success of his arms business, Eugene continued to experiment with improvements in firearms design and manufacture. On December 5, 1859 he was granted French patent number 24524, with subsequent additions being added on February 7th and 20th of 1860 (*see Plate 2-18*). A single-barrel rifle is shown, but as Eugene carefully worded his text,

> *The said invention relates to certain particular constructions and arrangements of muskets, fowling pieces, rifles and other fire-arms of that class, whether single or double barreled.*

Later he would describe and illustrate a pistol designed on this same principle. The frame, stock extensions, and butt are made in the form of a single metal skeleton, into which the lock and barrel are fitted and to which a two-piece wooden stock is added. This design provided for a lightweight yet rigid and sturdy carbine that was easy and inexpensive to manufacture. The fixed-barrel rifle, with its hinged breech and hammer which rotate on the same axis (*see Plate 2-21*) constituted an arm that, although single-shot, could be loaded and fired with rapidity and economy of motion. A single movement of the right-side lever up and back not only opens the breech, but moves the hammer rearward into the cocked position. With the breech thus open a cartridge can be inserted into the chamber; the lever is then moved forward and down to close and seal the breech while the hammer remains cocked until trigger pressure releases it for firing. To remove an unfired cartridge the lever is again raised up and back, and the force of gravity easily slides the cartridge out of the chamber on elevating the muzzle. For unloading a fired round, in the event that the brass cartridge case has expanded on discharge, a second lever placed on the left side of the frame is fitted with a small collar having a slot corresponding with the pin on the cartridge. Lifting the lever places slight upward pressure on the rear of the case, which is sufficient to effectively dislodge the

text continued on page 50

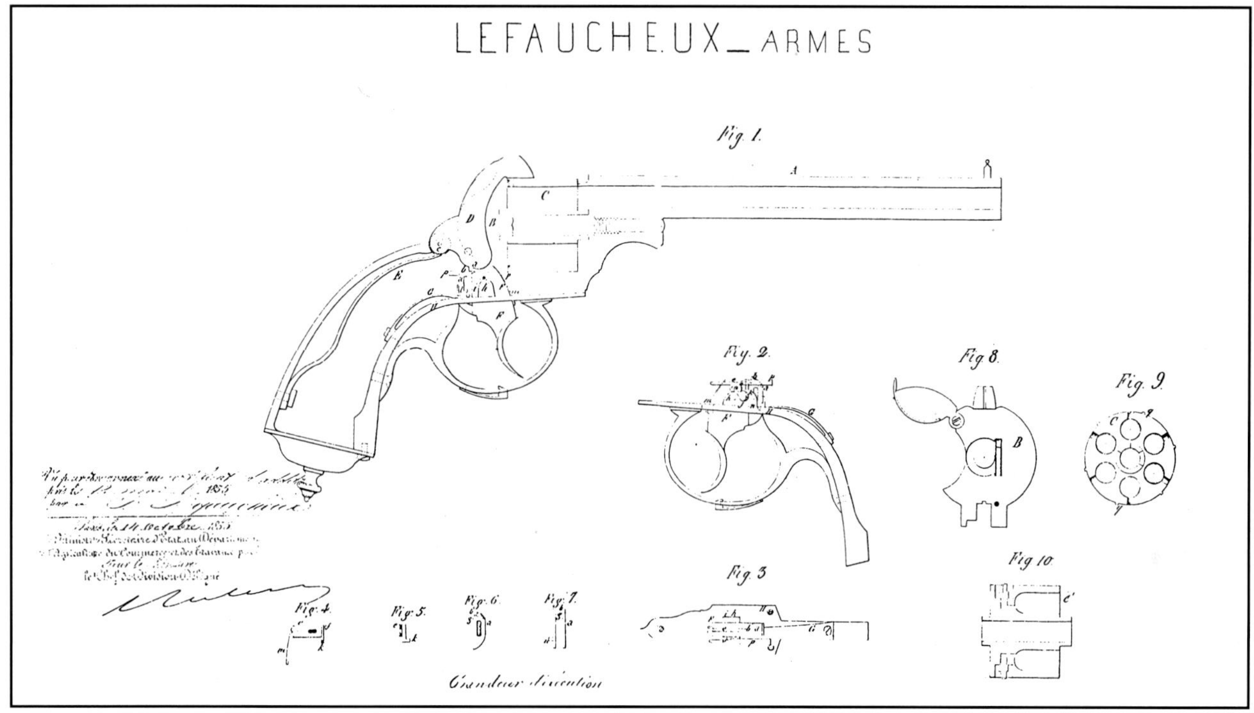

Plate 2-14. Drawings from the second certificate of addition to French patent number 19380, for a double-action, military-style revolver. *Chris C. Curtis collection*

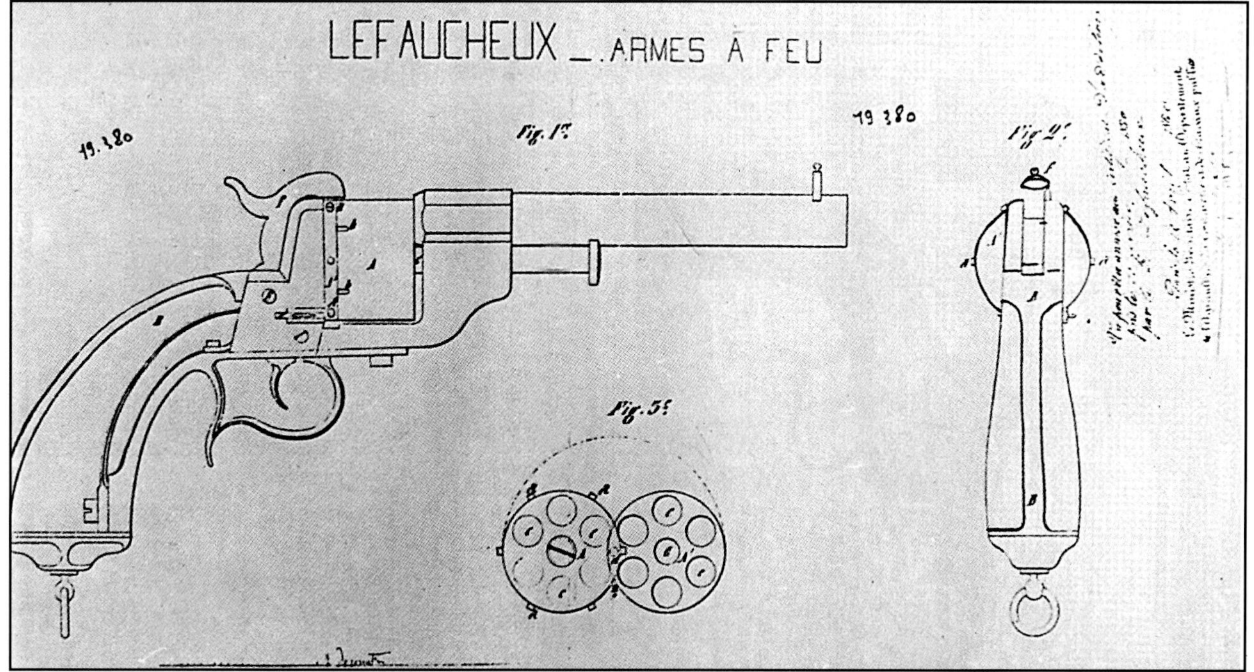

Plate 2-15. The final certificate of addition to French patent number 19380, granted in April of 1860. The basic Model 1854 revolver is illustrated, having improvements to the cylinder stops and chambers. Frame and cylinder were redesigned to allow cylinder to swing to side for loading or cartridge ejection after withdrawing cylinder pin, which doubles as an ejector rod. Swivel backplate with stops was added to cylinder. No example of this model is known. *Chris C. Curtis collection*

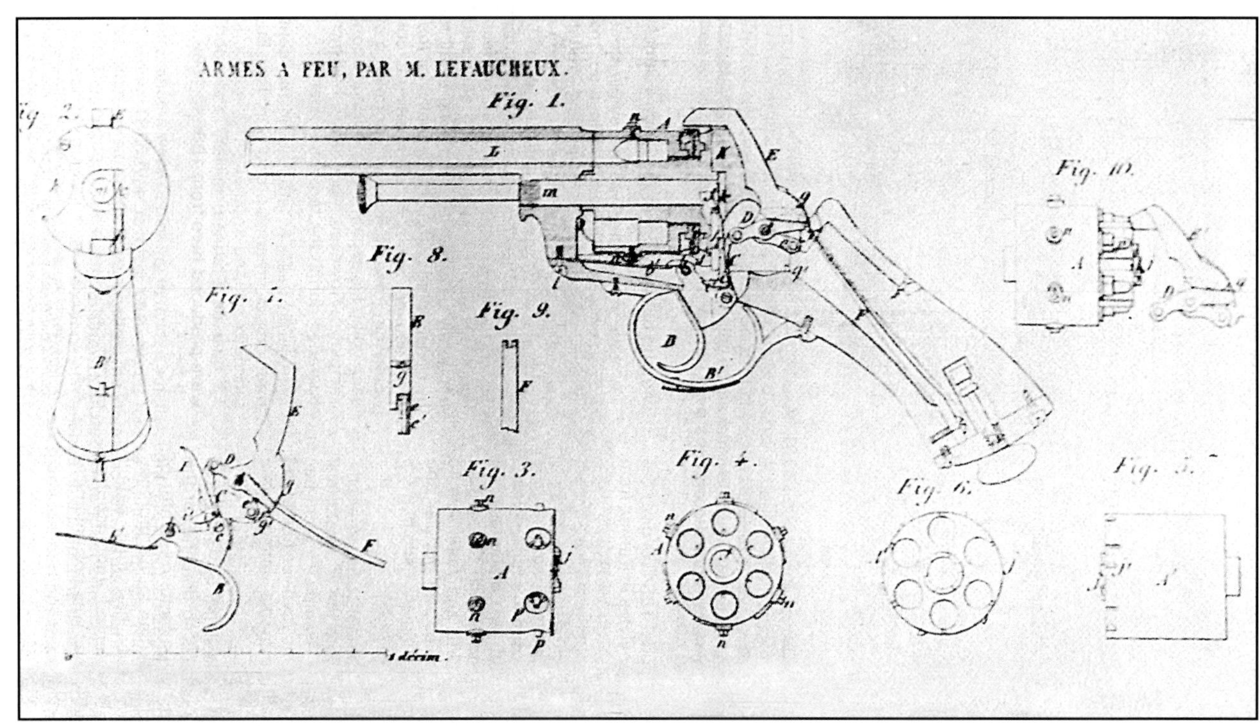

Plate 2-16. Drawings from Eugene Lefaucheux' French patent number 29055, of September 5, 1856, for another military-style, double-action revolver utilizing percussion-pinfire dual-ignition cylinders. Also included are other general improvements in firearms. *Chris C. Curtis collection*

Plate 2-17. An ornate example of the dual-ignition, double-action Lefaucheux revolver illustrated in the patent drawings shown in *Plate 2-16.* Barrel marked "*E. Lefaucheux Bte a Paris*"; the oval marking on the left side of the frame reads, "*Inv. Lefaucheux Brvt S.G.D.G. Paris.*" Serial number in the 4200 range; deluxe casing with spare percussion cylinder and accoutrements. *Courtesy George Wagoner*

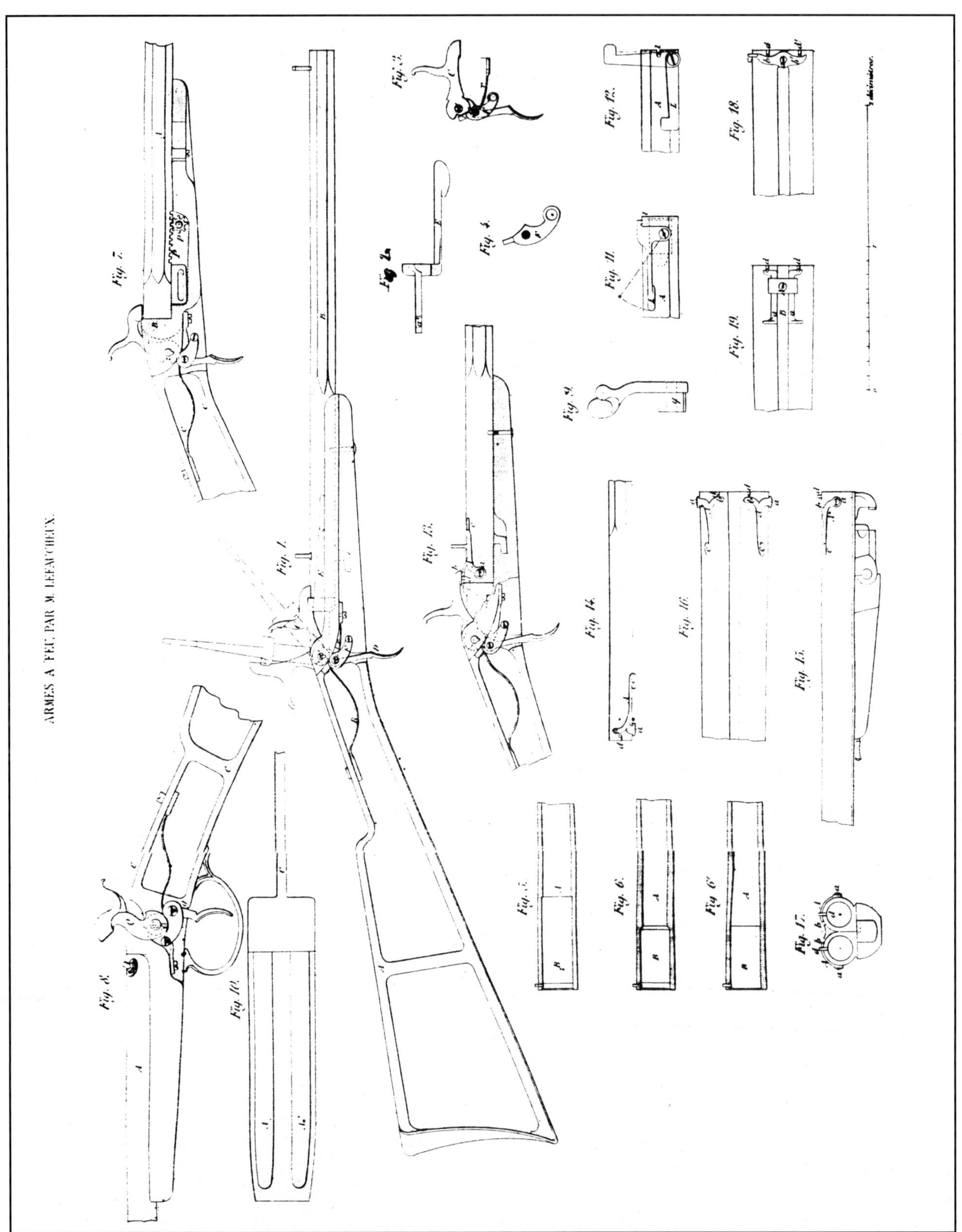

Plate 2-18. Drawings from Eugene Lefaucheux' French patent number 24524, of December 5, 1859, for metal skeleton-frame arms. Shown is a single-shot, breechloading pinfire carbine. *Chris C. Curtis collection*

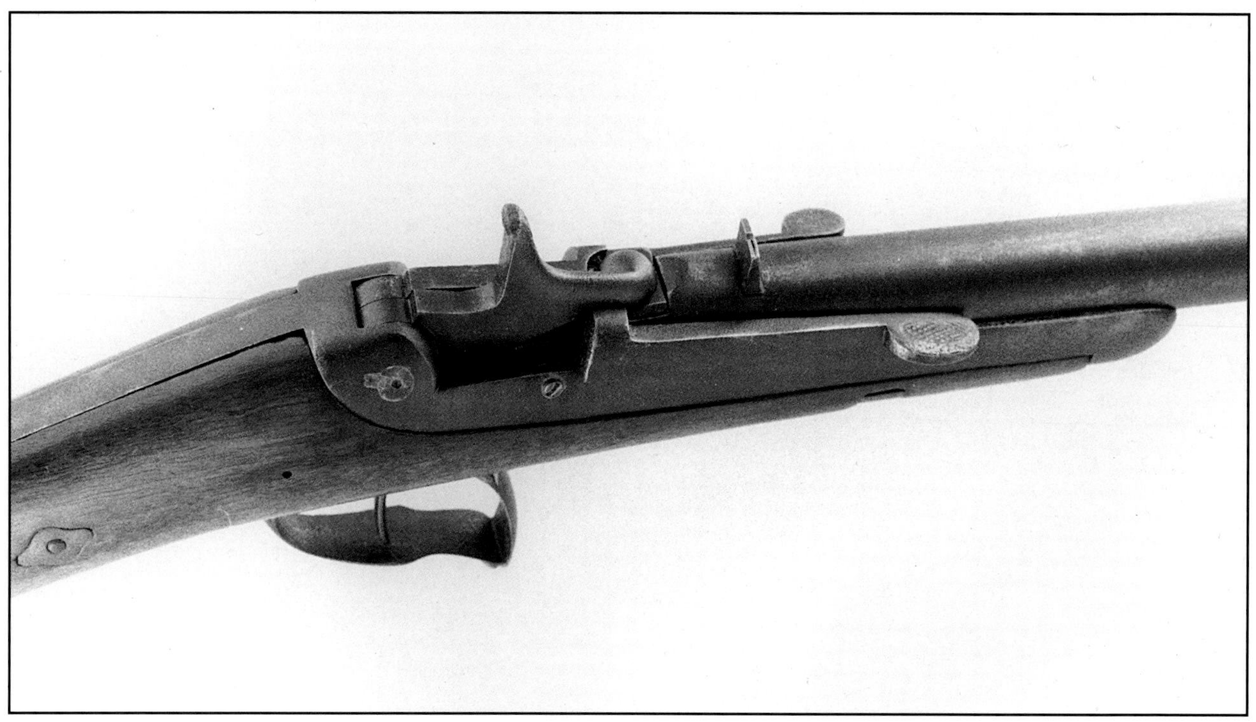

Plate 2-19. Detail view of the carbine illustrated in the patent drawings in *Plate 2-18,* showing cocking and ejection side levers of the breechloading 12mm caliber pinfire action. *Chris C. Curtis collection; Richard McMillan photograph*

spent casing. *See Plate 2-19* for the construction of these two side levers and their positions in relation to the hammer; *Plates 2-20 and 2-21* illustrate the construction and general features of this firearm. The rifle shown is chambered for the 12mm caliber pinfire cartridge, and is completely unmarked except for a single Liége proofmark.

At some later time during the production of the single-shot rifle model, the design and construction of the mechanism were altered and simplified to improve the cocking lever-ejection lever system, as shown in *Plate 2-22.* Here the hammer is located farther back on the frame, having been lengthened to compensate for its different positioning. The external extraction lever is eliminated, being replaced by internal components which are connected to the single (cocking) lever within milled openings in the frame. Thus, the two sepa-

rate functions of opening the breech while cocking the hammer, and manually raising the extraction lever to remove a fired cartridge, are combined into a single movement. Lifting the cocking lever and hammer to the half-cock position still opens the breech, as before, but continuing the upward motion of the lever to the full-cock position activates a collar at the breech opening to eject a spent cartridge. This simple economy of motion greatly reduced the amount of time needed to load and fire the weapon. Like the previous rifle, the rifle pictured in *Plate 2-22* also is chambered for the 12mm pinfire cartridge, and has both the Lefaucheux legend, "*E. Lefaucheux Bte a Paris*" on the barrel and the oval-style "*INVn E. Lefaucheux Brevete S.G.D.G. Paris*" on the frame. An unusual third marking is found on this particular rifle that is not found on previous Lefaucheux models: the letters "*ELF.*" surmounted by a small revolver (*see Plate 2-23*), stamped on the cocking lever.

Plate 2-24 illustrates a single-shot, 7mm caliber pinfire pistol manufactured to the same patent specifications. The curved hammer with its offset

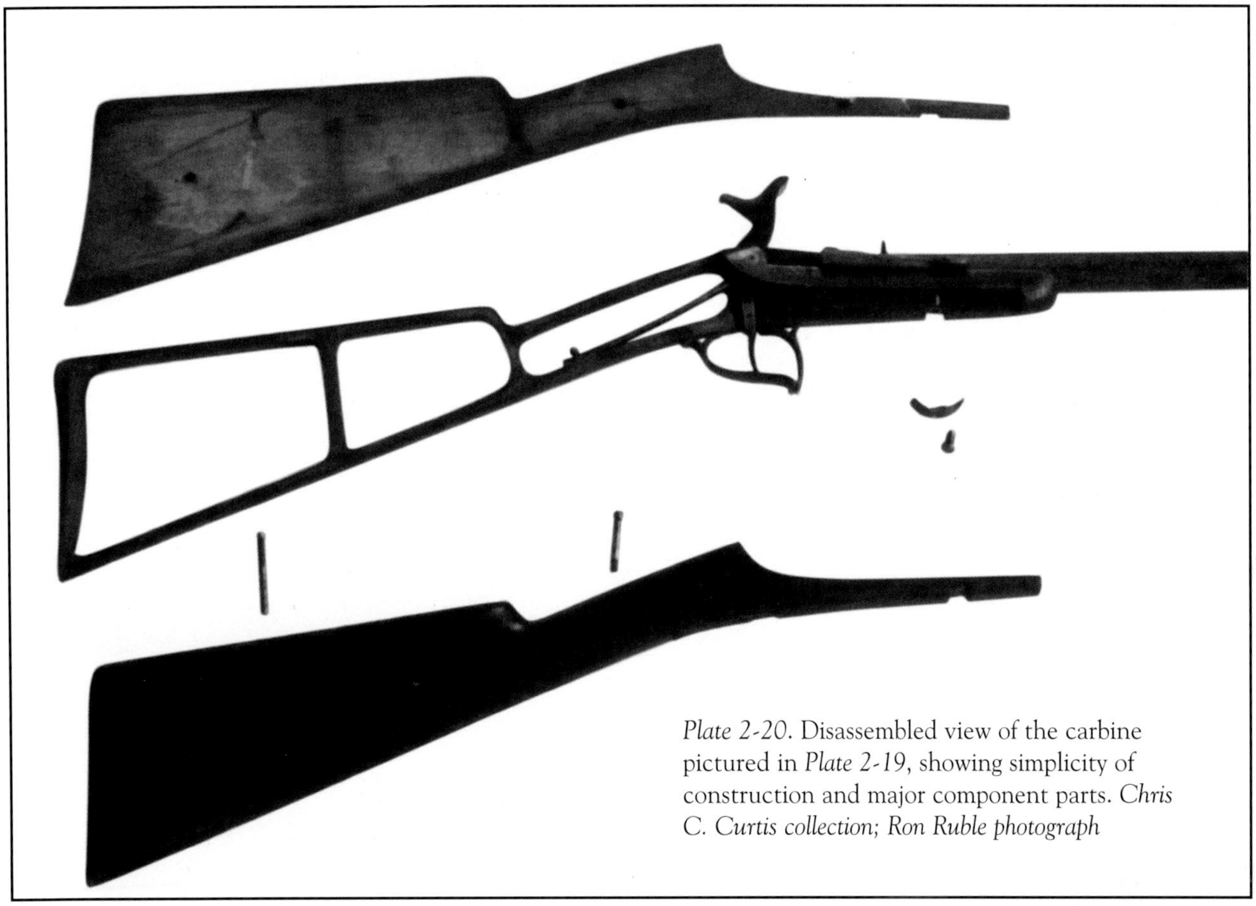

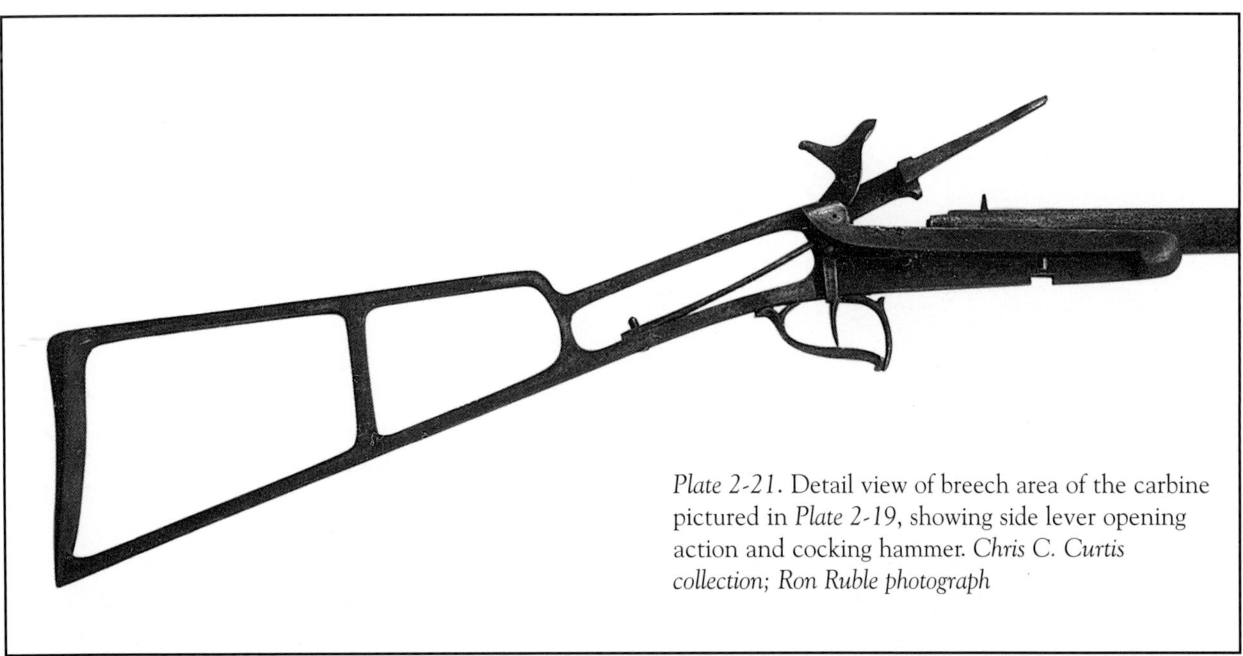

Plate 2-20. Disassembled view of the carbine pictured in *Plate 2-19*, showing simplicity of construction and major component parts. *Chris C. Curtis collection; Ron Ruble photograph*

Plate 2-21. Detail view of breech area of the carbine pictured in *Plate 2-19*, showing side lever opening action and cocking hammer. *Chris C. Curtis collection; Ron Ruble photograph*

striker is the same type utilized on the two rifles just discussed (*see Plate 2-19*), as are the cocking and ejection levers. The major difference between this pistol and the rifles is the unusual hinged trigger on the pistol, which folds sideways into a recess in the underside of the frame (*see Plate 2-25*). The pistol bears serial number "13"; its octagonal barrel is marked "*E. Lefaucheux a Paris*"; "*Invur E. Lefaucheux Brevete Paris*" is stamped in an oval configuration on top of the cocking lever.

Other large, 12mm caliber pistols have been observed which more closely resemble the drawings on the second page of the 1859 patent papers. The same patent was registered in the United States on March 26, 1861, and is the only patent found to have been granted to Eugene Lefaucheux in America (*see* Chapter Four for further discussion of this document). Doubtless the inventor, like many European men of commerce, was anticipating military orders for his arms in the upcoming American Civil War, and thus wanted to protect his new breechloading design against Yankee infringement.

In France Eugene Lefaucheux had ample patent protection for his double-action revolver designs, covered as they were by the second certificate of addition (of May 12, 1855) to patent number 19380 (of November 9, 1854), and by patent number 29055, of September 5, 1856 (*see Plates 2-14 and 2-16*). An interesting example of a Lefaucheux-made, double-action revolver is shown in *Plate 2-26*. It carries the usual Lefaucheux markings, and logo preceding the serial number "167." However, it is different from the earlier designs in that its cylinder has *ten* 12mm chambers. Lefaucheux produced very few arms of this type before the patent rights and manufacture of these large-capacity, single-ring cylinder style revolvers were assumed by J. Chaineux of Liége, Belgium.

Eugene Lefaucheux may have begun the man-

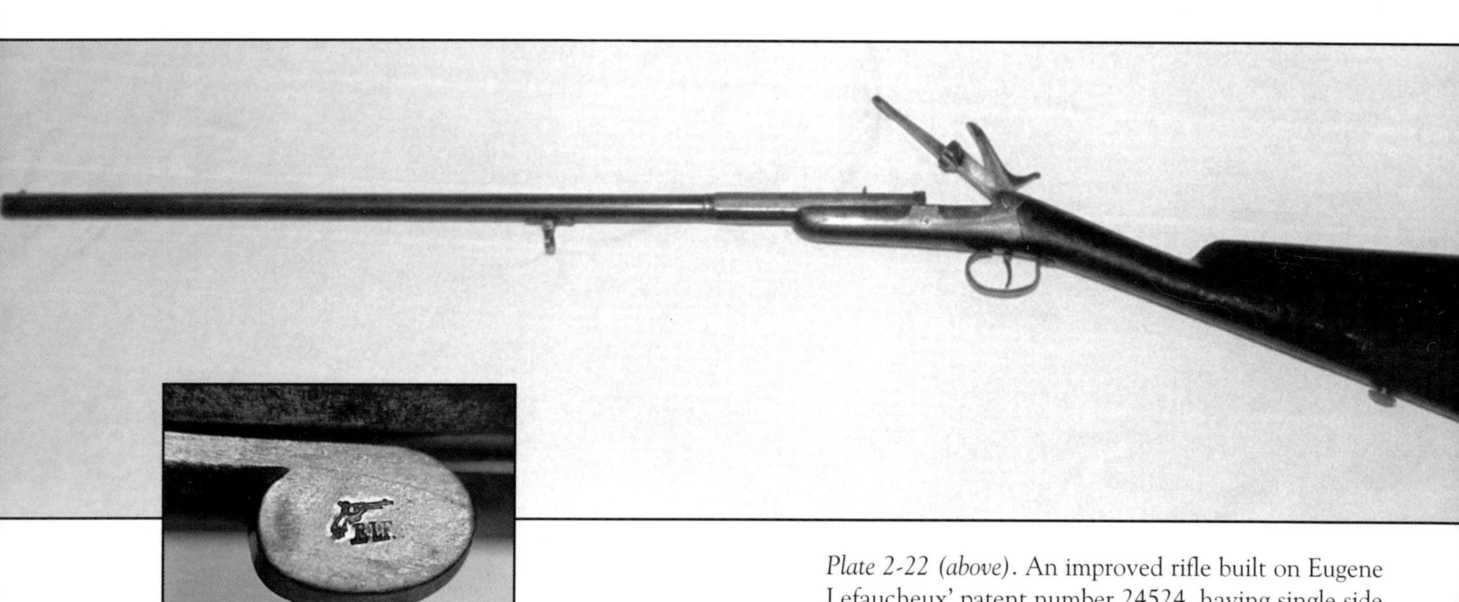

Plate 2-23 (inset). Detail view of single side lever of the improved rifle pictured in *Plate 2-22*, showing unusual "*revolver over ELF.*" marking. *Courtesy Larry Compeau; Mark Ingram photograph*

Plate 2-22 (above). An improved rifle built on Eugene Lefaucheux' patent number 24524, having single side lever for opening breech, cocking hammer, and cartridge ejection in one motion. Note the unusually long hammer striker. *Courtesy Larry Compeau; Mark Ingram photograph*

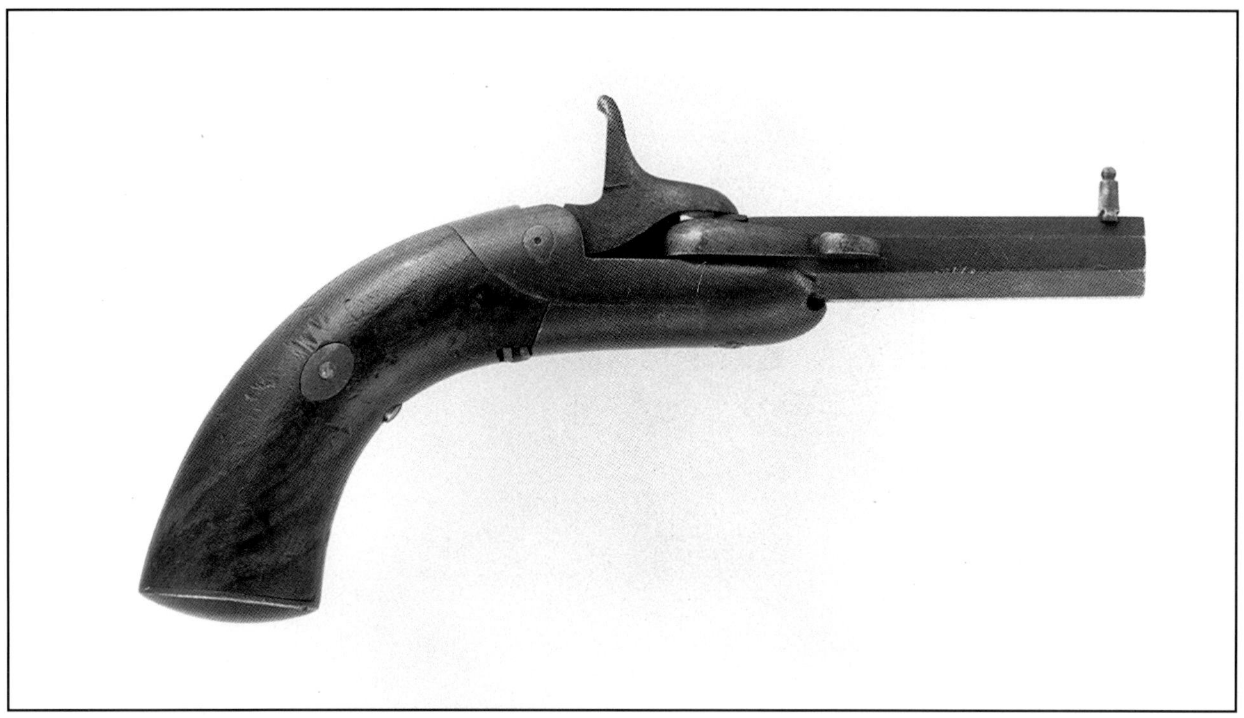

Plate 2-24. A single-shot, 7mm caliber pinfire pistol made on Eugene Lefaucheux' patent number 24524. Note side cocking lever and offset hammer. *Chris C. Curtis collection; Richard McMillan photograph*

ufacture of double-action arms in several different styles soon after his 1855 and 1856 patents were granted. But it was not until he had submitted application on September 27, 1862, and received the patent rights for French patent number 55784 on December 2, 1862, that we see illustrated the very familiar folding trigger (*see Plate 2-27*) that was to become a Lefaucheux trademark. In addition to its appearance on many Lefaucheux revolvers in the decades to come, the folding trigger was adopted by scores of other gunmakers who used it on countless styles and calibers of pinfire revolvers.

Following are illustrated several examples of Lefaucheux double-action pinfire revolvers. *Plate 2-28* depicts a 7mm caliber pistol which closely resembles the one shown in the 1862 patent drawing; it is deeply engraved with floral motifs, silver plated, and fitted with beautiful rosewood grips. Another highly-finished 7mm caliber example is shown in *Plate 2-29*. This particular piece bears Lefaucheux markings; the frame, cylinder, and octagonal barrel lug are acid-etched, the well-grained grips are carved and checkered, and it is cased in the French

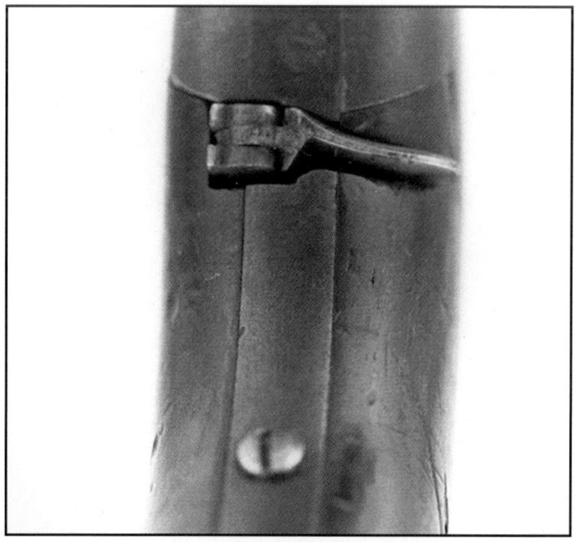

Plate 2-25. Detail view of side-folding trigger of the pistol shown in *Plate 2-24*. *Chris C. Curtis collection; Richard McMillan photograph*

Plate 2-26. An unusual Lefaucheux 12mm caliber, double-action revolver, having ten-shot cylinder; serial number "167." *Chris C. Curtis collection; Richard McMillan photograph*

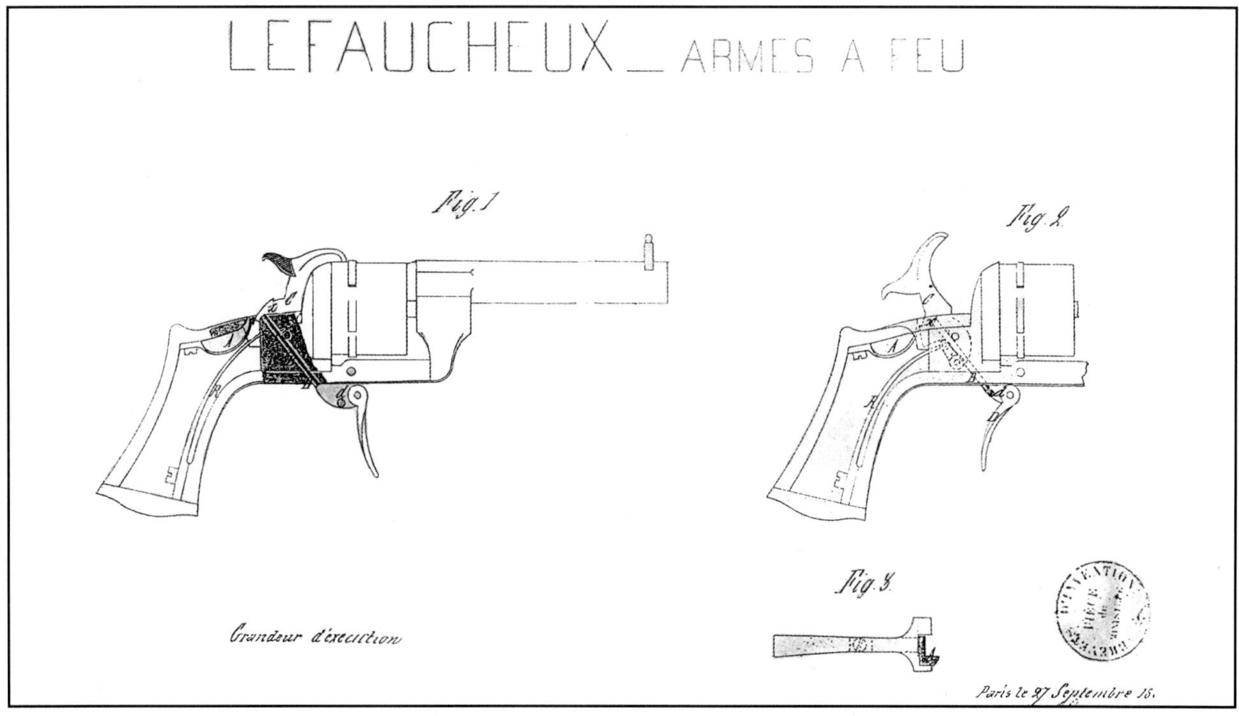

Plate 2-27. Drawings from Eugene Lefaucheux' French patent number 55784 of December 2, 1862, for what was to become a Lefaucheux trademark, the folding-trigger revolver. *Chris C. Curtis collection*

(recessed) style with all accoutrements. An even more ornate French-cased example in 9mm caliber is pictured in *Plate 2-30*. It too bears Lefaucheux markings, the frame and cylinder are scroll engraved, and the grips are relief-carved ebony wood, as are the handles of the numerous accessories. *Plate 2-31* shows another 7mm caliber example bearing Lefaucheux markings, including the oval logo stamp on the side of the trigger (*see Plate 2-32*). The frame, cylinder, barrel lug, and muzzle are acid-etched, and it is housed with several accessories and a tin of 7mm pinfire cartridges in an English-style (partition) casing.

cheux *Brevete S.G.D.G. Paris*", and was converted into a combination cutlass-pistol by Dumonthier of Paris, who had an arrangement with Lefaucheux and other armsmakers whereby he purchased pistols finished in all respects but without barrels. Dumonthier held a French patent for a knife blade bored through to form an integral barrel-blade assembly, which is marked "*Dumonthier Bte.*" The frame and cylinder of this cutlass-pistol are engraved, and it is chambered for the 7mm caliber pinfire cartridge. Of additional interest is the metal-mounted leather scabbard made by Dumonthier, that is fitted with an integral ejector rod.

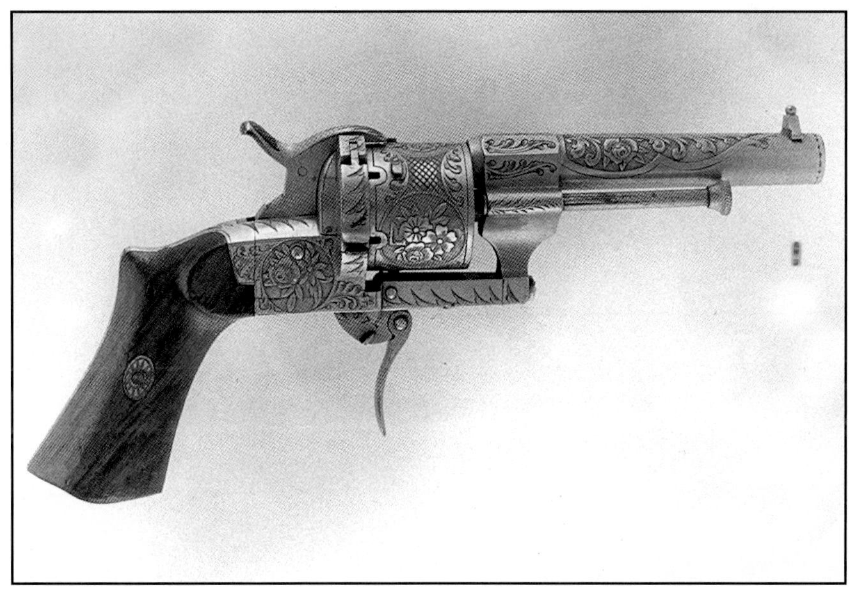

Plate 2-28. An ornate double-action, folding-trigger revolver made on Eugene Lefaucheux' patent number 55784. Engraved, silver plated, and fitted with rosewood grips; 7mm caliber pinfire. Chris C. Curtis collection; Richard McMillan photograph

Some of the subject revolvers have double-action mechanisms only, but variations such as those pictured in *Plates 2-28, 2-29, and 2-30* function either as single- or double-action arms. The revolver shown in *Plate 2-31* is nearly identical to the type illustrated in the 1864 catalog of famed New York military goods dealers, Schuyler, Hartley and Graham. Yet another fine example of the type is pictured in *Plate 2-33*.

Another variant of the Lefaucheux double-action, folding-trigger revolver is the example shown in *Plate 2-34*. It is marked "*Invon E. Lefau-*

Another somewhat different style of double-action, folding-trigger revolver was covered by Lefaucheux' 1862 patent, being larger and having a heavier frame and barrel assembly. Examples of this very sturdy arm most often are found in 9mm caliber pinfire, as is the example shown in *Plate 2-35*. It operates in both single- and double-action modes, and is unmarked except for an assembly number, which is unusual for a Lefaucheux-made gun. It might be an early production arm; perhaps even a prototype.

The similar example pictured in *Plate 2-36*

text continued on page 58

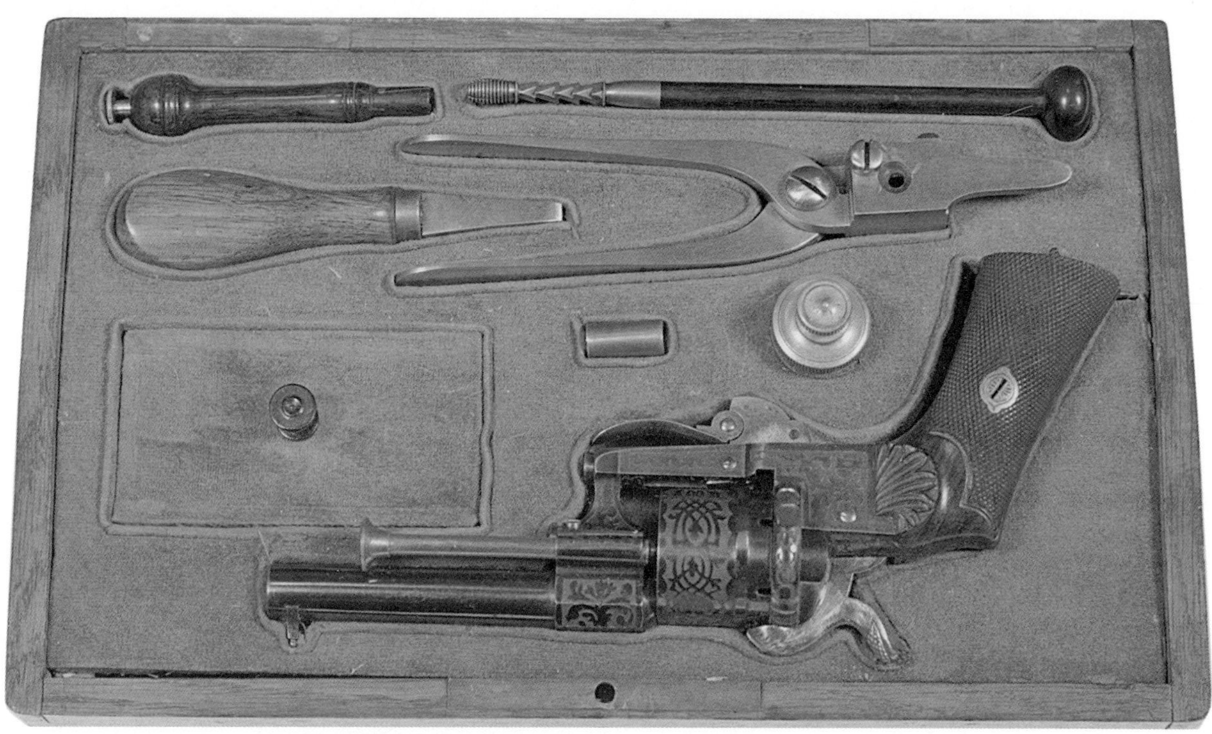

Plate 2-29. A beautifully finished Lefaucheux double-action, folding-trigger revolver, acid etched, having carved grips, and cased in the French style with accoutrements. *Courtesy James Lowther; John Calcany photograph*

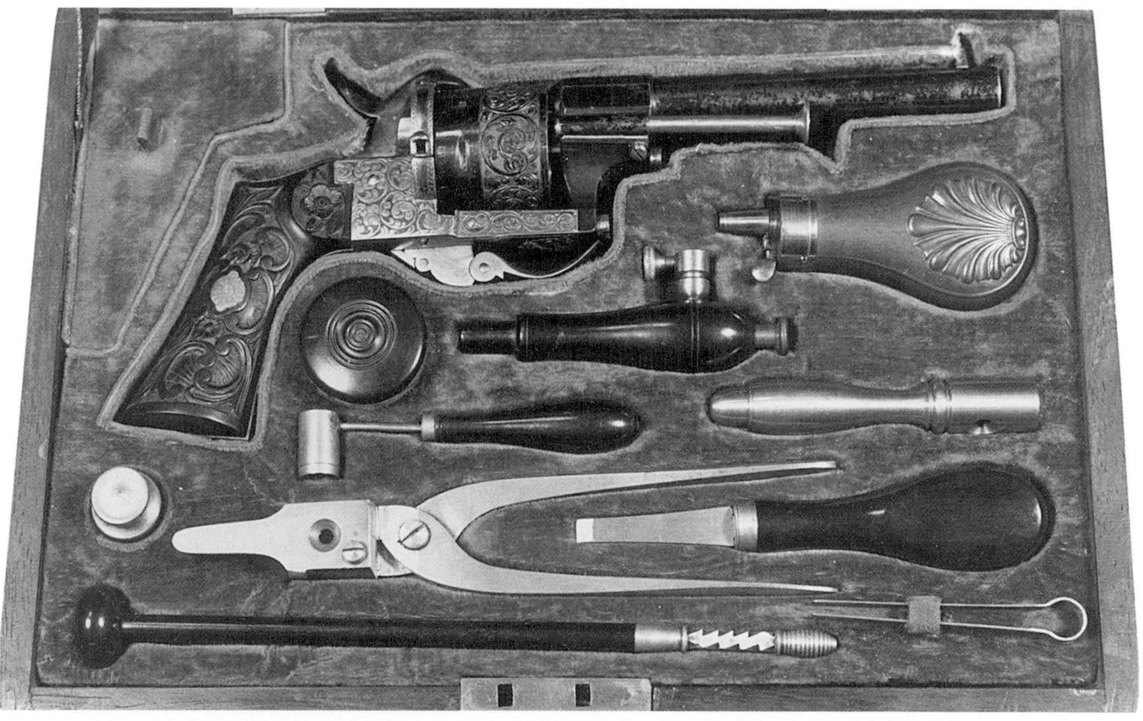

Plate 2-30. Another ornately embellished Lefaucheux double-action, folding-trigger revolver, finely engraved, having carved grips, and cased in the French style with full accoutrements. *Courtesy James Lowther; John Calcany photograph*

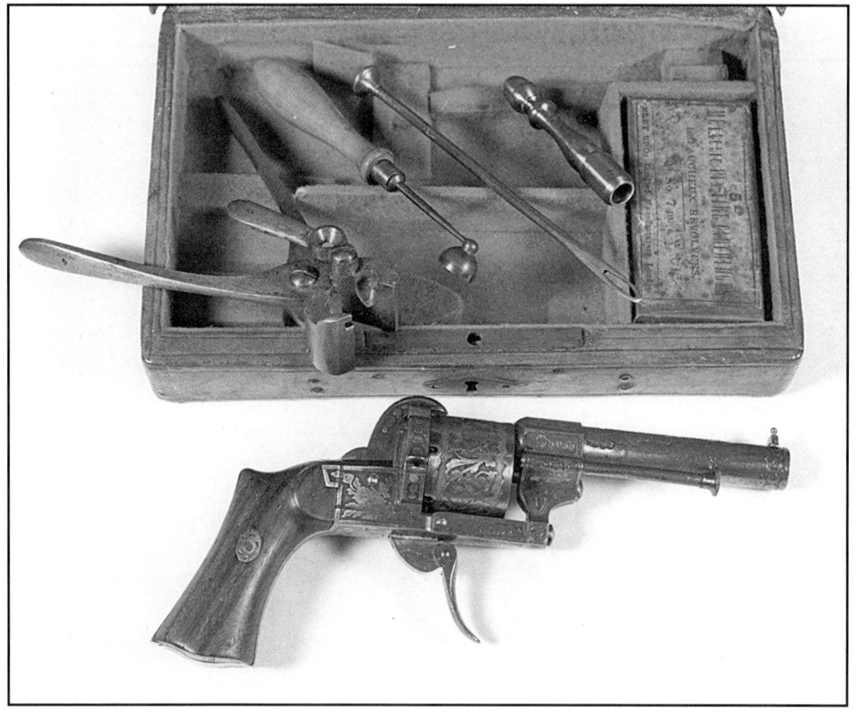

Plate 2-32. Detail view of folding trigger of the revolver pictured in *Plate 2-31*, showing oval *"Lefaucheux"* markings. *Courtesy Don Kramer; John Calcany photograph*

Plate 2-31. Another extra-finished Lefaucheux double-action, folding-trigger revolver, acid etched, and cased in the English partition style with accoutrements. *Courtesy Don Kramer; John Calcany photograph*

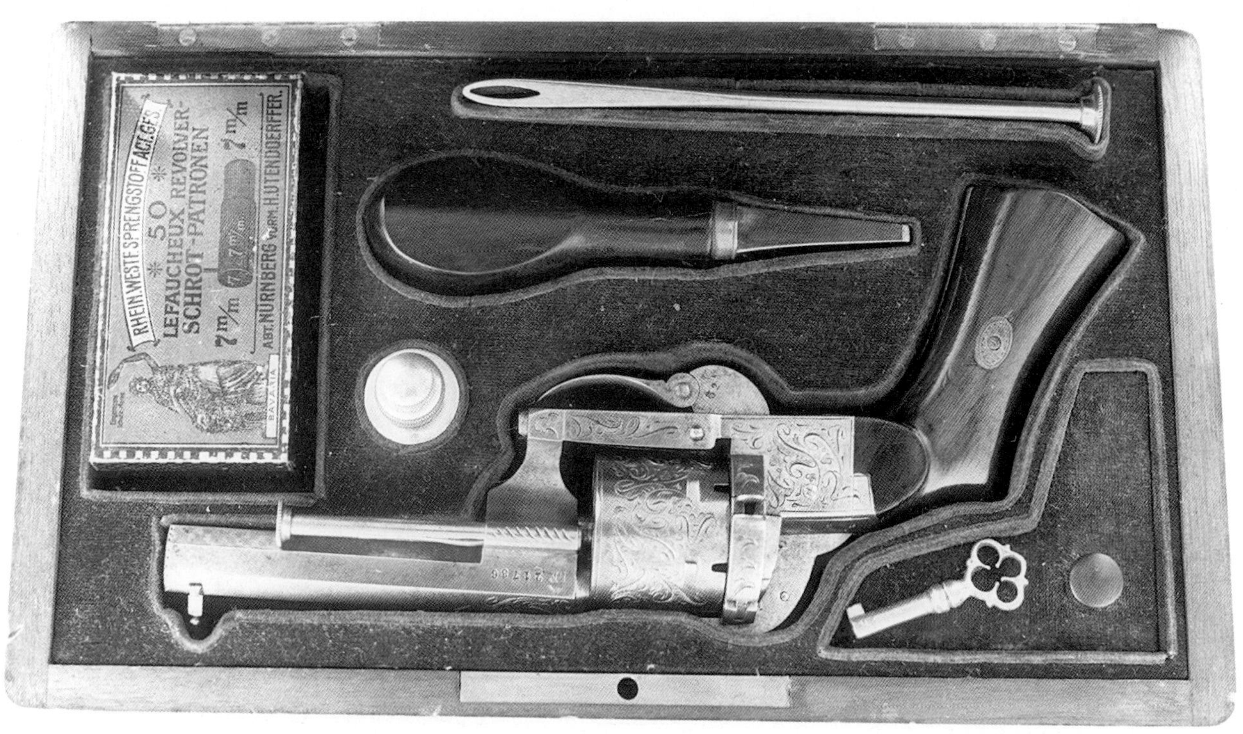

Plate 2-33. Yet another finely embellished Lefaucheux double-action, folding-trigger revolver, engraved, and housed in a *"Lefaucheux a Paris"*-marked casing in the French style with accoutrements. *Chris C. Curtis collection; Richard McMillan photograph*

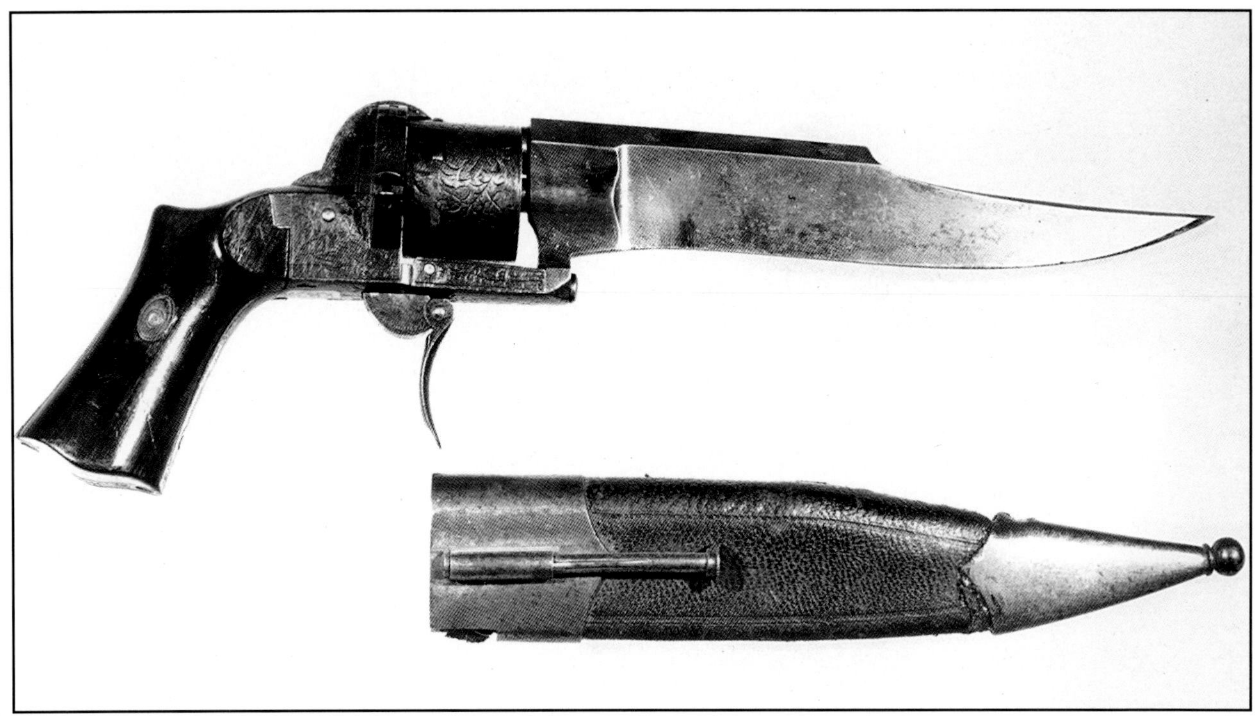

Plate 2-34. A rare variant Lefaucheux double-action, folding-trigger revolver, made into a cutlass-pistol by Dumonthier of Paris. Note original scabbard fitted with ejector rod.
Courtesy H. Gordon Frost

functions as double-action only, has a hammer-block safety lever on the left standing breech, and carries the standard Lefaucheux markings on barrel and frame. Examples of both of the above types have been observed elaborately engraved and fully marked.

The third and last type of revolver to emerge under the protection of French patent number 55784 did not closely resemble Lefaucheux' 1862 patent drawing. However, it did incorporate into its mechanical construction the significant improvements set forth in the text of the patent (*see Plate 2-27*). Once again, Eugene Lefaucheux had succeeded in improving on his previous ideas. By the inclusion of two additional components in the lockwork and another projection on the sear which acts as a delaying element, a mechanism which offered *three modes* of firing was made possible: first, by cocking the hammer with the thumb as in conventional single-action firearms; second,

by pulling the trigger rearward both cocking and firing are accomplished in one motion, as in conventional double-action firearms; and third, by pulling the trigger rearward with lighter pressure the hammer is arrested in the full-cock position, having the same effect as a set trigger.

This was Lefaucheux' finest double-action pinfire revolver, and it became famous in France as the Lefaucheux "Triple-Action." The example shown in *Plate 2-37* is chambered for the 12mm caliber cartridge, standard for the model, and carries full Lefaucheux markings. The revolver pictured in *Plate 2-38* also is fully marked, and additionally features acid-etched decoration. *Plate 2-39* illustrates a superior quality Triple-Action model. It has overall relief engraving and silver plating, and an unusual cloverleaf cylinder. Both the revolver grips and screwdriver handle are scrimshawed ivory, and the brass-bound, deluxe French-style casing features ivory knobs on two

text continued on page 61

Plate 2-35. A large-frame Lefaucheux single- or double-action, folding-trigger revolver, in 9mm caliber pinfire. *Chris C. Curtis collection; John Calcany photograph*

Plate 2-36. A large-frame Lefaucheux double-action only, folding-trigger revolver having hammer-block safety. *Chris C. Curtis collection; Richard McMillan photograph*

Plate 2-37. A Lefaucheux Triple-Action revolver in 12mm caliber pinfire. *Chris C. Curtis collection; Richard McMillan photograph*

Plate 2-38. A Lefaucheux Triple-Action revolver in 12mm caliber pinfire, having acid-etched decoration. *Courtesy Don Kramer; Ferrari Color photograph*

Plate 2-39. Another Lefaucheux Triple-Action revolver having unusual cloverleaf cylinder, acid etched decoration, and scrimshawed ivory grips and screwdriver handle, housed in a *"Lefaucheux a Paris"*-marked casing in the French style with accoutrements. *Courtesy James Lowther; John Calcany photograph*

covered compartments holding cartridges, tools, and the case key. An equally fine Triple-Action model having dual-ignition cylinders was previously pictured in *Plate 2-17*.

The final Triple-Action revolver in this study is illustrated in *Plate 2-40*. It bears full Lefaucheux markings as well as serial number "11044", and on casual inspection appears to be an unadorned standard model. But when viewed from the front it quickly becomes apparent that this is no standard production item: the cylinder and muzzle bores are *oval* in cross-section! Evidently this gun was created for an experiment in ballistics, as the milling of the oval portions of the cylinder chambers as well as the oval barrel bore with its straight rifling bear testimony to armory-quality engineering and fabrication. The alignment of cylinder face (*see Plate 2-41*) to barrel bore is, in itself, a remarkable achievement. The rear of the cylinder is pictured

in *Plate 2-42*; the abrupt change from round to oval bore can readily be seen in the photograph. This revolver is chambered for the short 12mm caliber pinfire cartridge. In order for the cartridge case to properly seat, the bullet must be round at its base and oval at the front. No example of such a round has been observed and it is doubtful that any was made, even to test fire the revolver. Adding to that logistical problem is the fact that a pinfire cartridge can be inserted into the cylinder in only one position: with the pin through the slot in the cylinder. It is possible that the soft lead bullet was compressed into shape in some sort of vise-like accoutrement that guaranteed its shape to be consistent with the position of the pin. Perhaps standard pinfire cartridges were intended to be used, the thought being that the sharp edges within the cylinder bores would shave the soft lead bullet into the requisite oval shape as it was fired. Or

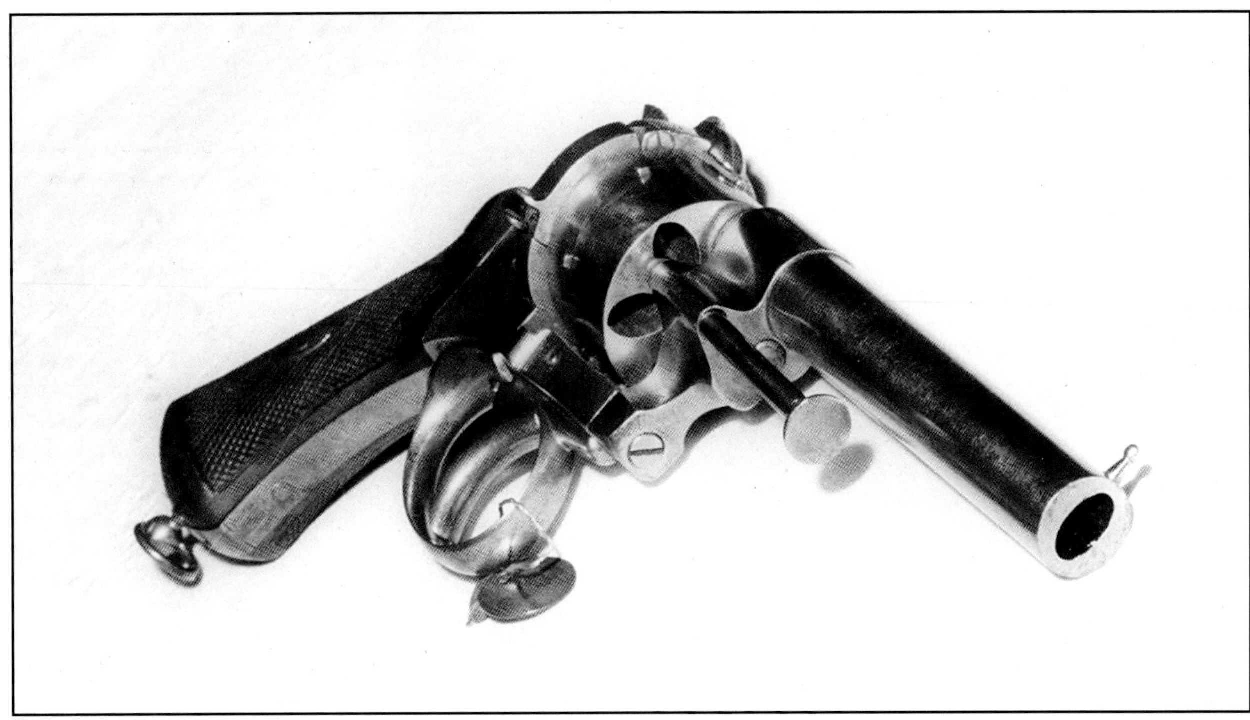

Plate 2-40. Unique variant Lefaucheux Triple-Action revolver having oval bore; likely a ballistics experiment. 12mm caliber pinfire, serial number "11044." *Courtesy Ruby Mann; Gene P. Smith photograph*

Plate 2-41. Detail view of front face of cylinder of the revolver pictured in *Plate 2-40,* showing oval chamber bores. *Courtesy Ruby Mann; Gene P. Smith photograph*

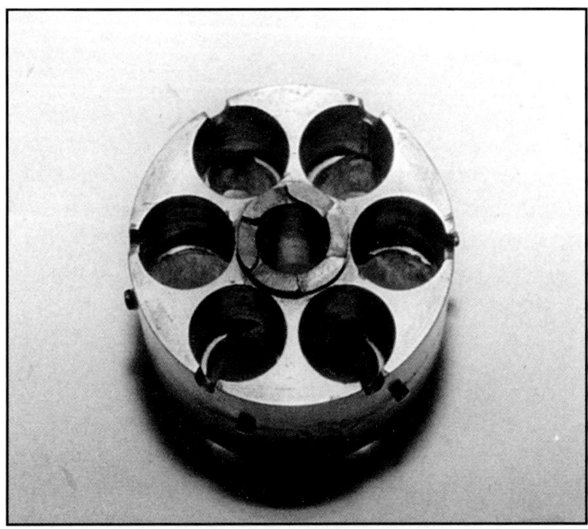

Plate 2-42. Detail view of rear face of cylinder of the revolver pictured in *Plate 2-40,* showing round chamber bores. *Courtesy Ruby Mann; Gene P. Smith photograph*

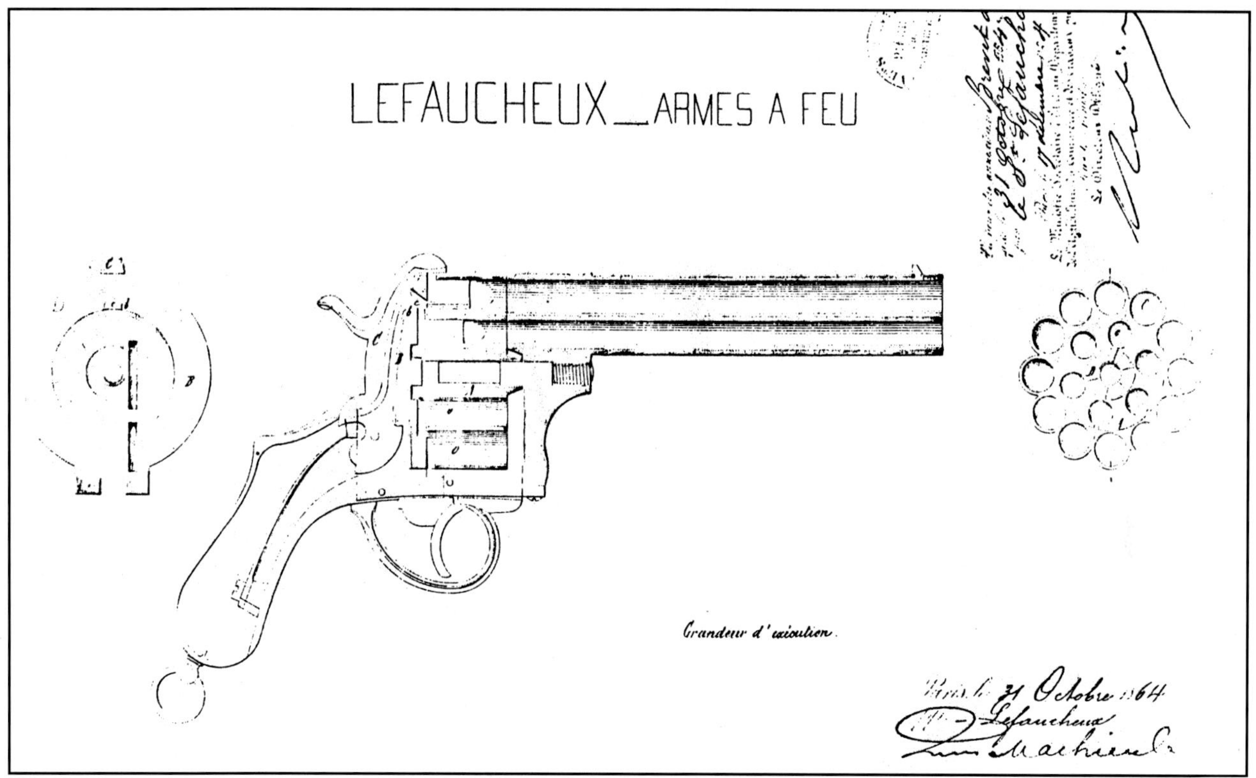

Plate 2-43. Drawings from Eugene Lefaucheux' French patent number 64960 of December 17, 1864, for a double-action, dual-caliber revolver having eighteen-shot, two-ring cylinder. *Chris C. Curtis collection*

this particular pistol may have been intended for use with shot cartridges, involving some sort of experiment in the lateral displacement of shot. Whatever its intended function, the oval bore revolver required a great deal of thought, engineering, and machining work. Whether the results expected were ever achieved is unknown today.

On November 9, 1862 Eugene Lefaucheux applied for yet another French patent, and number 56197 was issued to him on January 12, 1863. This patent covered the means to prevent the escape of gas in breechloading arms, used with or without a self-contained cartridge. To achieve the objective he proposed adding a recess at the rear of the chamber which would engage a corresponding projection serving as a stop valve (gas seal). As an alternative, the employment of a circular or polyg-

onal ring at the rear of the barrel was proposed, which in a like manner was to be engaged by the gas seal projection. At the time of this writing no firearms constructed on this design by Lefaucheux have been located for study.

By late 1864 Eugene Lefaucheux' well-established business was a complete success. Several foreign governments, as well as that of his native France, had adopted variations of his now-famous Model 1854 revolver. In addition to his military contracts, the large Lefaucheux workshop was kept continually busy filling orders from the civilian sector.

Never one to rest, Eugene Lefaucheux now introduced what was perhaps his greatest engineering achievement, for which he applied for patent rights on October 31, 1864 and was granted protection on December 17, 1864. Patent number 64960 (*see Plate 2-43*) illustrates a large, eighteen-shot revolver. No provision for ejection is shown, nor is the hammer clearly pictured; its cylinder has two concentric rows of chambers of different calibers, twelve in the outer ring and six in the inner ring, arranged around a central axis. The single hammer first strikes the pins of the cartridges in the cylinder's outer ring of chambers in the manner typical of all pinfire arms; the hammer then strikes a sliding vertical bar which in turn strikes the cartridge pins when the chambers of the inner ring are aligned with the lower barrel. Needless to say, the large-diameter cylinder and extra weight of this revolver made it bulky and cumbersome to handle, and very few were actually manufactured by Lefaucheux. One unmarked revolver of this type has been examined in the course of this study. It is very close in design to the patent drawing, except that all eighteen chambers take the 7mm caliber pinfire cartridge, as do the two superposed barrels. A large, Liége-made specimen is pictured in Chapter Ten.

Less than two months after he received patent number 64960, in early February of 1865 Eugene Lefaucheux was awarded a certificate of addition which depicts the now-familiar profile of his twenty-shot revolver. An ejector rod was illustrated for the first time, which was designed to swing out and away from the frame to align with either of the two rows of ten cylinder chambers. The hammer with its two striking projections is clearly illustrated (*see Plate 2-44*). This revolver incorporates Lefaucheux' folding trigger design, and functions as either a single- or double-action arm. The area encompassing frame and grip is extremely similar to the double-action revolvers built on his patent number 55784, granted in 1862.

Brilliantly conceived and designed, Eugene Lefaucheux' twenty-shot revolver was easy to handle and in fact weighs but a few grams more than most conventional six-shot revolvers of the period. Chambered for the popular 7mm caliber pinfire cartridge, it became a success almost immediately following its debut, and by the end of 1865 a significant number of them had been manufactured and had found their way into the market. It reaped high praise from the public sector, and numerous endorsements were received from other firearms inventors and armsmakers as well, most notably Auguste Francotte (*see Plate 2-45*). Although serial numbers in the five-digit range have been noted, examples of this revolver are rather scarce today and enjoy premier status in any firearms collection.

Plates 2-46 and *2-47* depict side and front views of this remarkable firearm. The example pictured bears the oval Lefaucheux markings and the logo preceding its serial number, "67"; it also is marked along the top of the barrel with the name of one of Lefaucheux' retail sales agents, "*Lepage Freres a Paris–12 rue d'Enghin.*" A single cocking of the hammer rotates the cylinder eighteen degrees, the top striker of the hammer aligns with a chamber in the outer ring of the cylinder, and the chamber in turn aligns with the uppermost of the two superposed barrels. The next cocking of the hammer brings the lower hammer striker into alignment with a slot cut into the rear of the frame, through which the striker hits the pin of a cartridge that has rotated into alignment with the lower barrel bore. Thus shots alternated between the top and bottom barrels until both cylinder rings of all twenty rounds were expended. The concept and design were simple, the mechanism intricate; yet it proved to be a sturdy and dependable arm over the passage of time.

Even more rare than the twenty-shot revolver is the Lefaucheux twenty-shot carbine, an example of which is shown in *Plates 2-48 and 2-49*. The only one of its kind to be examined for this study, the example pictured exhibits all features of the handguns. The 22-inch barrel is marked "*E. Lefaucheux Bte a Paris*"; the overall length of the arm is 38½ inches.

To more effectively appreciate the deadly efficiency of Eugene Lefaucheux' double-ring cylinder design, one need only remember that contemporary with its manufacture American soldiers were slaughtering each other on the battlefields of the Civil War with single-shot, muzzleloading percussion muskets. Troops armed with twenty-shot weapons firing self-contained metallic ammunition would have made those battles not only unequal in odds, but far more terrible in human cost.

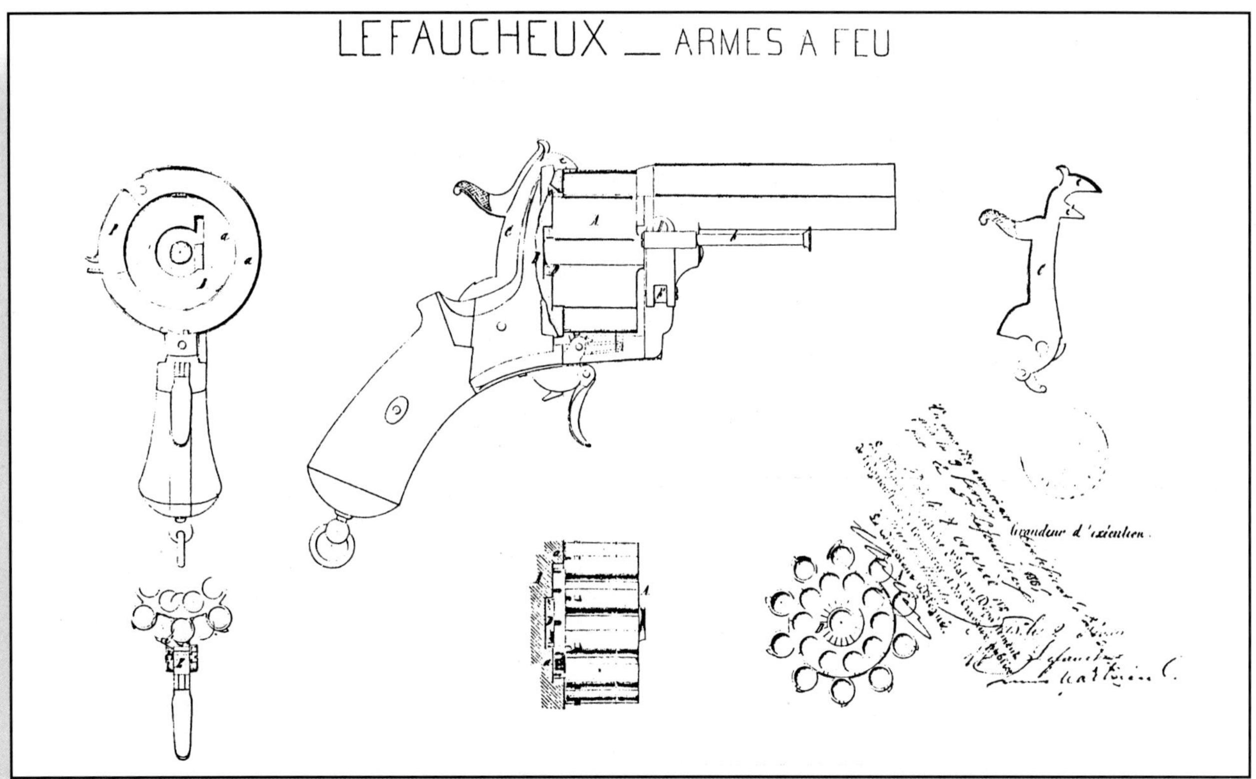

Plate 2-44. Drawings from certificate of addition to patent number 64960, for a double-action, folding-trigger, two barrel, twenty-shot, two-ring cylinder, 7mm caliber pinfire revolver. Note swing-out ejector rod. *Chris C. Curtis collection*

Plate 2-45. Handwritten letter from famed armsmaker Auguste Francotte, congratulating Eugene Lefaucheux on his revolutionary twenty-shot revolver. *Chris C. Curtis collection*

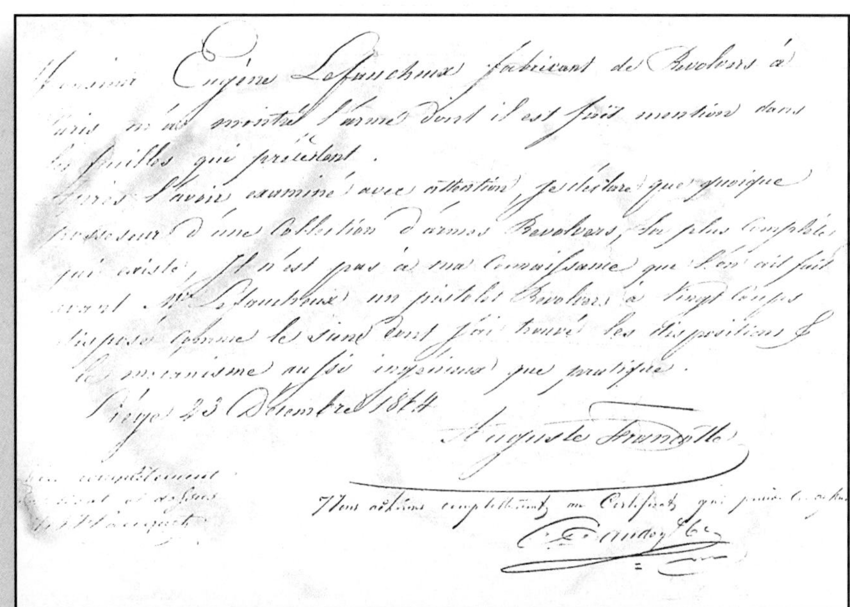

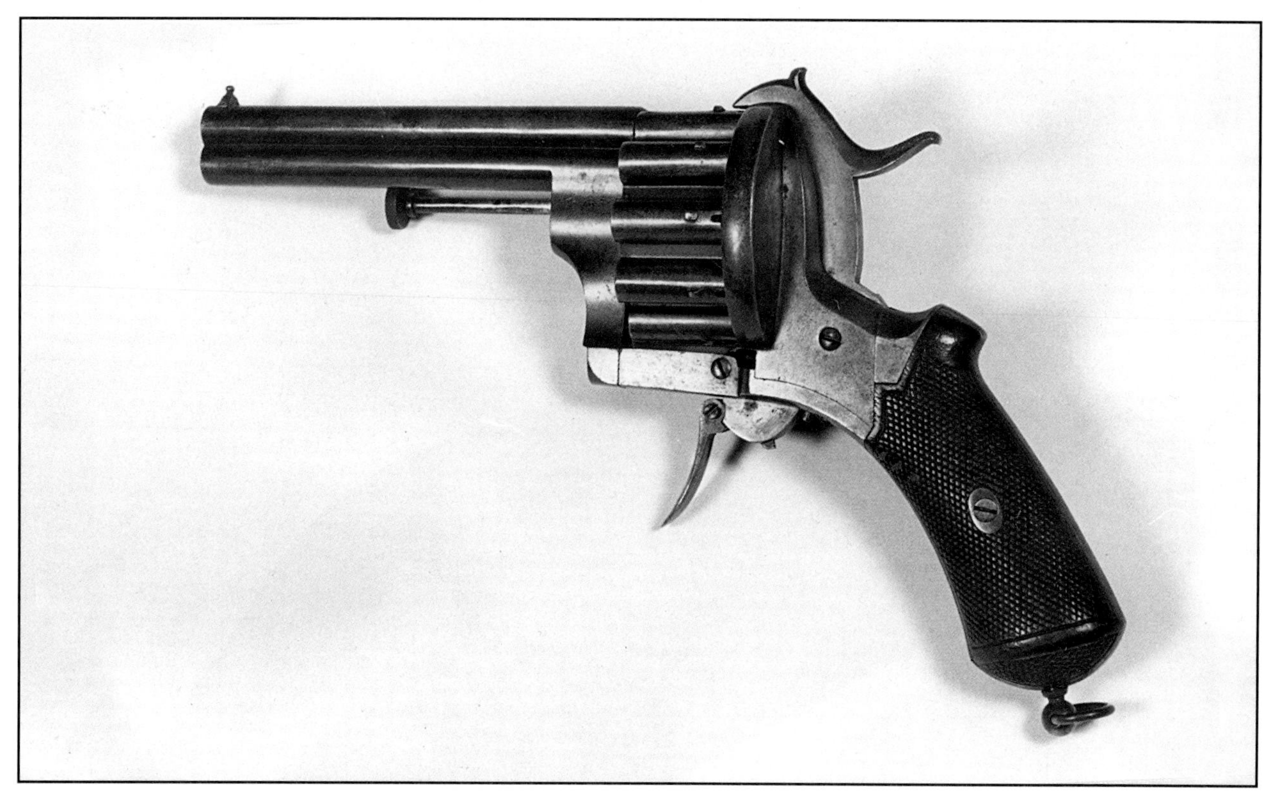

Plate 2-46. A Lefaucheux double-action, folding-trigger, two barrel, twenty-shot, two-ring cylinder, 7mm caliber pinfire revolver; serial number "67." *Chris C. Curtis collection; John Calcany photograph*

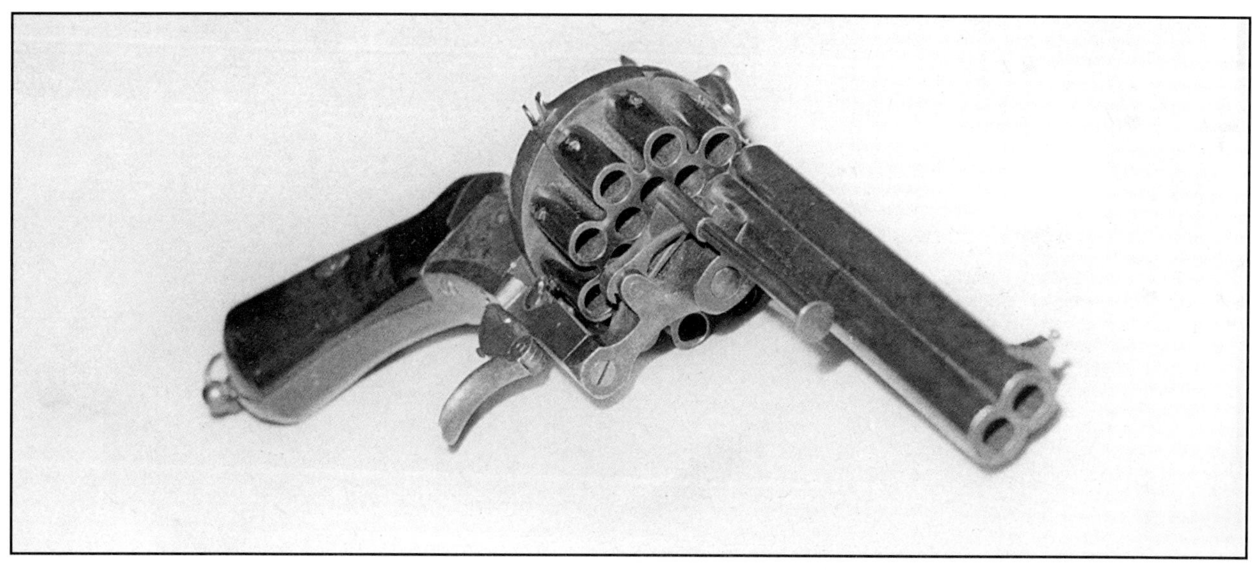

Plate 2-47. Front view of the revolver pictured in *Plate 2-46*, showing two barrels and two-ring cylinder arrangement. *Chris C. Curtis collection; John Calcany photograph*

Plate 2-48. Detail view of breech area of the revolving carbine pictured below in *Plate 2-49,* showing two-ring cylinder and swing-out ejector rod. *Courtesy Don Kramer; Ferrari Color photograph*

Plate 2-49 (below). A rare Lefaucheux double-action, two barrel, twenty-shot, two-ring cylinder revolving carbine. *Courtesy Don Kramer; Ferrari Color photograph*

Along with thirty other armsmakers, Lefaucheux displayed a new type of combination weapon at the Paris Universal Exhibition of 1867. While some of the other makers actually did hold patent rights to various types of combination revolver-sword arms, no evidence exists that Eugene Lefaucheux ever applied for such protection. Most likely he manufactured a line of such arms based on his existing patents for double-action revolvers utilizing the pinfire system. *Plates 2-50* and *2-51* illustrate a combination short sword-revolver with scabbard, chambered for the 7mm caliber pinfire cartridge. It is marked on the barrel, *"E. Lefaucheux Bte a Paris."*

Plate 2-52 depicts another Lefaucheux-marked combination short sword-revolver 30 inches in overall length. The barrel bears the same Lefaucheux legend as above, and is additionally

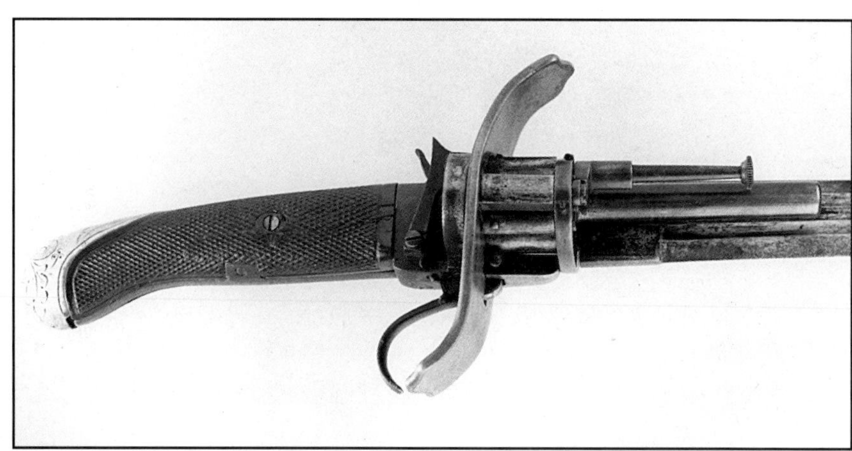

Plate 2-50. An unusual Lefaucheux short sword-revolver combination arm, 7mm caliber pinfire. *Chris C. Curtis collection; Richard McMillan photograph*

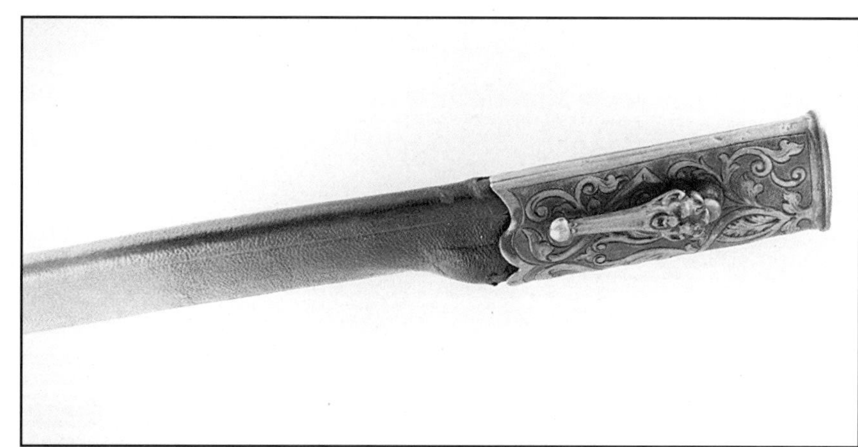

Plate 2-51. Detail view of hilt area of leather scabbard for the combination short sword-revolver pictured in *Plate 2-50*, showing grotesque mask on cast hanger. *Chris C. Curtis collection; Richard McMillan photograph*

marked with the name of a Peruvian importer-agent, "*Alfredo Herouard–Lima.*" The barrels of the longer cavalry-type sword-revolver combination arms rest in a corresponding depression on the outside of the scabbard, but on these short sword-revolvers the barrel usually is housed within the leather-and-brass scabbard, as shown here.

Plate 2-53 pictures another Lefaucheux-marked combination arm, similar in appearance to the previous one except for its straight blade 16 inches in length. It too is marked with the same South American agent's name, "*Alfredo Herouard—Lima*", both on the blade and on the inside of the case lid. All three of the combination sword-revolver arms just discussed have slightly offset cylinders and rear loading gates, and are chambered for the 7mm caliber pinfire cartridge.

The following group of Belgian-made firearms generally credited to Eugene Lefaucheux is the most difficult to positively attribute. The problem originates with the word "*Brevete*", or its abbreviations "*Brevet*", "*Bvt*", or "*Bte.*" The English equivalents of the word are "Patent", "Patent Pending", or "Patent of." When placed next to a maker's name it sometimes means that the maker holds patent rights to the type of firearm on which the legend appears, but it also can mean that the maker is producing the arm under license, and giving credit to the inventor or patent holder. To confuse the matter even further, it additionally can mean that the individual named, perhaps a sales agent or a retailer, has applied for one or more patents for different types of firearms, or improvements thereto. For example, one revolver studied

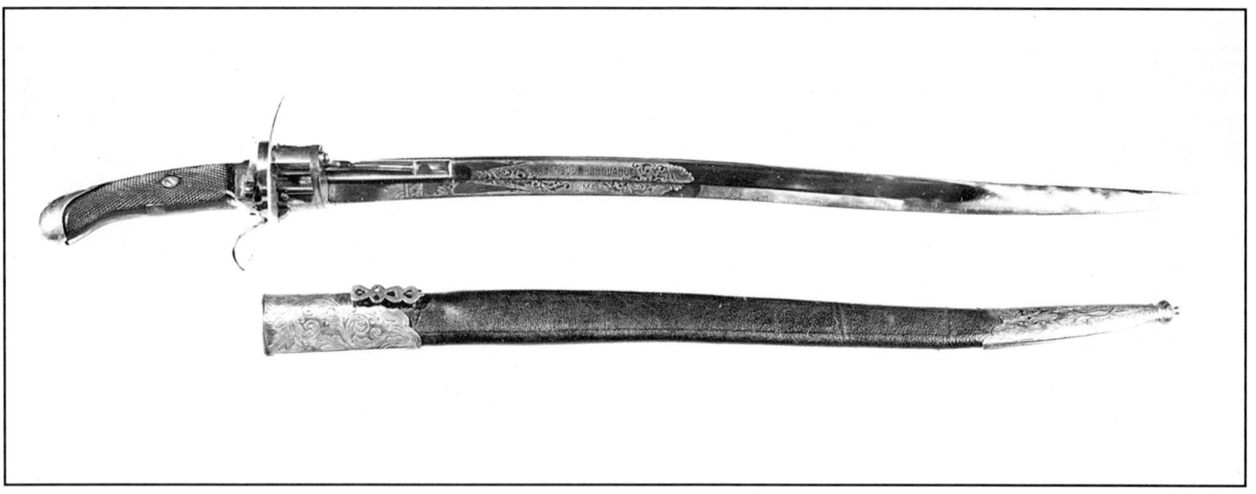

Plate 2-52. Another Lefaucheux short sword-revolver combination arm having a curved blade, marked with a South American agent's name and accompanied by matching scabbard. *Courtesy H. Gordon Frost*

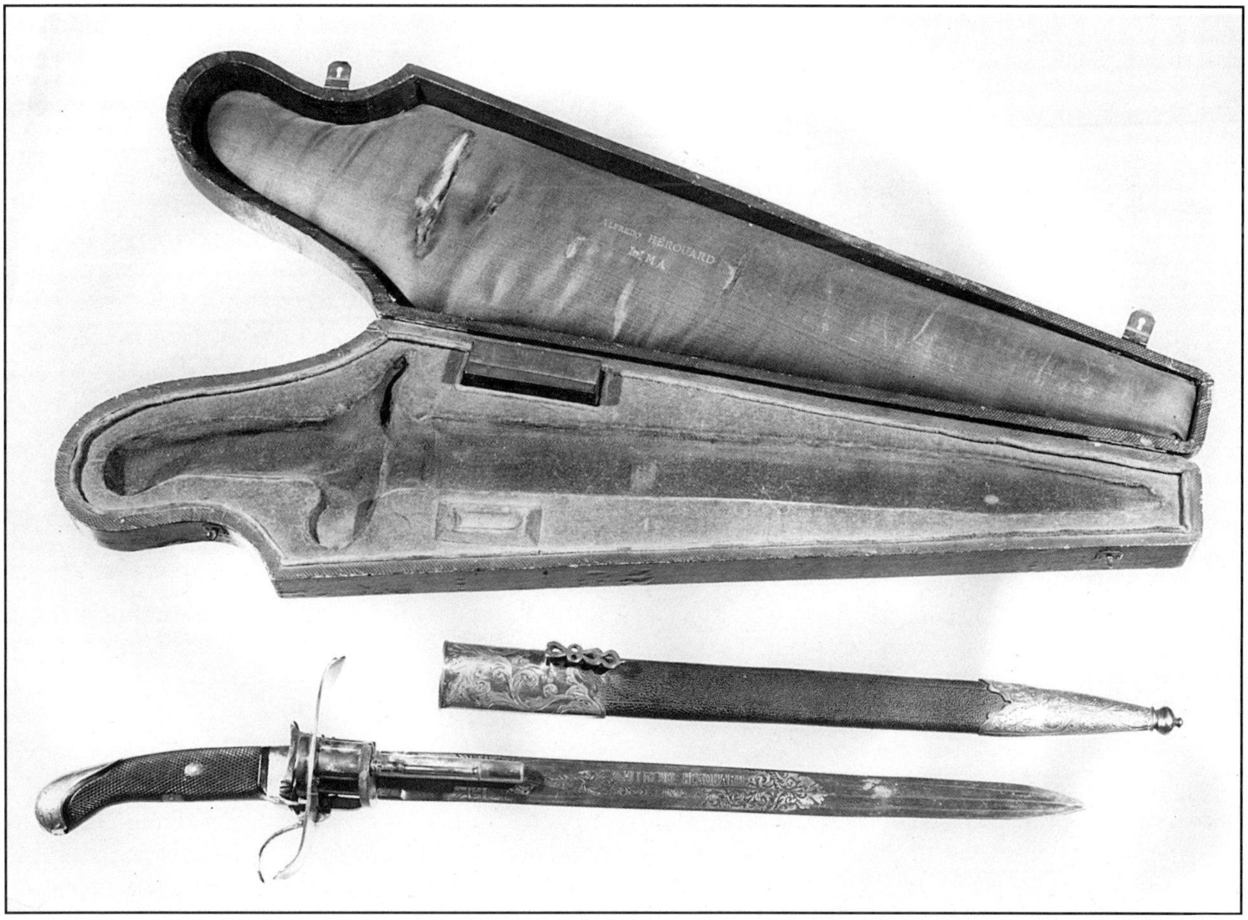

Plate 2-53. Yet another Lefaucheux short sword-revolver combination arm having a straight blade, also marked with a South American agent's name and accompanied by matching scabbard, housed with box of cartridges in a form-fitted, French-style case. *Courtesy H. Gordon Frost*

is marked on the frame "*E. Lefaucheux Inv Brevete*", and on the barrel "*Houllier Blanchard Brevete a Paris.*" In that case, Houllier Blanchard was the retailer, who also held different firearms-related patents; Lefaucheux was the manufacturer, and holder of the patents covering this particular arm. It is worthy of mention here, that in every case the word "*Brevete*" (or its variations) on a firearm was recognized as the mark of quality goods. It was especially true of the arms made in Belgium, where all firearms underwent rigorous testing at government proof houses.

During the historical period under discussion, the arms manufacturing center of Liége, Belgium offered a solution to many of the production problems encountered by Parisian gunmakers. It became standard practice for the French makers to have their prototypes and patent models perfected and then manufactured in Liége[3], and Eugene Lefaucheux was very familiar with that practice and with the quality workmanship of the Liége gunsmiths. There was no single, central arms factory in that city, but many small firms or individual gunmakers employing craftsmen who worked either at their facilities or in home shops on a piecemeal basis. Liége census records indicate over fifty barrel makers operating there in 1856, ninety-seven manufacturers of arms, and a total of 9,675 persons involved in the local arms industry.[4] Yet the figures quoted do not include the many women and children who frequently assisted in the work by completing small tasks, and by transporting parts between one shop and another. Occasionally, for the purpose of executing a large order, several competitors would temporarily join forces by forming a syndicate, each again going his separate way when the contract was completed. Each, however, kept his own firm open and in operation during the temporary business merger.[5]

It was in that city, steeped in the centuries-old traditions of firearms making as an art, that Eugene Lefaucheux opened another arms factory, located at 13 quai de Fragnee, to produce both military and sporting arms. The generally-accepted dates for the operation of this new facility are between 1866 and 1869.[6] If this time frame is

accepted at face value, a second series of problems in attributing the Belgian-proved "*Lefaucheux Brevete*" marked arms surfaces. Several variations of these types of firearms have been historically associated with events occurring prior to the accepted 1866 date of the beginning of Liége production, especially the Model 1854 designs. One such revolver is known to have been excavated from the Civil War battlefield at Gettysburg, several others have family provenance of having been owned and carried in battle by their Civil War forebears, and yet another was presented by Giuseppe Garibaldi[7] to an Italian countryman in 1863. Perhaps the best-known example in America is the variant-style Lefaucheux double-action revolver that was presented to Confederate General "Stonewall" Jackson[8] from a group of his officers (Jackson's revolver is pictured and discussed in detail in Chapter Four of this book).

As virtually all nineteenth century records of Belgian armsmakers were destroyed in the twentieth century's two world wars, at this time the definitive solution to the problem of absolute attribution is difficult, at the very least. It is possible that the accepted 1866 date for Lefaucheux' factory opening is incorrect, and that the facility actually began operation earlier; or that Lefaucheux subcontracted the manufacture of an early group of guns to another Belgian maker prior to the opening of his Liége armory.

While all of the arms in question are of good quality and workmanship, and similar in design and mechanics, they do not exactly match their French counterparts. All bear Liége proofmarks, including the pre-1877 inspectors' stamps. In most cases they are serial numbered on the left side of the frame forward of the trigger, and are marked "*Lefaucheux Brevete*", usually on the left barrel flat forward of the cylinder.

The Belgian-made *Brevete* revolvers fall into three general categories. The first and most often encountered type is, like their Paris-made counterparts, the folding-trigger model in 7mm and 9mm calibers. On the engraved example with an unusually long barrel pictured in *Plate 2-54* the front

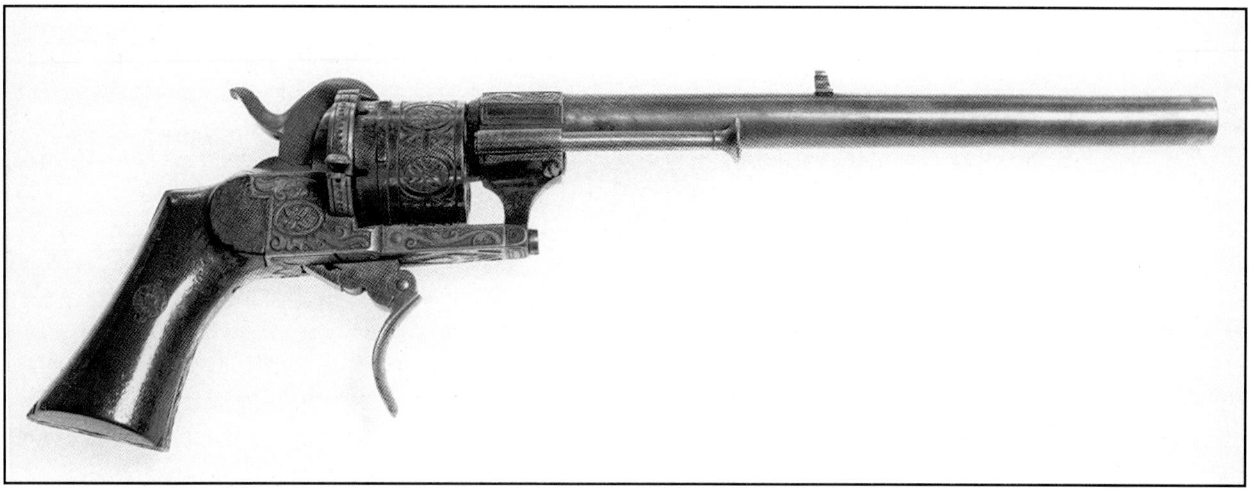

Plate 2-54. A first-type, Belgian-made *"Lefaucheux Brevete"* folding-trigger revolver having an unusually long barrel and tapered smoothbore for use with shot cartridges; note placement of front sight midway down barrel. *Chris C. Curtis collection; F.W. Hulbert photograph*

sight is positioned halfway down the barrel. Another unique feature of this arm is that while it is chambered for the 7mm caliber pinfire cartridge, the smoothbore barrel gradually increases in diameter to 9mm at the muzzle. This design was intended to fire shot cartridges, and the results of this "reverse choke" must have been quite interesting. A more standard example of this revolver in 7mm caliber is pictured in *Plate 2-55*, housed in a fitted "pipe-style" casing.

The second type of Belgian-made Lefaucheux *Brevete* revolver is the easily-recognized, single-action Model 1854 style. Although it too is similar to the Paris-made guns, this model differs slightly in configuration and structure. The triggerguard spur was retained, but the buttcap was changed to a flat oval form (having several variations within itself). The barrel-frame juncture has a more abrupt angle that is less graceful in appearance than the French-made version, and on most examples the screw joining barrel and frame enters from the front rather than from the bottom through the trigger-guard, as does the Paris standard. Other variations exist in the shape of the front sight, and some examples have a rear sight mounted atop the barrel lug in addition to the hammer groove sight. And

Plate 2-55. Another first-type, Belgian-made *"Lefaucheux Brevete"* double-action, folding-trigger revolver, housed in a fitted, pipe-style case. *Courtesy James Lowther; John Calcany photograph*

Plate 2-56. A second-type, Belgian-made *"Lefaucheux Brevete"* revolver of the Model 1854 pattern, 12mm caliber pinfire. *Chris C. Curtis collection; F.W. Hulbert photograph*

while most Belgian-made Model 1854 revolvers are chambered in 12mm caliber (*see Plates 2-56* and *2-57*) like their French cousins, some have been encountered in 9mm caliber. The 9mm caliber example shown in *Plate 2-58* is engraved, fitted with carved and finely-checkered grips, and nicely finished; note the addition of the fixed rear sight.

The third variation of the Belgian-made Lefaucheux *Brevete* revolver has its own distinct style. This 12mm caliber, double-action arm may have been manufactured under the protection of Eugene Lefaucheux' 1856 French patent number 29055. The frame design is dissimilar to his later models, but more like those shown in the patent drawings. Dubbed by collectors the "Stonewall Jackson model" (*see also* Chapter Four), this finely made revolver with its more modern-appearing rounded triggerguard and saw-handle grip was very advanced for its time (*see Plate 2-59*).

As the decade of the 1860s neared its end, so passed the golden age of the pinfire arm in Europe. Although pinfire guns were produced well past the turn of the twentieth century they were relegated to lesser standing than before, and many were very cheaply manufactured merely for export to developing countries. The military establishment that had been so quick to embrace the modern pinfire system now eagerly turned to its more advanced successor, the centerfire cartridge.

Fortunately, Eugene Lefaucheux had earlier experimented with the centerfire system. Despite overwhelming political and economic difficulties created by the Franco-Prussian War he managed to obtain sufficient materials and to retain his skilled workforce. The Lefaucheux double-action, centerfire cartridge revolver was adopted for use by the French Navy in 1870.

Manufactured in small quantities and in several minor variations known as the Models 1868,

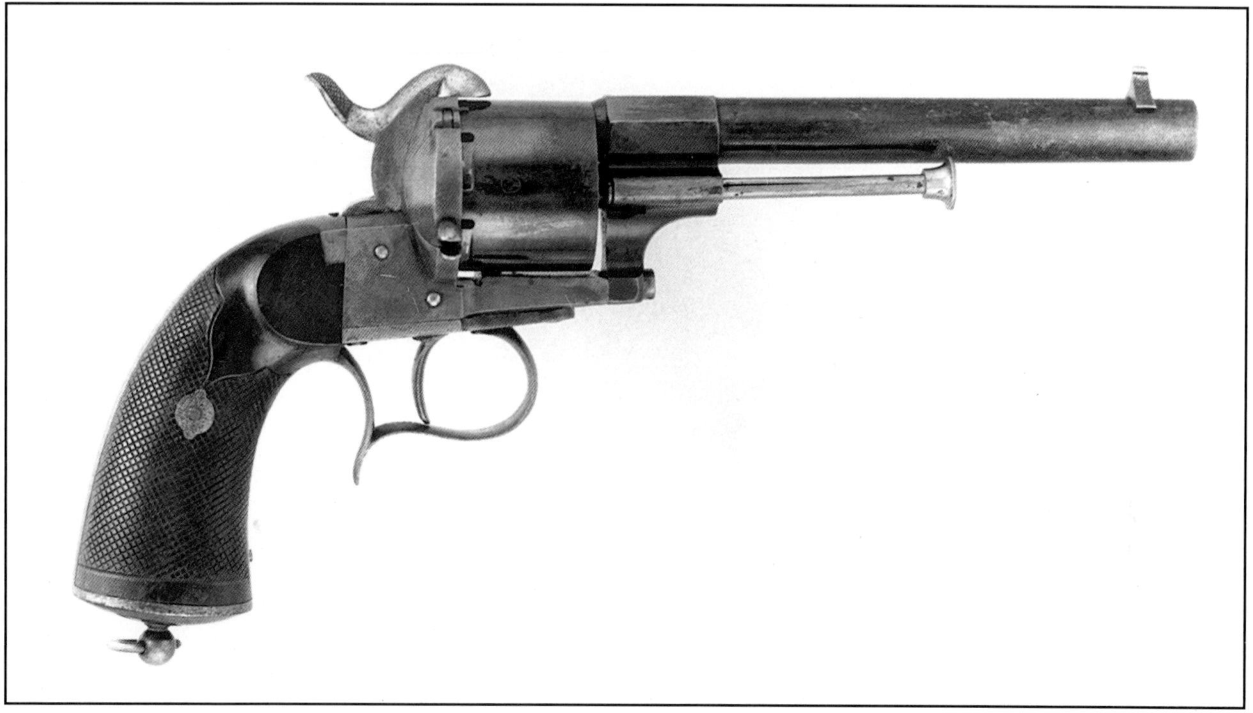

Plate 2-57. Another second-type, Belgian-made *"Lefaucheux Brevete"* revolver of the Model 1854 pattern, 12mm caliber pinfire. *Chris C. Curtis collection; Richard McMillan photograph*

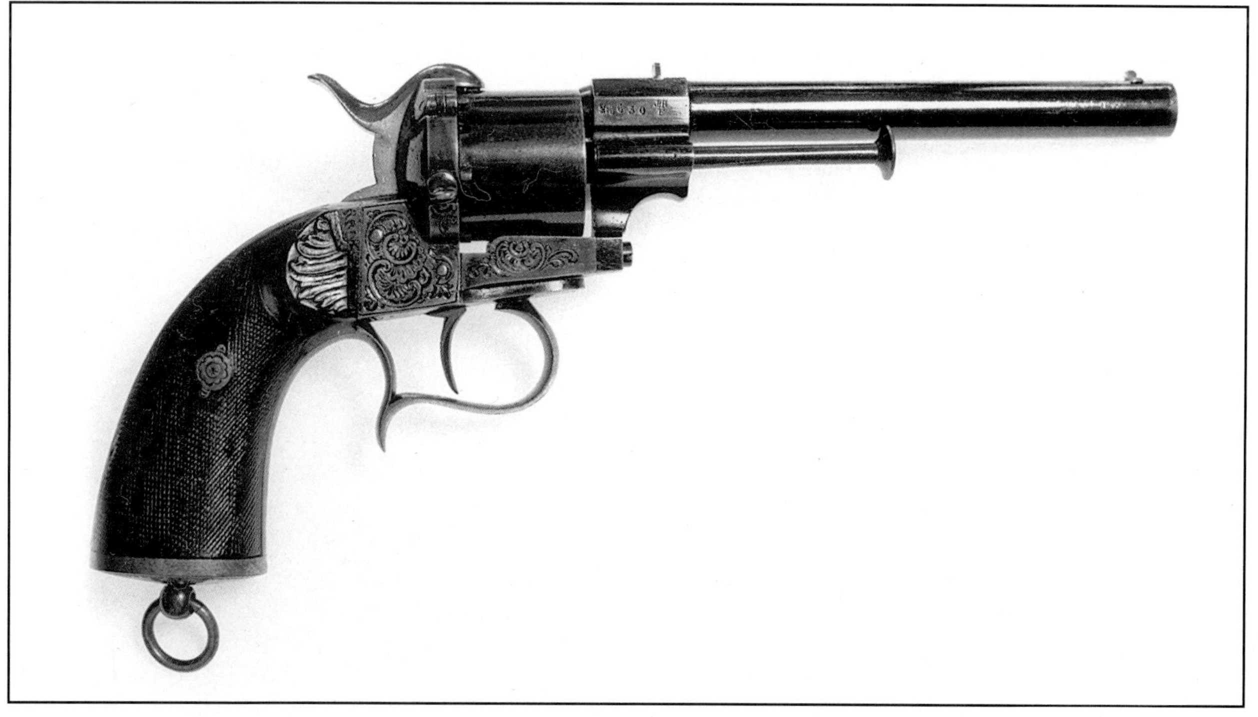

Plate 2-58. Yet another second-type, Belgian-made *"Lefaucheux Brevete"* revolver of the Model 1854 pattern, but in 9mm caliber pinfire. Note engraving, carved and finely-checkered grips, and rear sight atop barrel lug. *Courtesy F.W. Hulbert; F.W. Hulbert photograph*

Plate 2-59. A third-type, Belgian-made "*Lefaucheux Brevete*" double-action revolver, known as the "Stonewall Jackson" model; 12mm caliber pinfire. *Chris Curtis collection; F.W. Hulbert photograph*

1870, and 1871 for the civilian trade, the new arm met with only moderate success. Because the French government arsenal at St. Etienne was heavily committed to production of the Chassepot rifle, Lefaucheux produced the military version of his revolver for the navy in 11mm centerfire caliber, a very potent cartridge for its time.

During the decade that followed, Eugene Lefaucheux remained active designing and obtaining patents for many firearms and firearms improvements. French patent number 82358 covered the revolver design just described, and it was followed by others in 1869, 1870, three in 1872 (with a certificate of addition to the last), 1875, 1876, two in 1877, and a final patent for firearms improvement in 1878, for a new method of producing cartridge cases.

It is at about that time that Eugene Lefaucheux and his influence on the firearms world begin to fade from the historical record. It is unclear exactly why. He was in late middle age; perhaps his health was failing from years of overexertion, or maybe he had suffered a family loss or financial reverse. Perhaps the new firearms technology had simply passed him by. His manufacturing facility at 37 rue Vivienne was first taken over by Rieger, then by Mode, then by Verney Caron, and finally by Callens and Mode, who as late as 1987 operated the factory under the name *Armurerie de la Bourse*, though by then not much of the original establishment remained.

The pinfire system invented by Casimir Lefaucheux and advanced by his son Eugene had become a worldwide success within their lifetimes. During the era of percussion arms it was an idea far ahead of its time. The pinfire was a critical first step in the evolution of modern firearms ignition and ammunition manufacture. As that first step, however, it was only natural that given the springboard and the technology to improve upon it, other inventors in time would do just that. More efficient rimfire cartridges, followed by easily-reloadable centerfire cartridges, and the arms that used them, began to flood the markets. The pinfire cartridge fell victim to its own success, as the natural evolution of more improved systems made possible by the pinfire began to appear in greater numbers and variety.

Many were the fortunes made and lost during the halcyon years of the last half of the nineteenth century, by inventors and armsmakers who grew rich on one idea only to gamble and lose all on the next. These same men, of course, were fostering the rapid advance of firearms technology. Some of them managed to keep their wealth, and their names live on even today; many others were left behind, poor and forgotten to all but a few.

As was his father, Eugene Lefaucheux was a brilliant and prolific inventor. He was a shrewd businessman, also, pouring his profits back into the business for the improvement of his operations. Frugal with his personal and business expenditures, he nevertheless spent substantial sums where they would do the most good, as on gifts to obtain government contracts.

It has been written that at the time of his premature death Eugene Lefaucheux was forced to eke out a meager existence working as a painter for farmers in France's Sarthe district. To Sarthe, the birthplace of his father, he had returned in his declining years, and there he died in 1892. Eugene Lefaucheux was just fifty-nine years of age.

However modest his circumstances at the time of his demise, Eugene Lefaucheux was guaranteed a prominent place in the history of firearms invention. Long before 1892 the Lefaucheux name had become synonymous with the pinfire system. "Lefaucheux" was then, as it is today, commonly used as a generic term in the context of pinfire arms and ammunition, regardless of the actual maker.

Each of the many types of Lefaucheux guns was a great success in its own right. But in spite of

the great variety designed, patented, and manufactured, one stands head and shoulders above the rest. It is Eugene Lefaucheux' first, and greatest, effort: The Model 1854 revolver, the first metallic cartridge handgun to be officially adopted by a major military power.

Chapter notes.

1. In 1877 and 1879 Eugene Lefaucheux registered French patents addressing improvements to horse-drawn carriages, as his father had done before him in 1840.
2. French patent number 19380 is cross-indexed as patent number 10831 in the *American Catalog of Foreign Patents*.
3. Claude Gaier, *Four Centuries of Liége Gunmaking*. Liége, Belgium, 1976.
4. *Ibid.*
5. An example of this type of joint undertaking is the completion of a contract for the British government of 150,000 rifles between 1854 and 1863 by the "*Societe des Anglais*", which consisted of *Monsieurs* Ancion, Pirlot, Renkin, and Francotte.
6. Eugene Heer, *Der Neue Stockel*, Volume I. Herausgeber, 1978.
7. In 1860, Giuseppe Garibaldi (1807-1882) led the "Red Shirts" in conquest of Sicily and Naples in support of the policies of reunification architect Conte di Cavour and Sardinian King Victor Emmanuel II. As a result of that action the latter became king of a united Italy the following year.
8. A native of Clarksburg, Virginia (now West Virginia), General Thomas Jonathan Jackson (1824-1863) earned his enduring sobriquet during 1861's first Battle of Bull Run, where he and his Confederates staunchly defended Henry Hill against a superior Union force "like a stone wall." Two years later, at the Battle of Chancellorsville, Jackson was mortally wounded by his own men in a tragic case of mistaken identity, and died May 10th, 1863. Today, his Lefaucheux *Brevete* pinfire revolver is on display at the Museum of the Confederacy in Richmond, Virginia.

Plate 3-1. A group of French infantry soldiers displays the variety of colorful uniforms worn during the Franco-Prussian War (1870-1871). *Courtesy private collection*

Pinfire Arms
and the European Military

The pinfire system of firearms ignition designed by Casimir Lefaucheux and perfected by his son Eugene was adopted by many European powers during the latter half of the nineteenth century, and even tested by the U.S. military on the eve of the Civil War.

France

The French government was aware of the development of the new Lefaucheux pinfire cartridge revolver from its inception, and early recognized the new arm's suitability for military purposes. The French Navy was the first military branch to show real interest in the Lefaucheux arm, as it had begun a testing program in 1855 to replace the then-current service issue piece, a single-shot percussion pistol, with a new sidearm of the revolver design. The navy trials continued through 1857, during which time various types of percussion arms received rigid testing and thorough consideration. At the trials' conclusion, however, all of the percussion and combustible cartridge revolvers, including the highly esteemed Colt, were rejected as unsuitable for naval use.

As the testing progressed, the naval council became increasingly convinced that only a metallic cartridge revolver was worthy of serious further consideration. The reasons, later enumerated by military writer Colonel Jean Martin, were: more rapid and convenient loading, less danger of misfire or multiple cylinder discharge, no risk of the cylinder loads jarring loose when carried, and the fact that the new metallic cartridges were less fragile than pre-prepared cap-and-ball loads. In agreement, the officers on the French military testing board determined that a metallic cartridge revolver would be the only type of arm suitable for naval use.

As a matter of course the Lefaucheux Model 1854 12mm caliber pinfire revolver had been submitted to the trials. Being rugged and well-made, the modern arm proved very efficient, and Emperor of France Napoleon III (1808-1873) even test-fired the Lefaucheux as a courtesy. At a later date the emperor fired a Lefaucheux Model 1858 issue revolver at Chalons.

On October 27, 1857 the Council of Naval Armaments adopted the Lefaucheux Model 1854 revolver as the official standard sidearm of the French Fleets. It was the first cartridge handgun to be adopted by a major military power. The Model 1854 was to be produced at the Imperial Arms Factory at St. Etienne, in accordance with an agreement whereby all military armaments were to be manufactured by the French government. However, Lefaucheux would be allowed to continue manufacturing the same model for the civilian trade and for open-market military sales to foreign

Plate 3-2. Lefaucheux Model 1858 Navy revolver, serial number "21." *Chris C. Curtis collection; Richard McMillan photograph*

countries.

Production of the military model was begun at the St. Etienne Arsenal on March 4, 1858, and given the official designation "*Pistolet-Revolver de Marine Modele 1858*" (Navy Revolver Model 1858). Confusion has long existed as a result of the Model 1854-Model 1858 designations. But the Model 1854 correctly belongs to those revolvers manufactured by Lefaucheux and distributed to the civilian market or adopted by various foreign governments as a military sidearm (although those arms were sometimes given different model designations by the adopting power). The Model 1858 designation correctly belongs *only* to those revolvers made at the St. Etienne Arsenal for French naval use.

The total length of the Model 1858 revolver is 11⅝ inches (295mm); the barrel is 6⅛ inches (155mm) long, and has four-groove rifling (1.3mm grooves). The cylinder chambers are 12mm in diameter, tapering to 10.7mm at the rear; the caliber of the model is frequently listed as 11mm, but the 12mm diameter at the cylinder openings is the official caliber designation. Total weight of the revolver is 990 grams.

Plate 3-2 illustrates a Model 1858 revolver manufactured during the first year of production. Its serial number is "21", and all major parts (as well as some minor ones) are stamped with that number. The Lefaucheux name, logo, and serial numbering system were omitted from the military model; instead, the legend "Mre *Imple* ^{ale} *de* St *Etienne*" appears on the right side of the frame behind the cylinder (*see Plate 3-3*). On the right barrel flat the date of manufacture is stamped, preceded by the letters "MI" (*Manufacture Imperiale*), and the letter "S." (for *St. Etienne*).

The practice of using the "MI" stamp was discontinued in 1862; therefore earlier examples of the model will have the barrel markings "MI S.1859" as seen in *Plate 3-4*, and later-manufactured revolvers will have their barrels marked

Plate 3-3. Detail view of right side of rear frame area of the revolver pictured in *Plate 3-2*, showing St. Etienne Arsenal markings. *Chris C. Curtis collection; Richard McMillan photograph*

Plate 3-4. Detail view of right barrel lug area of an early-production Lefaucheux Model 1858 Navy revolver, showing "MI S.1859" marking. *Courtesy F.W. Hulbert; F.W. Hulbert photograph*

Plate 3-5. Detail view of bottom of buttcap of a Lefaucheux Model 1858 Navy revolver, showing "naval anchor" inspector's marking. *Courtesy F.W. Hulbert; F.W. Hulbert photograph*

Plate 3-6. Detail view of stampings on the left barrel lug of a Lefaucheux Model 1858 revolver, showing at left the arsenal *controlleur*'s initial "B" cartouche, and at right the steel maker's initial "F" cartouche. *Chris C. Curtis collection; Richard McMillan photograph*

"S.1865", for example, although some exceptions to this rule have been encountered.

Various other markings appear on parts such as the cylinder, hammer, and barrel, but as they are inspectors' initials they vary according to date of manufacture. Two initials will be found on the left barrel flat in an oval cartouche: the letter nearest the cylinder is that of the producer of the steel used in making the arm, the other is the first letter of the last name of the "*controlleur*", the officer in charge of the St. Etienne Arsenal at the time of manufacture. In the case of the revolver pictured in *Plate 3-2* it is that of *Commandant* Briand (*see Plate 3-6*), who was commanding officer from 1856 to 1862. Later examples bear the letter "*J*", for Lieutenant Colonel Jouffray (1862-1866), or "*B*", for Colonel Boigeol (1866-1873). A naval anchor appears on the buttcap (*see Plate 3-5*).

Minor changes to the revolver occurred throughout the early years of its production, but in 1862 a general revision of the arm included enough changes to warrant a new model designation. The first Model 1858 revolvers had the barrel, hammer, and ejector rod made from cast iron, which proved deficient because the rod was subject to bending or even breaking, and several screws had the tendency to work loose after heavy use. So in 1862 the barrel, hammer, and ejector rod were changed to cast steel construction. Some internal parts involved in the rotation and locking of the cylinder also were strengthened. The butt, butt strap, and triggerguard screws were reinforced by a system of interlocking parts called "hooks" by the French, which better secured the grip straps to the frame. By order of M. Dechambe, supervisor of arms production for the navy, these modifications were incorporated into all revolvers manufactured after 1862, and thereafter the revolver was designated the "Model 1858N" (for *neuf*, or new). The above modifications increased the weight of the arm slightly, to 1,010 grams.

Despite the change to steel, the problem of the ejector rod bending and jamming the cylinder continued, and in 1867 another modification was incorporated. A rod guide was soldered onto the side of the barrel, and the ejector rod head was altered to slide on a rib on the guide (*see Plate 3-8*). The guide both controlled the angle of the ejector rod, and supported it as well. All Model 1858 and Model 1858N revolvers regardless of their date of manufacture received this improvement modification when they were returned to the St. Etienne Arsenal for general refurbishment and repairs. Many arms that were in serviceable condition and still in current use escaped the modification, however.

Examples of the Model 1858 revolver have been observed dated "1869." It is doubtful that any were manufactured after that date, as in 1868 the French Navy already had begun to search for a replacement revolver chambered for the new, improved centerfire ignition system. During the later years of its production, a few variations of the Model 1858 began to appear. One such type bears proper St. Etienne markings, inspectors' stamps, and initials of the steel provider and the arsenal *commandant*, but the finish is blue instead of the usual bright polish and it has the multi-faceted buttcap common to the civilian Model 1854 revolvers. Another variation has a rear sight added atop the barrel flat ahead of the cylinder; yet another variant carries the St. Etienne commercial proof consisting of two laurel leaves and the initials "*SE*." During the later years of Model 1858 revolver manufacture under the authority of Felix Escoffier, then civilian arsenal director, it was the practice at St. Etienne to allow fabrication of arms for private sale to military officers. All of the above variations bear manufacture dates between 1865 and 1869.

Few period documents remain in existence that record the production activities of these years at the St. Etienne Arsenal. One piece of evidence does remain, however, a book written in 1900 by a French artillery captain named R. Debussy, titled *Historique de la Manufacture d'Armes de Guerre de St. Etienne*. While Debussy's main interests were in the areas of machinery, steam engines, and production capabilities, his fragmentary notes on the Model 1858 revolver at least give us some idea of the total number manufactured. His is only a partial list; in it he records only four of the twelve years of revolver production, and for those gives a total of 3,446 revolvers produced. Of that number, Debussy stated that 1,145 were the original Model 1858 revolver, and that the remainder were the improved Model 1858N. Production years and numbers manufactured are as follows: 1858—580; 1860—565; 1862—606; and 1864—1,695. Clearly, his report of the total number of revolvers manufactured is low, inasmuch as only one-third of the years of production was reported.

For years following its official adoption of the

Plate 3-7. Ready, aim, fire! Sailors of the French Navy practice shooting their Lefaucheux Model 1858 pinfire revolvers aboard ship. *Courtesy private collection*

Lefaucheux pinfire revolver, the French Navy unsuccessfully tried to persuade the War Department to test it. But the French Army stubbornly clung to its outdated traditions of early-nineteenth century warfare and consistently declined the opportunity to submit the superior arm to military trials.

Finally, however, in 1869 the army became interested in a cartridge handgun, when the Ordnance Commission at Vincennes tested a centerfire Perrin revolver against the new Lefaucheux double-action centerfire revolver. The army could arrive at no conclusion concerning the superiority of one over the other, but in its independent testing the French Navy again decided to adopt a Lefaucheux design.

Designated the Model 1870, this new revolver was adopted by the navy on February 3, 1870. Once again the French Navy made history, by becoming the first major military power to make a centerfire revolver official issue for its forces. The Model 1870 revolvers were manufactured by Lefaucheux; production began immediately and soon examples began to arm the fleet.

The Lefaucheux centerfire revolver was well accepted and performed up to expectations during the short Franco-Prussian War, resulting in the French Navy's decision to make the centerfire cartridge the standard type in their handgun arsenal.

Then in 1873, all Model 1858 and Model

Plate 3-8. Drawings of barrel areas of Lefaucheux Model 1858 Navy revolvers, showing (left, top) old style ejector rod assembly, and (left, bottom, and at right) ejector rod guide added to barrel in 1867. *Chris C. Curtis collection*

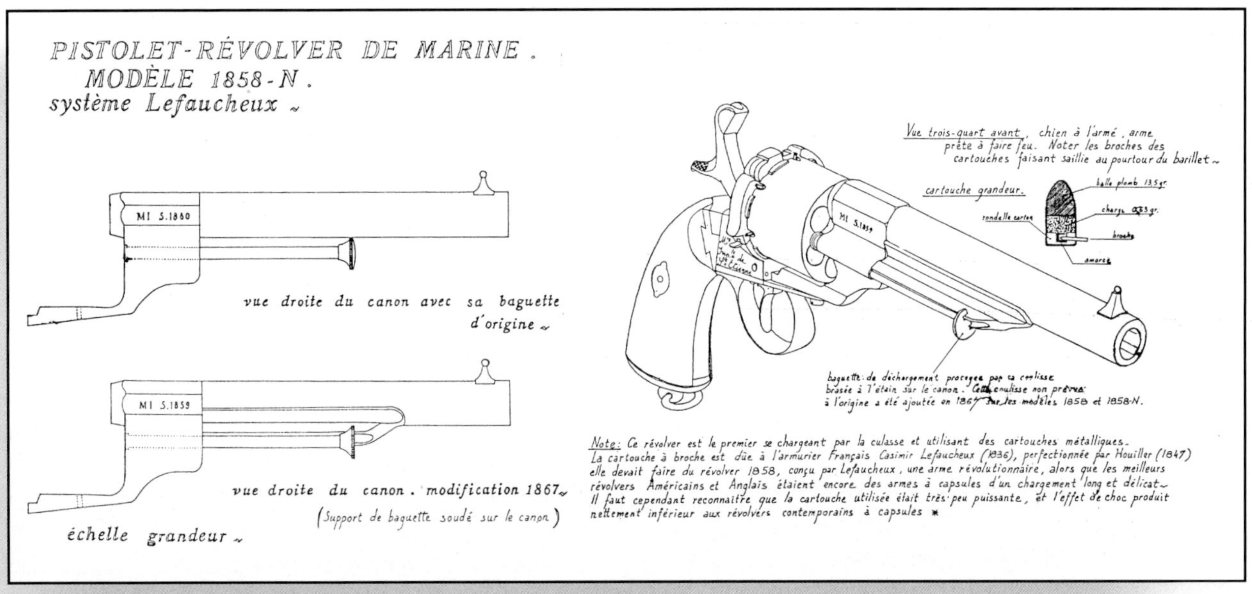

Plate 3-9. "French Foreign Legion" short-barrel variant of the Lefaucheux Model 1854 revolver. *Chris C. Curtis collection; Richard McMillan photograph*

1858N revolvers were ordered to undergo major modification, from single-action pinfire to double-action centerfire. As each ship returned to port, the officer in charge of the shipboard compliment of arms was required to make those arms ready for delivery back to the factory. Inventory control measures were strict, and very few revolvers escaped these changes. While the conditions associated with naval use had reduced the existing number of Model 1858 revolvers, this 1873 modification with its sweeping changes is what really made the Model 1858 and Model 1858N revolvers in original pinfire configuration very rare today.

For that modification the revolver's entire lock mechanism was replaced with one of double-action capability designed by Lefaucheux. Cylinders were not replaced, but their rear bore faces were grooved to accept the rim of the centerfire cartridge; the pin slots were left unchanged to act as visual indicators of whether the chambers were loaded. The front sight was changed from the ball type to a short, flatter type, and a rear sight was added on all barrels. The left barrel flat was stamped with a script letter "T", as were all parts of the lockwork involved in the conversion. The revolvers were then re-serial numbered, and many of their original markings were obliterated in the process of polishing them to a fine finish. Thus converted, the new centerfire revolvers were re-issued to the navy under a new designation—the Model 1858NT, the "T" meaning "*Transformé*."

Plate 3-9 illustrates a variation of the Model 1854 revolver manufactured in Paris by Lefaucheux for private purchase and distribution to the officers of the famed French Foreign Legion. It resembles Lefaucheux' civilian "Navy" revolver, but has a shorter barrel and forward frame assembly (120mm), and is shorter in overall length (250mm) compared to the regulation military Model 1854 and Model 1858 Navy revolvers (usually 295mm in overall length, having barrels 156mm to 158mm long). The Lefaucheux logo and serial number were placed on the right side of the barrel assembly forward of the cylinder. The French Foreign Legion Museum (*Le Museé de la Legion Etrangere d'Aubagne*) has one of these rare revolvers on display among other famous Legion artifacts. Another example is pictured in the April 1996 Camerone anniversary issue of the magazine *Kepi Blanc*. It has been reported that Lefaucheux revolvers accompanied French troops into Mexico during Napoleon III's attempt to expand his empire into the Americas between 1862 and 1867. On April 30, 1863, the French Foreign Legion fought its version of the Battle of the Alamo at the tiny Mexican village of Camerone, with sixty-five officers and men defending against the combined attacks of 1,800 Mexican cavalry and infantry troops. The commanding officer of the French, Captain Danjou, is said to have carried one of these short Model 1854 Lefaucheux revolvers into that fateful battle. Very few specimens have survived from that period, due to the harsh climates, fierce battles, and many campaigns the Foreign Legion was involved in throughout the French empire.

With but few exceptions, single- or double-barrel pinfire breechloading rifles never received serious consideration for testing or adoption by the military powers of Europe. One of the more interesting exceptions is the unusual, breechloading rifle adopted by the French government for a short period. This was the "*Mousqueton des Cent Gardes*" rifle. Sometimes it is called the "*Treuille de Beaulieu*", crediting the French artillery captain responsible for its design and subsequent adoption by the French military, *circa* 1862, as a weapon for the Imperial Palace Guards. Its special 9.5mm caliber cartridge was the smallest cartridge used by the French military until that time, and was inserted into the breech from the rear (*see Plate 3-10*) through a groove cut in the stock for that purpose. The cartridge had two pins, a short one (the ignition pin) which protruded only about one-eighth of an inch, and a longer pin on the opposite side that was utilized for extraction. On pulling the trigger (A) the combination sear and trigger spring (B) are activated, causing the sear (C), which is part of the triggerguard, to fly upward pushing the breechblock (D) into the closed position, thereby sealing the breech. The projection (E) on the breechblock strikes the ignition pin with sufficient force to detonate the cartridge.

This rifle was difficult to manipulate, and potentially dangerous, as the shooter aimed and fired the arm with the breech in the open position.

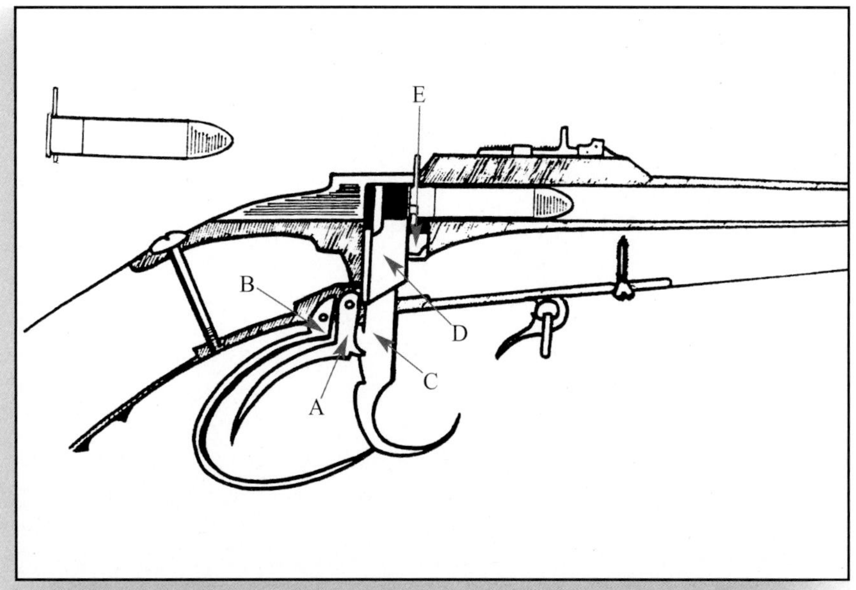

Plate 3-10. Sectional drawing of "*Mousqueton des Cent Gardes*" rifle, showing chamber with unusual cartridge having two pins, the top pin for ignition and the bottom pin for extraction. *Chris C. Curtis illustration*

The sling swivel (F) also acted as a guard, to keep the shooter's hand from becoming entangled in the mechanism. *Plates 3-11 through 3-14* picture a possibly unique, cut-away *Mosqueton des Cent Gardes* rifle, the only example of this scarce model made available for inclusion in this study. The specimen pictured was carefully cut in half down the centerline, to reveal the inner workings of this unusual action (*see Plate 3-13*). The rear leaf sight

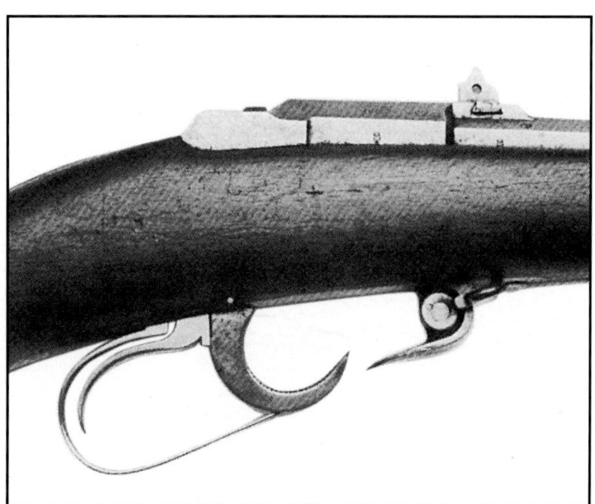

Plate 3-12. Detail view of right side breech area of the rifle pictured in *Plate 3-11*, showing relationship of unusual combination triggerguard-mainspring, cocking lever, and front guard. *Courtesy Martin B. Retting; Bob Steele photograph*

Plate 3-11. A likely unique, cut-away "*Mousqueton des Cent Gardes*" rifle. *Courtesy Martin B. Retting; Bob Steele photograph*

is missing, probably because it could not be fastened to the remaining half-base; or, possibly it was separated and lost over the passage of time. *Plate 3-14* pictures a detail view of the breech section of this cut-away rifle, with the various components lettered to correspond with the diagram shown in *Plate 3-10*; note how iron pins have been added to hold the parts to the stock (non-lettered arrows).

Any *Mousqueton des Cent Gardes* rifle is rare; this sectioned example surely is unique, likely having been made for training and familiarizing troops with the unorthodox principles of its action.

Spain

Spain was the first country to follow the example of the French Navy, when by order of Queen Isabella the Lefaucheux Model 1854 revolver was approved as the official sidearm of the Spanish armed forces, on April 30, 1858. The Lefaucheux replaced the British Beaumont Adams percussion revolver. It cost approximately twenty percent less and was judged to have a twenty-year life expectancy. By subsequent royal orders of March 29 and June 18, 1858, the Lefaucheux was declared the regulation arm for officers of the Spanish national guard, and of the fixed regiment at Ceuta, Spanish Morocco. Still later, by royal order of February 4,

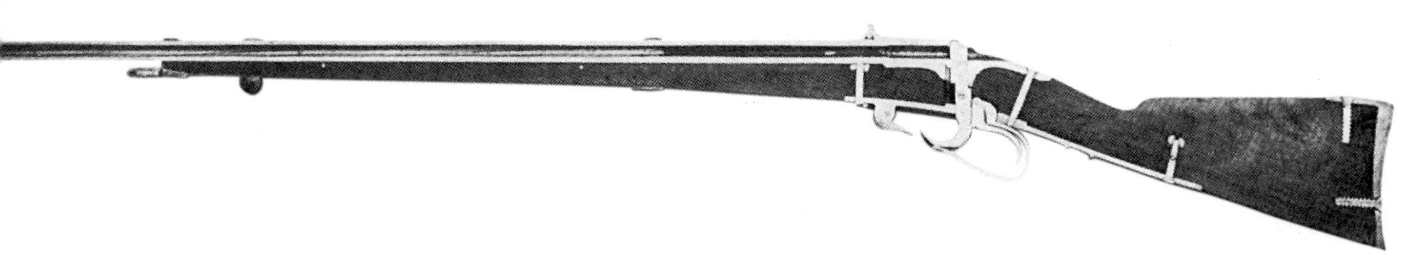

Plate 3-13. Left side of the rifle pictured in *Plate 3-11*, showing sectioned components open to view. *Courtesy Martin B. Retting; Bob Steele photograph*

1862, it was declared regulation equipment for all officers required to supply their own sidearms.

The fabrication of these Lefaucheux-designed Model 1854 revolvers was assigned to the Trubia Arsenal (*Fabrica Nacional de Trubia*), and to the firm of Orbea Brothers (*Orbea Hermanos*) in Eibar, Spain. Members of the Orbea family had been involved in the armsmaking business since 1538, but *Orbea Hermanos* was a separate company founded in 1858 by Juan, Manuel, Matthew, and Casimiro Orbea.

The Model 1854 revolvers produced in Trubia were marked on the barrel with the Trubia Arsenal name and the year of manufacture (*see Plate 3-15*). Examples have been observed bearing the dates 1860, 1861, and 1862, although production began prior to 1860. Serial numbers are located on the right side of the frame above the triggerguard.

The Orbea-made examples generally are of better quality and finish than those manufactured at the Trubia Arsenal. They are marked on the

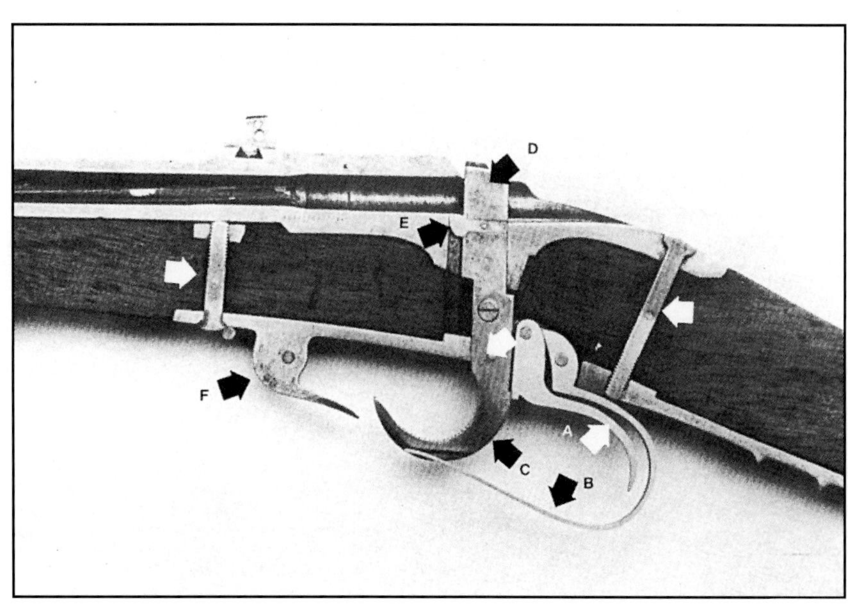

Plate 3-14. Detail view of left side breech area of the "*Mousqueton des Cent Gardes*" rifle pictured in *Plate 3-11*, showing component parts: (A) trigger; (B) triggerguard-mainspring; (C) cocking lever-sear; (D) breechblock; (E) firing pin; (F) front guard and sling swivel base. Unlettered arrows indicate pins holding sectioned parts in place. *Courtesy Martin B. Retting; Bob Steele photograph*

barrel *"Orbea Hermanos-Eibar"*, with the serial number of the arm stamped on the right flat of the barrel lug (*see Plate 3-16*). *Orbea Hermanos* produced the largest number of these Model 1854-style revolvers; all were chambered for the standard 12mm caliber pinfire cartridge.

In 1863 the Spanish government contracted with Eugene Lefaucheux to design a different and distinctly new revolver for the Spanish military. The result was the single-action *"Fabrica de Oviedo"* model pictured in *Plate 3-17*. This revolver, designated the Model 1863, was less graceful in appearance than the Model 1854 it replaced. By royal order of October 19, 1863, the new revolver

name and the year of manufacture.

Only two examples of this rare, Model 1854-style *Fabrica de Oviedo*-marked revolver were available for this study, serial numbers "360" and "369." Like the Trubia Arsenal-made arms, they also have the "N" prefix to their serial numbers, and both examples bear the "1864" date on their barrels.

Production of the new Model 1863 revolver evidently was begun in late 1864. The earliest recorded barrel date on a Model 1863 is "1864", on revolver serial number "N71", which reposes in the collections of the Spanish Army Museum. The next lowest recorded serial number is "N274", on

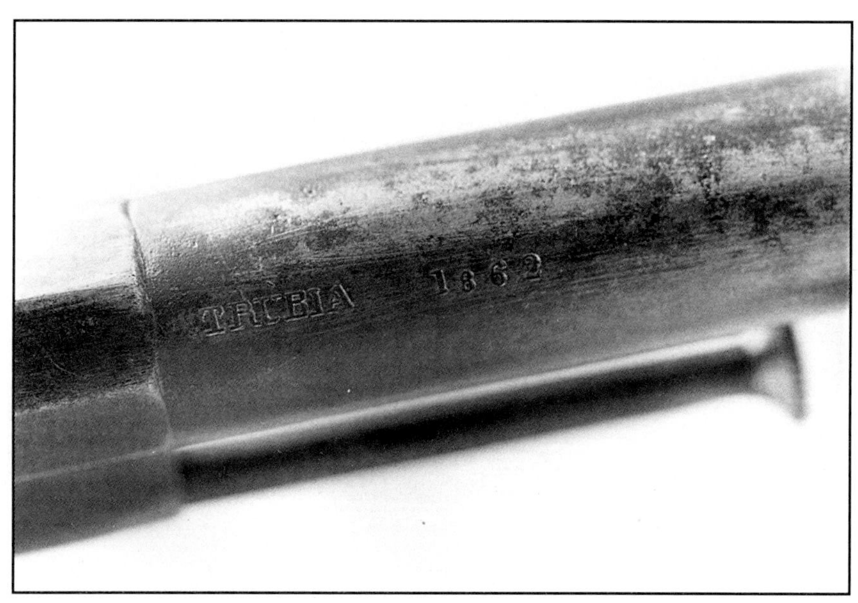

Plate 3-15. Detail view of top of barrel area of a Model 1854 revolver showing *"Trubia"* Arsenal name and date of manufacture. *Chris C. Curtis collection; Richard McMillan photograph*

was approved to supercede all Model 1854 types as the issue sidearm for officers. It was to be manufactured at the government arsenal at Oviedo, where all national revolver production had been assigned. Yet while preparations were being made for full production of the Model 1863 revolvers, a small number of Model 1854-style revolvers also was made there. Like the Trubia Arsenal-produced examples, these Model 1854 Oviedo-made arms are marked on top of the barrel with the arsenal

an example bearing the "1865" barrel date.

These Model 1863 revolvers were largely handmade, as the Oviedo Arsenal was not equipped with machinery adequate for the mass production of military arms. Due to that circumstance, by 1866 only about 1,500 revolvers had been manufactured, and less than 6,000 more by 1870. A specimen dated "1870" has a serial number in the 7,300 range, while another example with its barrel dated "1875" bears a serial number in the 8,400

Plate 3-16. Lefaucheux-design Model 1854 revolver manufactured by Orbea Hermanos of Eibar, Spain, showing serial number stamped on barrel lug. *Chris C. Curtis collection; Richard McMillan photograph*

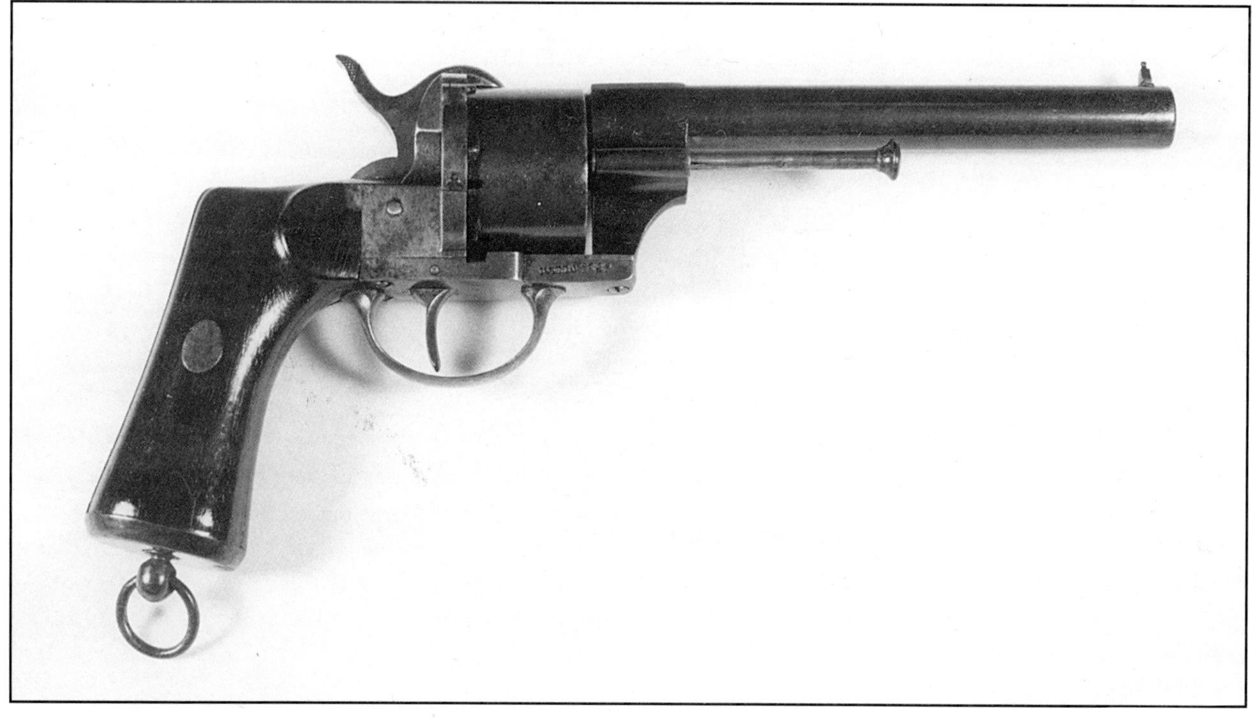

Plate 3-17. Lefaucheux-design Spanish Model 1863 *"Fabrica de Oviedo"* officer's revolver. *Chris C. Curtis collection; John Calcany photograph*

range. The fact that only 1,100 revolvers were fabricated in the intervening five years is indicative of the slow manufacturing processes involved, as well as their similarly slow distribution to the Spanish armed forces. Not many more than 8,500 Model 1863 revolvers were made in all, a very small quantity for a military-issue revolver.

The Oviedo Arsenal Model 1863 pistol is chambered for the 12mm caliber pinfire cartridge.

It measures 10.8 inches in overall length, and is fitted with a six-inch barrel having four-groove rifling. As with the French-made Model 1858, the Lefaucheux name is omitted from the Model 1863, being marked only "*Oviedo*" followed by the date of manufacture on the right side of the frame forward of the triggerguard. A proofmark consisting of an "*S*"-shaped line enclosed by a circle appears on the rear right side of the barrel and on

Plate 3-18. Detail view of right side breech area of a Spanish 15mm caliber pinfire rifle designed by Lt. Jose Ybarra, showing barrel release lever. *Courtesy Juan-Luis Calvó Pascual; Juan-Luis Calvó Pascual photograph*

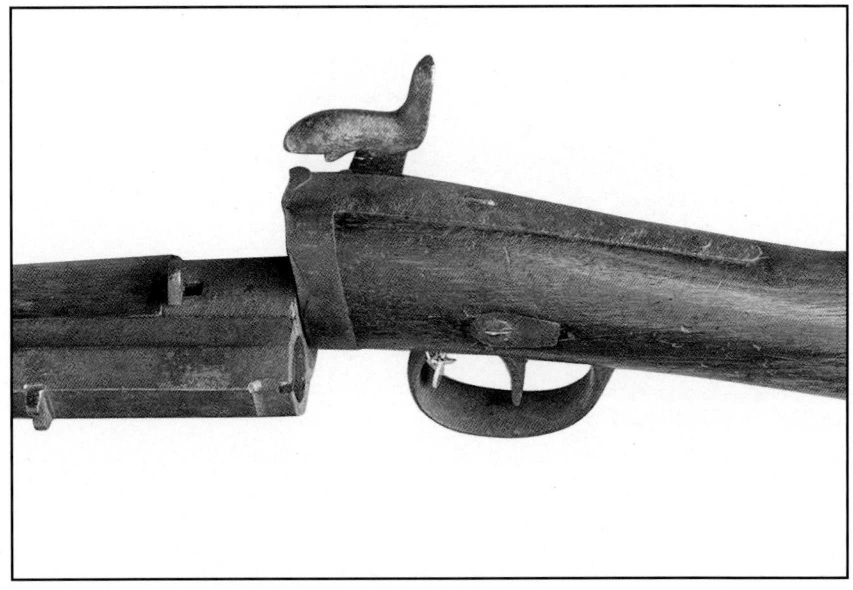

Plate 3-19. Detail view of left side breech area of the rifle pictured in *Plate 3-18*, showing barrel swiveled open for cartridge loading/extraction. *Courtesy Juan-Luis Calvó Pascual; Juan-Luis Calvó Pascual photograph*

the inner surface of the barrel lug. The last three digits of the serial number appear on all major parts, while the complete serial number is marked on the inside of the grips; the number on the frame is preceded by the letter "N." One exception to the foregoing has been noted: the serial number of the late-production Model 1863 revolver mentioned above, having the "1875"-dated barrel and serial number in the 8,400 range, lacks the "N" prefix. Unlike the French, the Spanish military authorities never modified or converted these revolvers to fire the improved centerfire cartridge, so surviving examples invariably are chambered for pinfire ammunition.

During 1884 a revolver of Smith & Wesson .44 Russian design, also manufactured by *Orbea Hermanos* of Eibar, replaced the Oviedo Arsenal-made pinfire arm as the official Spanish Army revolver. In addition to the new domestic model, officers of the army were allowed to choose their sidearms from a variety of makers, including the large-frame frontier revolvers made by Merwin, Hulbert & Co. of America.

Another interesting pinfire small arm used temporarily during this period by the Spanish armed forces is pictured in *Plates 3-18 and 3-19*. The 15mm caliber, single-shot rifles designed by Lieutenant José Ybarra were carried as issue equipment by the *Guipuzcoanos* Battalions during the Carlista War (1872-1876). Although manufactured at an arsenal located within the zone occupied by the Carlistas the factory site has not been identified, as surviving examples are not marked. The small lever located on the right side of the frame just ahead of the hammer unlocks the breech and allows the barrel to be swiveled to the left for cartridge loading and extraction.

Lieutenant Ybarra also designed an automatic cartridge extraction system adaptable to the standard Model 1863 Oviedo revolver; it was produced experimentally at the Oviedo Arsenal during 1874 only, but never officially adopted. An example of this rare conversion applied to a Model 1863 revolver resides in the collections of the Arms Museum in Madrid.

With the adoption of metallic cartridge sidearms by the two major European military powers, France and Spain, many neighboring countries now undertook to update the armament in their own arsenals.

Italy

In 1859 the Kingdom of Sardinia, ruled by King Victor Emmanuel II (1815-1898), included most of what is modern-day Italy. When Sardinia's Prime Minister Cavour (1810-1861) diplomatically maneuvered France into the Pact of Plombières in 1858, the latter country agreed to ally with Sardinia in the event of aggression by a foreign power. That done, Cavour cleverly engineered an attack by Austria against the Piedmont region, which he had built up economically as a magnet to attract the rest of Italy back into reunification.

With Austria's act of aggression French troops were quickly sent to the aid of Sardinia. During that campaign many advisors and regular troops of the French forces were armed with the Lefaucheux Navy Model 1858 issue revolver, while other officers and men carried with them Lefaucheux Model 1854 revolvers which they had purchased privately. Impressed by these advanced firearms, the Kingdom of Sardinia adopted the Lefaucheux revolver for its navy, and purchased small quantities from Eugene Lefaucheux in Paris. Because they were drawn from the firm's existing commercial inventory, those arms were not stamped with any identifying military markings.

By 1861 Italy had been almost completely reunited under King Victor Emmanuel, with Lombardy having come back into the fold during 1859, most of the Papal states during 1860, and the two Sicilys in 1861. There remained, however, great social and political unrest throughout the country, especially in the southern regions where poverty and generally poor living conditions created strife among the populace. There, too, existed the "*Brigandage*", large roving guerilla bands engaged in all manner of criminal activities. In response to the crisis the Italian *Carabinieri*, or state police force, was greatly increased in size and strength as well as in the scope of its operations. The agency requested that another new revolver design especially suited to their needs be studied and commissioned from Eugene Lefaucheux. But because modern arms were so urgently needed to control the rampant lawlessness, especially so in the hard-hit rural south, as a stopgap measure the Italian government ordered the purchase of another 3,000 commercial Model 1854 pinfire revolvers from Lefaucheux. Like the previous purchase those revolvers received no special markings, but were issued for immediate service with the *Carabinieri Reali.*

Soon, specifications for a new police handgun design had been agreed on: a shorter, lighter, and more compact 12mm caliber pinfire revolver based on the tried-and-true Lefaucheux Model 1854. In order to avoid the problems of bent and broken ejector rods, the entire fixed ejector assembly was eliminated from the new arms, a decision endorsed by the Italian Army.

By then, however, the situation in the south was approaching anarchy; even more small arms were urgently needed to equip the ever-growing ranks of the *Carabinieri.* In yet another stopgap move, Eugene Lefaucheux convinced the Italian authorities to purchase a version of his Model 1854 pinfire revolver which had been slightly modified by unscrewing the standard ejector rod head, removing the spring and rod entirely, and shortening the barrel from 155mm to 120mm in length. These modifications not only could be done quickly, but without making major alterations to Lefaucheux' existing factory or production equipment. The Italian government agreed to the proposal, and 5,000 so-modified Model 1854 revolvers were delivered into Italian arsenals within two months. Not all examples of the "new" short-barrel model had their ejector assemblies removed (*see Plate 3-20*), and others were altered even further by Glisenti, who ground off the integral ejector housing from the right side of the barrel lug.

While the long-barrel models retained their popularity with the Italian Navy, the modified short-barrel Model 1854 revolvers were used effectively not only by the *Carabinieri* but by military units as well.

Due to the country's continuing domestic unrest, soon production of the entirely new Italian Model 1861 revolver was undertaken. Called the "*Pistola a rotazione da Carabinieri Reali Modello 1861*" (Model 1861 Royal Police revolver), this six-shot, 12mm caliber pinfire arm measured 250mm in overall length and had a 120mm-long barrel; its total weight was 980 grams (*see Plate 3-21*). Not only was the barrel assembly shorter, but the gun was manufactured with no provision for an ejector rod; rather, a separate rod was issued with each revolver. At first the ejector rods were simply those that had been removed from the Model 1854 short-barrel revolvers discussed previously; later a thicker and stronger rod having a slot milled in its end for a cleaning patch was provided.

The Model 1861 *Carabinieri* revolver featured an oval shape to its triggerguard and buttcap, as well as a shorter front sight blade, and remained in service from 1861 until 1874. The example pictured in *Plate 3-21* has an unusual extra feature not noted on other Model 1861s: a 29mm-long piece of brass was fitted to the end of the barrel after it had been turned down, thereby lengthening the barrel by 15mm. No explanation has surfaced for this unorthodox modification; perhaps it was an attempt to create a signal gun, or an experiment with some type of pyrotechnics. The brass, cannon-style muzzle extension forms a cup larger than the bore, of approximately the outside diameter of the barrel.

In 1869 G. Glisenti of Brescia, Italy began producing under license approximately 5,000 Model 1854-style revolvers. Each was marked "*Acciajo Fuso*" along with a serial number on the right side of the frame above the triggerguard, and "G. *Glisenti—Brescia*" on the left side of the frame. The revolvers made toward the end of this contract additionally have a Glisenti logo stamped atop the barrel flat.

By that time the Italians had overcome their opposition to having an ejector rod made integral

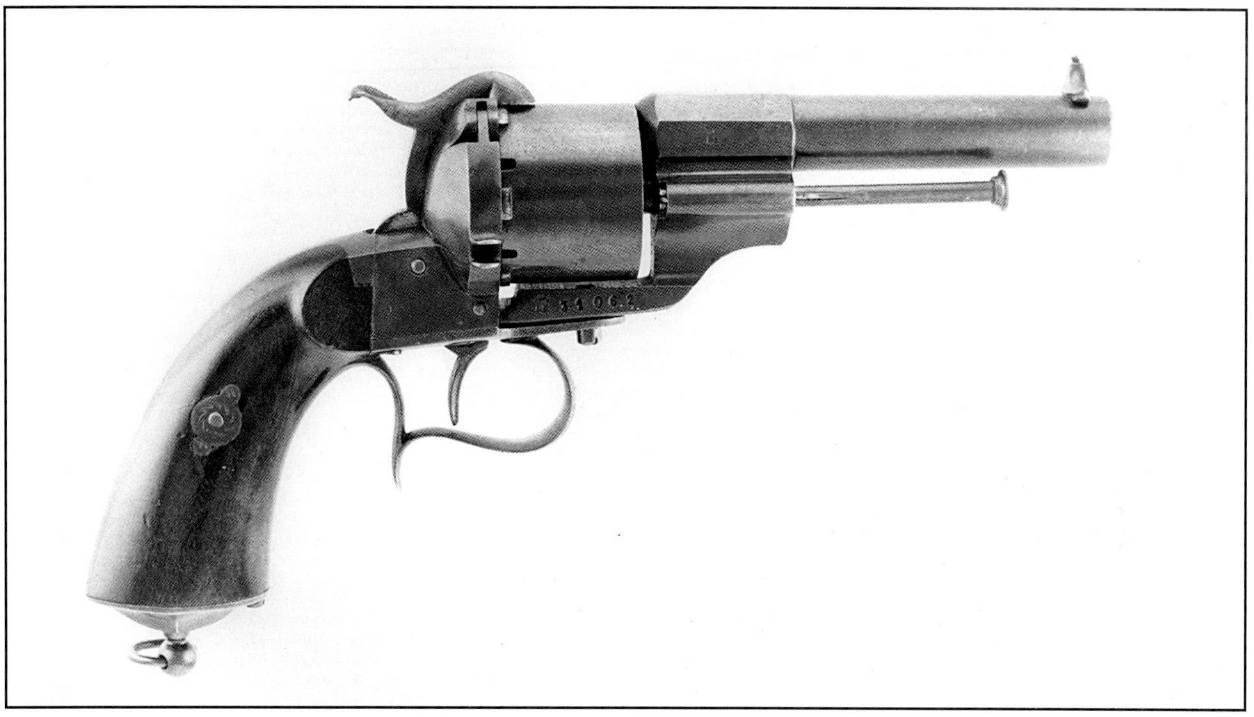

Plate 3-20. Lefaucheux-made Italian Model 1861 *"Carabinieri Reali"* modified revolver having ejector rod. *Chris C. Curtis collection; Richard McMillan photograph*

Plate 3-21. Lefaucheux-made Italian Model 1861 *"Carabinieri Reali"* modified revolver without ejector rod but having unique brass barrel extension fitted to muzzle. *Chris C. Curtis collection; F.W. Hulbert photograph*

with the arm. While the separately-issued rods had proved more durable, they also were lost with far greater regularity, especially under typically hard military use.

The Model 1854 revolvers manufactured by Glisenti were based on the Lefaucheux design, and examples of the Glisenti-made arm follow very closely the specifications of the French original. Intended to replace the Lefaucheux Model 1854 and the Model 1861 *Carabinieri* arms as they became unserviceable, the Glisenti revolvers were issued to Army and *Carabinieri* units in the field until 1872, and to the navy until 1876, when all pinfire arms were phased out of Italian service, including the original issue of Lefaucheux commercial revolvers.

Although the theme of this chapter is the official military adoption and use of the various types of pinfire small arms, a revolver made by the Mazzocchi Brothers fits into the category by virtue of its interesting para-military history. This type was approved for use by the Roman police force on November 26, 1867, and designated the *"Pistola da Gendarmeria Modello 1868"* (Pontifical Police Revolver Model 1868).

During the period of domestic unrest and conflict that raged throughout Italy, the opposing factions had acquired numerous types of pinfire arms. While the majority were of Lefaucheux' design, others also were represented, such as the later Models 8 and 9 of Chamelot & Delvigne manufacture. In turn those arms influenced the revolver design of the Mazzocchi Brothers firm. The four Mazzocchi brothers—Giovanni, Pietro, Luigi, and Giuseppe—were *Camerali*, exclusive official armsmakers for the Papal troops in the territory of Rome. Under that arrangement the brothers already had delivered 1,000 Model 1857 carbines to an elite unit of Papal sharphooters.

The Model 1868 revolver illustrated in *Plate 3-22* is very similar in physical appearance and mechanical function to the Chamelot & Delvigne models. Marked *"Flli Mazzocchi–Roma"* on top of the barrel, the Model 1868's cylinder revolves counter-clockwise, the loading gate is on the left side of the frame, and it is chambered for the 9mm caliber pinfire cartridge. The spur trigger is unusual for a pinfire revolver, however. The overall length of the Mazzocchi revolver is 185mm; its weight is 609 grams.

The Model 1868 revolvers remained in Papal service for only a short time, until late 1870, when

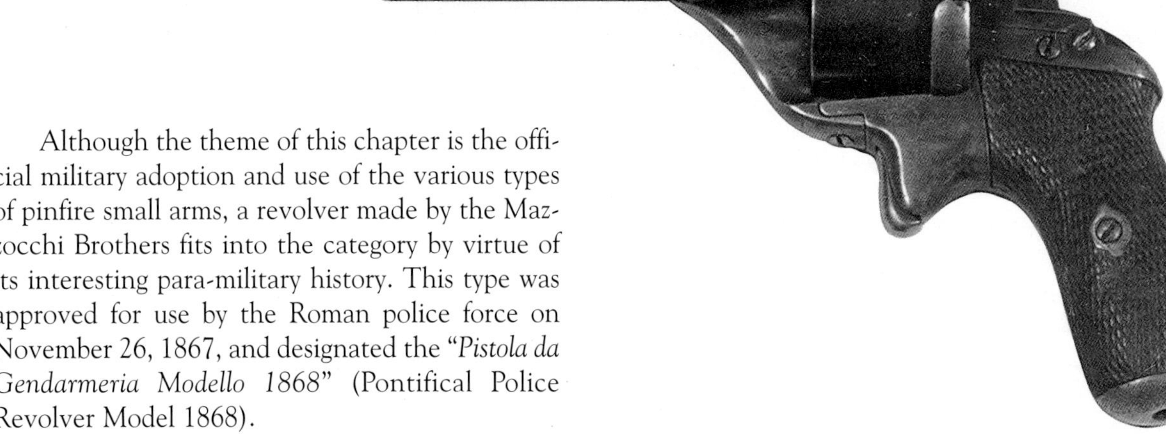

Plate 3-22. Lefaucheux-design Italian Model 1868 *"Gendarmeria"* revolver made by Mazzocchi Brothers in Rome for the Papal Police. *Courtesy James Lowther; John Calcany photograph*

all were delivered to the Italian Army troops then occupying Rome. The four Mazzocchi Brothers were allowed to continue in business under Italian rule, and on September 30, 1871 the firm received a license for perfecting and manufacturing Remington Rolling Block-type firearms which were later adopted for use by Papal troops.

Russia

The Russian infantry tactics utilizing musket and bayonet were similar to those employed throughout Europe during the first half of the nineteenth century. Although handguns were regarded as secondary weapons, the Russian government did consider replacing the outmoded, single-shot smoothbore pistol that had been standard issue since the mid-1800s with a newer, military style revolver. The Crimean war (1853-1856) clearly demonstrated that the need for modernizing Russia's small arms arsenal was imperative.

Plate 3-23. Detail view of top of barrel lug of the revolver pictured in *Plate 3-24*, showing crest of Czar Nicholas I of Russia stamped into metal. *Chris C. Curtis collection; Richard McMillan photograph*

Plate 3-24. Lefaucheux-design Model 1854 revolver made at the Tula Arsenal, Russia. *Chris C. Curtis collection; Richard McMillan photograph*

A military arms commission appointed for the purpose rejected all existing native revolver designs, and instead began to seek foreign types of superior quality. At that time the Russian government instituted a standard practice of small arms acquisition that would remain in use for many years to come: the purchase of small lots of arms suitable for testing, followed by copying and their subsequent manufacture at Russian arms factories, primarily the Tula Arsenal. The practice continued well into the 1880s, producing Russian versions of such notable revolver designs as the Beaumont-Adams, the Galand, and the Smith & Wesson 3rd Model Russian, in addition to the Lefaucheux Model 1854.

While the general appearance of the Model 1854 revolvers produced at the Tula Arsenal was the same, the workmanship in evidence on the Russian-made examples is clearly inferior to the French original. An example of the rare, Russian-manufactured Model 1854 revolver is pictured in *Plate 3-24*. The right barrel flat is stamped, in Russian, "*Under the Directorship of Lt. Col. Goltjakov.*"[1] The top barrel flat bears the crest of Czar Nicholas I (*see Plate 3-23*), who reigned between 1825 and 1855. Noteworthy is the fact that although the revolver was manufactured long after Nicholas I's rule had ended, the Russians were notoriously slow in changing firearms markings on the assumption of power by a new czar.

Plate 3-25 (above). Danish 12mm caliber pinfire Model
1861 Navy revolver serial number "190",
manufactured at the Copenhagen Arsenal, pictured
with its original issue holster. *Chris C. Curtis collection;
John Calcany photograph*

Plate 3-26 (above). Detail view of top of barrel lug of
the revolver pictured in *Plate 3-25*, showing crown
over "ST" ("*So Tojhuset*") stamp of the Copenhagen
Naval Arsenal. *Chris C. Curtis collection; Richard
McMillan photograph*

*Plate 3-27 (opposite page). Danish Model 1871/1882
double-action, 12mm caliber pinfire military revolver
manufactured by Auguste Francotte of Liége, Belgium.
Courtesy Robert E. Brooker, Jr.;
Robert E. Brooker, Jr. photograph*

Denmark

In 1861 Denmark adopted a six-shot, 12mm caliber pinfire revolver for navy use. The original model for the arm was fabricated by N.S. Jenssen, master armorer at the Danish Naval Armory. Actual production was begun under Georg Christensen, who at the time was armorer at the Copenhagen Arsenal. The Danish revolver featured a solid frame having a top strap into which the barrel was threaded. Other features of interest are the ring trigger, and the lanyard loop made integral with the backstrap, the latter feature being in common with later army-issue revolvers.

The example pictured in *Plate 3-25* is accompanied by its issue holster. The revolver is marked on cylinder, frame, and barrel with the serial number "190", and on the right side of the frame at its juncture with the top strap "GC" in large letters, for armorer Georg Christensen. At the top front of the top strap are the initials "ST" surmounted by a crown (*see Plate 3-26*), which stand for "*So Tojhuset*", or naval arsenal. The example pictured in *Plate 3-25* has a rounded hammer without cocking spur; two other examples observed during the course of this study had hammers with cocking spurs.

Production of the Model 1861 Danish pinfire revolver was very limited, being a mere 201 pieces. As they remained in service over thirty years, until 1891, obviously surviving examples are very scarce.

A decade after the former design was adopted, in 1871 the Danish Navy adopted another double-action, 12mm caliber pinfire revolver. It was manufactured by Auguste Francotte of Liége, and bears his logo comprised of the letters "AF" beneath a crown, and the letters "SA" for "*So Artilleriet*", or Naval Artillery. Francotte's name and/or the words "*Acier Fondu*" ("cast steel") also may be found atop the barrel.

Designated the Model 1871, this new revolver type remained in service until 1882 when it was modified to use centerfire cartridges. That was accomplished by redesigning the upper portion of the hammer, adding a firing pin striker, and boring

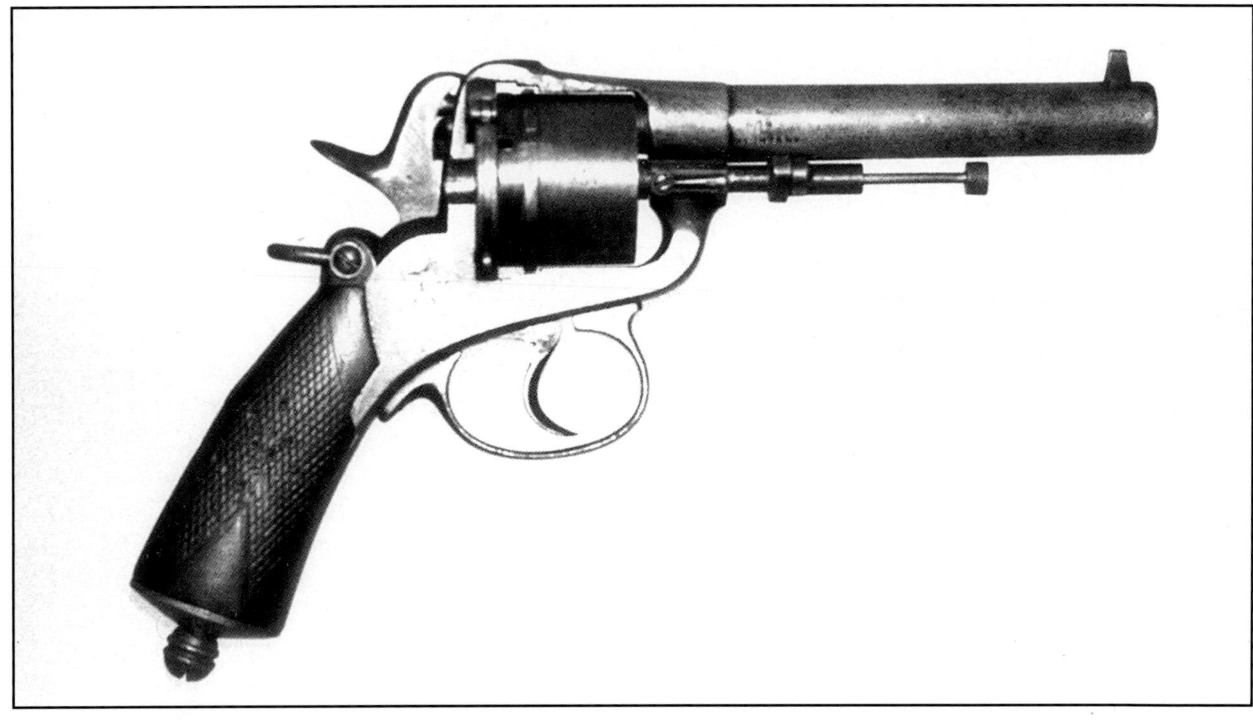

Plate 3-28. Danish Model 1865/1897 revolver made to use the 11.44mm centerfire metallic cartridge. *Courtesy Robert E. Brooker, Jr.; Robert E. Brooker, Jr. photograph*

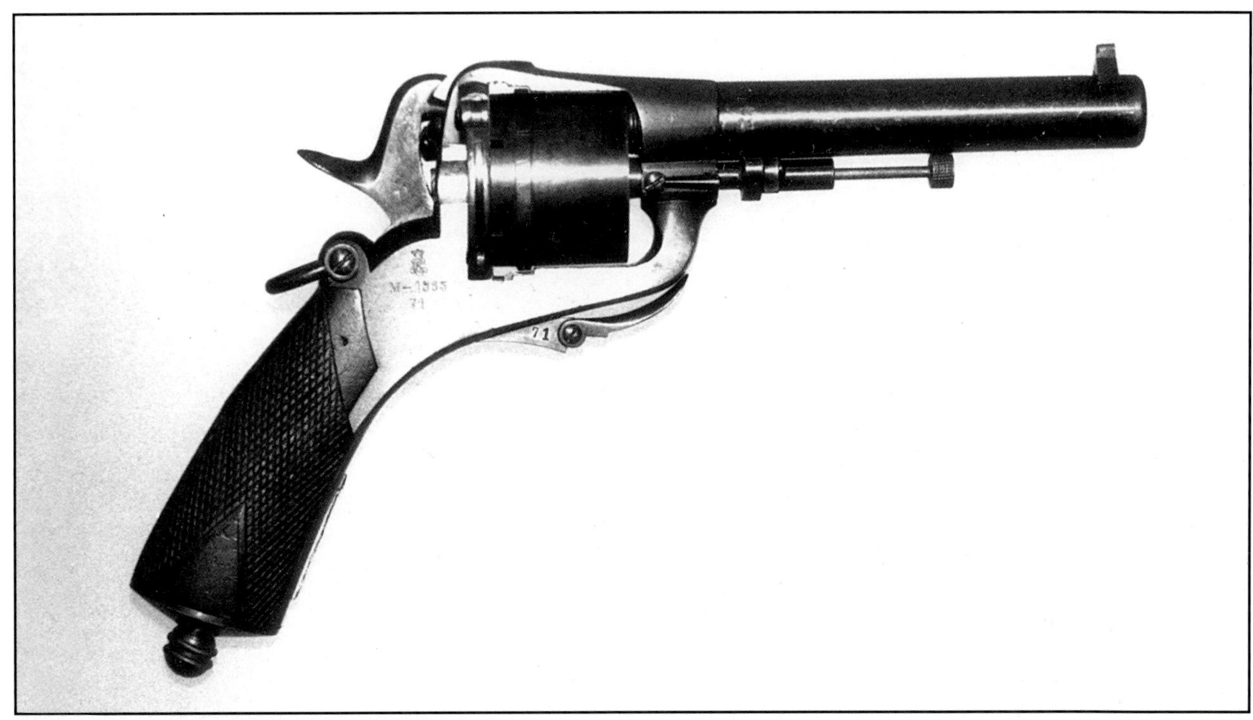

Plate 3-29. A rare variant (only 52 made) Danish Model 1865/1899 revolver altered for use in the Danish colonies. *Courtesy Robert E. Brooker, Jr.; Robert E. Brooker, Jr. photograph*

through the frame to accept the firing pin. Subsequently redesignated the Model 1871/1882 (*see Plate 3-27*), the type was not phased out of Danish naval service until 1910.

A 12mm caliber pinfire revolver was adopted by the Danish Army in 1865. It was similar in appearance to the Model 1861 Navy revolver, with the exception of having a folding trigger rather than the latter type's ring trigger. The army revolvers were manufactured at the *Kronborg Gevaerfabrik* (Kronberg Rifle Factory), and are so marked, in addition to being marked on the right side of the frame with the model designation, "M-1865." Some examples also are marked with a crowned, intertwining "CR" and the small Roman numeral "IX", which refers to the then-King of Denmark, Christian IX. Regimental markings are sometimes found stamped on buttcaps, and all major parts bear the serial number of the arm.

This well-made revolver has a hammer-block safety located on the left side of the frame behind the cylinder. Another noteworthy design feature is the movable left sideplate which swivels downward to expose the internal trigger and hammer lockwork (a Lefaucheux-Chaineux design), after the wood grips have been removed. The Danish Army Model 1865 revolver remained in active military service until 1897.

That year, the model was redesigned and modified to utilize an unusual 11.44mm centerfire round having a wooden projectile and nickel casing. The folding trigger was replaced with the standard fixed style, and a triggerguard was added. Also added was an integral ejector rod, and the hammer safety block lever was redesigned and enlarged. Newly designated the Model 1865/1897 (*see Plate 3-28*), this Danish Army revolver remained in service well into the twentieth century, until 1919.

Another style of modification of the Danish Model 1865 revolver is pictured in *Plate 3-29*. It also features an ejector rod and redesigned safety lever, but retains the old-style folding trigger. This very rare alteration, of which only fifty-two examples were made and designated the Model 1865/1899, was intended for use in the Danish

colonies. Like the previous model it too remained in service until 1919.

Egypt

The *Khedive* of Egypt during the early 1860s, Ismail Pasha, was a great admirer of France and all things Gallic, as had been his uncle, Said Pasha, who had made Egypt an unofficial satellite of France. That alliance had been further strengthened during the planning, promotion, and construction of the Suez Canal between 1859 and 1869 by French diplomat and engineer Ferdinand Marie de Lesseps (1805-1894). In return for the boost to the national economy and employment for tens of thousands of local workers that the canal project provided, Egypt hired French military advisers to assist in the training of Egyptian troops, and in 1864 sent token artillery forces into Mexico on one of Napoleon III's ill-fated expeditions to expand his French Empire into the Americas.

As many of those French military advisers carried Lefaucheux Model 1854 revolvers as their personal sidearms, it was inevitable that the Egyptians would notice and admire that handsome pistol. Soon afterward, an order was placed with Lefaucheux for approximately 250[2] Model 1854 revolvers of a unique design to be supplied to Egyptian cavalry troops. They were 12mm caliber pinfire Model 1854s fitted with special extended-length barrels having long-range folding-leaf rear sights, and fixed (non-detachable) skeleton shoulder stocks (*see Plate 3-30*). The Lefaucheux address legend appears on the barrels, but not on the frames; all serial numbers observed have been very low, not exceeding 2,000. In addition, a secondary number, either an issue or armory rack number, is stamped on both the grip and left side of the frame. A few civilian examples have been observed; obviously Eugene Lefaucheux produced a small batch of commercial revolvers concurrent with the Egyptian military contract arms. Of interest is the fact that while both civilian and military examples bear very low serial numbers, both styles also embody later-production Model 1854 features, doubtless indicative of their being numbered

Plate 3-30. Variant Lefaucheux Model 1854 revolver made for the Egyptian cavalry, having an extra-long barrel with folding-leaf rear sight and a fixed shoulder stock. *Chris C. Curtis collection; Richard McMillan photograph*

in a special serial number block.

Rather than being removable as with their civilian counterparts, shoulder stocks of the Egyptian cavalry revolvers are permanently fastened with screws at the rear of the slightly oversize wrap-around-style wood grips. A lanyard ring is fitted to the buttcap, which attaches a chain to a corresponding ring on the underside of the stock. The chain has a sliding ring to provide a point of attachment for a shoulder sling or saddle scabbard, to prevent loss when in use by a mounted horseman.

By 1867 the French had fallen out of favor with the Egyptian viceroy. Modern machinery had replaced the thousands of unskilled Egyptian laborers working on the Suez Canal, and the project's stockholders would firmly exert European control over the canal for the next ninety-nine years. That unpleasant situation, in addition to the humiliating expulsion of Napoleon III from Mexico, provided Ismail Pasha good enough reason to fire all of his French military advisers. They were immediately replaced by battle-hardened Americans, Union and Confederate veterans who had fought so bitterly against each other in the late Civil War.

The French were gone from Egypt. The special Lefaucheux cavalry revolvers were all that remained as their legacy.

Sweden

In 1863 a decision was made by the Swedish government to purchase a quantity of 12mm caliber pinfire cartridge revolvers from the Lefaucheux factory. The style of these revolvers was similar to the civilian version of Lefaucheux' French Model 1858 revolver. Two thousand revolvers were purchased and delivered into Swedish arsenals; all were stamped with the country's official acceptance mark, three crowns, on the right barrel lug (*see Plate 3-32*). The Lefaucheux logo and the serial number of the arm are stamped on the right side of the frame, along with the Lefaucheux oval marking on the left side of the frame and the Lefaucheux address on top of the barrel.

The serial number range of these revolvers—designated the Model 1863—falls between 78,000 and 80,500. Eleven hundred and ten of them were delivered to the Swedish Army for distribution among cavalry and artillery units, and the remaining 890 went to the navy. Serial numbers were not assigned in blocks; rather, guns were distributed randomly between the two service branches. Included with the original purchase was one hundred rounds of 12mm caliber pinfire ammunition to accompany each revolver. The cartridges were provided by the French firm Gevelot.

Plate 3-31 pictures a Lefaucheux Model 1863 Swedish Navy revolver which has an additional mark resembling a crown stamped on the right side of the frame ahead of the serial number. This mark is occasionally accompanied by yet another mark, a cross within a circle, that is the official dismissal stamp of the Swedish Navy. The latter mark was applied when the Model 1863 revolvers were phased out of service in 1884, and replaced by the double-action centerfire French *Modele* 1873 (designated the Model 1884 by the Swedish authorities). Examples are found both with and without the dismissal stamp.

On April 19, 1871 the Swedish Army adopted the new 11mm caliber centerfire revolvers, called the Model 1871, of Lefaucheux-Francotte design, which were purchased from the French government arsenal at St. Etienne.

Although by 1879 some Swedish cavalry units had turned in their single-shot percussion pistols for the Model 1871, that same year all units were ordered to surrender their pinfire revolvers for arsenal modification to utilize centerfire ammunition. Thus the Model 1863 Army revolvers were altered to use the same 11mm centerfire cartridge as the Model 1871. These changes included cutting off the forward portion of the hammer which had struck the pin of the old pinfire round, and

Plate 3-31 (below). A single-action Swedish Model 1863 Navy revolver. *Chris C. Curtis collection; Richard McMillan photograph*

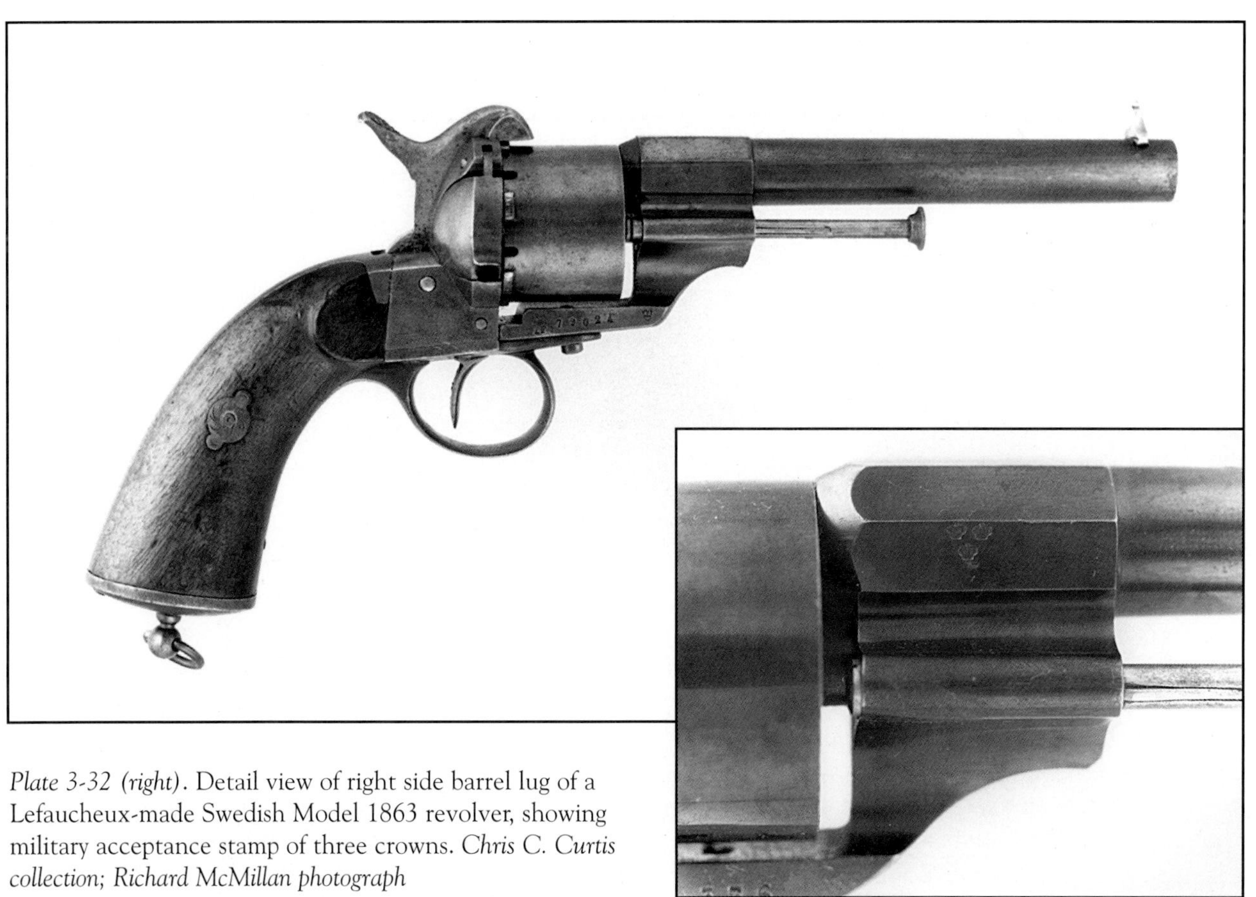

Plate 3-32 (right). Detail view of right side barrel lug of a Lefaucheux-made Swedish Model 1863 revolver, showing military acceptance stamp of three crowns. *Chris C. Curtis collection; Richard McMillan photograph*

adding a firing pin, then milling recesses into the rear of the cylinder chambers to seat the rim of the centerfire cartridge.

These converted guns were redesignated the Model 1863/1879 revolver, and remained in service until 1890. Following their alteration they were reissued to cavalry and artillery units, and occasionally unit markings will be found stamped on the right side of the frame just ahead of the grip juncture. Because very few Swedish Army Model 1863 revolvers escaped the 1879 recall and modification process, examples in original pinfire configuration are considered scarce among collectors.

Norway

In 1859 a small number of Lefaucheux Model 1854 12mm caliber pinfire revolvers were purchased for testing by the Norwegian Navy. They were standard civilian revolvers (having the spur triggerguard and fluted buttcap) that had been randomly drawn from regular commercial production stores; no military markings were applied. Serial numbers were in the 14,500 to 16,000 range.

Called the Model 1859 (sometimes referred to as the Model 1862 by collectors), the Lefaucheux revolvers remained the property of the navy until 1893 when they were replaced by the 7.5mm caliber centerfire Nagant revolver.

Early in 1864 the Norwegian parliament allocated funds to purchase 1,500 Lefaucheux revolvers of a pattern similar to the Swedish Model 1863 contract arms. Delivery was fulfilled during the months of April, May, and June of that year. Eleven hundred of the 1,500 revolvers ordered were identical to the Swedish revolvers (see *Plate 3-33*); they were destined for delivery to the enlisted personnel of Norwegian cavalry and artillery units. Four hundred of the remaining contract arms were intended for issue to officers, who could select their personal sidearm from three versions according to individual preference in barrel style and mechanism: 200 were single-action revolvers similar to the guns above, except for full-octagonal barrels; the remainder were double-action revolvers made on Eugene Lefaucheux' 1862 "Triple-Action"

patent, 100 with full-round barrels, and 100 with full-octagonal barrels (see *Plate 3-34*).

All four variations of the Norwegian contract Lefaucheux revolvers were designated the Model 1864, including both officer and enlisted classes. Serial numbers of the single-action arms range between 80,000 and 82,000; those of the double-action variety are in the 31,000 to 32,000 range.

All 1,500 of the Norwegian Model 1864 revolvers carry standard Lefaucheux markings, logos, and serial numbers, plus the official military acceptance stamp of Norway—a rampant lion holding a raised battle axe—on the right barrel lug (see *Plate 3-35*). The gothic letters "AR" are stamped into the wood of the right grip (see *Plate 3-36*) approximately in line with the serial number on the frame. The latter marking, which oftentimes has been worn away as a result of the revolvers' hard military use, signifies acceptance by the armorer responsible for the inspection process, Anton Rasmussen.

In 1867 the Norwegian government opted to manufacture their own version of the single-action Lefaucheux Model 1864 revolver having a round barrel, and that same year production was commenced at the Konigsberg Arms Factory. Full-scale manufacture was never achieved, however, and only 200 revolvers were delivered to the army the following year. All bear low serial numbers in the usual right frame location, in addition to a controller's mark and a crowned "K" stamped on the right rear of the frame behind the cylinder.

These revolvers were noteworthy for their longevity, especially in light of their military purpose, and they remained as issue arms from 1864 to 1898 when all of the single-action variations (of both Lefaucheux and Konigsberg manufacture) were recalled to the Konigsberg Arms Factory for modification. There, a reinforcing top strap having an integral rear sight was added; redesignated the Model 1864/1898, the revolvers were reissued. Beginning in 1883 they were gradually replaced with newer Nagant models of both the single- and double-action varieties, which continued until 1910 when all single-action Model 1864 Norwegian revolvers were declared obsolete.

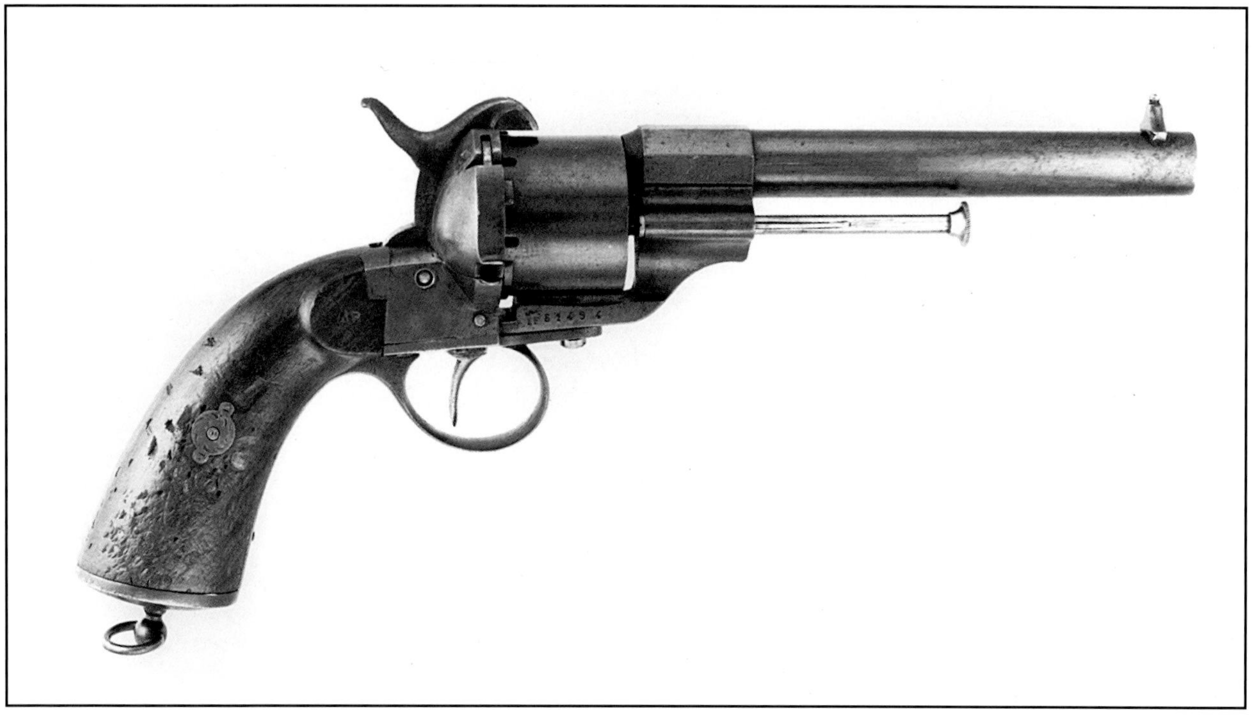

Plate 3-33. A single-action, Lefaucheux-made Norwegian Model 1864 revolver for use by enlisted troops. *Chris C. Curtis collection; Richard McMillan photograph*

Plate 3-34. A double-action, Lefaucheux-made "Triple-Action" Norwegian Model 1864 officers' revolver. Note octagonal barrel. *Chris C. Curtis collection; Richard McMillan photograph*

Plate 3-35. Detail view of right side barrel lug of a Lefaucheux-made Norwegian Model 1864 revolver, showing "rampant lion with battle axe" military acceptance mark. *Chris C. Curtis collection; Richard McMillan photograph*

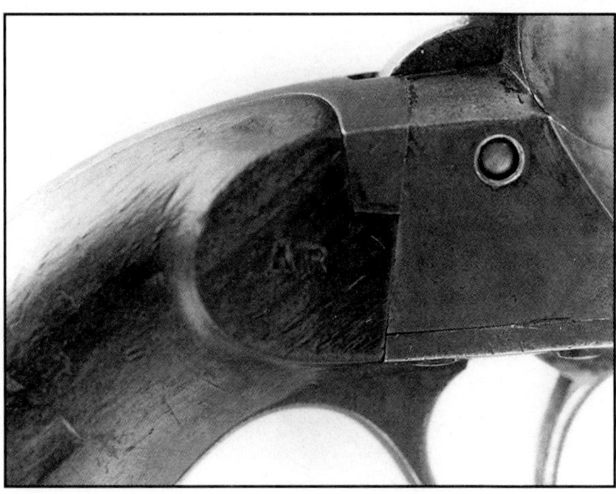

Plate 3-36. Detail view of right side of wood grip of a Lefaucheux-made Norwegian Model 1864 revolver, showing "AR" stamp of military inspector Anton Rasmussen. *Chris C. Curtis collection; Richard McMillan photograph*

The issue and use in Norway of all double-action Lefaucheux officers' models were discontinued in 1898, at the time of the modification of the single-action revolvers.

Other Countries

During 1866 a small number of double-action, 9mm caliber pinfire revolvers manufactured by Beuret Freres of Liége was issued to Swiss Army officers on an experimental basis. They were marked with the Beuret Freres name and the company trademark, "*BF*" surmounted by a crown, in addition to "*Lefaucheux Bte*" and "*Acier Fondu.*" This transition-era revolver features a unique but impractical design, in that it is chambered to utilize both pinfire and rimfire ammunition. Unfortunately, the quality of workmanship did not approach that of the arms made by Eugene Lefaucheux in Paris.

With the possible exception of France, many more pinfire arms were manufactured in Belgium than in any other country. Oddly, though, the Belgian armed forces never were officially equipped with pinfire arms. A Belgian government trial was conducted in 1859, in which a Lefaucheux re-volver that had been slightly modified by A. Janssen[3] was tested, but no decision to adopt a pinfire revolver of any design was ever made.

It has been reported that Romania purchased 4,000 revolvers from the Lefaucheux factory in Paris during 1864.[4] The contract was for arms of the civilian "navy" style, in the serial number range between 99,000 and 110,000. They were not stamped with military markings. In 1876 many were converted to use the new centerfire cartridge. While the author found no primary historical evidence to substantiate the existence or details of such a contract, examples do exist which fall into this serial number range and which bear the modification mentioned.

As late as 1870, with the coming of age of improved centerfire ammunition and the revolvers to use it, the Dutch military establishment issued a small number of 12mm caliber pinfire revolvers to certain units for experimentation and testing. *Plate 3-37* pictures such a revolver. It is well made, having a solid top strap with integral rear sight, and is marked "*Meyers Bte*" in addition to bearing pre-1877 Belgian proofmarks.

Plate 3-37. A 12mm caliber pinfire Dutch military revolver marked *"Meyers Bte."*, made in Liége, Belgium. *Chris C. Curtis collection; F.W. Hulbert photograph*

Plate 3-38. A double-action, Chamelot & Delvigne Model 8 12mm caliber pinfire revolver. Note bayonet lug on right barrel flat. *Courtesy Don Loughery; F.W. Hulbert photograph*

During the late nineteenth century, high military officers generally followed established tradition and went into battle armed only with a sword or cane with which to direct the combat action, but not to participate in it directly with a firearm.

Many European officers were beginning to be more practical, however. Although their governments did not officially issue sidearms to officers, they chose to arm themselves with privately purchased equipment, often the very best that the market had to offer. Regulations concerning officers' individual sidearms tended to be rather lax, and some chose to carry the fancier grades of revolver, many of which were ornately engraved and had grips of ivory, bone, or rare woods. Not all were chambered for the large 12mm caliber pinfire cartridge, either, as the lighter 9mm caliber revolvers were then coming into more popular use.

As the demand for military style pinfire revolvers increased, the armsmakers of Europe began producing many varieties of the arm. The result was a profusion of revolver types in 9mm and 12mm calibers (having both single- and double-action mechanisms, fixed triggers with triggerguards, and lanyard rings) that were acceptable to the military tastes and standards of the day. Shown here in *Plates 3-38 through 3-44* are a few representative examples, both plain and ornate, from the vast variety of military style pinfire cartridge small arms then available.

Plate 3-38 pictures a Chamelot & Delvigne 12mm caliber revolver referred to by the maker as their Model 8, which was patented in May of 1864. As with all arms made by that firm the cylinder of this specimen revolves counter-clockwise, and the loading gate is on the left side of the frame. Examples of this fine revolver in both 9mm and 12mm calibers were tested in France by the permanent Ordnance Commission at Vincennes on August 2, 1867. The results of the trial, announced in January of 1868, in which the Chamelot & Delvigne revolver was tested against the Lefaucheux-designed Model 1858 revolver then currently in use, clearly favored the 12mm caliber Chamelot & Delvigne. The overriding factors in the panel's decision were the latter revolver's double-action mech-

anism, and the ease with which it could be pointed and aimed. In addition, its overall design was judged to be sturdier, having fewer delicate pieces, resulting in less need for field maintenance. The French Ordnance Commission recommended an extensive field trial by army troops for the Chamelot & Delvigne revolver, but such a practical test failed to materialize and no official purchase was forthcoming. Note the bayonet lug on the right side of the barrel on the example illustrated, perhaps yet another experimental feature designed to attract potential military contract purchases.

Plate 3-39 pictures a well-made military style revolver, also in 12mm pinfire caliber. Its features include a top strap for added strength and a pin shield to improve functional safety. It is stamped on top of the barrel, "*A. Francotte A Liége*", in addition to Francotte's logo, the letters "*AF*" beneath a crown. Other markings appearing on this sturdy arm include "*Lefaucheux Bte*" and "*Acier Fondu*", as well as pre-1877 Liége proofmarks.

Plate 3-40 pictures a 12mm caliber pinfire revolver marked "*Dumonthier Bte*" on the side of the barrel, and on top of the barrel with the Paris address of the arms retailer, LePage. This standard style of revolver exhibits the one-piece horn grip and same types of frame and cylinder that are found on some of the better-known Dumonthier cutlass-pistols.

Plates 3-41 and 3-42 picture an extremely well-made 12mm caliber revolver of unknown origins. The external appearance of this example is similar to the Model 1854 Lefaucheux, but the internal mechanism is different. It is double-action only, counter to the single-action Lefaucheux. In collector condition and ornately embellished, it has an unidentified family crest surmounted by a crown engraved and gold inlaid on top of the six-inch barrel, which exhibits a beautiful damascus pattern along the greater portion of its length.

Plate 3-43 pictures a rare LeMat revolver, its cylinder chambered for the 12mm caliber pinfire cartridge and having the customary shotgun barrel beneath the revolver barrel. The pinfire LeMat revolvers are believed to have been manufactured

Plate 3-39. A double-action, military style 12mm caliber pinfire revolver made by Auguste Francotte in Liége, Belgium. Note top strap and pin shield. *Courtesy F.W. Hulbert; F.W. Hulbert photograph*

Plate 3-40. A double-action, military style 12mm pinfire revolver made by Dumonthier in Paris, having grip of dark animal horn. *Chris C. Curtis collection; F.W. Hulbert photograph*

Plate 3-41. An unmarked as to maker, but well-made 12mm caliber, double-action pinfire revolver resembling the Lefaucheux Model 1854. Note damascus pattern on barrel, and embellishments to metal and wood. *Courtesy John Mullen; John Mullen photograph*

Plate 3-42. Detail view of top of barrel lug of the revolver pictured in *Plate 3-41*, showing unidentified, gold inlaid family crest. *Courtesy John Mullen; John Mullen photograph*

only after the American Civil War, but Dr. LeMat had a patent registered and the technology and manufacturing facilities available to produce arms during that turbulent period. Dr. Alexandre François LeMat and his firearms are discussed in detail elsewhere in this study (*see* Chapter Four).

The popularity of military style pinfire revolvers during the latter half of the nineteenth century was not confined just to the European continent, and in fact many saw use in locales far removed from the birthplace of the pinfire system. Some were gifts presented to persons of high rank or other importance in distant countries, and many more were put to use in everyday encounters. The revolver pictured at the top of *Plate 3-44* was manufactured by Comblain of Liége, Belgium, but bears a Japanese inscription that when translated reads, "*Gifu Ken—District of Tokyo 1885*", being a police arm that was marked for use by a district law enforcement unit.

The 12mm caliber revolver pictured at the center of *Plate 3-44* is of French manufacture, and is marked "*Javelle*." In addition it bears the inscrip-

Plate 3-43. A LeMat combination revolver chambered for the 12mm caliber pinfire cartridge, with shot barrel beneath. *Courtesy private collection; John Calcany photograph*

tion (in Korean), "1884 Warrior Storage Tank Company", possibly indicating a handgun that was issued to a guard by his employer or military unit.

The 12mm caliber pinfire revolver pictured at the bottom of *Plate 3-44* is unmarked except for Liége proofmarks; the original owner's name appears in Chinese characters.

Other pinfire arms manufactured in continental Europe found their way to still different corners of the globe, to Mexico and the countries of Central and South America. Little information exists with regard to the fabrication of pinfire arms in Latin America, and it is assumed that all were imported rather than produced locally. An ornate late-nineteenth century pinfire revolver of exceptional quality was owned by Pedro II, Emperor of Brazil, and many are known which bear the markings of South American agents or retail dealers, sure testimony to the great popularity of pinfire arms in those countries.

Plate 3-45 pictures a fine, 12mm caliber pinfire revolver housed in a fitted French-style casing complete with screwdriver, oil bottle, case key, and

one hundred rounds of ammunition in a covered compartment. Called the "Stonewall Jackson" model after the type used by famed Confederate General Thomas J. Jackson during the American Civil War (*see* Chapter Four), the example illustrated is engraved and bears London proofmarks.

Finally, the 12mm caliber pinfire revolving rifle pictured in *Plate 3-46* has a distinctly military appearance, and several features uncommon to similar revolving rifles. First is the long, wood forestock beneath the smoothbore octagonal barrel. Second is its extended-length cylinder, which was intended to fire a long, brass base, paper-body cartridge carrying a slug projectile. Adding to the rifle's military flavor is the bayonet lug affixed to the muzzle adjacent to the blade front sight. While it is stamped with Liége proofmarks the rifle is unidentified as to maker, and perhaps was a prototype or experimental piece.

Military style pinfire revolvers were renowned in many countries as rugged and reliable firearms that were far advanced in technology over their percussion counterparts. Where not officially adopted by armed forces, pinfire small arms nevertheless found their way into military circles on the strength of reputation. Those privately purchased sidearms were as highly esteemed by their original owners then, as they are in collector circles today.

Privately acquired pinfire arms, as well as those adopted and issued to regular military troops, saw action in countless campaigns around the world, from Europe to the Americas, Africa to the Orient, in Crimea and the Franco-Prussian War.

And pinfire arms were used in far greater numbers in one arena of combat than in any other—perhaps one of the most legendary conflicts known to world history—the American Civil War.

Plate 3-44. Top: A pinfire revolver made by Comblain in Liége, Belgium, having Japanese police markings. Center: A 12mm caliber pinfire revolver made by Javelle, in France, having Korean markings. Bottom: A 12mm caliber pinfire revolver bearing proofmarks for Liége, Belgium, having Chinese owner's name. *Courtesy Robert E. Brooker, Jr.; Robert E. Brooker, Jr. photograph*

Plate 3-45 (left). A fine example of the 12mm caliber pinfire revolver known as the "Stonewall Jackson model", cased with accoutrements and 100 rounds of ammunition. *Courtesy Don Kramer; Ferrari Color photograph*

Plate 3-46 (below). A perhaps experimental 12mm caliber pinfire, military style, smoothbore revolving rifle bearing proofmarks for Liége, Belgium, but unidentified as to maker. *Courtesy private collection; John Calcany photograph*

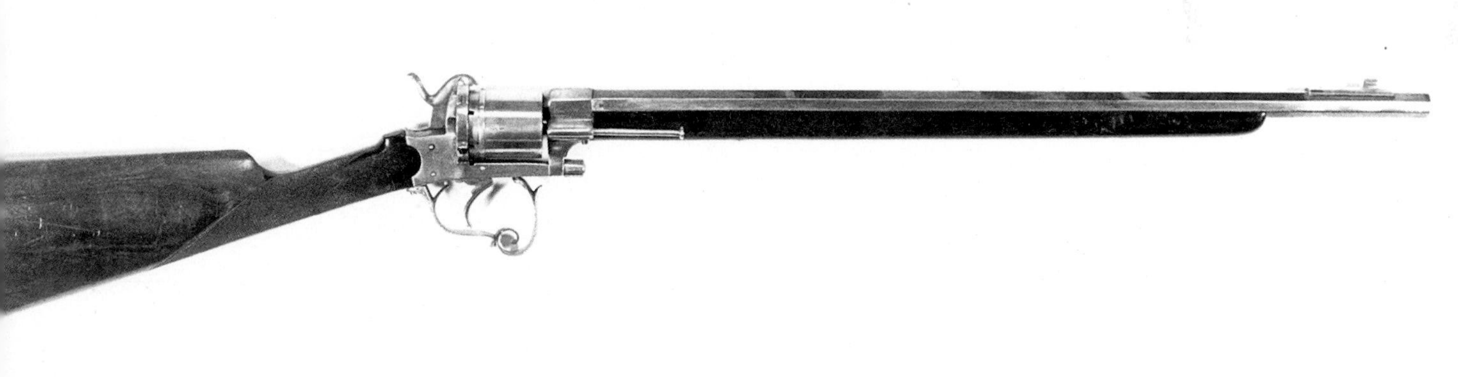

Chapter notes.

1. Lt. Col. Nikolai Ivanov Goltjakov was active at the Tula Arsenal between the years of 1860 and 1880.
2. This low production figure was arrived at through examination of the serial number range and military unit markings of extant specimens.

3. Gunmaker A. Janssen was involved with the Brussels firearms industry from the mid-1850s until 1884. Janssen received Belgian patents for pinfire revolver designs, as well as for improvements to the same, in both 1856 and 1859.
4. Rolf H. Muller, *Geschichte und Technik der Europaischen Militarrevolver.*

Plate 4-1. This unidentified but steely-eyed young Civil War Union soldier posed for the photographer in uniform with his sword at his side and a pinfire revolver tucked into his belt. *Courtesy Herb Peck, Jr.*

Pinfire Arms and the American Civil War

Any serious effort to research even general primary information concerning the arms and equipment used during the American Civil War virtually mandates a visit to the National Archives in Washington, DC. Once there, however, the researcher is seriously challenged in his or her attempt to find information on specific, more narrow subjects, such as the Lefaucheux revolver. Even the considerable amount of material made available to the author at the time of his visit to the Archives clearly was not sufficient to document every record concerning the purchase or use of pinfire arms and ammunition during the Civil War.

Much of the information presented in this chapter was located and verified during the author's four full days spent searching through seemingly countless volumes of *related* historical material. Some of that material, such as the partially-surviving records of purchases of arms and ammunition, has been published previously. But other, previously undiscovered records came to light during the author's search that substantially increase the available body of knowledge on the subject. For instance, a *single purchase* of 12mm pinfire cartridges was found to have been *one million rounds*, many times the amount formerly believed to have been the total quantity of pinfire ammunition used during the entire war!

Pinfire Arms used by Union Forces

The United States government had been an interested observer at the London Exhibition, held in 1851, during which many advances in the field of firearms were displayed to an international audience. Nevertheless, at the outbreak of the War Between the States ten years later, Federal forces largely were still equipped with semi-obsolete muskets of a style dating back to the Revolutionary War.

Throughout the decade which preceded the Civil War, the U.S. Ordnance Department experimented with many firearms designs while seeking to update and modernize the nation's armory. Countless experiments were made with, and to, varied types of guns in initial efforts to eliminate unsuitable firearms and to advance the more promising types to the next level, the official ordnance trial. During the trial a competition was held between the previously-qualified arms of various manufacturers, and Department of the Army contracts usually were awarded to the maker of the arm or arms that performed best at the trial. During the decade of the 1850s four major trials were held, but inasmuch as nineteenth-century bureaucratic "red tape" was as thick then as now, modernization of military equipment was slow in becoming a reality.

As reports began arriving from Europe that Eugene Lefaucheux' Model 1854 revolver was the front-runner in highly competitive tests for potential adoption by the French Navy, the U.S. Ordnance Department began to take notice and the new Lefaucheux arm was given preliminary consideration in May of 1857. After testing a Lefaucheux revolver (supplied by John C. Palmer, president of the Sharps Rifle Mfg. Company, from a small batch also being tested by that firm), Major Bell of the Washington Arsenal submitted a report stating that the Model 1854 revolver would be a most desirable arm for cavalry use. Following subsequent tests during April of the next year, Major Bell again praised the Lefaucheux' accuracy and efficiency, claiming that it performed exceedingly well for the limited amount of firing it had completed.

Plate 4-2 reproduces a letter (in the collections of the National Archives) describing another of these experiments with Lefaucheux revolvers. Written to Colonel H.K. Craig, Chief of Ordnance, and received by the Ordnance Department on 8 April 1858, the letter expresses the opinions of John C. Palmer following Sharps' testing of the Lefaucheux Model 1854 revolver. Palmer, one of the original stockholders in the Sharps Rifle Mfg. Company, had been elected its president and treasurer in 1851. From that time on

Plate 4-2. Copy of an 1858 letter from President J.C. Palmer of the Sharps Rifle Mfg. Co. to Colonel H.K. Craig of the U.S. Army Ordnance Department, concerning military tests of the Lefaucheux Model 1854 revolver. *Courtesy the National Archives*

Hartford Ct April 6. 1858.

Col. H. K. Craig.
Chief of Ordnance.
Dr Sir.

I beg leave to present you with my views of the LeFaucheaux Pistols —

On examination we found the Rifling defective and the bbls rusted, consequently in firing balls that were not patched or greased, the range and accuracy as well as the penetration was perceptibly affected —

The Charge of Powder is too small, but with all these drawbacks, the Pistols did extremely well, and I have no doubt can be made a most acceptable and serviceable Arm, using a metallic Cartridge, 35 grains of powder, and greased ball.

The paper tube for Cartridge would be a failure. The first one tried (paper tube) drove about half its length into the barrel and effectually prevented revolving the Cylinder until it was removed — Thirty more of the same sort were fired without any such result, and the wonder is that such a Circumstance should occur on the first trial and not afterwards — In my opinion the difficulty would be likely to occur, and should be avoided by using only the Metallic Cartridge —

Your Very Obedt Servt
J. C. Palmer.

he handled the bulk of correspondence between that firm and the Ordnance Department, most of which concerned possible arms contracts between the two. While Colonel Craig's original request authorizing the Sharps Company's testing of an unknown number of Lefaucheux revolvers could not be located, Palmer's reply is most revealing:

Col. H.K. Craig
Chief of Ordnance

Dear Sir:

I beg leave to present you with my views of the Lefaucheux Pistols.

On examination we found the Rifling defective and the bbls. rusted, consequently in firing balls that were not patched or greased, the range and accuracy as well as the penetration was perceptibly affected.

The charge of powder is too small, but with all these drawbacks, the Pistols did extremely well, and I have no doubt can be made a most acceptable and serviceable arm, using a metallic cartridge, 25 grains of powder, and greased ball.[1]

The paper tube for cartridge would be a failure. The first one tried (paper tube) drove about half its length into the barrel and effectively prevented revolving the cylinder until it was removed. Thirty more of the same sort were fired without any such result, and the wonder is that such a circumstance should occur in the first trial and not afterwards. In my opinion the difficulty would be likely to occur, and should be avoided by using only the Metallic Cartridge.

Your Very Obed't. Svn't.,
J.C. Palmer

One might wonder why paper cartridges were used in the testing process at all. Some early pinfire handguns were designed having a chamber diameter slightly larger than the barrel bore, creating a rim at the junction of the paper cartridge tube and the projectile which prevented the tube from following the ball down the barrel when the arm was discharged. However, the Lefaucheux Model 1854 revolver did not have that feature. By the time of its debut the metallic cartridge had been improved to the point that paper tubes were rendered obsolete, and from then on all pinfire handguns were designed to fire the less troublesome metallic cartridge. Today, examples of paper rifle cartridges can be found in collections, and cardboard shotshells are fairly common, but the true early paper pinfire revolver cartridge as illustrated on Casimir Lefaucheux' 1835 patent drawing is considered extremely rare, with examples being found in only the most advanced collections.

No definite conclusions were drawn from either the Ordnance Department or Sharps Rifle Company tests, and no procurement orders for the Model 1854 revolver were placed until the outbreak of the Civil War in early 1861. While the overall results of the various experiments reflected favorably on the Lefaucheux, the Ordnance Department decided against including the Model 1854 in its subsequent test trials; perhaps that was done on the strength alone of Palmer's letter reporting the failure of the paper cartridge, but more likely it was due to the strong and insular nationalism then prevalent in America. The long-range result was that American military arms contracts went to American companies that made weapons utilizing the outdated percussion ignition system. After the fall of Fort Sumter three years later, however, the Lefaucheux Model 1854 revolver became a popular and widely-used martial sidearm.

The War Between the States would become a proving ground for scores of new and untried weapons and tactics that were destined to alter the pattern of warfare for generations to come. At the war's outbreak the North possessed numerous arms factories within its borders, most of which quickly secured government contracts for manufacturing military arms. Production quotas could not be filled soon enough to equip the troops in the field, let alone to arm the steadily increasing numbers of men in uniform resulting from the Fed-

Plate 4-3. Sheet 1 of Eugene Lefaucheux' only United States patent, number 31,809 of March 26, 1861, for his breechloading pinfire action. *Chris C. Curtis collection*

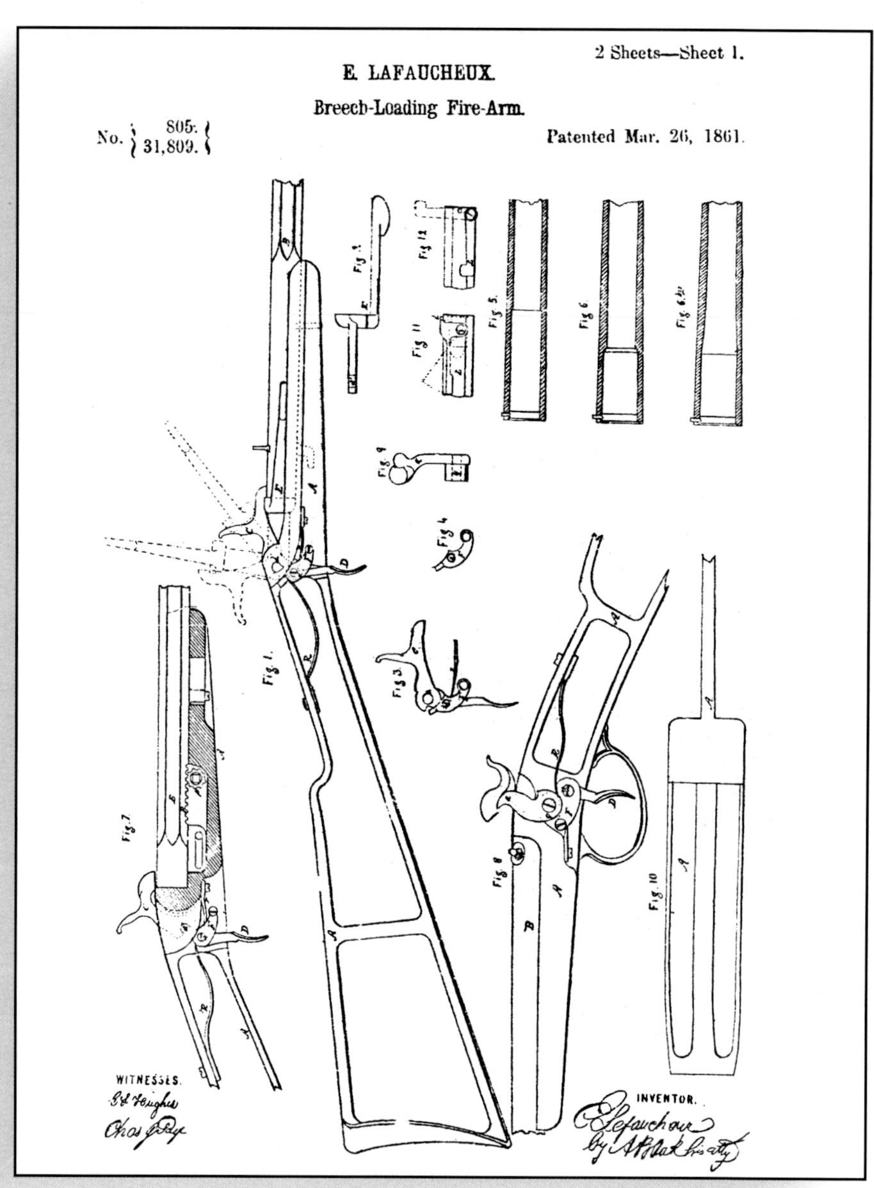

eral draft system and the surge of patriotic enlistments. Thus the U.S. government was forced to resort to a policy of making purchases of whatever arms were available from civilian munitions dealers. From this wide variety of purchases, numerous pinfire arms were acquired for use by troops loyal to the Union.

Eugene Lefaucheux was only one of the many foreign gunmakers who attempted to profit from this sudden rush to obtain U.S. contracts for existing as well as new types of military arms. In fact, the Civil War had not yet begun when Lefaucheux registered his U.S. patent number 31809, on March 26, 1861 (*see Plates 4-3 and 4-4*). This is the only patent known to have been applied for or granted to Lefaucheux in the United States. Previously recorded in France in 1859 (as patent number 24524), the American version illustrated

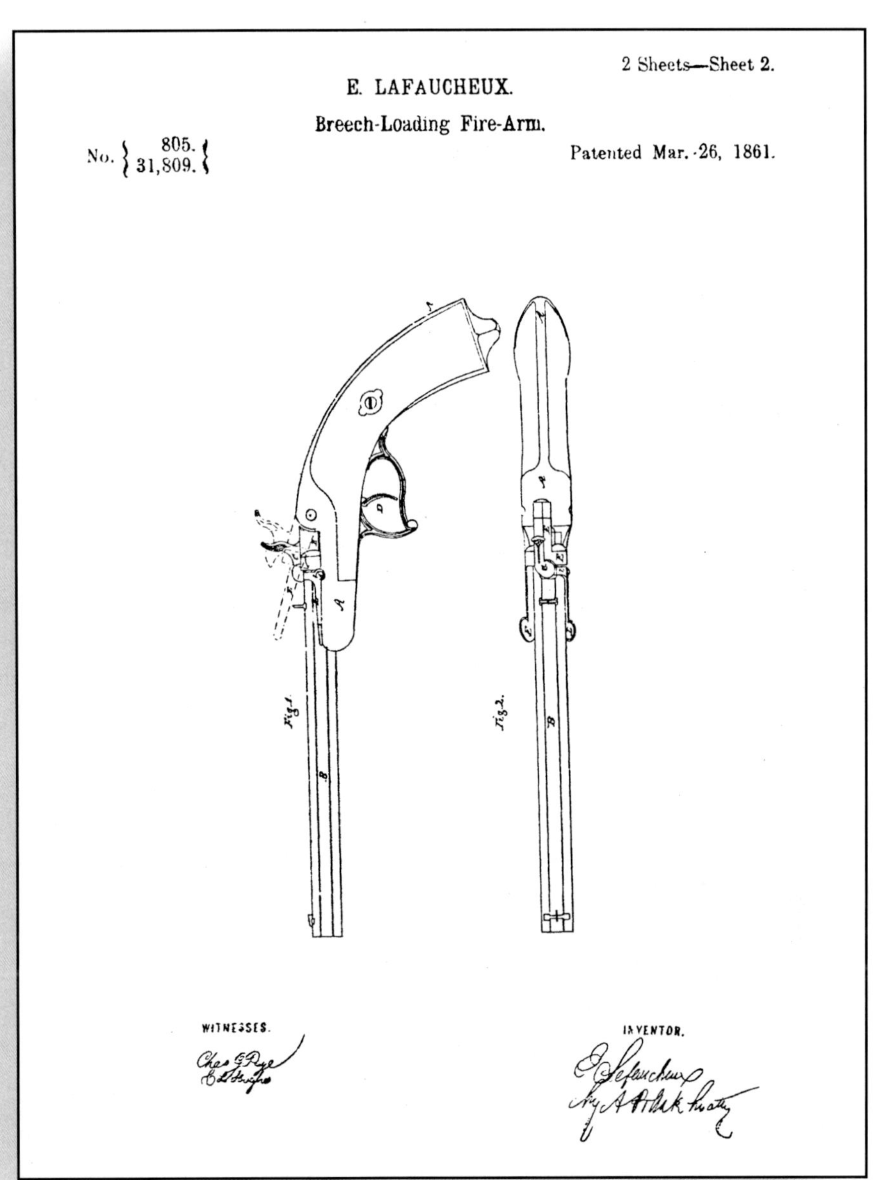

Plate 4-4. Sheet 2 of the Lefaucheux 1861 American patent, showing the breechloading pinfire action as adapted to pistols. *Chris C. Curtis collection*

the design principles as applied to both rifle and pistol. Lefaucheaux also pictured a variation incorporationg the movable, forward-sliding breech, a design his father Casimir had earlier experimented with.

The simplicity of Lefaucheux' designs and the ease of their manufacture should have propelled his arms into the forefront of any group of firearms being considered by a nation on the brink of a major military conflict. The rifle's solid, one-piece buttstock and frame rendered unnecessary several components made in the traditional fashion, such as triggerguard, lockplate, and false breech with screws, resulting in production costs considerably less than those of the guns that were eventually adopted. The Lefaucheux rifle would have made an excellent cavalry carbine: it was short and light, and the examples examined were chambered for the standard 12mm caliber pinfire metallic cartridge that was soon to be purchased in large numbers for use with the Model 1854 revolver. The efficiency of its operation (as described in Chapter Two) would have greatly increased the firepower of any unit armed with it.

Unfortunately for Eugene Lefaucheux, no official attention or consideration was given his longarms, or their possibilities. His name was even spelled incorrectly on the U.S. Patent Office papers! Although the Lefaucheux breechloader was an advanced design for its time the U.S. government elected to continue using older, more traditional systems. Not until the Civil War was over, and in the face of newer repeating arms that already had proved their worth in battle, in 1866 the government adopted a breechloading longarm similar in design to Eugene Lefaucheux'. The Allin system converted obsolete muzzleloading muskets into breechloaders which fired metallic cartridges, but even at that it was not as simple or efficient as the Lefaucheux arm. Yet American toops were armed with that rifle, and the Springfield "Trapdoor" model that followed it, until near the end of the nineteenth century when the U.S. military establishment finally caught up with its European counterparts and adopted a bolt-action rifle.

One of the first recorded munitions transactions of the Civil War took place on September 28, 1861, when the Herman T. Boker Company of 50 Cliff Street in New York City sold the U.S. government fifty-two Lefaucheux revolvers, plus "appendages" (probably ammunition), for the price of $20.04 each. Boker would go on to supply the government with some $2,000,000 worth of guns during the course of the war, almost all of which were foreign-made arms.[2]

In April of 1861 Colonel Ripley of the U.S. Ordnance Department wrote to General Winfield Scott, to suggest that the government consider obtaining arms from abroad to supplement its domestic purchases in fulfilling the needs of the ever-expanding Union military. Already the government realized that then-current domestic arms

Plate 4-5. This formidable-looking Yankee cavalryman was well armed, with a brace of Lefaucheux Model 1854 revolvers and saber. *Courtesy Tom Bowen*

manufacturing capacity, even coupled with private-sector purchases, could not keep up with demand. Although the practice of private purchases would continue, the government soon turned to the purchase of arms directly from manufacturers and sales agents in Europe.

General Scott indeed did consider Ripley's recommendations, and passed them along up the chain of command. On July 29, 1861, Secretary of War Simon Cameron notified New York State Militia Colonel George L. Schuyler by letter that President Lincoln had appointed the colonel as the government's sole purchasing agent for the procurement of small arms in Europe:

The President relies upon your integrity and discretion to make such purchases of arms as you may deem advisable upon the very lowest terms compatible with the earliest possible delivery.

For his task at hand, Colonel Schuyler was provided with a $2,000,000 line of credit with Baring Brothers Bank in London. With it he was to purchase 100,000 infantry rifles complete with bayonets, 10,000 cavalry carbines, 10,000 sabers, and 10,000 revolvers. His instructions allowed his discretion as to the exact models of arms required.

After experiencing difficulties in England, not only those caused by the activities of Confederate purchasing agent Caleb Huse, but by the sheer numbers of other New York buyers, Schuyler sailed to France to acquire his 10,000 revolvers. That October in Paris he was able to purchase directly from Eugene Lefaucheux 10,000 Model 1854 revolvers at $12.50 each, along with 200,000 rounds of 12mm pinfire cartridges at a cost of $17.45 per thousand. No reasons were stated for Colonel Schuyler's decision to purchase Lefaucheux revolvers. Perhaps he had previous knowledge of them, or was aware of the 1857 Sharps Rifle Company tests; perhaps it was Eugene Lefaucheux' persuasive salesmanship. More likely, it was the availability and immediate delivery of such a large number of revolvers from a single source.

Soon after, on December 17, 1861 the U.S. government purchased twenty Lefaucheux revolvers from the firm of Schuyler, Hartley & Graham of New York, one of the largest suppliers of military goods during the Civil War era. Colonel Schuyler, the Army's purchasing agent, was not related to Mr. Schuyler of the firm, but in July of 1862 he was replaced in his duties by Marcellus Hartley, who was an active partner in that very busy retail arms outlet.

Another New York City firm, Howland and Aspinwall, sold a group of ninety-two Lefaucheux revolvers for $22.00 each to the government on January 10, 1862, included as part of a large and varied order of munitions. One week later Tiffany and Company of the same city supplied the government with six Lefaucheux revolvers at the same price. Obviously, the New York arms houses were emptying their showcases and warehouses of all the small arms they had acquired, taking advantage of the buying frenzy while at the same time turning their patriotism into handsome profits. On March 8, 1862, 138 more Lefaucheux revolvers were purchased from New York arms importer George Raphael, at the significantly lower price of $16.00 each.

When General John C. Fremont was assigned the task of creating a Western Department of the Army during the war, he too turned to the gunmakers of Europe for a solution to his arms problem. Some of his first purchases were made on a trip to the Continent in 1861. Among the mixture of handguns, muskets, and cannon Fremont obtained through Henry Stanford, United States Minister to Belgium, were twenty-five Lefaucheux Model 1854 revolvers. Neither the price or final destination of those arms is known today, but it is likely that they were intended to arm one of the Great Pathfinder's colorful cavalry units.

On December 20, 1861 Ordnance Major P.V. Hagner signed a contract to purchase 2,000 Lefaucheux revolvers, each with fifty rounds of pinfire ammunition, from Alexis Godillot of Paris and Liége. Godillot's representative in the United States was agent J.B. King. Six revolvers from that group were personally taken by Major Hagner, while the rest were readied for shipment to the U.S.A. By May 31, 1862 only 1,500 pistols had been received in America; the remaining 500 were sent on another ship but never reached their destination, having been either lost at sea or seized by a Confederate raider. As the arms had not been delivered according to agreement, the contract expired by limitation. Before that occurred, however, 600 pinfire revolvers of a different specification, valued at $15.90 each, were shipped, but there is no record of their receipt and they do not appear on the lists of arms purchased. Perhaps the revolvers in this second shipment did not meet the standards agreed to in the original contract, and were refused by Colonel Ripley.

Ten days after the above contract was initiated, on December 30th the following letter was sent to Major Hagner from the Ordnance Office in Washington:[3]

Sir,

The four 6pdr guns ordered from NS Alger should not be rifled. Agreeably to your suggestion I have this day sent one of the French pistols with some cartridges to Lt. Treadwell with the request that he will have proper cartridges made. You may retain the Godillot pistols until further orders.

Jas. W. Ripley, Br. Gen.

There had been some interest shown in the pinfire cartridge system after the brief testings of the Model 1854 revolver during 1857 and 1858.

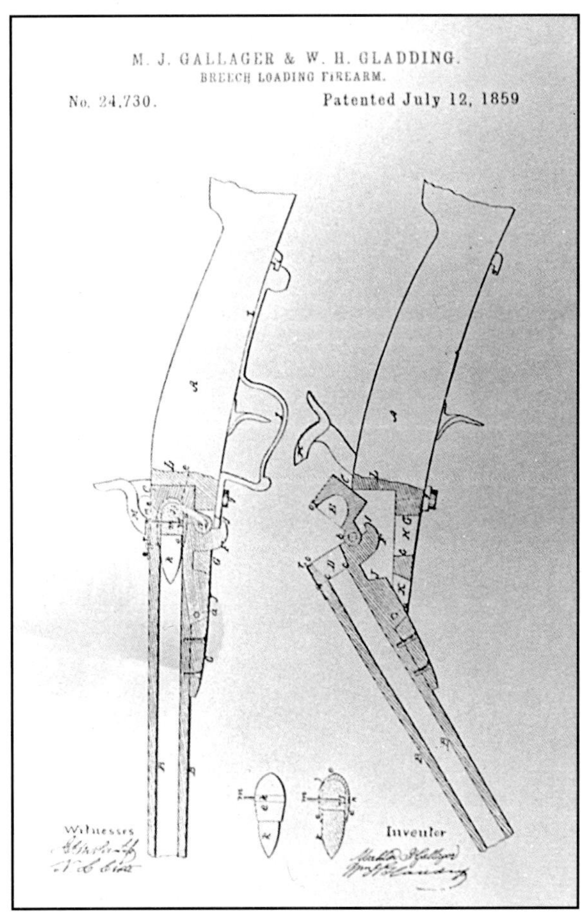

Plate 4-6. United States patent number 24730, granted to Gallager & Gladding on July 2, 1859, for a tip-up breechloading pinfire action and corresponding pinfire cartridge. *Chris C. Curtis collection*

Two of the initial American arms inventors to show such interest were M.J. Gallager and W.H. Gladding of Savannah, Georgia, who secured United States patent number 24730 on July 12, 1859 for a single-shot breechloading rifle and a pinfire cartridge (*see Plate 4-6*). The cartridge case of the Gallager-Gladding pinfire round was ovoid in cross-section, rather than cylindrical, and the breech was correspondingly concave. The ignition pin was placed almost in the middle of the case, which was made of either metal, paper, or wood, the latter two having a light metallic band in the area of the pin.

Another American cartridge inventor was Christian Sharps, of longarm fame. Although during the time the Lefaucheux Model 1854 revolver was being tested Sharps was no longer affiliated with the rifle manufacturing company that bore his name, he became one of the few Americans who secured patent protection for the domestic manufacture of pinfire cartridges. Sharps' patent of April 15, 1862, number 34987 (*see Plate 4-7*), describes his improvement of the pinfire cartridge as having a thicker base to prevent possible bulging of the case when fired, which could interfere with rotation of the revolver's cylinder. The base also was of sufficient thickness to allow for an opening of proper size to admit the detonating primer and pin.

American arms inventor Ethan Allen later started manufacturing 12mm pinfire cartridges under the Sharps patent. The "thick base" of his cartridge consisted of a disk of lead, and the priming material was contained in a small percussion cap. The Allen pinfire cartridge case measures .770" in length, known as the "U.S. case length" because it falls midway between the European 12mm long and 12mm short cases. Lacking any headstamp, Allen cartridges are identifiable only by their case length and the presence of three (occasionally four) short, indented lines at the head of the case.

Another American to patent a pinfire cartridge during the Civil War was Charles Edward Sneider of Baltimore, Maryland. His patent number 45210 of November 22, 1864 (*see Plate 4-8*)

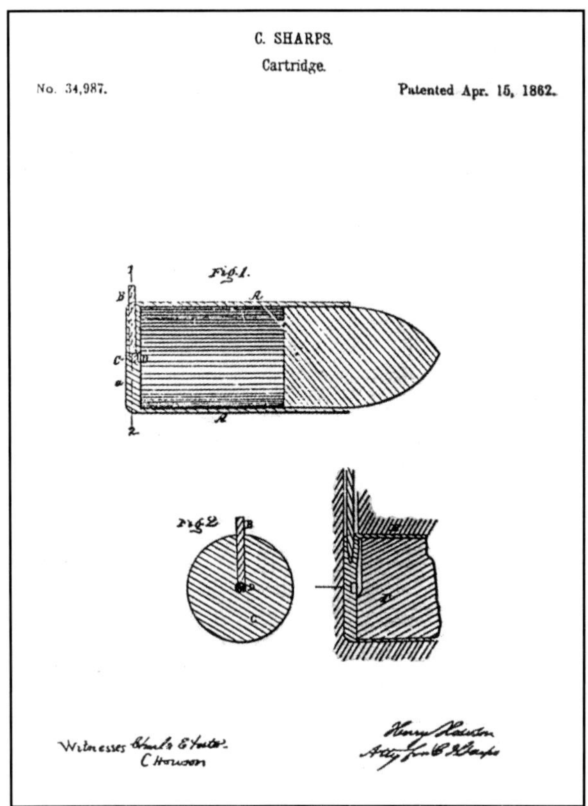

Plate 4-7. United States patent number 34987, granted to Christian Sharps on April 15, 1862, for an
improved pinfire cartridge design. *Chris C. Curtis
collection*

Plate 4-8. United States patent number 45210, granted to Charles E. Sneider on November 22, 1864, for a
two-piece pinfire cartridge using percussion cap
detonation. *Chris C. Curtis collection*

was for a cartridge consisting of a case made of any
suitable material having a pin, perforated to permit
the fitting of a common percussion cap at its end,
passing through one wall of the case nearly to the
opposite wall. After loading it with powder and
lead ball, the cartridge was inserted into an outer
metal sleeve and twisted about one-quarter turn
to lock the pin into place within an "L"-shaped
groove. Unique and complicated, Sneider's cartridge was an early attempt at making an easily
reloadable pinfire cartridge.

The manufacture of pinfire ammunition in the
U.S. has a very checkered history. Sharps made
only a very limited number of cartridges, Allen did
not begin manufacture of his until the end of the

war, the Sneider came too late and was too complex, and the Gallager & Gladding cartridge was
too fragile to enter quantity production.
Nevertheless, C.D. Leet & Company of Springfield, Massachusetts did in fact produce pinfire
ammunition in significant amounts during the
Civil War, the only American manufacturer to do
so. An employee of Smith & Wesson at the time of
that firm's initial and continuing success with the
rimfire system, Leet foresaw a future for the pinfire
system, as well. He left S&W's employ in 1860,
and within a few months had formed the cartridge
manufactory of Leet, Goff and Company. Less
than a year later Leet became the sole owner, and
the name of the firm was changed to C.D. Leet &

Company. Cartridges made by this firm are copper cased and, like Allen's, bear no headstamp.

On February 28, 1862, Captain Silas Crispin attempted to purchase 250,000 12mm caliber pinfire cartridges from C.D. Leet. For some reason only 112,000 rounds from that order were delivered, at a total cost of $1,848.00. But on December 10, 1863 Captain Crispin again placed an order, for 75,000 rounds at a cost of $1,520.00; that time 76,000 were delivered.

It is unknown under what patent protection, if indeed there was any, that C.D. Leet manufactured his ammunition. He may have chosen to forego that formality altogether, as being the first to begin production he quickly capitalized on the government's shortage of arms and ammunition during the early years of the rebellion. While C.D.

Leet's pinfire cartridges were similar to those of Allen and Sharps, they could not have been produced under the latter's patent as Leet delivered his first government-contract ammunition order two months before Christian Sharps' patent was recorded. Like Ethan Allen's 12mm cartridges, Leet's have the U.S. case length. Each holds 25 grains of black powder (*see Plate 4-10*), which was the load originally suggested to the Ordnance Department in 1858 by J.C. Palmer. Pinfire cartridges manufactured by C.D. Leet were packaged 25 to a box, and wrapped in brown paper (*see Plate 4-11*). They were supplied to Federal soldiers for use in their government-issued Lefaucheux Model 1854 revolvers.

These wartime government purchases ensured the success of C.D. Leet and Company. The firm was in business on Market Street in Springfield until 1866 when it moved to 29 and 31 Hillman Street, and it continued to be listed as an ammunition manufacturer until 1876. Brothers Charles S. and Herbert A. Leet joined the firm in 1872 as successors to their father, then formed the Rock Drill Company in 1877, which was the last year they were listed in the Springfield city directory. During its varied career the company also manufactured patent medicines between 1867 and 1868.

The Lefaucheux Model 1854 revolver proved itself to be a sturdy and dependable sidearm, and it remained in service throughout the entire Civil War. Government puchases of pinfire ammunition began early in that conflict, when the first small supplies of cartridges were issued to Federal troops to accompany each Model 1854 revolver. On December 20, 1861, Major R.H.K. Whitely ordered from munitions dealer John Holy 500,000 rounds of Lefaucheux 12mm pinfire ammunition, and Holy received $10,272.00 for the 428,000 rounds actually delivered. One million Lefaucheux pistol rounds were ordered by Major T.T.S. Laidley from William P. Wilstach on March 25, 1862; the sum of $19,992.00 was paid Wilstach for the 999,680 cartridges received from that purchase.

Then, on May 3, 1862 Captain Silas Crispin

Plate 4-9. This Union lad in tarred cap carried a Sharps carbine in addition to a pinfire revolver stuck into his belt. *Courtesy Jacques Salzedo*

purchased 200,000 Lefaucheux pistol cartridges from Schuyler, Hartley & Graham of New York City, paying $3,300.00 when the full order was delivered. On that date Marcellus Hartley of the firm had not yet replaced Colonel Schuyler as army purchasing agent. But Hartley had received

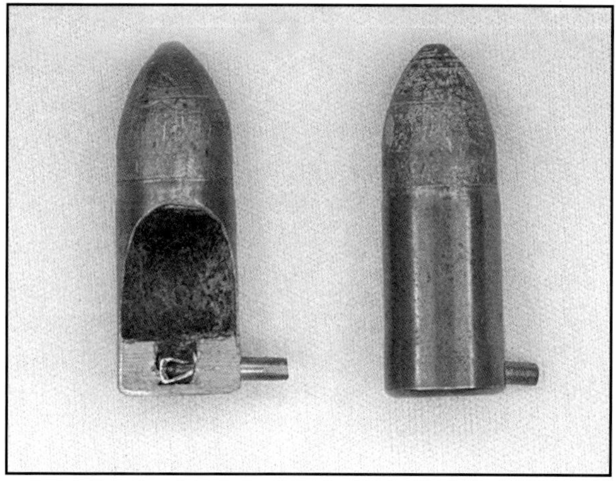

Plate 4-10. Detail view of a 12mm caliber pinfire cartridge holding 25 grains of black powder, manufactured by C.D. Leet & Co. of Springfield, Massachusetts during the Civil War. *Chris C. Curtis collection; Ed Prentiss photograph*

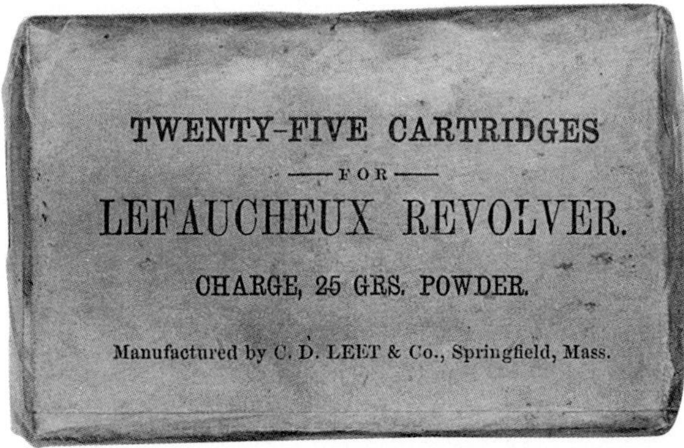

Plate 4-11. Detail view of the paper label on a box of twenty-five 12mm pinfire metallic cartridges, manufactured for use with the Lefaucheux Model 1854 revolver by C.D. Leet & Co. of Springfield, Massachusetts. *Chris C. Curtis collection; Richard McMillan photograph*

ample exposure to the pinfire system on frequent buying trips to Europe, and as a major importer of pinfire arms and ammunition before, during, and after the war. Hartley also was instrumental in establishing the Union Metallic Cartridge Company following the war's end, and it is no coincidence that U.M.C. was one of only three American firms to manufacture pinfire cartridges in quantity.

Apparently the Ordnance Department found it more desirable to buy its pinfire ammunition from American manufacturers whenever possible, as shown in the following portion of a letter from Brigadier-General J.W. Ripley, Chief of Ordnance in Washington, to Schuyler, Hartley & Graham. The letter is dated May 26, 1862, shortly after Captain Crispin's purchase of 200,000 rounds of pinfire ammunition from SH&G.

> *In answer to your letter of the 23rd inst., I have to say that this Department has made arrangements for all the Lefaucheux pistol cartridges that will be required....*

Because of the better availability of suitable ammunition, pinfire revolvers were used more extensively and for a longer time by troops of the Northern armies than by their Southern counterparts. As quickly as the Lefaucheux revolvers arrived at United States ports, they were dispersed among the various Federal arsenals. A report dated December 18, 1861 shows 3,241 Model 1854 pistols on hand at the Washington Arsenal. Many of those arms were destined for use in the Western Theater, and by July of 1863 most of them had been delivered to the St. Louis and other arsenals, as well as to numerous army posts such as Forts Marcy, Randall, Larned, and Riley. One of the Western units which was slated to receive the new pistols was Company A of the 2nd Regiment Kansas Volunteer Cavalry, and on March 16, 1862 it was issued Lefaucheux Model 1854 revolvers along with Austrian and U.S.-made Hall carbines.

Following the 1862 Confederate foray into New Mexico Territory that was intended to isolate distant California from the rest of the Union, cav-

Plate 4-12. Tintype photograph of Private George F. Haas of Company A, 2nd Kansas Cavalry, which was outfitted with the Lefaucheux Model 1854 pinfire revolver for Civil War service. *Courtesy John Peter Beckendorf*

alry Companies A, C, and D were detailed from Kansas to escort a large supply train sent to reinforce Federal troops in the territory. The three units left Ft. Riley on May 22nd and arrived at Ft. Union, New Mexico on June 22nd; while on duty there some one hundred men were detailed to pursue a marauding band of Navajo Indians. After duty in New Mexico the troopers returned east, where they saw heavy Civil War action in both Missouri and Arkansas.

Plate 4-12 depicts Private George F. Haas, a German immigrant who along with his brother Louis enlisted in the Union Army at Minneola, Kansas on December 14, 1861. George Haas was assigned to Company A of the 2nd Kansas Volunteer Cavalry, and served with that unit throughout the entire war until his regiment was

mustered out on April 15, 1865. Haas participated in over a dozen battles with the 2nd Kansas, the only unit to capture a Confederate artillery battery in the Western Theater, in addition to surviving numerous skirmishes with bushwackers, guerilla raiders, Rebel regulars, Indians, and disease. It is a sad comment that when the 62-year-old veteran passed away peacefully at his farm on March 13, 1905, much of his estate had to be sold in order to settle debts and pay the funeral expenses. Always proud of his service to his adopted country, a copy of the tintype portrait of George Haas' shown here was displayed next to the coffin at his wake.

Yet another account of the activities of the 2nd Kansas Cavalry was reported in a letter originally published in the April 26, 1862 issue of the *Big Blue Union* newspaper of Marysville, Kansas.[4] The writer was a cavalry trooper stationed at a temporary military outpost called Camp Blair. Existing only from March 12th to April 20th of that year, during that time Camp Blair was home to all ten companies (870 men) of the 2nd Kansas Cavalry. The trooper's letter, dated April 14th, related a chase and subsequent fight with Quantrill's Raiders. With 300 troopers in the field, each man having been issued only six cartridges, the 2nd Kansas killed eight raiders and captured six, although leader William Quantrill and eight others of his band managed to escape.

Continuing with his account, the cavalryman spoke of the forming-up already taking place at Ft. Riley for the upcoming expedition into New Mexico Territory, and of his regiment's excellent outfitting with horses, clothing, and especially "guns and pistols." After complaining about the carbines, he gave this description of their Lefaucheux revolvers:

> *The pistols are six-shooting revolvers of French manufacture, quite similar to Colt's pattern, except that they load at the breech with a cartridge encased with copper.*

The anonymous, accidental historian signed his name simply "Soldier."

Plate 4-13. Tintype photograph of Private Eltora Dye of Company E, 5th Kansas Volunteer Cavalry, shown holding one of the eighty-five Lefaucheux Model 1854 revolvers issued to that Civil War unit. *Courtesy U.S. Army Military History Institute, Carlisle Barracks*

Surviving photographic images of Civil War soldiers armed with Lefaucheux revolvers are very rare, and when the individual is identified, they are even rarer yet. *Plate 4-13* illustrates such an identified Western cavalry trooper, Private Eltora Dye of Company E, 5th Kansas Volunteer Cavalry, shown brandishing a Lefaucheux pistol in his right hand.

Stationed in Kansas, Missouri, and Arkansas throughout the war, young Private Dye's regiment, like the 2nd Kansas, fought in numerous battles and skirmishes against both irregular guerilla forces and regular Confederate units, including the 15th Texas Cavalry under Colonel Smith.

On the July 1, 1863 inventory of arms the 5th Kansas was listed as having eighty-five issue Lefaucheux revolvers on hand, but the 2nd Kansas

had only thirty revolvers remaining out of its original full company issue. Hard frontier use and the gradual replacement with American-made arms accounted for the Lefaucheux' dwindling numbers. On the same date the 6th Kansas showed seventeen Lefaucheux revolvers in inventory, but the 1st California had only one, probably the personal sidearm of the company commander.

Another report made mention of Lefaucheux revolvers being in the possession of men of the 2nd Colorado. Missouri regiments also issued those arms included the 11th Missouri Volunteers. The 1st, 4th, 7th, and 8th Missouri Cavalrys were equipped with eighty-three, two, four, and eighty-five Lefaucheux revolvers, respectively, while the 9th Missouri State Militia reported 612 then currently in its inventory.

Other Western units included the 1st Dakota and the 3rd Michigan, listing ninety-two and six revolvers, respectively; the 3rd and the 6th Kentucky showed eight and three as having been issued; the 2nd Ohio, three. The 1st Wisconsin had seventy-four Lefaucheuxs, the 2nd Wisconsin twenty-five, and the 3rd Wisconsin had ninety-five issued; those pinfire revolvers had been carried during operations out from Ft. Scott, Kansas and against Quantrill's Raiders.

While on July 1st, 2nd, and 3rd, 1863 the Battle of Gettysburg was raging far to the east, reports for the period showed nearly 1,600 Lefaucheux Model 1854 revolvers listed in inventory of the just-mentioned cavalry units. Far more than that number were in the hands of other cavalry, infantry, and artillery regiments throughout the U.S. Army, as well.

Many tales are told of the Lefaucheux revolver in battle during the Civil War, such as the Union artillery lieutenant who carried a matched pair at Gettysburg. During the battle one became lost, and much later the surviving pistol was donated to the Gettysburg Museum. Ironically, ninety years later the missing revolver was recovered from a group of battlefield relics and donated to the same museum, once again to take its place alongside its mate of nearly a century ago.

The use of other Model 1854 revolvers at the Battle of Gettysburg is well-documented in the Quarterly Ordnance Reports for June 30, 1863, now in the National Archives. On the third day of battle, Confederate General J.E.B. Stuart's cavalry attacked the Union flank in an audacious maneuver designed as a diversion to allow further penetration of the now-famous Pickett's charge on the center of the Union lines. East of town Stuart's troops were met by the 1st Brigade units, the 1st New Jersey, 3rd Pennsylvania, and the Purnell Legion, Company A. The latter was armed with one-hundred Merrill carbines, ninety-five sabers, and one-hundred-ten Lefaucheux revolvers. As the battle grew in intensity Union reinforcements were called up, and the 2nd Brigade under General George Armstrong Custer engaged Stuart's 1st Virginia Cavalry in a violent clash. Custer's flank held, the Rebel forces were forced to retire from the field, and the Union won the day.

Plate 4-14 pictures another Gettysburg veteran. Corporal Absalom S. Talmadge was mustered in with his regiment, the 11th New Jersey Volunteer Infantry, on August 18, 1862. He saw fighting at Fredericksburg and Chancellorsville before suffering a severe wound to the head during the Battle of Gettysburg. By February of 1864 he had recovered sufficiently to rejoin his unit at Brandy Station, Virginia; he again was wounded during the Battle of the Wilderness, May 5 to 7. After miraculously recovering from his second serious wounding, Talmadge was stationed in the Commissary Department in Washington until Lee's surrender in April of 1865. Only then was Corporal Talmadge mustered out with his regiment—which had been engaged in thirty battles, from Fredericksburg to Appomattox Courthouse.

In a magazine called *The Cannoneer*, a Union artilleryman named Augustus Buell wrote of his experiences with a Lefaucheux Model 1854 at Cedar Creek during General Sherman's Valley Campaign:[5]

The usual revolvers for the cannoneers was the navy Remington or the Colt, but the one I had was a "French Tranter", as they were called,

which I had bought from Corp'l. Ray, of the 10th New York Cavalry, who had taken it from the body of a Confederate lieutenant killed at Brandy Station the year before. I used to say that "I captured it", but as a matter of fact I captured it with a $5 bill. However, it was a captured weapon, by proxy if not in person.

In the article Buell sketched his revolver (it definitely was a Lefaucheux Model 1854). He noted its speed of firing, then went on to tell of how during a lull in one battle he began to reload his pistol, only to find that his cartridge box had been shot away! "It was a serious loss to me because my revolver used the pinfire metallic cartridge, which I had to buy, as the Government did not issue

Plate 4-14. Tintype photograph of Corporal A.S. Talmadge of the 11th New Jersey Volunteer Infantry, shown formidably armed with his Lefaucheux Model 1854 pinfire revolver and a U.S. percussion musket. *Chris C. Curtis collection*

them, and I had recently filled the cartridge box at a cost of 10¢ per cartridge."

Buell's last statement was a result of his having privately purchased both the pistol and the cartridges for it, as it is established fact that the Federal government purchased large quantities of pinfire ammunition as late as December of 1863. However, that ammunition obviously was provided only to units that used government-issued Lefaucheux Model 1854 revolvers.

By late 1863 the Northern munitions factories had reached full production. Large numbers of varied types of firearms were now arriving at the front, and Ordnance Department authorities no longer felt the pressing need to import foreign-made arms. A letter from Chief of Ordnance Brigadier-General J.W. Ripley to Captain E.F. Townsend, acting ordnance officer in Nashville, Tennessee, on August 24, 1863 stated that,

> *Parts for the U.S. Holster pistols Cal. .54 and the Harpers Ferry rifles Cal. .58 are not ordered as these arms are no longer manufactured and the parts could only be furnished at great inconvenience and expense.*
>
> *The same remark applies to the parts asked for Joslyn's Carbine and the Lefaucheux, Adams and Savage revolvers. As far as practicable these arms should be repaired by parts made specially for them in the Shops of the Depot.*

For many years historians have tried to accurately account for the amount of funds spent on arms and other war matériel during the Civil War, in addition to the exact numbers and types of weapons purchased.

Two tables[6] originally published in the 1970s were compiled using many Congressional Record and National Archives documents as primary sources of information. The first table, titled "Records of Ordnance [pistols] purchased from Jan. 1, 1861 to June 30, 1866", lists 12,374 Lefaucheux revolvers purchased. The second table, "United States Government purchases between April 13, 1861 and April 3, 1866", reflects the purchase of

---

Federal Purchases of Pinfire Revolvers and Ammunition

<u>Revolvers</u>

September 28, 1861	52 Revolvers, plus "appendages" (possibly ammunition)
October, 1861	10,000 Revolvers
December 17, 1861	20 Revolvers
December 20, 1861	2,000 Revolvers
Late 1861	25 Revolvers
January 10, 1862	92 Revolvers
January 17, 1862	6 Revolvers
March 8, 1862	138 Revolvers

<u>Ammunition</u>

October 1861	200,000 Rounds
December 20, 1861	10,000 Rounds
December 20, 1861	500,000 Rounds
February 28, 1862	250,000 Rounds
March 25, 1862	1,000,000 Rounds
May 3, 1862	200,000 Rounds
December 10, 1863	75,000 Rounds

The chart above records the quantities of pinfire arms and ammunition officially purchased by the Union during the Civil War. In many cases, however, the amounts actually delivered were different than the amounts purchased.

11,833 Lefaucheux revolvers. While researching "Executive Document 99",[7] the latter number was confirmed as exactly 11,833 Lefaucheux revolvers purchased by the government. The serial number range of these Model 1854 revolvers is believed to fall between 25,000 and 37,000.[8]

Likewise, a new total of 1,815,680 12mm caliber pinfire cartridges was established as having been delivered to the government during the war years. Over ten percent of that number (188,000) cartridges were supplied to the Ordnance Department by the American manufacturer, C.D. Leet & Co.

After reviewing the historical material it becomes easy to understand the discrepancy between the two tables of government small arms purchases. In fact, neither of the figures quoted above may be entirely correct. In one entry, a number of Lefaucheux revolvers is listed as purchased at a specific price; on the very next line is a number of revolvers listed simply as "French", at exactly the same price. It is quite possible that both categories listed *Lefaucheux* revolvers, but the vague description in the second line leaves too much doubt for us to consider them as such.

There are other cases with similarly elusive descriptions, as well. However, we can accept the number positively identified in the National Archives, 11,833 Lefaucheux revolvers, as accurate. To the number of officially purchased revolvers must be added a large, but unknown, quantity of privately purchased pinfire arms which were carried into battle by military men as their own personal sidearms, or given as gifts by relatives and friends who had purchased them through the many Eastern arms retailers and importers.

Even without this latter category, the total number of Lefaucheux revolvers purchased was surpassed only by those from the large American arms companies, Colt, Remington, and Starr, making the Lefaucheux Model 1854 the fourth most-numerous U.S. martial revolver to see service during the Civil War. That alone should ensure it a permanent (if yet largely unrecognized) place in history!

Pinfire Arms used by Confederate Forces

At the outbreak of the Civil War neither side was well equipped with modern military arms, and munitions factories in both North and South immediately were pressed into full-scale production. It was a challenge much easier met by the industrial North than by the agrarian South.

Nevertheless, the Confederate States authorities hastily set up armories for the manufacture of firearms, and awarded military contracts to qualified—and some not-so-qualified—firms to produce small arms for the Southern cause. One example of the Confederacy's ability to adapt from peacetime to wartime needs was the firm of

Griswold & Gunnison, which in 1862 was converted from the fabrication of cotton gins into producing brass-frame revolvers on the Colt "Navy" pattern.

Most arms factories in the South operated under great handicaps, ranging from constant shortages of raw materials to persistent danger of attack by Yankee raiders. Many, such as the Rigdon & Ansley revolver factory in Macon, Georgia, organized their own private defense forces, which consisted of employees who were expected to put down their tools of commerce and take up the tools of war when the occasion demanded.

Realists in the Confederacy—those who had traveled abroad, or at least had traveled north— knew the limited industrial output of Southern factories could never hope to equal the pressing need imposed by the war. They turned their eyes and hopes toward Europe, relying heavily on the importation of firearms and other military goods to make up the difference. Thus during 1861 Captain Caleb Huse, chief purchasing agent for the Confederate States of America, arrived in London, his mission to obtain small arms and ordnance using cotton warrant promissory notes.

At the age of thirty-one Huse was the keystone of the Confederate Ordnance Department's purchasing system, and he bore sole responsibility for making contracts and subsequent purchases throughout all of Europe. Captain Huse was successful in his purchasing endeavors, and the armsmakers and military dealers of Europe kept up a steady supply of goods flowing through the Union blockade and into Confederate ports.

His most successful ventures were with the London Armoury Company. From that firm alone Captain Huse acquired over 80,000 Enfield rifles and muskets by February of 1863, in addition to approximately 9,000 Kerr percussion revolvers. While no record of specific purchases of pinfire arms from the London Armoury Company can be located from the period, it is known that the firm did import and sell them in the U.S. both before and during the Civil War. So if Huse did obtain pinfire arms in England for the South, it is likely that they came from the London Armoury

Plate 4-15. This half-smiling young Confederate wearing what appears to be a white seaman's blouse took his weaponry seriously, firmly grasping a pike as well as his pinfire pistol. *Courtesy George P. Law*

September of 1863 the South had imported 350,000 small arms alone from Europe.

By comparison, a total of only about 10,000 pistols was made in Southern factories during the entire war. Through the existence of fragmented records from the government of the C.S.A. and private firms it is estimated that about 250,000 pistols of various makes were imported from England, France, and Belgium during the same period. Even that number was not nearly enough to supply the demand from troops in the field, and handguns became regarded as the great prize of the battlefields.

Confederate General John Hunt Morgan ordered all the men of his command to carry two revolvers in their belts. The pistol was the weapon of choice carried by all officers, many musicians (who were in the thick of most major battles), and by the field artillery units who were fortunate enough to obtain them. They were the units most often overrun, having but little defense against mounted cavalry.

The types of pinfire revolvers most favored by both Union and Confederate soldiers were those of 12mm caliber, because of their superior firepower, but 9mm and even 7mm caliber revolvers were used by Confederates when the larger caliber arms were unavailable to them.

Company. Many of those arms were retailed having the company's name on the case only, not marked on the gun itself.

Importing arms and other war matériel into the Confederacy was an extremely hazardous, albeit highly remunerative, task. In addition to the numerous privately-owned craft so engaged, the Confederate Ordnance Department purchased five fast steamers of its own to run goods through the Union blockade. The ships were named the *Banshee*, the *Banshee II*, the *Don*, the *R.E. Lee*, and the *Chameleon*. In just one year those shallow-draft coastal steamers carried in four times as many small arms as were produced at the Southern armories at Richmond, Fayetteville, and Asheville, together. In addition, the ships delivered much-needed explosives, heavy goods, and uniforms to the Confederacy. So successful were they, that by

As the war dragged on and the Union naval blockade tightened its stranglehold on the Confederacy, potential blockade runners became increasingly less willing to have their ships and arms cargoes lost to the Federal raiders, exhorbitant profits notwithstanding. So a new method of transshipment was devised by Captain Huse and the C.S. Ordnance Department, whereby arms shipments destined for the South were labeled as "hardware" or "merchandise" (*civilian*, as opposed to military goods), and shipped first to Bermuda. There they were stored until arrangements could be made to have them conveniently run through the blockade. But even that ruse was only a temporary expedient, and eventually the Union blockade of Southern ports became almost totally effective. As one by one Southern ports were sealed off from incoming goods, the fate of the Confederate States of America was likewise ultimately sealed.

In addition to completed pinfire pistols, apparently component parts for them also were entering the Confederacy through the blockade. In 1974 a wooden crate containing rough, unfinished castings for 9mm caliber pinfire revolvers was discovered in Texas (*see Plate 4-16*), evidently having been intended for final finishing and assembly at some Southern armory. It is well known that many pinfire revolvers were purchased by Southern sympathizers at New York from Schuyler, Hartley & Graham, as well as from other arms dealers, and smuggled southward through the Union lines.

Very few pinfire revolvers have adequate authentication to conclusively prove them as genuine Confederate arms, and the authors recommend the use of caution and sound judgement when purchasing one so attributed. It does not help that no consistent markings were applied to Confederate handguns, as usually was the case with Federal government purchases, nor were the handguns themselves all of one type. If done at all, such markings were applied by individual units or soldiers, many of whom were not skilled in the fabrication of tools for the metal stamping process.

Plates 4-17 through *4-19* illustrate Southern markings applied to several pinfire revolvers, none of which has been positively traced to actual Confederate ownership or use. Thus the marks are not presented here as authentic, but rather to illustrate the variety of such markings to be found. It has been reported that during the late 1950s a number of antique pinfire revolvers had "C.S.A." markings applied by a large western arms importer to enhance their salability, increasing their value from around $2.50 to $7.50 each. The practice not only resulted in a number of pinfire revolvers bearing spurious "C.S.A." markings, but served to cast doubt on *all* Confederate-marked pinfires. Many of those revolvers bear contradictory post-1877 Belgian proof and inspector's marks, thereby exposing the illegitimate origins of these "C.S.A." markings. Other examples only coincidentally bear proofmarks of the proper Civil War period. In every case, let the buyer beware![9]

One of the most convincing Confederate-marked pieces, although without any proven authentication, is illustrated in *Plate 4-20*. The maker is unknown; it bears English proofmarks and "*improved Pat.*" stamped on the left rear side of the barrel, and the number "*1*", and "C.S.A." within a border on the right frame flat.

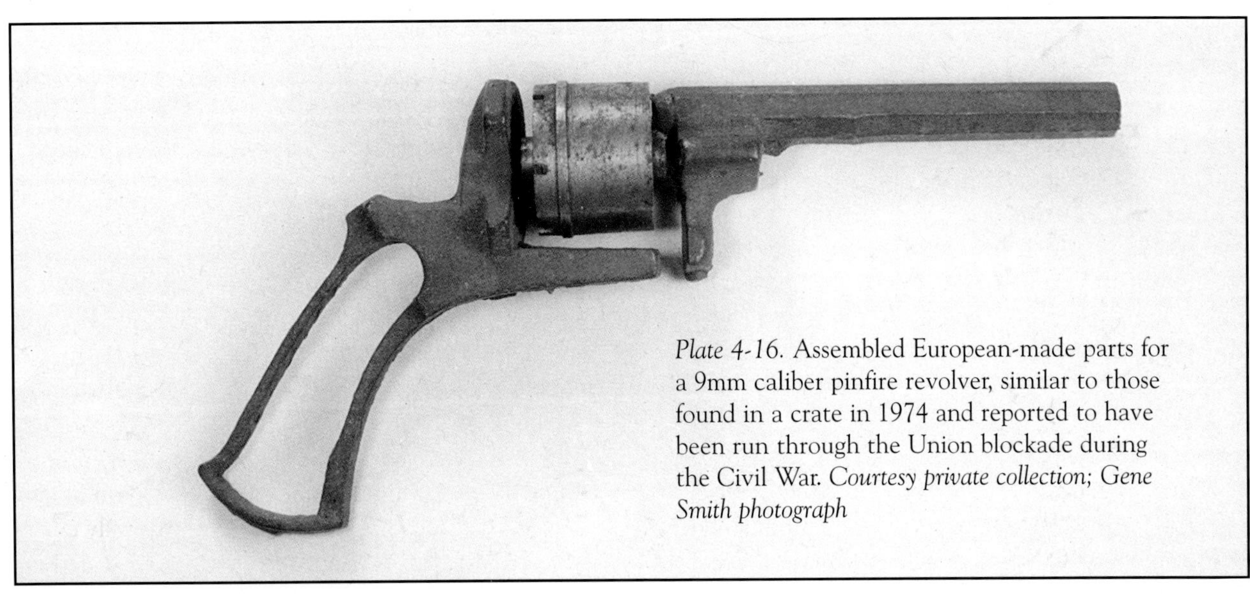

Plate 4-16. Assembled European-made parts for a 9mm caliber pinfire revolver, similar to those found in a crate in 1974 and reported to have been run through the Union blockade during the Civil War. *Courtesy private collection; Gene Smith photograph*

Plate 4-17. Detail view of the left side of a Belgian-made pinfire revolver, showing spurious "C.S.A." markings stamped on frame and post-1877 Liége proofmarks on cylinder. *Courtesy private collection; F.W. Hulbert photograph*

Plate 4-18. Detail view of the top of a European-made pinfire revolver, showing spurious "CSA" stamped (or engraved) on flat of barrel lug, likely applied during the 1950s. *Courtesy private collection; Gene Smith photograph*

Another convincing, possibly Confederate-used specimen is a Lefaucheux Model 1854 revolver stamped "CSA 9 VA." on the top flat of its barrel lug (*see Plate 4-22*). The serial number of this particular pistol falls within the range of revolvers known to have been purchased by the Federal government. Thus, it is feasible that it might have been captured from a Yankee soldier in battle, stamped with the "C.S.A." markings, and reissued to this Southern unit. Like the previously described revolver, this piece has no authentication other than its appearance and serial number. It is not in fine original condition, which would tend to rule out later alteration or faking. But when first found the pistol was in a box of junker "parts" guns, its action was defective, the ejector rod was missing, and the loading gate spring was broken, conditions that strongly suggest contemporary use with the "chimney" cap-and-ball cartridge adaptor (*see Plate 4-27*).

There are no complete records of Confederate arms purchases extant that can be made available

Plate 4-19. Detail view of the right side of a European-made pinfire revolver, showing spurious "CSA" stamped (or engraved) on right flat of barrel lug, virtually identical to that illustrated in Plate 4-18. *Courtesy private collection; Gene Smith photograph*

Plate 4-20. An unattributed to maker, but fine-condition pinfire revolver bearing English proof marks and "C.S.A." stamped within a cartouche on its frame flat; right side. *Courtesy Gene Smith; John Calcany photograph*

Plate 4-21. Detail view of right frame flat of the revolver illustrated in *Plate 4-16*, showing "C.S.A." stamping within a cartouche. *Courtesy Gene Smith; John Calcany photograph*

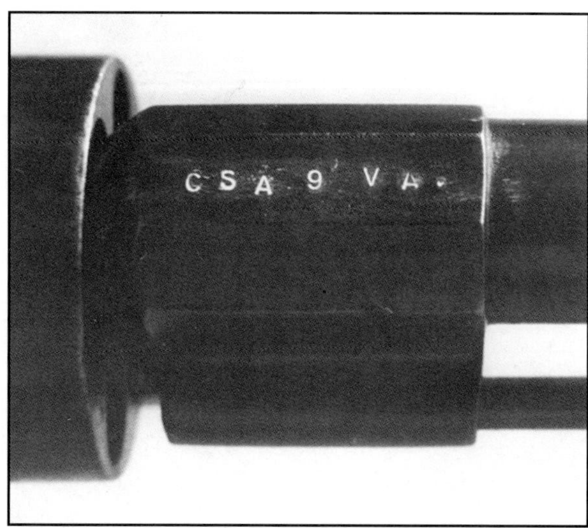

Plate 4-22. Detail view of a Lefaucheux Model 1854 pinfire revolver, showing "CSA 9 VA." markings stamped on the top flat of its barrel lug. The serial number of this pistol falls within the range known to have been imported for Union troops during the Civil War. *Chris C. Curtis collection; F.W. Hulbert photograph*

for study by researchers today. Nearly all arms importation into the South during the Civil War was considered a criminal act against the United States government, so many arms merchants and agents, as well as those transporting weapons, were understandably reluctant to preserve any detailed records that could be used against them at a later time. As previously discussed, many such purchase records were intentionally misleading, and arms crates were labeled "farm equipment" or "hardware." Unfortunately for today's researchers, the situation leaves us with little but speculation and conjecture to work with when attempting to establish the numbers of pinfire arms imported by the Confederacy. Nevertheless, it is certain that many types of pinfires were bought and used there.

One documented indication of the use in significant numbers of pinfire revolvers in the South during the Civil War is found in a letter written on August 13, 1864 by Lieutenant-Colonel J.L. White, commandant of the arsenal at Selma, Alabama. Writing in reply to an inquiry from his commanding officer in Mobile, Major-General D.H. Maury, Colonel White stated that there were but twenty to forty arms then present, all currently undergoing repair, and which according to their condition were being rendered servicable daily. He went on to report various types and amounts of rifle and pistol ammunition on hand in the arsenal as of that date. Among the dozen or so entries listed appears one "For French Pistol (LeFaucheux) caliber .472k— 52,800 rounds."[10]

Yet another report, this one from an arsenal in Louisiana during 1863, recorded over 45,000 rounds of 12mm ammunition on hand.[11] Obviously, these quantities are far in excess of what might be considered battlefield captures, or even government purchases from civilian firms, as was the practice of Federal authorities for some time. The two foregoing ammunition reports, though just fragments of the surviving evidence, would indicate that substantial Confederate purchases of pinfire arms were made during the war.

Many U.S. government contracts for revolvers specified a certain number of rounds of ammuni-

Plate 4-23. A Civil War-era ambrotype likeness of an unidentified Confederate soldier, shown holding a pinfire revolver tucked into his waist belt. *From* Confederate Faces; *Courtesy William A. Albaugh*

tion to accompany each gun bought. For instance, the purchases Schuyler, Hartley & Graham made from Lefaucheux called for twenty rounds per gun, whereas Alexis Godillot's contract called for fifty rounds to each revolver. While it is true that to date no record of a large Confederate government purchase has been found, by utilizing the ratios above it is easy to assume that somewhere between 2,000 and 5,000 pinfire revolvers would have been acquired.

The Confederate troops under Thomas J. "Stonewall" Jackson presented their general with a fine, highly-engraved pinfire revolver. *Plate 4-24* depicts Jackson's large, double-action revolver, which measures twelve inches overall. Its proofmarks indicate Belgian origins, and the top of the round barrel bears Lefaucheux markings along almost its entire length. Engraved on the underside of the barrel is the inscription, "Presented to Major General Thomas J. Jackson by his Officers, Camp Near Richmond."

While unfortunately not all of the pinfire arms used by Southern forces during the Civil War are so well authenticated as Stonewall Jackson's, the fact remains that whether marked or unmarked, the Confederacy utilized sizeable quantities of pinfire cartridge arms. Nor were they all revolvers, necessarily, for Rebel soldiers took privately acquired sidearms of many types to the war with them.

The Confederacy was not without its share of arms dealers in the major Southern cities, and arms of all types were routinely purchased wherever and whenever possible. Some of those cities, especially the sea ports like New Orleans, retained strong business and cultural ties to Europe, and surely more than just a few French pinfire shotguns could be found on hand in merchant's show-cases and local homes. Too, many commercial sporting rifles as well as shotguns had their barrels shortened, and were subsequently issued to Confederate cavalry units.

War Surplus

With the arrival of the inevitable and tragic end to the Civil War in early 1865, vast quantities as well as varieties of military and civilian arms were accumulated on both sides of the Mason-Dixon Line. In particular, the North had come into possession of thousands of small arms, formerly the property of the Confederate Ordnanace Department. Those it began to sell off to American and foreign arms merchants, and thus many European-made arms returned to the very governments from which they had been purchased just several years earlier.

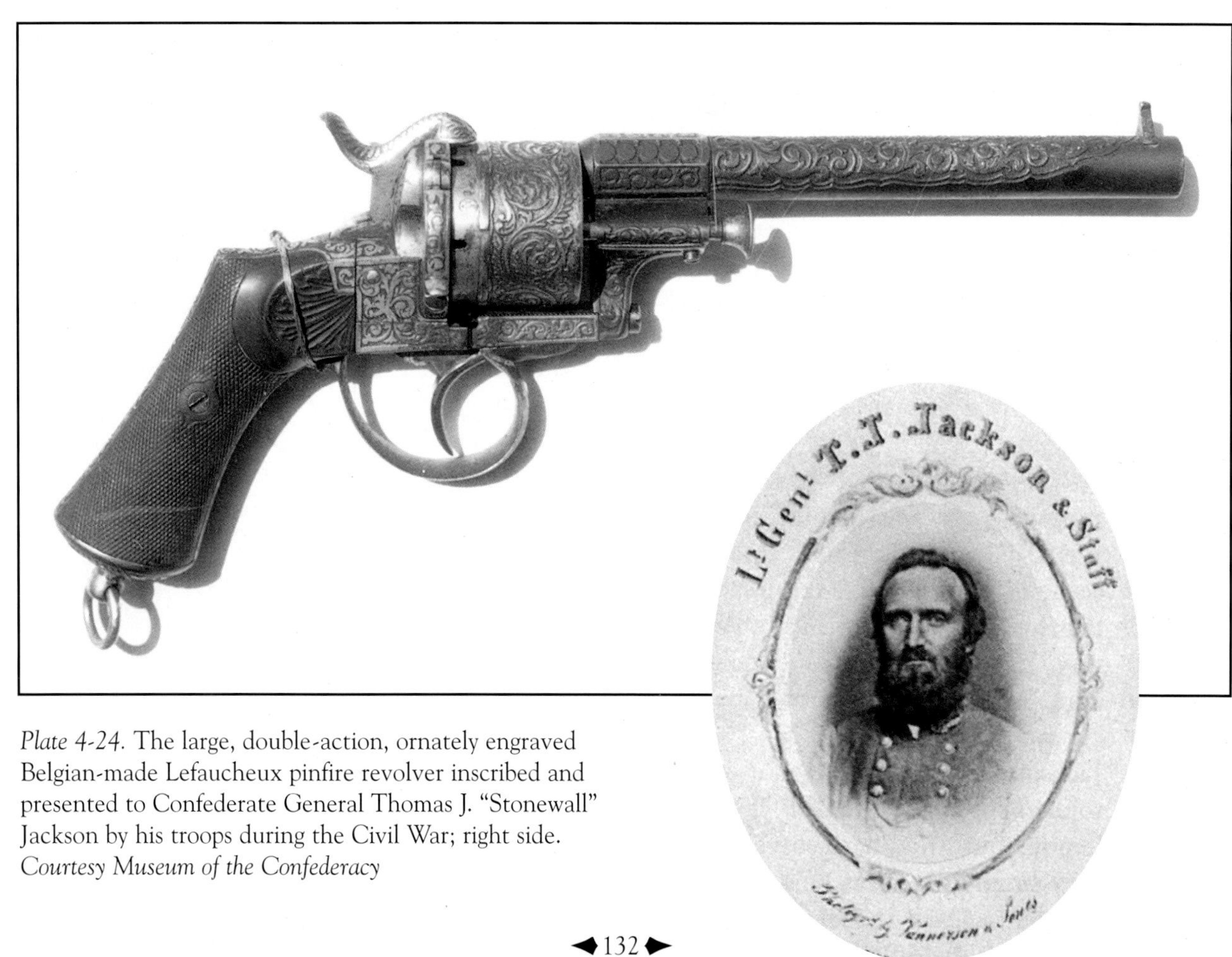

Plate 4-24. The large, double-action, ornately engraved Belgian-made Lefaucheux pinfire revolver inscribed and presented to Confederate General Thomas J. "Stonewall" Jackson by his troops during the Civil War; right side. *Courtesy Museum of the Confederacy*

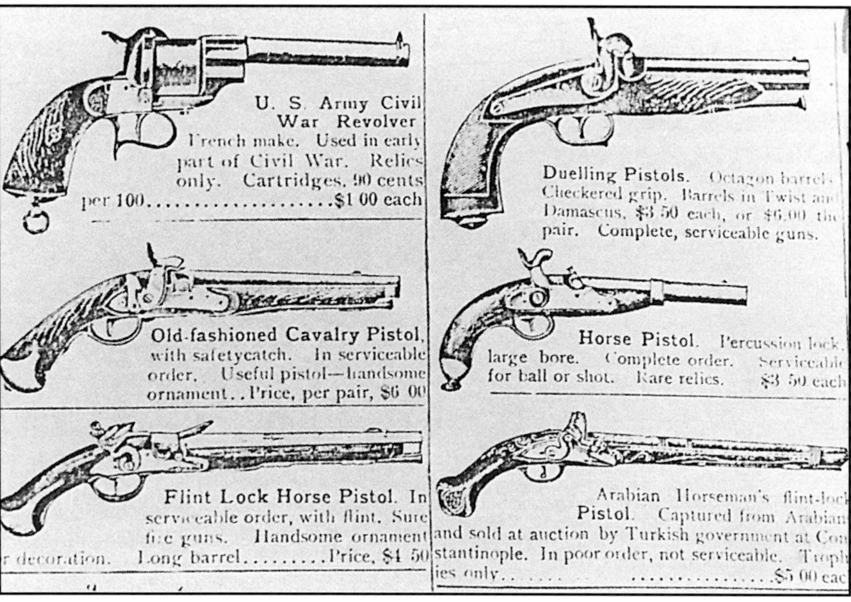

Plate 4-25. Reproduction of a page from New York military surplus dealer Francis Bannerman's 1909 catalog, offering "relic" Lefaucheux Model 1854 revolvers, "Used in early part of Civil War", for only one dollar each; cartridges 90 cents per hundred, extra. *Courtesy Konrad F. Schreier, Jr.*

Serviceable pinfire weapons were included in sales on both sides of the Atlantic. On November 25, 1867 a group of 19,551 ordnance-condemned small arms was sold off at the Leavenworth Arsenal, in Kansas, and Lefaucheux pistols were among the items listed for sale. Large numbers of these veteran firearms found their way to the American West, to see action once again on the new frontier.

Many of the government-surplus Lefaucheux Model 1854 revolvers were purchased by the large New York arms dealers such as Schuyler, Hartley & Graham. Another dealer, Francis Bannerman, stored literally tons of surplus arms at his famed island arsenal in the Hudson River, and was one of the greatest munitions dealers of the time. In the largest post-Civil War government surplus arms sale Bannerman bought from the New York Arsenal 1,925 Lefaucheux revolvers, at prices ranging between eight and twenty-two cents apiece. In the 1904 Bannerman catalog those revolvers were listed for sale at $1.95 each, including a box of 25 "sure fire" cartridges, and additional pinfire ammunition was available at ninety cents per hundred rounds. In his descriptions, Mr. Bannerman was careful to state that neither the Civil War-era revolvers or their "sure fire" cartridges was guaranteed to shoot!

Also advertised were an additional 20,000 Lefaucheux revolvers of different patterns, for European delivery only, at eighty cents each. By the time his 1909 catalog was produced the remaining Lefaucheux Model 1854 revolvers were reduced to only one dollar each (*see Plate 4-25*). Until interest in old guns on the part of collectors began to increase following the end of World War Two, Bannerman's had difficulty disposing of their old, obsolete pistols.

The U.S. government, from which Francis Bannerman had obtained his pinfire revolvers, had purchased them from Alexis Godillot during the early part of the war. Following the war other firms also sold pinfire revolvers bought at government surplus arms auctions. In his 1902 catalog Charles J. Godfrey of New York listed a Lefaucheux revolver model for sale that purportedly had seen Confederate use (*Plate 4-26*). Inasmuch as Godfrey's catalog was published nearly four decades after the close of the Rebellion, perhaps he was attempting to stimulate some interest in those slow-moving surplus foreign-made revolvers by advertising them as having been "imported by the Southern Confederacy for use in the Civil War."

Beginning in the years immediately following

the end of the Civil War, and right up to the present time, military-style pinfire revolvers have been offered for sale in the catalogs of arms dealers. For countless legions of land seekers, emigrants, and rootless war veterans who cast their eyes and destinies westward in the decades after the cessation of hostilities, such surplus arms provided inexpensive protection while one began a new life on the frontier. Doubtless many of the westering ex-soldiers took their army-issue Lefaucheux Model 1854 revolvers with them as authorized by General Order No. 101 of June 1865, which allowed enlisted men to keep their personal sidearms. But the vast majority were obtained indirectly through the government military surplus sales. Those pinfire revolvers would play a role in the new chapter of American history just then being opened.

The "Chimney" Adaptor

Many 9mm and 12mm caliber revolvers were capable of employing the "chimney" cartridge adaptor (*see Plate 4-27*), which enabled a pinfire revolver to be fired as a conventional cap-and-ball arm. Prior to capping with a percussion cap, the adaptor's small metal chamber would be loaded with black powder and a .36 or .44 caliber lead ball. The balls were interchangeable with 9mm or 12mm bullets, respectively, and although the .44

caliber soft lead ball was of slightly greater diameter than 12mm it would be "shaved" when ramming it into the bore of the revolver's steel cylinder. The chimney adaptor was then inserted into the cylinder, and the arm was fired in the conventional manner. The adaptor could be used until the owner was able to acquire more pinfire cartridges, which in the Confederacy were in very short supply.

All revolvers manufactured on the pinfire system were constructed with a slot milled into the frame (and top strap, if present) at the rear of the cylinder, which accommodated the protruding cartridge pin and allowed the cylinder to rotate. However, revolvers designed to utilize chimney adaptors have wider and deeper top strap slots, in addition to enlarged pin slots in their cylinders, to facilitate insertion of the adaptor and its percussion cap. While the enlarged cylinder slots oftentimes are difficult to detect, both features will be found on many Lefaucheux Model 1854 revolvers, as well as on other early military-style revolvers.

Loading a pinfire revolver with the chimney cartridge adaptor probably accounts for their high incidence of missing or bent ejector rods, which were often used as a rammer to push the ball into the chamber. The cartridge-ejector rods on pinfire revolvers were not designed for the same purpose as a percussion revolver's loading lever, which

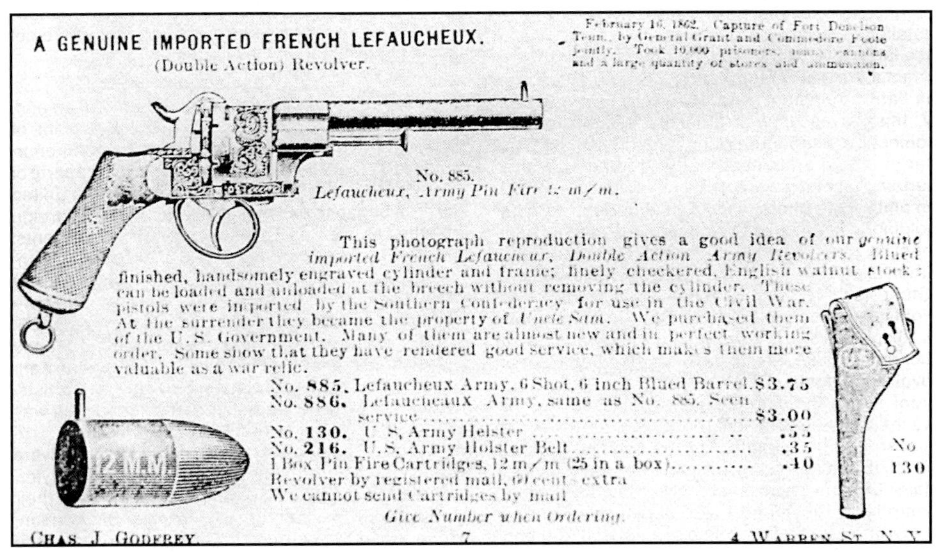

Plate 4-26. Reproduction of page seven from New York military surplus dealer Chas. J. Godfrey's 1902 catalog, showing "handsomely engraved" Lefaucheux Model 1854 12mm revolvers, "imported by the Southern Confederacy for use in the Civil War" and "in perfect working order", for $3.75 each. *Courtesy Konrad F. Schreier, Jr.*

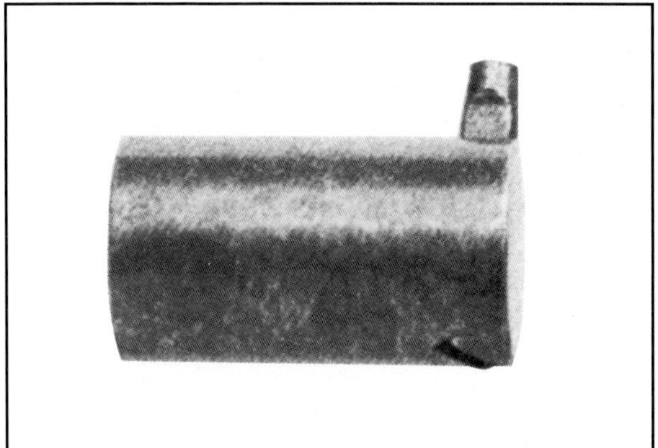

Plate 4-27. The "chimney" adaptor, a field expediency for loading a pinfire revolver for use as a cap-and-ball percussion gun when pinfire cartridges could not be obtained. *Chris C. Curtis collection; Bob Steele photograph*

obtained the great force necessary to seat a ball in the chamber through the use of leverage and thus had to be stronger.

The same mistake doubtless also accounts for the high rate of broken loading gates, which in most cases are located directly behind the ejector rod and are a recognized weak point in the design of most pinfire revolvers. The loss of a loading gate might render the operation of the gun unreliable, as pinfire cartridges are normally smaller in diameter than the cylinder chambers and can slide rearward and jam the action, or fall completely out of the cylinder.

The "Rogue's Gallery" in *Plates 4-28* through *4-33* on the following page depicts a cross-section, in age and battle experience, of Civil War soldiers from both sides of the conflict armed with large military-style pinfire revolvers. "Billy Yank" (*Plate 4-28*) carries a Colt "Navy" pistol as backup; the gent in homespun (*Plate 4-29*) is believed to be Confederate; the grizzled Union veteran in *Plate 4-30*'s family scene looks ready to "mix it up" at a moment's notice; the bearded Yank (*Plate 4-31*) holds a pinfire revolver across his chest; the lefthanded soldier (*Plate 4-32*) holds his sword and pinfire revolver; as does the young artillerist (*Plate 4-33*). *Plates 4-28, 4-32, 4-33 courtesy Herb Peck, Jr.; Plate 4-29 courtesy John Delph; Plate 4-30 courtesy Bill Gillespie; Plate 4-31 courtesy John H. Luckey.*

Chapter Notes.

1. It is surely no coincidence that the label on a packet of C.D. Leet & Co. pinfire cartridges reflects a 25 grain charge of black powder, and that the case length of the "American" pinfire cartridge was made longer to accomodate the increased powder charge.
2. In 1862 Herman Boker was successfully sued by Smith & Wesson, for selling handguns manufactured by the Manhattan Firearms Co. that infringed on the Rollin White patent (owned by S&W) for bored-through cylinders taking rear-loading metallic cartridges. Due to his long association with the European arms market, and exposure to the pinfire system, Boker must have considered the Rollin White patent as without merit. In France, Eugene Lefaucheux had been producing pinfire revolvers with rear-loaded, bored-through cylinders for some time before White's patent was recorded in the U.S., and he continued to manufacture them in France and Belgium for several years afterward. For Boker that may have obscured the fact that in America the features of the Rollin White patent were not only legally protected, but rigidly defended in court, by Smith & Wesson.
3. Letters to Ordnance Officers, June 13, 1861 to February 12, 1862, National Archives, Washington, DC.
4. Republished in the "Old Shawnee Days" edition of the Shawnee (Kansas) *Journal-Herald*, Wednesday June 3, 1992.
5. William B. Edwards, *Civil War Guns* (Stackpole Books, Harrisburg, PA, 1962).
6. Catalog No. 124, Dixie Gun Works, Union City, Tennessee.
7. Ordnance Contracts, Ex. Doc. 99, 40th Congress, 2nd Session.
8. *Op. Cit., Civil War Guns.*
9. One collector of pinfire arms succinctly remarked, "If you saw a Confederate soldier stamp a gun 'C.S.A.', you know it's right. If you didn't see him do the stamping, assume the mark is a fake!"
10. U.S. War Department, *The War of the Rebellion: A Compilation of the Official Records of the Union and Confederate Armies* (Government Printing Office, Washington, DC, 1880-1901), Volume 39, Part 2.
11. Richard Taylor Hill and William Edward Anthony, *Confederate Longarms and Pistols* (The Authors, Charlotte, NC, 1978).

Plate 4-28

Plate 4-29

Plate 4-30

Plate 4-31

Plate 4-32

Plate 4-33

Pinfire Arms in the Commercial Market: Shotguns and Rifles

The idea of breechloading arms is surely not a recent one, as breechloading guns have been built almost from the inception of the age of firearms.

Most early breechloaders, however, were as dangerous to their users as to their quarry, and none was successful until the appearance of the Pauly gun in France during the early nineteenth century.

The admittedly limited success of the Pauly gun was due to its reloadable cartridge. Despite its fragile construction of a pasteboard tube containing powder and shot held within a brass shell, the Pauly cartridge was far ahead of its time and served as an inventive springboard for the next generation of arms designers and manufacturers.

The breechloading firearm, like most inventions, was not the result of just one man's genius. Instead, it was the synthesis of many attempts toward an end, and a collection of workable ideas amassed during the search for a gas-tight seal at the breech of the gun. Due to the limited resources of material, and especially the limitations of technology during the gun's early days, the solution to the problem of gases escaping from the breech juncture of a breechloading gun was initially directed toward the construction of the firearm itself. Prior to the advent of the self-contained cartridge, the loose and separate components of primer, powder, and shot afforded no provision to

contain those gases. Many early patent papers described mechanical methods of creating a positive gas seal. When put into actual practice, however, most succumbed to the problems of metal fatigue and continuous loosening of parts caused by the stress of the powder explosion on ignition, in addition to the complications caused by black powder fouling.

While Casimir Lefaucheux was working to improve the design of his pinfire shotgun (French patent number 5525 of 1833, based on the Pauly theory), he too was plagued by the problem of gases escaping at the breech. But rather than following the lead of others seeking to solve the problem by modifying the breech of the gun itself, Lefaucheux instead chose to direct his inventive efforts toward the cartridge. The result was the first true pinfire cartridge, already discussed in Chapter One. Lefaucheux' cartridge, although less than perfect, was to open the door to some of the most revolutionary developments in the whole history of firearms.

Casimir Lefaucheux' original intent was to use his new cartridge in shotguns, and his 1833 invention of the pivoting action shotgun (*see* Chapter One, *Plate 1-5*) was easily modified to utilize the

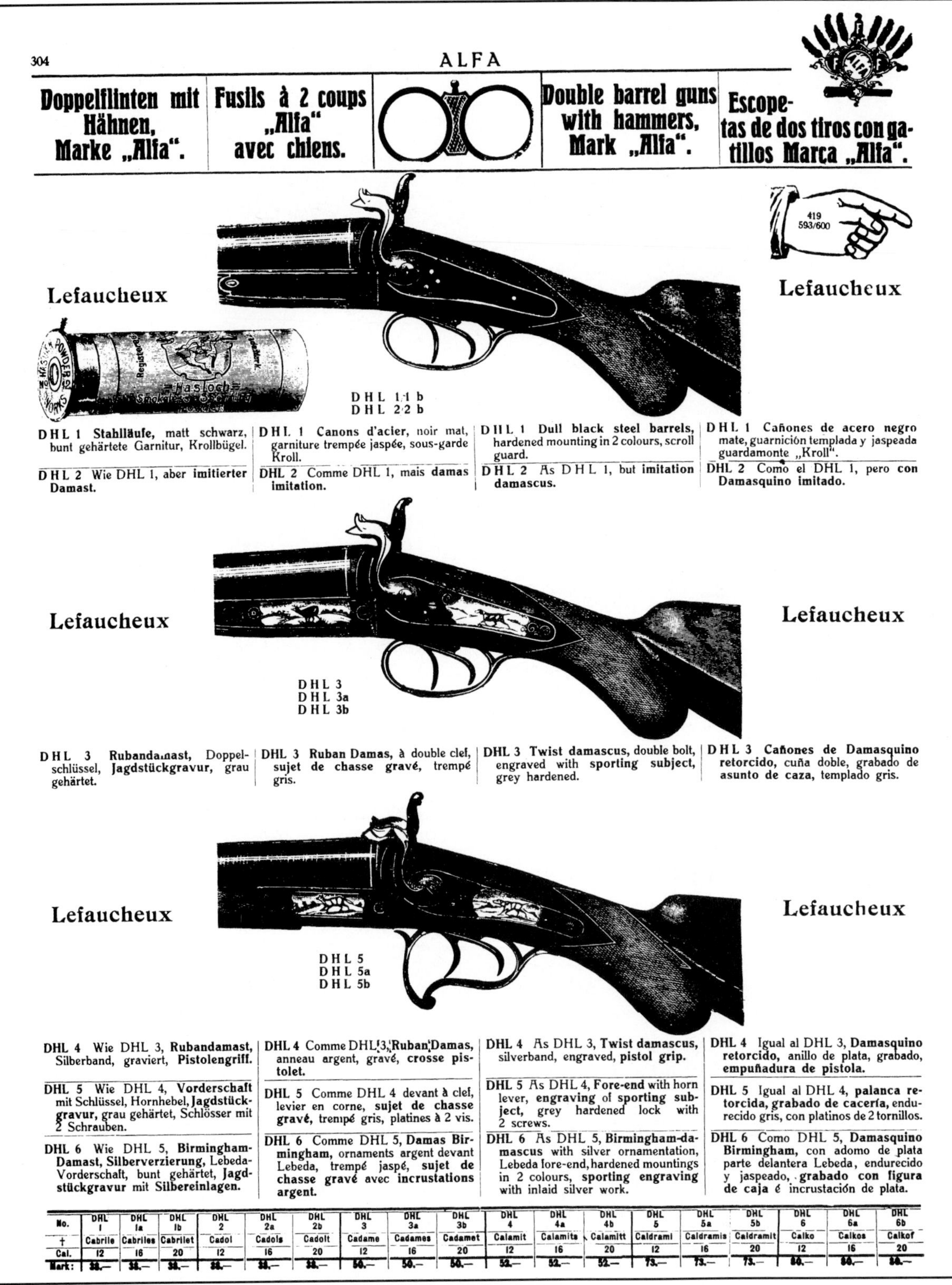

Doppelflinten mit Hähnen, Marke „Alfa".	Fusils à 2 coups „Alfa" avec chiens.		Double barrel guns with hammers, Mark „Alfa".	Escopetas de dos tiros con gatillos Marca „Alfa".

Lefaucheux — DHL 1-1 b / DHL 2-2 b — Lefaucheux

419
593/600

DHL 1 Stahlläufe, matt schwarz, bunt gehärtete Garnitur, Krollbügel.	DHI. 1 Canons d'acier, noir mat, garniture trempée jaspée, sous-garde Kroll.	DHL 1 Dull black steel barrels, hardened mounting in 2 colours, scroll guard.	DHL 1 Cañones de acero negro mate, guarnición templada y jaspeada guardamonte „Kroll".
DHL 2 Wie DHL 1, aber imitierter Damast.	DHL 2 Comme DHL 1, mais damas imitation.	DHL 2 As DHL 1, but imitation damascus.	DHL 2 Como el DHL 1, pero con Damasquino imitado.

Lefaucheux — DHL 3 / DHL 3a / DHL 3b — Lefaucheux

DHL 3 Rubandamast, Doppelschlüssel, Jagdstückgravur, grau gehärtet.	DHL 3 Ruban Damas, à double clef, sujet de chasse gravé, trempé gris.	DHL 3 Twist damascus, double bolt, engraved with sporting subject, grey hardened.	DHL 3 Cañones de Damasquino retorcido, cuña doble, grabado de asunto de caza, templado gris.

Lefaucheux — DHL 5 / DHL 5a / DHL 5b — Lefaucheux

DHL 4 Wie DHL 3, Rubandamast, Silberband, graviert, Pistolengriff.	DHL 4 Comme DHL 3, Ruban Damas, anneau argent, gravé, crosse pistolet.	DHL 4 As DHL 3, Twist damascus, silverband, engraved, pistol grip.	DHL 4 Igual al DHL 3, Damasquino retorcido, anillo de plata, grabado, empuñadura de pistola.
DHL 5 Wie DHL 4, Vorderschaft mit Schlüssel, Hornhebel, Jagdstückgravur, grau gehärtet, Schlösser mit 2 Schrauben.	DHL 5 Comme DHL 4 devant à clef, levier en corne, sujet de chasse gravé, trempé gris, platines à 2 vis.	DHL 5 As DHL 4, Fore-end with horn lever, engraving of sporting subject, grey hardened lock with 2 screws.	DHL 5 Igual al DHL 4, palanca retorcida, grabado de cacería, endurecido gris, con platinos de 2 tornillos.
DHL 6 Wie DHL 5, Birmingham-Damast, Silberverzierung, Lebeda-Vorderschaft, bunt gehärtet, Jagdstückgravur mit Silbereinlagen.	DHL 6 Comme DHL 5, Damas Birmingham, ornaments argent devant Lebeda, trempé jaspé, sujet de chasse gravé avec incrustations argent.	DHL 6 As DHL 5, Birmingham-damascus with silver ornamentation, Lebeda fore-end, hardened mountings in 2 colours, sporting engraving with inlaid silver work.	DHL 6 Como DHL 5, Damasquino Birmingham, con adomo de plata parte delantera Lebeda, endurecido y jaspeado, grabado con figura de caja é incrustación de plata.

No.	DHL 1	DHL 1a	DHL 1b	DHL 2	DHL 2a	DHL 2b	DHL 3	DHL 3a	DHL 3b	DHL 4	DHL 4a	DHL 4b	DHL 5	DHL 5a	DHL 5b	DHL 6	DHL 6a	DHL 6b
+	Cabrile	Cabriles	Cabrilet	Cadol	Cadols	Cadolt	Cadame	Cadames	Cadamet	Calamit	Calamita	Calamitt	Caldrami	Caldramis	Caldramit	Calko	Calkos	Calkof
Cal.	12	16	20	12	16	20	12	16	20	12	16	20	12	16	20	12	16	20
Mark:	38.—	38.—	38.—	38.—	38.—	38.—	50.—	50.—	50.—	52.—	52.—	52.—	73.—	73.—	73.—	80.—	80.—	80.—

Plate 5-1. Reproduction of page 304 of the ALFA (A.L. Frank Company) 1911 arms catalog, which offered eighteen variations of pinfire shotguns at prices ranging from DM38 to DM80 (US$9.05 to US$19.05). Primed paper shotshells (page 419) cost DM47 to DM68 per hundred for 10 gauge, DM22 to DM48 for 28 gauge. This Hamburg, Germany firm's catalog was reprinted as *Arms Of The World 1911*, by Digest Books, Inc., in 1972. *Chris C. Curtis collection*

pinfire cartridge. Patent number 5525 covered his earlier experimental ignition pin detonating a cartridge within the chamber. Also protected by the same patent were the pivoting breech action and the double-bite locking system, developments that were to become the standard on longarms made and used on the European continent for well over half a century. Oddly, the double-bite locking action placed well to the rear of the barrels was later replaced by a single-bite system much nearer the pivot point, which became one of the major causes of criticism of Lefaucheux' overall design.

The 1833 Lefaucheux patent continued in force for ten years, during and after which time he continued to make improvements to his shotgun design. One of Casimir Lefaucheux' concerns during those initial trial years was the difficulty with which guns were dismantled for cleaning, storage, or field repairs; most were permanently fastened at the hinge and could not be easily taken down. Then, on October 2nd, 1849 Lefaucheux was granted a fifteen-year patent, number 4839, which provided an improved hinge and pivot design with levers for dismantling the gun. It was an important step in the evolution of the breechloading shot-gun, and it soon was being copied throughout all of Europe. Other improvements covered by the same patent included the design of the locking hook, length of the butt, and methods for the modification of existing arms to the new version.

On November 22, 1849 a certificate of additions was granted to patent number 4839, describing the practical application of the techniques set down in the original with regard to pivoting-action rifles and shotguns. Another certificate of additions was granted on December 15th of the same year, covering the improvements to the gas seal around the ignition pin of the cartridge (which Casimir Lefaucheux referred to as having been "invented by me in 1835").

There were many other attempts by French inventors to improve on the pivot design, which was considered by many as the weak point in Lefaucheux' concept for tip-down breechloaders. One such design was patented by Brun of Paris, patent number 5975 of October 19, 1850. This patent, shown in *Plate 5-2*, is concerned with the placement of the reintroduced double-bite locking system located midway between the breech and pivot point.

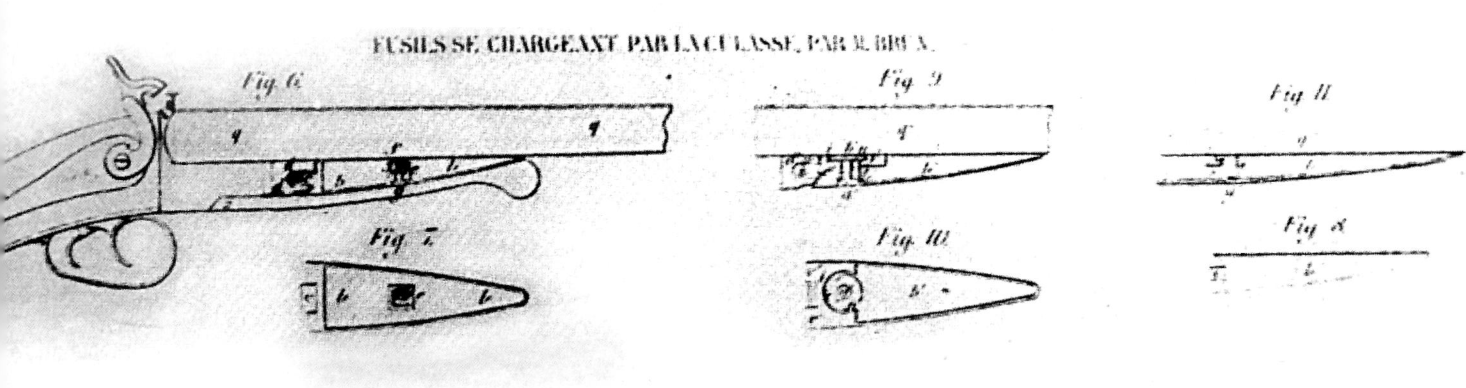

Plate 5-2. Reproduction of a drawing from Brun's French patent number 5975 of October 19, 1850. *Chris C. Curtis collection*

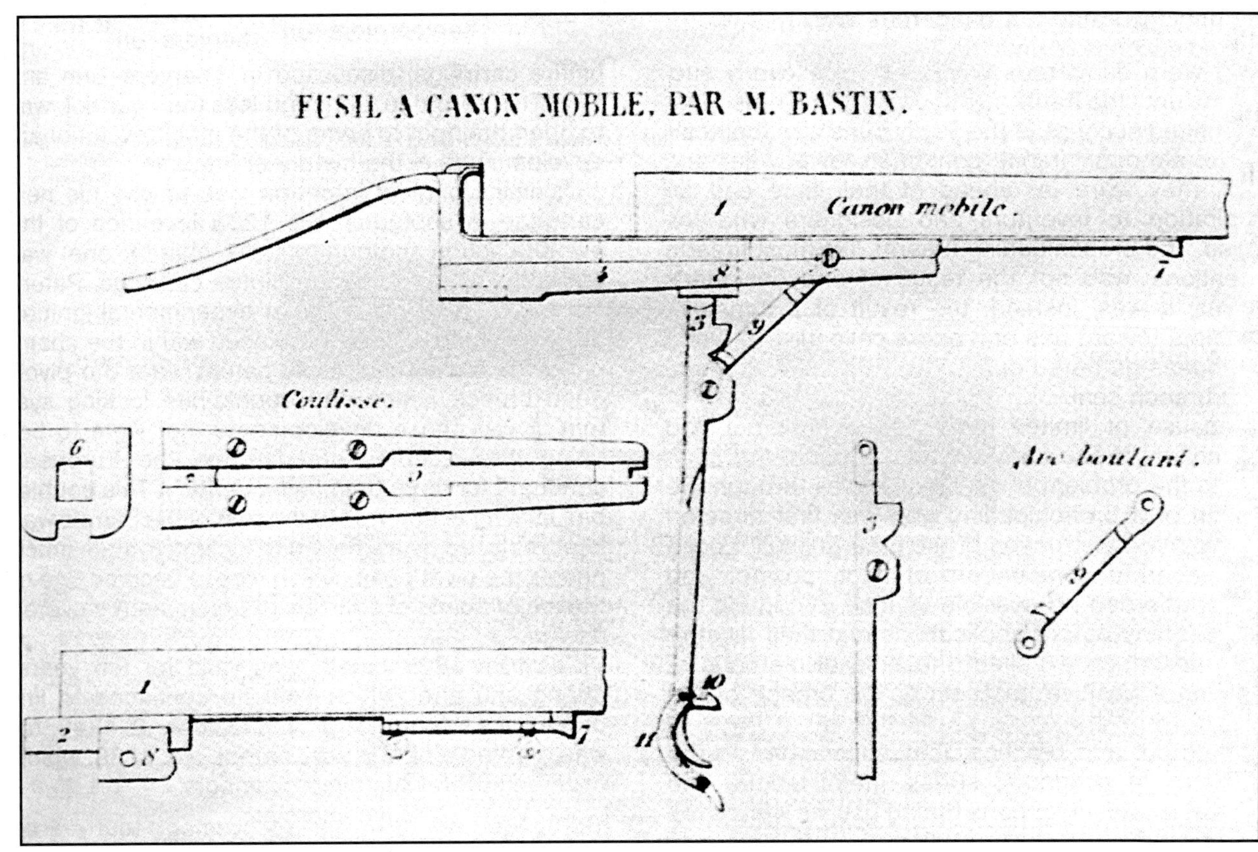

Plate 5-3. Reproduction of a drawing from Bastin's French patent number 16042, of 1856. *Chris C. Curtis collection*

From the late 1820s on, there was increasing interest by the French gunmakers in breechloading firearms. Many versions of such weapons, along with their special cartridges, appeared on the market, both before and after the pinfire shotguns and ammunition introduced by Lefaucheux. The Lefaucheux inventions, however, provided the foundation that inspired all other related efforts. What resulted were newer and more practical firearms designs. It frequently has been said that imitation is the sincerest form of flattery; if true, Casimir Lefaucheux must have felt highly complimented. For, many were the firearms inventors that followed in his initial footsteps, copying, modifying, and building on his designs, in essence confirming the practical usefulness of his ideas many times over.

text continued on page 144

Plate 5-6 (opposite page, bottom). Another example of the double-underlever, take-down system applied to a pinfire shotgun made in Belgium. This high-quality arm is gold-washed over engraved birds against foliate and geometric designs; the rearmost 4½ inches of the barrels also feature gold-wash over scroll engraving. "*A. Francotte Bte*" is script engraved and gold-washed on top of the barrels; a "*crown over AF*" mark appears on either side of the locking mechanism; in addition it bears Liége proofmarks, and inspector's marks indicating pre-1877 manufacture. The French-style case, with its intricate locking mechanism that activates four bolts simultaneously, contains a bullet mold, chamber reamer, three-piece wooden cleaning rod, bore swab, pin puller, primer seater, powder flask with automatic measure, shot measure, screwdriver, and a tool the purpose of which is unknown. The empty spaces in the deluxe casing are for a wad cutter, wad setter, crimper, wire brush, and an oil can. *Courtesy James Lowther; John Calcany photograph*

Plate 5-4 (above). An unmarked as to maker, Liége proofed 16-gauge shotgun of high quality. Profusely engraved and inlaid with animals in gold, it is a fine example of the Belgian gunmakers' art of the period. The forward underlever which releases the tip-down action is similar to Lefaucheux' early design. *Courtesy James Lowther; John Calcany photograph*

Plate 5-5 (right). Detail view of open breech of another Liége-made 16-gauge shotgun, unmarked as to maker. This copy of a Lefaucheux gun bears post-1877 inspector's marks; the small lever forward of the action opening lever releases the lock on the pivot and allows removal of the barrels. Popular for half a century, this is the type most often found today. *Courtesy private collection; Gene Smith photograph*

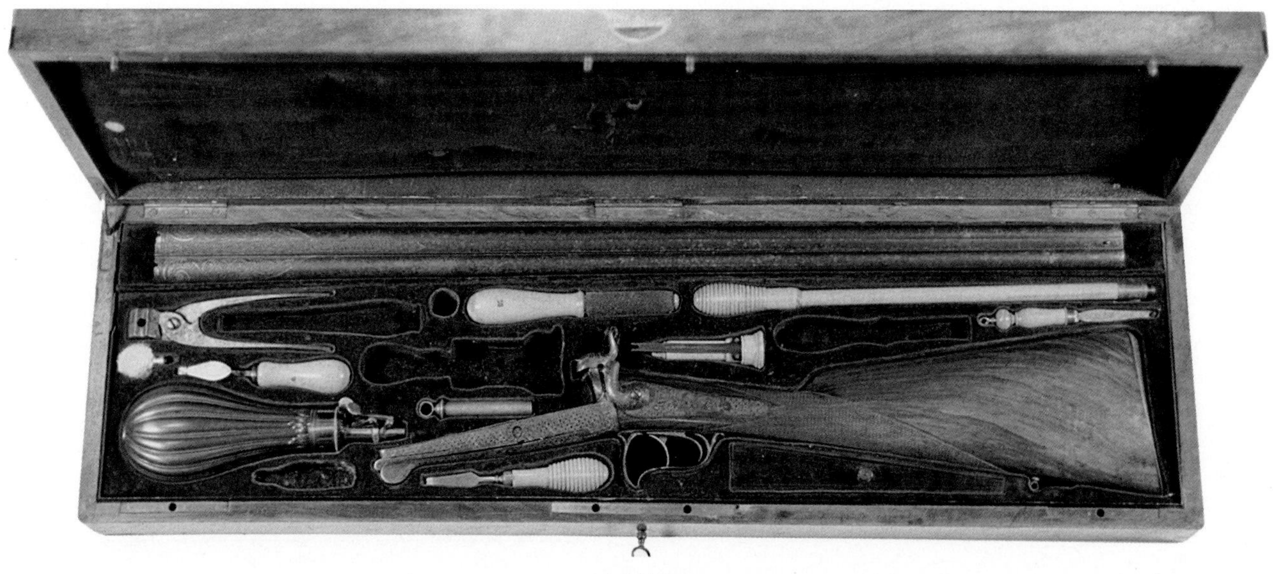

Plate 5-7 (right). Detail view of a Spanish-made, 16-gauge pinfire shotgun marked on the barrels, *"Fa de B. Echeverria Vitoria-Damasquine Bernard."* The date of this shotgun is unknown, as the Spanish system of proof testing was voluntary during the period, yet it bears marks indicating manufacture prior to 1910. The cocking lever is located beneath the triggerguard on this relief-engraved and nickel-plated example. Shown out of its leatherette casing, this gun represents the better firearms produced in Spain during the pinfire era. Bonifacio Echeverria, a descendant of the maker of this shotgun, produced the "Star" 9mm caliber Bergmann semi-automatic pistol, which has remained the standard sidearm of Spanish armed forces since 1946. *Courtesy Mike Gibbons; Gene Smith photograph*

Plate 5-8 (above). A French-made, 14-gauge pinfire shotgun with damascus barrels. The barrel rib is marked, *"Chenevier ARQ St. Quentin"*; under the barrel are, *"Leopold Bernard"* and *"Chenevier A St. Quentin."* The date "1873" precedes the serial number. Both lockplates bear Chenevier's name and address. Beneath the breech opening lever is an unusual pull-down lever that releases the barrels from the frame. *Courtesy James Lowther; Gene Smith photograph*

Plate 5-9 (right). This type of combination arm is generally known as a "cape gun." The left barrel is 12-gauge smoothbore; the right is chambered for a cartridge of approximately 18mm (70 caliber). Both barrels have rifle sights, the name of the retailer, *"C. Densell in Breslau"*, Liége proofmarks, and pre-1877 inspector's marks. *Courtesy private collection; Gene Smith photograph*

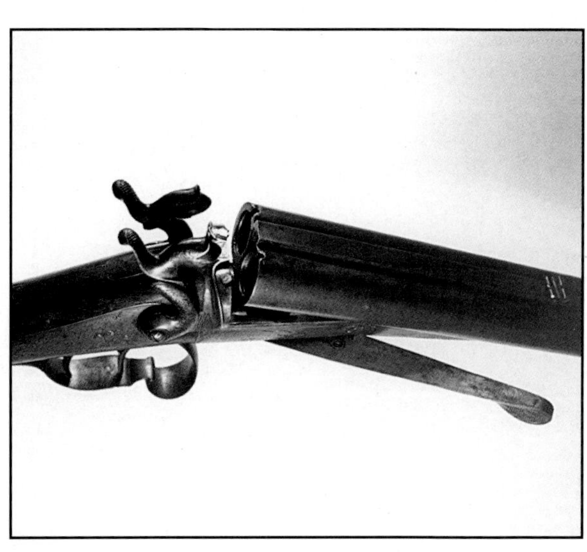

Plate 5-10 (right). Detail view of breech area of a high-grade, 16-gauge, Belgian single-barrel pinfire shotgun. The locks and frame are engraved with game and hunting scenes; the tops of the 27-inch barrels have the maker's name, *"A. Francotte"*, inlaid in gold. *Courtesy Don Kramer; Ferrari Color photograph*

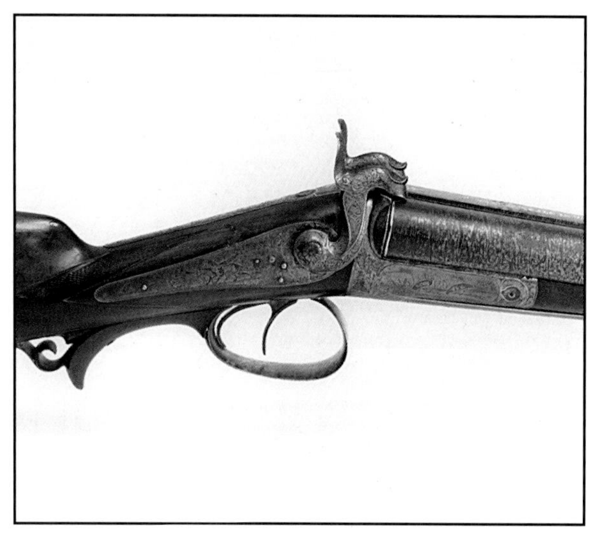

Plate 5-11 (below). A single-barrel, 28-gauge pinfire shotgun. The steel barrel is stamped *"Guss Stahl"* and has the maker's name and location, *"V. CHR. Schilling in Suhl"*, marked on top. Valentin Christoph Schilling was an important German armsmaker whose career began in 1847. The firm he founded has supplied the German government with arms and munitions ever since. *Courtesy James Lowther; John Calcany photograph*

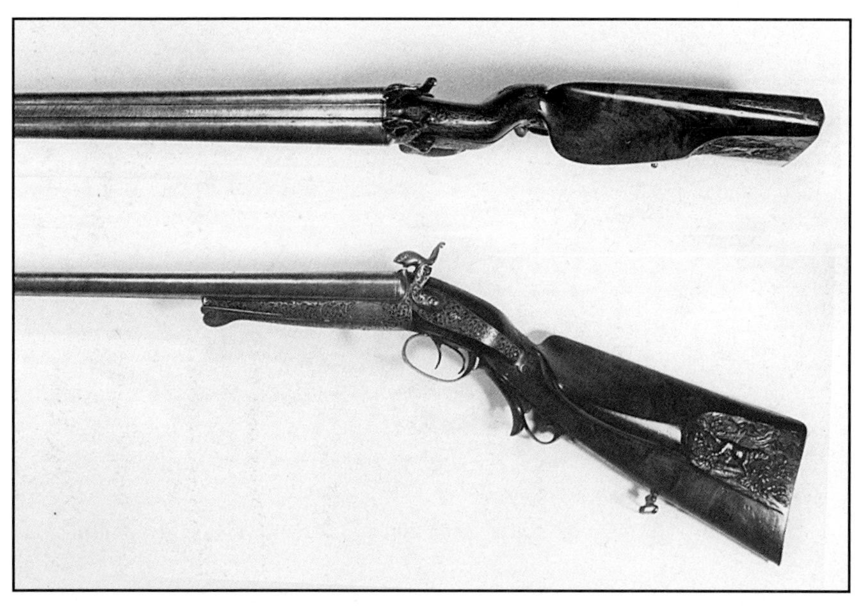

Plate 5-12 (left). A 16-gauge pinfire shotgun. Offset stocks were made for right-handed shooters who had lost the sight of their right eye; when put to the right shoulder the offset stock allows sighting down the barrel using the left eye. This gun bears German proofmarks: inlaid in gold in the top of the barrel rib is the maker's name and location, *"Eust. Sick in Gunzburg."* Relief-engraved; animals are relief-carved into the stock; a coat of arms appears behind the breech. This high-quality shotgun has a double-lever barrel break beneath the metal forearm. *Courtesy James Lowther; John Calcany photograph*

The Bastin action was one such attempt to improve on Lefaucheux' design, as discussed elsewhere in Chapter One. Bastin's patent, number 16042 of 1856 (*see Plate 5-3*), was just one in a steady stream of firearms improvements to reach the French Patent Office. Another was Houllier's improved pinfire cartridge with its expanding base wad that created a positive gas seal. Prior to Houllier's improvement, pinfire breechloaders were made in very limited quantities, the majority in France, with only a few originating elsewhere in Europe.

The breechloading pinfire shotgun, on the other hand, found more ready acceptance by their cartridges. By then sportsmen around the world had acknowledged the pinfire as a superior system of firearms ignition, and the percussion, muzzle-loading shotgun was gradually replaced by the more advanced breechloaders. Gunmakers were producing varying types and styles of guns to fill the growing demand for modern arms.

During the early period of breechloading arms development (1835-1860), the sportsmen and gunmakers of Great Britain all but ignored the strides being made in arms technology on the Continent. Even after these new Continental arms were shown to the British public at the London

Plate 5-13. This French-made, single-barrel pinfire shotgun fits into the category of a "poacher's gun", as it folds at the breech pivot point for easy concealment or more convenient transport. The arm bears no maker's name but the barrel is marked, "*N.A. St. Etienne 16.0*", which dates its manufacture after 1900. *Courtesy James Lowther; John Calcany photograph*

European sportsmen, and even before 1850 it had attained a high level of popularity on the Continent. During the following two decades many improvements were made to the design and general construction of both the shotguns and Exhibition of 1851, no great demand was engendered for the pinfire breechloading shotgun. Articles appearing in the sporting publications of the day largely ignored the breechloader's presence, as well, while others spoke of it only in disparaging terms. The English remained steadfast in their belief that the traditional muzzleloading shotgun was best, and saw no need to replace it.

However, some progressive-minded British sportsmen did import the early French pinfire shotguns, and a very few English gunmakers experimented with the idea of manufacturing them at home. One was Joseph Lang, who, if not the first Englishman to construct a pinfire shotgun, was the first to recognize the breechloader's potential advantages on the sporting field.

The controversy over which of the two systems was better continued unabated. As early as 1856, it was the subject for debate in a correspondence column in *The Field*, a weekly English publication catering to country gentlemen and sportsmen. Finally, in 1858 John Henry Walsh, editor of *The Field*, organized a series of public gun trials to be held that year, and again in 1859 and 1866. The tests were completely impartial, with several rules being strictly enforced. Guns, both pinfire and percussion, were separated into individual categories and divided into classes according to their weight and length of barrel. Inspectors chosen by the exhibitors were to inspect targets and supervise loading of the firearms. Powder, shot, and cartridges were furnished by *The Field*, and all guns were loaded in the presence of either editor Walsh or the inspectors. The size of shot and measure of powder also were regulated, and the types of targets and firing distances were determined and then recorded by judges from both sides. All records and scores were kept by *The Field*, and published soon after the contest concluded.

In the first trials, 1858, six of the twenty-six entries were breechloading shotguns; the highest place earned by a pinfire breechloader was fifth.

In 1859, fifteen of the twenty-nine entries were breechloaders, although only five of the fifteen employed pinfire ignition (centerfire and Needham's cartridge guns also were entered). A pinfire shotgun entered by Egan of Bradford placed fourth in the competition.

By 1866, however, all thirty-five entries were breechloaders, twenty-three of which were pinfires. Five of the top ten awards went to pinfire arms, with both first and second places going to pinfire shotguns made by W.R. Pape.

During all three of *The Field*'s competitions breechloading arms had clearly demonstrated their superiority over the muzzleloader. As British sportsmen began to accept the pinfire breechloading principle, English armsmakers responded with

a steady stream of applications to the British Patent Office.

The primary concern of the British gunmakers was the weakness inherent in the breech area of breechloading guns, both those made on the Continent and their close English copies. Inventors set out to correct the basic flaw in Lefaucheux' design, that of the single-bite locking lug located close to the pivot point, and variations of the breech opening lever system are many among British guns manufactured during the latter years of the nineteenth century.

text continued on page 155

Plate 5-14. A youthful European sportsman posed with his favorite pinfire shotgun, in this *carte de visite* photograph dating from the latter half of the nineteenth century. *Chris C. Curtis collection*

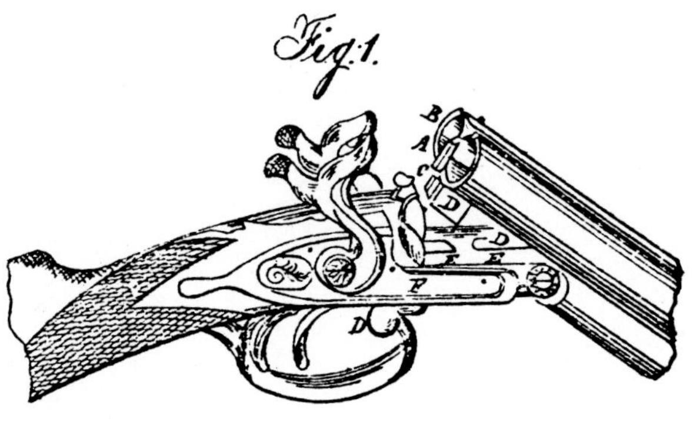

W. R. PAPE.

Breech-Loading Fire-Arm.

No 70,463.   Patented Nov. 5, 1867.

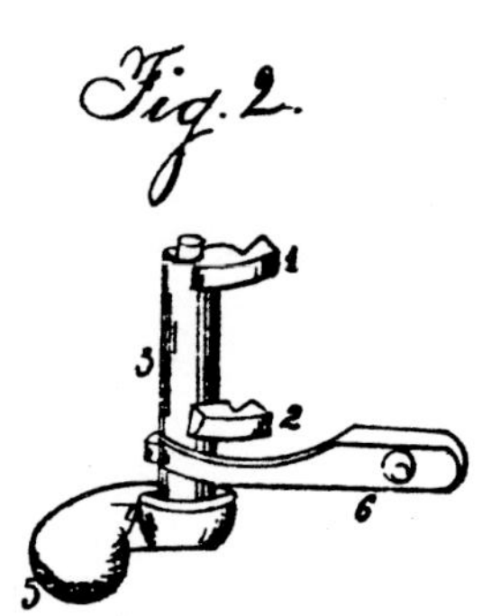

Plate 5-15. Reproduction of W.R. Pape's British gun patent number 70463, of November 5, 1867, showing his vertical spindle breech locking system. *Chris C. Curtis collection*

Plate 5-16. Detail view of the open breech of an English-made, 10-gauge pinfire shotgun marked on its barrel rib, *"W.R.Pape—Newcastle On Tyne—Winner of the London Gun Trials in 1858, 1859, and 1866—Patent 210."* The barrels of this arm are 33¼ inches long, and its overall length is 48 inches. The small thumb lever ahead of the triggerguard when pushed forward frees a curved bolt moving on a vertical spindle which rotates to one side and clears the bite at the rear of the lug, allowing the barrels to tip downward. The snap spring is a leaf type, set in the forward area of the action bar; it bears on the vertical spindle. In 1866 Pape won the test trials with a breechloading pinfire shotgun; in 1858 and 1859 Pape muzzleloaders claimed the prizes. This was one of many attempts by British gunmakers to improve on the single-bite breech locking system. W.R. Pape was part of the English firearms industry from the 1850s until his accidental death in 1923 at the age of 91. *Courtesy private collection; Gene Smith photograph*

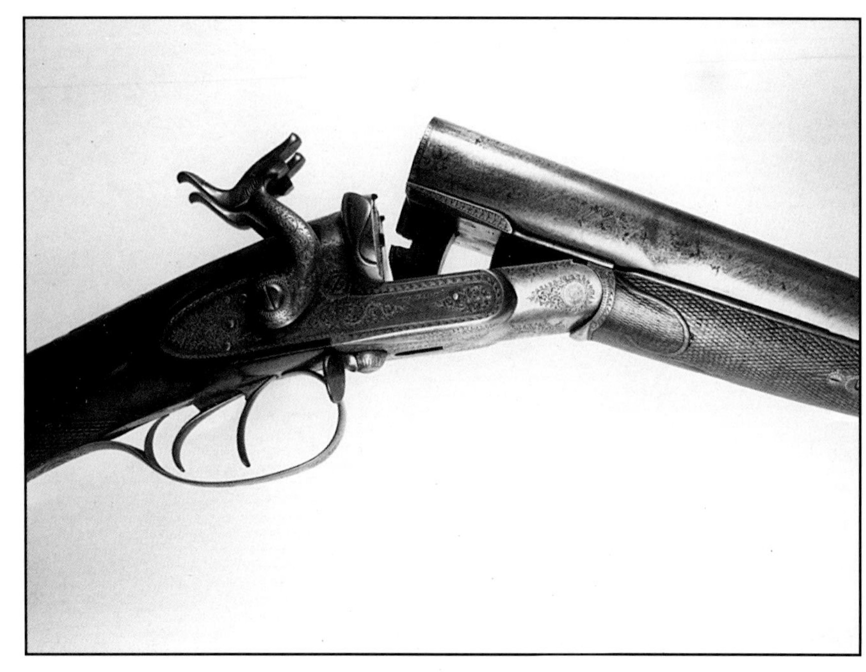

Plate 5-17 (below). A Scottish-made, 16-gauge pinfire shotgun from the mid-1860s marked *"Edward Paton"* on the locks, *"Edward Paton, 11 Geo. St. Perth, Maker to H.R.H. The Prince Consort"* on the barrel rib, and bearing London proofmarks. The lever under the triggerguard turns to free the single-bite action by moving a sliding bolt. Paton also converted muzzleloading shotguns to the breechloading system by securing the barrels to the action by a single stud held in place and released by a lever extending through the frame ahead of the triggerguard. It is not known if he patented his method of conversion. *Courtesy James Lowther; John Calcany photograph*

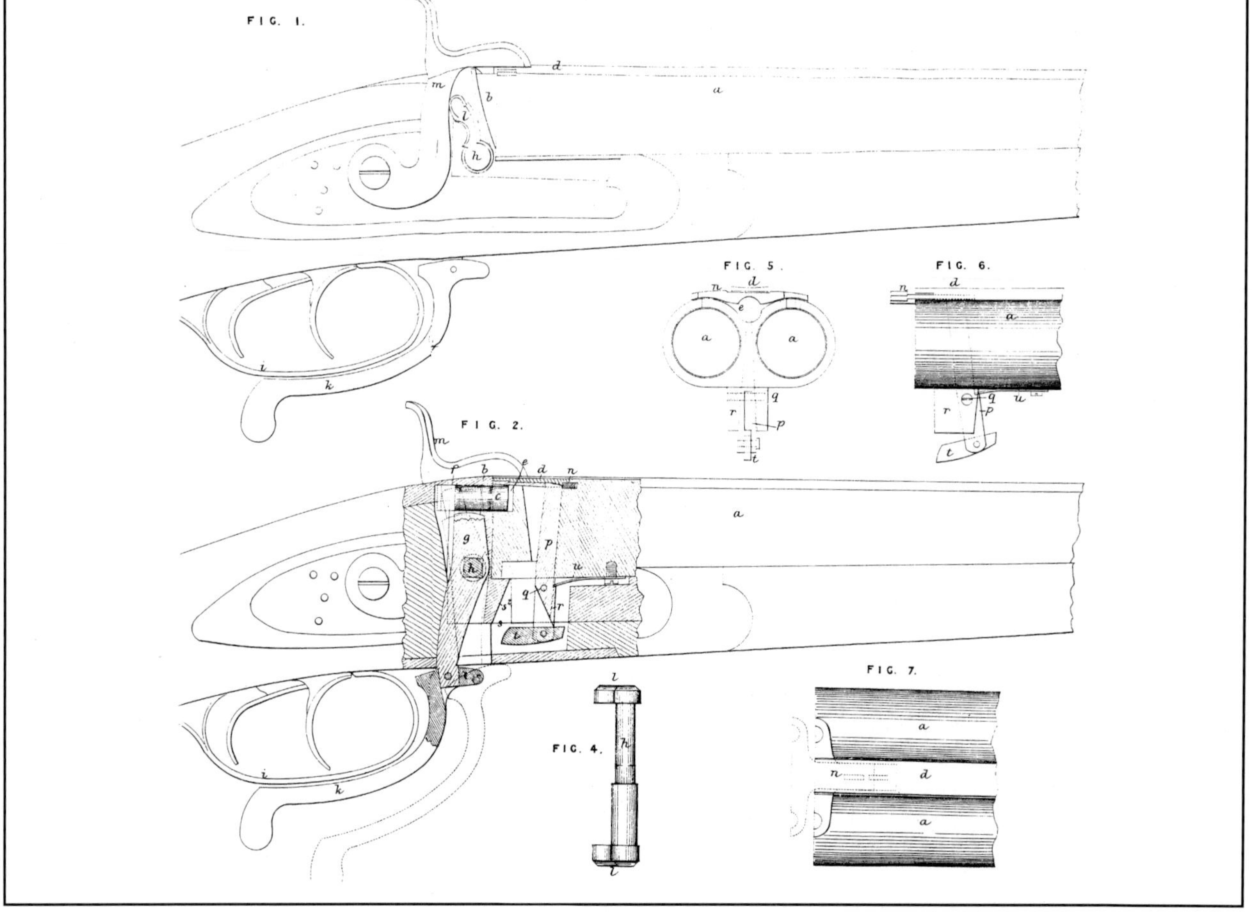
FIG. 1.
FIG. 2.
FIG. 4.
FIG. 5.
FIG. 6.
FIG. 7.

W. W. GREENER,
GUN RIFLE & CARTRIDGE MANUFACTURER,
BIRMINGHAM.

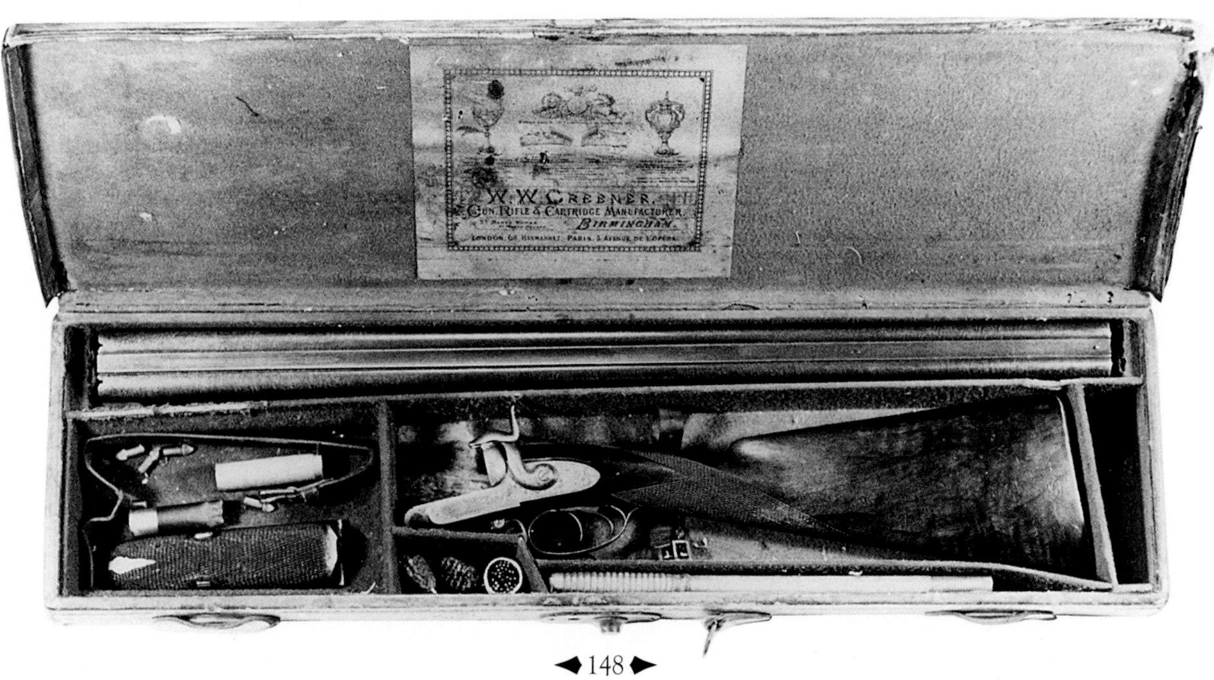

Plate 5-18 (opposite page, top). Reproduction of fine gunmaker W.W. Greener's British gun patent number 2231, of September 10, 1863. Illustrated are Greener's modifications to the locking system of shotgun actions. *Chris C. Curtis collection*

Plate 5-19 (opposite page, bottom). An English-made, 10-gauge pinfire shotgun engraved on the barrel rib, *"William W. Greener, 48 Duke St. St. James London, Stub Damascus."* Under the forearm both barrels are marked with the serial number of the arm, Birmingham proofmarks, and the Greener registered trademark: a small elephant. The barrels are 29 3/8 inches long, the overall weight of the arm is seven pounds, and the action-break lever is located beneath the triggerguard. The lettering of the award label affixed inside the lid of the leather paved, trunk-style casing has *"W.W. Greener"* composed of guns. It advertises the many trophies won by Greener arms, some of which were the London Field Trials of 1875, the London Choke Bore Match of 1877, and the

Melbourne Gold Medal of 1881. Guns made by Greener are invariably of high quality, and were much sought-after by discerning individuals who appreciated fine arms. An example of the prices commanded by Greener firearms is found in the 1873 catalog of J.H. Johnson of Pittsburgh, Pennsylvania, which offered 10-gauge shotguns made by W.W. Greener for $120.00 each. Higher grades brought $125.00 to $200.00, depending on their materials and finish. These were extremely high prices when compared to the prices asked for other arms of the period: for instance, a Lefaucheux shotgun was $40.00 in the same catalog, and a Stevens single-barrel shotgun was listed for just $16.00. *Courtesy James Lowther; John Calcany photograph*

Plate 5-20 (right). Detail view of the action of an English-made, 12-gauge pinfire shotgun marked *"William Powell & Son, 12 Carr's Lane, Birmingham"* and with Birmingham proofmarks on the barrels. The side of the action is marked *"Powell's Patent No. 685."*[1] The locking bolt design of this gun was protected by English patent number 1163, granted to Powell in 1864. The lever located between the hammers is lifted to release the locking bolt, which acts as the forward end of the release lever. The simplicity of Powell's system made it very popular, and it is used today on some European shotguns. It was invented by William Powell, Jr., who joined his father's business in 1843, and later served as a Guardian of the Birmingham Proof House between 1862 and 1901. *Courtesy Larry Compeau; Gene Smith photograph*

Plate 5-21. Another version of the "poacher's gun", this unmarked, 12-gauge single-barrel pinfire shotgun quickly disassembles for ease of carrying or concealment. The three parts are secured by locking lugs. *Courtesy James Lowther; John Calcany photograph*

Plate 5-22 (below). An English-made, 12-gauge double-barrel shotgun marked on top of the damascus barrels, *"J. Purdey, 314½ Oxford Street, London."* An accompanying letter from James Purdey & Sons Ltd. confirms the 30-inch barrel length and dates its manufacture to 1857, early for an English pinfire breechloader. Engraved action; select wood stocks. A label in the lid of the oak case gives the firm's particulars, and loading specifications. *Courtesy James Lowther; John Calcany photograph*

Plate 5-23 (opposite page, top). Reproduction of James Purdey's British gun patent number 1104 of May 2, 1863, encompassing new designs for an underlever shotgun breech locking mechanism. *Chris C. Curtis collection*

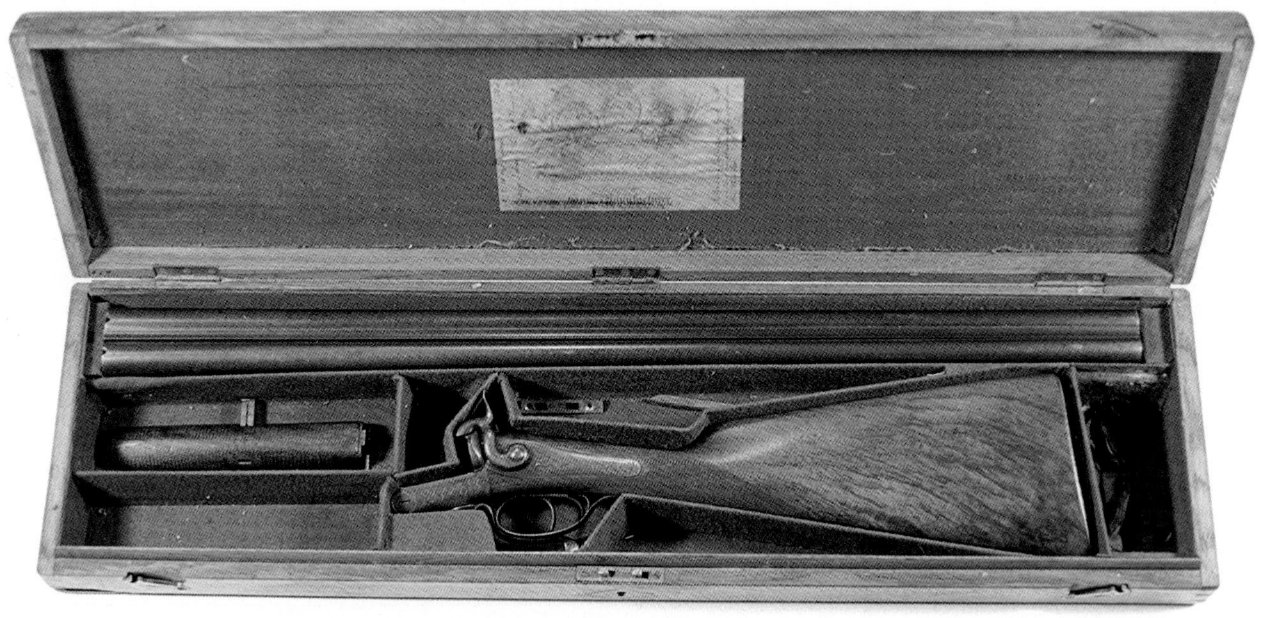

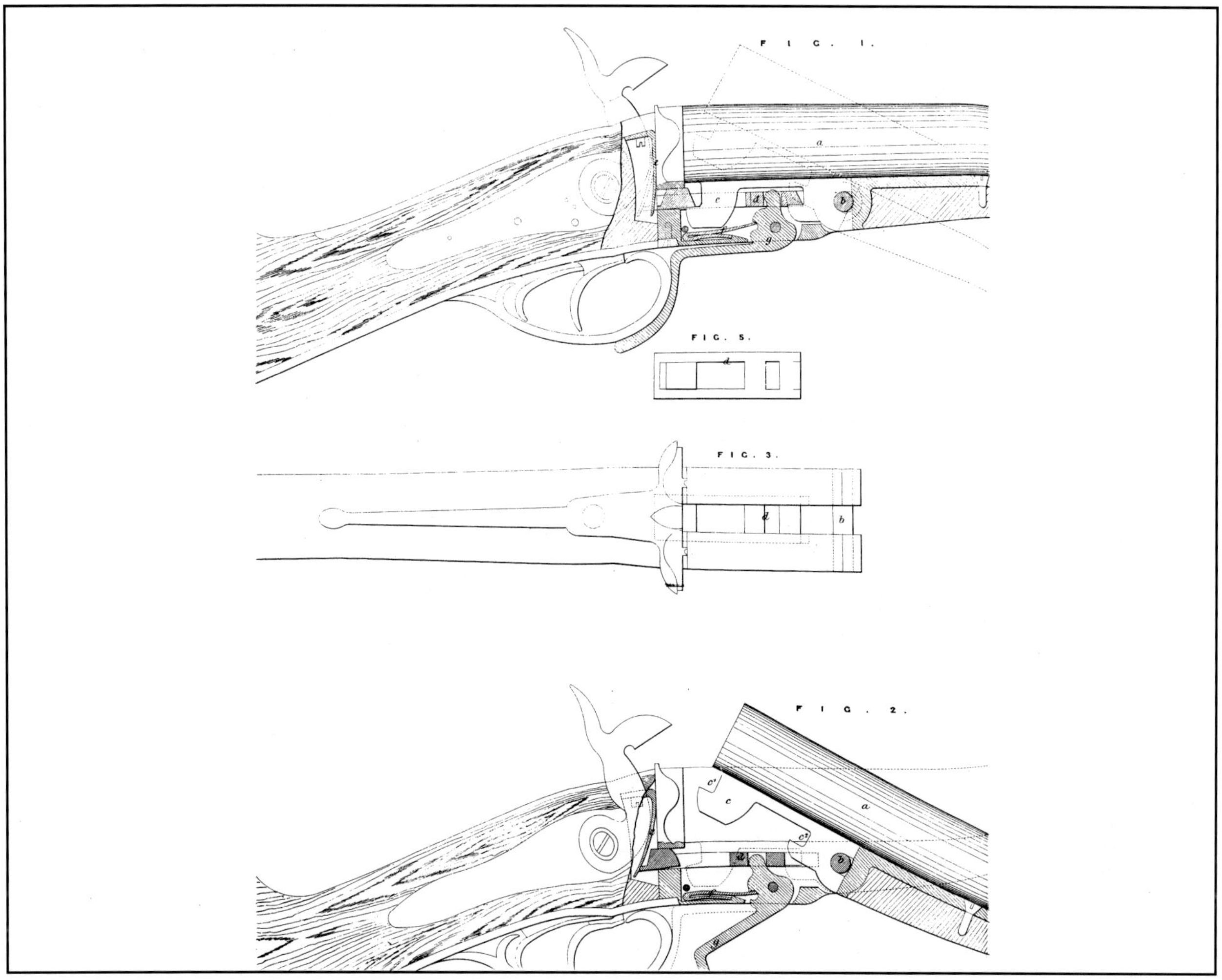

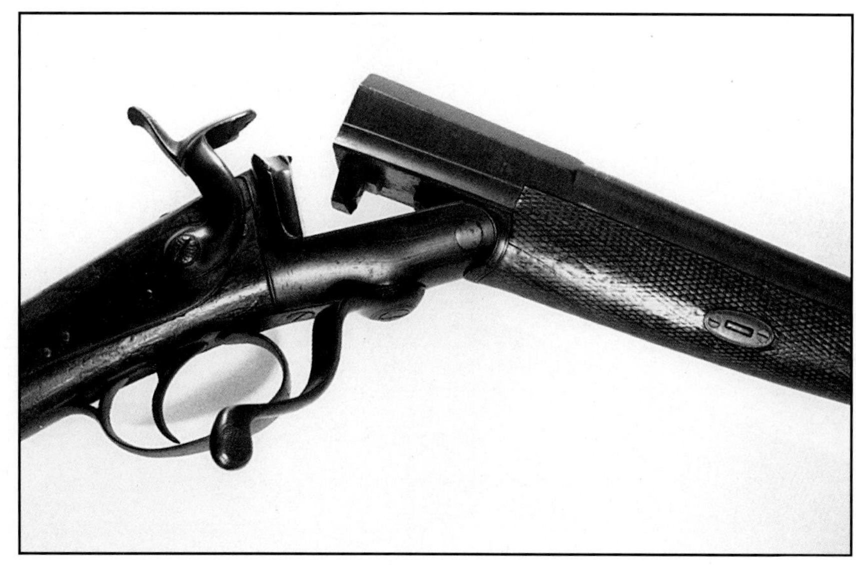

Plate 5-24 (right). Detail view of the open breech of an English, 12-gauge single-barrel shotgun marked on the 31¾-inch barrels, *"Poultney & Trimble—Baltimore."* The firm made Gilbert Smith breechloaders under U.S. patent number 17644, of June 23, 1857, and Snider breechloaders under U.S. patent number 27600, of March 20, 1860. This shotgun bears Birmingham proofmarks, demonstrating how markings can identify the origins of a gun. *Courtesy private collection; Gene Smith photograph*

T. W. WEBLEY.
BREECH LOADING FIREARM.

No. 65,783.   Patented June 11. 1867.

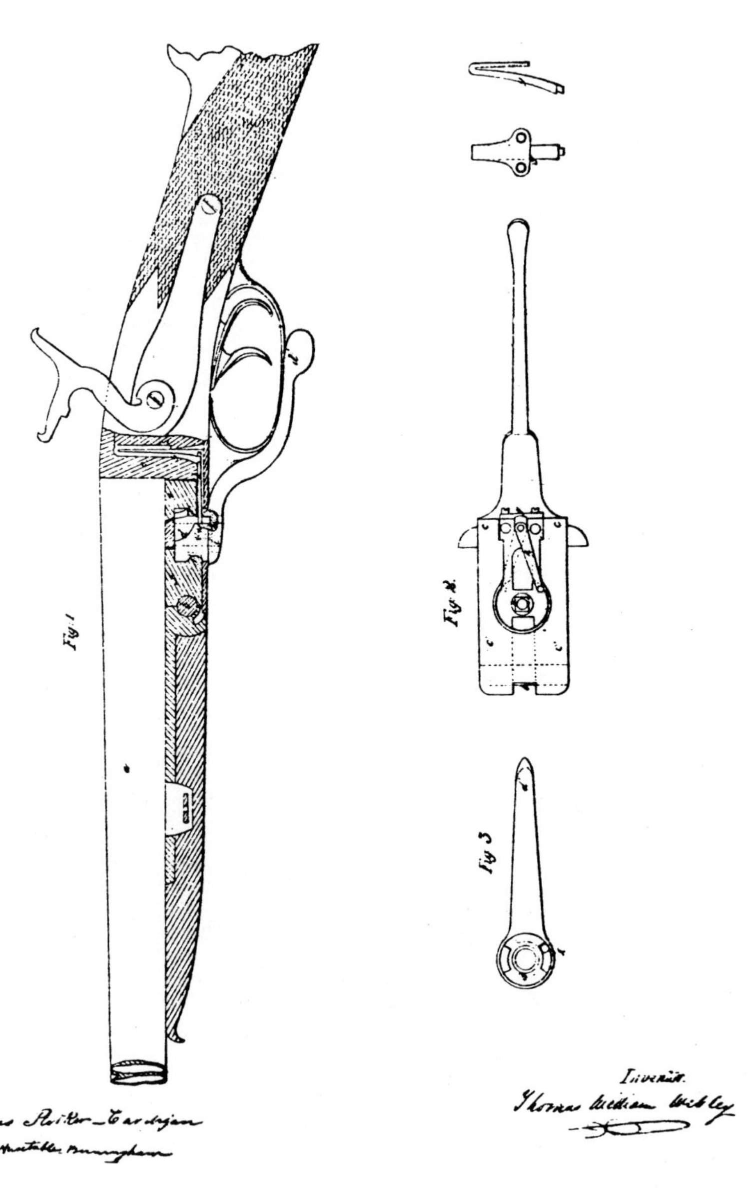

Plate 5-25 (opposite page). Reproduction of T.W. Webley's British gun patent number 65783, of June 11, 1863. Note the similarity of the shotgun shown in *Plate 5-24* to this patent drawing. *Chris C. Curtis collection*

Plate 5-26 (right). Reproduction of a letter from James Purdey & Sons Ltd., detailing the specifications of the shotgun pictured in *Plate 5-22. Courtesy James Lowther*

Plate 5-27 (below). Detail view of the left side of a 12-gauge, double-barrel pinfire shotgun marked on the barrel rib, "M.J. Chaumont." The action is beautifully engraved, and the hammers and lockplates border inlaid in gold. *Courtesy Don Kramer; Ferrari Color photograph*

JAMES PURDEY & SONS LTD.

(INCORPORATING JAMES WOODWARD & SONS)

GUN, RIFLE AND CARTRIDGE MAKERS

REGISTERED OFFICE:

AUDLEY HOUSE, 57-58 SOUTH AUDLEY STREET, LONDON W1Y 6ED

TELEPHONE: 01-499 1801/2.
TELEGRAMS: PURDEY—LONDON, W.1.

SHOOTING SCHOOL

AT WEST LONDON SHOOTING GROUNDS, NORTHOLT, GREENFORD, MIDDLESEX.

REGISTERED IN ENGLAND COMPANY REG. NO. 200759

DIRECTORS:
HON. RICHARD BEAUMONT (CHAIRMAN)
LAWRENCE SALTER (MANAGING DIRECTOR)
A.J.R. COLLINS, C.V.O.
HON. ANTHONY TRYON
H.L.C. GREIG, C.V.O.
C.H. LAWRENCE, M.B.E.

CHL/AGS.

James Lowther,   13th. July 1976.

U.S.A.

Dear Mr. Lowther,

    Thank you for your letter of 29th. June, in reference to the two pin fire weapons that you have acquired.

    The double pin fire 12 bore No.5944, was built by us in 1857. The original specification simply states that it had 30" barrels.

    The double pin fire 40 bore Rifle No.6439, was built by us in 1863 and the only other mention is that it had 29" barrels.

    The pin fire gun was one of the earliest forms of breech loading weapons. We started building these in 1855 and were popular until 1861, when the centre fire cartridge took over, but there was still a demand for the pinfire weapon until circa 1866. I hope this information has been of some help to you.

    Yours sincerely.

JAMES PURDEY & SONS LTD.

Harry Lawrence

DIRECTOR.

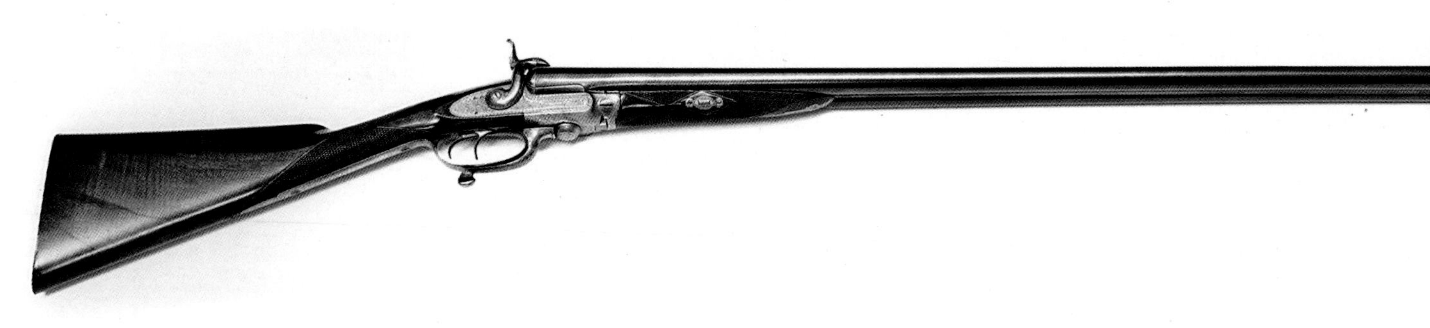

Plate 5-28 (above). A Scottish-made, 12-gauge, double-barrel pinfire shotgun marked *"John Dickson & Son"* on the lockplates. All metal surfaces are delicately engraved in the "English banknote" style, with the exception of the 30-inch barrels. The firm of Dickson & Son was in business in Edinburgh from 1820 well into the 1930s, and was always known for its fine-quality arms. *Courtesy Don Kramer; Ferrari Color photograph*

Plate 5-29 (above). Detail view of breech area of the shotgun pictured in *Plate 5-28*, showing the fine foliate engraving, breech-opening lever under the triggerguard, double-set triggers, checkered deluxe-wood stocks, and overall high quality of the workmanship. *Courtesy Don Kramer; Ferrari Color photograph*

Plate 5-30 (opposite page). An English-made, 4-gauge, double-barrel pinfire shotgun by E.M. Reilly & Company of London. Contained in the leather, trunk-style casing are several reloading tools for the massive shot cartridge. Edward M. Reilly & Company was located at 502 New Oxford Street, with a branch office at 315 Oxford Street. The firm exhibited double guns, rifles, air gun canes, and pistols at the 1851 London Exhibition, as well as at the 1862 London Exhibition, and shotguns and express rifles at Philadelphia in 1875. Earlier, in 1860, Reilly had advertised himself as "Maker of Reilly's Pinfire Shotgun on the Lefaucheux System." He was active until the turn of the twentieth century. *Courtesy Don Kramer; Ferrari Color photograph*

One pinfire shotgun occupies its own unique niche in the field of variant firearms, that being the horizontal box magazine shotgun invented by P. J. Jarre of Paris. Its cartridges are held firmly in place by a plate which swivels down on a hinge at the rear of the magazine (*see Plate 5-31*). As the action is cocked, an internal mechanism advances the box magazine, one chamber at a time, horizontally through the frame from left to right. Jarre's original patent illustration described a "fowling piece", but he carefully added that "the object of my invention is to so construct, arrange and combine the operative parts of guns, pistols, cannon, carbines or other firearms, as to enable them through one barrel to be fired successively a given number of times without any time being consumed for the loading, swabbing, cocking, etc." Jarre received his patent protection on April 21, 1859 under French patent number 23287, and later was granted two additions to the original patent, on April 23, 1860 and July 5, 1861, for improvements to the action. Jarre also patented his invention in the United States on June 24, 1862 (U.S. patent number 35685).

A variation of Jarre's "harmonica" long gun exists, which seems to have an earlier mechanism than the example illustrated and described in the patent drawing. Its chief difference lies in a separate operating lever that extends down through the trigger to release the hammer; it appears to have been produced before Jarre's improvements to the cocking mechanism were implemented.

As earlier noted, the original design for the hinged-action shotgun was far from perfect, its main weakness being in the "bar" of the action. The bar, lying forward under the barrels, not only lacked strength but was machined with a sharp corner at the juncture of the barrels and standing breech. As a result of this construction, after considerable use a gap appeared at the breech, and the bar was known to break under the stress of continued firing. As demonstrated by only a few of the myriad systems invented during that era for locking the actions of shotguns, improvement of the original design was uppermost in the minds of many arms inventors. Despite the weakness inherent in his original design, Casimir Lefaucheux' shotgun not only survived but flourished in the

text continued on page 160

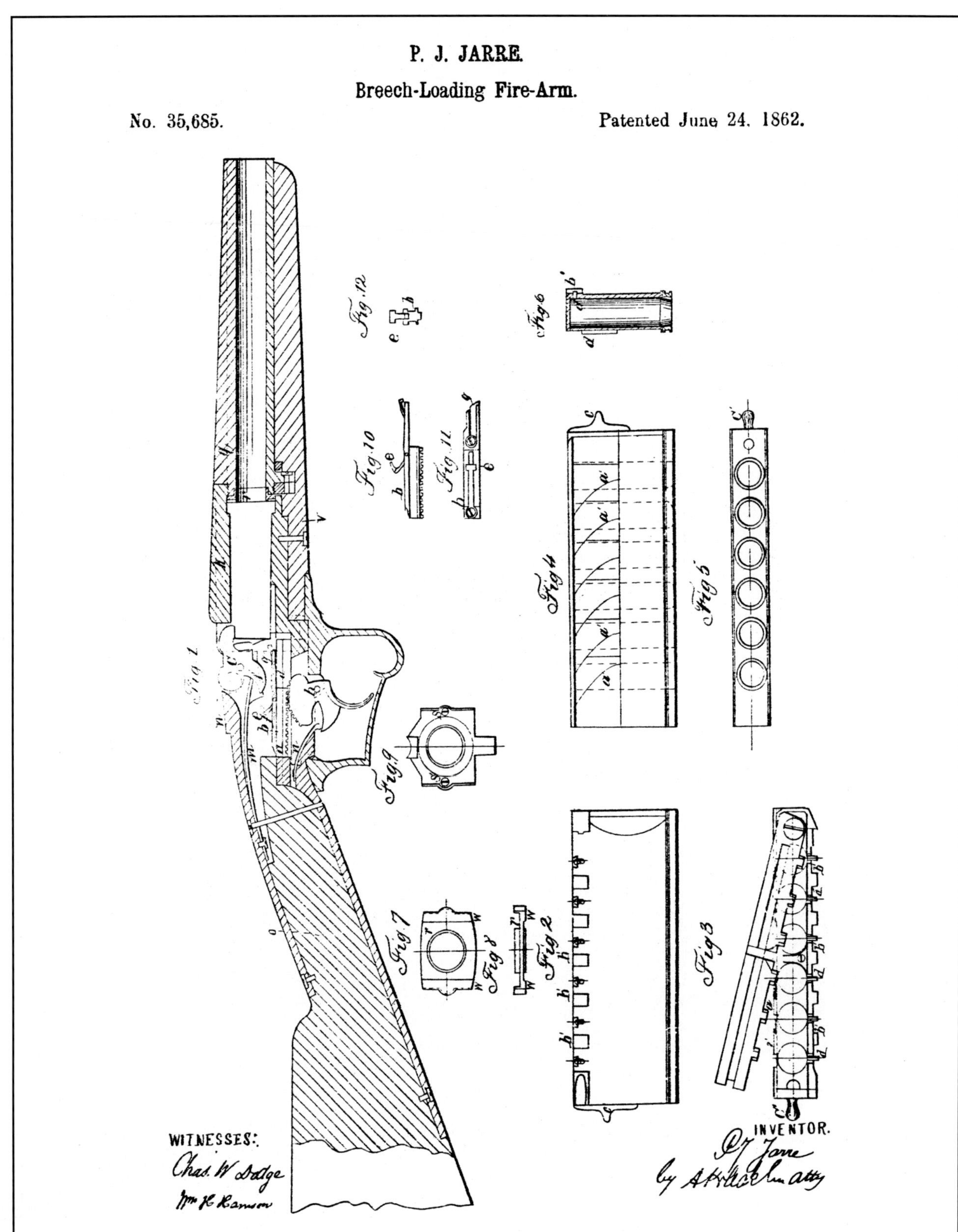

P. J. JARRE.
Breech-Loading Fire-Arm.
No. 35,685.
Patented June 24. 1862.
Fig.1
Fig.2
Fig.3
Fig.4
Fig.5
Fig.6
Fig.7
Fig.8
Fig.9
Fig.10
Fig.11
Fig.12
WITNESSES:
Chas. W. Dodge
Wm H. Ranson
INVENTOR.
P. J. Jarre
by A. Pollock atty

Plate 5-31 (opposite page). Jarre's United States patent number 35685, of June 24, 1862, showing his horizontal box magazine shotgun. *Chris C. Curtis collection*

Plate 5-32 (right). Shown at left in the photograph is a massive, English-made pinfire punt gun marked "*Chas Osborne*" on the back-action lockplate. The name and proofmarks date its manufacture to between 1855 and 1876, at the firm's 12-13 Whittal Street shops in Birmingham. Osborne was one of that city's prominent gunmakers until after the turn of the twentieth century. He served a large colonial market and was one of a very few gunmakers specializing in heavy-caliber game rifles and punt guns. The latter were designed to be fired from a specially-fitted boat which was aligned (or "punted") to the game. The charge was huge (from 6 ounces to 1½ pounds of BB or No. 1 shot, together with black powder having the same bulk); the boat absorbed the heavy recoil. A well-placed shot fired at sitting waterfowl might kill as many as fifty ducks. Punt guns usually had barrels ranging in length between five and nine feet, and weighed 50 to 250 pounds; the example pictured here measures 9 feet 4 inches overall, and weighs 130 pounds. It is shown alongside a standard 12-gauge shotgun. The manufacture of punt guns was discontinued when game laws were passed which outlawed professional market hunting. *Courtesy James H. Marsh; James H. Marsh photograph*

Plate 5-33 (above). Detail view of the barrel breech of the punt gun pictured in *Plate 5-32*, showing the massive No. 2 (1.325 inch) bore swallowing a modern 12-gauge centerfire shotgun shell made by Kynoch. *Courtesy James H. Marsh; James H. Marsh photograph*

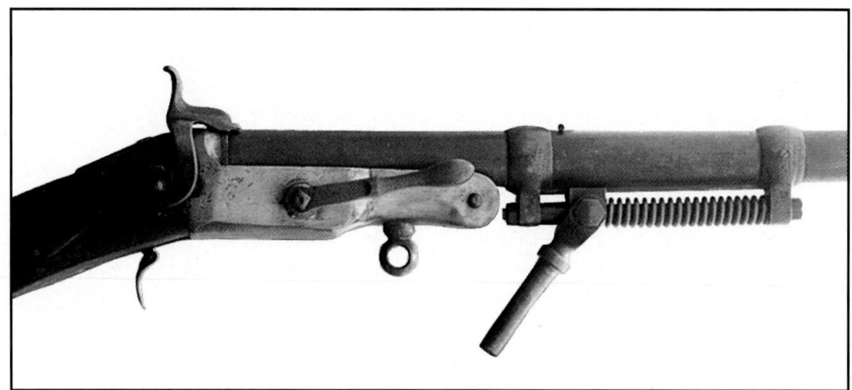

Plate 5-34 (right). Detail view showing the breech area of the punt gun pictured in *Plate 5-32*. Illustrated in addition to the gun's heavy construction are the recoil device and swivel mount. *Courtesy James H. Marsh; James H. Marsh photograph*

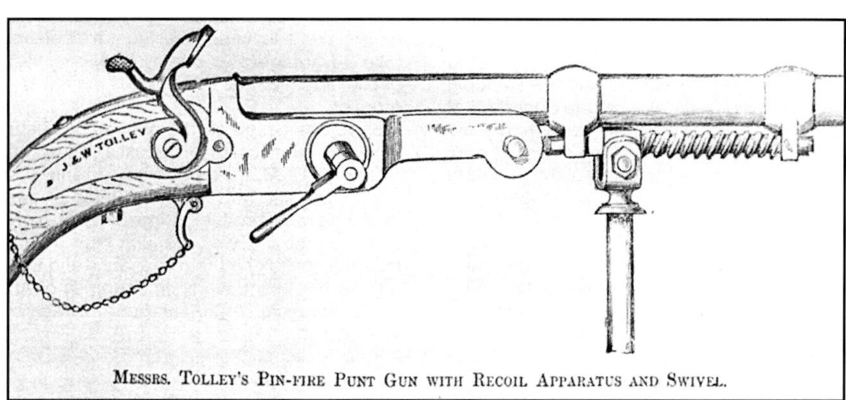

Plate 5-35 (right). Catalog illustration of an English pinfire punt gun made by James and William Tolley. The firm operated in Birmingham between 1859 and 1900 as "Gun, rifle and pistol manufacturers. Contractors for military arms, breechloading guns and all guns suitable for African markets." This punt gun, with a recoil device and swivel mount, probably was the largest pinfire arm ever produced. *Courtesy D.J. Baker*

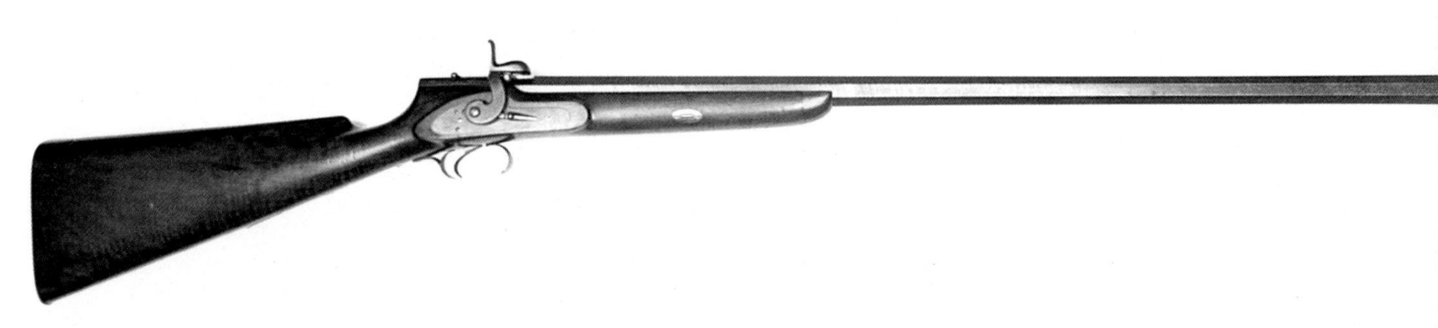

Plate 5-36. An unmarked as to maker, single-barrel, 16-gauge pinfire shotgun built on British patent number 2081, of August 21, 1863, petitioned by Edmond Pope of Clonmel, Ireland. This gun differs only slightly from the patent drawing illustrated in *Plate 5-38*. An elongated square dovetailed bolt, moving parallel with the barrel, slides in an open chamber. On top of the bolt a semicircular gauge having two inclined planes to its cavity slides forward with the bolt. The bolt has a projection that inserts a cartridge into the chamber, accurately aligning it with the pin slot without manual assistance. On discharge, the escaping gases automatically effect recoil of the bolt assembly which ejects the spent cartridge, leaving the chamber empty for reloading. A rifled version of this gun marked "*Alexander Henry*" (likely the retailer) has been observed. *Courtesy private collection; John Drake photograph*

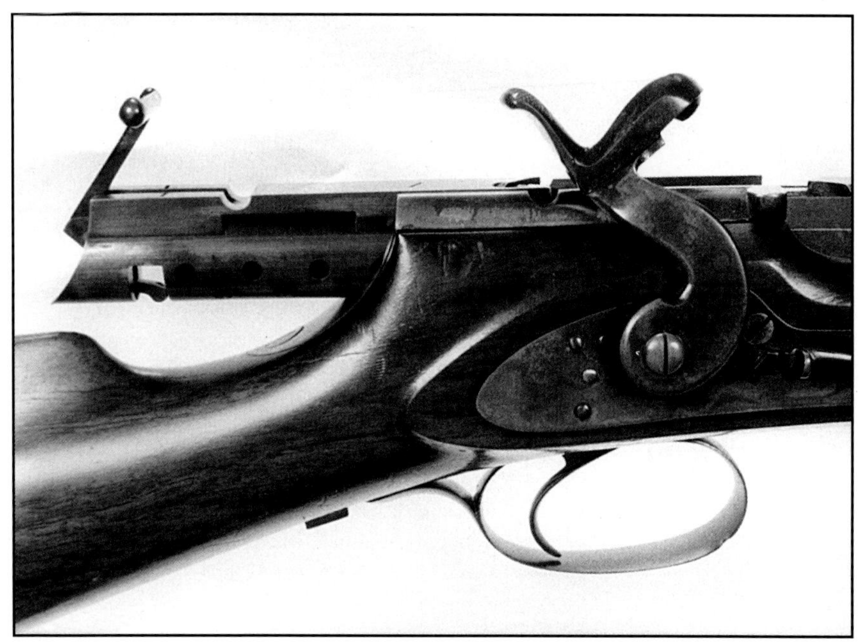

Plate 5-37. Detail view of the lock area of the shotgun illustrated in *Plate 5-36,* showing the hammer cocked and the bolt drawn back with the action open for loading. The holes along the side of the bolt were to be packed with grease to automatically lubricate the action during use. This was a very advanced design for its time—the early 1860s. *Courtesy private collection; Chris C. Curtis photograph*

Plate 5-38 (below). Reproduction of Edmund Pope's British gun patent number 2081, of August 21, 1863. *Chris C. Curtis collection*

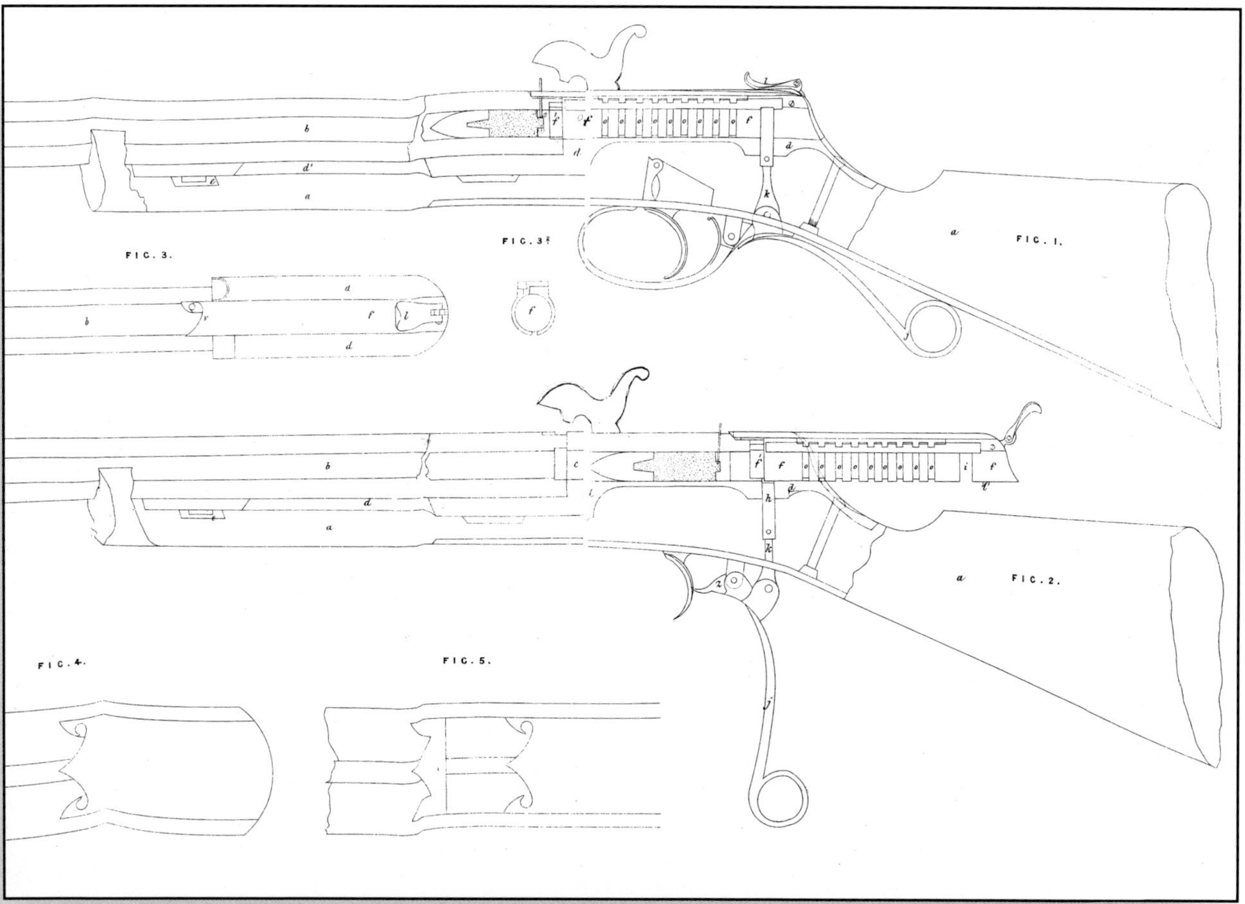

Plate 5-39 (below). An unmarked as to maker, but probably of Spanish origins, 16-gauge revolving pinfire shotgun. The barrel length is 25 inches, and the arm measures 43 inches overall; the massive cylinder and frame help account for its weight of over eight pounds. A notch cut into the top of the hammer creates a rear sight; a small post front sight is mounted at the barrel muzzle. A very rare example of one gunmaker's approach to increasing the firepower of the pinfire shotgun. *Courtesy Larry Compeau; Bob Steele photograph*

highly competitive firearms trade of the mid-nineteenth century. This simple, tip-down breechloader, needing no extractors, was one of the few really fundamental inventions in firearms to emerge from that period.

Over the years the name "Lefaucheux" fell into generic use in reference to pinfire shotguns. It was applied to the type of firearm, not just to those manufactured and marked by the original inventor, and the practice of grouping all pinfire arms under the Lefaucheux heading continues to this day. While the lack of markings and of specific knowledge relating to the various shotgun makers constituted the main reason for the generalization,

Plate 5-40 (right). Detail view of the shotgun illustrated in *Plate 5-39*, showing the massive size of the frame and cylinder. *Courtesy Larry Compeau; F.W. Hulbert photograph*

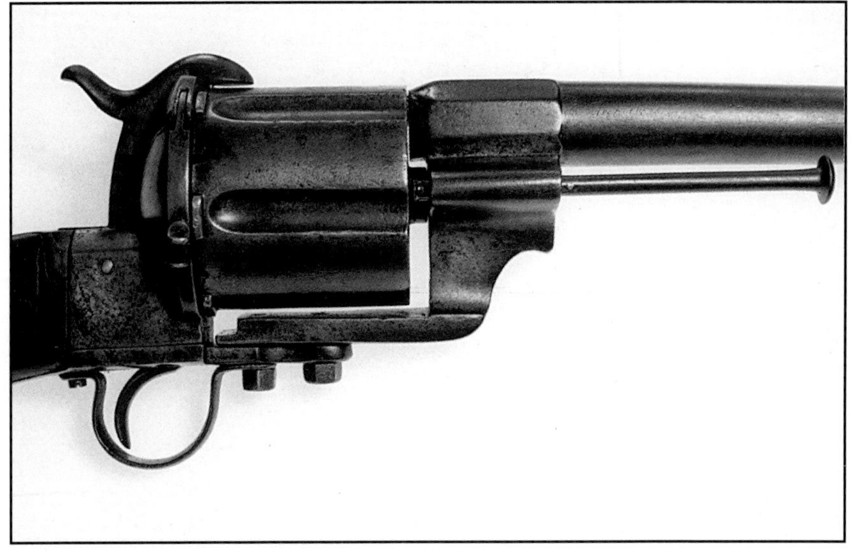

the lure of increased profits also was a factor. Many nineteenth century firearms makers described their merchandise as "Lefaucheux" to take advantage of a name already accepted by the public, and to increase the sales of their guns.

Shotguns based on the original Lefaucheux system have been in use for almost a century-and-a-half. As late as 1938, Beretta illustrated and offered a pinfire shotgun in their catalog of arms. Husqvarna was producing inexpensive pinfire shotguns for use in Sweden even much later, and in fact may still be making them. In France and England, as well as in the less developed countries of Africa and South America, pinfire shotguns see considerable use even today.

Despite its popularity, and the widespread use of the pinfire shotgun throughout Europe, it never was accepted in America. Pinfire handguns and shotguns sometimes, but rarely, are encountered bearing American names, which on closer examination can be identified as those of retailers or sales agents, not the actual arms makers. On disassembly these "American" pinfires invariably exhibit Belgian, Spanish, or British proofmarks. It is true that pinfire shotguns and their component parts were imported and then assembled in the United States, but pinfire guns almost *never* were manufactured entirely by an American maker.

The single exception to the above rule are the examples made by the firm of N.R. Davis of Assonet, Massachusetts. Nathaniel R. Davis had worked at the Springfield Armory, and for Colt as well, before forming a partnership with David C. Thrasher for the purpose of manufacturing firearms. In 1866 Davis became the only known American maker of pinfire shotguns, three different types of which were introduced by the company. The first was of the tip-down barrel style having a curved opening lever at the front of the triggerguard (*see Plate 5-41*). The third type also was of the tip-down style, but having the opening lever on the left side of the frame. The second type was patent-protected by Thrasher and Aiken (a company employee) on July 16, 1867, and featured a forward-sliding barrel action, with the release button located between the front of the double triggers

and the front of the triggerguard (*see Plate 5-42*). N.R. Davis & Co. also made percussion shotguns, but by 1872 the firm had abandoned both the pinfire and percussion systems in favor of the new and far more popular centerfire cartridge arms.

A majority of the pinfire shotguns made were sturdy but devoid of decoration. Yet, as with all other types of pinfire arms, some shotguns were elaborately decorated works of art. Magnificent examples of the type were commissioned and owned by many members of European royalty, including Queen Victoria of England. U.S. President Theodore Roosevelt's first long gun was a Lefaucheux pinfire shotgun, presented to him by his father prior to T.R.'s fourteenth birthday. It was while practicing marksmanship with his shotgun that Roosevelt discovered and corrected his nearsightedness; later he would recall that it was "an excellent gun for a clumsy and often absent-minded boy."[2]

Another well-known enthusiast of pinfire arms was Britain's Sir John Everett Millais. He is shown in an 1884 photograph (*see Plate 5-43*) posing in his favorite role, as a sportsman, and is pictured in *Plate 5-44* with members of his hunting club. A close friend of influential English author and critic, John Ruskin (1819–1900), Millais (1829–1896) was considered one of the most naturally gifted fine artists of his age.

From its infancy in the 1830s, and right up to the present, the improved Lefaucheux breechloading system has produced simple, sound, and functional weapons which were reliable in the field. That fact alone may account for their longevity.

For an in-depth study of the pinfire shotguns patented and manufactured in Great Britain, and their makers, the reader is referred to *The British Shotgun Volume I 1850-1870*, by I.M. Crudgington and D.J. Baker.

By 1860 the pinfire cartridge had proven itself to the world's gunmakers and gun users, and the pinfire shotgun had passed countless tests of its design, strength, and reliabilty. It was in the natural course of firearms progression, then, that a similar weapon would be created to fire a single projectile, while retaining the basic design. The results were single- and double-barrel pinfire rifles.

The majority of breechloading pinfire double rifles were of very high quality in their materials as well as construction, and were made in very limited numbers. Ammunition for the big game double rifles usually was of a large caliber, frequently made for the specific arm at hand, and for the most part, of the brass case and cardboard tube design. Rifles made to utilize the oversize cartridges had right, left, or straight-groove rifling, depending on the particular ballistic beliefs of their maker, owner, or user.

text continued on page 171

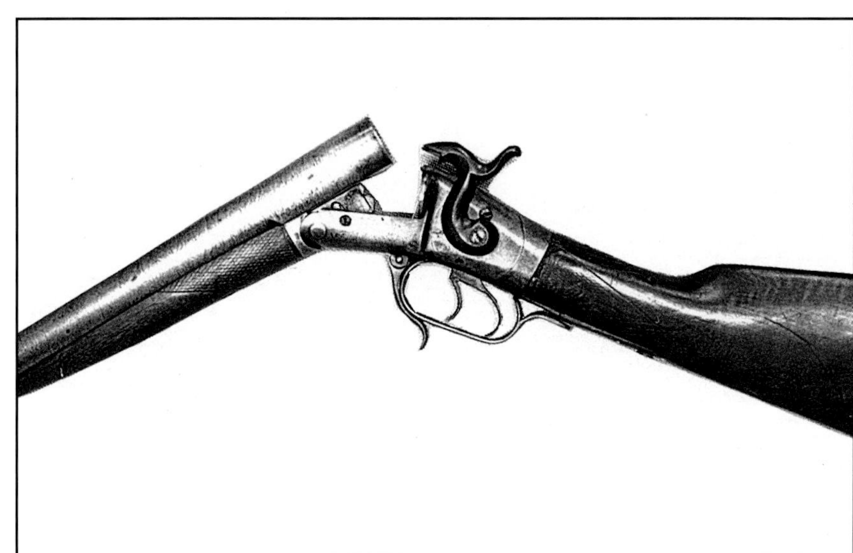

Plate 5-41. Detail view of a tip-down, single-barrel pinfire shotgun made by N.R. Davis of Assonet, Massachusetts. A first type, it has the curved opening lever under the open breech. *Courtesy Charles Carder; Charles Carder photograph*

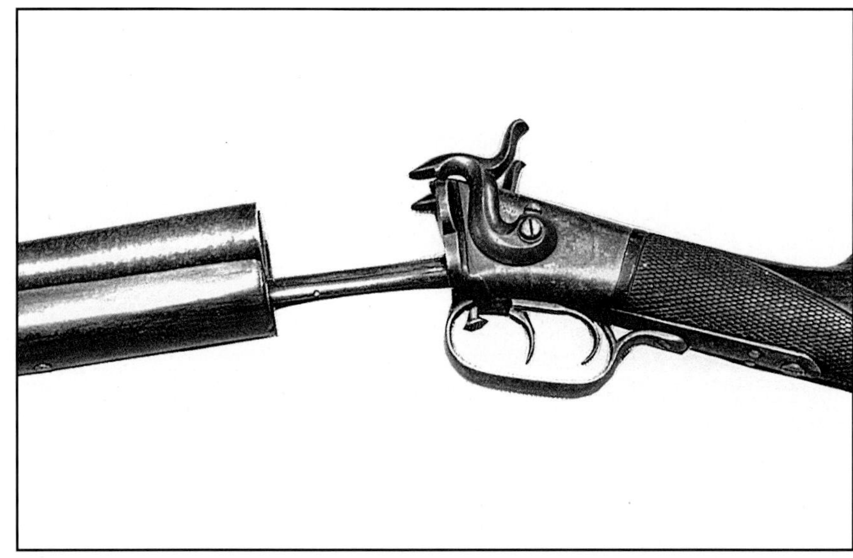

Plate 5-42. Detail view of a forward-sliding, double-barrel pinfire shotgun patented by Thrasher and Aiken and made by N.R. Davis. A second type, it has the barrel-release button located ahead of the double triggers inside the triggerguard. *Courtesy Charles Carder; Charles Carder photograph*

Plate 5-43 (left). British artist, sportsman, and hunting enthusiast Sir John Everett Millais, pictured in 1884 with his favorite arm—a pinfire shotgun. *Courtesy David J. Baker*

Plate 5-44 (below). Sir John Everett Millais (second from left, wearing dark bowler hat), pictured in the field with a group of hunting companions. *Courtesy David J. Baker*

Plate 5-45. A German-made, double-barrel pinfire rifle of approximately 28-gauge (14mm caliber) gold inlaid on the rib of the damascus barrels, "*U. Roos and Sohn in Stuttgart*", either the maker or retailer. Each barrel has six lands and grooves: the right with right-hand twist, the left with straight-groove rifling. The thumb lever under the forearm turns to the side to open the action; a second lever located beneath the first also turns to the side to release the locking lugs and allow removal of the barrels. *Courtesy James Lowther; John Calcany photograph*

Plate 5-46. A Belgian-made, double-barrel pinfire rifle of unknown caliber but having a bore diameter of 28 gauge (14mm caliber); inlaid in gold on the rib of the barrels, "*Canon Acier Fondu Lt Ghaye a Liége.*" Both barrels have eight-land, right-hand twist; a bayonet lug is mounted beneath the muzzle; the long-range rear sight has two leaves. Shown with the "Bastin" breech open; a lever beneath the forearm is pulled down and forward to release the barrels, which then slide forward. *Courtesy James Lowther; John Calcany photograph*

Plate 5-47. A double-barrel pinfire rifle of 14mm caliber marked on the barrels, *"Jackson. Maker. New York."* The damascus barrels have three-land, right-hand twist rifling; the rear sight has five leaves marked from 100 to 500; the breech opening lever is located beneath the triggerguard; both lockplates are marked *"Jackson."* This rifle might be attributed to either of two American gunmakers: S. Jackson of Palmyra, New York, who made large-caliber percussion rifles marked with his name on the barrels and lockplates, *circa* 1860, or Jay Jackson of Pine Plains, New York, who worked between 1878 and 1882, although the type of guns he produced is not known. A single "crown over V" proofmark is stamped on the barrel, ruling out the possibility that this rifle is wholly of American manufacture; rather, Jackson likely imported the barrels which he assembled to locks, stock, and furniture that he made or purchased locally. Although purists might discount the Jackson rifle as not truly being an American gun, it nevertheless would be the centerpiece in any collection of pinfire cartridge arms. *Courtesy James Lowther; John Calcany photograph*

Plate 5-48. An English-made, double-barrel pinfire rifle marked on the damascus barrels, *"J. Purdey 314½ Oxford St. London."* The barrels have six lands and grooves, with gain twist in the right bore. The rear sight has three leaves; the locks are equipped with sliding safeties; the breech release lever is mounted beneath the forearm. A 1976 letter from the Purdey firm in reply to an inquiry about this rifle is pictured in *Plate 5-26.* James Purdey & Sons Ltd. has been producing some of the finest arms in the world since the 1850s, and the gunmaker's production methods and standards of quality have varied little from that time to the present. *Courtesy James Lowther; John Calcany photograph*

Plate 5-49 (right). Detail view of a German-made, 16-bore (16.8mm caliber) double-barrel pinfire rifle inlaid in gold on the barrel rib, "*H. Barella Konigl: Hof + Buchsenm. in Berlin.*" Three engraved hunting scenes; locks, frame, hammers, tang, and triggerguard are deeply relief engraved with a geometric scroll; forearm, stock wrist, and takedown lever are finely checkered. Double-set triggers and pin guides at the breech attest to the quality and workmanship of this piece. The barrels were crafted by Bernard, the most important maker of damascus barrels. Gunmaker Heinrich Barella (1819-1893) in 1871 became "Gunmaker to the King of Prussia." *Courtesy private collection; F.W. Hulbert photograph*

Plate 5-50 (right, center). Detail view of an unusual English-made, single-shot pinfire rifle marked on the barrel, "*J. Lang, 22 Cockspur St. London.*" The tip-down barrel is chambered for the 12mm caliber long cartridge. A practical sportsman and a quality gunmaker, Joseph Lang recognized the potential of breechloading pinfire arms when he saw the Lefaucheux exhibit at the 1851 London Exhibition. He is credited with pioneering the manufacture of pinfire arms in Great Britain, and was a staunch supporter of the system during its early years of rejection by most British gun users. Lang received two British patents for gunlock improvements; later his son James took over the business. *Courtesy private collection; Gene Smith photograph*

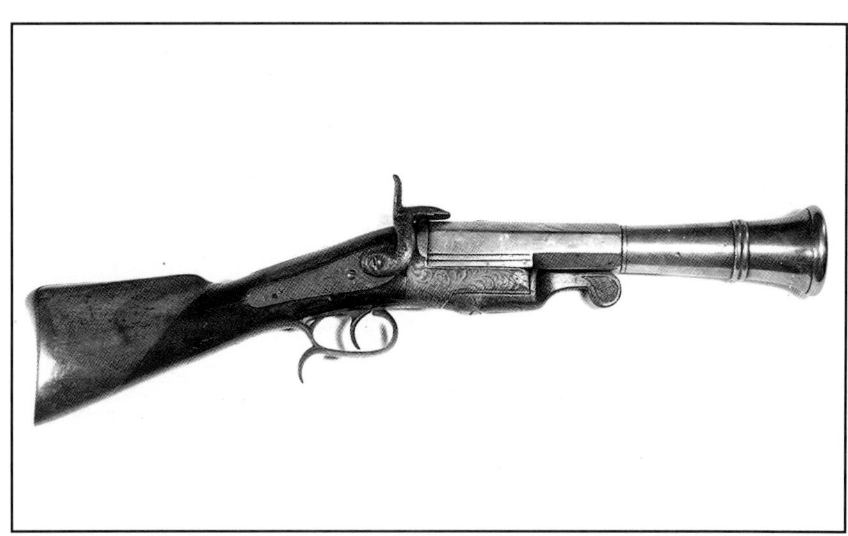

Plate 5-51 (pictured on opposite page, bottom). An unmarked as to maker, but Belgian-made 16-gauge tip-down barrel blunderbuss. While chambered for a shotshell, the bore is rifled from breech to the beginning of the bell. The 9³/₈-inch brass barrel bears Liége proofmarks and post-1877 inspector's marks. A large thumb lever under the barrel releases the breech; the gun is just 19½ inches in overall length. The style of this arm was already half a century outdated at the time of its manufacture, probably for export to South America (most likely Argentina). In most of South America the ownership and use of firearms were officially discouraged. But the citizenry nonetheless wanted to be armed, and the short, bell-muzzle blunderbuss was one of the most popular types employed during the period. Many were imported, utilizing flintlock, percussion, and pinfire ignition systems, and collectively were referred to as *"Trabuco"*, Spanish for "blunderbuss", the favored weapon of the gauchos. These curious, anachronistic guns are another example of the endless variety found in firearms which utilize the pinfire ignition system. *Courtesy Larry Compeau; Gene Smith photograph*

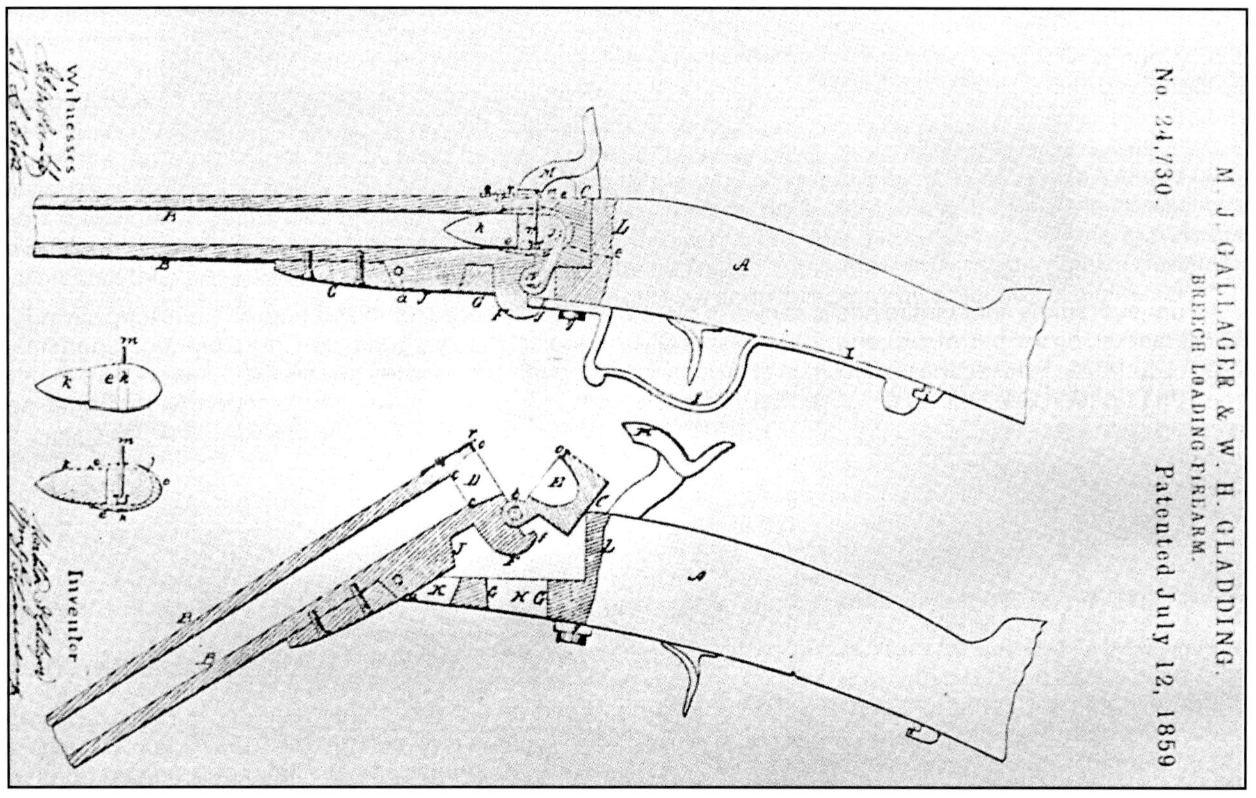

Plate 5-52 (above). On July 12, 1859, United States patent number 24730 was granted to M.J. Gallager and William H. Gladding of Savannah, Georgia, for a tip-down breechloading rifle. The patent was not for the general design of the rifle, but for the breech which breaks open on a hinge to expose the chamber. The latter is shaped like two frustums of a cone and a section of parabolic spindle, whose bases meet at the joint between barrel and breech. The triggerguard also serves as the locking lever, which pivots to the side to open the action. The chamber was designed to accept the special pinfire cartridge previously discussed in Chapter Two. The shapes of the chamber and cartridge did create an effective gas seal, but such arms enjoyed only limited production. *Chris C. Curtis collection*

Plate 5-53. A single-shot breechloading pinfire rifle marked on top of the single barrel, "*T. Richardson & Son—Cork.*" The barrel is 30 inches long, and chambered for the large 15mm caliber pinfire cartridge. *Courtesy Don Kramer; Ferrari Color photograph*

Plate 5-54. Detail view of the right side of a Belgian-made 12mm caliber pinfire revolving rifle marked on the barrel, "*Fabrique de Lepage Freres A Liége Maison A Paris.*" It operates single-action only. The barrel has pre-1877 inspector's marks; the overall length of the piece is 42 inches. As far back as the matchlock, attempts were made to increase the firepower of long guns. Additional barrels were the most common answer, but their increased weight rendered them clumsy; next came the multi-shot breech (or cylinder) containing multiple charges that could be fired successively through a single barrel. As the former were sturdier in construction but heavier, and the latter more complicated, the search was continued for a weapon that could fire multiple times without reloading. Revolving rifles provided one solution to the problem, and examples are found in matchlock, wheellock, flintlock, percussion, pill lock, and cartridge ignition systems. With the advent of the self-contained cartridge gunmakers could create safer and far more dependable firearms. Revolving cylinder pinfire rifles generally are well-constructed, but their popularity waned rapidly. The majority were produced in the two decades spanning 1855 and 1875, and it has been reported that a small number was acquired by the Confederacy in its purchases of European arms necessitated by the South's lack of wartime industrial capacity. Although most pinfire revolving rifles appear suited for military use, sufficient data has not yet been found that clearly records military adoption by a major power. Some may have been utilized on a more local level, as by national guard or militia units. One 12mm caliber pinfire revolving rifle examined by the authors is marked "AGM 13" on its barrel and stock, in the fashion of unit markings or rack numbers. *Courtesy private collection; Gene Smith photograph*

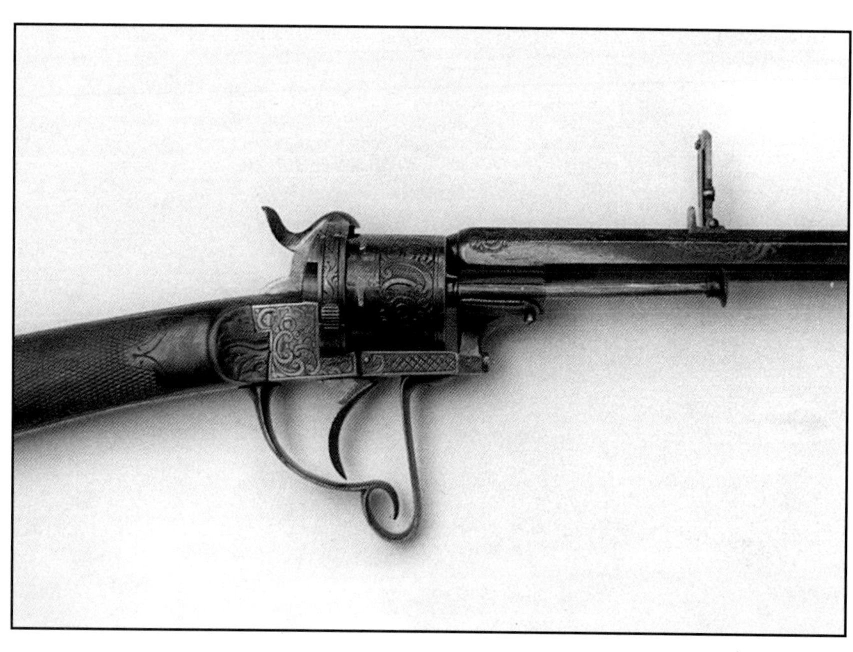

Plate 5-55 (right). Detail view of a Belgian-made, six-shot 12mm caliber pinfire revolving rifle marked on top of the barrel, *"Victor Collette—Liége."* The left-rear side of the 23¼-inch long, octagonal barrel is marked, *"E. Lefaucheux—Brevete"*; in addition it bears Liége proofmarks and pre-1877 inspector's marks, and has a long-range flip-up rear sight. The rifle measures 39 inches overall, and is nicely engraved. Its maker, Collette, was engaged in the Liége firearms industry between 1836 and 1909, making better-than-average rifles and handguns that are sought after by antique arms collectors today. *Courtesy private collection; F.W. Hulbert photograph*

Plate 5-56 (below). Another six-shot, likely Belgian-made 12mm caliber pinfire revolving rifle. The example pictured is marked on the frame, *"Meyers Brvt."* This sturdy rifle has the reinforcing top strap over the cylinder common to most Meyer-marked guns, an integral ejector rod mounted on the right side, and fancy scrollwork triggerguard, but no folding leaf rear sight. *Courtesy James Lowther; John Calcany photograph*

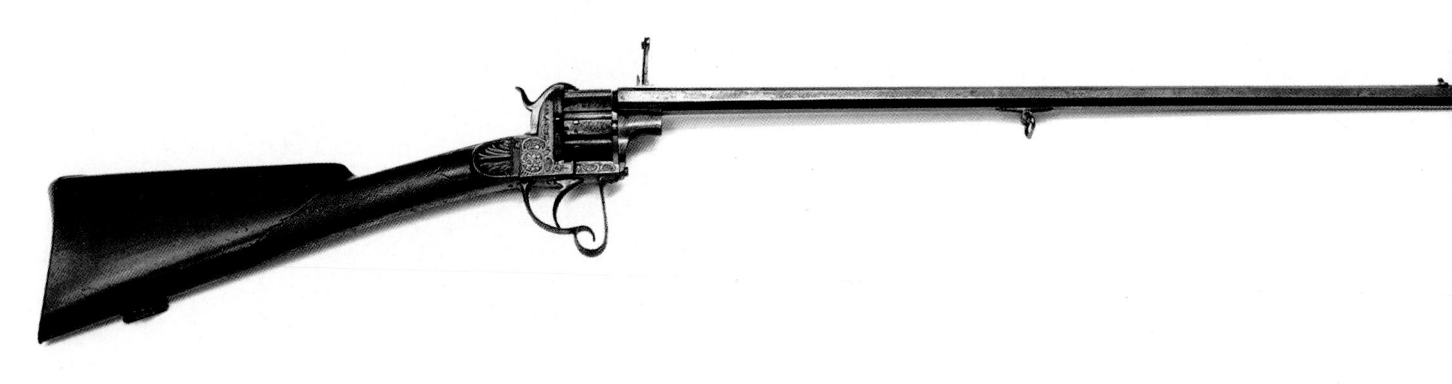

Plate 5-57. Considerably greater firepower was provided by the ten-shot cylinder of this Belgian-made 12mm caliber pinfire revolving rifle, marked on the barrel, "*E. Lefaucheux— Bvt.*" The barrel bears Belgian proofmarks and pre-1877 inspector's marks, with no provision for a side-mounted ejector rod. The frame and cylinder are beautifully engraved, and the gun is fitted with a carved and checkered stock. *Courtesy Don Kramer; Ferrari Color photograph*

Plate 5-58. An even more ambitious attempt at maximum firepower, the cylinder of this Belgian-made 12mm caliber pinfire revolving rifle has twelve chambers! As few makers of revolving rifles of the period deviated from the standard six-shot cylinders, rifles like the one pictured here and in *Plate 5-57* are quite rare. The maker of this piece is unknown, but the octagon barrel bears the familiar marking "*Acier Fondu*", Liége proofmarks, and has a long-range leaf sight. *Courtesy James Lowther; John Calcany photograph*

The Pilon Pinfire Rifle

"I, Martín Regul Pilon, Citizen of the United States, residing in Aguas Calientes, Mexico, and actually in Brussels, in the Kingdom of Belgium, Merchant, do hereby declare…as follows:—
I propose to control the recoil, to secure precision of aim, and to increase the facility of loading firearms."

So begins the specification of Martín Pilon's British patent, number 1911, of August 23, 1858. Neither this nor his two other British patents mentions his use of pinfire cartridges. Rather, they all specify a type of cartridge similar to the Pauly case mentioned in Chapter One of this work. It is thought that this is one of Pilon's last rifles, in which he utilized the best cartridge available at the time (*circa* 1863) to give his gun the best possible chance of success. That even this move did not help is suggested by the fact that his name appears in no list of American gunmakers or inventors, nor in any list of such men in Europe. Pilon apparently held no patents in the United States.

It seems rather unfair that Pilon should be so forgotten, as his improvements to firearms have merit. He proposed to control recoil by installing a spring in the forestock of a gun, which also allows the barrel to recoil against the standing breech thus aiding obturation. He secured precision of aim by moving the trigger to the top of the gunstock, and he increased ease in loading by making a breechloading arm which opened at the breech by means of a rod located near the trigger.

Plate 5-59 illustrates the pinfire cartridge version of Pilon's rifle. It has a chamber diameter of 14.5mm, and a bore diameter of 12mm, suggesting that it was intended to fire a 14mm caliber paper cartridge similar to the larger one chambered in the military rifle previously discussed here. The top of the barrel is marked, *"Pilon Brevete S.G.D.G."* This gun represents a fine example of the novel thinking being done in arms development during the mid-nineteenth century.

Our study of pinfire revolving rifles ends with an illustration of one of the most interesting combination firearms ever devised. *Plate 5-60* pictures a LeMat carbine having a nine-shot, 12mm caliber pinfire revolving cylinder, and a 28 gauge, 17¾-inch long percussion shotgun barrel beneath the 20-inch long rifled top barrel. The left side of the barrel is marked, *"Col. A. LeMat Brvte"*, and the cylinder bears Liége proofmarks.

This very scarce example has the hammer which employs a rotating pin in the center, which when moved into position fires the percussion shotgun barrel. The metal shotgun ramrod is mounted on the left side between the barrels.

Confederate Colonel Jean Alexandre François LeMat was known simply as Dr. LeMat of New Orleans, when in 1856 he first patented his unique revolver in England. In his patent papers LeMat described both pinfire and percussion models, and he was granted three additional patents in the following years for various improvements to his design. A post-Civil War English patent covered LeMat's breechloading concepts, as well as an improved hammer design. It is this latter patent which has generated the belief that LeMat did not manufacture any arms chambered for pinfire cartridges until after the American Civil War.

Although it would have been possible to build some models under his 1859 patent, no evidence exists that the same was done. Colonel LeMat was an inventor and a business agent. His partner, C. Giraud of Paris, actually did the manufacturing of the LeMat firearms in France, with perhaps some having been made in Belgium.

Chapter notes.

1. "No. 685" indicates that this was the 685th gun made by William Powell under his 1864 British patent, number 1163.
2. R.L. Wilson, *Official Price Guide to Gun Collecting* (New York, NY: House of Collectibles (Ballentine Publishing Group), 1998), p. 250.

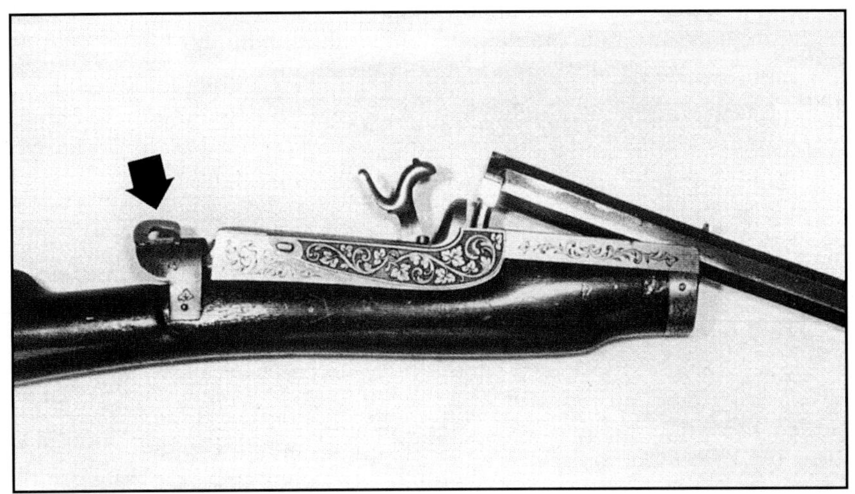

Plate 5-59. Detail view of Martín Pilon's unusual recoil-absorbing single-shot, 14mm caliber pinfire breechloading rifle, with tip-down barrel breech in the open position and hammer cocked. The thumb-operated trigger is concealed under a safety shield atop the stock wrist at back of action; above it, an arrow points to the barrel-release thumb lever. *Courtesy Dr. E.W.C. Houser; Bob Steele photograph*

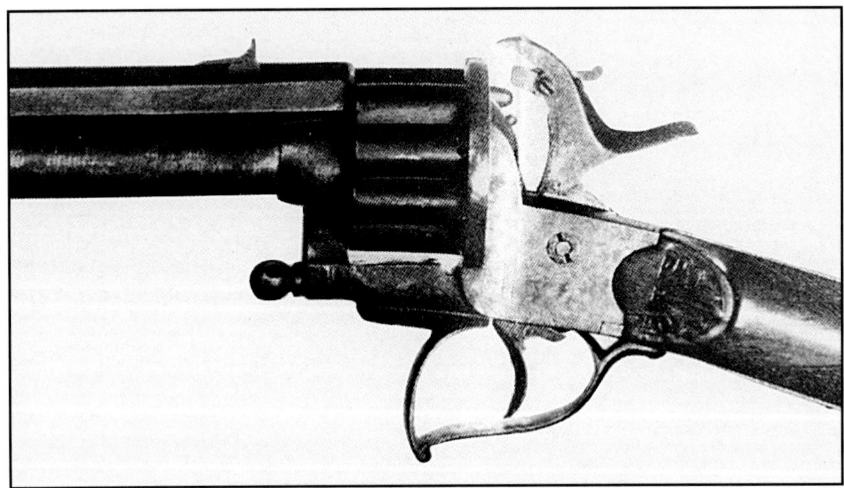

Plate 5-60. Detail view of the lock area of a combination 12mm caliber pinfire/28-gauge percussion LeMat revolving carbine. *Courtesy Frank Russell; Frank Russell photograph*

Plate 5-61. Last, and by far the least, of the pinfire rifles shown in this chapter are these 2mm caliber rifles. At top is a military rifle with knife bayonet; below is a sporting arm fitted with "imitation ivory" stock and forearm; it measures about 3½ inches in overall length; both are working miniature firearms. *Chris C. Curtis collection; F.W. Hulbert photograph*

Pinfire Arms in the Commercial Market: Revolvers and Pistols

This chapter discusses and illustrates examples from the broad spectrum of handguns primarily designed for and sold within the civilian market. For the most part, these are the most common types of pinfire handguns, recognizable to anyone having even a general knowledge of firearms.

However, the role they have in the history of the pinfire system is easily equal to those played by the rare variations, oddities, and military pinfires.

Civilian Pinfire Handguns

Numerous types of pinfire arms were being manufactured, and accepted and used by sportsmen, long before the military adoption of the Lefaucheux revolver in 1858. But it was the success of the Model 1854 revolver, both in its adoption by the French Navy and by the military forces of other nations, that created a surge of private interest in the new cartridge arms.

Eugene Lefaucheux, like many armsmakers before and after him, had early-on cast his eyes toward the lucrative potential of government contracts for his revolver design. The financial stability that followed its military acceptance in turn gave Lefaucheux the wherewithal to expand into the civilian arms segment. Of course, Lefaucheux was not the only armsmaker aware of the vast new market created by the pinfire cartridge. Many others set out to capture their fair share, and inventors introduced scores of new gun designs based on and improving on the basic Lefaucheux revolver.

The Patents of Guerriero, and Chamelot & Delvigne

The majority of the new pinfire revolver designs which appeared on the commercial market at the time were different in their outward appearances only; very little was done to improve the operation of the revolver mechanism, or to address the inherent weaknesses in its operation and safety. Of course, in the study of pinfire arms there is at least one exception to every rule, and in this case it is the American patent issued to A. Guerriero of Paris. It was registered during 1863 in the United States as patent number 39645, by H. Gross. Claiming several improvements to the design of revolvers, an expanded version of this patent was issued in England as number 628 of 1863 by W. Clark, a British patent agent in Guerriero's employ (*see Plate 6-2*). In his application Guerriero claimed eight improvements to the Lefaucheux revolver designs then currently being manufactured, three of them improvements in the design and construction of the arm. The first added a spring safety on the hammer yoke which held the hammer away from the cylinder, to prevent accidental discharge during the loading process. The second made the hammer nose narrower, so the cartridge pin would be struck only if the cylinder chamber was accurately aligned with the barrel. The third claim added a removable breech plate to the rear of the cylinder, to simultaneously protect all six cartridge pins when the arm was loaded. Narrow slots cut in the plate permitted the hammer to strike the pin only if the cylinder and barrel were properly aligned. The breech plate prompted the fourth improvement, as its addition to the rear of the cylinder caused the chambers to be slightly recessed. If the base of a cartridge bulged on firing, it would not impede the cylinder's rotation and thus render the arm inoperable. The fifth improvement also addressed cartridge failure, with the addition of another plate covering the face of the cylinder that prevented jamming in the event of a bullet dislodging from its cartridge case. The sixth improvement called for machining the butt portion of the revolver from a solid piece of steel, rather than from several parts pinned or screwed together. The seventh claim called for constructing of the revolver so that it could be disassembled in the field into four major components, without the use of tools. Guerriero's eighth and final improvement replaced Lefaucheux' method of turning the barrel on a threaded cylinder pin held in the frame by a screw, with a lever-operated eccentric cam which moved the barrel assembly longitudinally along a polished cylinder arbor, and which locked the barrel-cylinder-frame assembly in place. His design provided for less operating friction, resulting in reduced wear to the parts and a longer working life for the arm.

The Guerriero patent is given special attention here, for although his designs probably never were put into actual production, his ideas influenced the construction of a number of revolvers that followed. Guerriero's lever-operated eccentric cam principle, for instance, did not escape the notice of Europe's patent agents and arms inventors, and with slight modification to prevent patent infringement it is found on several revolvers pictured in Chapter Ten. His provision for protecting the exposed cartridge pins also is found, altered to be part of the frame itself rather than a removable plate on the cylinder, on many revolvers made virtually to the end of the pinfire era.

The evolution of the pinfire system was no different from that of most firearms, in that it involved continuing experimentation which produced innumerable variations on a central theme, copying, improving, altering, and expanding it. Often it is difficult to distinguish between the original idea and its successors, and in certain cases the difference may never be known. In all fairness to *Monsieur* Eugene Lefaucheux, it must be noted here that several of Guerriero's "improvements" had already been patented by Lefaucheux in France, and incorporated into his designs in some

Plate 6-1. Two nineteenth century dandies enjoy a good cigar, a glass of dark beer, and a "friendly" game of cards—with revolvers cocked and at the ready. On the table at left appears to be a 12mm caliber Lefaucheux-style pinfire pistol. *Courtesy Frank Rietta*

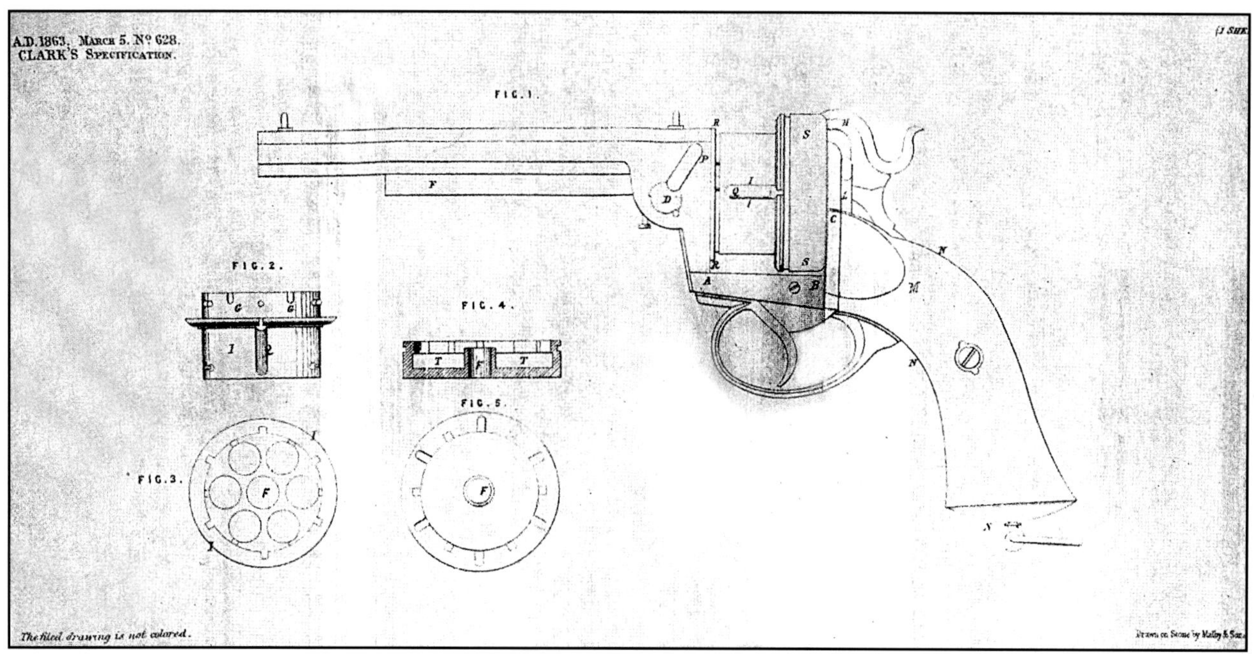

Plate 6-2. An illustration from A. Guerriero's 1863 patent, number 628, as registered in Great Britain by patent agent W. Clark. *Chris C. Curtis collection*

slightly different form. For instance, in the certificate of addition to his patent number 19380, dated February 10, 1860, Lefaucheux illustrated a hinged (or swivel) cylinder plate on a proposed improved version of the Model 1854 revolver, and a narrowed hammer is present on most Lefaucheux double-action revolvers. Though the narrow hammer was not protected by any known Lefaucheux patent, it nevertheless was utilized on some of his arms.

There exists another series of patents that also warrant special attention here, for they differ from all other pinfire revolvers in design and function, as well as in external appearance. *Monsieur* J. Chamelot was a Belgian arms manufacturer, and H. Delvigne a French infantry officer. In July of 1862 the Liége-based firm of Chamelot & Delvigne registered in Brussels the first of their eleven patents relating to firearms.

The first patent was for a pocket-size, 7mm caliber six-shot revolver having a horizontal-acting button trigger, with a stationary stud behind to provide a better grip on this diminutive pistol. A removable guard in front of the trigger provided a safety feature; in addition, another guard in front of the cylinder prevented injury to the user's hand from burning powder or from lead shavings emitting from the juncture of the barrel and cylinder. The cylinder, as with all Chamelot & Delvigne handguns regardless of size or caliber, revolves counter-clockwise. A loading gate is on the left side; on the first model it slides to the rear. A removable ejector rod is threaded into the butt.

In September of 1862 the second patent was registered, making improvements to the original. This second model operated both single- and double-action, and had a folding trigger; the internal springs were improved, as well as the locking device which had been patented by Chaineux. Apparently Chamelot & Delvigne had an agreement with Chaineux to use his locking system, as mention of it is made in their patent applications. The left-side sliding loading gate design was retained, as was the threaded ejector rod; the shield in front of the cylinder became an integral part of the frame.

The following month another patent was regis-

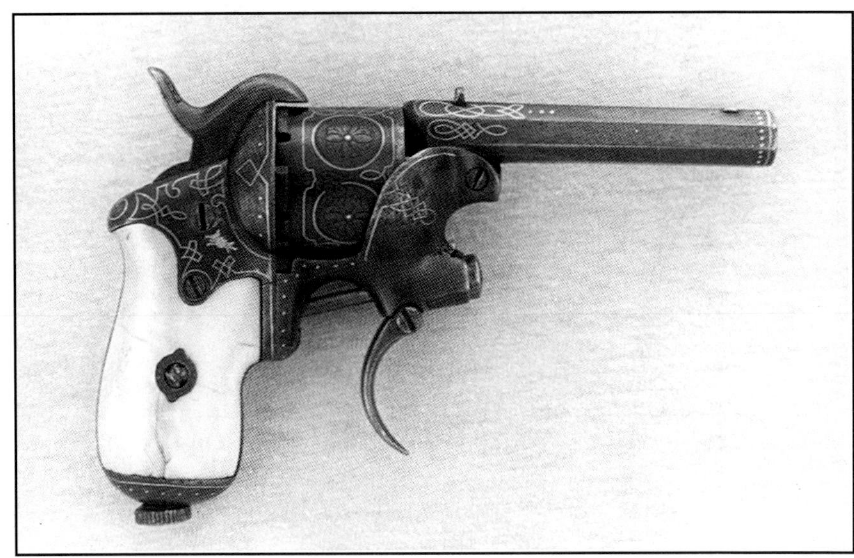

Plate 6-3. An engraved and gold-inlaid fourth model Chamelot & Delvigne 7mm caliber pinfire revolver, having the guard in front of the cylinder. *Courtesy private collection; F.W. Hulbert photograph*

Plate 6-4. A nicely engraved Chamelot & Delvigne 7mm caliber pinfire revolver, made under their tenth patent of December, 1865. *Courtesy private collection, F.W. Hulbert photograph*

tered, which created the third model. It was similar in appearance to the second model, except that the mechanism was altered so the folding trigger now cocked the hammer, and the reintroduced button trigger released the hammer for firing.

In December of 1862 the fourth patent created yet another similar but slightly different model, a revolver operated single-action only and fired by a button trigger. Again, the folding false-trigger was used only for gaining a better grip on the pis-

tol. In some ways this fourth model was a step backward almost to the first model, inasmuch as although the ejector rod threading into the butt was retained, the sliding loading gate was replaced by a solid hinged gate that rotated back and up to a ninety-degree angle. This design was to remain on all subsequent Chamelot & Delvigne models. *Plate 6-3* illustrates one of these early fourth model revolvers. The example pictured is caliber 7mm pinfire, is nicely engraved and gold-inlaid, and

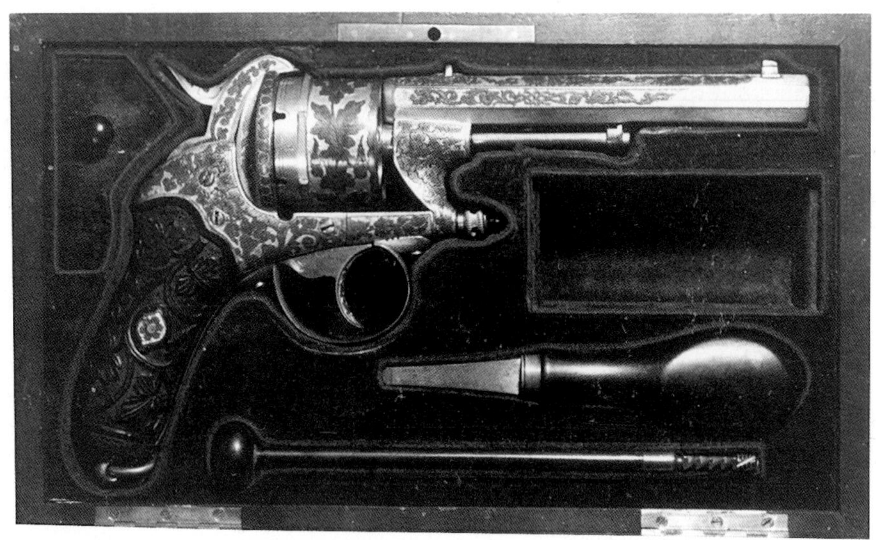

Plate 6-5. An ornately embellished Chamelot & Delvigne eighth model revolver, 12mm caliber pinfire. The top of the barrel bears the name of the retailer, *"Lepage Moutier et Janie a Paris"*, and a plate in the outside lid of the French-style casing is marked, *"Courses de Courtalain Prix des Dames 1866." Courtesy G. Lautissier; G. Lautissier photograph*

bears Liége proofmarks and pre-1877 inspector's marks. As with all Chamelot & Delvigne arms, the hammer is slightly offset from center.

The fifth model, patented in April 1863, is similar to the third model, having only minor internal improvements; it operates as both single- and double-action. The sixth model is a slight variation on the fifth, operating double-action only. Most of the pepperboxes manufactured by Chamelot & Delvigne follow this later pattern.

The registration of Chamelot & Delvigne's seventh patent in September of 1863 brought yet another change to their basic design. The ejector rod in the butt was replaced by a side-mounted rod; actually two rods, one fixed beneath the barrel which created a track for the second rod to slide in. This fixed rod design provided stability for the moving ejector rod, and is the reason why this type of rod was rarely broken or lost as were so many others.

The eighth Chamelot & Delvigne model, created by a later patent of May 1864, has already been discussed and pictured in Chapter Three. One of its major design alterations was the discontinuation of the shield ahead of the cylinder. This model was chambered for the 12mm pinfire cartridge, whereas all prior Chamelot & Delvigne

arms (except for some pepperboxes made under the sixth patent) fired the 7mm cartridge.

The ninth patent, of June 1864, was for improvements to the locking mechanism which were quite similar to those of the fifth model.

The tenth patent and model were to follow in December of 1865. Revolvers made on this design were chambered to fire the 7mm, 9mm, and 12mm pinfire cartridges. A folding trigger and the absence of a triggerguard constituted the main changes implemented. *Plate 6-4* illustrates a 7mm revolver of this type, which is significantly larger than any of the Chamelot & Delvigne first through seventh models. The larger size of the eighth and higher models afforded a better grip, thus negating the need for the front shield. The folding trigger was standard on all tenth models, regardless of caliber.

The eleventh and final Chamelot & Delvigne patent was registered in 1869, and claimed further improvements to the ejector rod design. Some eighth and tenth model revolvers have been noted with a coil spring on the stationary shaft of the ejector rod, creating a spring-loaded effect when the rod is pushed back and released. Perhaps it was the only reason for this final patent.

2mm Caliber Commercial Pinfire Arms

Our study of pinfire handguns designed primarily for the civilian trade begins with the diminutive 2mm pinfire "charm pistols." These tiny handguns, averaging 1¼ inches in length, were manufactured in several European countries during the late nineteenth and early twentieth centuries, as well as in a variety of styles and configurations. They were referred to as *"Breloque"* or *"Berloque"*, literally meaning "charm" or "trinket." Later, the post-World War Two industrial rebirth of Japan saw the production of large quantities of charm pistols, though generally of lower quality. Many

were sold in the United States as cufflinks, tie tacks, and key chain fobs.

All single-shot, tip-down barrel charm pistols were chambered to actually fire the 2mm pinfire blank cartridge. A small shot pellet could be placed in the end of the blank cartridge, and on firing was propelled with considerable force.[1] One cased charm pistol set observed by the authors contained tiny, needle-like darts, considerably adding to the "weapons" ability of the innocent-looking "toy gun." While the barrels of the earlier-made European pistols were bored-through to allow actual firing of projectiles, as consumer safety became a popular issue that type of construction was abandoned in favor of a solid (closed) barrel having a top vent, which permitted the firing of blank cartridges only.

Plates 6-6 and 6-7 illustrate several kinds of 2mm pinfire charm pistols, as well as cartridge containers. All pistols are single-shot, with the

Plate 6-6. A grouping of 2mm caliber pinfire "charm pistols." Those at top left and right center are marked "Austria"; at bottom and left center, "Japan." The modern (circa 1960s) six-shot, double-action revolver at center is marked, "Xythos." Courtesy private collection, Gene Smith photograph

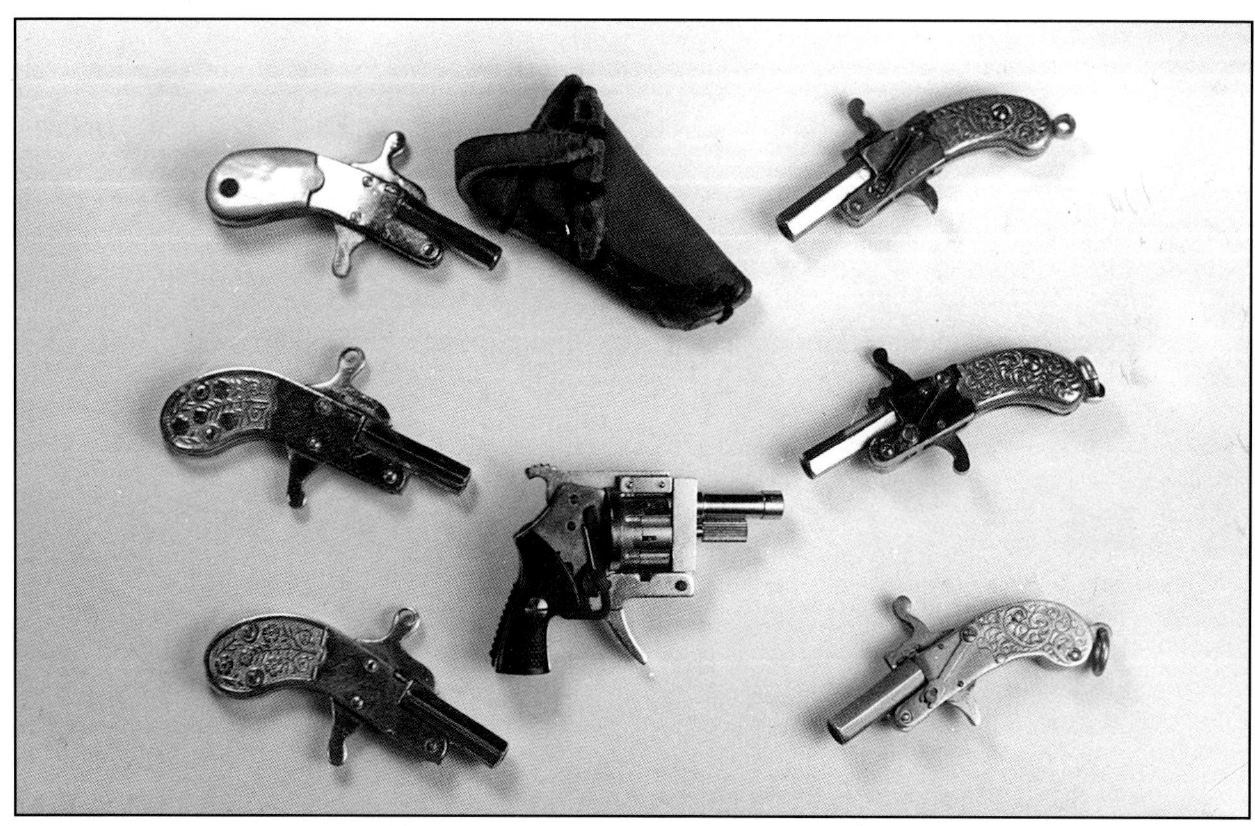

exception of the "*Xythos*" revolver at the center of *Plate 6-6*.

Charm pistols have been manufactured for more than a century in far-flung locales such as Austria, Japan, Germany, Belgium, and the United States. A very few of those made in America were manufactured under L.S. Chilson's 1931 patent: while appearing to be revolvers, they actually are 2mm single-shot pistols.

The making of functioning, miniature firearms has presented challenges to armsmakers literally for centuries, and for just as long these little arms have been considered prizes by collectors. During the late nineteenth century a limited number of miniature revolvers was made; like the toy pistols they too were chambered to fire 2mm caliber pinfire cartridges. The revolvers ranged in quality from the most basic to examples of exceptional craftsmanship and beauty. *Plate 6-8* illustrates an unadorned specimen, probably of French origin. This example measures 3¾ inches overall, although most miniature arms are less than half its size.

The appeal and life span of pinfire arms have been considerably extended, thanks to these "charming" little pistols.

Plate 6-7. Round pasteboard boxes containing twenty rounds each of Austrian 2mm blank cartridges, and an Austrian-made pistol measuring 1½-inches overall. *Courtesy private collection; Gene Smith photograph*

Plate 6-8 (below). This may be the largest 2mm caliber pinfire revolver ever made. It measures 3¼ inches in overall length. *Courtesy James Lowther; John Calcany photograph*

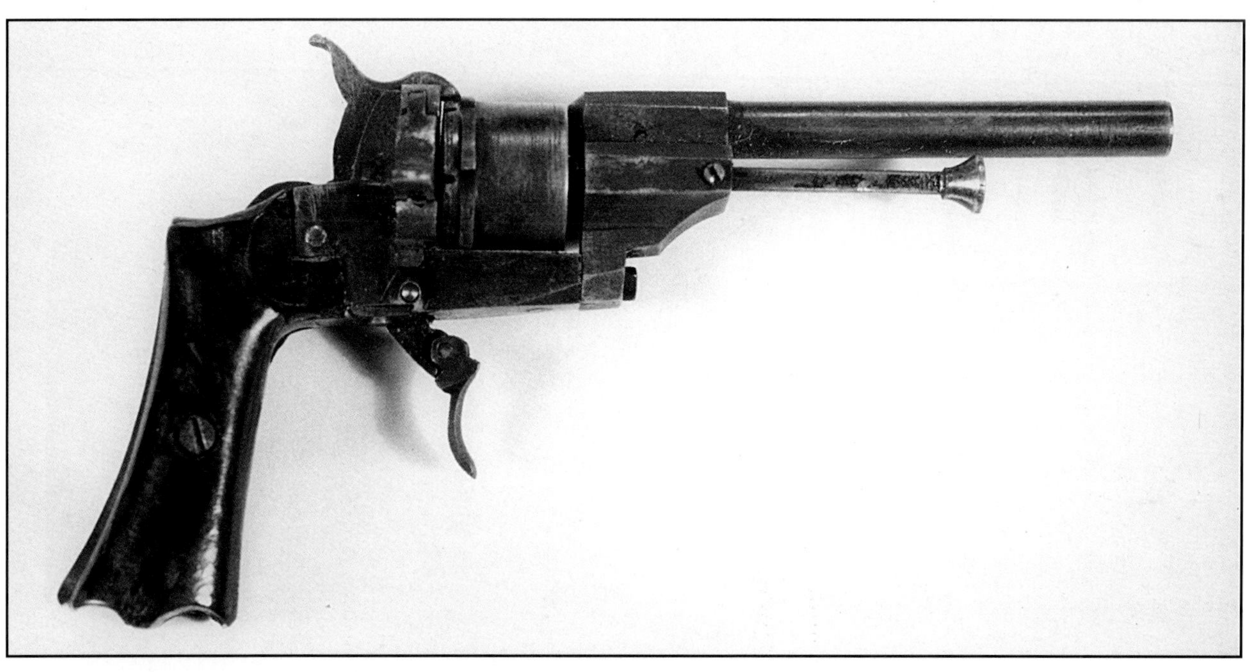

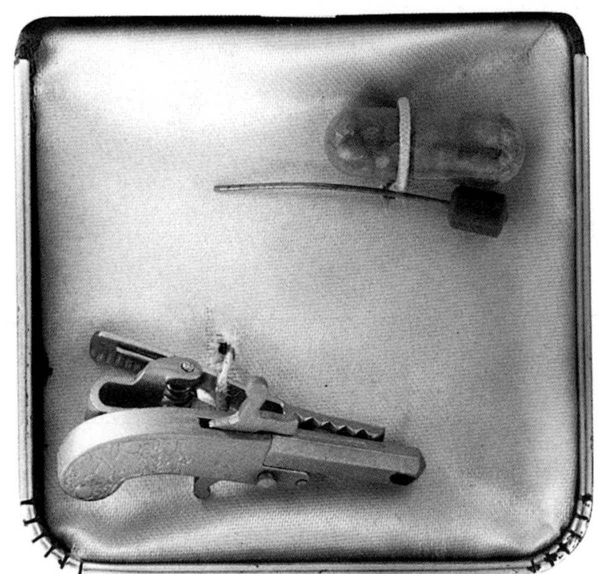

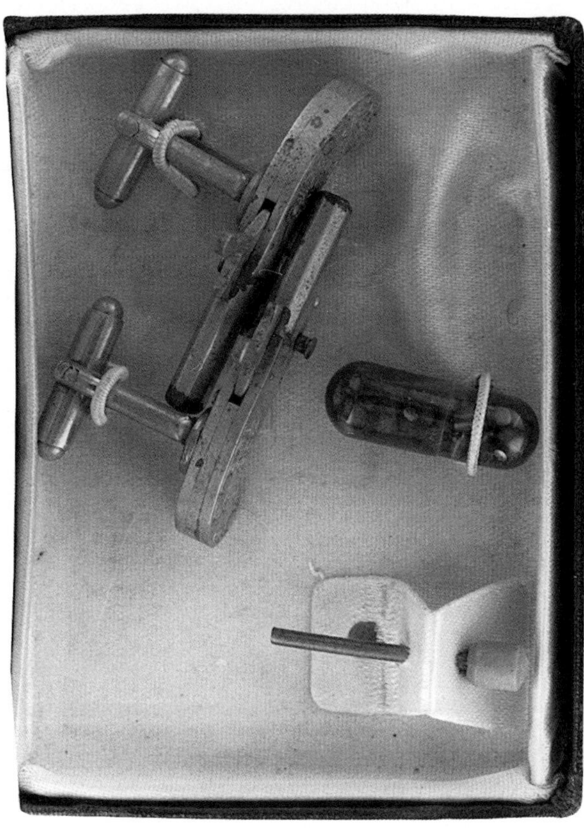

Plate 6-9 (left). A 2mm caliber pinfire "charm pistol" made as a tie-tack, cased with blank cartridges and an ejector rod. *Chris C. Curtis collection; Richard McMillan photograph*

Plate 6-11 (above). A single-shot, 2mm caliber pinfire pistol with muzzle flare adaptor, cased with flares and other accessories for use as a survival signal gun. *Chris C. Curtis collection; Richard McMillan photograph*

Plate 6-10 (above). A pair of pinfire "charm pistols" made as men's cufflinks, similar to the one shown in Plate 6-9, and cased with accessories. *Chris C. Curtis collection, Richard McMillan photograph*

Plate 6-12 (below). An Austrian-made "*Xythos*" 2mm caliber pinfire revolver, cased with muzzle flare adaptor and flares. Cast into the top of the grip is the word, "*Automatic.*" *Chris C. Curtis collection; Richard McMillan photograph*

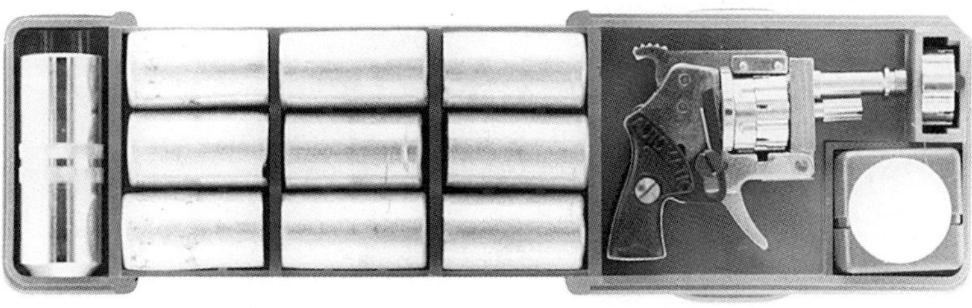

5mm Caliber Commercial Pinfire Arms

The next-larger pinfire handguns manufactured for the civilian trade were six-shot, 5mm caliber revolvers. Designed to function either single- or double-action, most examples average about five inches in length. *Plate 6-13* illustrates a 5mm caliber pinfire revolver having the standard folding trigger; it was made in Liége, Belgium between 1877 and 1893.

The top pistol pictured in *Plate 6-14* is a 5mm revolver fitted with bag-style grips. It also was produced in Liége, although its inspector's marks date its manufacture before 1877. Below it is pictured a Liége-proofed 5mm revolver designed to fire either pinfire or rimfire cartridges, and fitted with birds-head shape grips. This example is of later manufacture, as it bears inspector's marks not in use until 1894.

Plate 6-13. A standard 5mm caliber pinfire revolver having a folding trigger. Made in Liége, Belgium between 1877 and 1893. *Courtesy private collection; John Calcany photograph*

The 5mm caliber pinfire revolver was produced in a great variety of styles from about 1860 until the turn of the twentieth century. They were made by a great variety of armsmakers, most of whom were not troubled to mark their products with their names, and in many nations of the Western world. No standard model of 5mm pinfire revolver bearing a maker's name has been observed by the author.

Although these arms fire a virtually ineffective cartridge—weaker by far than today's .22 caliber short—they enjoyed popularity with the general public enough to warrant many years of production. During their era of use their diminutive size made them attractive to women and others who desired an easily concealable firearm. Today these little guns are becoming scarce, because they were made in countless styles and varying qualities, and because they fit into any number of collecting categories: miniature arms, ladies' arms, and so forth. Some specimens are elaborately engraved, inlaid with gold and/or silver, and fitted with ivory, ebony, or ornate gutta percha grips.

Plate 6-14. Pictured at top is a sparsely-engraved 5mm caliber pinfire revolver made in Liége, Belgium prior to 1877; shown at bottom is another revolver having more engraving and birds-head grips, made after 1894. *Courtesy private collection; F.W. Hulbert photograph*

The style of 5mm caliber pinfire revolver pictured in *Plate 6-15* is known among collectors as the "change purse" revolver. This first example bears Belgian proofmarks and inspector's marks indicating manufacture after 1877.

Another change purse revolver is housed in a hard case which was constructed to hold spectacles and cigars within two separate compartments in one half, and the revolver in the other. The gun is equipped with lovely ivory grips, and has gold inlay on the frame and cylinder (*see Plate 6-16*). It also was made in Belgium, with inspector's marks indicating pre-1877 manufacture. The average size

of these "cigar-style" pistol cases is approximately three by five-and-a-half inches.

The engraved and silver-plated revolver pictured in *Plate 6-17* also has bag-shape ivory grips and decorative engraving. The case has two compartments, with a hinged, metal-framed silk divider shown standing vertically between them. One side holds cigars, the other the revolver and its ammunition. While many of these cigar cases and guns appear nearly identical, they will not interchange. Each case was made specifically for its own revolver, and all have slightly different dimensions.

Plate 6-15 (right). A 5mm caliber pinfire revolver, unmarked but for Liége proofmarks, shown with its soft leather "change-purse" casing. *Courtesy private collection; John Calcany photograph*

Plate 6-16 (above). A gold-inlaid, ivory-gripped 5mm caliber pinfire revolver, housed in a hard case which holds the gun in one half and cigars and a pair of spectacles in the other. *Courtesy private collection; John Calcany photograph*

Plate 6-17 (right). Another 5mm caliber pinfire revolver in its "cigar case", having a hinged divider separating the gun from the cigars. *Courtesy Don Kramer; Ferrari Color photograph*

7mm Caliber Commercial Pinfire Arms

Revolvers chambered for the larger 7mm caliber pinfire cartridge also are found cased in a variety of styles. The unmarked but Liége-made example pictured in *Plate 6-24* is housed in a "pipe-style" casing having a hard-shell exterior and a fabric-lined interior. This high-quality arm is fitted with ivory grips, and features gold line inlay on its cylinder and frame.

The familiar Liége proofmarks are the only markings to be found on the revolver pictured in *Plate 6-25*. This somewhat scarcer type of pipe-style casing has provision for carrying six 7mm caliber pinfire cartridges in addition to the revolver.

Plate 6-26 illustrates a Belgian-made revolver having birds-head grips. On the cylinder it is impressively marked, "*New English Pattern Pinfire Pistol, Sept. 20th 1876*", and bears post-1877 inspector's marks.

The small revolver pictured in *Plate 6-27* has no front sight, the relatively uncommon feature of a full-fluted cylinder, and an ejector rod threaded into the butt. The gun itself is unmarked except for London proofmarks, but the ornate label in the lid of the English-style case reads, "*Frederic T.*

text continued on page 189

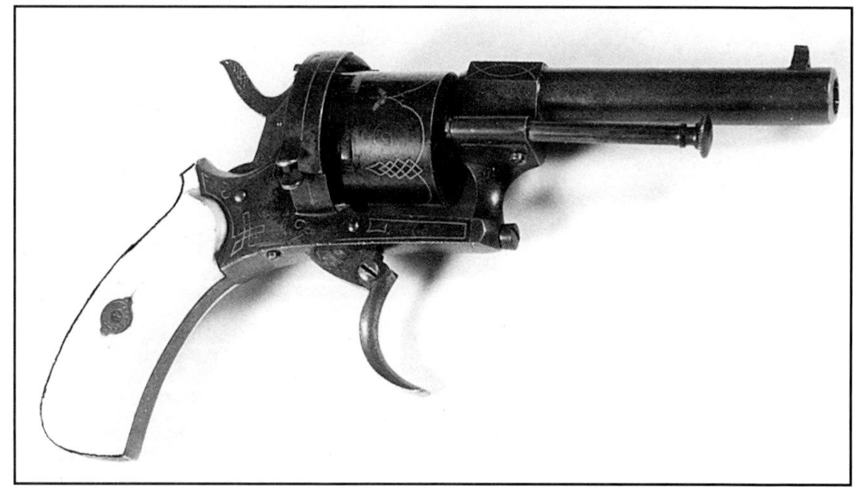

Plate 6-18. A Liége-made, 7mm caliber pinfire revolver having gold-line inlay and ivory grips, and a pin shield at the rear of the cylinder. *Courtesy private collection; John Calcany photograph*

Plate 6-19. An English-made, double-action 7mm caliber pinfire revolver having Birmingham proofmarks and marked on top of the barrel, "*Thos. Bradburn and Sons, London.*" *Courtesy private collection; F.W. Hulbert photograph*

Plate 6-20 (right). An unusual, solid-frame 7mm caliber pinfire revolver having a Liége proofmark "*ELG*" on its frame rather than at the typical cylinder location, and inspector's marks dating its manufacture before 1877. In addition, it has an uncommon full-fluted cylinder, and an ejector rod mounted in the butt rather than alongside the barrel. *Courtesy James Lowther; John Calcany photograph*

Plate 6-21 (right). A small 7mm caliber pinfire revolver having a solid frame and a spur trigger, features common to American-made cartridge handguns of the period but rarely found on pinfire revolvers. Also unusual, it is completely devoid of marks, even proofmarks, except for a "*1*" on the side of the frame. *Courtesy Don Kramer; F.W. Hulbert photograph*

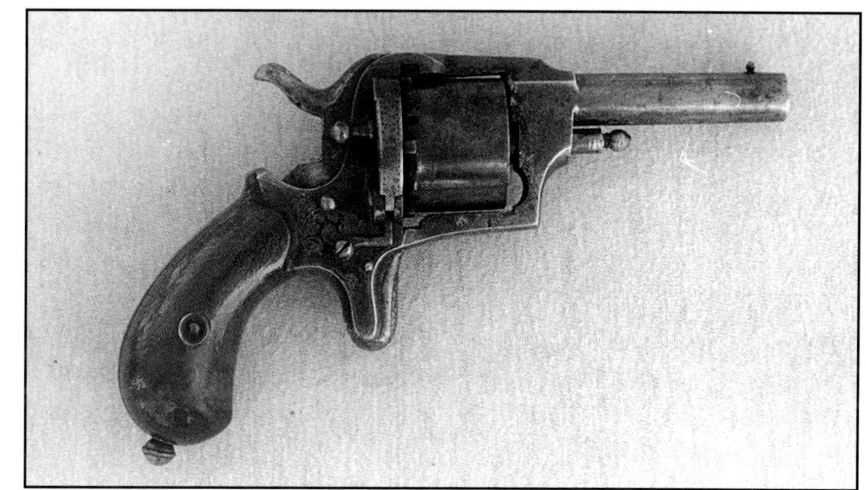

Plate 6-22 (below, right). A 7mm caliber pinfire revolver marked "*Meyers Bte.*" "*Meyers*" arms are difficult to identify, as several makers and sales agents used the name during the period. Ferdinand Meyers worked in Zurich, Switzerland in 1876-77, and Meyer & Co. of Innsbrück, Austria displayed at the 1851 London Exhibition; some "*Meyers*"-marked guns bear both British and Liége proofmarks, as does this example. Most revolvers marked "*Meyers Bte.*" share some similarities, but it is unclear what improvements his patent claimed. The ejector rod mount and cylinder pin are the same, but they also have an integrally-machined rear sight on the top strap, which may constitute at least part of his patent claim. *Courtesy private collection; F.W. Hulbert photograph*

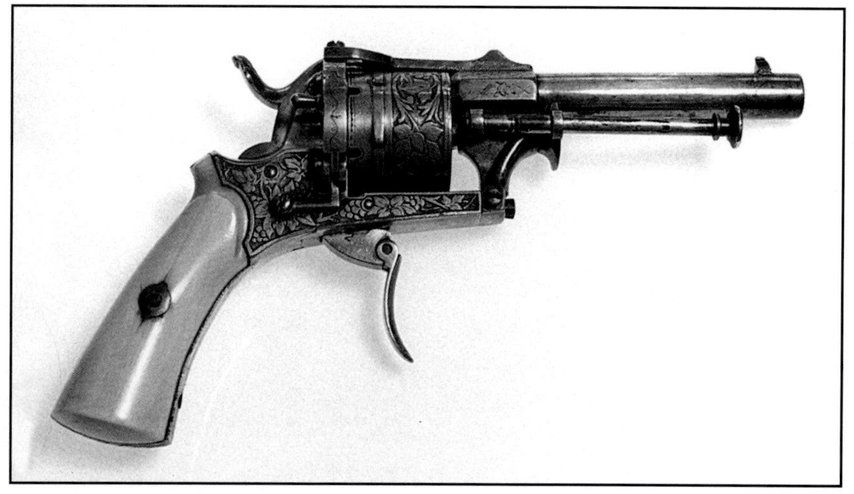

Plate 6-23 (above). A group of 7mm caliber pinfire revolvers having longer than usual barrels. Note the front sights on the upper two examples; their mid-point locations gave rise to the term "extended barrel" to describe this variation. All bear Liége proofmarks. Only the revolver at top left bears a maker's name: "*Lefaucheux*"; however, that may refer to the system rather than its manufacturer. All six examples have a pin shield at the rear of their cylinders, although it is not standard on long-barrel arms. *Courtesy James Lowther; John Calcany photograph*

Plate 6-24 (right). This pipe-cased 7mm caliber pinfire revolver is unmarked except for Liége proofmarks, but has decorative gold-line inlay and ivory grips. *Courtesy private collection; John Calcany photograph*

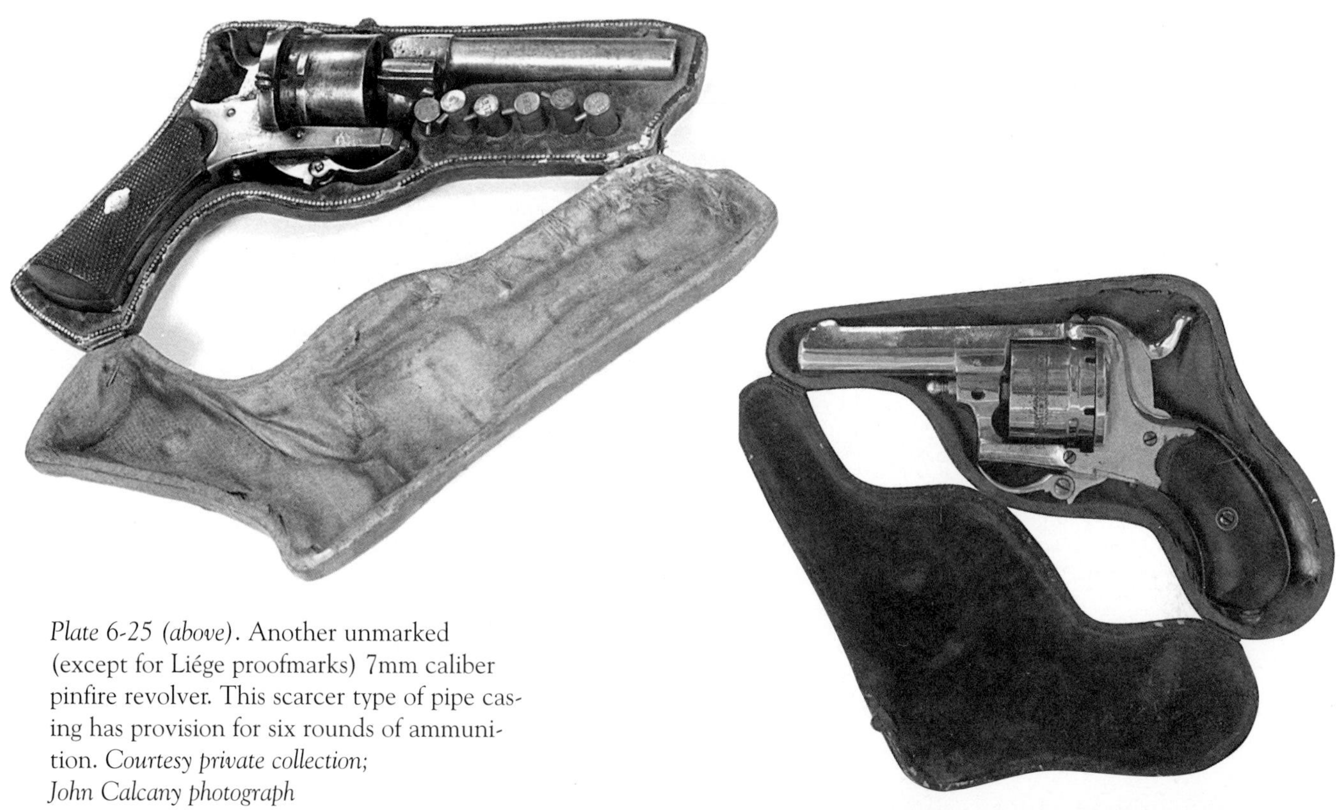

Plate 6-25 (above). Another unmarked (except for Liége proofmarks) 7mm caliber pinfire revolver. This scarcer type of pipe casing has provision for six rounds of ammunition. *Courtesy private collection; John Calcany photograph*

Plate 6-26 (above, right). Another pipe-cased pinfire revolver, nickel-plated, with birds-head grips, and marked "*New English Pattern Pinfire Pistol…*." *Courtesy private collection; F.W. Hulbert photograph*

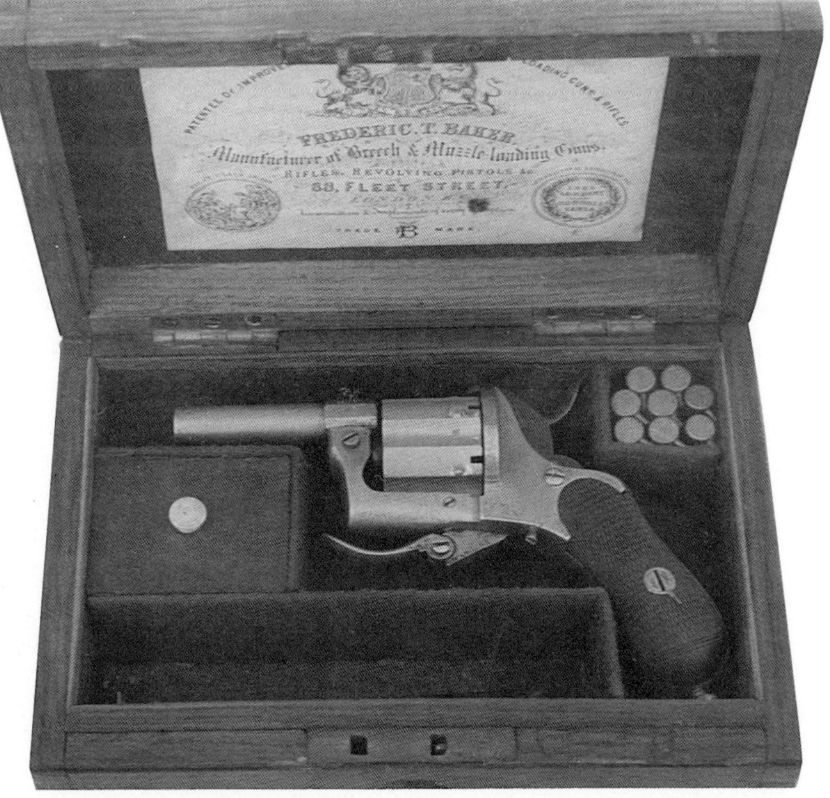

Plate 6-27 (right). A small 7mm caliber pinfire revolver unmarked except for London proofmarks, and cased in an English-style case with London maker's label in lid. Note rare full-fluted cylinder and lack of a front sight. *Courtesy private collection; F.W. Hulbert photograph*

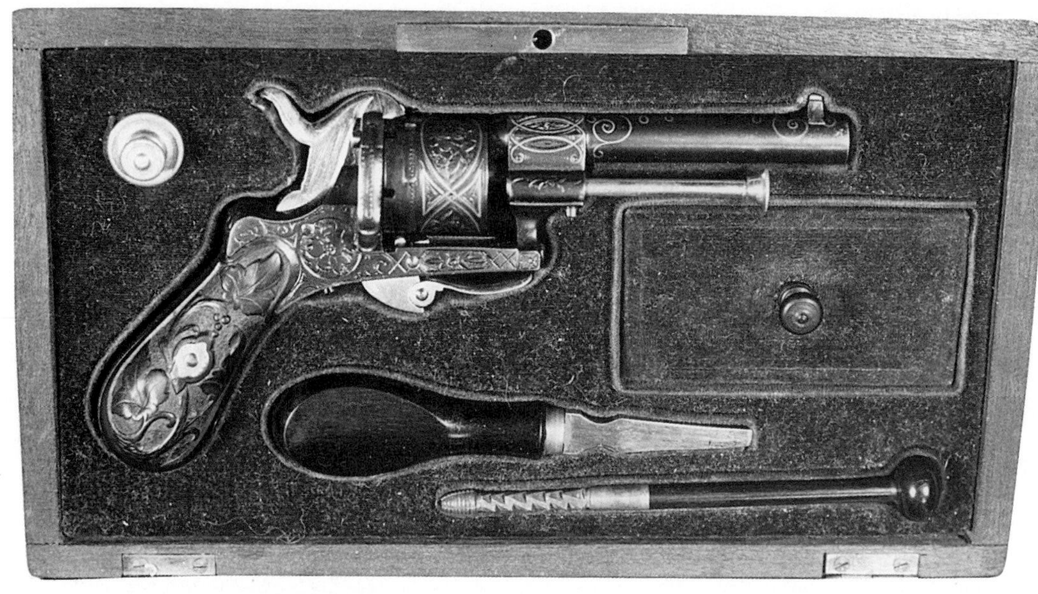

Plate 6-28. An ornately-embellished 7mm caliber pinfire revolver, engraved, gold-line inlaid, and having carved ebony grips, housed in a French-style case with accoutrements. The gun is unmarked but for Liége proofmarks. *Courtesy private collection; John Calcany photograph*

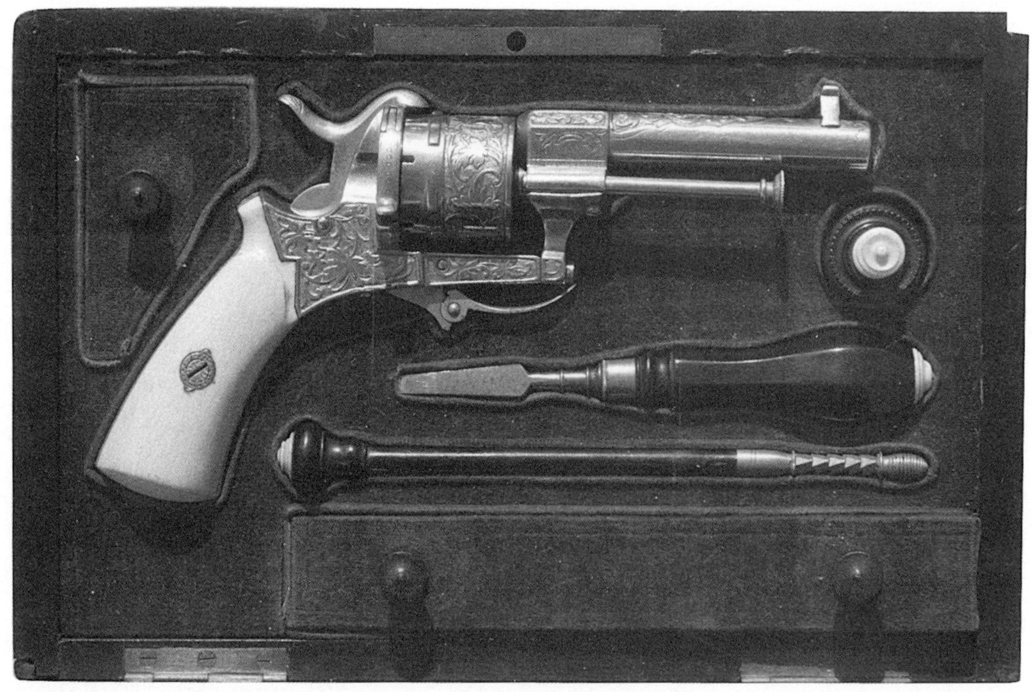

Plate 6-29. Another ornate 7mm caliber pinfire revolver, engraved, gold-plated, and fitted with ivory grips. Housed in a French-style case with full accoutrements. The gun is unmarked but for Liége proofmarks. *Courtesy private collection; F.W. Hulbert photograph*

Baker, 88 Fleet Street, London." Baker occupied this address *circa* 1860-1862.

Because of their variety, completeness, and beauty, cased sets have always attracted more collector attention, and thus are more valuable than the same arm uncased. Certainly this is true of the style of casing shown in *Plate 6-28*, known as the "French-style" case. The term applies to cases that have form-fitted interior recesses in which the gun and its loading and cleaning accoutrements lay. It is opposed to the "English-style" of casing shown in *Plate 6-27*, which has partitioned open compartments which conform to the general size and shape of the gun and its accessories. The revolver pictured in *Plate 6-28* is unmarked with the exception of Liége proofmarks and inspector's marks. The lid of the French-style case is marked "*Souvenier—L. De Rasquinet—par Victor Lejeune.*"

Plate 6-29 illustrates another 7mm caliber pinfire revolver housed in a French-style casing. The gun is relief engraved and overall gold-plated, but unmarked except for Liége proofmarks. The accessories have ebony handles with ivory tips matching the ivory grips of the revolver. In the covered compartment at the bottom of the picture is an integral container holding thirty pinfire cartridges.

9mm and 12mm Caliber Commercial Pinfire Arms

The next-largest caliber found among commercial pinfire revolvers is 9mm, roughly equivalent to the American .38 caliber cartridge (9mm is equal to .354 inch, *vs.* .357 inch for most U.S.-made .38 caliber cartridges). Both the 9mm and 12mm caliber pinfire cartridges (the latter measures .472 inch, roughly comparable to the U.S. .44/.45 caliber cartridges) were used in military and civilian handguns during the second half of the nineteenth century.

Eugene Lefaucheux was not the only armsmaker at the time to realize the sales potential of a handgun designed to fire both the newly-emerging metallic cartridge, and the tried-and-true, cap-and-ball percussion system.

Five years after Lefaucheux was granted a French patent for his double-action revolver having the combination-ignition capability, John Adams of King William Street, London, designed a similar revolver. In his 1861 English patent, number 1758, Adams described his barrel design as being one solid piece which attached to a frame containing the mechanism and the grip. The purpose of Adams' patent was to provide a revolver capable of using interchangeable cartridge and percussion cylinders. It utilized a metal backplate at the rear of the cylinder which revolved on the base pin with the cylinder. The pin, held in place by a spring, could be withdrawn slightly to allow the backplate to move to the side, thus permitting the cylinder to be loaded from the rear. Completely withdrawing the pin allowed the cartridge cylinder to be removed, and be replaced with a percussion cylinder.

In his patent papers Adams illustrated an early type of centerfire metallic cartridge, and in the main patent drawings he depicted his gun as a centerfire revolver. However, Lefaucheux cartridges are mentioned numerous times in Adams' patent text, and a pinfire cylinder is illustrated and described in a series of drawings. In one part, his explanation reads, "So that the chambers may be suitable for receiving and exploding the charges contained in cases or cartridges somewhat similar to those known as Lefaucheux cartridges." Mr. Adams definitely believed in covering all his bases!

The Adams Patent Small Arms Company was formed in 1864 to manufacture revolvers based on his 1861 patent. Only a few Adams revolvers having the dual-ignition system are known to collectors, and none is chambered for the pinfire cartridge.

John Adams had worked in some unknown capacity for the London Armoury in the late 1850s. That company was a major importer and exporter of European arms during the American Civil War, most notably of Kerr's revolvers and Enfield rifles. During that period, Adams clearly had the opportunity to study the varied designs of pinfire revolvers which were part of the company's trade, as well.

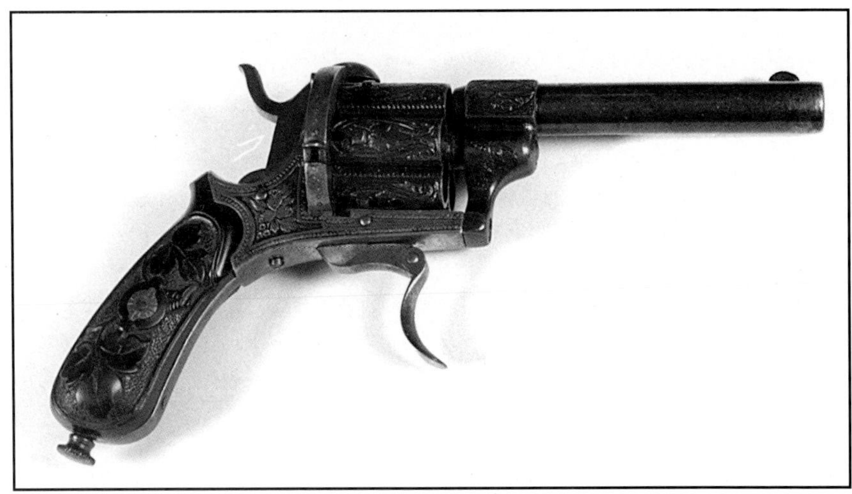

Plate 6-30. A fine-quality 9mm caliber pinfire revolver, having a rare "cloverleaf" cylinder and the ejector rod in butt. The gun is unmarked but for Liége proof-marks. *Courtesy private collection; John Calcany photograph*

Plate 6-31. A 9mm caliber pinfire revolver made by Arendt prior to 1877, having silver-line inlay and unusual features. Arendt worked in Liége from 1857 until 1889. This revolver has a removable ejector rod, and front and rear sights. A pin safety shield is at the rear of the cylinder and a side-mounted safety bar that when pushed through the frame prevents the hammer from falling. The bar is pushed back from this safe position to fire. *Courtesy private collection; F.W. Hulbert photograph*

Plate 6-32. Another 9mm caliber pinfire revolver manufactured in Liége. It dates from between 1877 and 1893, and has a nicely-engraved frame and cylinder. *Courtesy Jack Robbins; F.W. Hulbert photograph*

Plate 6-33. A 9mm caliber pinfire revolver housed in an unusual style of leather-paved, fitted casing. It was expertly engraved, and left "in the white", which is quite unusual; in addition, it bears no maker's name, only Liége proofmarks. *Courtesy private collection; Gene Smith photograph*

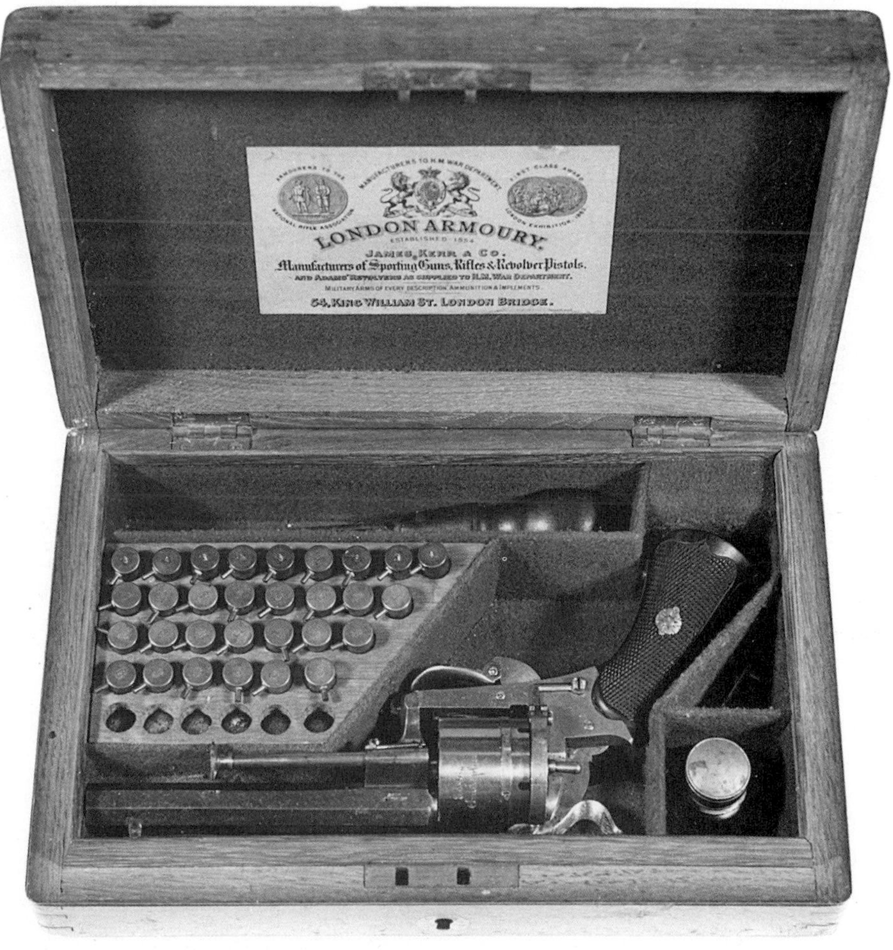

Plate 6-34. A French-made 9mm caliber pinfire revolver, marked "*Fabrique St. Etienne*" and "*Acier Fondu*" on the barrel and bearing proofmarks indicating manufacture after 1869. Like the previous piece, it too was left unfinished "in the white." However, it was shipped to the London Armoury, whose label appears inside the case lid, where it was engraved and cased with accoutrements. The cylinder is marked, "*Edwin Christopher.*" *Courtesy private collection; John Calcany photograph*

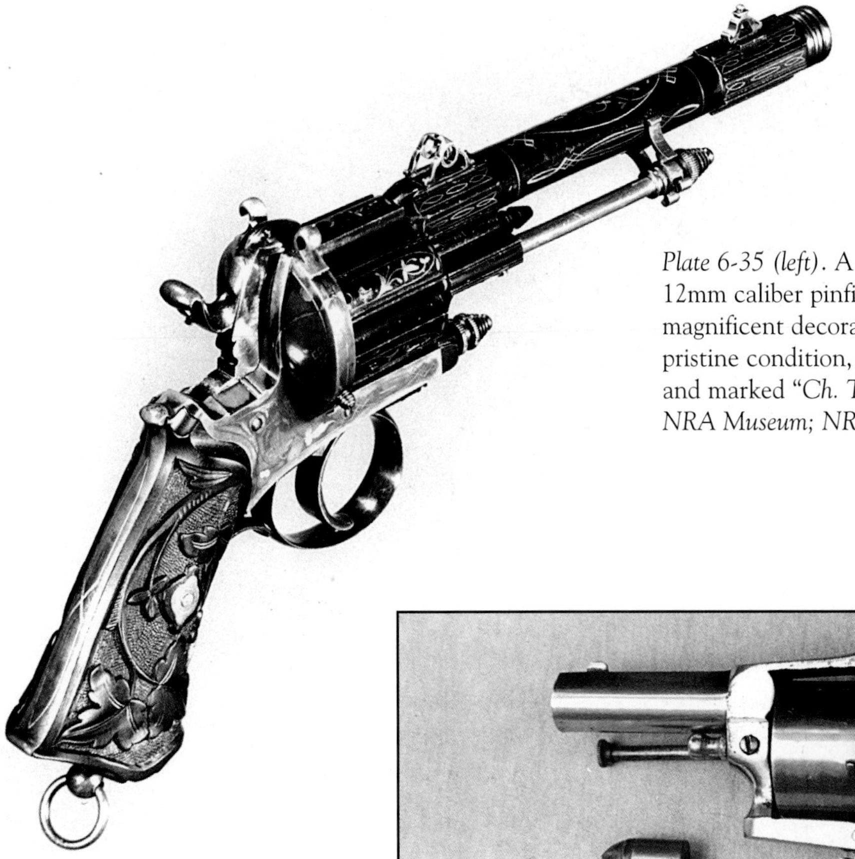

Plate 6-35 (left). A large, high-quality 12mm caliber pinfire revolver having magnificent decoration and displaying pristine condition, made in France by and marked *"Ch. T. Colard." Courtesy the NRA Museum; NRA Museum photograph*

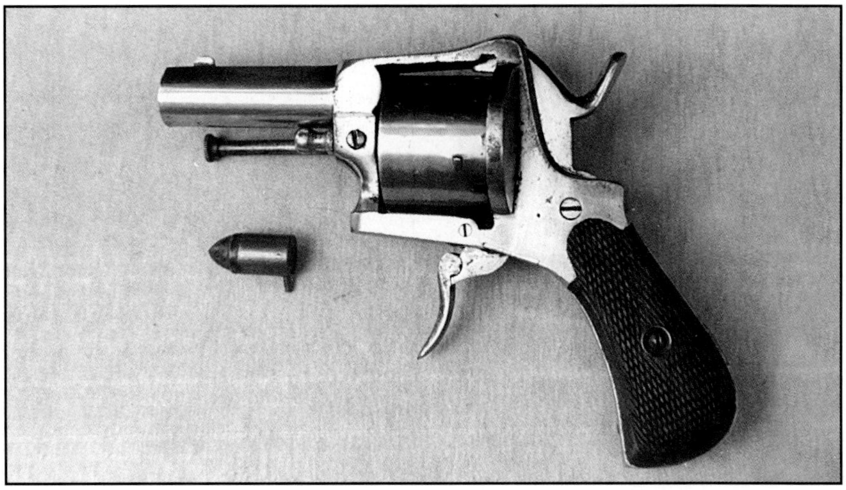

Plate 6-36 (right). A nickel-plated, 12mm caliber pinfire revolver of unknown origins. It is five-shot, solid frame, and quite small for a gun chambered for this large-caliber cartridge. *Courtesy private collection; F.W. Hulbert photograph*

Plate 6-37 (right). A large 12mm caliber pinfire revolver, marked *"Kirschbaum Solingen"* on the right side of the barrel, *"Sme Lefaucheux"* on the left side, and *"12mm"* atop the barrel. German maker's marks are on the cylinder, which has counterbored chambers common to dual-ignition revolvers of the period for firing either pinfire or centerfire ammunition. *Courtesy private collection; F.W. Hulbert photograph*

Plate 6-38. A large Meyers-type, 12mm caliber pinfire revolver bearing Birmingham proofmarks and "*London No. 65397*" markings on its frame. Note the integral lanyard ring. *Courtesy private collection; F.W. Hulbert photograph*

Plate 6-39. A high-quality, French made 12mm caliber pinfire revolver marked "*A. Francotte.*" It is engraved and inlaid with gold and silver; note the finely-checkered, bag-style grips. *Courtesy Don Kramer; Ferrari Color photograph*

Plate 6-40. Another 12mm caliber pinfire revolver, floral engraved on the frame and with a rare "cloverleaf" cylinder, marked, "*E. Lefaucheux Brvt.*" It bears Liége proofmarks and pre-1877 inspector's marks. *Courtesy Don Kramer; Ferrari Color photograph*

Another firm, Adams & Co., operated at 9 Finsbury Place in London between 1870 and 1880 under the leadership of Henry Adams. Probably Henry Adams was related to gunmakers John and Robert Adams, and in fact his company contracted for much of their work. In addition to the percussion, rimfire, and centerfire revolvers the Adamses are known to have manufactured, the brothers are credited with having made twelve-shot pinfire revolvers.

The 12mm caliber pinfire revolver pictured in *Plate 6-41* does not bear Adams markings, nor does it have British proofmarks. It is marked with the legend, "*Inventor—Lefaucheux*", in English, however, and included here because of its strong outward resemblance to the revolvers manufactured by Adams during the period.

The advent of the greatly improved centerfire military revolver hastened the decline in popularity of the pinfire system in the military market during the 1870s. Nevertheless, the manufacture of inexpensive pinfire ammunition for the private sector did not decline during the same period. Rather, it witnessed a dramatic increase through the end of the century, by which time the market was flooded with countless numbers of pinfire arms.

The variety in the design and external appearance of those firearms seems endless even to those who collect them, and the contrasts found in their workmanship are noteworthy. During the late nineteenth century period of almost-frantic pinfire arms production, the quality of the guns manufactured ranged from vastly inferior to some of the finest arms ever produced in Europe. Masterpieces of exceptional beauty and quality found their way into the possession of the world's wealthiest arms owners and collectors. On the other hand, cheap and lowly pinfire revolvers of every size and shape filled the needs of the less well-heeled, and in some cases, less reputable, citizenry.

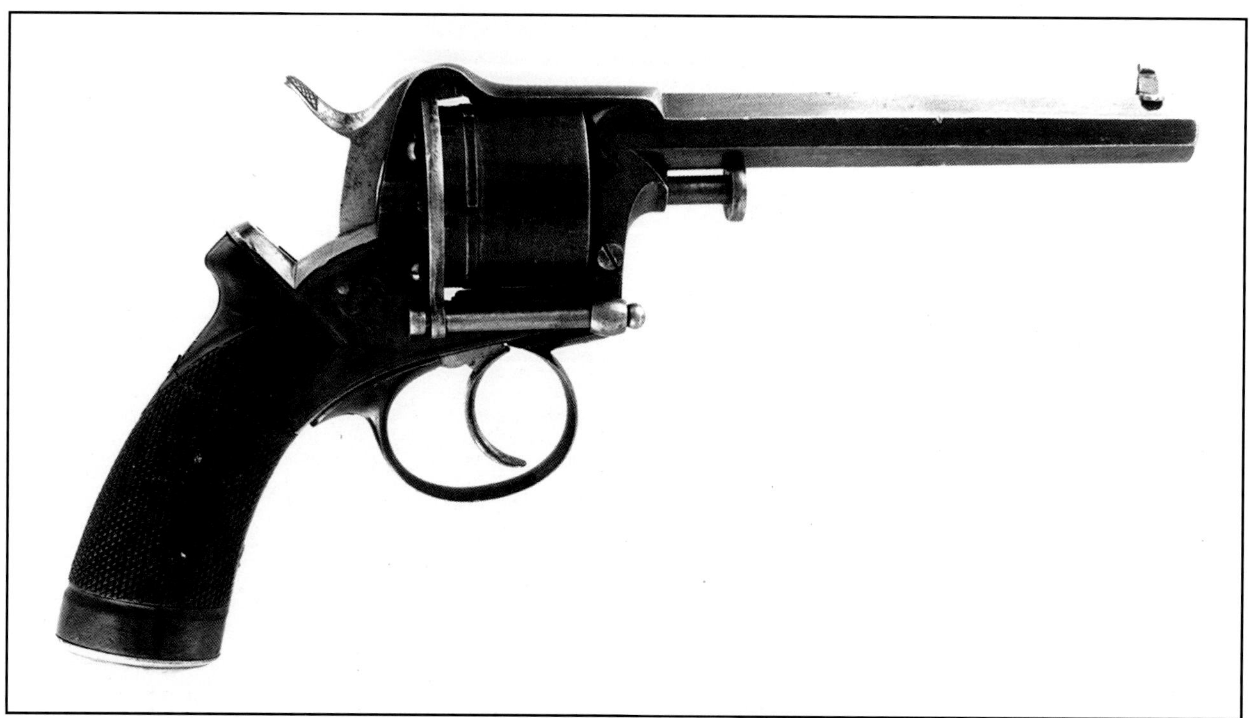

Plate 6-41. A large 12mm caliber pinfire revolver which resembles the English Adams revolvers of the period. It is marked, "*Inventor—Lefaucheux.*" *Courtesy Jacques Salzedo; Richard McMillan photograph*

Other Types of Pinfire Pistols

Besides revolvers, there were many types of pinfire handguns produced for sale in the civilian marketplace. One style is the double-barrel pistol. When the two hammers are pulled back to the half-cock position, the barrels can be released and tipped down for loading or cartridge ejection.

Opening the action is accomplished by moving a lever or button which releases a locking lug. When the hammers are moved to full-cock, the folding triggers spring down into firing position.

The majority of double-barrel pinfire pistols were made in either Belgium or Spain, and most were intended for export to South America and other foreign markets. When examples of better

Plate 6-42. A 15mm caliber pinfire revolver, unmarked except for Liége proofmarks. These largest-caliber pinfire arms are very rare. *Courtesy James Lowther; John Calcany photograph*

Plate 6-43. Another 15mm caliber pinfire revolver, unusual in that it was marked on the barrel by the retailer, *"Tarbert Arq Marseille"*, although manufactured in Belgium and bearing Liége proofmarks. *Courtesy private collection; John Calcany photograph*

quality are encountered they often exhibit the marks of French manufacture.

Other types among the vast variety of pinfire handgun styles are illustrated on the following pages.

The casing shown in Plate 6-62 is equally as interesting as the pistol it houses. When the upper drawer of this ladies' sewing box is removed, a fine-quality 7mm caliber, double-barrel pinfire pistol is revealed. Engraved and fitted with ivory grips, the pistol is unmarked except for Liége proofmarks and inspector's marks indicating manufacture after 1877. Atop the barrels is a combination rear sight and sliding pin protector. The recessed portion of the case is shallower than commonly encountered, but still falls into the category of a French-style casing. This interesting ladies' outfit probably was made as a traveling set.

An unusual single-shot pistol is pictured in *Plate 6-63*. At first it appears to be a standard, large-frame 12mm caliber pinfire revolver. But in place of a cylinder there is a hinged, swing-out breechblock. When the ejector rod is pulled forward the breechblock rolls over to the side so that it can be loaded, or a spent cartridge ejected. The block is then moved back into the closed position and the ejector rod slides rearward into a milled opening, thus locking the breech in the firing position. The pistol is marked *"Mariette Brevete"*, and bears pre-1877 Belgian inspector's marks. The Mariette name is often found on double-action underhammer pepperboxes; its meaning on this single-shot pistol is unclear. By its outward appearance, students of modern arms might be reminded of the short-lived Ruger Hawkeye pistol of 1963-64.

The 14mm caliber dueling style, single-shot pinfire pistol illustrated in *Plate 6-64* originally was in the very large arms collection of Carlos Amadoes, an Argentine aristocrat descended from Spanish nobility. The gun is marked with "558", to correspond with page 558 of Amadoes' detailed late-nineteenth century personal record book. Translated into English, the description of this pistol reads,

> *Lefaucheux single shot pistol—smooth octagon barrel, 265mm long and 14mm caliber. On top of the barrel is etched "BRUN Bte a Paris"—on the bottom of the barrel the number 354, on the barrel closure is the inscription "INVENTION LEFAUCHEUX A PARIS 412"—Silver butt plate, hair pin trigger—all of the steel parts have been finely engraved. The firing pin has been modified from that of the first Lefaucheux.[2]*

> *I saw this dueling pistol and its companion piece along with its corresponding case in the year 1887 in Goth's Armory "Arsenal"—from there it went to Pedro Worms from whom one was stolen. They first had belonged to General Luelo Mansilla, from whom Goth bought them, according to what I was told.*

Chapter notes.

1. Examples of rare, factory-loaded 2mm caliber pinfire ball ammunition also are known among collectors.
2. This sentence may be the result of an error in translation from the old Spanish as written by Amadoes. The hammer of this pinfire pistol appears to be an unaltered, standard Lefaucheux part.

Plate 6-44 (opposite page, top). These four, double-barrel pinfire pistols range from the small 7mm caliber pictured at bottom, through 9mm and 12mm calibers, to the large 15mm caliber example at top. Measurements range between 6½ inches overall (7mm caliber) and 11 inches overall (15mm caliber). None bears proofmarks, and only the 12mm caliber example is marked with a maker's name, *"Jarranaga—Eibar"* (Spain). *Courtesy private collection; F.W. Hulbert photograph*

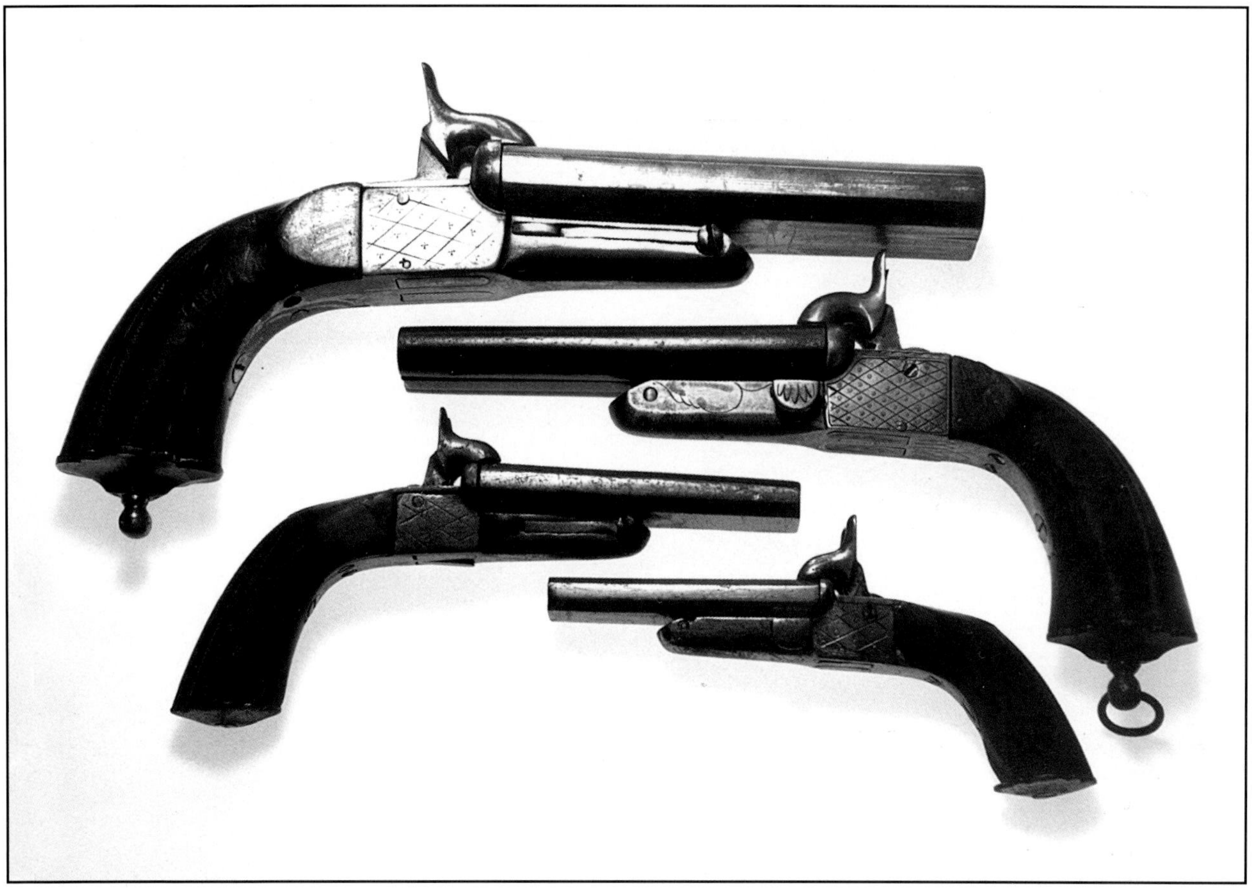

Plate 6-45 (right). Pictured at top is a German-made 9mm caliber double-barrel pinfire pistol. The 3½-inch barrels are rifled and marked "*Guss Stahl*" at the breech. The lever at the trigger-guard bow is pushed forward to release the tip-down barrels for loading or extraction. Pictured at bottom is an English-made, 7mm caliber double-barrel pinfire pistol. The 3½-inch barrels are smoothbore, and bear Birmingham proofmarks. The lever at the front of the frame swings to the side to release the tip-down barrels. *Courtesy private collection; F.W. Hulbert photograph*

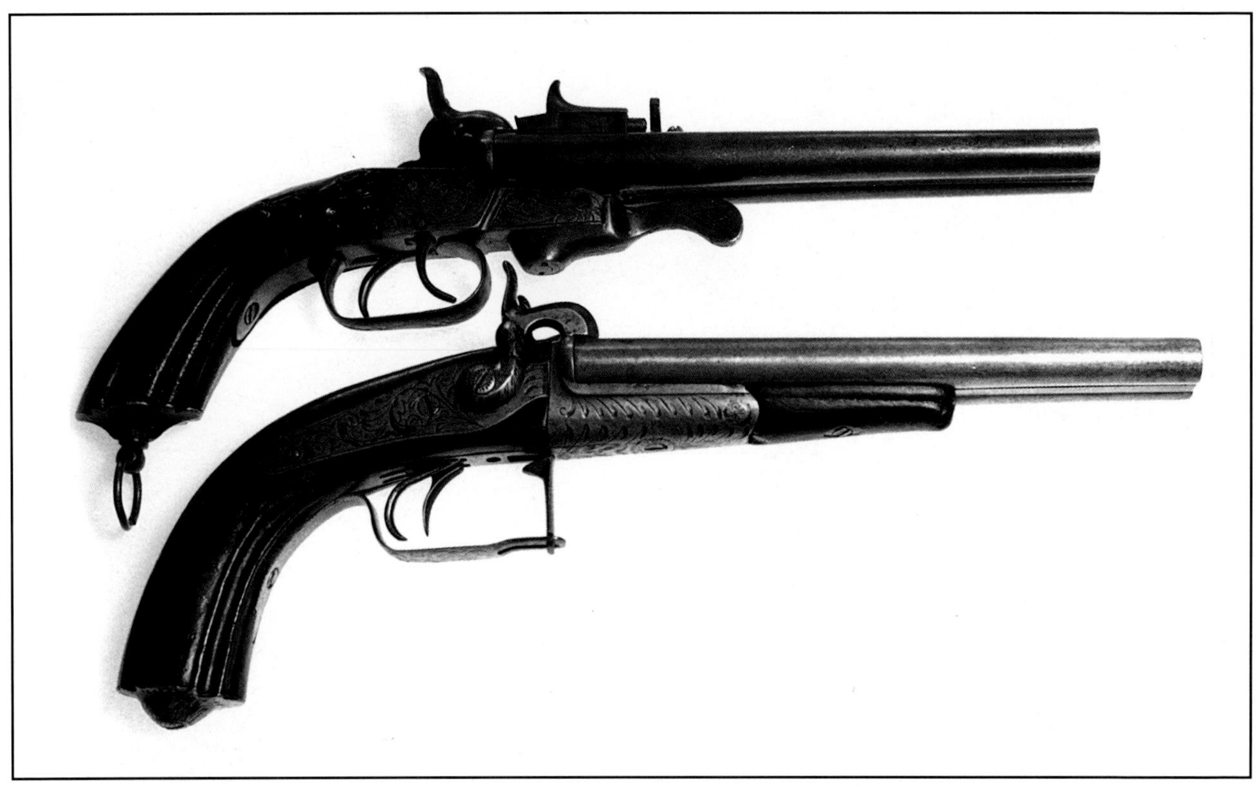

Plate 6-46. Pictured at top is a 12mm caliber, double-barrel pinfire pistol manufactured in Belgium after 1894. The 7-inch rifled barrels at the top rear are fitted with a combination rear sight, manual cartridge extractor, and spring-loaded pin protector. When the hammer is lifted and the protector moved rearward, slots in the protector align with the cartridge pins protruding through slots in the breech. The hammers are lowered onto the protector and the pistol may be safely carried while loaded. When the hammers are raised to full-cock position the protector springs forward, exposing the cartridge pins and allowing the arm to fire. Pictured at bottom is a double-barrel pinfire pistol probably of early French origin. The 7-inch smoothbore barrels calibrate 12mm at the breech, tapering to 9mm at the muzzle; the bore choke must have been very effective at close range using shot cartridges. When the front edge of the triggerguard is pulled rearward the tip-down barrels release for loading or extraction. *Courtesy private collection; F.W. Hulbert photograph*

Plate 6-47. A most unusual 12mm caliber over-and-under double-barrel pinfire pistol, unmarked except for what appear to be spurious Belgian proof and inspector's marks. The 3-inch rifled barrels, held by friction, swivel 90 degrees for loading; a 180-degree turn aligns the second barrel in firing position. A spur-trigger makes this scarce pistol, probably of Spanish origin, even more intriguing. *Courtesy Larry Compeau; F.W. Hulbert photograph*

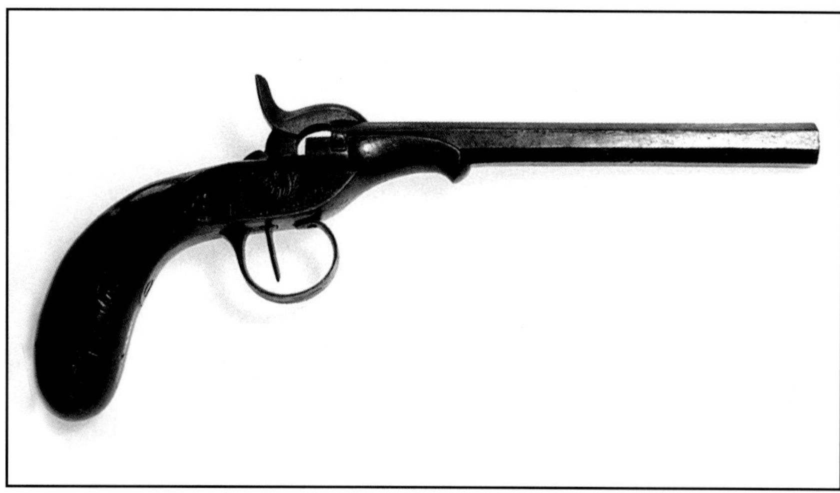

Plate 6-48 (right). An unusual 12mm caliber, single-barrel pinfire pistol manufactured in Belgium. The 7-inch barrel bears Liége proofmarks and pre-1877 inspector's marks; the frame is marked, *"Pirlot Fréres—Brevete"*, and has a lifting breechblock. This pistol and the pistol illustrated in *Plate 6-47* were offered in the 1927 catalog of famed New York surplus military goods dealer Francis Bannerman. *Courtesy private collection; F.W. Hulbert photograph*

10 SHOT REVOLVER. Cylinder holds 9 ordinary pin fire revolver cartridges, while the large bore under barrel can be loaded with duck shot or large sized ball cartridge, the barrels are 3½ inches long, all in fine order, cleaned and blued equal to new. Price, $15.00.

This pattern revolver fired with powder and ball was used extensively by Southern Army officers, delivered to the South by blockade running steamers in exchange for cotton during the period of 1861-1865.

10878. **BREECH-LOADING PIN-FIRE PISTOL.** For European cartridge, 6¼-inch octagonal barrel. Engraved frame; blue finish; good working order; dark-colored hard wood stock. Offered without cartridges. Valuable only to collectors. Price, $3.65.

10878A. Same pistol with 4½-inch barrel. Price, $2.95.

Plate 6-49 (above). An illustration from page 120 of military goods dealer Francis Bannerman's 1920 catalog, showing the pistol pictured in *Plate 6-48* offered for $3.65 (right). Note also the ten-shot pinfire LeMat revolver at left, priced at $15.00! *Chris C. Curtis collection*

Plate 6-50 (right). A 9mm caliber, double-barrel pinfire pistol manufactured in Belgium. The stationary barrels are marked, *"C. Dandoy a Liége"*; a lifting and turning breechblock opens the chambers for loading, but without provision for extraction. *Courtesy James Lowther; John Calcany photograph*

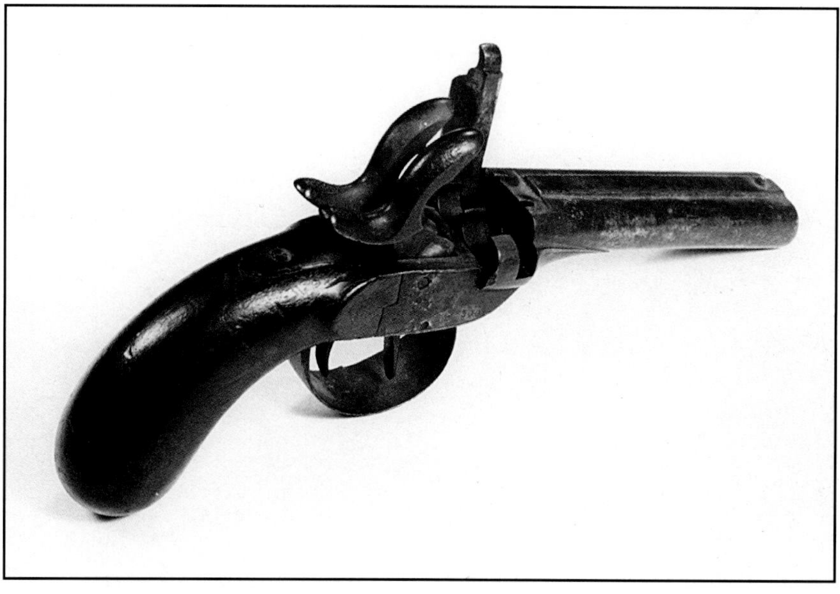

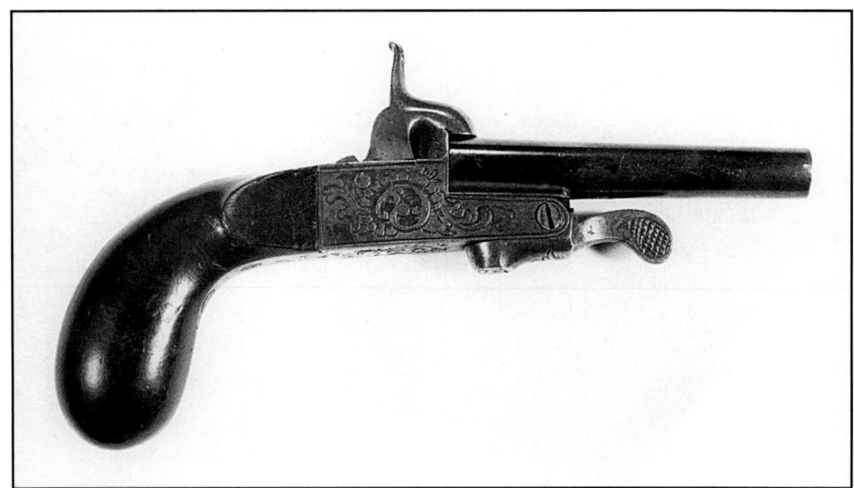

Plate 6-51 (right). A fine quality 7mm caliber, single-shot pinfire pistol manufactured in France, marked with St. Etienne proofmarks. When the locking lever at the front of the frame is turned to the side, the tip-down barrel opens for loading or extraction. *Courtesy James Lowther; John Calcany photograph*

Plate 6-52 (right, center). A 12mm caliber, single-shot pinfire pistol probably of French origin. The 2-inch barrel has straight rifling and swivels to the right for loading. Its underside is marked, *"T 13 Dse"*, and lacks proofmarks. Overall length is under 4 inches. *Courtesy Larry Compeau; F.W. Hulbert photograph*

Plate 6-53 (below). A French-made, 12mm caliber, single-shot pinfire pistol designed to fire shot cartridges. The long barrel has St. Etienne proofmarks and is marked *"12.6"* underneath near the front support handle; the barrel tips down for loading and extraction. *Courtesy James Lowther; John Calcany photograph*

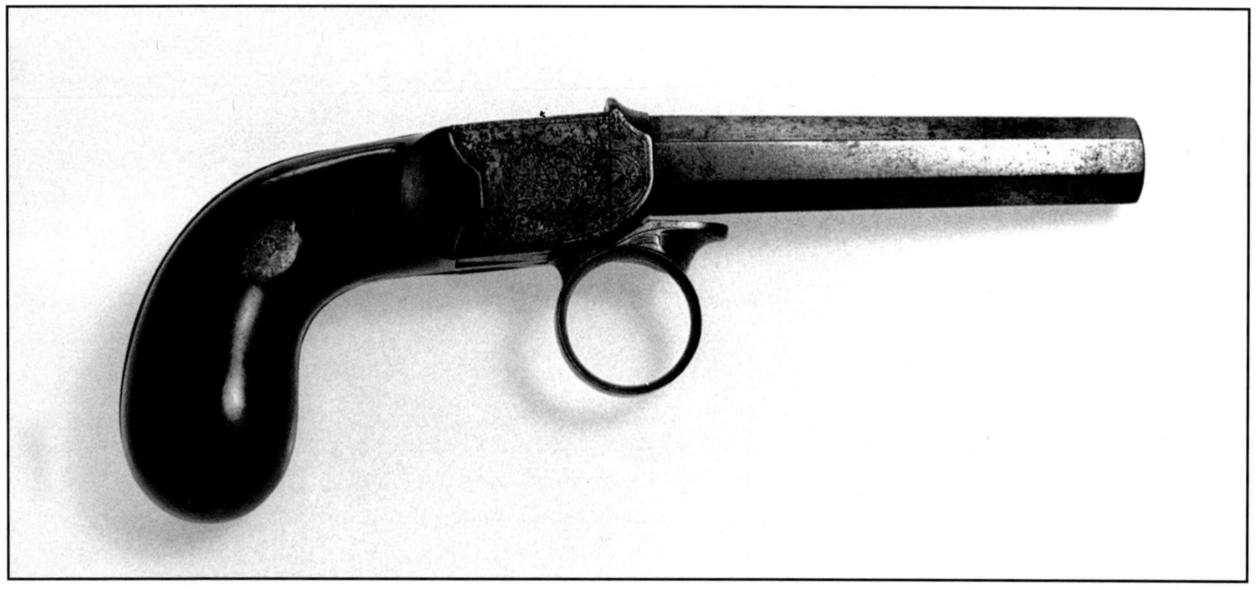

Plate 6-54. A 12mm caliber, single-shot pinfire pistol similar in design to the example pictured in *Plate 6-55*, but having an underhammer action with ring trigger. This pistol, like the example below, is of early production; both are desirable additions to a collection of pinfire arms. *Courtesy Don Kramer; F.W. Hulbert photograph*

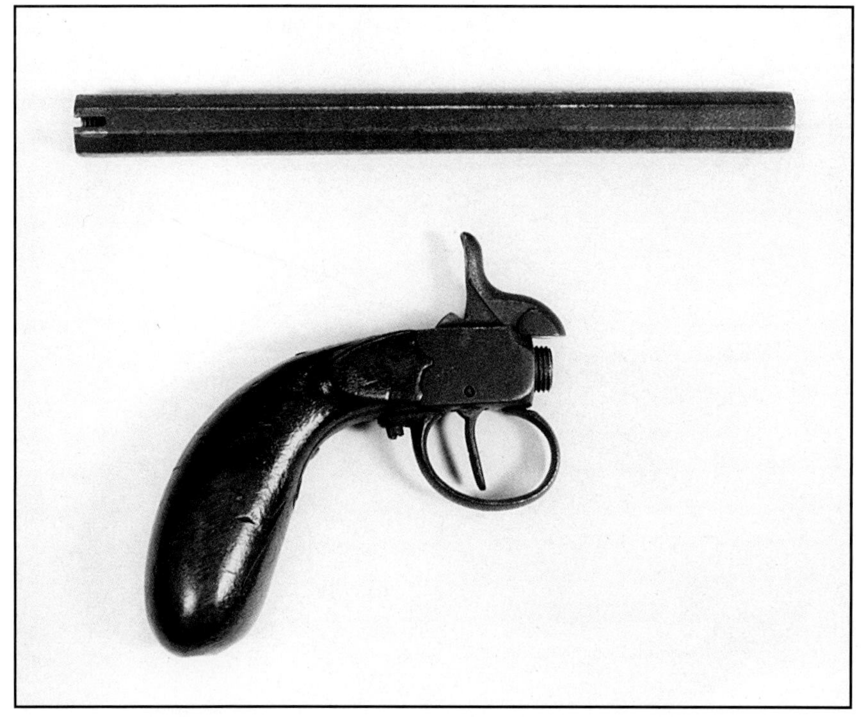

Plate 6-55 (left). A Belgian made, 9mm caliber, single-shot pinfire pistol. The barrel bearing Liége proofmarks is unscrewed for loading; a cartridge is placed into the chamber, and the barrel re-screwed onto the short threaded breech. Single-action operation only, it is similar to earlier percussion pistols with screw-off barrels, but of higher quality. *Courtesy James Lowther; John Calcany photograph*

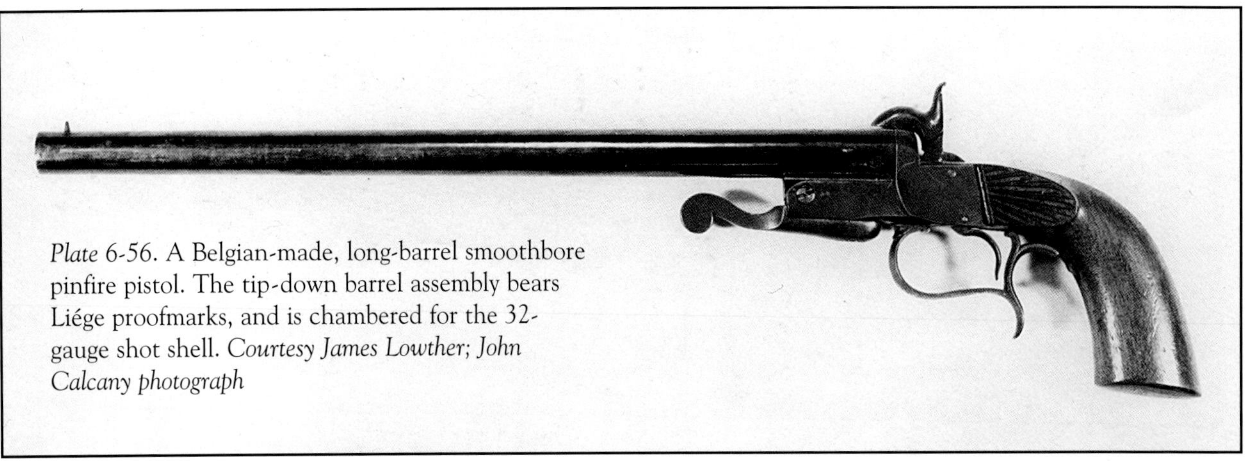

Plate 6-56. A Belgian-made, long-barrel smoothbore pinfire pistol. The tip-down barrel assembly bears Liége proofmarks, and is chambered for the 32-gauge shot shell. *Courtesy James Lowther; John Calcany photograph*

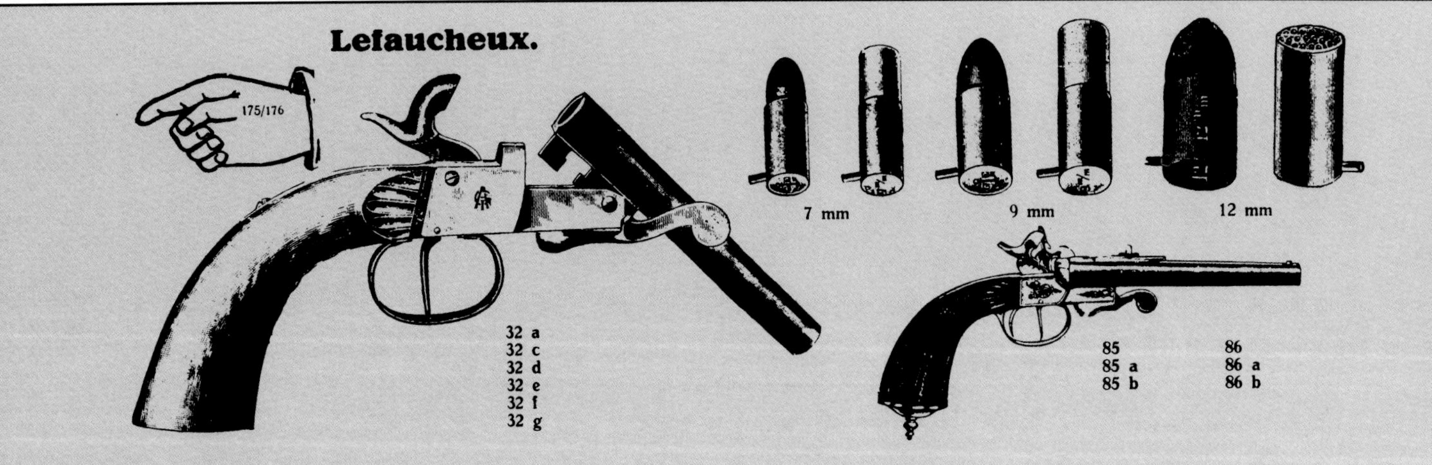

Plate 6-57 (above). From the 1911 ALFA arms catalog (Germany): "*Pin-Fire-Pistols Mark 'Kropp'.*" Those at left range in price from DM6 (US$1.43) for a 7mm pistol without cartridge ejector, to DM9 (US$2.14) for a 12mm pistol with ejector. The fancier pistols at right cost DM9.5 to DM10.8. Pinfire cartridges in 7mm caliber cost $6.07 per thousand. *Chris C. Curtis collection*

Plate 6-58 (right). Circa 1864, this illustration is from the catalog of New York military dealer Schuyler, Hartley & Graham. Among the many offerings is this fancy tip-down, double-barrel 7mm caliber pinfire pistol. *Chris C. Curtis collection*

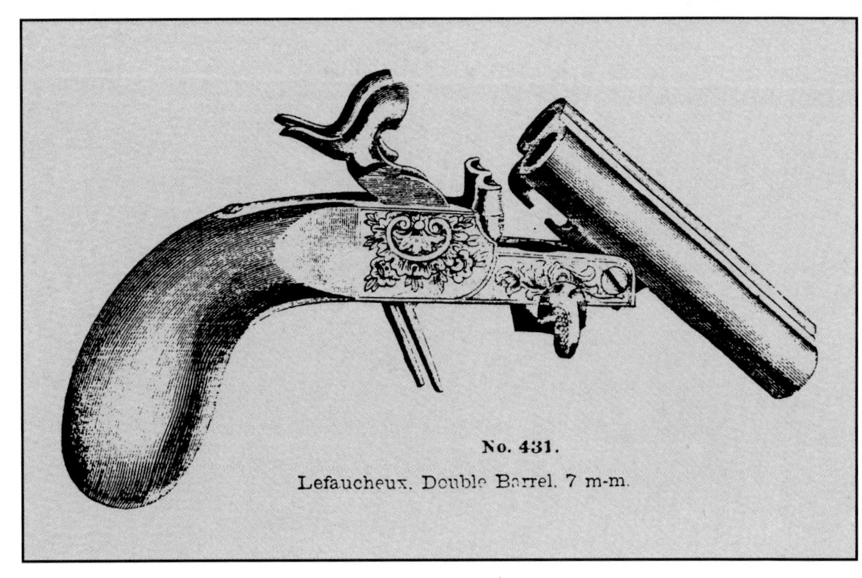

Plate 6-59 (left). A French-made, single-shot pinfire pistol. The barrel bears St. Etienne proofmarks indicating manufacture between 1879 and 1885, and also is marked *"F. Voytier"* and *"15.0"* (for the 15-gauge shot shell). *Courtesy private collection; John Calcany photograph*

Plate 6-60 (right). An unusual, single-shot *"Trabuco"* or blunderbuss pinfire pistol. The 6½-inch belled brass barrel is 16-gauge, having a rifled section 1½-inch in length; it bears pre-1877 Belgian proof and inspector's marks. The pistol measures 11 inches overall. *Courtesy Larry Compeau; F.W. Hulbert photograph*

Plate 6-61 (left). A cased pair of French-made, double-barrel 9mm caliber pinfire pistols. The barrels are marked *"Boissy"*, and bear pre-1868 St. Etienne proofmarks. The common type of tip-down barrel pistols having folding triggers which drop down when the hammers reach full cock, this pair is engraved and fitted with flute-carved ebony grips indicating better than average quality. The label in the case lid reads, *"Edward London—Gun Maker. 51 London Wall, London. Merchants, Captains, and Others Supplied with all Kinds of Firearms, Ammunition, etc. for Exportation on the Lowest possible Terms. N.B. An assortment of Rifles for Canada and the East Indies."* This maker worked in London *circa* 1870-1872. *Courtesy James Lowther; John Calcany photograph*

Plate 6-62 (left). An engraved, double-barrel, 7mm caliber pinfire pistol having ivory grips and the rare combination rear sight and sliding pin safety. Concealed at the bottom of a lady's traveling sewing box, this constitutes an unusual variant cased set. *Courtesy Mario Pancino; F.W. Hulbert photograph*

Plate 6-63 (left). Another rare variant, this Belgian-made, 12mm caliber single-shot pinfire pistol at first appears to be a standard revolver. Note the swing-out breechblock which is locked in place by the ejector rod. The barrel is marked, *"Mariette Brevete"*, and bears pre-1877 inspector's marks. *Courtesy private collection; F.W. Hulbert photograph*

Plate 6-64 (right). A French 14mm caliber, single-shot pinfire pistol, high-quality, floral-engraved, and fitted with a finely-checkered grip having silver buttcap. The tip-down octagonal barrel is marked, *"Brun Bte a Paris"*, and *"Invention Lefaucheux a Paris 412."* Originally one of a cased pair. *Courtesy Don Kramer; Ferrari Color photograph*

Identifying and Collecting Pinfire Arms

ost of us become antique firearms collectors due to a love of history and a desire to possess something with historical signficance, along with perhaps an appreciation for firearms as art, or as simple mechanical curiosities. One of the most satisfying facets of antique arms ownership is the study of the origins and use of the pieces comprising our collection.

We might ask, "What was the state of the world on the day this gun left the factory? What did its original owner do with it during the time he owned this piece? What historical events might this gun have been a witness to?" These and similar questions arise in our minds as we contemplate the different pieces in our collection, or consider the purchase of something new to add to it.

Identification

Unfortunately for collectors of pinfire arms, serial numbers, dates of production, quantities of guns produced, and even information about the manufacturers themselves—data generally available to collectors of Colt firearms and many other makes, in particular those made in America—simply is not readily obtainable. Between the era of the pinfire system and the present day Europe has experienced three major wars, in addition to several periods of lesser social upheaval, and as a result many armsmakers' records were destroyed or so scattered as to make systematic research almost impossible. Then, too, European gun manufacturers of the latter half of the nineteenth century were more concerned with producing low-cost arms to fill the enormous demands placed on them by various governments, the military, and the civilian markets, than with preserving accurate records for the convenience of today's collectors and historians. The manufacturers of pinfire arms in Europe were many, and prolific, producing countless thousands of guns annually. Their halcyon years—the latter half of the nineteenth century—roughly correspond to the same period in America when numerous firearms makers were flooding the market with cheaply made spur-trigger, solid-frame, top-break "Saturday Night Special" revolvers in vast numbers.

Most pinfire cartridge arms were not marked with their makers' names, country of origin, or a date that would allow the establishment of the time period during which they were made. However, some were so marked, and bear names both familiar and not-so-familiar to the collecting world. Adding to the confusion, occasionally a gun will be marked with *two* names, that of its maker as well as that of the retailer. Because it was not customary for European manufacturers to market their own products, they relied on others to sell the finished goods. Thus many retailers and sales agents marked firearms with their names, as well.

When an abbreviation of the French word *"Inventor"* (*"Invr"*, *"Ivon"*, or *"Ivion"*) precedes or follows a name found on a certain firearm, it usually identifies the individual named as having been directly associated with the design, invention, and/or manufacture of that arm. The word *"Brevete"* (or its abbreviations *"Bte"* and *"Bvte"*) is not quite as helpful. As explained in Chapter Two, this marking, while giving some insight into the origin of the firearm, does not positively identify the person named as the designer or manufacturer.

In many cases, the inventor or patentee of a pinfire arm would subcontract, or license, the production of his gun to another firm. Many pistols marked *"E. Lefaucheux Brevete"* were manufactured in Belgium and bear Liége proof marks, and thus are not the true products of Lefaucheux. Still other Belgian arms were marked *"Systeme Lefaucheux"*, possibly to credit Lefaucheux as the inventor and to avoid any potential legal action resulting from patent infringement. Many Lefaucheux arms also bear the letters *"S.G.D.G."*[1] within the usual barrel or frame markings, which was typical practice for many firearms inventors and manufacturers (as well as others) in France. The *S.G.D.G.* marking was a formality which notified the public that the French government, while it granted a patent, neither guaranteed the quality or the priority of the patent, nor claim of invention of an object or medicinal remedy (law of July 5, 1844), and thus the term refers not just to firearms but to other goods, as well.[2] Many early-production Lefaucheux revolvers bear this *S.G.D.G.* marking, in addition to the markings of other makers of the era, such as Javelle of St. Etienne, and Jarre of Paris.

While many French firearms, especially those made by Lefaucheux, are well-marked, it is unfortunate indeed that not all pinfire arms may be so easily identified as to their maker or country of origin. In many cases only the sales agent's or retailer's name (if even that) appears on a weapon, rendering it difficult if not impossible to identify the actual maker of the gun.

Perhaps this is an appropriate place to eliminate the two "famous European gunmakers", *"Acier Fondu"* and *"Guss Stahl"*, from our list of known pinfire manufacturers. Many Belgian, French, and German arms are so marked; rather than being their makers' names, however, the terms instead mean "Cast Steel"! It also is apropos here to clarify another mistaken idea concerning pinfire arms numbering. Lefaucheux used a consecutive serial numbering system, as did the majority of British gun and pistol makers; if an English shotgun, for instance, bears serial number "100", in most cases it was the one hundredth of its type made. The same does not hold true for the vast majority of pinfire revolvers, especially those manufactured in Belgium, where firearms were individually crafted in small shops. There, when individual guns were disassembled for finishing and/or embellishing, their major components were stamped with Arabic (sometimes Roman) letters to avoid mixing parts during reassembly. The practice resulted in guns often bearing one- or two-digit "assembly"—not serial—numbers. Although many collectors prefer to own low serial number guns, in the case of the common pinfire revolver it is nothing more than a random number assigned to a gun that was completed in a particular day or week.

Now that the question of "who" (the name of the maker or retailer) has been to some degree answered, we can next move to the questions of "where" and "when." For these answers we look to the European system of proofmarks, which can be helpful at least with the partial attribution of unmarked firearms.

Proofmarks in General

It is not the authors' intent here to create a standard reference for, or a history of, all European proofmarks. But in addition to a discussion of the proofs used during the pinfire arms period, a listing of all proofmarks used during that era also will be attempted.

The application of proofmarks to firearms dates back to the sixteenth century, local with guild and city marks going back even earlier. The purpose of proofmarking a firearm was to ensure public safety, by controlling the quality of all arms produced and sold within a given geographic area or political entity. A proof house was a government-established or approved organization "for the purpose of insuring the proper and careful manufacture of firearms and for making provision for proving the barrels of such firearms...."[3] This was accomplished by a series of tests involving the actual firing of the gun and barrel during several stages of manufacture and assembly. After the barrels alone were tested by firing them into a bed of sand, *provisional* proofmarks were applied to each barrel that had successfully passed the test. The firearm was then completely asssembled and tested again; included were the lock mechanism and the general operation of the gun. At that time a *definitive* (final) proofmark was stamped onto the gun (in the case of revolvers, usually on the cylinder).

Thus proofmarks are helpful in identifying the country, and sometimes even the city, of origin for a firearm. Establishing a precise date of manufacture is more difficult and, in most cases, impossible, as many proofmarks were used over long periods of time. Given the lack of a uniform serial numbering system, or factory production records, we are forced to accept a *period*, as opposed to an actual *date*, of manufacture.

French Proofmarks (*Figures a through q*)

Inasmuch as France was the birthplace of the pinfire system, our study of pinfire arms proofmarks rightly begins with that country.

While the gunmakers in the city of St. Etienne had been using a voluntary proof system since the early sixteenth century, the official adoption of firearms proofing in France did not take place until the year 1700. The practice was not strictly enforced until December 14, 1810, however, when Napoleon issued an executive order decreeing a compulsory proofing system, and from that date all firearms manufactured within the French Empire were subjected to varying degrees of proof testing.

The St. Etienne city proofmark, prior to the compulsory proofing law of 1810, appeared as a variation of the city's coat of arms. That mark

came to be regarded as a symbol of quality, and was easily recognized even in the remoter areas to which St. Etienne arms were exported and sold (see *Figures a* through *d*).

Then, on August 5, 1885, as the result of a court decision, the president of France signed into law an act abolishing compulsory proofing. Voluntary proof testing of arms once again became the norm, but the industry did not vary from its established procedure for proving firearms. Gun manufacturers felt that customers would be hesitant to buy firearms without proper proofmarks, and the St. Etienne proof house continued normal operations under government supervision, using the marks from the 1868 law.

A new proof house was established in Paris by official decree in November of 1895. At the same time proof charges were approved, which became effective on July 30, 1897.

Belgian Proofmarks (*Figures r through ee*)

At the time Napoleon issued his mandatory proof regulations in France, the area of Belgium in which the city of Liége is located had been recently conquered by the French Army and incorporated into the French Empire. But Liége gunmakers were reluctant to accept the St. Etienne regulations governing proof testing. Although proofmarks had been in general use in Belgium since as early as 1672, many Liége manufacturers enjoyed a flourishing trade selling unmarked arms to foreign merchants who in turn stamped their own names onto the weapons. Beginning in 1810, however, no one argued with success against Napoleon, and his rules of proof became law in Belgium as well as in France.

When Belgium was returned to being an independent kingdom in 1830, gun manufacturers there attempted to resume their former policy of avoiding identifying marks. But the government of King Leopold issued its own proof law, very similar to Napoleon's decree of 1810, which went into effect on March 29, 1836. Various additional decrees were issued during the succeeding years, and on December 20, 1849 existing Belgian proof

text continued on page 211

French Proofmarks

Figure a	February 19, 1824 to April 30, 1856		Definitive proofmark for St. Etienne arms.
Figure b	April 30, 1856 to April 22, 1868		Definitive proofmark for St. Etienne arms. *Replaced proofmark "a".*
Figure c	1869 to 1886		Definitive proofmark for St. Etienne arms. *Replaced proofmark "b".*
Figure d	April 20, 1879 to August 1885		Provisional proofmark for unfinished arms manufactured at St. Etienne.
Figure e	April 20, 1879 to August 1885		Provisional proofmark for unfinished arms made elsewhere, and imported into France.
Figure f	April 20, 1879 to August 1885		Provisional proofmark for arms made in France, other than by St. Etienne.
Figure g	1886 to July 30, 1897		Definitive proofmark for finished arms. *Replaced proofmark "c".*
Figure h	1892 to 1923		St. Etienne proofmark for unfinished barrels.
Figure i	October 18, 1893 to July 30, 1897		Definitive proofmark applied to St. Etienne arms which had undergone stronger testing.
Figure j	July 30, 1897 to 1923	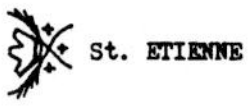	St. Etienne proofmark for finished barrels.
Figure k	July 30, 1897 to 1923		Paris proofmark for unfinished barrels.
Figure l	July 30, 1897 to 1923		Paris proofmark for finished barrels.

Figure m	July 30, 1897 to 1923		St. Etienne proofmark for guns tested in a finished state. *Replaced proofmark "g".*
Figure n	July 30, 1897 to 1923		Paris proofmark for finished arms.
Figure o	July 30, 1897 to 1923		St. Etienne proofmark for arms given reinforced testing in a finished state. *Replaced proofmark "i".*
Figure p	July 30, 1897 to 1923		Paris proofmark for arms given reinforced testing in a finished state.
Figure q	1901 to 1923	N.A.	Proofmark indicating finished but not joined barrels; also for arms exported in an unassembled state. Used in conjunction with the proofmark for finished barrels by both the St. Etienne and Paris proof houses.

Belgian Proofmarks

Figure r	February 20, 1811 to July 11, 1893		Definitive Liége proofmark.
Figure s	December 21, 1852 to December 30, 1853		Inspector's proofmark; mainly applied to arms in stock when the new mark was introduced by the Board of Administration.
Figure t	June 16, 1853 to Present		Provisional Liége barrel proofmark.
Figure u	December 30, 1853 to January 26, 1877		Inspector's proofmark applied after arm left proof house; ensured against weakening modifications. *Replaced proofmark "s".*
Figure v	June 16, 1853 to Present		Liége "Perron" or lower proofmark, used on barrels of breechloading, tip-down arms.
Figure w	January 26, 1877 to Present		Inspector's proofmark. *Replaced proofmark "u"* (changed to this configuration after complaints from London proof house claiming a similarity of marks).

Figure	Date	Mark	Description
Figure x	April 16, 1878 to January 30, 1897	NON POUR BALLE	Barrel proofmark for choke-bored shotguns.
Figure y	July 11, 1893 to Present	(ELG with crown)	Definitive Liége proofmark indicating stronger testing; eliminated the need for further testing by countries importing Belgian arms. *Replaced proofmark "r".*
Figure z	July 11, 1893 to 1924	CH B RAYE	Barrel proofmark for wholly- or partially-rifled choke bores.
Figure aa	January 30, 1894 to 1924	NON RAYE	Used on the unrifled barrels of Flobert arms, multi-shot pistols, and revolvers; caliber marking used with this proofmark.
Figure bb	January 30, 1894 to Present	R (with crown)	Proofmark stamped on rifled barrels of above-described arms.
Figure cc	January 30, 1897 to 1910	(16 C in diamond)	Chamber gauge for barrels given compulsory black powder proofmark.
Figure dd	January 30, 1897 to October 4, 1898	CHOKE	Proofmark for choke-bored shotguns. *Replaced proofmark "x".*
Figure ee	October 4, 1898 to 1910	CHOKE 17.0 16.2	Proofmark for choke-bored shotguns; added marks for muzzle diameter and barrel diameter, 22cm from breech. *Replaced proofmark "dd".*

regulations were again confirmed. At the same time additional provisional proof regulations were added, and all firearms destined for commerce, both those imported into Belgium and those manufactured locally, were subjected to the existing proof laws.

With the introduction in 1852 and 1853 of inspectors' marks, additional assurance was added that a firearm had not been tampered with after definitive proof testing. The intent of inspection following final testing was to prevent any modification which might weaken the structure of the firearm. The marks were to be applied by independent inspectors, each of whom was assigned an identifying letter of the alphabet to be stamped on the firearm, plus a crown over the letter. The identity of the individual inspectors and the letters assigned to them were kept secret, to such a degree that the names of the inspectors and the dates that they worked have never been revealed. If at some time that information surfaces, the task of attributing dates of manufacture to Belgian firearms will be made much easier.

It is interesting to note here that some Belgian proofmarks were adopted and used by the proof house for a period of time before becoming officially adopted by royal order. Others were abandoned long before a royal decree made their termination official. Thus it is possible that a firearm might be older than the official date listed for adoption of the proofmark it bears; conversely, it could never be newer than the date listed for abandonment of a mark found on it.

British Proofmarks (*Figures ff through ss*)

On the 14th of March 1637, several gunsmiths joined together by order of England's King Charles I to found "The Worshipful Company of Gunmakers of the City of London." At that time they also established their own proofmark, which remains in use today in essentially unaltered form (*see Figure ff*).

In the year 1670 the Worshipful Company's charter was confirmed, and its powers were extended. It was then that the London "view" mark (*see Figure gg*) was adopted, to be applied during the inspection following proof. In 1813 the jurisdiction of the London proof house was expanded to encompass all of England and Wales, and during the same year an additional proof house was founded in the city of Birmingham, which had long been a major armsmaking center. The proofmark selected by the Birmingham firearms-making trade was one of crossed scepters (a mark in use for many years prior by one of Birmingham's leading makers, Ketland), plus the letters "BCP" (Birmingham Company Proof) to indicate provisional proof testing. The letter "V" was added for the final "view" test (*see Figures hh and ii*).

A new proof law passed in 1855 confirmed the two separate proof houses, in London and Birmingham, and their respective marks. The same law also defined the types of arms required to undergo proof testing.

In 1868 another revision of the British proof laws was enacted by Parliament, but with no major additions to the existing laws in the areas of firearms testing or marking. The enforcement powers of the proof laws were strengthened, however, to impose a penalty of twenty pounds sterling as punishment for selling a gun barrel without proofmarks, or for incorrectly representing a foreign-made barrel as being British manufactured. Neither imported barrels or complete arms were required to be tested, if they already had been tested and marked by a foreign proof house acceptable to the British regulators.

A series of additions kept the Proof Act of 1868 current until 1875, when the rules for proof testing choke-bored barrels were first introduced (*see Figures nn through qq*). Further rules were added in 1887 and 1896, providing new marks and a table to indicate bore diameter in thousands of an inch, for all gauges. Those rules, with the addition of new proof rules in 1904, were later modified to keep abreast of the modern developments in firearms and nitro powder.

British Proofmarks

Figure ff	March 14, 1637 to Present		Provisional proofmark of the London proof house.
Figure gg	1670 to Present		"View" proofmark applied at inspection following final testing; definitive proofmark of the London proof house.
Figure hh	1813 to 1904		Provisional proofmark of the Birmingham proof house.
Figure ii	1813 to 1904		Final or definitive proofmark of the Birmingham proof house; "V" stands for "View."
Figure jj	1855 to Present		London provisional proofmark for unfinished barrels.
Figure kk	1855 to Present		Birmingham provisional proofmark for unfinished barrels.
Figure ll	1868 to 1925		London proofmark indicating single final test using load strength of definitive proof test.
Figure mm	1868 to 1925		Birmingham proofmark indicating final proof, bypassing provisional proof but using load strength of definitive proof test.
Figure nn	1875 to 1887		London proofmarks for choke-bored barrels.
Figure oo	1875 to 1887		Birmingham proofmarks for choke-bored barrels.
Figure pp	1887 to 1904		London proofmarks for choke-bored barrels. *Replaced proofmark "nn".*

Figure qq	1887 to 1904		Birmingham proofmarks for choke-bored barrels. *Replaced proofmark "oo".*
Figure rr	1887 to 1904		Birmingham proof house provisional proofmark. *Replaced proofmark "hh".*
Figure ss	1904 to 1925		Birmingham proof house definitive proofmark. *Replaced proofmark "ii".*

German Proofmarks

Figure tt			Applied to domestic and foreign arms made prior to 1893 but in stock when 1893 proof law took effect.
Figure uu			Optional definitive proofmark; used after 1893.
Figure vv	1893 to 1939		Definitive proofmark used on revolvers.

Spanish Proofmarks

Figure ww			Provisional proofmark for shotgun barrels.
Figure xx			Provisional proofmark for shotgun barrels tested with black powder; also final proofmark for muzzleloading shotguns.
Figure yy			Definitive proofmark for breechloading shotguns; usually accompanied by the above two marks.
Figure zz			Final proofmark for breechloading shotguns having a lever under forestock, usually accompanied by proofmarks "ww" and "xx".
Figure aaa			Final proofmark for breechloading shotguns having two or more locking lugs; usually accompanied by proofmarks "ww" and "xx", and occasionally all four above proofmarks.

German Proofmarks (*Figures tt through vv*)

The history of proof testing and marking firearms in Germany dates to the year 1600. Although the country has long been a major producer of arms, no mandatory system of proof testing existed until Germany's *Reichstag* passed the Proof Law of May 19, 1891, which became effective on April 1, 1893. The law stated that no firearm of any type was to be sold within Germany's borders without its lock and barrel bearing the prescribed proofmark. Exempted from the rule were imported arms already proof tested and marked by a foreign proof house whose standards were recognized and accepted by the German proof establishment.

Military small arms sold in Germany were exempted as well, unless they had undergone some type of alteration, such as rechambering for a different caliber or type of cartridge. A finished gun could be submitted for a single proof test, but the proof load had to be the strength of the first proof rather than the customary lighter load used for testing finished arms.

Many German firearms bear the mark shown here as *Figure tt*, the "V" denoting "*Vorrat*", or "supply." This mark was applied to both domestic and foreign arms produced prior to 1893, and in stock or in the possession of dealers when the proof rules became effective that year. Firearms stamped with this mark were not actually proof tested, and were not required to undergo any further proof. But many gun owners and dealers voluntarily submitted their arms for proof firing to increase their salability at a time of heightened consumer awareness of the protection provided by firearms proof laws.

The mark shown as *Figure uu* is the final definitive proofmark applied on revolvers after 1893. It was applied to arms tested in the finished state, accompanied by the stamp shown in *Figure vv*. The "*Crown over U*" occasionally is seen with the German "*Eagle*" mark, but in the case of the markings found on most German pinfire revolvers a second crown also is present, indicating a second proof as required by the 1893 law. This "*Double Crown over U*" mark was used on revolvers from 1893 until new proof regulations were introduced in 1939, and is the final German proofmark of any value to collectors in identifying pinfire arms of the period.

Spanish Proofmarks (*Figures ww through aaa*)

According to the accepted belief of many firearms historians, proof testing in Spain was first conducted during the sixteenth century at the Royal Arsenal in Palencia. However, the first government sponsored proof houses were not established until 1844 in the city of Eibar, which even today remains Spain's major armsmaking area. As was the case in France, proof testing in Spain was voluntary during the pinfire era, and until established in 1923 the country did not enforce any compulsory firearms proof laws. The following illustrate the Spanish proofmarks in use prior to 1910. Yet the majority of Spanish-made pinfire arms will not bear proofmarks, especially the low-cost handguns made for export.

Figure ww shows the provisional proofmark used on shotgun barrels. *Figure xx* represents the provisional proofmark used on shotgun barrels tested with black powder; it was the final proof for muzzleloading shotguns. *Figure yy* was the definitive proofmark for breechloading shotguns; usually it is accompanied by the two preceding marks. *Figure zz* was the final proofmark for breechloading shotguns having a lever under the forestock; it also will be accompanied by the first two marks. *Figure aaa* shows the final proofmark for breechloading shotguns with two or more locking lugs; those arms also bear the first two proofmarks, and in some cases, all four.

Proofmarks in Use Elsewhere

The existing records of armsmakers in the remaining countries of Europe in which pinfire arms were manufactured and sold provide little or no information about the origins of unmarked pinfire arms.

The proofmarking of firearms in Italy remained on a voluntary basis until 1923, when as in Spain the first compulsory proof laws were established by royal edict. Relatively few pinfire arms were fabricated in Switzerland, and during the pinfire era the country proof-tested only its military arms. Norway manufactured military pinfire revolvers in small numbers, but no mention has been noted of their proof testing or marking.

Pinfire arms made in South America were mostly copies of the European guns imported there during the period. On occasion, rough castings were imported to be assembled and finished, but like the arms manufactured in South America they bear no identifying features or proofmarks, and cannot be accurately traced to their origins.

As a consequence, it must be assumed that pinfire arms which lack proofmarks either are of late French manufacture, after the compulsory French firearms proofing laws had expired, or are the products of European countries operating with non-compulsory proof laws.

Another possible explanation, albeit a remote one, is that an unmarked pinfire arm is the product of American manufacture, where the proof testing and marking of firearms have never been accepted practices. It is established fact that pinfire *ammunition* was fabricated in the United States, both during and after the Civil War, and that surplus arms used in that conflict were utilized in America for many years afterward. Add to that the fact that many immigrants brought their pinfire arms with them to the New World, and we can state with some certainty that nineteenth century American shooters were familiar with the pinfire system. Yet it is doubtful that American arms manufacturers gave serious consideration to producing firearms chambered for pinfire cartridges, while superior rimfire and centerfire ammunition was readily available. Whereas in Europe the pinfire system was an intermediate step between the percussion and the rimfire/centerfire cartridge systems, American armsmakers made the transition directly from percussion arms, which remained in vogue longer, into the modern era of rimfire/centerfire ammunition.

Collecting Pinfire Arms

Only recently has the significance of the pinfire cartridge system in the evolution of firearms been acknowledged by the gun collecting world. Today, firearms designed for the pinfire cartridge are rising from the depths of obscurity to become desirable collector's items. This growing interest on the part of collectors has been accompanied by a resultant increase in values, and pinfire guns which until recently were practically without value now are found on the sales lists of prominent antique firearms dealers. Many of them are becoming expensive.

Yet in the overall scope of gun collecting, pinfire arms are still reasonably priced. A fairly comprehensive and sizable collection of them might be assembled in a relatively short period of time, and at relatively modest cost. A fascinating and seemingly-endless array of styles, sizes, calibers, and variations awaits the collector who devotes his interest and energies to the pinfire system.

The calibers to be found in pinfire handguns range from the diminutive 2mm, through 5m, 7mm, 9mm, and 12mm, to the huge 15mm caliber cartridge. Shotgun bores range in size from 4 gauge through 28 gauge to 14mm, with some unusual odd sizes falling between the standard gauges.

A great variety of frame styles and barrel designs can be found among the profusion of pinfire arm types. Included are designs which attempted to speed up the loading and cartridge ejection processes, which in themselves make for an interesting collection. Pinfire firepower begins with modest single-shot weapons, continues with two- to four-shot capacities, and from there to revolvers having cylinders chambered with five, six, seven, eight or ten shots, and reaches its zenith with the twin-ring cylinder revolvers having twelve, fifteen, eighteen, twenty, twenty-one, and even thirty shots! While pinfire arms of all the usual configurations will be found, a great many firearms considered to be "oddities" were designed to utilize the pinfire cartridge, and these too have captured the attention of specialized collectors.

Within the broad category of pinfire arms are

numerous areas of more specific interest, in which collectors may choose to concentrate their attention and efforts. Revolvers might be the least expensive avenue for one to assemble a representative collection, as many styles, calibers, and sizes of pinfire revolvers exist. An excellent collection of them could number sixty or seventy-five pieces, without duplication, and consist of military models as well as examples by the important makers and from all the principal pinfire arms-producing countries. A revolver collection might be expanded to include pinfire pepperboxes, being basically revolvers having rotating multi-barrel groups instead of separate cylinders and barrels. Such a collection might number specimens in all the many pinfire calibers, the most expensive of which would be the rare 15mm caliber models, the all-brass revolvers, the scarce 5mm caliber revolver, and 12mm caliber pepperboxes. Other revolvers which bring premium prices include the Lefaucheux Model 1854, because of its known use by soldiers on both sides during the American Civil War.

Yet the collector might opt to narrow his scope while staying within the specialty category of pinfire revolvers, concentrating on just pepperboxes or guns of just one style, caliber, or manufacturer. An example is the "Guardian-American Model of 1878" revolver; it is a fairly common model and can be obtained at rather modest cost (excepting the uncommon 9mm and 12mm calibers). *Plate 7-1* illustrates three sizes and three slightly different configurations of the Guardian revolver. All three are 7mm caliber, and bear Liége proofmarks. *Plate 7-2* pictures a better-quality example of the Guardian in the scarce 9mm caliber; it possesses fine engraving, fancy carved grips, an extended-length barrel, and pre-1877 Liége inspector's marks.

The Guardian revolvers display a wide range of grip styles, barrel lengths, and calibers, providing enough variety to form an impressive "collection within a collection." While their actual manufacturer is unknown, the Belgian armsmaker, Clement, is a likely candidate. As Clement and Company, and later under his name alone,

Clement produced firearms in Liége between 1862 and 1904. Though not all were pinfire arms, Clement marked a number of them in English with Americanized names, such as "The Washington .38", "The White House .38", "The Bad To Beat American Model of 1887", and "The American Settler."

The "Guardian-American Model of 1878" enjoyed considerably more success than did others in the highly-competitive field of low-cost handguns during the late nineteenth century, and Clement produced them throughout the entire pinfire era. Examples are known having Liége inspectors' marks indicating manufacture during the pre-1877 period, during the 1877 to 1893 period, and during the later post-1893 period of pinfire production. While the name "Guardian-American Model of 1878" would indicate that the model was manufactured solely for export to America, in fact it was widely distributed in England and throughout all of Europe by such notable agents as H. Gotz of Berlin, L. Chobert of Paris, and L. Ancion Marx Company of Liége.

In recent years one prominent collector of pinfire arms from San Diego, California decided to specialize even further within the field. He chose the area of pinfire arms fabricated entirely from "brass" (although when tested by a metallurgist, the majority of them proved to be made of bronze). While certainly scarcer than those made from the more standard materials, he managed to assemble an impressive collection of revolvers in calibers 5mm, 7mm, 9mm, and 12mm, both plain and engraved models, and added pepperboxes to the final mix for a most impressive array.

A number of theories exist surrounding these all-brass (or bronze) pinfire revolvers. Some experts proclaim that they were destined for naval use, or for customers residing near the sea, as a bronze material is less susceptible to the corrosive effects of saltwater. Some state they were in fact salesmens' samples, while still others lean toward the possibility of their being the work of arms apprentices, a sort of "final exam" to be submitted to the master gunsmith. None of these theories has

Plate 7-1 (above). The "Guardian" Belgian-made 7mm caliber pinfire revolver, shown in three sizes. Note the non-folding trigger (and perhaps missing triggerguard) of the top example. Folding triggers are the most common feature of pinfire pocket revolvers. *Courtesy private collection; John Calcany photograph*

Plate 7-2 (right). Another "Guardian" revolver, this one of military configuration. It is engraved, fitted with carved grips, and chambered for the scarce 9mm caliber cartridge. *Courtesy private collection; John Calcany photograph*

been proven, or is embraced by the author, due to a lack of evidence. Most bronze pinfire revolvers are nicely made, and are found both plain and embellished. Some have bronze frames only, with the high-wear parts such as hammers, triggers, springs, and ejector rods made of steel, proving that they were indeed intended for actual use.

If a collector's interest leans in the direction of shotguns, enough variety in styles, gauges, action variations, and makers exists to assemble a most interesting specialty collection. Another area, pinfire oddities, might make for a fascinating and educational display; but as collectors have long pursued "curiosa-type" weapons their prices are much higher.

A general collection, which would number all types of firearms designed to use pinfire ammunition, might have the broadest appeal, but would require more time to assemble and would be more expensive due to the wider variety of guns needed. Included in this type of collection would be single- and double-barrel pistols, single- and double-barrel rifles, revolving rifles, single- and double-barrel shotguns, pepperboxes, and perhaps several types of oddities. All of these guns would compliment a basic collection consisting of a large and varied group of pinfire revolvers.

When the new collector of pinfire arms has decided on a general category, the next logical step is to locate and purchase guns that fall within his specific area of interest. Fortunately, pinfire cartridge arms of all types, sizes, descriptions, and price ranges are available at gun shows, auctions, in the listings of arms dealers, and now on the World Wide Web. Prices can range from modest to breathtaking, depending on a gun's quality, condition, and historic value, on the seller's needs, and of course on the personal preferences and budget of the buyer.

Always it is difficult to accurately judge the value of individual arms, and occasionally a very desirable or important piece has been allowed to slip away. Both dealers and collectors of antique arms have the need to determine as nearly as possible the accurate value of every item in their possession, and every buyer and seller, certainly one contemplating the sale of a significant ancestor's firearm, needs to be aware of the fair market value of the item in question.

Economic inflation and the growing interest in pinfire arms both in Europe and America are factors which render impractical the construction of an accurate price guide for them. But collectors may rest assured that values are increasing rapidly. Any attempt to establish value guidelines would be outdated virtually before publication.

Rather than a price guide, the authors believe a sliding scale of pinfire arms rarity and desirability is of more value to collectors, such as the one presented on the facing page. Beginning with Level 1, which the most common pinfire arms occupy, it progresses in numerical stages to Level 10, which encompasses the rarities. The almost unlimited variety found within the pinfire collecting field prevents listing every type, but general categories are given into which most examples fall.

Nor does this rarity guide seek to replace the National Rifle Association's standard condition ratings. While condition does factor heavily into the value of an arm, the various levels in this guide are to be used only to determine an individual type's rarity. Condition, maker, model, embellishment, provenance and other factors can elevate a particular arm to a higher level, as will an additional and/or scarce feature (a twelve-shot cylinder on a 15mm caliber revolver, one fitted with an attached knife blade, or a gold-inlaid shotgun, for example). Cased sets were omitted from the guide, as their level will vary depending on the style and rarity of the casing as much as that of the firearm.

Chapter notes.

1. *Sans Garantie Du Gouvernement* (without government guarantee).
2. *Encyclopedia Larousse*, Volume 5, page 363; *see also* Volume 8: "Property."
3. "An Act of Parliament: Proof House, Birmingham, England, July 10, 1853", in Clive Harris, *The History of the Birmingham Gun Barrel Proof House*, 1945.

Pinfire Arms Rarity and Desirability Chart

Level 1 (Most common types)
a. 7mm revolvers with folding triggers
b. 9mm revolvers with folding or solid triggers, and triggerguards
c. 9mm double-barrel pistols
d. 12mm double-barrel pistols
e. 15mm double-barrel pistols

Level 2
a. 12mm revolvers with folding or solid triggers, and triggerguards
b. 7mm double-barrel pistols
c. Double-barrel shotguns
d. 7mm revolvers with extended-length barrels
e. 5mm revolvers
f. 5mm double-barrel pistols
g. 7mm revolvers with solid triggers, and triggerguards
h. Single-barrel pistols
i. Ring-trigger revolvers

Level 3
a. 7mm pepperboxes
b. Lefaucheux Model 1854 revolvers
c. Lefaucheux Model 1862 revolvers
d. Double-barrel pistols with attached folding knife blades
e. Single-barrel shotguns
f. 9mm pepperboxes
g. Factory combination pinfire/rimfire revolvers
h. Factory combination pinfire/centerfire revolvers

Level 4
a. Lefaucheux Model 1854 revolvers with 4¾" barrels
b. 5mm pepperboxes
c. 12mm pepperboxes
d. 5-, 8-, 10-, and 12-shot revolvers

Level 5
a. Revolvers with attached folding knife blades
b. 12mm revolving rifles
c. Over-and-under pistols

d. All-brass (or bronze) revolvers
e. Pepperboxes with screw-off barrel groups
f. Underhammer (Mariette style) pepperboxes

Level 6
a. Dolne "Apache" pistols
b. Double-barrel rifles
c. Military-marked revolvers
d. 15mm revolvers
e. 20-shot revolvers (double-barrel, double-row chambers)

Level 7
a. Delhaxhe solid-frame knuckledusters
b. Single-barrel rifles
c. 18-shot revolvers
d. 10-, 12-, and 15-shot pepperboxes
e. Cutlass pistols and revolvers made by Dumonthier (and others)
f. Harmonica pistols

Level 8
a. LeMat revolvers
b. Combination sword-pistols, sword-revolvers
c. Rifles with attached knife blades
d. Lefaucheux Model 1854 revolvers with exceptionally-long barrels, and shoulder stocks
e. American agent-marked arms

Level 9
a. 15mm revolving rifles
b. Revolving shotguns
c. 20-shot revolvers (single-barrel, single-row chambers)
d. *Trabuco* (blunderbuss) arms
e. LeMat rifles
f. Harmonica rifles and shotguns

Level 10 (Rarest types)
a. French Navy Model 1858 revolvers (unaltered)
b. Polain revolvers
c. Any arms made by Casimir Lefaucheux

Plate 8-1. A fine engraved pinfire revolver manufactured by Prosper Polain, of Liége; left and right sides. The lower view shows the barrel and inner cylinder assembly drawn forward for loading or extraction. *Courtesy Musee d'Armes de Liége; Francis Niffle photograph*

Pinfire Loading and Ejection Systems

The invention of the self-contained, waterproof cartridge constituted a significant step forward in the evolution of firearms. But progress inevitably is accompanied by new problems. The chapter that follows is devoted to the many attempts to solve two of the major hurdles encountered by the inventors of pinfire arms: loading and ejection.

The percussion system required the shooter to follow a prescribed series of steps to ready a firearm for operation, and little but constant practice and increased familiarity with the weapon could be done to speed up that process. With the advent of the pinfire system, however, it became possible to design arms mechanically suited to the rapid loading and ejection of cartridges.

Many of the firearms pictured in this chapter, however, proved not to be the answer. Indeed, most were cumbersome contraptions, if not glaring failures, and not all differ from the simple loading gate and push-rod ejector system patented by Eugene Lefaucheux. As the simplest method very often proves to be the best, so it was with the push-rod ejector, and the vast majority of pinfire revolvers were designed to utilize the loading gate and ejector rod method of cartridge loading and ejection.

Many of the revolvers illustrated in this chapter were serious attempts at improving on Eugene Lefaucheux' basic design. The majority were manufactured during the early years of commercial handgun production, roughly between 1860 and 1877. Many of those designs very likely were attempts to circumvent the patents granted to

Eugene Lefaucheux, which restricted the manufacture of cartridge revolvers to those gunmakers licensed by him.

One of the first attempts to diverge from the then-current pattern of arms convention was made by Prosper Polain of Liége, Belgium, in 1865. His revolver is often referred to as the sole pinfire evasion of Rollin White's American patent for a bored-through cylinder. It is Polain's unique side-loading cylinder design that sets his revolver design completely apart, not only from conventional pinfire revolvers, but all other loading-ejection systems as well. Polain's design actually is two cylinders, one inside the other. The inner cylinder consists of a number of short chambers screwed into openings in a circular disc at their forward ends. This disc with the chambers attached, slides forward or back on the central axis pin, which also passes through the outer cylinder. The outer cylinder has side openings through which cartridges are loaded; that done, the inner cylinder is moved to the rear and the open ends of the individual chambers enter into circular grooves on the backplate, thus effecting a successful gas seal at the breech. After firing the Polain revolver, the process is reversed. A locking screw at the forward base of

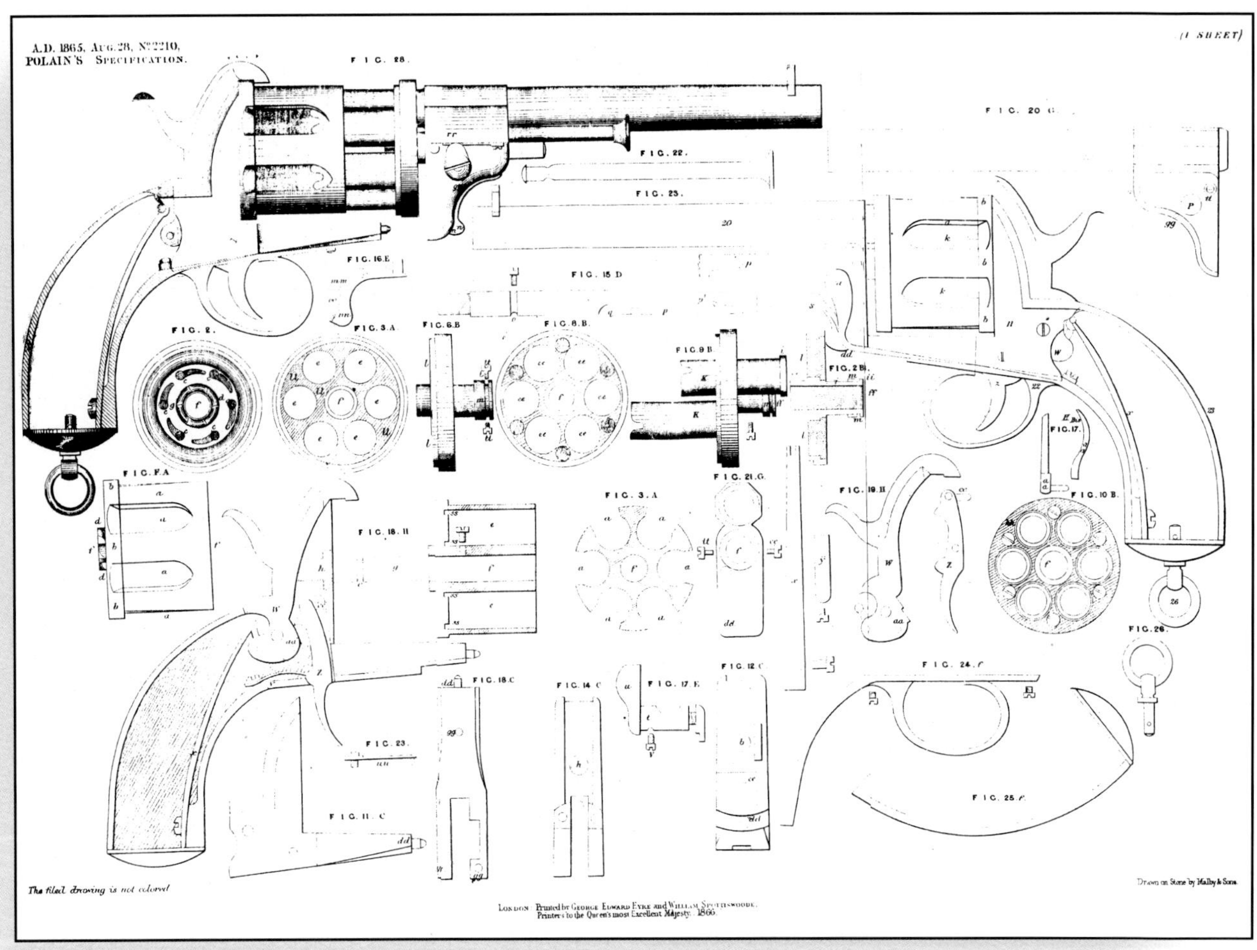

Plate 8-2. An illustration from Prosper Polain's British patent number 2210, of August 28, 1865.
Chris C. Curtis collection

the frame is loosened, allowing the barrel, forward frame section, and inner cylinder chambers to be drawn forward and exposing the spent cartridges for ejection with the aid of the side-mounted ejector rod.

Plate 8-1 illustrates the Polain revolver from both sides, with the bottom figure showing its mechanism in the open position. In his British patent number 2210, of August 28, 1865, Polain illustrates the process differently (*see Plate 8-2*). Instead of a locking screw, a lever is used to rotate the forward portion of the revolver to the open position. The actual working model, however, employed the locking screw, and the forward end is moved forward manually. As the Polain revolver pictured in *Plate 8-1* is one of only two examples

known, it must be regarded as one of the rarest of all patented pinfire arms.

A design from the same period and similar in concept to the Polain is the rimfire revolver patented in the United States by American inventor Frank Slocum. Slocum's patent number 38204, issued in 1863, features a cylinder having sliding sleeves to permit loading from the side rather than from the rear. The rear-loading, bored-through cylinder was the primary design protected by Rollin White's revolutionary patent.

The engraved 7mm caliber pinfire revolver pictured in *Plates 8-3 and 8-4* was manufactured by

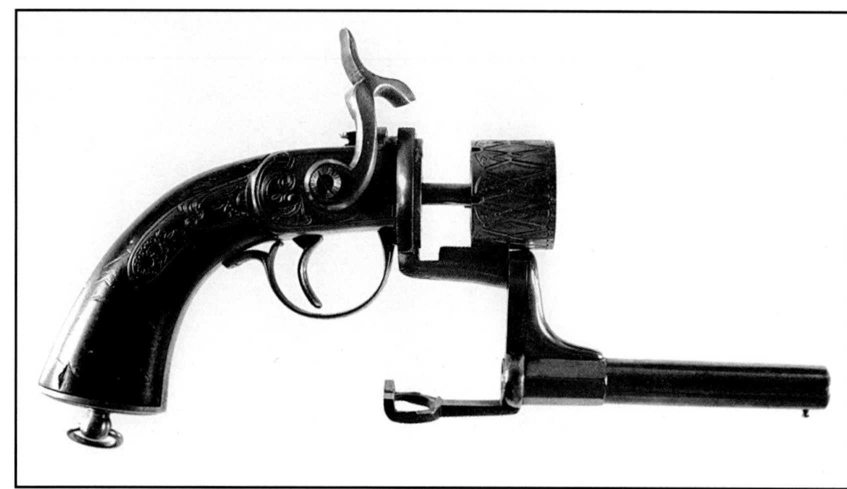

Plate 8-3. An unusual sidehammer pinfire revolver manufactured by John Batiste Eyraud, under French patent number 38649 of November 15, 1858. Note the barrel swung to the side to allow removal of the cylinder. *Courtesy Don Kramer; Ferrari Color photograph*

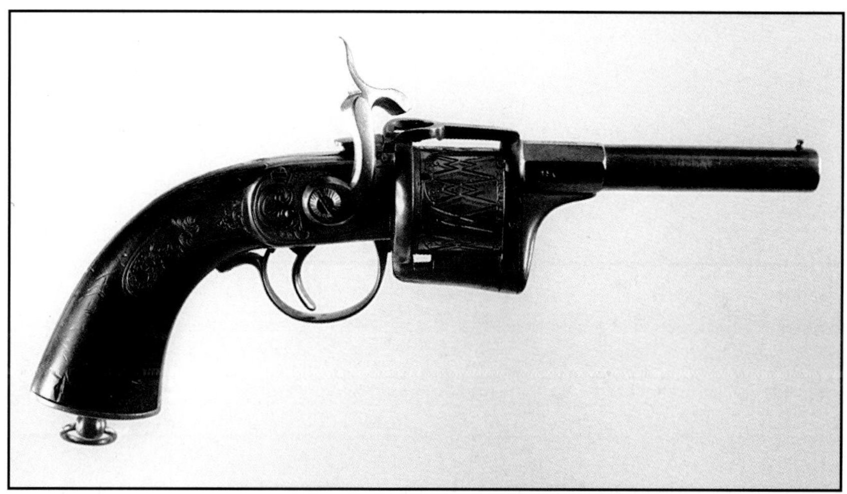

Plate 8-4. Another view of the Eyraud sidehammer revolver, assembled and ready for firing. *Courtesy Don Kramer; Ferrari Color photograph*

John Batiste Eyraud, under the protection of his French patent number 38649 of November 15, 1858. When a catch on top of the frame is depressed, it releases the top strap. The barrel assembly then swivels to the side and down to allow removal of the cylinder for cartridge loading or ejection. Note the side hammers on both the revolver pictured and on Eyraud's patent drawing shown in *Plate 8-5*; it is a most unusual feature for a pinfire revolver.

The engraved 7mm caliber Eyraud revolver illustrated in *Plate 8-6* is marked only with St. Etienne proofmarks, as is the undecorated exam-

ple shown at the top of *Plate 8-7*. A lever located forward of the trigger on the underside of the frame swivels to allow the barrel assembly to tip down and the cylinder to be removed for loading. The cylinder pin may then be used as a simple ejector rod. Eyraud's French patent, number 71170 of April 26, 1866, pictured in *Plate 8-8*, illustrates this design.

The pistols pictured at center and bottom in *Plate 8-7* are 9mm and 12mm caliber pinfire revolvers made by Javelle. The 9mm caliber revolver is nicely engraved and is marked "*Javelle Bte S.G.D.G.*" In addition, its barrel carries the enigmatic marking *"Brun Brevete a Paris."* The piece is unmistakably a Javelle product, and no mechanical feature is known to warrant the latter marking. Brun did patent improvements to firearms, but this particular revolver bears no obvious modifications to the Javelle system. However, on occasion Brun did act as a sales agent for Javelle, and the guns he retailed were so marked. Perhaps it is best explained as credit being taken for a patented design when it was not deserved, but that was granted as a sales incentive.

M. Javelle is known to have manufactured arms at St. Etienne, France, during the two decades between 1860 and 1880. The larger revolver pictured at the bottom of *Plate 8-7* is marked *"Javelle Bte. S.G.D.G. St. Etienne."* It bears proofmarks indicating manufacture after 1869, whereas the previous piece does not. In addition,

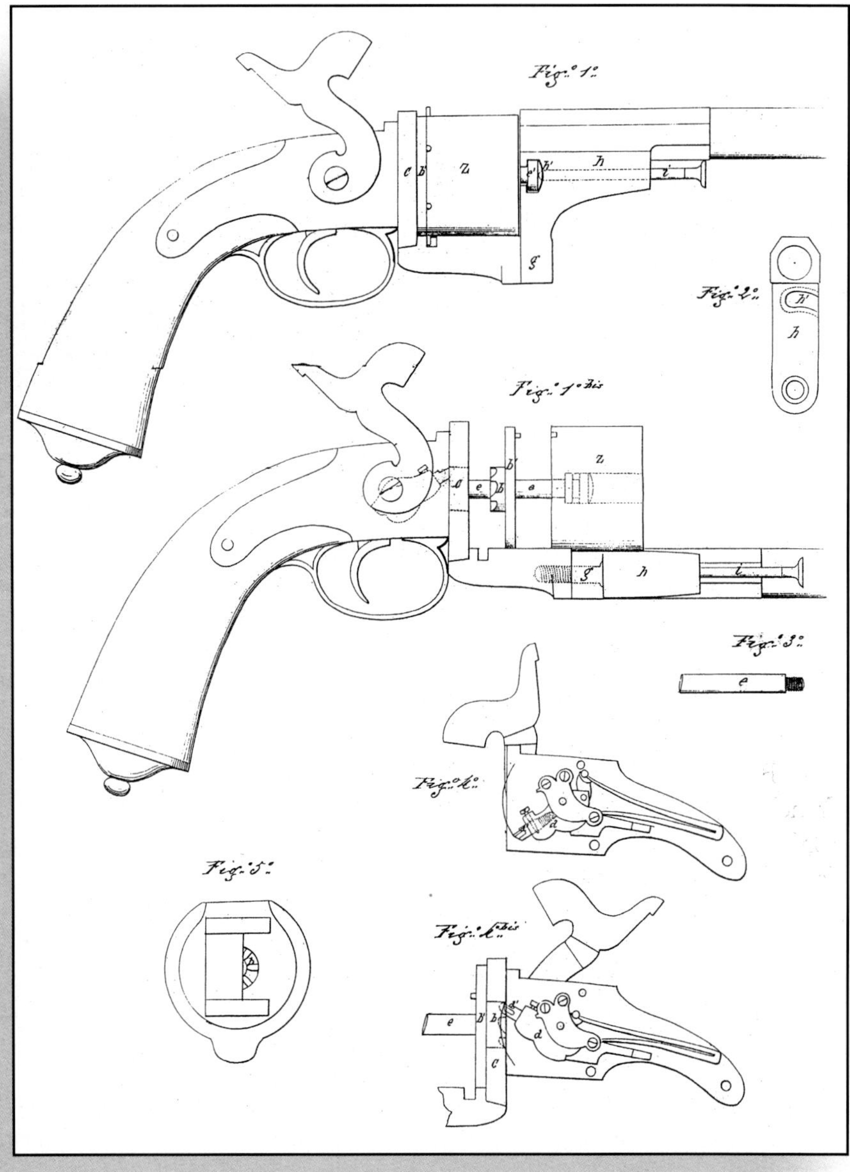

Plate 8-5. An illustration from John Batiste Eyraud's French patent number 38649, showing details of his sidehammer revolver mechanism. *Chris C. Curtis collection*

the barrel of the larger piece is marked with Korean characters reading "*1884 Warrior Storage Tank Co.*"

Both of the above revolvers operate as previously described, and both have an additional feature that sets the true Javelle gun apart from other, Javelle "types": the Javelle frame is hinged not only ahead of the cylinder, but also at the juncture of the forward frame and barrel. When the barrel is tipped down grooved rings are exposed inside the

the gun can be loaded from the rear of the cylinder; spent cartridges are extracted using the side-mounted ejector rod.

The seven-shot, solid-frame 12mm caliber pinfire revolver pictured in *Plate 8-12* is marked "*A. Fagnus Invr Brevete #1698.*" It is shown with its unusual cylinder pin drawn forward to permit removal of the cylinder for loading. A chain attached to a slip-ring at the rear of the cylinder connects to a corresponding ring around the bar-

Plate 8-6. An engraved (but unmarked), French-made 7mm caliber pinfire revolver showing its hinged tip-down method of cylinder removal for loading or extraction. *See Plate 8-8 for J.B. Eyraud's French patent illustrating this design. Courtesy private collection; F.W. Hulbert photograph*

locking assembly below the barrel, corresponding to grooves cut into the cylinder pin. Both sets of rings engage to create positive locking when the two halves of the revolver are rejoined after loading or ejection (*see Plate 8-9*).

Plate 8-10 illustrates drawings from Javelle's French patent. Although the revolver and cartridges shown are centerfire, the mechanical design features are identical to those found on the Javelle pinfire revolvers just described.

Pictured in *Plate 8-11* is a variation of the standard pinfire revolver. It is an engraved and gold-inlaid example which is unmarked except for having Liége proofmarks and inspector's marks indicating pre-1877 manufacture. Here, the reinforcing top-strap and loading gate comprise one integral unit that is hinged at the top rear part of the barrel. When the top-strap is tipped upward

rel which is attached to the cylinder pin; the perpendicular bar rests against the front of the frame when assembled, and acts as an ejector rod. *Monsieur* Fagnus produced arms in Liége between 1870 and 1877, working both as an independent gunsmith and as part of the armsmaking firm he founded.

The revolver illustrated in *Plate 8-13* is unmarked except for bearing Liége proofmarks. The loading gate tilts backward for loading from the rear of the cylinder, but extraction of fired cartridges is most easily accomplished by removing the unitized cylinder, cylinder pin, and ejector assembly attached to the frame by a single large screw, which is hand-adjustable. Note the beautifully carved hardwood grips on this example.

The revolver pictured at the top of *Plate 8-14* is of the Fagnus type, but bears London proof-

Plate 8-7. Top: Another unmarked French-made pinfire revolver having J.B. Eyraud's tip-down barrel design, but in 9mm caliber. Middle: An engraved, Javelle's patent 9mm caliber pinfire revolver marked "*Javelle Bte S.G.D.G.*" and "*Brun Brevete a Paris*" on the barrel. Bottom: A post-1869 manufactured, 12mm caliber pinfire revolver marked "*Javelle Bte. S.G.D.G. St. Etienne*", and on the barrel in Korean, "*1884 Warrior Storage Tank Co.*" Both of the latter revolvers employ Javelle's patented grooved locking mechanism and tip-down barrel design. *Courtesy James Lowther; John Calcany photograph*

marks. Interestingly, it features dual ignition, being designed to fire either pinfire or centerfire self-contained metallic cartridges.

The revolver pictured immediately below in *Plate 8-14* is marked "*GHIV Brvt. System Italien.*" It bears no proofmarks, but probably is of Italian origins. When a spring-loaded catch on the left side is depressed, the cylinder pin is freed and may be drawn forward. The cylinder, attached to the frame by a yoke similar to modern Smith & Wesson revolvers, swings out to the side allowing a hinged backplate to flip aside and exposing the rear of the chambers for loading. Once loaded, the backplate (which has ratchets for rotating the cylinder) is moved downward, the cylinder is replaced in the frame, and the arbor pin is pushed back into the frame to hold the assembly together. Cartridge ejection is accomplished in the same

Plate 8-8. An illustration from J.B. Eyraud's French patent number 71170, of April 26, 1866, showing details of his tip-down barrel design. *Chris C. Curtis collection*

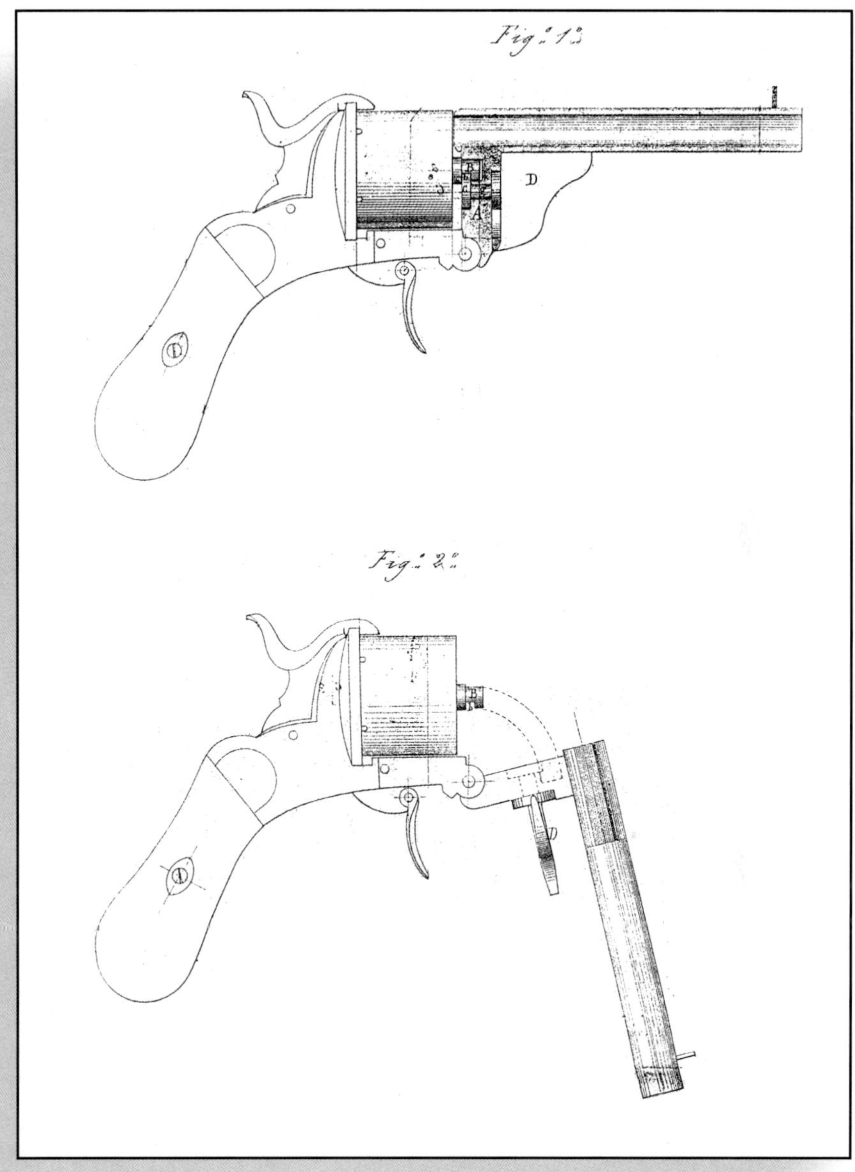

manner, utilizing the cylinder pin as an ejector rod. The mechanical features of this revolver are similar to the improvements illustrated in the certificate of addition to Eugene Lefaucheux' patent number 19380, of February 8, 1860. While no evidence has surfaced to indicate that Lefaucheux ever produced revolvers of this type, examples in both 9mm and 12mm calibers have been observed bearing Liége proofmarks. One such pinfire revolver in 9mm caliber is marked "C.M. *Venzi no 2963.*" All were manufactured under the provisions of Breuer's French patent number 71326, of April 6th, 1866 (*see Plate 8-15*).

The sidehammer revolver pictured in *Plates 8-16 and 8-17* is marked "*J. Peuvel Brevete S.G.D.G.*" and bears St. Etienne proofmarks for the 1856-1868 period. The lever on the side of the frame turns downward to unlock the barrel, which

Plate 8-9. Detail view of M. Javelle's patented revolver locking system, showing the split rings under barrel and corresponding rings on cylinder arbor. *Courtesy private collection; F.W. Hulbert photograph*

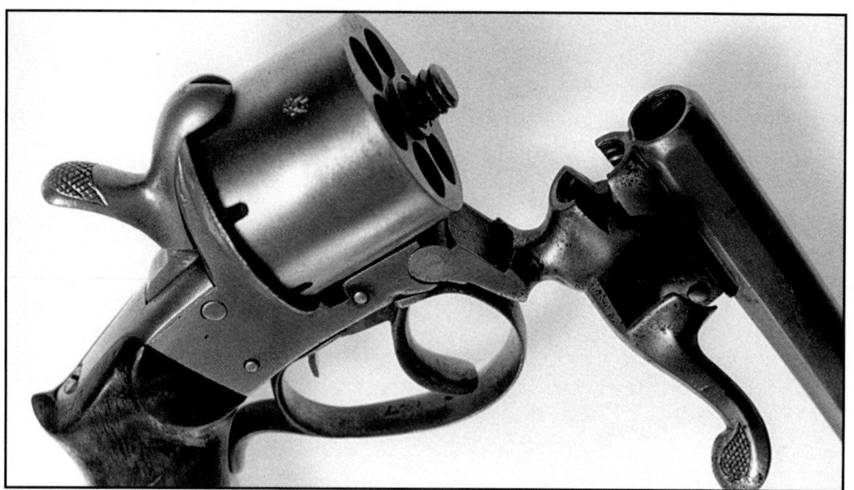

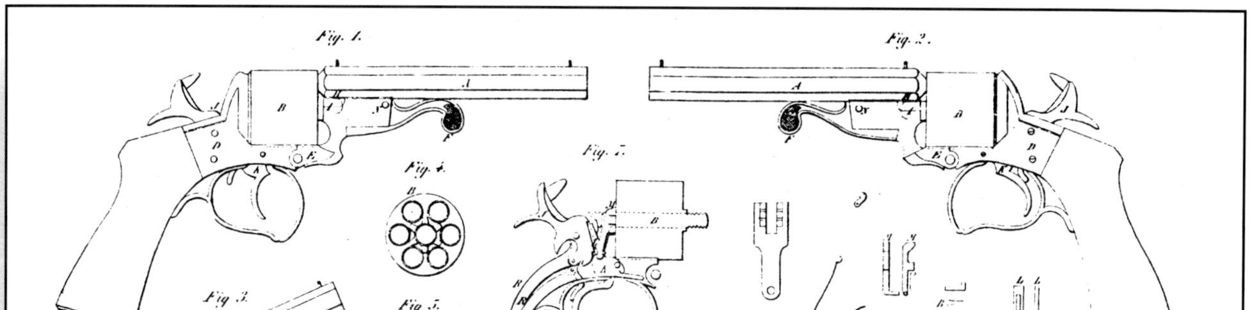

Plate 8-10. An illustration from Javelle's French patent, showing details of his unique grooved barrel locking mechanism. *Chris C. Curtis collection*

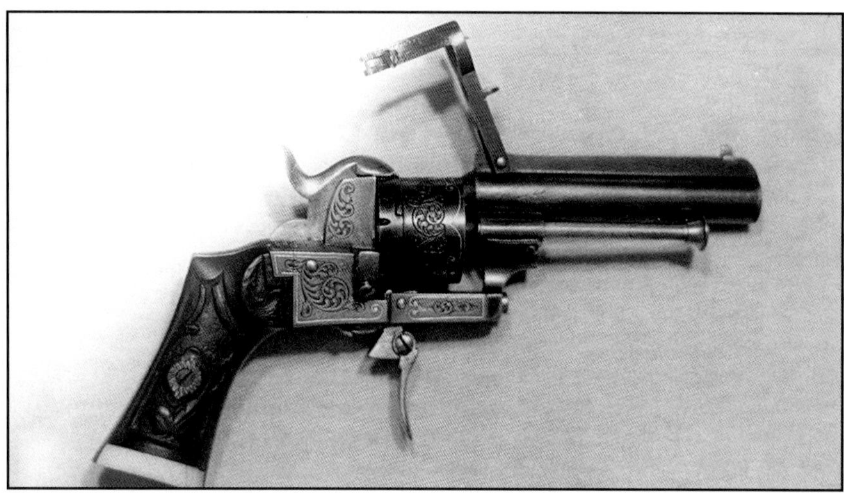

Plate 8-11. An unmarked, pre-1877 Belgian-made pinfire revolver having Liége proofmarks, an unusual hinged combination top-strap and loading gate, and integral ejector rod. *Courtesy Larry Compeau; F.W. Hulbert photograph*

Plate 8-12. A seven-shot, double-action 12mm caliber pinfire revolver marked "*A. Fagnus Invr Brevete #1698*", having an unusual cylinder pin that slides forward on a barrel-mounted slip-ring attached to the removable cylinder. *Courtesy private collection; F.W. Hulbert photograph*

Plate 8-13. An unmarked, Belgian-made 9mm caliber pinfire revolver having its cylinder-cylinder pin assembly held in place by a large screw. *Courtesy private collection; Gene Smith photograph*

then pivots sideways to allow removal of the cylinder. Note also the separate recoil plate behind the cylinder.

Marked *"Mariette Brevete"*, the double-action revolver pictured in *Plate 8-18* bears Liége proofmarks and inspector's marks indicating its manufacture before 1877, as do the great majority of revolvers featuring this loading-ejection design variation. A large knurled knob ahead of the ring trigger turns to release a lock on the cylinder pin, allowing both cylinder and barrel assembly to slide forward along the arbor for either loading or ejection. However, the major components of this revolver do not disassemble completely, as with other variations on this design. The pin protector to the rear of the cylinder acts as an effective safety feature; the locking knob resembles that of Polain's patent (*see Plate 8-1*).

The 9mm caliber pinfire revolver with triggerguard pictured in *Plate 8-19* is nicely engraved and

Plate 8-14. Top: Unmarked as to maker, but London proofmarked, this 12mm caliber Fagnus-type revolver was designed to fire both pinfire and centerfire cartridges. Bottom: A pinfire revolver manufactured on Breuer's 1866 patent. It is marked *"GHIV Brvt. System Italien"*, and employs a unique swing-out cylinder with hinged backplate for loading and ejection, utilizing the cylinder arbor as ejector rod. *Courtesy James Lowther; John Calcany photograph*

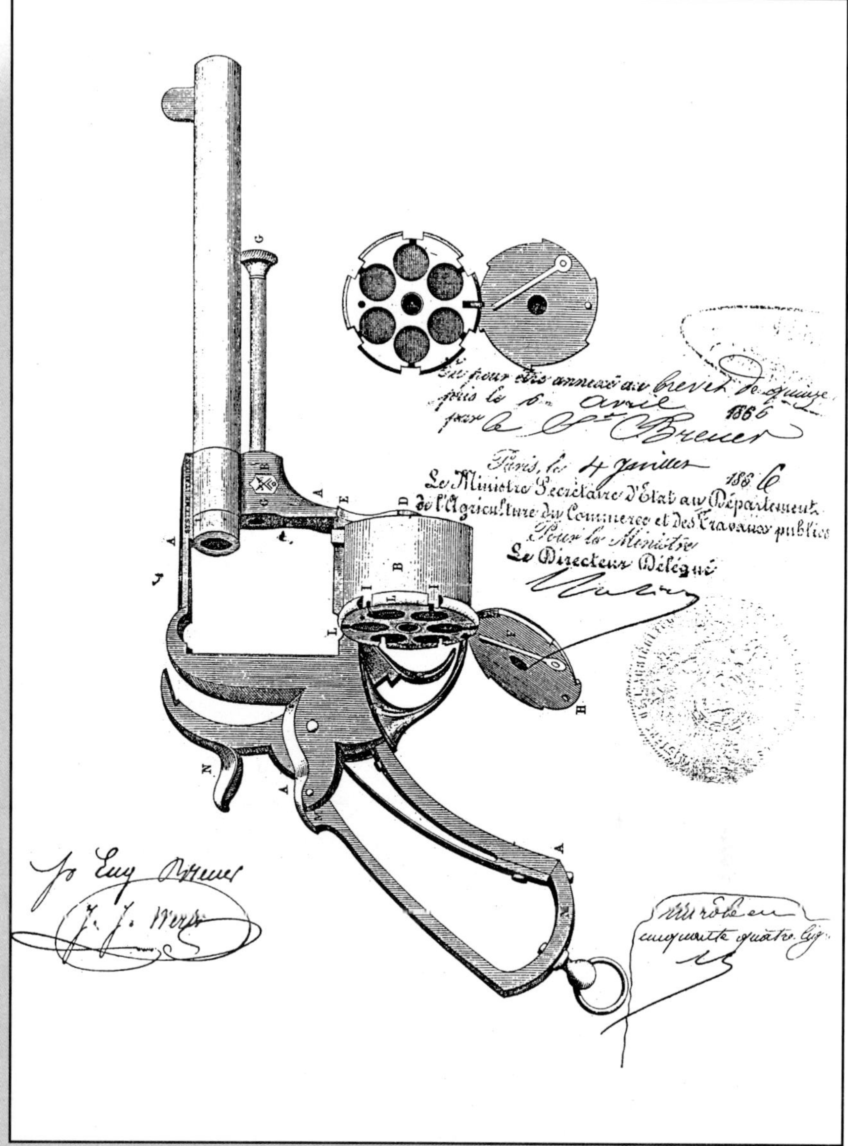

Plate 8-15. An illustration from Breuer's French patent number 71326, of April 6, 1866, showing the swing-out cylinder with hinged backplate. *Chris C. Curtis collection*

bears inspector's marks dating its manufacture prior to 1877. Otherwise, it is marked only "N.V.P.", the initials of its maker. A lever mounted at the upper rear of the frame releases a locking lug and permits the barrel assembly to tip down. After the cylinder is removed from the arbor pin the latter is used as an ejector rod. This pistol is equipped with the popular Lefaucheux Model 1854-style spur triggerguard, but the angle and style of the grip have a very American "Western" look. While it bears Belgian proofmarks, the design of this revolver was patented in France by Nicolas Vivario Plomdeur. Plomdeur's patent, number 49166 of April 6, 1861, is illustrated in *Plate 8-20.*

Plate 8-21 illustrates an unusual 12mm caliber pinfire revolver having bag-style grips and a triggerguard; it is marked "*Drivon Bvt.*" Pierre Drivon was granted French patent number 66991 on April

text continued on page 235

Plate 8-16. Disassembled view of a unique, 12mm caliber pinfire revolver having swing-out barrel and bored-through cylinder with separate recoil plate. *Courtesy G. Lautissier; G. Lautissier photograph*

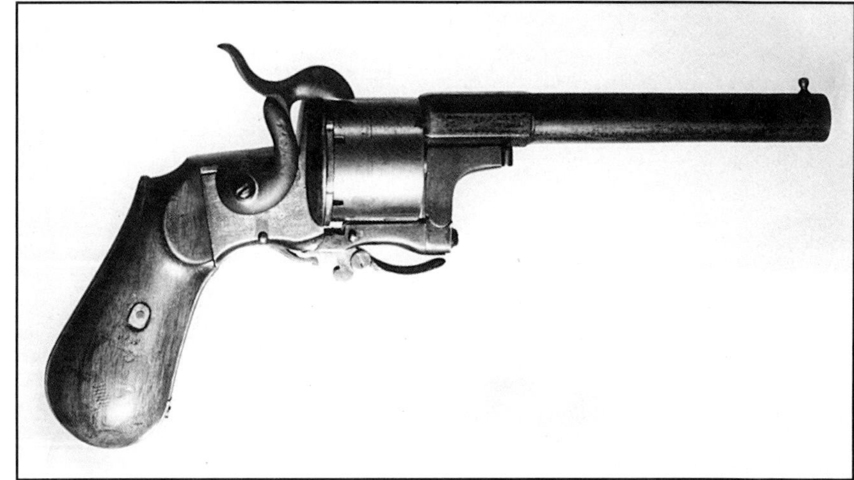

Plate 8-17. Assembled view of the revolver pictured in *Plate 8-16,* showing sidehammer design. The barrel is marked *"J. Peuvel Brevete S.G.D.G." Courtesy G. Lautissier; G. Lautissier photograph*

Plate 8-18. A pre-1877 Belgian-made, double-action, ring-trigger pinfire revolver marked *"Mariette Brevete."* A large knob releases the barrel assembly and cylinder to be drawn forward for loading and extraction. *Courtesy private collection; F.W. Hulbert photograph*

Plate 8-19. A pre-1877 Belgian-made, 9mm caliber pinfire revolver having tip-down barrel and cylinder assembly. Manufactured under N.V. Plomdeur's 1861 French patent. *Chris C. Curtis collection*

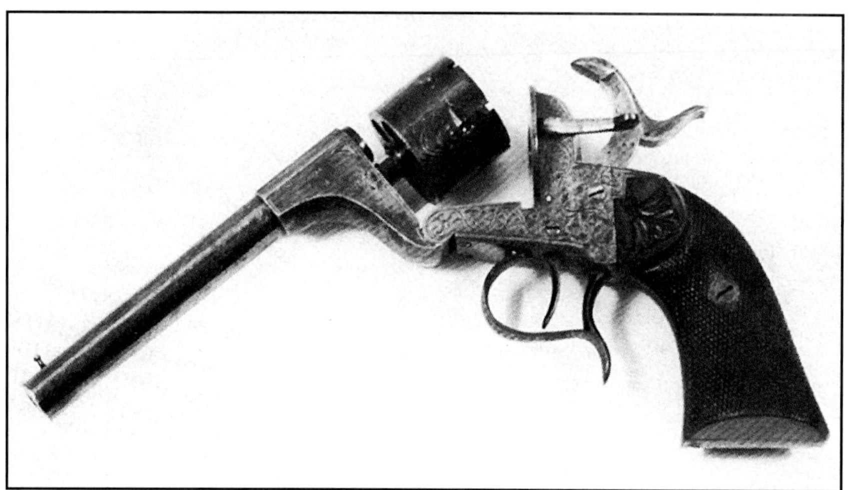

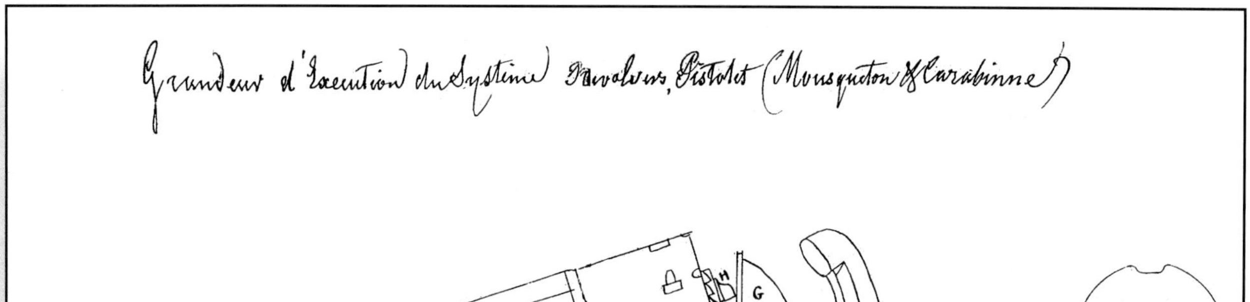

Plate 8-20. An illustration from N.V. Plomdeur's French patent number 49166, of April 6, 1861, showing his tip-down barrel design. *Chris C. Curtis collection*

Plate 8-21. A French-made 12mm caliber pinfire revolver marked *"Drivon Bvt."*, having a tip-down barrel-cylinder assembly and integral automatic ejector ring. *Courtesy G. Lautissier; G. Lautissier photograph*

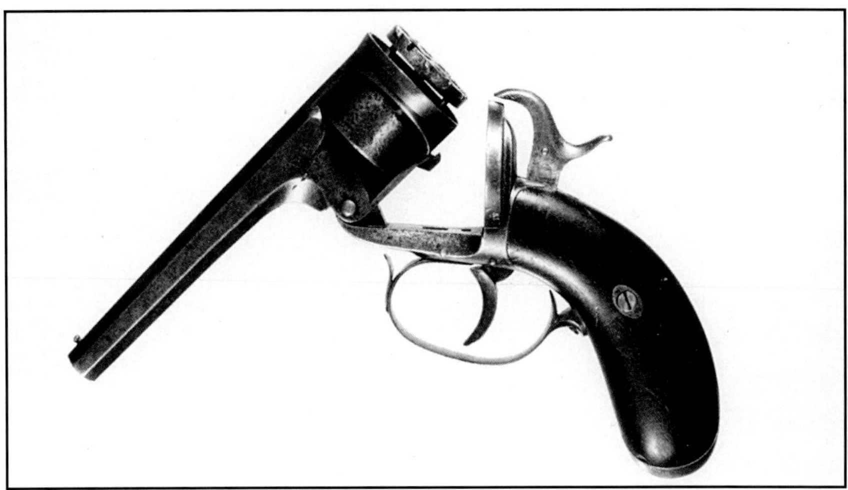

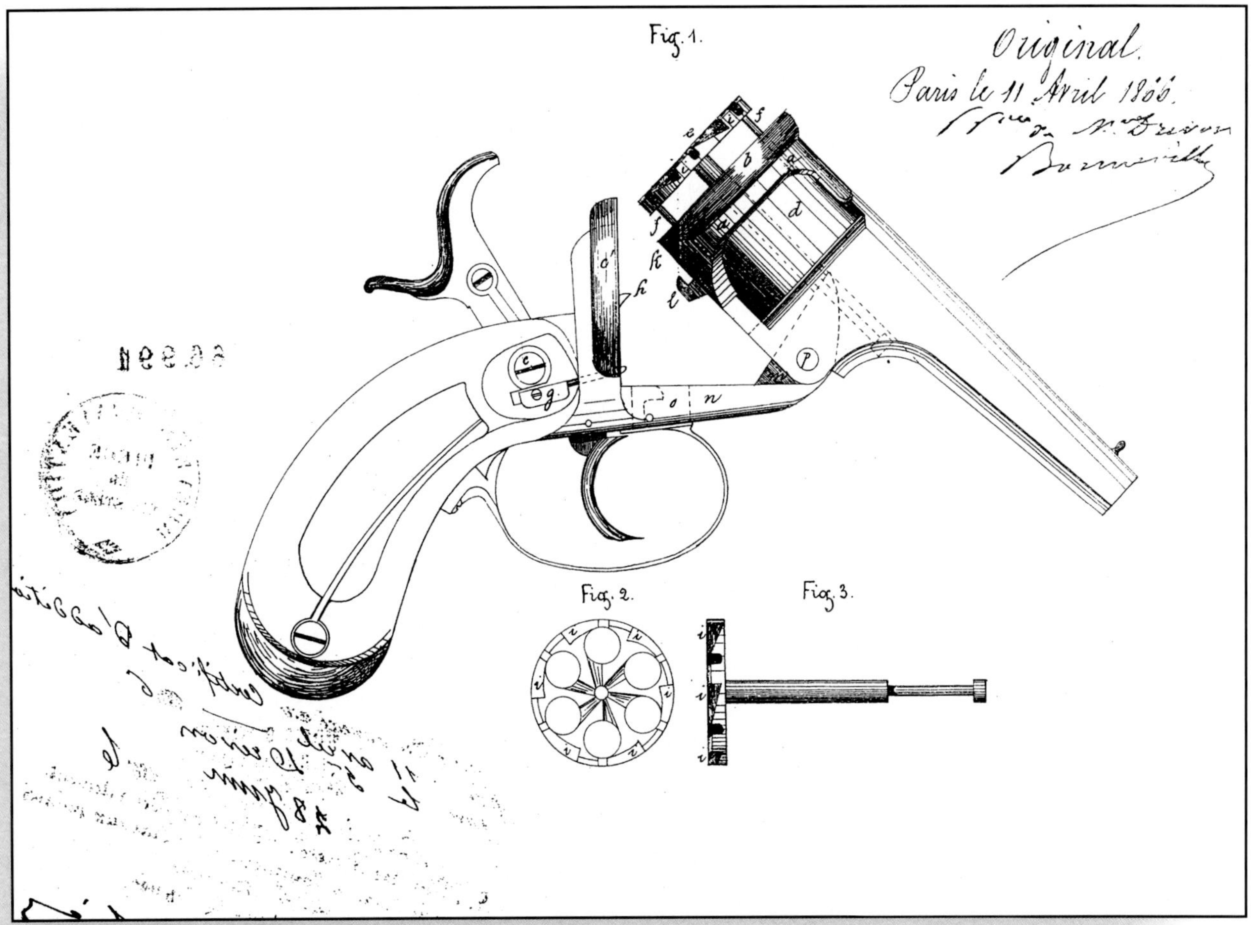

Plate 8-22. An illustration from the second certificate of addition to P. Drivon's French patent number 66991, of April 11, 1866, showing his tip-down barrel-cylinder assembly with automatic ejector ring. *Chris C. Curtis collection*

4, 1865 for this design, and subsequently issued certificates of additions on May 16, 1865 and April 11, 1866 (*see Plate 8-22*). Note the movable ring mounted behind the cylinder, which automatically ejects spent cartridges after firing.

Pictured in *Plate 8-23* is a 7mm caliber pinfire revolver made by Comblain. Like the previous example, it too bears Liége proofmarks and pre-1877 inspector's marks. On the barrel appears the name of an English sales agent, "*E.M. Reilly & Co. New Oxford St. London.*" Again similar to the pistol just above is its disassembly process, except that the locking lever is located on the right side; it turns upward and forward to release the barrel

assembly. Pins on the underside of the barrel and on the cylinder arbor and forward frame ensure proper alignment of all components when this arm is reassembled. Comblain was actively engaged in the Belgian firearms industry between 1855 and 1877, and in 1866 was appointed "Gunmaker to the Court of Brussels." Between 1857 and 1860 Comblain was awarded three patents for breech-loading revolvers and various improvements thereto, one being the takedown-loading system described and illustrated here.

The large and unusual 12mm caliber pinfire revolver pictured in *Plate 8-24* is marked on the right side of the frame "*London 86141*", and bears

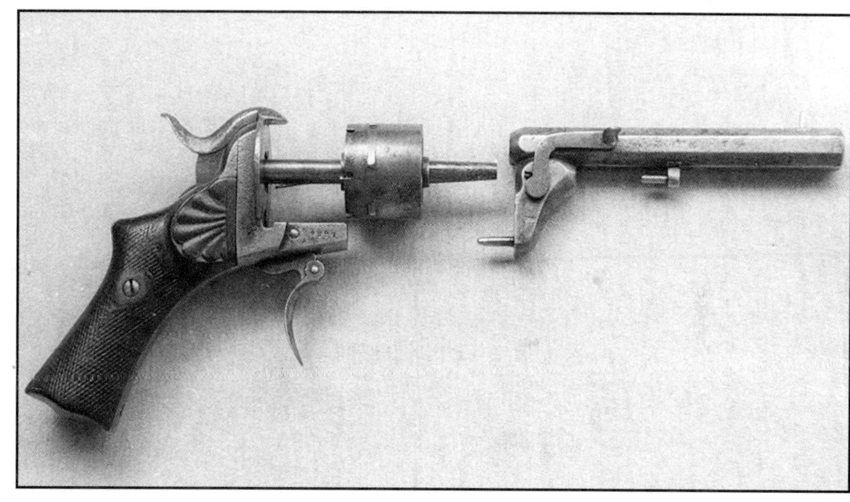

Plate 8-23. Disassembled view of a pre-1877 Belgian-made Comblain patent revolver marked on the barrel "*E.M. Reilly & Co. New Oxford St. London.*" Note the aligning pin on bottom of barrel lug, and shell-carved wood grips. *Courtesy private collection; F.W. Hulbert photograph*

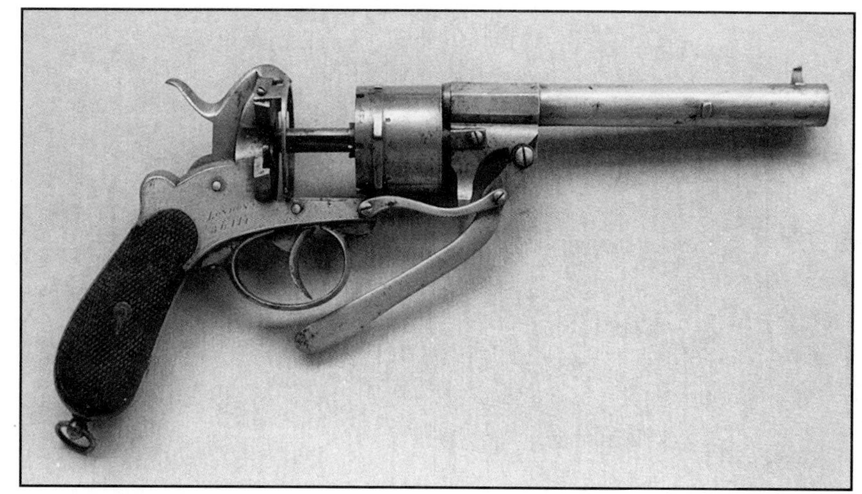

Plate 8-24. A large, 12mm caliber pinfire revolver marked on the frame "*London 86141.*" The cylinder is loaded with action closed; the long lever is drawn down and back to open the action for automatic cartridge ejection by a ring located behind the cylinder. *Courtesy private collection; F.W. Hulbert photograph*

London proofmarks. Loading is done while the action is in the closed position; for extraction, the long lever which normally rests alongside the right side of the barrel is pulled downward and to the rear, after which the cylinder, barrel, and forward frame assembly moves along the cylinder pin. A stationary ring located behind the cylinder catches the protruding cartridge pins as the cylinder slides forward, automatically extracting all six cartridges simultaneously. As the lever is moved back into position alongside the barrel the forward assembly returns back to the closed and locked position, and the arm is again ready for firing.

The Belgian-made revolver illustrated in *Plate 8-25* is marked "*T. Leclercq*", and bears Liége proofmarks along with pre-1877 inspector's marks. A lever mounted on the left side of the barrel lug, when pushed down and forward, releases a locking lug on the cylinder pin, which after removal of the barrel and cylinder is used as an ejector rod. When the cylinder is loaded and the process is reversed, this single-action revolver is again made ready for use. Its maker, Leclercq, produced firearms in Liége between the years 1871 and 1874.

Another 7mm caliber pinfire revolver, the example shown in *Plate 8-26* is unidentified as to maker but also bears pre-1877 Belgian proofmarks and inspector's marks. Its outward appearance

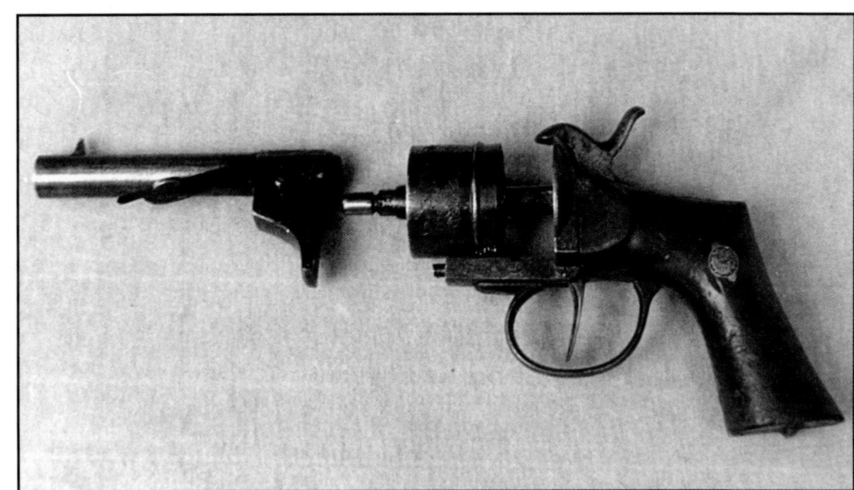

Plate 8-25. A pre-1877 Belgian-made, 7mm caliber single-action pinfire revolver marked "*T. Leclercq.*" The long barrel-mounted lever unlocks the action for disassembly and loading. *Courtesy private collection; F. W. Hulbert photograph*

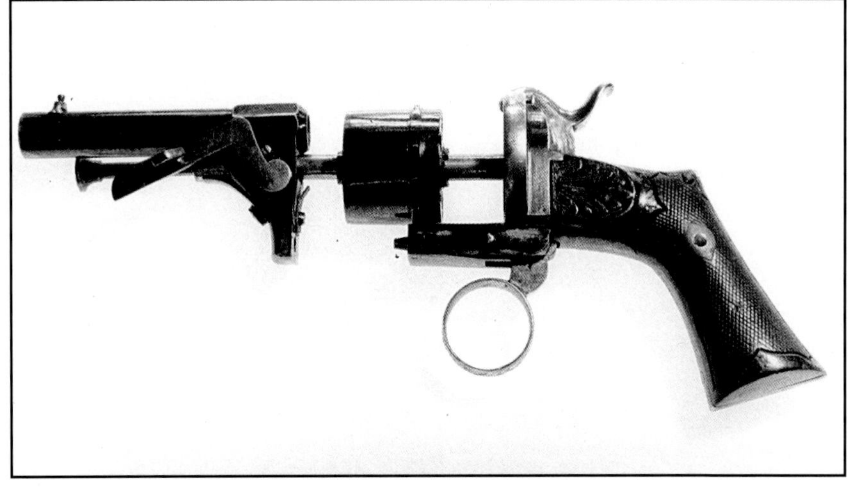

Plate 8-26. An unidentified as to maker, pre-1877, Belgian-made 7mm caliber pinfire revolver. Its design is similar to the Leclercq revolver pictured in *Plate 8-25.* Note ring trigger, carved and checkered wood grips. *Courtesy private collection; F.W. Hulbert photograph*

suggests manufacture by T. Leclercq, and with the exception of the ring trigger it is strikingly similar to the revolver just discussed. The lever on the left barrel lug swings down to release the barrel assembly, allowing it and the cylinder to slide forward along the cylinder arbor. Those components do not completely disassemble as on the previous example, but the cylinder moves far enough forward to permit the loading or extraction of cartridges. Ejection is assisted by an integral ejector rod. Equipped with a pin safety shield, this example can be operated in either single- or double-action mode.

Plate 8-27 illustrates a Belgian-made 12mm caliber pinfire revolver made by C.H. Loron, who was engaged in St. Etienne as an arms manufacturer between 1843 and 1880. In the early 1870s Loron produced a small number of revolvers in Liége, all employing this system for loading and ejection, for which he held the patent rights. This piece bears Liége proofmarks, and has pre-1877 inspector's marks. A lever mounted on the left barrel lug, when turned down and toward the rear, releases the barrel assembly and allows it and the cylinder to move forward along the length of the stationary cylinder arbor. Like the previous example, this pistol does not completely disassemble. Note the modern-looking trigger and triggerguard.

The pistol pictured at the top of *Plate 8-28* also is a product of *Monsieur* Loron, but chambered for the smaller 7mm pinfire cartridge, and having the more typical folding trigger. The revolver shown at center is marked "*Comblain.*" It is 12mm caliber pinfire, and was manufactured in Liége. On this example the loading gate and ejector rod are cleverly combined into a single unit. When a spring catch above the loading gate is depressed the unit is released and swivels down and to the front, from which position it is used as an ejector rod. The revolver illustrated at the bottom of *Plate 8-28* is marked "A. Pliers", and "L. Ghaye" on the front of the cylinder, and "*Maisongrande Arq. Limoges*" along the barrel. It is chambered for the 9mm caliber pinfire cartridge. The long ejector rod rotates 180 degrees when released from its retaining catch under the forward end of the barrel, and slides through a pivoting block recessed into the frame, moving it into position for use along the side of the frame. A spring release allows the cylinder backplate to revolve to an opening through which cartridges are loaded or extracted. Although it bears no external proofmarks, this fine-quality piece probably is of French manufacture.

The 12mm caliber, Belgian-made pinfire revolver pictured in *Plate 8-29* is marked "*Jongen Freres Brevete.*" Its action opens in a manner almost diametrically opposite that of Javelle's: the solid frame is hinged at the top rear, and the barrel

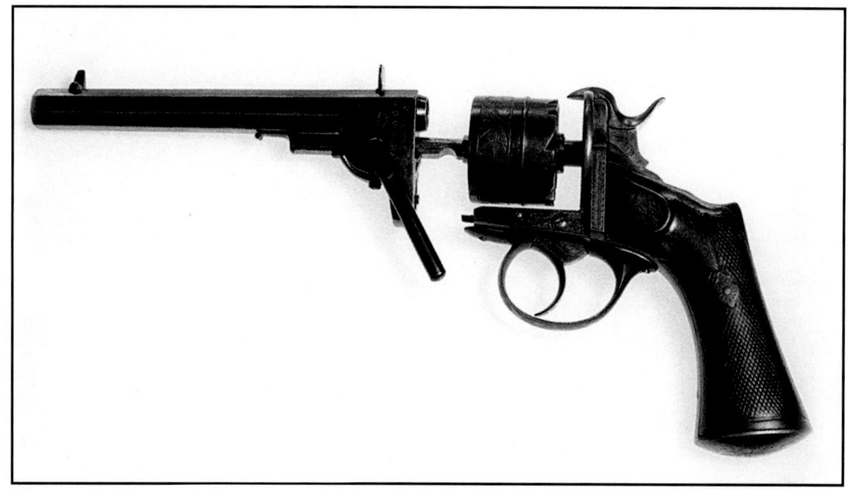

Plate 8-27. A pre-1877 Belgian-made, 12mm caliber pinfire revolver manufactured under C.H. Loron's French patent. The barrel and cylinder slide forward for loading and extraction, but do not remove from the cylinder arbor. *Courtesy private collection; F.W. Hulbert photograph*

Plate 8-28. Top: A 7mm caliber pinfire revolver manufactured by Loron, having the usual folding trigger. Center: A Belgian-made 12mm caliber pinfire revolver marked *"Comblain."* Note the combined loading gate-ejector rod assembly. Bottom: A likely French-made, 9mm caliber pinfire revolver marked *"A. Pliers"*, *"L. Ghaye"*, and *"Maisongrande Arq. Limoges."* Note the integral ejector rod, carved and checkered grips, fine engraving and finish. *Courtesy James Lowther; John Calcany photograph*

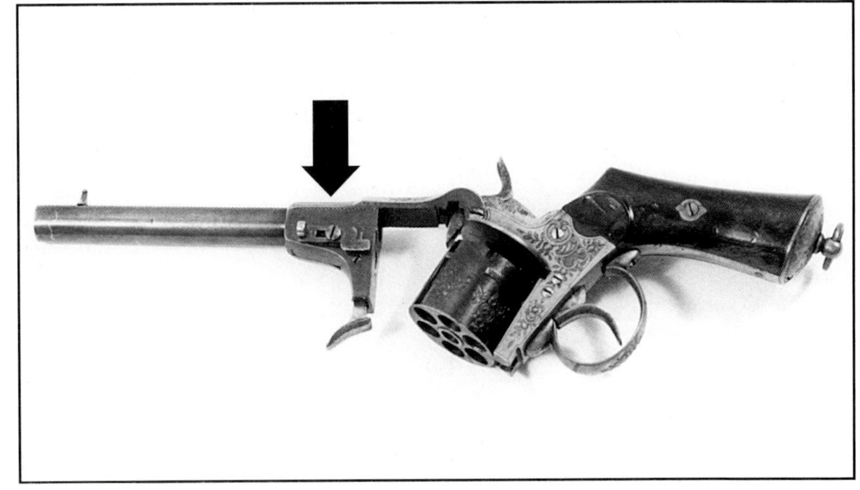

Plate 8-29. A Belgian-made, solid-frame, 12mm caliber pinfire revolver marked *"Jongen Freres Brevete."* Note tip-up barrel assembly which releases the cylinder for loading and ejection utilizing the cylinder arbor, and the unique sliding positive safety (arrow). *Courtesy private collection; F.W. Hulbert photograph*

assembly tips upward when a spring catch located at the forward bottom of the frame is depressed. The cylinder slides off the arbor, which then is used as an ejector rod. After loading the cylinder the process is reversed, the barrel assembly is locked back into place, and the gun is again ready for firing. A crude but effective safety (shown at the arrow) is provided by a small steel lever attached to the left-side barrel lug. When moved to the rear, it slides into the facing chamber and prevents rotation of the cylinder. Thus the hammer cannot be cocked, and the gun cannot be fired. Jongen Freres worked in the Liége armsmak-

ing business between 1856 and 1873. In 1863 and 1864 the firm was granted patents for improvements to breechloading revolvers.

Plate 8-31 pictures an unmarked, 12mm caliber pinfire revolver that obviously was constructed on the French patent of A. Guerriero, which was granted on January 30, 1864 (*see Plate 8-32*). Note the unusual adjustable front sight, and details of the barrel-release assembly. In addition to seeking patent protection in both France and the United States, Guerriero acquired protection in Great Britain where he was granted English patent number 628 on March 5th, 1863.

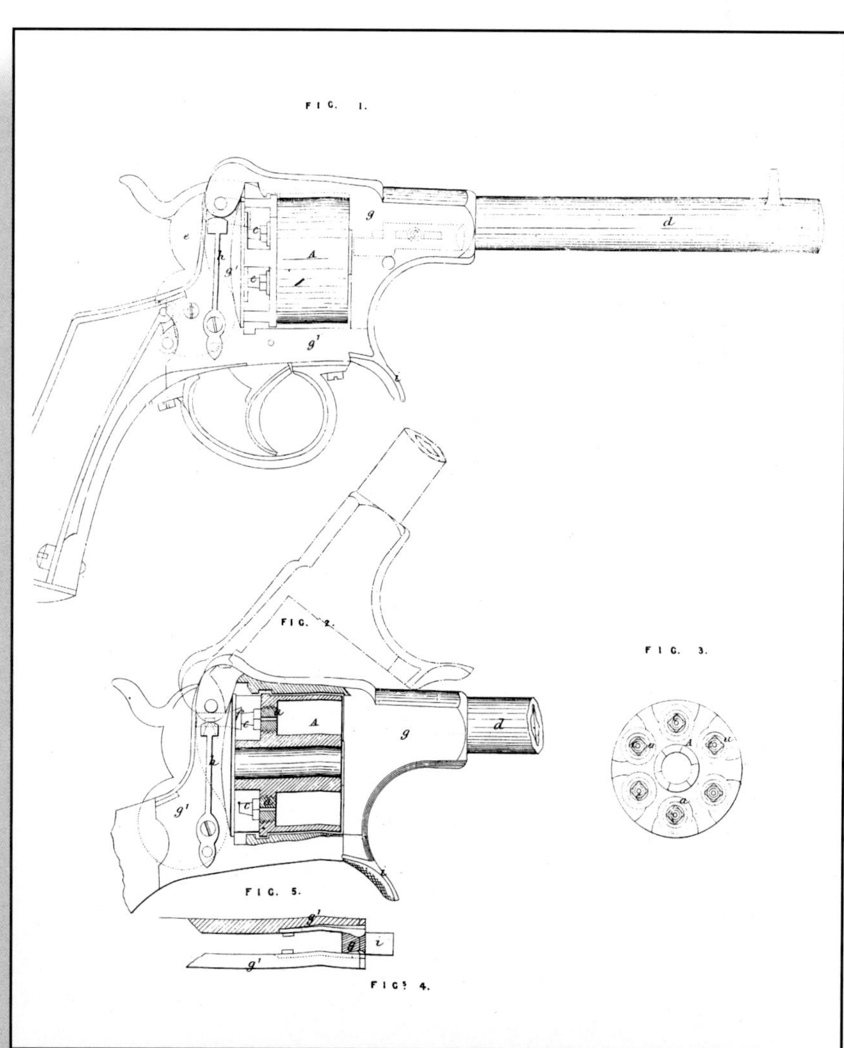

Plate 8-30. An illustration from Belgian gunmaker J. Freres' French patent number 2383, of September 28, 1864, showing details of his tip-up barrel design. *Chris C. Curtis collection*

Plate 8-31. An unmarked, 12mm caliber pinfire revolver manufactured under A. Guerriero's 1864 French patent. Note the unique adjustable front sight. *Courtesy G. Lautissier; G. Lautissier photograph*

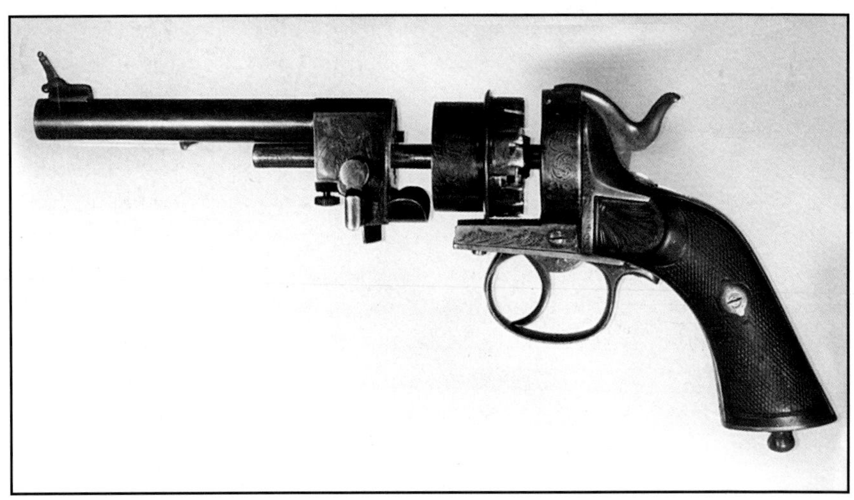

Plate 8-32. An illustration from A. Guerriero's French patent of January 30, 1864. *Chris C. Curtis collection*

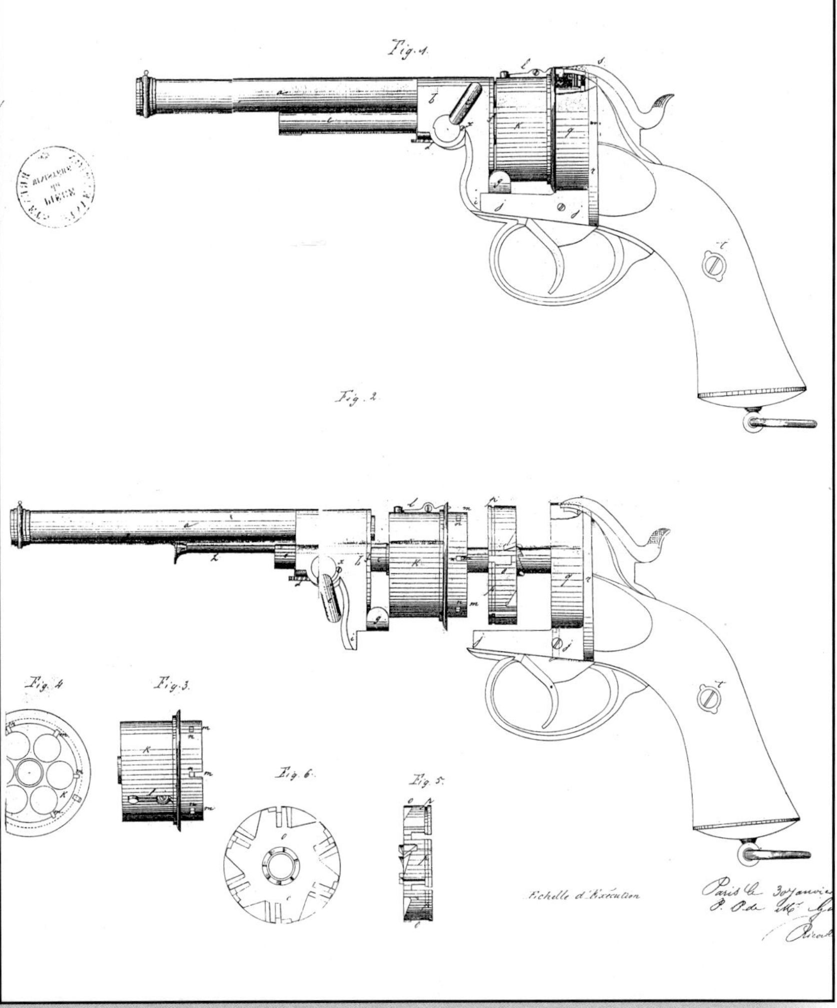

Pinfire
Pepperbox Pistols

The so-called "pepperbox" was one of the earliest forms of revolving pistol, and the first practical solution to the challenge of increased firepower. Pepperboxes were introduced during the late sixteenth century, and stubbornly refused to fade into obsolescence until early in the twentieth century.

During the period of their greatest popularity, pepperboxes were referred to as "revolving pistols." But that term was discarded during the nineteenth century when revolvers as we know them today became both practical and commonplace. The multi-barrel pistols also were known as "peppermills" and "fist pistols", but it is the term pepperbox that remains in use among collectors today. Their revolving multi-chambered barrels reminded many people of the rotating containers used for grinding peppercorns during the 1800s, and thus the slang name pepperbox came to be coined. In Germany they were known by the name *"Bundelrevolver"*, an equally vivid description.

The term pepperbox encompasses all firearms having three or more barrels, either fixed or rotating around a central arbor. Some pepperboxes have more than one striker, although most, including all known pinfire examples, employ only a single hammer.

At the time pinfire cartridges were being developed for use in hand arms, pepperboxes had evolved to their practical limits in both design and mechanical function. The new pinfire cartridge allowed firearms inventors to create arms that were more easily and quickly loaded, more trouble-free, and more compact and thus easily concealed. These smaller pistols found immediate favor with gamblers, women, and others who felt the need to be armed, yet not conspicuously so.

Revolvers could be sturdier, more accurate, larger in caliber, and generally more practical than pepperboxes, and the latter arms rapidly lost favor in the United States. The same was not true in Europe, however. There, pepperboxes were still being manufactured and used long after the introduction of the more advanced revolver designs, and even into the era of modern semi-automatic pistols.

Relatively few patents for pepperbox pistols were issued to individual firearms designers or companies, and due to the resultant free-borrowing of ideas and cross-fertilization of designs the variations found in pinfire pepperboxes are many. Some types have the standard rear loading gate and separate ejector rod screwed into the butt, others must be disassembled to load or extract cartridges, and numerous varieties exist of take-down systems. The stationary cylinder pin or arbor usually was employed as an ejector rod on most pepperbox arms.

Pepperboxes having more than six chambers

are uncommon. Examples are known with up to twelve or even fifteen chambers, but the much larger size of their barrel groups or cylinders makes them inherently unwieldy, and despite their increased firepower, essentially negates one primary reason for the popularity of the pepperbox gun: its concealability. The same holds true for pepperboxes made in the larger 9mm and 12mm calibers. Their increased bulk was not popular, and those types are seldom encountered by collectors today. Neither are the tiny 5mm caliber pinfire pepperboxes, as their very smallness rendered them ineffective. Early-on, most pepperbox manufacturers realized that the 7mm cartridge was best suited for use in these relatively small pistols, and the vast majority are found to be chambered in that caliber.

Casimir Lefaucheux concentrated his original efforts on building shotguns, and constantly strove to improve on his basic designs within the context of the pinfire shotgun and its cartridge. But, while working at the 10 rue de la Bourse location in Paris, Lefaucheux made other types of guns in limited numbers. One style was a pepperbox, which he displayed at the 1851 London Exhibition.

These were the first handguns manufactured by Casimir Lefaucheux, and in making them he borrowed heavily from the designs of Gilles Mariette. While no records exist to tell us how many were made by Lefaucheux, the quantity certainly had to have been small. Lefaucheux experimented with handguns only to the extent of designing and making a few examples which all were similar in style, appearance, and function. One of Casimir Lefaucheux' early pepperbox pistols is pictured in Chapter One.

The high-quality, double-action 7mm caliber pinfire pepperbox illustrated in *Plate 9-1* is from a slightly later date of manufacture. While it bears no proofmarks, the forward gripstrap is stamped *"Mariette Bte"*; the distinctive ring trigger, underhammer, and bag-shape grip readily identify it as the product of Gilles Mariette, who produced revolving arms in France between 1832 and 1865. The acorn-shaped knob at front unscrews to allow the barrel group to be drawn forward and off the cylinder arbor, which then may be used as an ejector rod.

Plate 9-2 illustrates an unmarked 9mm caliber pinfire pepperbox. Its ring trigger operates either as single- or double-action; the bores of the six-shot barrel group are rifled. A pin shield is made integral with the engraved German silver frame. The round device in front of the barrels, when threaded into the chamber opposite it, forms a crude but effective positive safety by blocking rotation and cocking of the arm. A lever (not shown in photograph) on the front barrel support flips open, allowing the barrel support to rotate to the side, in

Plate 9-1. A Mariette *Brevete* pepperbox having finely-engraved frame and barrel group. The ring trigger, underhammmer, and bag-style grip are typical of the type. *Courtesy Don Kramer; Clearwater Color photograph*

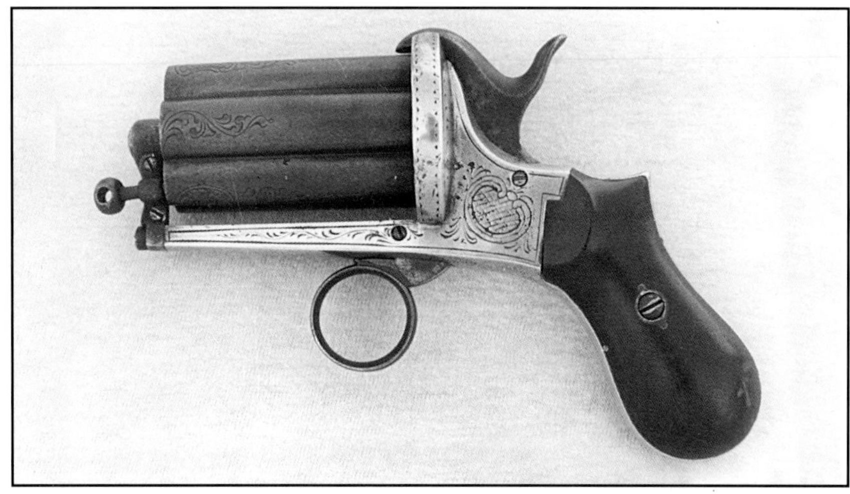

Plate 9-2. A 9mm caliber pinfire pepperbox, completely unmarked even to proofmarks. The engraved German silver frame, screw-in positive safety device, and either single- or double-action operation are its most distinctive features. *Courtesy private collection; F.W. Hulbert photograph*

turn permitting the barrel group to slide forward off the stationary cylinder pin.

In *Plate 9-3* we see an English-made pinfire pepperbox having a folding trigger and bearing London proofmarks. The front knob unscrews to allow the hinged front barrel support to tip down, after which the barrel group can be removed for loading or extracting spent cartridges, using the cylinder arbor as an ejector rod.

The Spanish-made pepperbox pistol pictured in *Plate 9-4* is marked "*Orbea Her.—Eibar*" on the trigger. It operates as a double-action arm only. The front lever unscrews to withdraw the cylinder arbor, permitting removal of the barrel group for

loading or ejection utilizing the arbor.

Plate 9-5 illustrates another English-made pepperbox, this double-action example being chambered for the 7mm caliber pinfire cartridge. It has an integral pin shield, and bears both London proofmarks and the marking "*London Patent No. 58471.*" The lever, comprising the portion of the frame under the barrel group and the front barrel support, swivels downward to expose the front of the cylinder arbor and then back and down to release the cylinder arbor. The cylinder is then free to slide off the arbor.

Plate 9-6 illustrates a Spanish-made 7mm caliber pinfire pepperbox which can be operated

Plate 9-3. An English-made pepperbox pistol having London proofmarks on the barrel group; it operates double-action, has a folding trigger, and fully-checkered grips. *Courtesy James Lowther; John Calcany photograph*

Plate 9-4. A double-action pepperbox pistol of Spanish manufacture, marked *"Orbea Her.—Eibar." Courtesy James Lowther; John Calcany photograph*

Plate 9-5. A 7mm caliber, double-action pinfire pepperbox pistol manufactured in England, marked *"London Patent No. 58471"* and bearing London proofmarks. *Courtesy James Lowther; John Calcany photograph*

Plate 9-6. A compact, 7mm caliber pinfire pepperbox pistol of Spanish manufacture, marked *"Zolar Cia Eibar"* but without proofmarks. *Courtesy private collection; F.W. Hulbert photograph*

either single- or double-action. It bears no proof-marks, but is marked *"Zolar Cia Eibar"* on the trigger. The short barrel group features gold inlay in a floral motif; this arm also features an engraved frame and a rear loading gate, but has no provision for an ejector rod.

The compact but high-quality, Belgian-made 9mm caliber pinfire pepperbox illustrated in *Plate 9-7* was manufactured in Liége by Chamelot & Delvigne. The cartridge pins protruding from the silver-inlaid barrel group are protected by a pin shield made integral with the engraved frame. On the forward right frame it is marked "C&D" within an oval, which was a typical practice among makers of the era who seldom marked their products with the whole firm name but occasionally employed a monogram for the purpose. Another well-known Belgian armsmaker, Auguste Francotte, marked the guns he made with his trademark "AF" initials surmounted by a crown.

Plate 9-8 illustrates the left side of the pepperbox pistol just described, showing the rearward-hinged cartridge loading gate necessitated by the left-hand rotation of the barrel group. While counter-clockwise cylinder rotation is contrary to the majority of revolving arms, it is common to all of the small arms manufactured by Chamelot & Delvigne. Note the separate ejector rod, which is

Plate 9-7. A fully-embellished 9mm caliber pinfire pepperbox pistol made by Chamelot & Delvigne of Liége. Note the compact form, making it well-suited to pocket use. *Courtesy Don Kramer; John Calcany photograph*

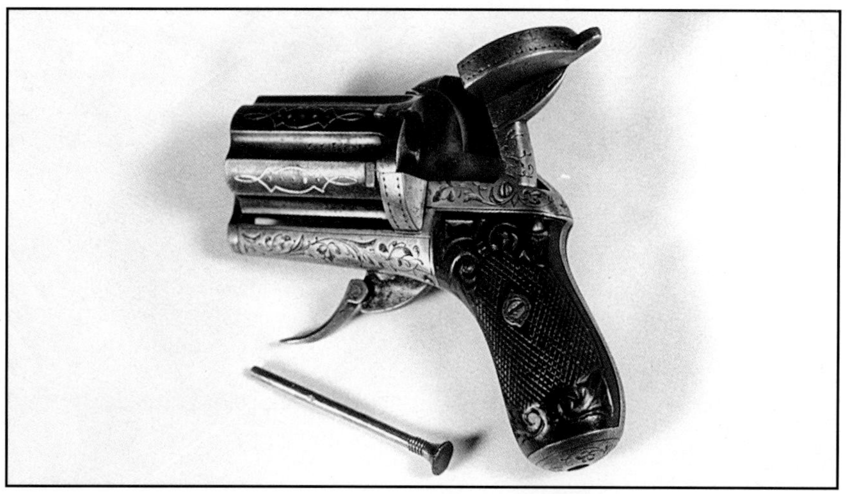

Plate 9-8. Left side of the pepperbox pistol pictured in *Plate 9-7,* showing its hinged left-side loading gate in the open position and the separate ejector rod removed from buttcap. *Courtesy Don Kramer; John Calcany photograph*

withdrawn after unscrewing it from the buttcap.

The pistol shown at the top of *Plate 9-9* is a French-made 7mm caliber pinfire pepperbox marked on the rear of the pin shield "*F. Decortis Bte.*" The spring-loaded forward barrel support is released when a latch (not shown in photograph) is depressed, thus allowing the barrel group to be withdrawn off the cylinder arbor. F. Decortis and Sons made quality arms between the years 1877 and 1884, and this piece is a fine example of their work. The pepperbox pistol shown at the bottom of *Plate 9-9* is unmarked, even to lacking proofmarks. It has the standard rear loading gate, but no provision for an ejector rod.

Plate 9-10 illustrates an English-made 7mm caliber pinfire pepperbox unidentified as to its maker, but marked "*Meyers*" on the left rear recoil shield and "*#1081 London*" on the frame. This pistol also bears Birmingham proofmarks, where Meyers likely was a retail sales agent. Note the single spearpoint grip escutcheon, a feature found on pinfire handguns of all types manufactured in England.

The pre-1877 Belgian-made pepperbox pistol shown at top in *Plate 9-11* is marked "*A. Francotte a Liege A.O.*", and bears Liége proofmarks. The knob at front unscrews and drops down with the hinged front cylinder support, allowing removal of

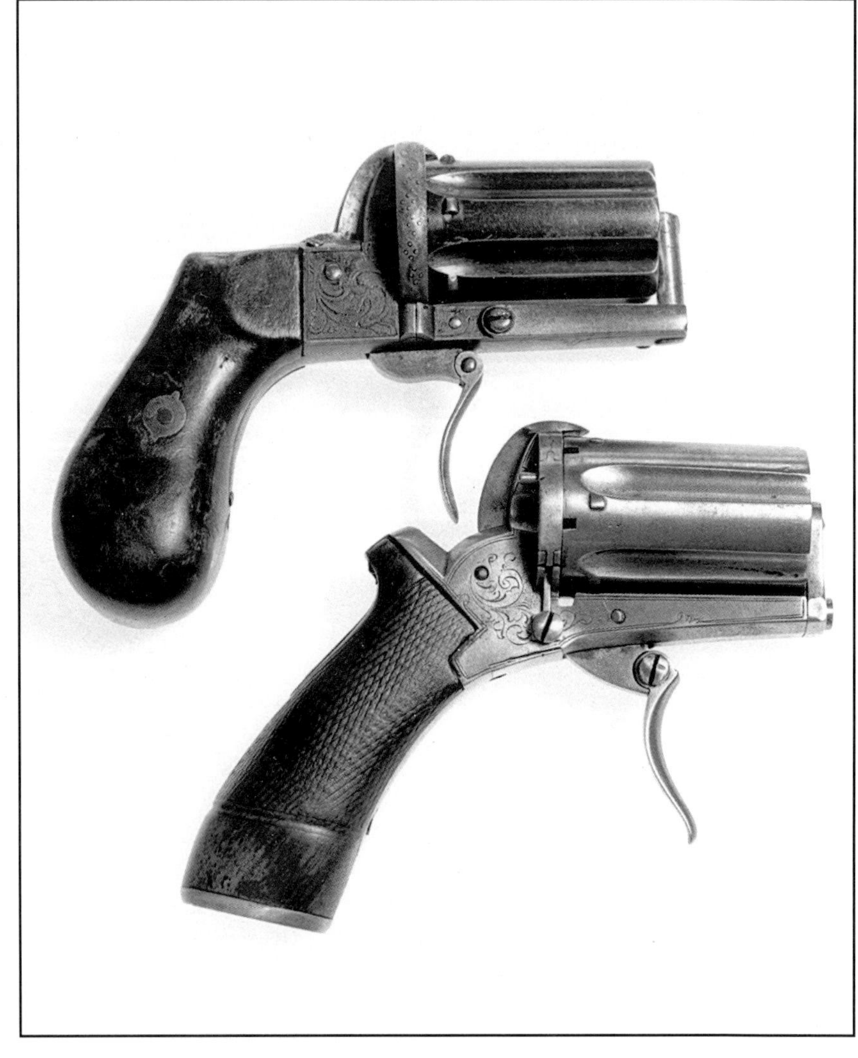

Plate 9-9. Shown at top is a French-made pepperbox pistol marked "*F. Decortis Bte.*" and having appropriate proofmarks. Shown at bottom is a 7mm caliber pinfire pepperbox pistol unmarked even to proofmarks. Note the lack of ejector rods on both pieces. *Courtesy private collection; F.W. Hulbert photograph*

Plate 9-10. A 7mm caliber pinfire pepperbox revolver unknown as to maker but marked "*Meyers*", the retailer. Note the full checkering on grips, typical of English-made examples. *Courtesy private collection; John Calcany photograph*

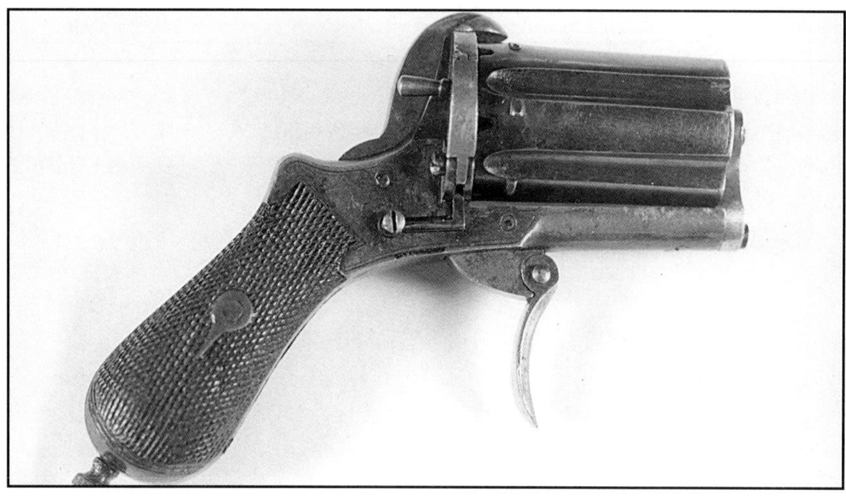

Plate 9-11. Shown at top is a 7mm caliber pinfire pepperbox pistol made in Belgium and marked "*A. Francotte a Liege A.O.*" The unusual mechanism was designed to fire either pinfire or rimfire cartridges. Shown at bottom is a German-made 7mm caliber double-action pepperbox pistol marked "*V.C.S. 1736*" and "*Guss Stahl.*" *Courtesy private collection; F.W. Hulbert photograph*

the barrel group. This interesting pistol was designed to fire either 7mm caliber pinfire or rimfire cartridges. The standard pinfire hammer has a rimfire firing pin machined on its underside, and the cylinder chambers are counterbored to allow pinfire cartridges to seat deeper in the chamber to avoid being struck by the rimfire firing pin as it passes through the pin slot in the rear of the cylinder. Rimfire cartridges are seated flush with the rear cylinder face. The Francotte family began their involvement with the Liége arms industry in 1810. The master, Auguste Francotte, began producing arms there in 1868, and the firm he established manufactured fine-quality arms for over half a century.

At the bottom of *Plate 9-11* is pictured a German-made 7mm caliber pinfire pepperbox, marked on the frame "*V.C.S. 1736*", possibly the initials of Valentin Christoph Schilling, and "*Guss Stahl*" on the barrel group. When the lever at front is rotated 180 degrees the cylinder pin is released, and the barrel group can be removed for loading or extraction of spent cartridges.

The lovely, Belgian-made pepperbox pistol having ivory grips shown at the top of *Plate 9-13*, is the standard 7mm caliber pinfire model equipped with a loading gate and a separate ejector rod that screws into the buttcap. It bears Liége proofmarks, and inspector's marks indicative of pre-1877 manufacture. The pinfire pepperbox pistol pictured at the bottom of *Plate 9-13* also is fitted with ivory grips, a loading gate, and an ejector rod in the butt, and bears Liége proofmarks and pre-1877 inspector's marks. Additionally, it is marked "*Deprez Bte*" for either Joseph Deprez, who manufactured firearms in Liége, Belgium from 1874 to 1886, or the firm of F&J Deprez, in which Joseph was a partner, which made guns in that same city between 1874 and 1876.

Plate 9-14 illustrates a French-made 7mm caliber pinfire pepperbox marked "*Acier Fondu*" on the barrel group and having proofmarks dating its manufacture to sometime after 1894, proof of the enduring popularity of the pinfire pepperbox in Europe. It is fitted with an ejector rod of unusual style that is reminiscent of those found on some cartridge revolvers. The rod is permanently attached to a swivel on the right side of the frame. When the rod is drawn forward its full length it is able to pivot upward into position at the front of the barrel group, directly opposite the hinged loading gate.

The Swedish-made 7mm caliber pinfire pepperbox pistol illustrated in *Plate 9-15* is of all-brass construction but for its hammer, trigger, and internal springs. The frame is marked "*J. Engh*", the mark of Johan Engholm of Odestugu, Smaland, Sweden. According to author Claude Blair in *Pistols of the World* (New York, 1968), Engholm (b. 1820; d. 1920) was a caster of brass candlesticks

Plate 9-12. This illustration reproduced from a Civil War-era catalog of New York arms dealer Schuyler, Hartley & Graham shows a pepperbox pistol almost identical in construction and appearance to the example pictured at top in *Plate 9-11*. *Chris C. Curtis collection*

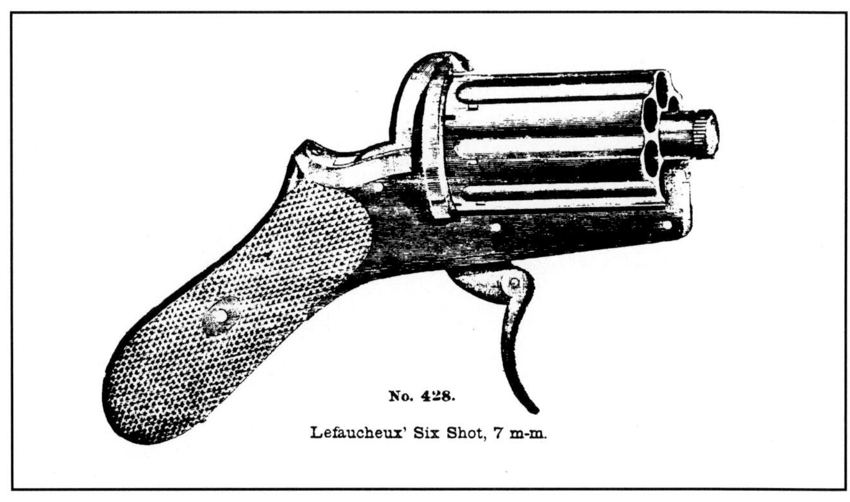

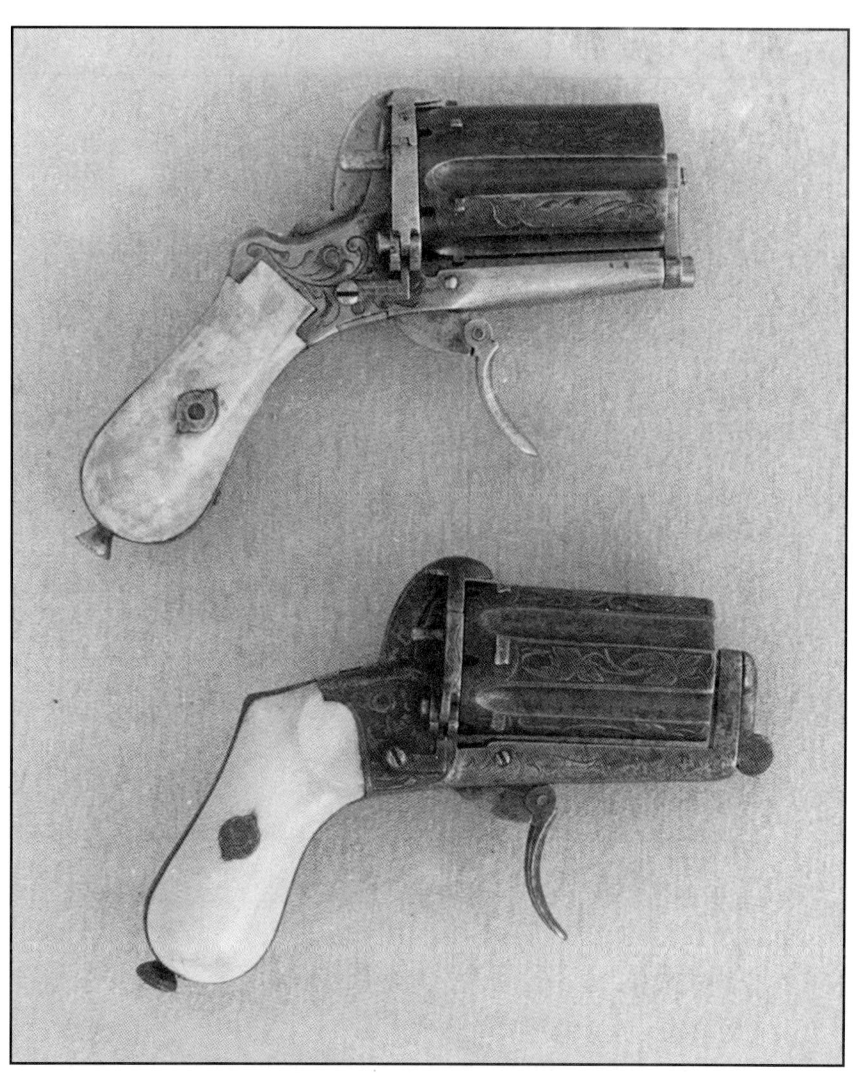

Plate 9-13. Shown at top is a 7mm caliber pinfire pepperbox pistol having Liége proofmarks, manufactured before 1877. Shown at bottom is a similar 7mm caliber pinfire pepperbox pistol marked *"Deprez Bte."* and with Liége proofmarks, also made pre-1877. Note the engraving on frames and barrels, and ivory grips on both. *Courtesy private collection; F.W. Hulbert photograph*

Plate 9-14. A very late French pepperbox, made after 1894, marked *"Acier Fondu"* on the barrel group. Note the unusual swivel ejector rod. *Courtesy Don Kramer; F.W. Hulbert photograph*

Plate 9-15. An all-brass pepperbox pistol of Swedish manufacture marked "*J. Engh*" on the frame, previously thought to be of American origin. *Courtesy Ron Ruble; F.W. Hulbert photograph*

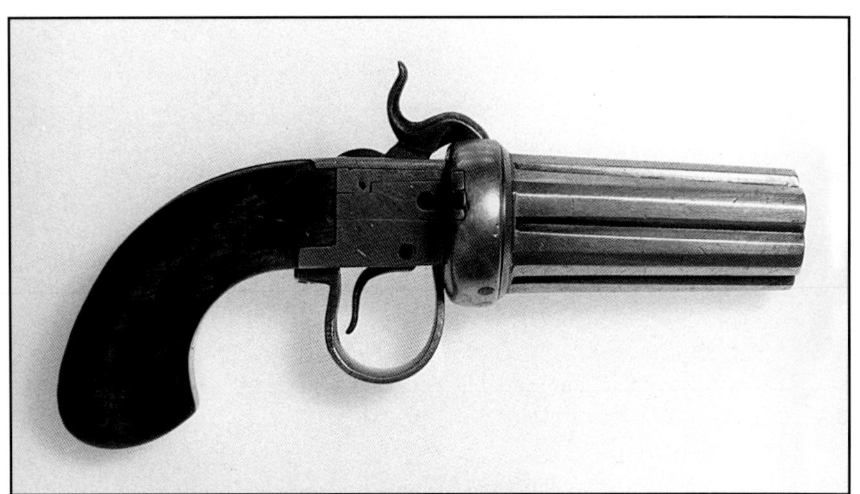

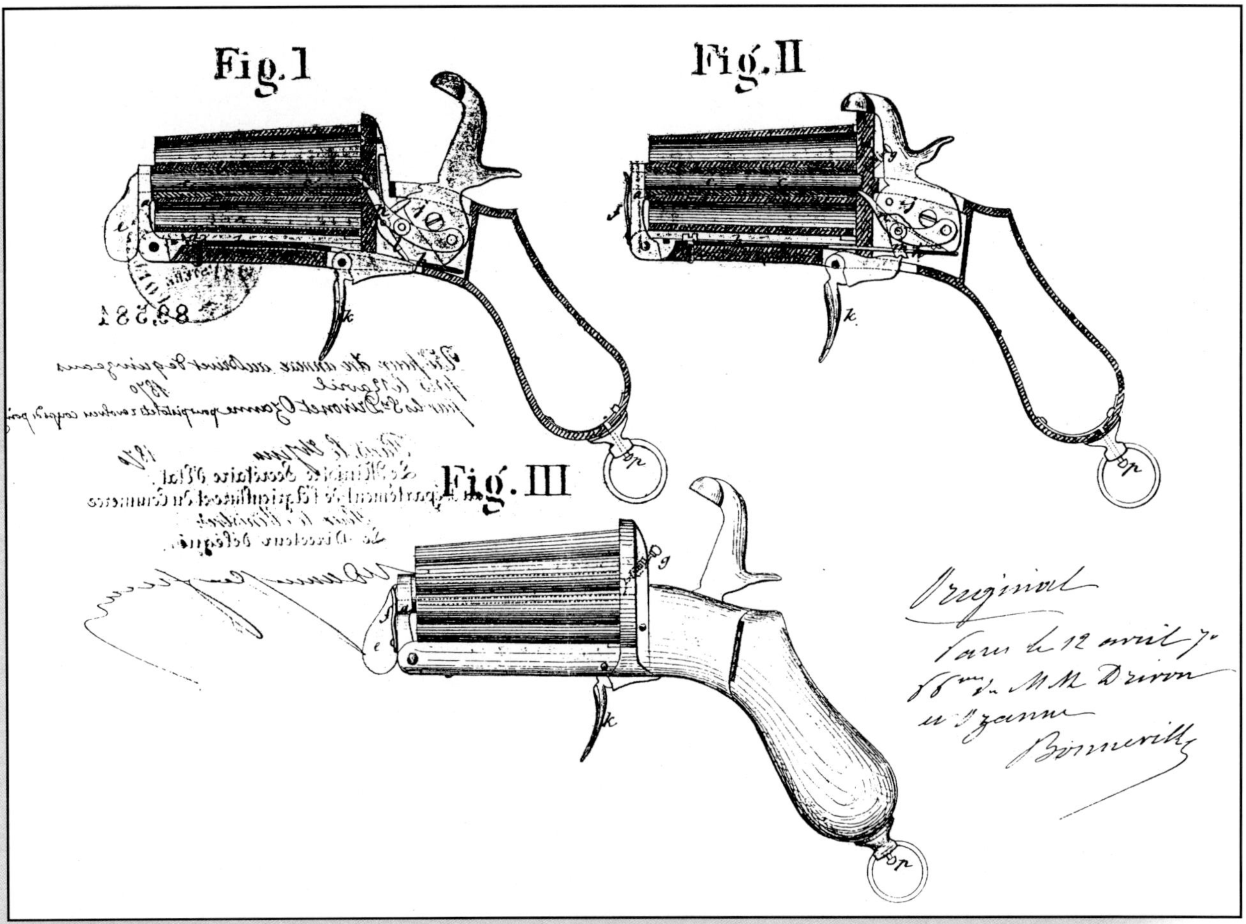

Plate 9-16. An illustration from Drivon and Ozanne's French patent number 89581, of April 12, 1870, showing details of their designs for pepperbox pistols. *Chris C. Curtis collection*

Plate 9-17. This short-barreled pinfire pepperbox has the unusual features of a revolver-style trigger and triggerguard. Note also fine floral engraving on the frame, and separate ejector rod screwed into the butt. *Courtesy private collection; F.W. Hulbert photograph*

Plate 9-18. A Belgian-made 5mm caliber pinfire pepperbox pistol of smallest proportions having a folding trigger; it functions in double-action operation only. *Courtesy Don Kramer; Ferrari Color photograph*

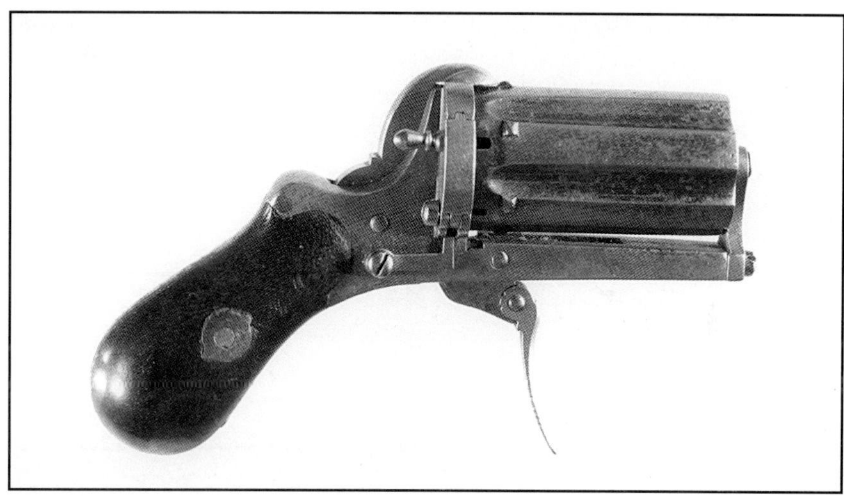

and chandeliers as well as of gun frames and barrels, who worked at his craft between the years 1840 to 1868 and perhaps even later. The style of this pistol is similar to the American percussion pepperboxes made in the 1830s by brothers Burton and Benjamin Darling of Woonsocket, Rhode Island. For many years collectors believed these all-brass pepperboxes with their hand-rotated percussion (or far-scarcer pinfire) cylinders were the products of gunsmith J. Englehart of Nazareth, Pennsylvania, perhaps working under license from the Darling brothers. Research in more recent times, however, has proven their European, not American, origins.

Plate 9-18 pictures a diminutive, Belgian-made 5mm pinfire pepperbox pistol bearing Liége proofmarks. It also is illustrated at the top of *Plate 9-21*, for the purpose of comparing the range of sizes of pinfire pepperboxes made in Europe during the nineteenth century.

The French-style burlwood casing pictured in *Plate 9-19* contains a 7mm caliber pinfire pepperbox along with various tools. The lovely little pistol bears London proofmarks and is equipped with a pin shield made integral with the frame. Note the fine engraving, the carved wood grips, and the same take-down lever system as well as overall shape and style shown on the London-made pepperbox pistol illustrated in *Plate 9-5*.

Plate 9-20 pictures a most unusual 12-shot, Spanish-made 7mm caliber pinfire pepperbox pistol marked with a maker's name that is too worn to decipher, making definite identification impossible. It does bear markings of the gunmaking center of Eibar, however. Pepperboxes having cylinders with this number of chambers are decided rarities.

Plate 9-21 illustrates the four standard calibers found in European pinfire pepperbox revolvers, in addition to their dramatic size differences. From top to bottom: 5mm, 7mm, 9mm, and 12mm calibers.

The following four plates illustrate an interesting concept on the part of the maker of these pepperbox revolvers. The identity of their inventor is unknown, as no specimen of the type as yet examined by the authors has been marked with a maker's name. Nonetheless, there exist a few clues to their origins, as well as to the general period of their manufacture. The central idea behind this type was a simple one: to combine two popular features into one pistol. The result was a pepperbox pistol having a removable revolver-type barrel.

With the barrel fitted in place it was a standard revolver; with the barrel removed it was an easily-concealed pocket pepperbox pistol.

Plate 9-22 shows a 7mm caliber pinfire pepperbox revolver, which operates either in single- or double-action. Both barrel and cylinder are smoothbore, and it is fitted with the standard ring trigger, loading gate, and ejector rod in the butt. The threaded barrel as well as the corresponding frame have key slots milled in at corresponding points, should the user wish to lock the barrel into place.

Plate 9-23 illustrates a pistol similar to that shown in *Plate 9-22*, except the caliber is 9mm pinfire. Like the previous piece it operates in either single- or double-action, has a smoothbore barrel and cylinder, ring trigger, and a pin shield integral with the frame. On this ivory-gripped piece, however, the barrel is locked in place utilizing a setscrew through the forward frame.

A Belgian-made pepperbox revolver having the standard folding trigger, and which operates double-action only, is pictured in *Plate 9-24*. This example is chambered for the 9mm caliber pinfire cartridge; the barrel and cylinder are smoothbore, and it is fitted with a loading gate but has no pro-

Plate 9-19. An English-made 7mm caliber pinfire pepperbox pistol bearing London proofmarks, cased in the French style with appropriate tools. Note the take-down lever similar to other British pinfire pepperboxes. *Courtesy Don Kramer; Ferrari Color photograph*

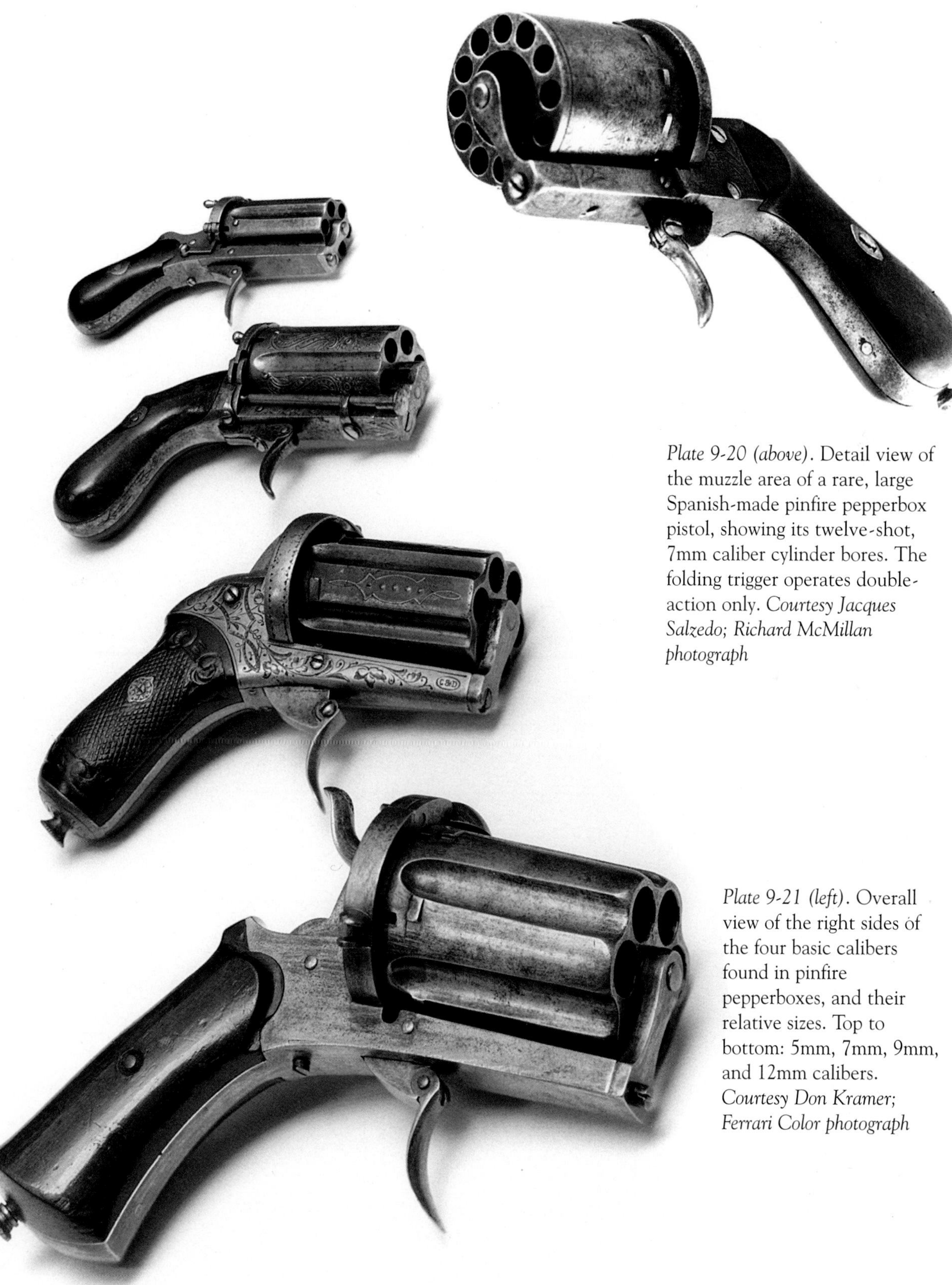

Plate 9-20 (above). Detail view of the muzzle area of a rare, large Spanish-made pinfire pepperbox pistol, showing its twelve-shot, 7mm caliber cylinder bores. The folding trigger operates double-action only. *Courtesy Jacques Salzedo; Richard McMillan photograph*

Plate 9-21 (left). Overall view of the right sides of the four basic calibers found in pinfire pepperboxes, and their relative sizes. Top to bottom: 5mm, 7mm, 9mm, and 12mm calibers. *Courtesy Don Kramer; Ferrari Color photograph*

vision for an ejector rod. It bears Liége proofmarks, and inspector's marks on the cylinder which date its manufacture to sometime before 1877.

Plate 9-25 pictures a brass-frame combination pepperbox revolver which in itself constitutes yet another variation of the type. Not only is the barrel removable, but it separates into two halves, creating not only a pepperbox but a revolver having both long and short barrel lengths. It is 7mm caliber. The barrel and cylinder both have straight rifling; the cylinder is "cloverleaf" in shape, having the rear area around the pin slots cut away to permit the hammer maximum striking force. This arm is fitted with the typical loading gate, and an ejec-

tor rod threaded into the butt. A large percentage of these scarce pepperbox revolvers are completely unmarked, even to proofmarks, as is this example. Of those having proofmarks, Belgium is the only country of manufacture to have been noted. One 7mm caliber example examined by the authors is marked with Liége proofmarks and Belgian inspector's marks on the cylinder, and all major parts including the barrel are stamped with matching assembly numbers. This tends to substantiate the theory that this type of pepperbox revolver was originally manufactured this way, and not made up or converted at some later time utilizing unrelated parts.

Plate 9-22. A 7mm caliber pinfire pepperbox revolver having detachable barrel. Note the ring trigger, and the hammer spur for single- or double-action operation. *Courtesy Larry Compeau; F.W. Hulbert photograph*

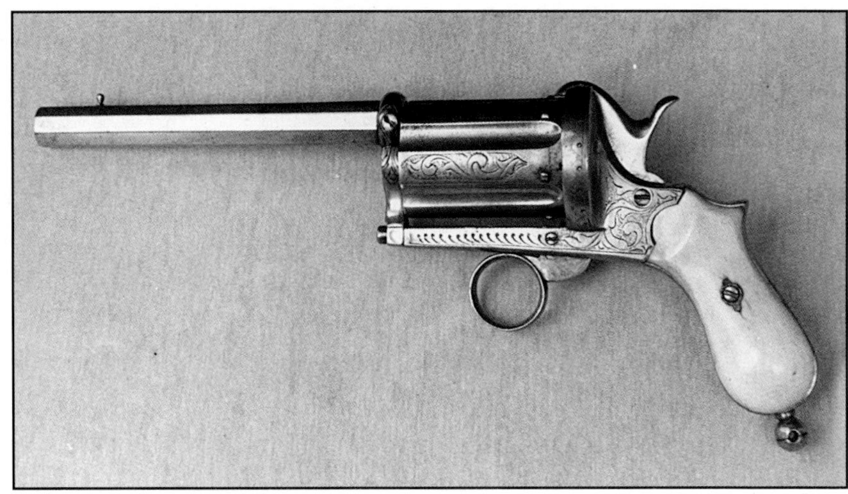

Plate 9-23. A 9mm caliber pinfire pepperbox revolver having many features similar to the example pictured in *Plate 9-22. Courtesy Don Kramer; F.W. Hulbert photograph*

Plate 9-24. A Belgian-made 9mm caliber pinfire pepperbox revolver having a short detachable barrel, and ivory grips. *Courtesy private collection; F.W. Hulbert photograph*

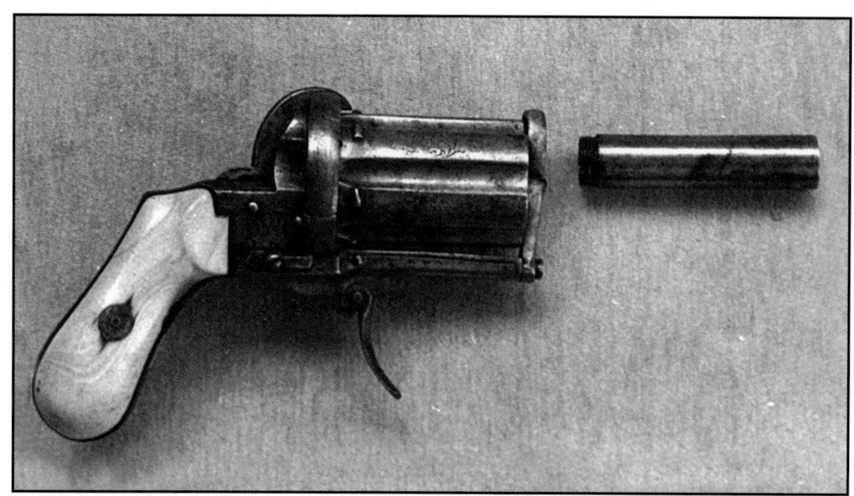

Plate 9-25. An unusual 7mm caliber pinfire pepperbox revolver having a jointed barrel. It may be used as a standard barrelless pepperbox, or as a revolver with either short or long barrels. The arm is unmarked, even to proofmarks. *Courtesy private collection; Gene Smith photograph*

Plate 9-26. Another 7mm caliber pinfire pepperbox revolver, having overall engraving and ivory grips. Note the unusual large, revolver-style triggerguard. *Courtesy Don Kramer; Ferrari Color photograph*

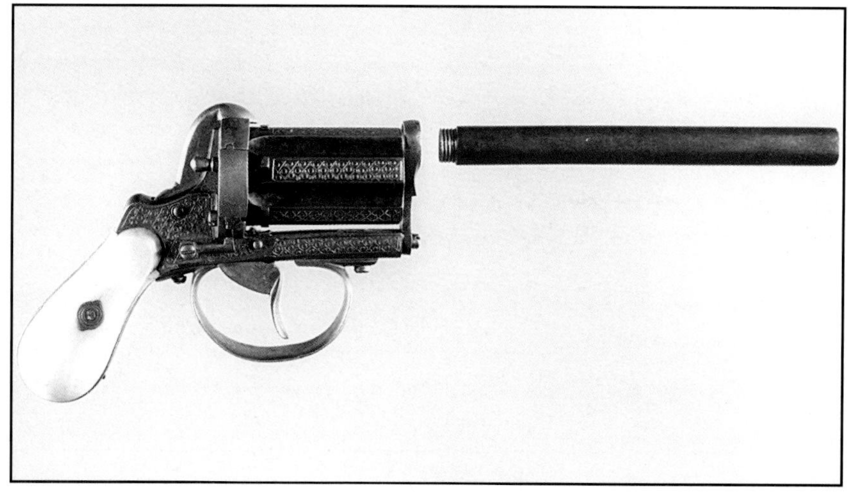

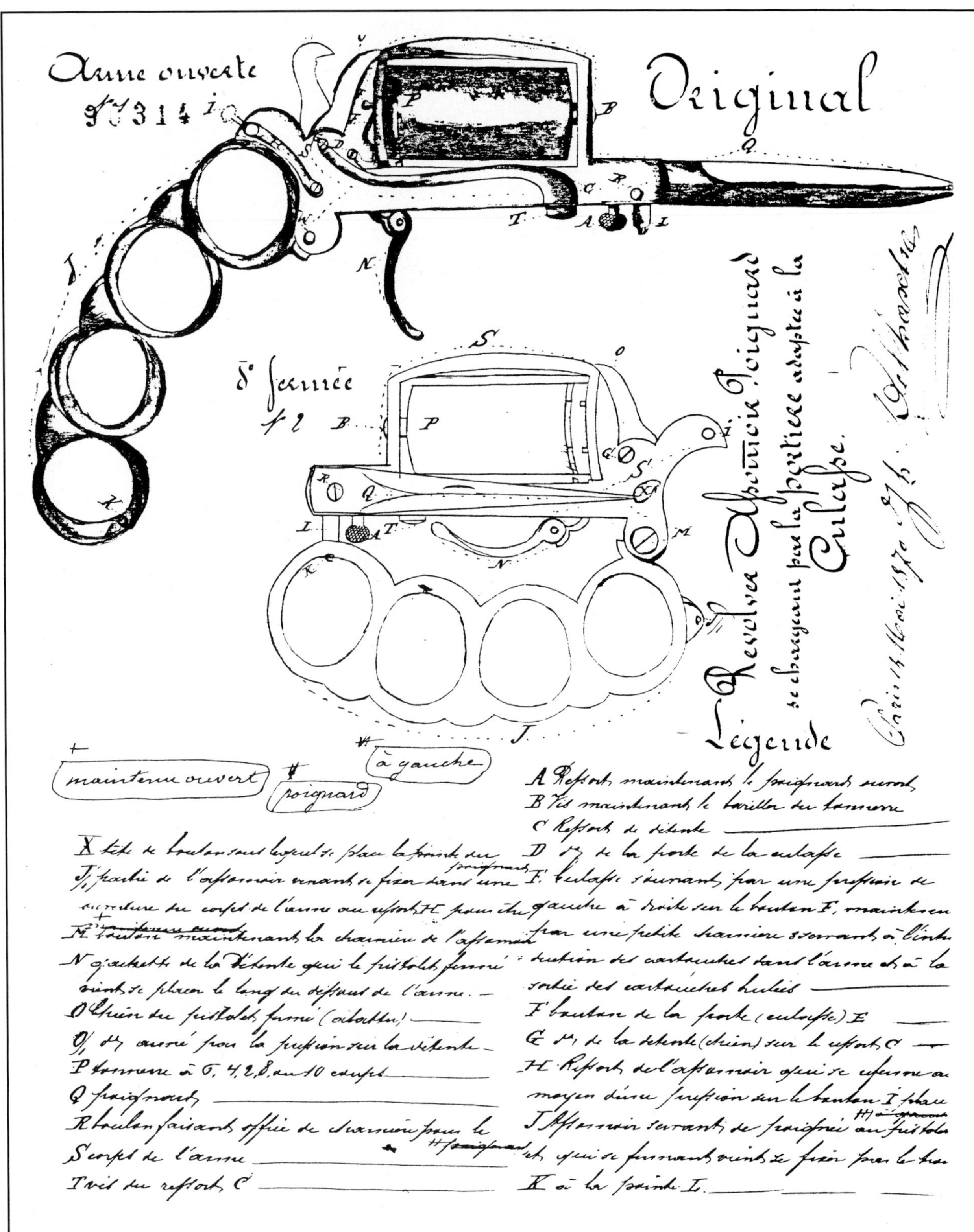

Plate 10-1 (see text on page 269). An illustration from J. Delhaxhe's French patent number 90314 of May 14, 1870, showing details of his designs for an *Apache* knuckleduster pistol. *Chris C. Curtis collection*

Peculiar Pinfire Arms

Each of the strange and unfamiliar firearms illustrated and described in this chapter is a tribute to the creative and inventive energy of the minds of the men who made it.

On its introduction to the gunmaking world the pinfire cartridge opened new doors for many of the nineteenth century's most imaginative firearms designers, particularly those practicing their trade in Western Europe. The self-contained metallic cartridge allowed even the most bizarre concepts in weaponry to become reality, and the development of unusual arms was limited only by the boundaries of their inventors' imaginations.

Because the pinfire cartridge was the first practical self-contained ammunition, many firearms oddities were chambered for that ignition system. During the pinfire era, many inventors constructed new firearms designs in the hope that theirs would be "the" idea that would alter the course of weapons development. A few realized limited commercial success, but most of those designs were soon discarded as impractical. Yet all had one thing in common: at the time, they seemed like good ideas!

Some of these firearms are, in fact, practical solutions to the problems their designers faced. At times the solutions took the form of improved methods for loading and extracting spent cartridges; others were attempts to generate more firepower from a single source. Many of the guns shown in this chapter, however, appear to have been the realization of some inventor's nightmare taking material form. It is these latter arms that we refer to as firearms oddities, curiosa, and combination weapons. But, grouped together, one statement describes them all: "Peculiar Pinfires."

Revolvers

Between the percussion era and the present day the six-shot revolver became the most accepted type of hand arm the world over. There are a few notable exceptions, however, and the guns illustrated in this chapter constitute deviations from that norm.

A seven-shot Fagnus revolver was pictured in Chapter Eight, while the revolver shown in *Plate 10-2* has an eight-shot cylinder chambered for the 12mm caliber pinfire cartridge. This revolver, of English manufacture, was made very late in the period of pinfire production, as it bears Birmingham proofmarks which did not come into use until 1904.

Plate 10-3 illustrates a French-made revolver having St. Etienne proofmarks. On this gun the cylinder is chambered to accept *ten rounds* of

12mm caliber pinfire ammunition, and the unusual attached, swivel-mounted ejector rod pivots out from the barrel into position for use.

Each of the three revolvers pictured in *Plate 10-4* is a *twelve-shot* model. All bear pre-1877 Belgian inspector's marks and Liége proofmarks. The revolver shown at top is chambered for the 7mm caliber pinfire cartridge; its barrel is 4¾ inches in length. At center, the revolver is chambered for the 9mm caliber pinfire cartridge; its barrel is 3½ inches long. The example shown at bottom is in 12mm caliber pinfire, with a barrel 6½ inches in length.

The highly-embellished revolver illustrated in

Plate 10-5 is not only beautifully engraved and fitted with carved ebony-wood grips, but the top of the barrel bears the engraved inscription, *"Ferdinand Maximilian von Oesterreich"*, along its rounded surface. Additionally, this unusual piece features *two barrels*, and is chambered to fire *eighteen rounds* of the 9mm caliber pinfire cartridge, arranged in two concentric rows in the cylinder! In use, the hammer first strikes the pins of the outer ring of cartridges, which fire through the upper barrel; then, the hammer falls on a sliding vertical bar working on much the same principle as the transfer bar found in some modern revolvers, which strikes the pins of the inner ring of car-

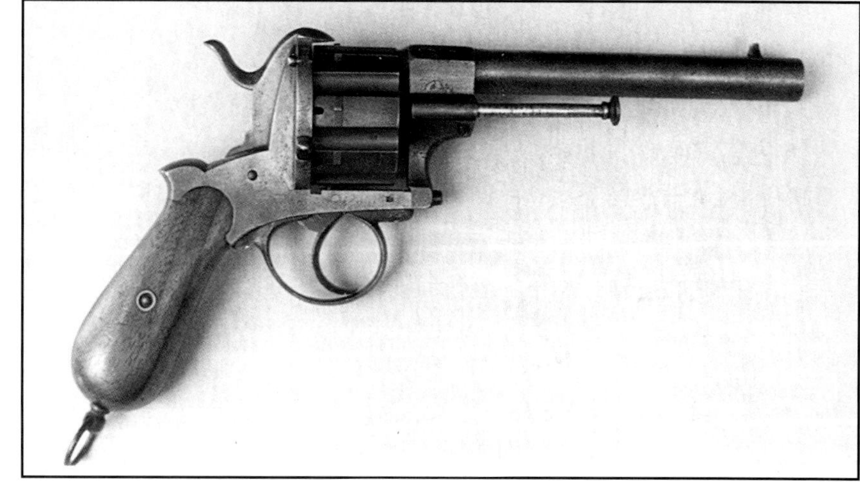

Plate 10-2. A large, eight-shot, 12mm caliber pinfire revolver having post-1904 English proofmarks. Note the unusual feature of eight tiny rear sights corresponding to each chamber, made integral on cylinder periphery. *Courtesy private collection; F.W. Hulbert photograph*

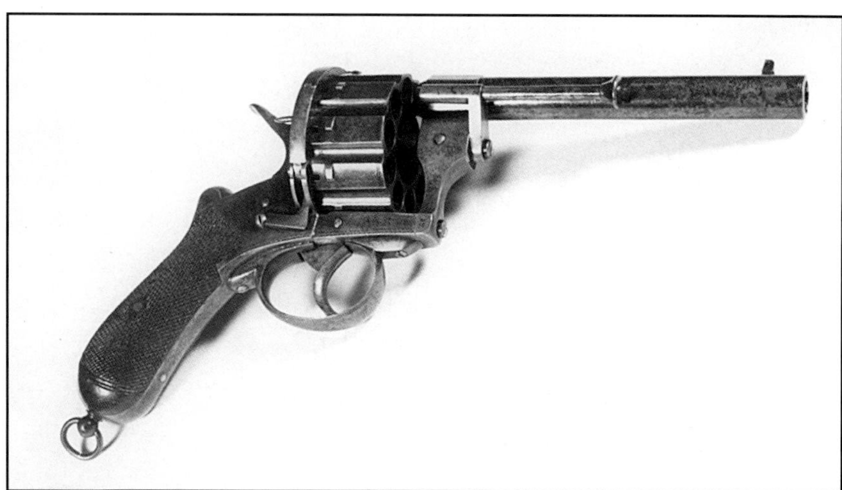

Plate 10-3. Another large, 12mm caliber pinfire revolver, but of French manufacture, this example having a ten-shot cylinder. *Courtesy private collection; John Calcany photograph*

Plate 10-4. Three sizes and calibers of pinfire revolvers manufactured in Liége, Belgium, all having twelve-shot cylinders. From top: 7mm, 9mm, and 12mm calibers. *Courtesy Don Cramer; Ferrari Color photograph*

Plate 10-5. A beautifully embellished, Belgian-made pinfire revolver having eighteen, 9mm caliber cylinder chambers arranged in two concentric rows, firing through two over-and-under barrels. *Courtesy private collection; Gene Smith photograph*

Plate 10-6. Detail view of the barrel of the revolver pictured in *Plate 10-5,* showing *"Ferdinand Maximilian von Oesterreich"* script-engraved along its top surface. *Courtesy private collection; Gene Smith photograph*

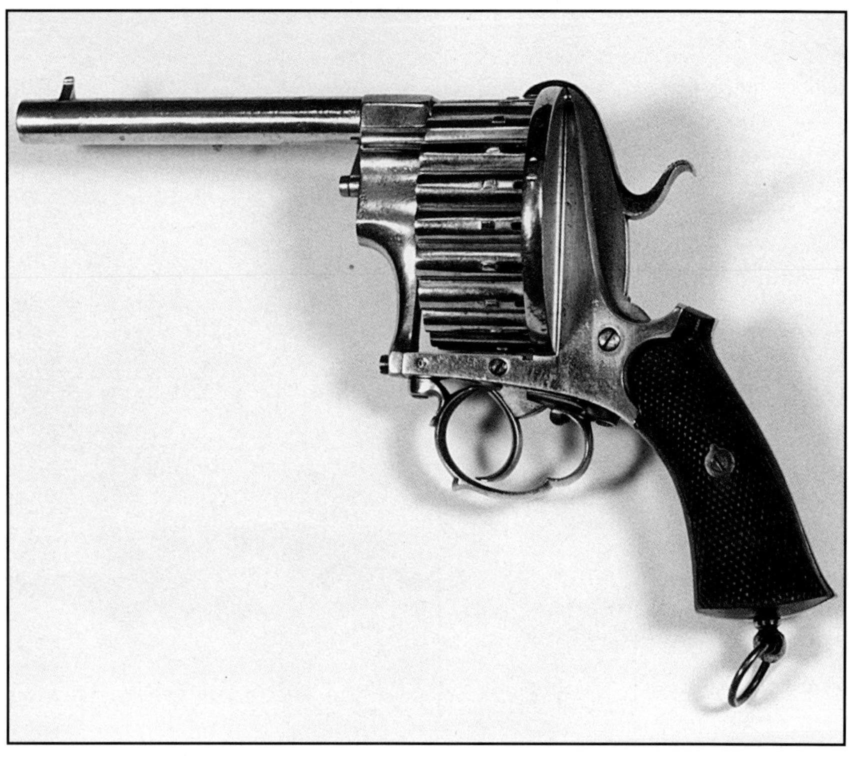

Plate 10-7. A large, twenty-shot, 7mm caliber pinfire revolver made by Chaineux of Liége, having all chambers arranged in a single row about the circumference of the cylinder. *Chris C. Curtis collection; John Calcany photograph*

tridges as they turn into alignment with the lower barrel. This particular revolver was made on the principle of Eugene Lefaucheux' French patent number 64960, of December 17, 1864. While unmarked as to maker, it does bear proofmarks indicating manufacture in Liége, Belgium prior to 1877.

Plates 10-7 and 10-8 picture another unusual Liége-proofmarked revolver, this one marked "*J. Chaineux.*" Quite different from the previous example, however, is the cylinder of this "beast", which has *twenty* 7mm caliber chambers arranged in a single row about its periphery! As shown in *Plate 10-8*, the center of the cylinder was machined out in a novel attempt to reduce the overall weight of this large and cumbersome piece. As on the example pictured in *Plate 10-3*, the side-mounted ejector rod swivels out to align with the chambers. The maker produced revolvers in Liége during the decade between 1860 and 1870. Chaineux had been granted firearms patents in 1858, 1859, 1863, and 1864, most of which dealt with the development of multi-shot revolvers hav-

ing 8, 10, 12, and 20-shot cylinders.

The multi-shot "harmonica"-style pistol shown in *Plate 10-9* is marked "*Ion* [Invention] *Jarre A. Paris.*" Its horizontal-sliding bar magazine automatically moves through the frame as the double-action mechanism is operated and cartridges are fired. A hinged face plate retains the ten 9mm caliber pinfire cartridges within the loaded magazine; when removed from the frame as illustrated, the face plate lifts up for loading or extraction of cartridges. Gunmaker J. Jarre of Paris received a United States patent, number 35685, for this type of firearm on June 24, 1862, over three hundred years after the Jarre family began their involvement with the French arms trade.

Another "harmonica pistol" is pictured in *Plate 10-10*. Quite similar in design to the pistol just shown, this piece, while unmarked, is almost certainly of Jarre's manufacture as well. In addition to pistols such as this, pictured with its magazine in place and ready to fire, Jarre also made rifles and shotguns utilizing the same principle in extremely limited numbers. The design earned its nickname

Plate 10-8. Frontal view of the Chaineux revolver pictured in *Plate 10-7,* showing hollow center area of cylinder. *Chris C. Curtis collection; John Calcany photograph*

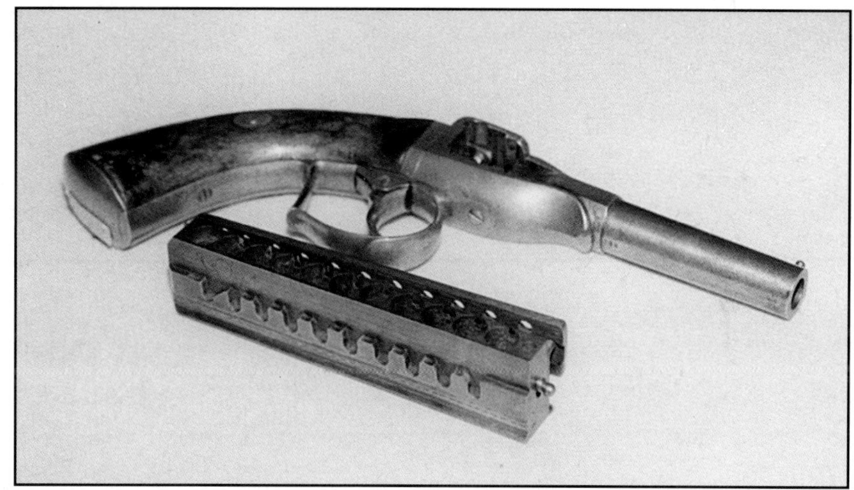

Plate 10-9. A ten-shot, 9mm caliber pinfire "harmonica" pistol patented and manufactured by J. Jarre of Paris. *Courtesy private collection; Gene Smith photograph*

Plate 10-10. Another sliding-bar magazine or "harmonica" pistol, unmarked but likely also made by Jarre. *Courtesy private collection; Gene Smith photograph*

Plate 10-11. A variant on the "harmonica" pistol, this example has a swiveling, ten-shot magazine combining 7mm caliber pinfire chambers and barrels into one unit. Made by A.E. and P.J. Jarre, successors to J. Jarre of Paris. *Courtesy private collection; F.W. Hulbert photograph*

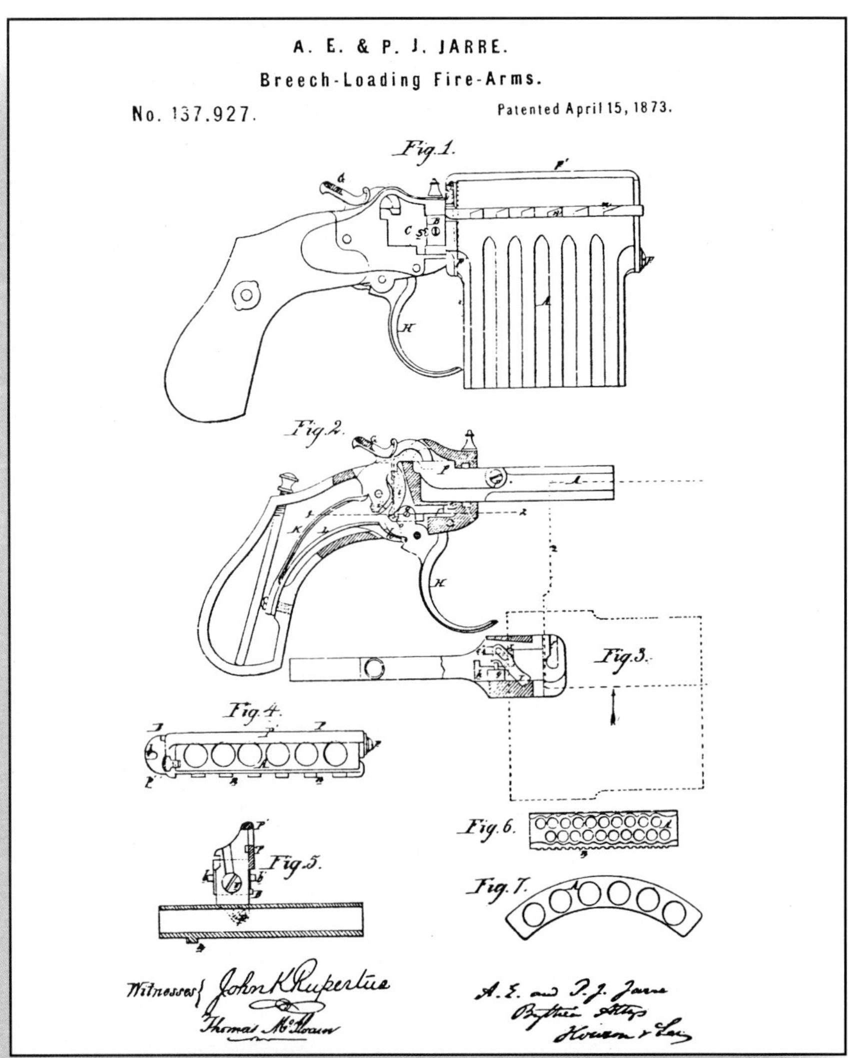

Plate 10-12. An illustration from A.E. and P.J. Jarre's United States patent number 137927 of April 15, 1873, showing their designs for a swivel-magazine pistol similar to the example pictured in *Plate 10-11. Chris C. Curtis collection*

among historians and collectors as a result of its similarity to the musical "mouth organ", or harmonica.

Still another type of harmonica pistol is illustrated in *Plates 10-11 and 10-12*. This arm was constructed on an entirely different principle, having an integral magazine-barrel group chambered for the 7mm caliber pinfire cartridge. The cartridges are retained by a hinged face plate similar to those on the pistols illustrated previously, however, and like the others, the barrel group moves horizontally through the frame as cartridges are successively fired. This pistol is marked "*A. Jarre Bte. S.G.D.G.*" Its design was protected under Jarre's French patent number 90883, first certificate of additions, of December 2, 1871, as well as United States patent number 137927, granted on April 15, 1873 to Alphonse Etienne Jarre and Pierre Joseph Jarre, successors to and most likely sons of J. Jarre. The pair operated at 28 boulevard Poissonierre in Paris from 1873 to 1890, manufacturing various arms in addition to pistols of this type having barrel groups with either six or ten chambers.

Plate 10-13 illustrates a pistol contained within a pocket change purse. One side consists of an accordian-style compartment for coins or other small items, and the other holds a diminutive six-shot, 5mm caliber pinfire revolver made integral with the metal frame. On first impression the gun appears to be a pepperbox, but it actually is a stub-barrel revolver which fires through a hinged port on the end. The port, closed when the arm is not in use, automatically pivots to the open position at first pull of the folding double-action trigger, which drops out of the bottom for firing. The gun compartment must of course be opened for loading and ejection of cartridges, but remains closed during use, concealing the revolver. This type of combination arm was popular during the last half of the nineteenth century, having been patented during 1877 in both the United States and England. This particular example was manufactured in Liége by O. Frankenau, and is so marked.

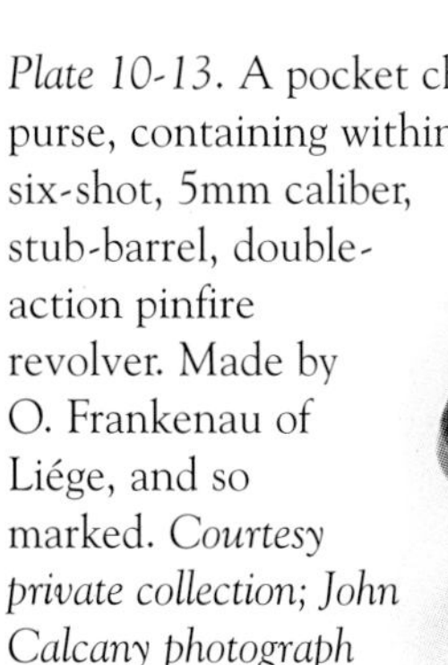

Plate 10-13. A pocket change purse, containing within a six-shot, 5mm caliber, stub-barrel, double-action pinfire revolver. Made by O. Frankenau of Liége, and so marked. *Courtesy private collection; John Calcany photograph*

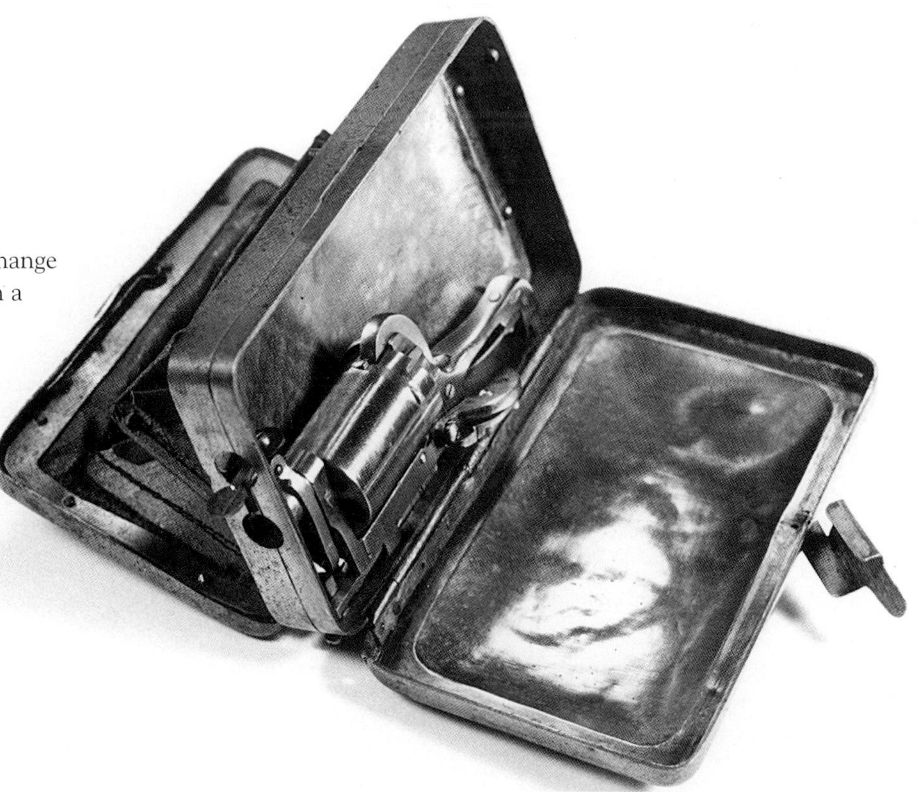

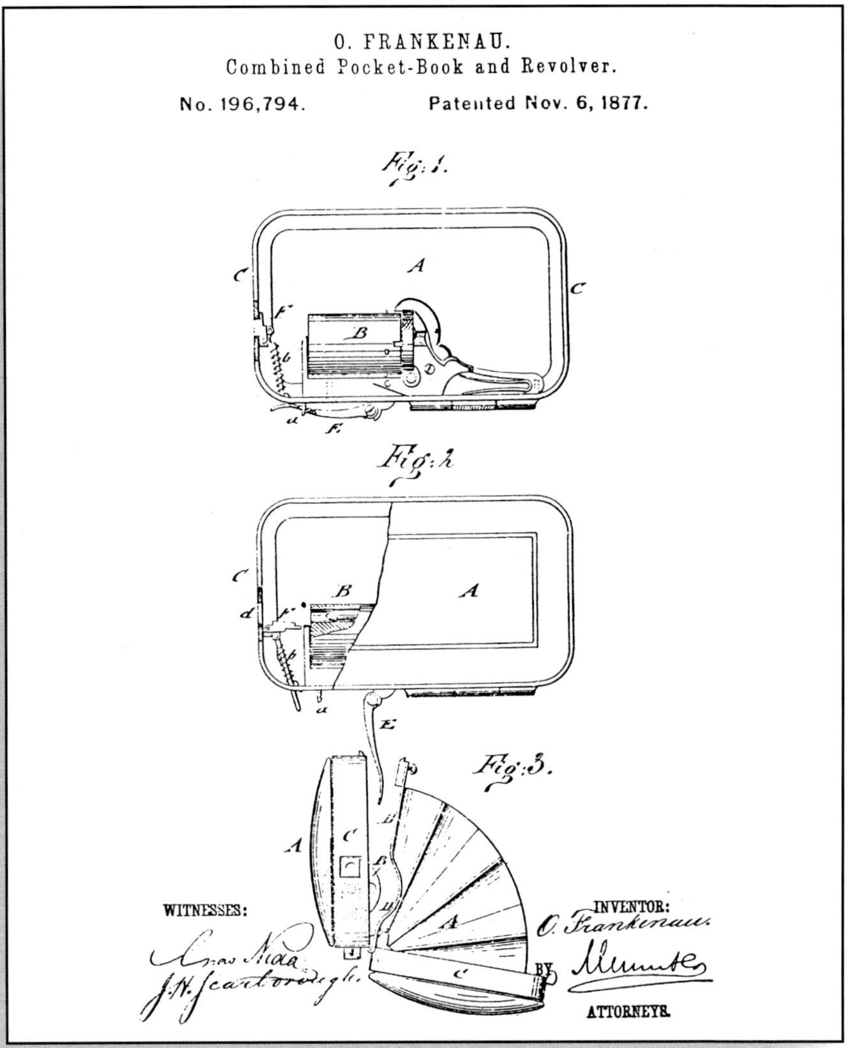

Plate 10-14. An illustration from Frankenau's United States patent number 196794 of November 6, 1877, showing designs for the change purse-revolver pictured in *Plate 10-13. Chris C. Curtis collection*

Trap Guns

During the same era other types of firearm devices also were conceived and made, which fall into the category of "trap guns." While some trap guns were intended to scare away or even kill predatory animals, others were designed to discourage human intruders. Each was different in appearance and function, but all were identical in one respect: namely, that the arm need not be manually discharged, nor the operator even be present.

Some trap guns were single-barrel devices permanently mounted in line with a door or window, which when opened activated a trip-wire connected to the firing mechanism. Others were fitted with clamps, which allowed the trap gun to be moved among different locations, while still others had stakes which were driven into the ground for use outdoors. All were fired in the same manner.

Plate 10-15 illustrates an all-metal animal trap gun, which utilized a long stake attachment to secure the device in the ground. A breechblock lifts to open the chamber for loading a single, 32-

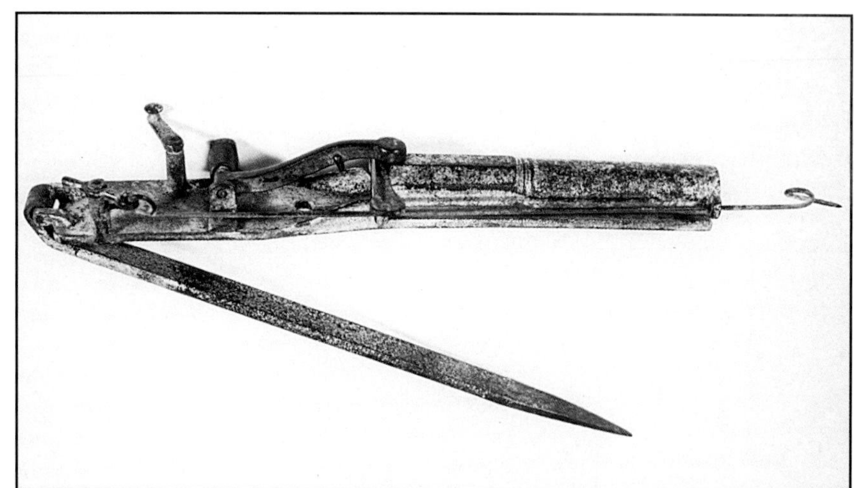

Plate 10-15. An all-metal, single-shot, 32-gauge pinfire animal trap gun. *Courtesy private collection; John Calcany photograph*

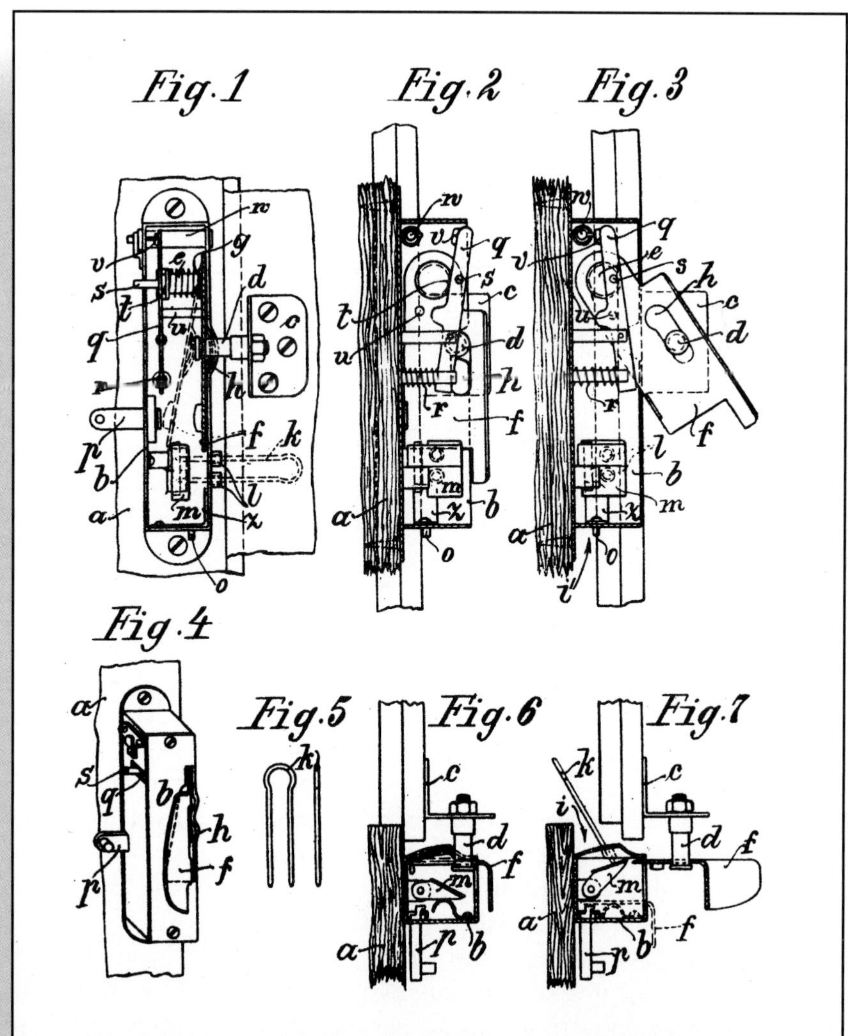

Plate 10-16. An illustration from Lamberg's British patent number 29786 of December 20, 1909, for an animal trap gun. *Chris C. Curtis collection*

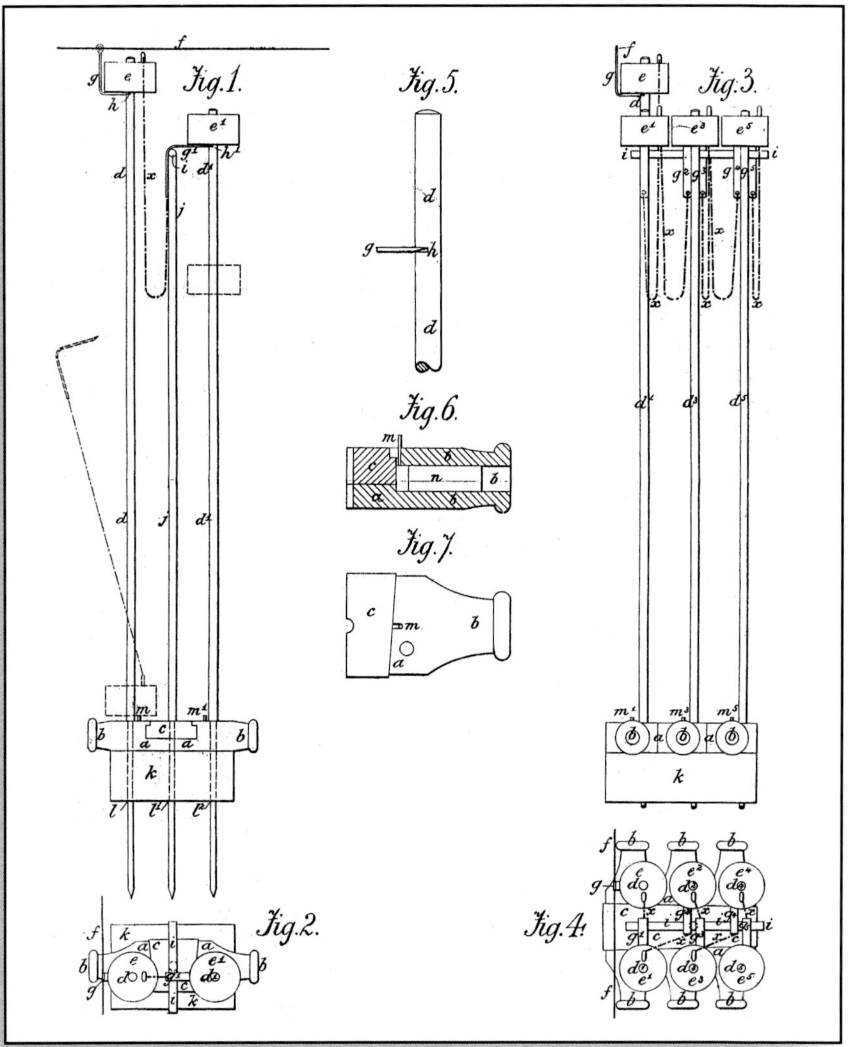

Plate 10-17. An illustration from Cank's British patent number 16318 of October 14, 1890, for an animal trap gun. *Chris C. Curtis collection*

gauge pinfire shotgun shell. The hammer pivots back and is held in "set" (firing) position by a swivel bar. When an animal pulls at a piece of meat or other bait on the wire visible at the front, the swivel bar moves out of the way and releases the hammer. Note the second swivel bar, which when moved under the cocked hammer acts as a positive safety while loading and setting the trap.

The patent drawings reproduced in *Plates 10-16, 10-17, and 10-18* illustrate just three of many attempts by British inventors to improve on the design and function of trap guns during the late nineteenth and early twentieth centuries.

The curious contraption illustrated in *Plates 10-19, 10-20, and 10-21* at first looks very much like a common rural mailbox when the cover is in the closed position over its mechanism. While this particular example is unmarked, others have been observed stamped "*Millichamp & Sons Fox Scarer*", and "*Kingster's Patent Rook Scarer.*" The purpose of this device was to frighten rooks (a large, crow-like English bird), foxes, and other varmints away from crops and henhouses by firing a discharge at timed intervals. The key-wound mechanism can be ad-

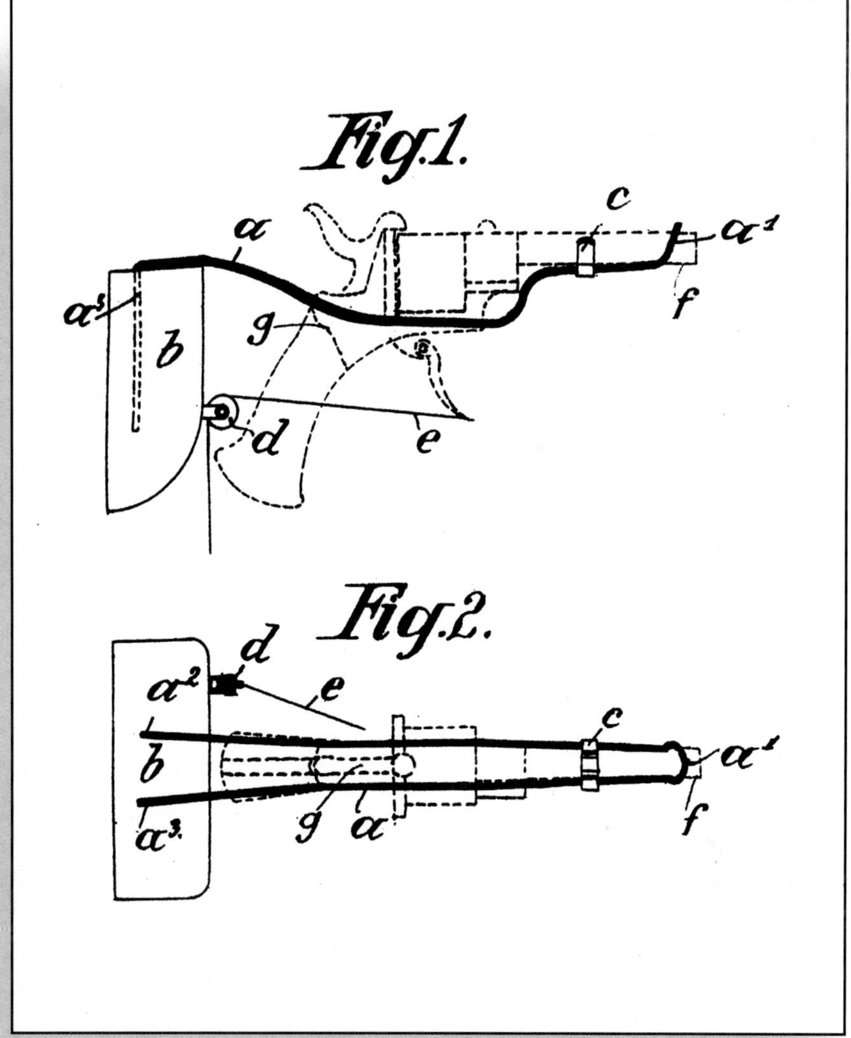

Plate 10-18. An illustration from Wachsmuth's British patent number 16418 of July 17, 1911, for another animal trap gun design. *Chris C. Curtis collection*

justed to automatically fire at between thirty and sixty minutes by sliding a weight higher or lower along the shaft of a pendulum. As the series of gears turns, the hammer is slowly raised off a cam, drops, and fires one round through the porthole in the side of the cover. The loaded cylinder then turns, is locked into position, and the device is again ready to fire.

The animal scarer pictured here fires a special short, 14-gauge blank, but standard 14-gauge blank cartridges also could be used. The device is

secured to a base by screws through the support feet, moved into position near the property to be protected, and then activated. Interestingly, as the hammer rises it pushes a rod up through a hole in the top of the protective cover; the rod serves as a visual safety signal to the operator, effectively informing him as to the firing-cycle stage should he approach to re-load or re-wind the mechanism. The majority of these "mailbox-type" animal scaring devices were made and used in Great Britain.

Plate 10-19. Top frontal view of an all-metal "rook scarer", showing its lid opened to reveal the inner clockwork mechanism. *Courtesy private collection; John Calcany photograph*

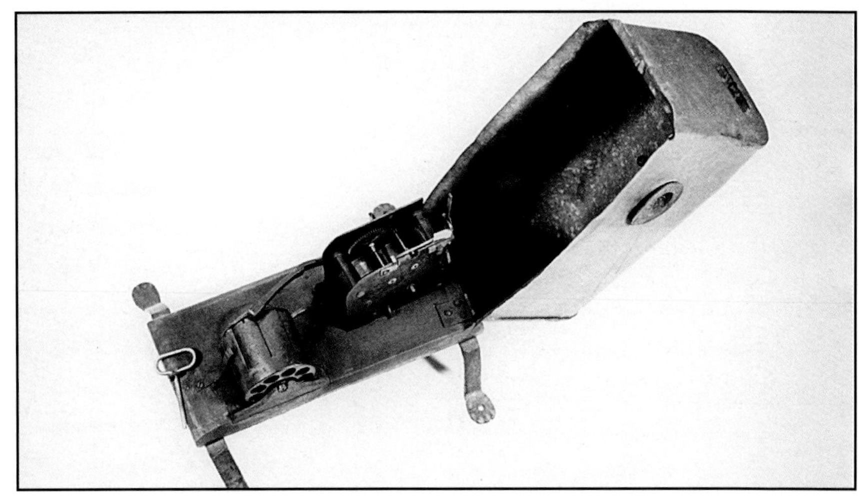

Plate 10-20. Detail frontal view of the adjustable, key-wound timing mechanism, hammer, and revolving, nine-shot cylinder of the rook scarer illustrated in *Plate 10-19*. *Courtesy private collection; John Calcany photograph*

Plate 10-21. Detail view of rear of the revolving cylinder and timing mechanism with winding key, of the rook scarer pictured in *Plate 10-19*. *Courtesy private collection; John Calcany photograph*

Combination Weapons

Plate 10-22 illustrates two variations of another peculiar pinfire: the triple-threat *Apache* "knuckleduster" combination weapon. Named after the violent Paris street gangs of the nineteenth century who favored their use, the lethal-looking *Apache* (pronounced "*Uh-pahsh*") combined a barrelless revolving pinfire cylinder with hinged brass (or iron) knuckles and a folding, *kris-*style dagger blade. The brass-frame *Apache* pistol shown at top is marked, "*L. Dolne Invur.*", and the cylinder is chambered for the 7mm caliber pinfire cartridge. The example shown below, also Dolne marked, has an iron frame, and it is 5mm caliber pinfire. The similarities between the two pistols, as well as their differences, make for an interesting study.

Plate 10-23 pictures an *Apache* knuckleduster in the folded, or closed, position, ready to be used as a set of brass knuckles. The popularity of these strange arms among collectors, due to their bizarre appearance and deadly purpose, has created high values despite their being fairly common in the collector marketplace.

While Dolne lists himself as "inventor" on the frame markings of the majority of *Apache* knuckledusters, the patent papers reproduced in *Plates 10-1 (see page 256) and 10-24* cast doubt on his claim. The French patent which covers this type of firearm, number 90314, of May 14, 1870, clearly was granted to J. Delhaxhe of Liége, Belgium. Perhaps Dolne, who is known to have manufactured firearms in France between 1873 and 1895, was acting as a sales agent for Delhaxhe, or possibly producing them in the role of subcontractor. Note that the patent drawing shown in *Plate 10-24* illustrates an *Apache* pistol fitted with a revolver-type barrel; this is the sole reference noted by the author for a removable barrel mounted on pepperbox-style handguns such as those illustrated in Chapter Nine.

The combination weapons shown in *Plate 10-25*, both of which fire the 7mm caliber pinfire car-

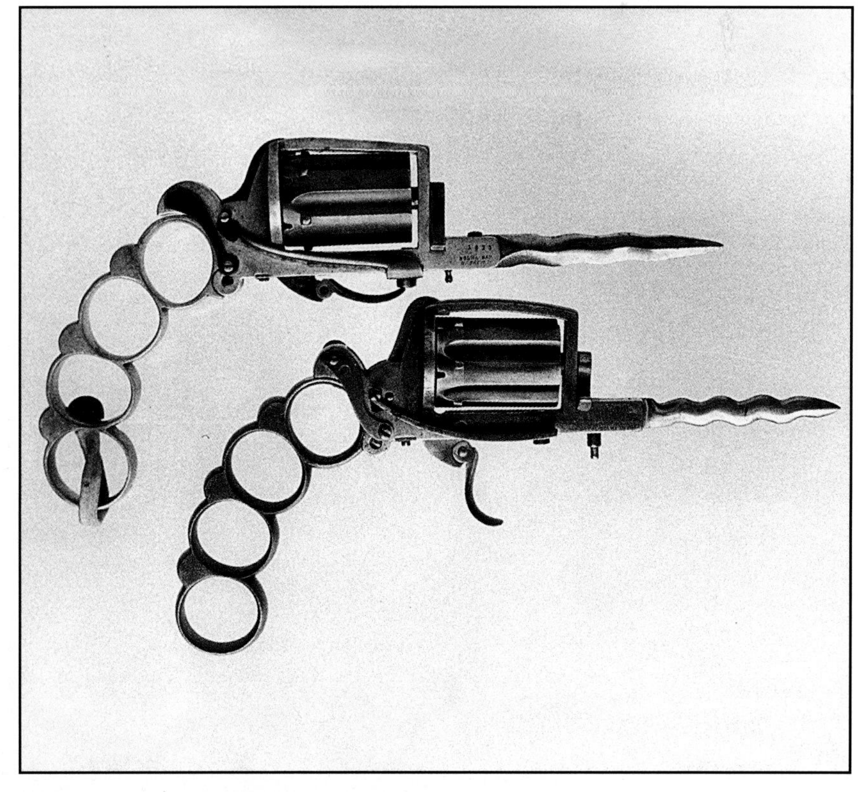

Plate 10-22. Two Apache "knuckleduster" pistols manufactured and marked by Dolne, having their folding knife blades and knuckle grips in the extended position. Top: brass frame, 7mm caliber pinfire. Bottom: iron frame, 5mm caliber pinfire.
Courtesy private collection;
F.W. Hulbert photograph

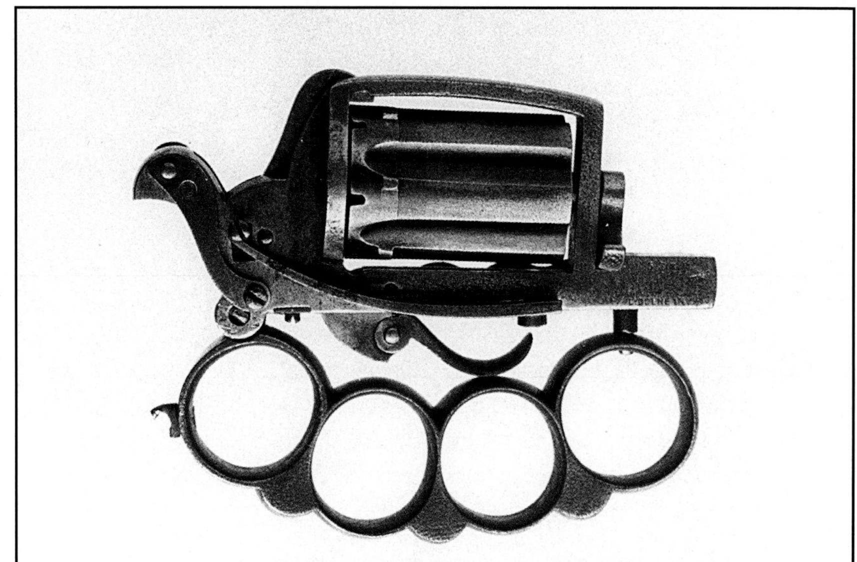

Plate 10-23. A Dolne-made *Apache* knuckleduster in the folded position, ready for use as a set of knuckles. *Courtesy private collection; F.W. Hulbert photograph*

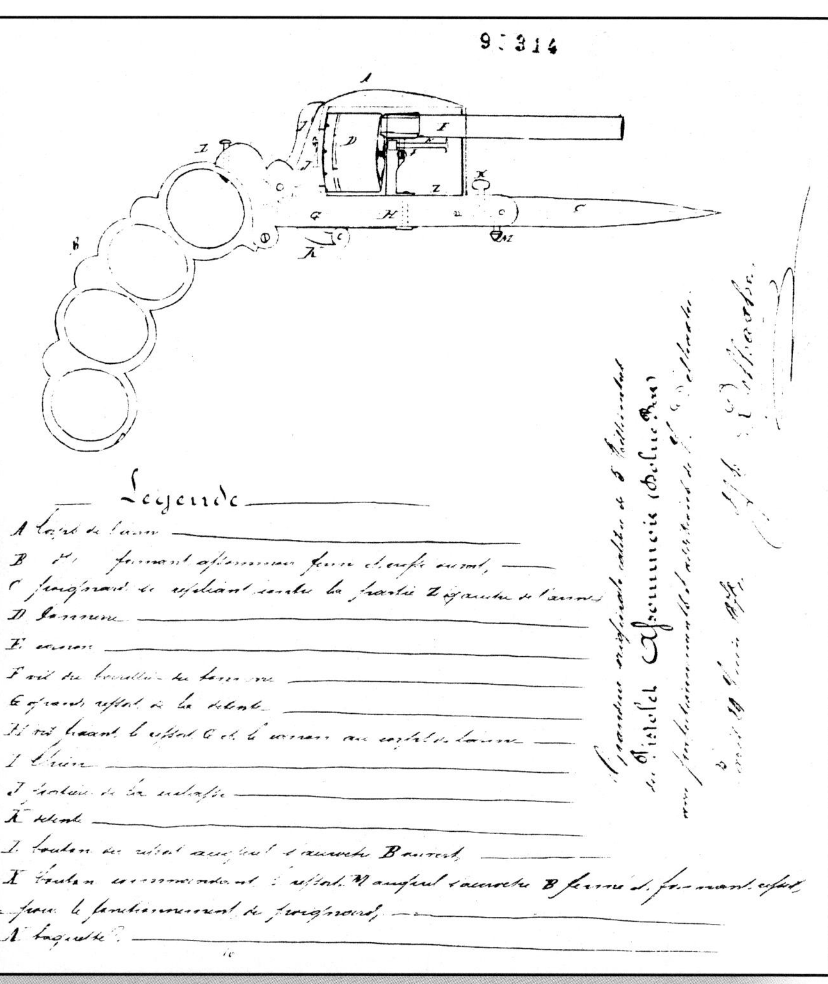

Plate 10-24. Another illustration from J. Delhaxhe's French patent number 90314, for an *Apache* knuckleduster pistol having a revolver-type barrel. *Chris C. Curtis collection*

tridge, are the product of J. Delhaxhe, whose manufacture of this style of arms ended in 1896. These square-frame knuckledusters are the rarest of the type. Their solid-frame construction enabled the arm to be utilzed as one, two, or a combination of all three weapons at any time, whereas the design of the *Apache* pistol allowed it to be used only in any two modes simultaneously. The engraved Delhaxhe arm shown at left has a brass frame, and a slightly wavy dagger blade; the specimen at right has an iron frame and a straight blade. Different combinations of frame materials, blade designs, and styles of loading gates were offered by this maker, and models having both unadorned and engraved frames are encountered by collectors.

The pocket knife-pistol shown in *Plate 10-26*

measures 3½ inches in overall length and has a 1½ inch barrel chambered for the 5mm caliber pinfire cartridge. This small combination arm has three blades, one of which is a nail file, buffalo horn grip scales, and all metal surfaces are nickel plated. The barrel is marked "*D.R.Pa.*", and the larger knife blade is marked "*Christians Solingen*", preceded by a logo in the form of a fork.

Plate 10-27 pictures another single-shot pocket knife-pistol combination arm, the barrel of which is chambered for the 7mm caliber pinfire cartridge. This French-made combination arm was manufactured by Marti, sometime around 1880. The barrel tips up for loading, as shown; after the gimlet trigger is pulled rearward and the barrel is fired, the knife blade snaps open.

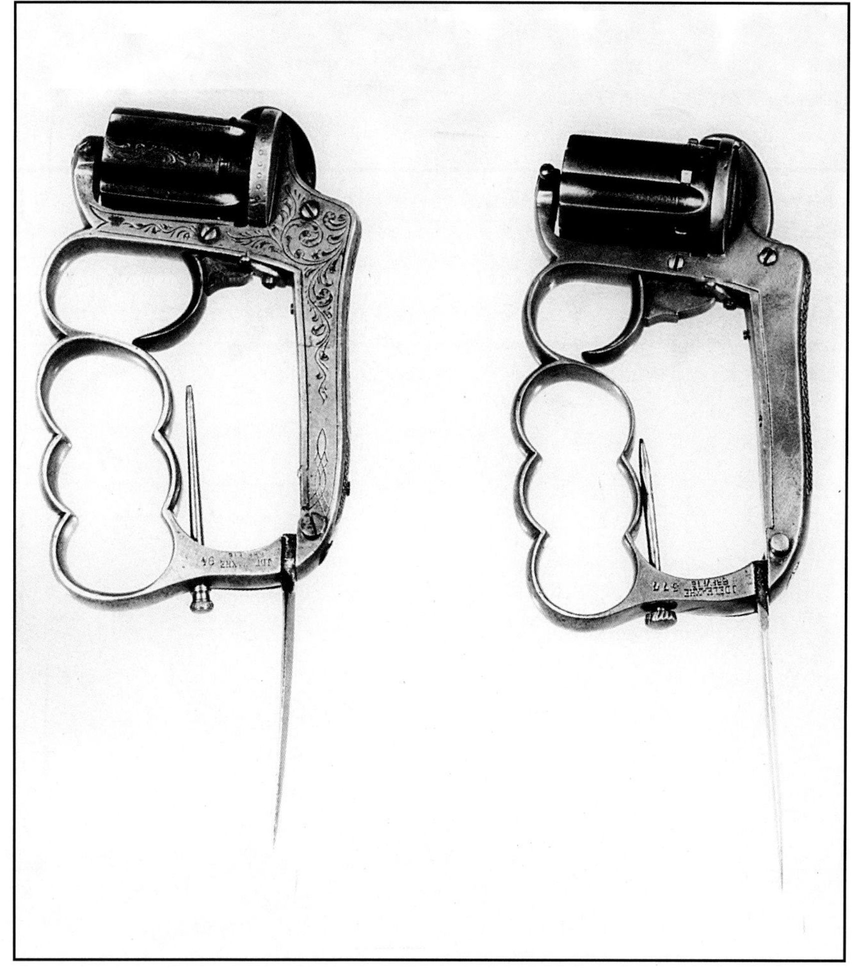

Plate 10-25. Two rare, square-frame, 7mm caliber pinfire knuckleduster pistols manufactured and marked by Delhaxhe, both bearing French proofmarks. Left: engraved brass frame, having a slightly wavy blade. Right: plain iron frame, having a straight blade. *Courtesy H. Gordon Frost; H. Gordon Frost photograph*

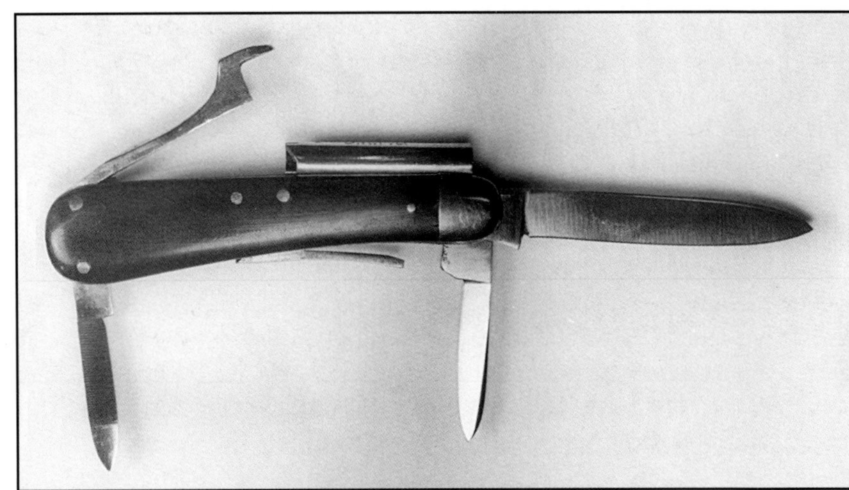

Plate 10-26. A small pocket knife-pistol combination weapon. The barrel fires the 5mm caliber pinfire cartridge. *Courtesy private collection; Gene Smith photograph*

Plate 10-28 illustrates a similar pistol-shape combination knife-pistol. Marked "*H. Cromwell, Criterion*", this English-made piece features ivory scales and grips; its barrel is chambered for the 7mm caliber pinfire cartridge, as are numerous other examples by the same maker.

The combination pocket knife-revolver pistol shown in *Plate 10-29* also is fitted with beautiful ivory grips. Belgian made, it has Liége proofmarks; its octagonal barrel is chambered for the 5mm caliber pinfire cartridge, and the overall length of the piece is 5³/₈ inches.

The elaborately etched, single-shot cutlass-pistol shown in *Plate 10-30* is the product of the firm Dumonthier et Charton, which was located at 194 rue St. Martin, in Paris, *circa* 1850. This large example measures fifteen inches in overall length and is fitted with horn grips. As was the case with many other models of combination weapons produced by this maker, the ejector rod is mounted on the separate blade sheath instead of on the weapon itself.

Plate 10-31 illustrates a combination pocket knife-revolver similar in style to the example shown in *Plate 10-29*. In common with that arm it was Belgian made and bears Liége proofmarks, and its octagonal barrel is chambered for the 5mm caliber pinfire cartridge. On the left side is an undec-

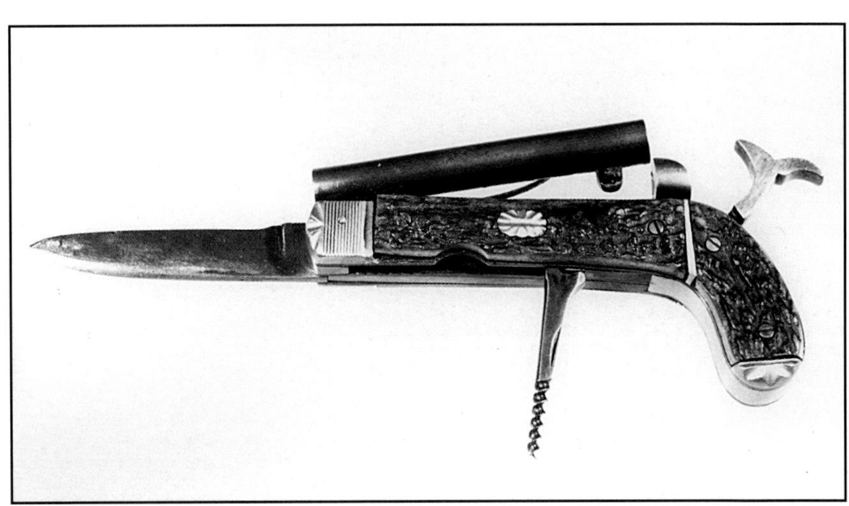

Plate 10-27. A French-made combination jackknife-single-shot pistol, chambered for the 7mm caliber pinfire cartridge. *Courtesy H. Gordon Frost; H. Gordon Frost photograph*

orated metal nameplate. The top of the barrel is marked *"Eprouve"*, *"S.G.D.G."*, and *"S.B."*; the knife blade is stamped *"Au Etoile d'Ager"* within a comet logo.

The single-shot cutlass pistol pictured in *Plate 10-32* is marked *"Dumonthier"*, although its style is more reminiscent of the early arms made by Eugene Lefaucheux: note the Model 1854 revolver shape of its grip. The blade-barrel assembly, which swings to the side for loading, is chambered for the 12mm caliber pinfire cartridge. After the pistol barrel has been fired, the triggerguard serves as a handguard when the weapon is used as a sword.

Plate 10-33 illustrates the open and closed positions of the spring-activated folding daggers mounted atop the octagonal barrels of a pair of Belgian-made double-barrel pistols. While unmarked as to maker, their 12mm caliber pinfire barrels bear Liége proofmarks. This is one of the more common types of combination arms.

The 12mm caliber pinfire revolver having a folding bayonet-type blade shown in *Plate 10-34* was manufactured in Liége, Belgium; it also is unmarked as to maker. The blade is released by finger pressure on the spring-activated catch mounted in front of the triggerguard. It may be that this blade assembly was a period gunsmith addition

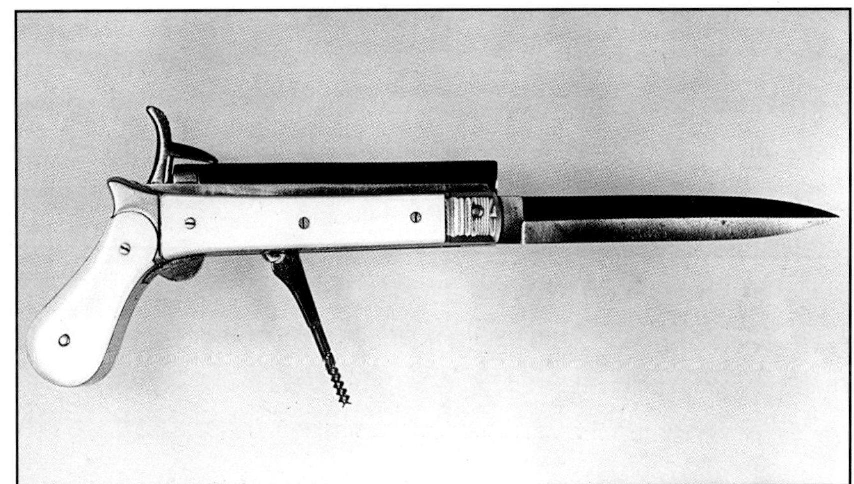

Plate 10-28. A combination knife-pistol similar to the example pictured in *Plate 10-27,* but having ivory grip scales and made in England by Cromwell. *Courtesy H. Gordon Frost; H. Gordon Frost photograph*

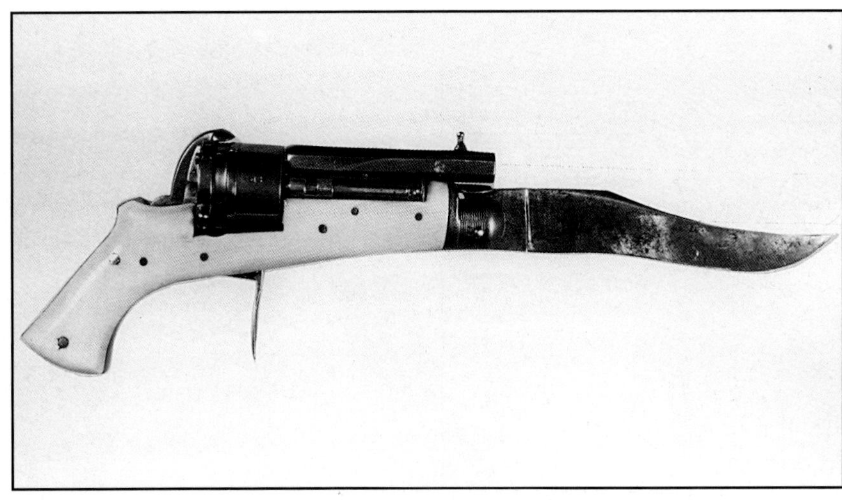

Plate 10-29. A Belgian-made, combination folding knife-revolver chambered for the 5mm caliber pinfire cartridge. *Courtesy H. Gordon Frost; H. Gordon Frost photograph*

Plate 10-30. A large, elaborately-etched cutlass-pistol made by Dumonthier of Paris. The overall length of this arm is 15 inches. *Courtesy H. Gordon Frost; H. Gordon Frost photograph*

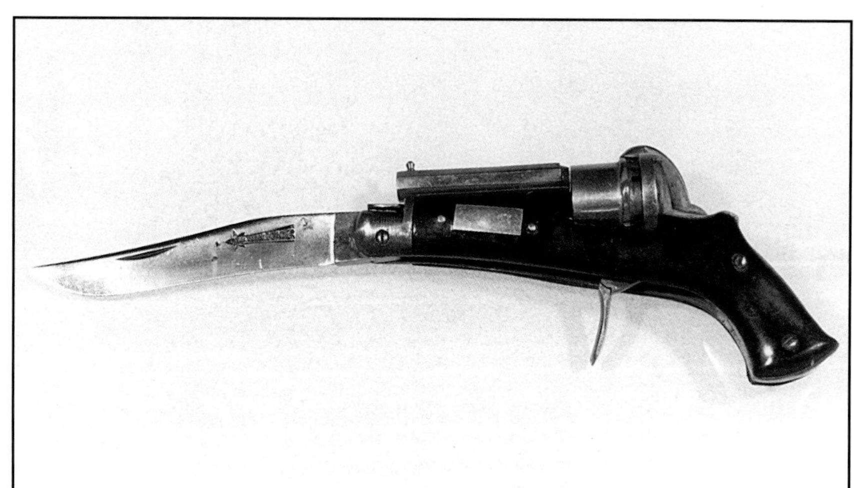

Plate 10-31. Another combination folding knife-revolver similar to the example illustrated in *Plate 10-29,* also chambered for the 5mm caliber pinfire cartridge, having maker's marks and Liége proofmarks. *Courtesy H. Gordon Frost; H. Gordon Frost photograph*

Plate 10-32. A single-shot cutlass pistol chambered for the 12mm caliber pinfire cartridge. Note the combination triggerguard-hand-guard, and Lefaucheux Model 1854 revolver-style grip. *Courtesy H. Gordon Frost; H. Gordon Frost photograph*

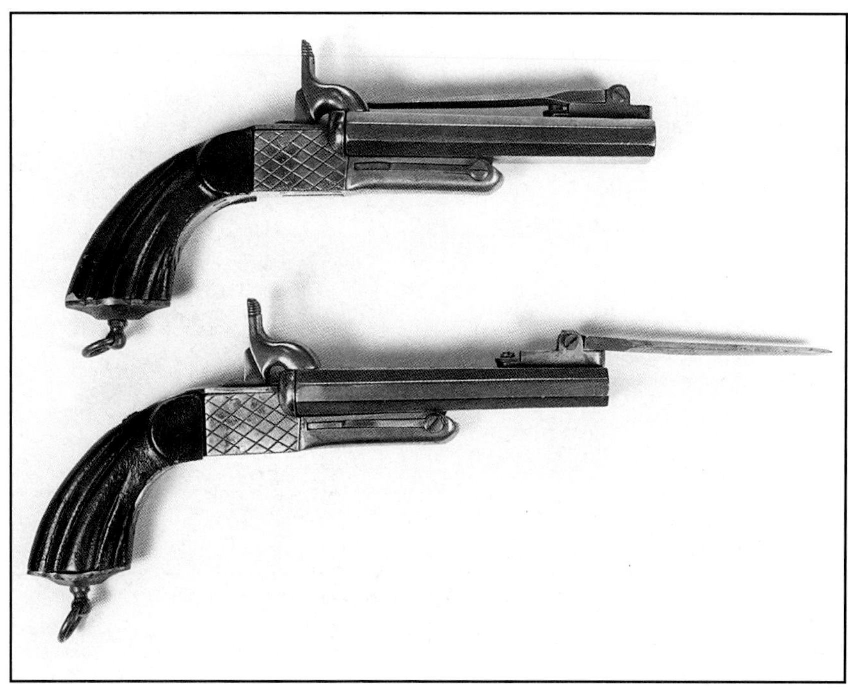

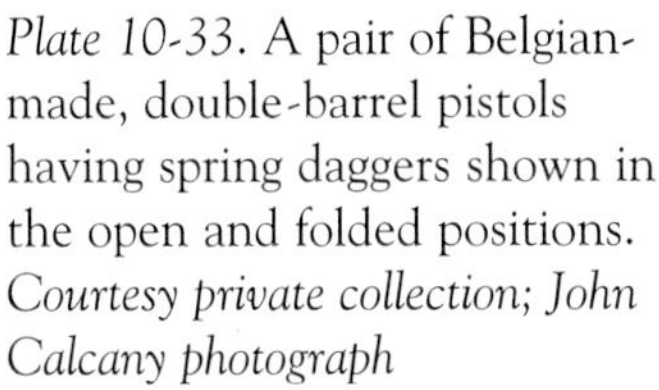

Plate 10-33. A pair of Belgian-made, double-barrel pistols having spring daggers shown in the open and folded positions. *Courtesy private collection; John Calcany photograph*

done without benefit of patent protection, as many firearms were so altered by agents acting on customer requests.

Plate 10-35 illustrates a 9mm caliber pinfire revolver having a spring-loaded folding dagger blade similar to the preceding example. The barrel of this twelve-shot pistol is marked "*C. Wagner A Berne*"; "*Improved Pat*" is marked on the frame. In the case of this revolver, C. Wagner of Berne, Switzerland, was the retail arms seller.

Another revolver having a spring-activated knife is the massive specimen shown in *Plate 10-36*, which measures 11⅝ inches in overall length with its blade folded. The retaining-release lever attached to the trigger on the left side activates the blade, which springs open automatically on firing; note that the cutting edge of the blade faces up, suggesting that the maker knew something about knife fighting as well as firearms manufacture. The piece is decorated with floral engraving, combined with gold inlay work. This particular revolver is the only known example chambered for the 15mm caliber pinfire cartridge. Its huge bore diameter and almost six-inch, Bowie-style blade doubtless had an intimidating effect on anyone

unfortunate enough to have been on the wrong end of this formidable weapon.

The pinfire revolver pictured in *Plate 10-37*, having a cutlass-type blade beneath the barrel, is marked "CSA" within a box on its frame. While collectors must always view any Confederate markings with a measure of skepticism, it should be noted that the markings on this example are identical to those on another pinfire revolver pictured in Chapter Four. The unusual holster-scabbard shown was constructed from a lightweight metal, probably tin.

Plate 10-38 reproduces an illustration from English patent number 130, granted on January 18, 1864 to British patent agent Henri Adrien Bonneville acting for Leon Lambin and Toussaint Theate, both of Liége, Belgium. The patent specification notes that "This invention consists in a system of adjustment of daggers to revolvers and other pistols, by means of which they may be taken off and put on without the use of any tool whatever." First, however, the revolver had to be altered with grooves and lugs to correspond to the type of blade being fitted. Note the similarity of the top figure in the patent drawing to the revolver illus-

Plate 10-34. A Belgian-made revolver chambered for the 12mm caliber pinfire cartridge, and fitted with added bayonet-type folding blade. Note blade release lever at front of the triggerguard. *Courtesy private collection; John Calcany photograph*

Plate 10-35. A twelve-shot, 9mm caliber pinfire revolver fitted with a spring-loaded dagger blade. The barrel of this arm was marked by the retailer, *"C. Wagner A Berne."* *Courtesy private collection; John Calcany photograph*

Plate 10-36. A large, German-made revolver chambered for the 15mm caliber pinfire cartridge, and fitted with a folding, Bowie knife-style blade. Note lever attached to the trigger, which activates the spring-loaded blade on firing. *Courtesy H. Gordon Frost; H. Gordon Frost photograph*

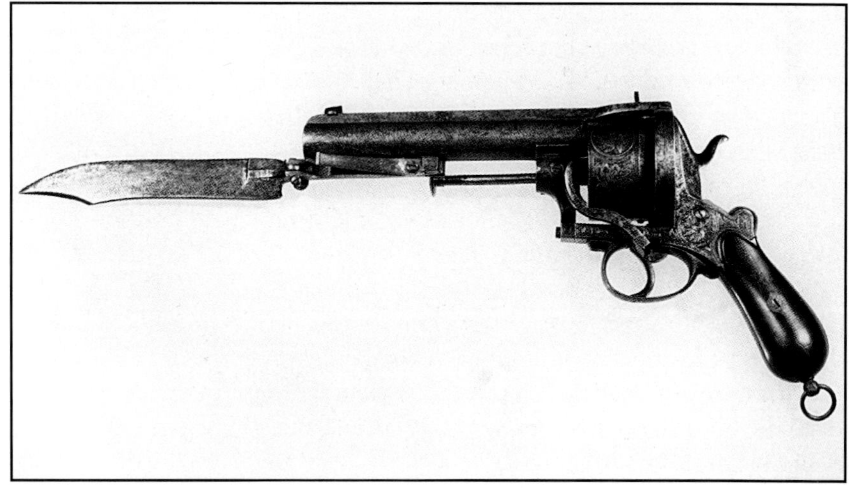

Plate 10-37. A combination cutlass-revolver marked "CSA" on its frame. Note the massive blade, and scabbard made of tin-like metal. *Courtesy Larry Compeau; Mark Ingram photograph*

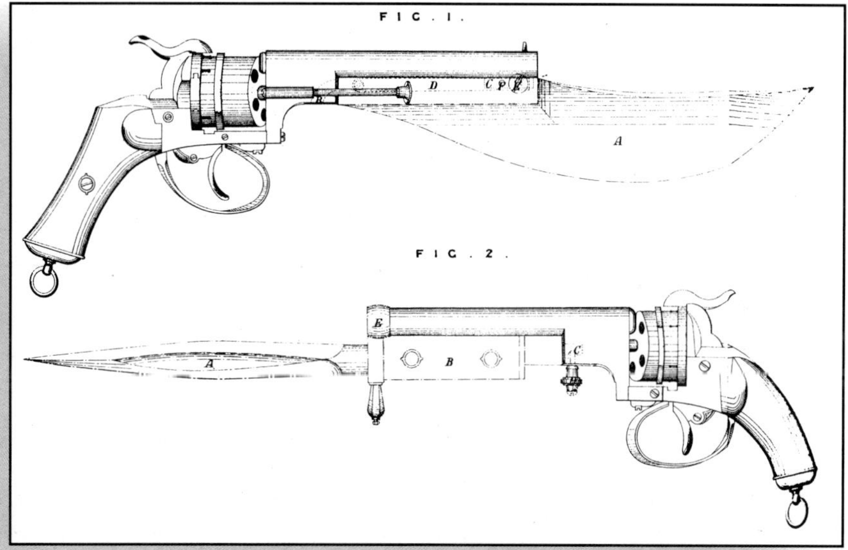

Plate 10-38. An illustration from H.A. Bonneville's British patent number 130, of January 18, 1864, showing designs for a cutlass-pistol similar to the example pictured in *Plate 10-37. Chris C. Curtis collection*

trated in *Plate 10-37.*

In 1867 a grand arms exhibition was organized in Paris, for essentially the same reasons that the London Exhibition had been held in 1851. Many of the Continent's premier gunmakers, including Lefaucheux, Dumonthier, LePage, and Devisme, were represented at the Paris Universal Exhibition that year, and there were at least thirty types of sword-revolver combination weapons on display. Combining the advanced offensive technology of the pinfire cartridge revolver with the traditional sword as defensive weapon was a temptation few

European armsmakers of the era could resist. Indeed, the sword-revolver found much favor among the officer corps of many nations, although it was never officially adopted by the military as an issue service weapon.

Plate 10-39 pictures a combination sword-9mm caliber pinfire revolver manufactured by "A. Rauh and Co. Solingen", and so marked along the top of its $32^3/_8$-inch long blade. The cylinder is loaded with cartridges through the ornate german-silver handguard; the revolver barrel is mounted along the right side of the sword blade and thus

text continued on page 280

Plate 10-39. Detail view of the hilt area of a combination sword-revolver marked "*A. Rauh and Co. Solingen*" atop the blade. This revolver is chambered for the 9mm caliber pinfire cartridge. *Courtesy H. Gordon Frost; H. Gordon Frost photograph*

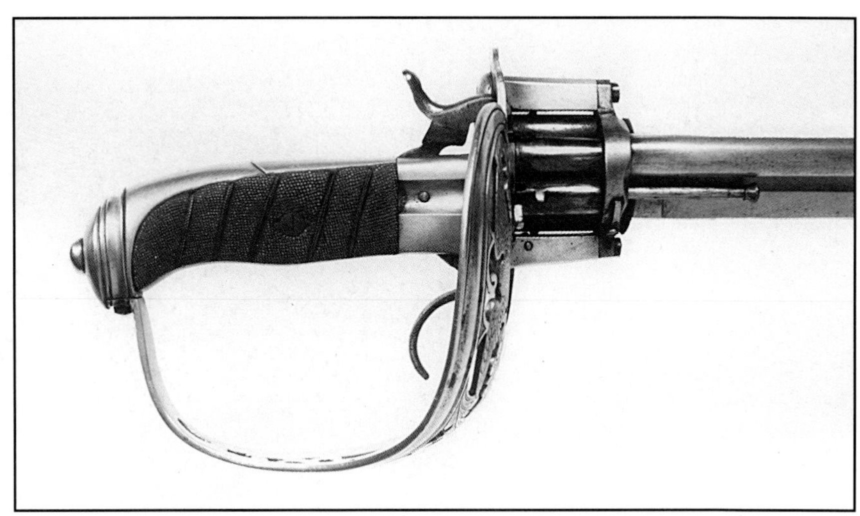

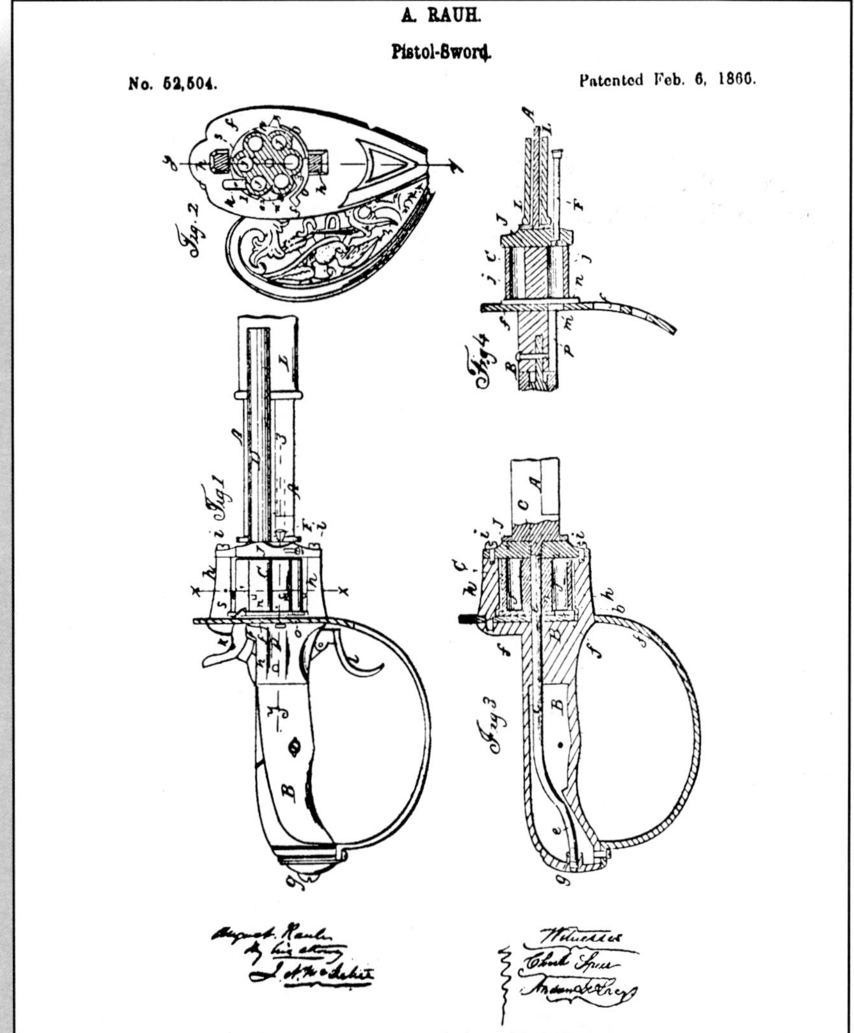

Plate 10-40. An illustration from A. Rauh's United States patent number 52504 of February 6, 1866, showing designs for a combination sword-revolver like the example pictured in *Plate 10-39. Chris C. Curtis collection*

Plate 10-41 (above). An unmarked, military-style combination sword-revolver and its original steel scabbard. This revolver is chambered for the 9mm caliber pinfire cartridge. *Courtesy private collection; John Calcany photograph*

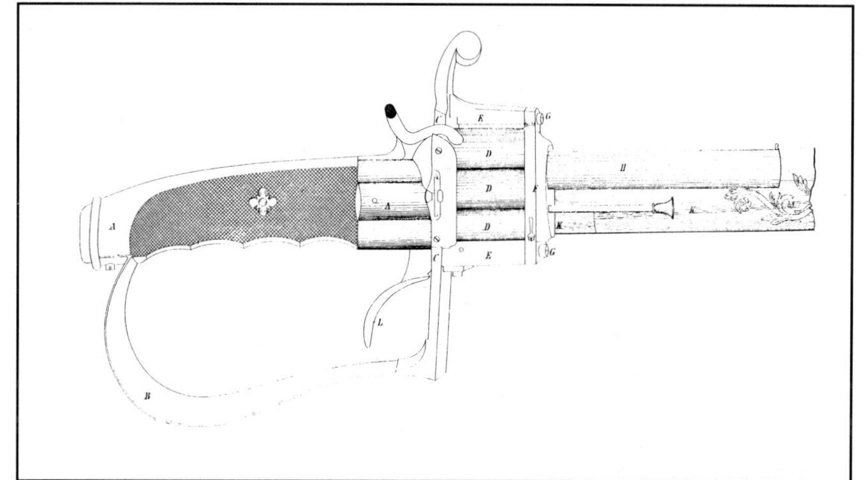

Plate 10-42 (above right). An illustration from Williams' British patent number 2513 of October 12, 1864, showing designs for a sword-revolver similar to that pictured in *Plate 10-41*. *Chris C. Curtis collection*

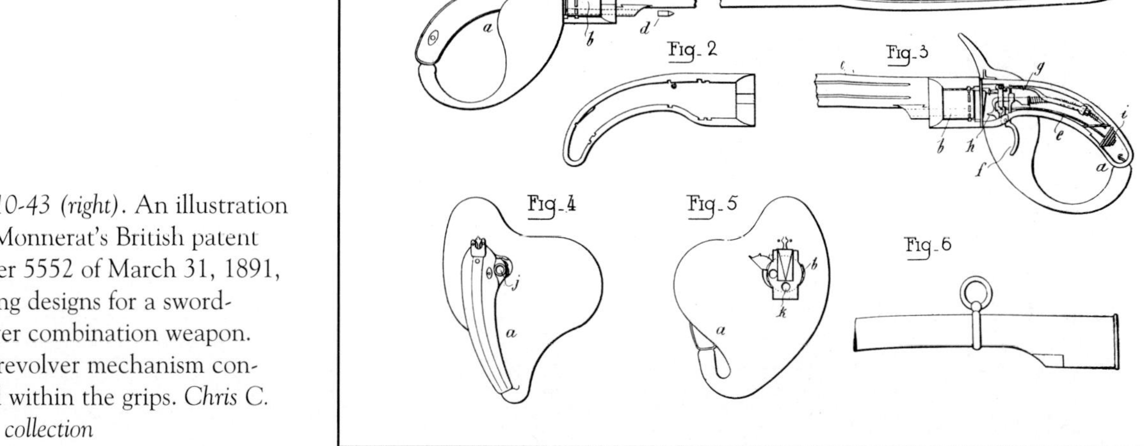

Plate 10-43 (right). An illustration from Monnerat's British patent number 5552 of March 31, 1891, showing designs for a sword-revolver combination weapon. Note revolver mechanism contained within the grips. *Chris C. Curtis collection*

the firearm is easily aimed and fired.

Plate 10-40 reproduces illustrations from United States patent number 52504, of February 6, 1866, which protected Rauh's designs for the combination sword-pistol shown in *Plate 10-39*, on page 278.

A similar combination sword-pinfire revolver is shown in a full-length view with its scabbard in *Plate 10-41*. Measuring 39 inches in overall length, the 9mm caliber example shown bears neither proofmarks nor a maker's name. Note the depression present on the right side of the scabbard near the throat; when the sword is sheathed it allows the revolver barrel to lie outside the scabbard, leaving the pinfire pistol instantly ready for use.

Plates 10-42 and 10-43 reproduce illustrations from two additional English patents that were intended to protect other sword-revolver combination weapon designs.

Last, but certainly not least in our examination of unusual combination weapons, is the pepperbox revolver with dagger concealed in the handle of a walking cane shown in *Plate 10-44*. The frame of the six-shot, 5mm caliber pinfire pepperbox is marked "*Paris A.J. Brevete*"; the barrel group bears French proofmarks. Cane guns such as the example pictured are among the very rarest combination weapons.

The preceding plates illustrate only a fraction of the peculiar variations and deadly features which flowed from the fertile imaginations of nineteenth-century European arms designers and manufacturers. For a more in-depth look at combination weaponry, the reader is referred to *Blades and Barrels: Six Centuries of Combination Weapons*, by H. Gordon Frost (El Paso, Texas: Walloon Press, 1972).

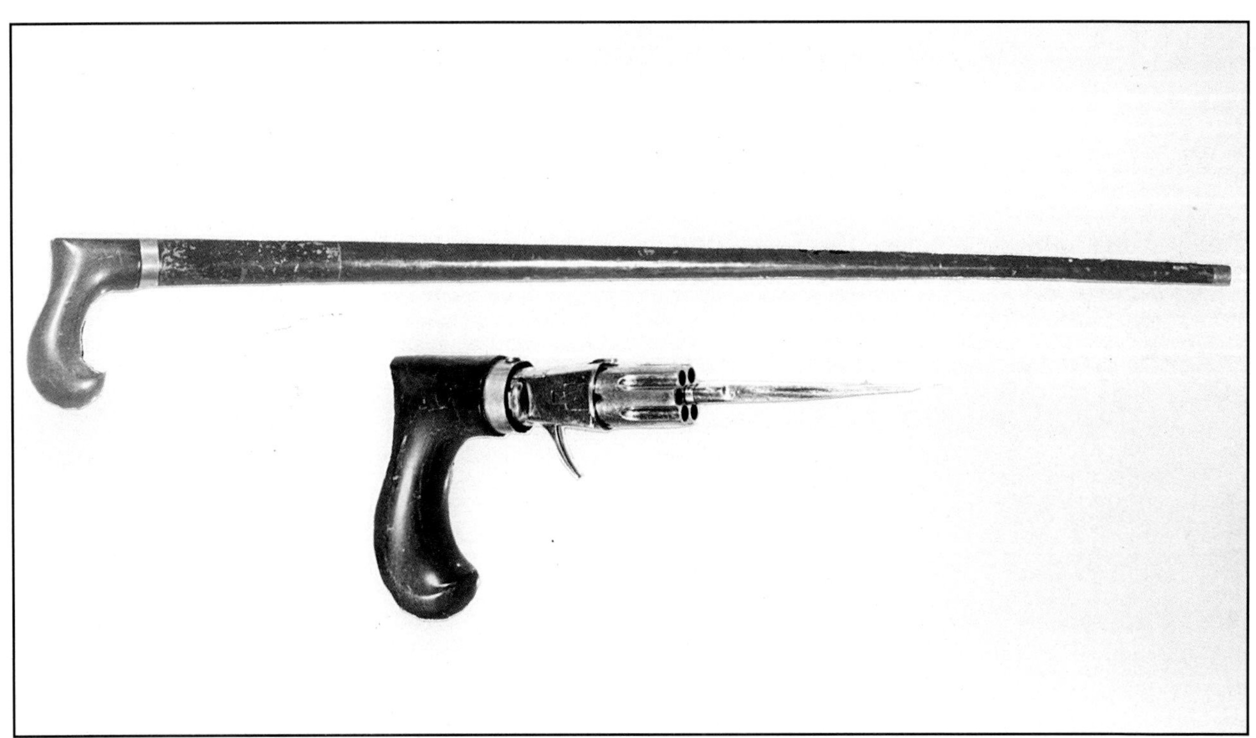

Plate 10-44. A rare, French-made walking cane which conceals a six-shot, 5mm caliber pinfire revolver fitted with a dagger within its shaft. *Courtesy H. Gordon Frost; H. Gordon Frost photograph*

Pinfire Cartridges
and Reloading Apparatus

Whether used with shotgun, rifle, or pistol, the pinfire cartridge is the unique feature of this type of firearm, as pinfire arms themselves do not essentially differ from the rimfire or center-fire arms of the same period. Our study of the pinfire system, then, necessarily begins and ends with a study of the pinfire cartridge.

A functional breechloading weapon requires ammunition which fulfills three basic and very important requirements. First, the charge must be a single fixed unit consisting of case, primer, powder, and projectile. Secondly, the casing of the charge must be constructed of an easily-shaped material which will expand instantly but briefly within the chamber of the arm when it is fired, creating a seal which prevents gases from escaping back along the sides of the case. The case must then immediately shrink back to its near-normal size after the gas pressure is relieved, to allow easy extraction of the spent cartridge. Third, the primer or priming material must be in a stationary position within the case to allow the firing pin to strike and crush the primer to detonate the charge. In the case of the pinfire cartridge, the firing pin is part of the cartridge itself, rather than part of the firearm.

A slot cut into the breech or the cylinder chamber of a pinfire arm allows for the proper positioning of the cartridge, as well as for the pin to protrude through the chamber in firing position. Thus the cartridge may be loaded in one position only, for if the pin does not seat in its corresponding recess the cartridge will neither fit into the breech nor chamber deeply enough to permit closing the action.

This ignition pin, which normally projects at a right angle from the base of the cartridge, rests within the cartridge base on a cup containing the priming mixture. When the hammer falls, it strikes the exposed pin and drives it into the case. The force of the hammer blow drives the pin into the primer, creating the spark which detonates the main powder charge.

It is possible to reload the pinfire cartridge case. Pulling the pin upward causes the fired primer to fall out, after which a new one may be inserted with a tool. When the pin is thus reset, the case may be reloaded with powder and projectile.

In 1835 Casimir Lefaucheux began making cartridges for use in the breechloading pinfire arms of his manufacture. In the text of the fourth addition to his patent number 5525[1] of that same year, Lefaucheux described the cartridge tube as being constructed of cardboard material, with base and pin of copper (*see Plate 1-6*, Chapter One). However, the copper pin soon was replaced by one of brass, as copper proved to be unsatisfactorily soft.

The cartridge itself closely resembles a modern shotgun shell, with its metallic base being crimped

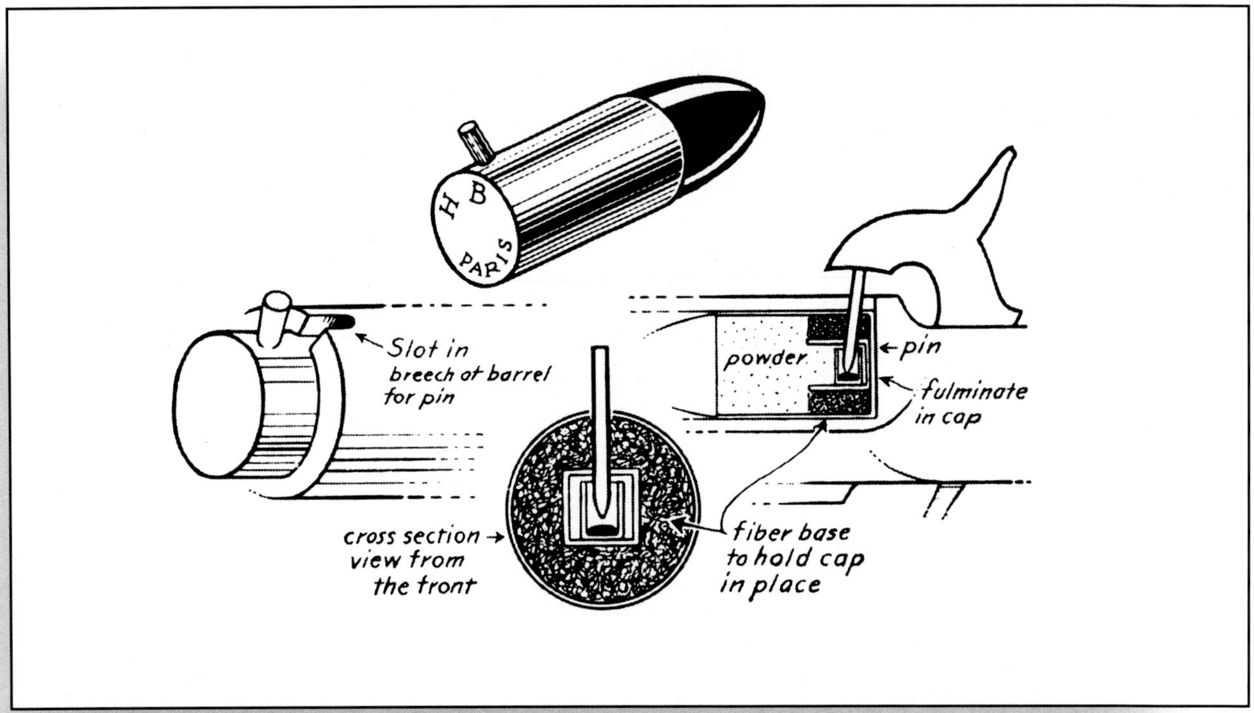

Plate 11-1. This reproduction of a drawing by arms author and artist, Herschel C. Logan, graphically explains the principles and components of the pinfire cartridge. *Reprinted from the January, 1966 issue of* The American Rifleman, *with permission of the artist and publisher.*

around the cardboard tube. The original bottle-neck pin (*see Plate 1-6*, Chapter One) used in these early cartridges was replaced by one having a straighter configuration, for greater ease in manufacture and loading. To date, no example of this very early, bottle-neck pin Lefaucheux cartridge is known by the author to exist.

Casimir Lefaucheux manufactured the cardboard pinfire cartridge for at least fifteen years. The cardboard cartridge was displayed in a hand-gun caliber at the 1851 London Exhibition, and one example is illustrated with a pinfire pepperbox pistol in *Plate 1-21*, Chapter One.

Eugene Lefaucheux inherited the family's gun-making business following his father's death in 1852. As late as 1858, Eugene shipped a quantity of cardboard pinfire cartridges and metallic cartridges along with a group of Model 1854 revolvers to the United States, for test trials and potential adoption by the American military authorities.

Lefaucheux, however, was not the only manufacturer of cardboard tube cartridges; examples by other makers are illustrated in *Plate 11-3*.

After Casimir Lefaucheux' original patent expired in 1845, the following year Houllier of Paris was granted patent number 1936 for an improved pinfire cartridge. It was Houllier's improvement that opened the door to the mass production of metallic pinfire ammunition, and thereby ensured the commercial and sporting success of breechloading pinfire arms.

Houllier's cartridge design was nearly the same as Casimir Lefaucheux', even to utilizing the bottle-neck pin that had been discarded earlier by Lefaucheux. Nevertheless, in his patent Houllier provided for the entire cartridge case to be made of thin copper or brass drawn from a circular blank. The expansion of the whole case at the instant of firing thus created a positive, gas-tight breech seal. His patent also included an internal improvement, in the form of a heavy fiber or cardboard wad placed in the head of the case to hold the ignition pin and primer cap more firmly in place (*see Plate 11-4*).

A few early Houllier patent cartridges are known to exist, but none has the bottle-neck pin shown in his original 1846 patent. Some of those very early cartridges may yet come to light, but

Plate 11-2. This pinfire pistol cartridge with paper tube and brass base was described in the fourth addition to Casimir Lefaucheux' 1835 French patent number 5525. The 12mm caliber specimen shown is marked *"Chaudun Bte Paris."* Compare it with the example illustrated in *Plate 1-6*, Chapter One. *Courtesy George Hoyem; George Hoyem photograph*

their absence likely indicates that Houllier, as had Lefaucheux, soon discarded the bottle-neck pin for the straight pin, the former's near-perfect gas seal being abandoned in favor of the latter's easier manufacture and reloading. Although minute amounts of gas escaped through the case opening around the straight pin, it was discovered that the expansion of the cartridge case on firing created a sufficiently gas-tight seal in the gun's breech.

Houllier was not the only French arms inventor attempting to improve on the design of Lefaucheux' pinfire cartridge. In 1847 Chaudun of Paris was granted patent number 3601, which introduced a case made of copper, brass, or paper having a base disk of type metal covered by a copper base cup. The cap containing the priming mixture was rendered waterproof by the application of resin. Chaudun also received additions to his original patent, in continuing attempts to improve the interior construction of the pinfire cartridge.

The year following Chaudun's patent saw another French arms inventor, Beringer, receive patent number 4909 for a shell of zinc, or a lap-jointed tube of thin metal, which in turn was lap-jointed to a metal base. The cap containing the priming mixture was in a perforated wad of pasteboard and metal in the base, or between the inside diaphragm of the metal case and the cartridge base.

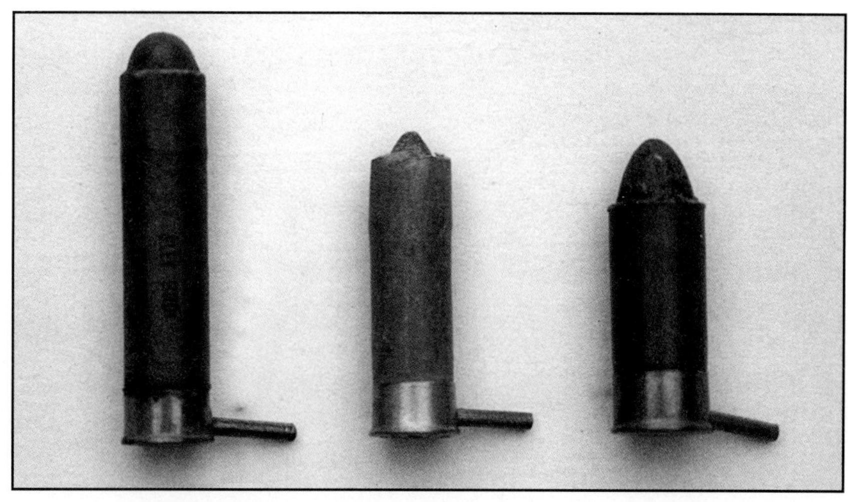

Plate 11-3. Three interesting British-made pinfire cartridges. From left: .360 caliber, 10.5mm caliber, .410 gauge. *Courtesy David Kendrew; David Kendrew photograph*

Realizing the advantages of the all-metal cartridge design, Casimir Lefaucheux attempted to circumvent Houllier's patent with a distinct variation of the metal case. In an addition to his patent number 4839 of 1849 (granted in 1850), Lefaucheux described and illustrated a copper cartridge case having a separate copper base that could be screwed in, or removed to disarm the round for shipping or reloading. A later addition to this

patent provided for an internal reinforcing ring between the base cup and the tube. But for once Lefaucheux' design proved to be impractical. It was more expensive to manufacture, and the threads of the cartridge base would occasionally freeze in position, preventing its unscrewing and removal. Houllier's one-piece metallic cartridge became the accepted norm.

It is worthy of note here, that nearly two decades later a cartridge design strikingly similar to Lefaucheux' reached the United States patent office. U.S. patent number 96373 was granted to Friedrich Wohlgemuth in November of 1869, for a cartridge made of brass having a screw-in base

Plate 11-4 (below). An illustration from Houllier's French patent number 1936, the certificate of addition of April 1850, for an improved pinfire cartridge. *Chris C. Curtis collection*

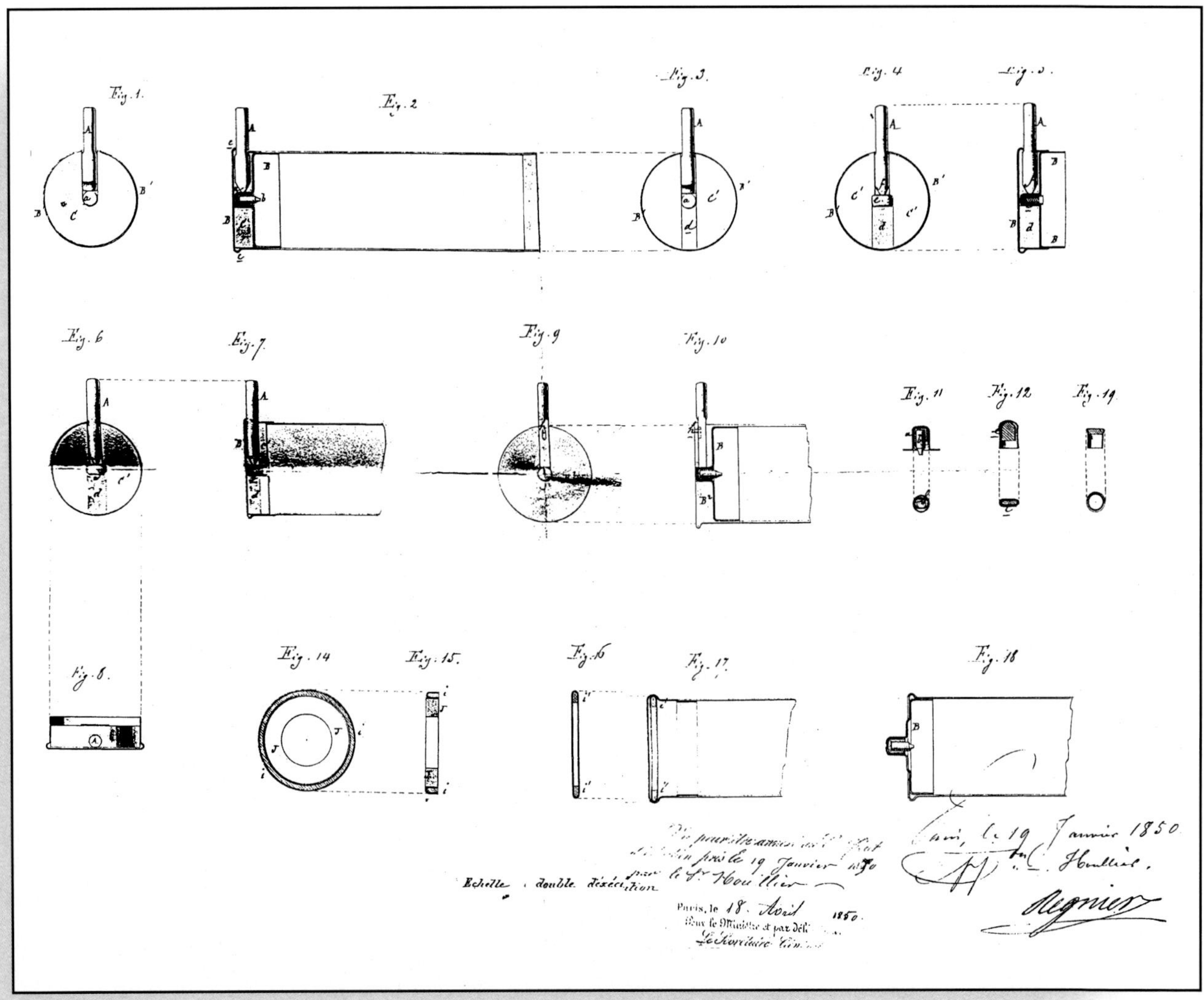

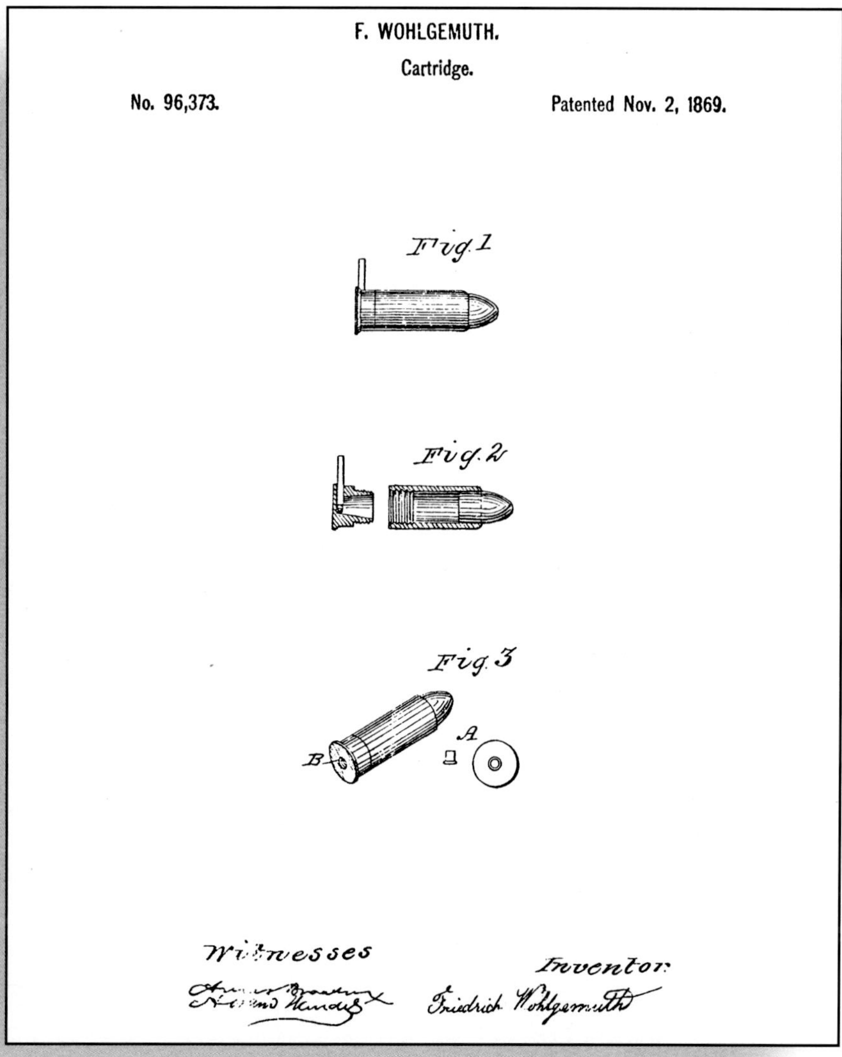

Plate 11-5. An illustration from Friedrich Wohlgemuth's United States patent number 96373 of November 2, 1869, showing the removable pinfire and centerfire heads for a brass case. *Chris C. Curtis collection*

that held the primer (*see Plate 11-5*). Also illustrated in Wohlgemuth's patent drawing was a centerfire base designed to be removed in the same fashion. Durability was the claim of the inventor, along with the facility with which it could be cleared of a defective cap; the claim also stated that the cases could be reloaded as often as the owner chose. Ironically, a similar, all-plastic shotgun shell was patented in the U.S. more than a century later—apparently there is nothing too old to be called new!

During the mid-nineteenth century, firearms patent applications continued to flood the French patent office. In 1853 Gevelot received patent number 9335 for another improved pinfire cartridge. His design featured a crown of paper between two copper cups, as the area designated to contain the priming mixture.

That same year Boche was granted patent number 9686 for a pinfire cartridge, the base of which was metal, with the case and wad made of wound paper. Also in 1853, patent number 8340 was granted to Devoir and Leclercq, whose drawing indicated the base of the powder chamber could be made conical in shape by introducing a wad having a central cavity. In their design the tube was to be made of either paper or metal, with a metal base.

During the following year Gevelot and Lemaire received patent number 10482, which covered a cartridge having a paper case and a metallic base cup (*see Plate 11-6*). And in 1854, Chaudun made an addition to his 1847 patent for an improved pin and wad, as well.

Vincent was granted patent number 14572 in 1855, covering a paper case cartridge with a metallic cap. The interior of the powder chamber was made concave by means of shaped internal reinforcing of the case. That same year, Gevelot received another patent, number 12603, for a pin-

fire cartridge having a paper tube and a reinforced metal base cup. A wad of paper was added inside, to surround the base cup.

Also in 1855, Needham received patent number 13210 for an original idea in cartridge design and manufacture: his tube and base were made of vulcanized rubber. Needham's patent additionally covered the design whether constructed of paper or metal. The latter specification was prophetic. Evidently his rubber case met with little success, although metallic cartridges made by Needham are known in collections today. Two years later, on June 30, 1857, Gilbert Smith of Buttermilk Falls, New York was granted United States patent num-

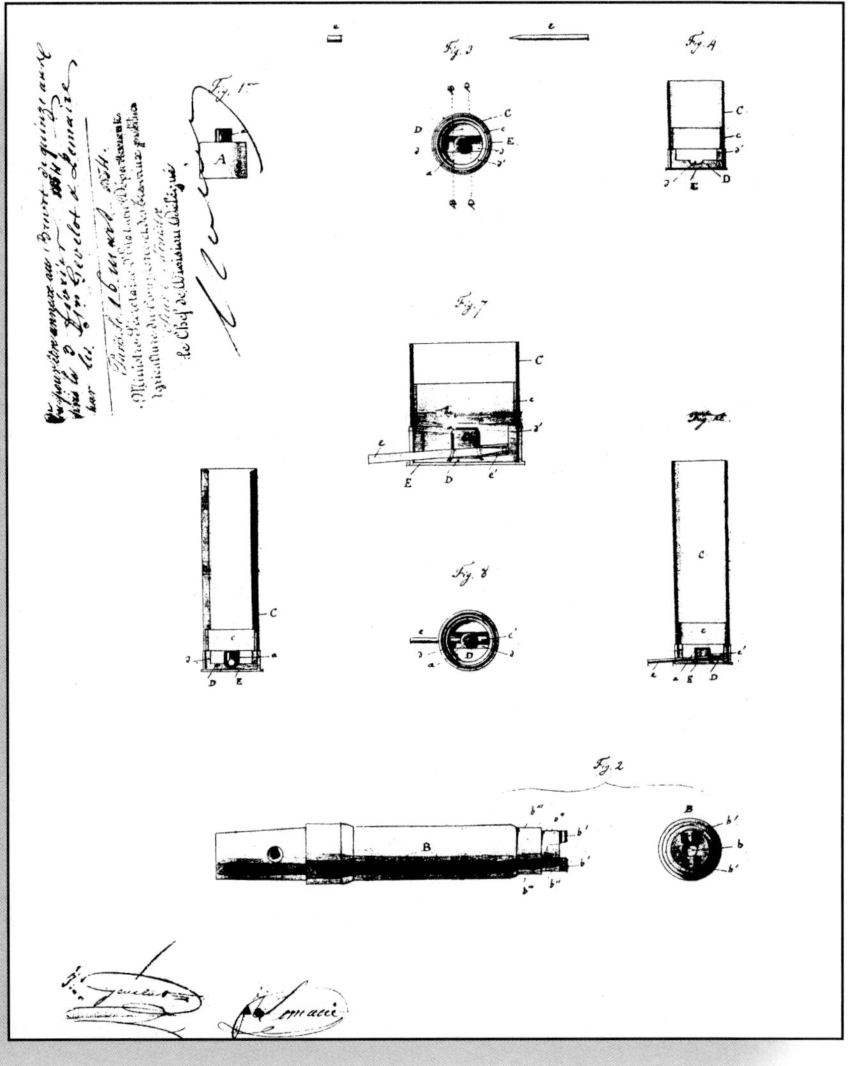

Plate 11-6. An illustration from Gevelot and Lemaire's French patent number 10482 of March 16, 1854, for a pinfire cartridge having paper case and metallic base cup. *Chris C. Curtis collection*

ber 17702, for a cartridge similar to Needham's.

Patent number 14550 was issued in 1855 to Boche, Tordeux, and Ouarnier, covering their design for a pinfire cartridge having the usual paper case and metal base. However, their primer was located between a stationary pin within the base and the familiar pin protruding from the base.

The next year, 1856, saw patent number 17741 granted to firearms designer Perrin, for a pinfire cartridge having shot and powder held in separate compartments within the case.

Houllier again led the field in innovations during 1857, with his patent number 20108 that introduced the simple idea, still in use today, of rolling over the open end of the cardboard tube to retain in place a cardboard disk that in turn holds the shot within the case.

The following year, 1858, Thomas introduced the idea of a cartridge having ratchet teeth on one side that were to engage sprockets in a magazine. His idea was protected by patent number 21830, though just what magazine-fed weapon the cartridges were intended for use with, if any existed, is unclear. The same year patent number 22370 was granted to Ouarnier, the former partner of Boche and Tordeux. Ouarnier's cartridge tube was of paper, as was the wad and reinforcing material; a screw entered the base of the cartridge from the side opposite the pin, holding the various components together and acting as an anvil beneath the primer.

The year 1859 brought a virtual torrent of new applications into the French patent office. Boche's patent number 22099 covered a pinfire cartridge consisting of a wound paper tube with a metallic cup in its base to form a partly conical powder chamber. The base wad was to be made of paper, gelatin, or some similar substance. Patent number 23200 was granted to Roy, for a cartridge also having a paper tube. Its priming cap was held within a metal-lined enclosure in the base wad; in addition, there was to be a metal reinforcement between the case and wad. Chaleyer received patent number 23421 during 1859, which covered a pin passing completely through the base to aid in removing the cap after firing, in much the same manner as Casimir Lefaucheux' original patent.

1859 also saw patent number 23439 granted to Varlet, whose design shows the pin passing through an external iron opening in the copper base cup. Lejeune and Chaumont received patent number 24035 that year, as well: it was for a paper cartridge having a steel, copper, or brass base. Boche was granted a second patent in 1859, number 24521, which was for a pinfire cartridge described simply as being bottle-necked, possibly referring to the shape of the primer cup within the metal base.

1860 saw Chaleyer being granted yet another patent, number 26478, for a cartridge having a base reinforced by a perforated base wad of non-oxidizable metal, with the priming cap being held in the perforation. Two additional firearms ammunition patents were granted in France during 1860, both of which were for cartridges having their shot and powder separated within the case: number 26422, to Robert Adams, who also patented his cartridge in England that year (number 285); and number 26927, to Leme.

Still more attempts were made toward improving the pinfire cartridge during subsequent years. But the basic design of Houllier prevailed for pistol cartridges, while the Lefaucheux design predominated in shot cartridges. One noteworthy concept was patented by Herbert in 1862, as patent number 55123. This all-metal cartridge had a hinged "trapdoor" in the base which swiveled down to expose the primer cap, greatly simplifying the reloading process. Herbert's cartridge was not commercially successful, however, and today examples are seldom encountered; a single specimen is illustrated in *Plates 11-7* and *11-8*.

For almost a decade, the all-metal cartridge had been the most popular choice for use with shotguns. Yet, by 1860 the many improvements in the design and construction of the cardboard cartridge had returned public favor back to widespread use of the latter type. The cardboard tube cartridge having a metal base was to remain in use until the pinfire shotshell cartridge era ended, although all-metal cases were used concurrently, as well.

During those formative years for the pinfire cartridge, many parallel developments were taking

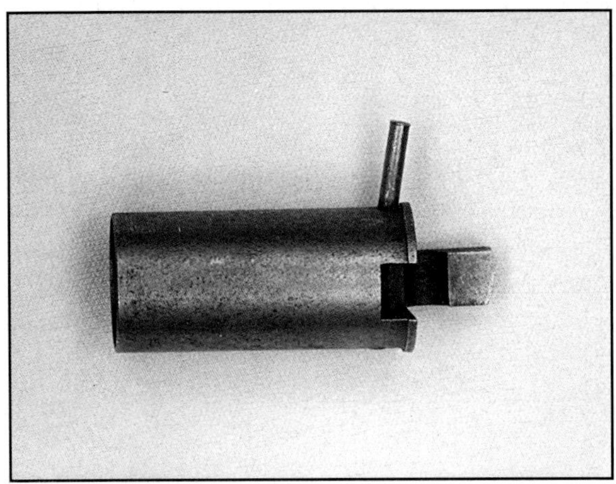

Plate 11-7. Made under Herbert's French patent number 55123 of 1862, this pinfire cartridge has case and pin made of iron, and a unique "trapdoor" in its base. *Chris C. Curtis collection; Ed Prentiss photograph*

Plate 11-8. Detail bottom view of the hinged "trapdoor" in the base of Herbert's pinfire cartridge shown in *Plate 11-7. Chris C. Curtis collection; Ed Prentiss photograph*

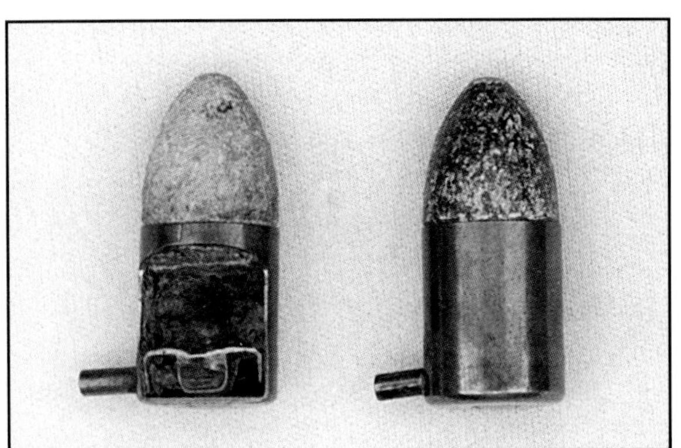

place in the quest for the perfect firearm cartridge. A substantial number of patents were issued for rimfire and centerfire designs; the same collection of ideas also spawned the needlefire cartridge.

One interesting cartridge design did attain limited production. The horizontal pinfire cartridge is a hybrid of the pinfire and needlefire systems, having the ignition pin in line with the length of the case and protruding slightly from a recess at the rear of the base. When struck from the rear the pin is propelled forward into the primer to detonate the cartridge. Manufactured by Gevelot for an experimental military rifle designed between 1860 and 1870, the horizontal pinfire cartridge had a cardboard tube case with a brass base.

It is equally interesting to note here, that nearly a decade earlier Eugene Lefaucheux had briefly experimented with a similar idea. In an addition (number 19380) to his 1854 patent, Lefaucheux illustrated two variations on the internal pinfire cartridge. In the first variation the cap was positioned opposite the pin inside the case at the base; in the second variation the cap was located opposite the pin on the rear of the bullet. How Lefaucheux intended for the percussion cap to be held in place was not explained in the patent. Apparently the idea was abandoned, and Lefaucheux continued producing conventional pinfire arms designed to use the cartridges already available.

The popularity of the breechloading pinfire shotgun was largely confined to Continental Europe prior to 1860, with France of course being at the center of those activities. In England, only the most progressive sportsmen of the time imported arms and ammunition utilizing the pinfire system. There, the combined effects of the great London Exhibition of 1851 and the famed

Plate 11-9 (left). Detail view of two 12mm caliber pinfire pistol cartridges manufactured in the United States by the Union Metallic Cartridge Company. The cartridge on the left was cut-away to show its internal components. *Chris C. Curtis collection; Ed Prentiss photograph*

field trials of 1858, 1859, and 1860 were that pinfire breechloading arms began to be taken seriously by English gunmakers. Many British inventors began submitting patent applications as the popularity of the new system grew. A brief summary of a number of their patents may be seen in the chart on this page, below.

The only American company to undertake the manufacture of pinfire ammunition in quantity following the Civil War was the Union Metallic Cartridge Company, of Bridgeport, Connecticut. The cartridges illustrated in *Plate 11-9* are 12mm caliber rounds having brass cases .577 inch in

length, and with the same impressed "U" headstamp as the rimfire cartridges made by U.M.C. The company also made pinfire ammunition in 7mm, 9mm, and 12mm short calibers. All have brass cases; the 9mm and 12mm versions bear the "U" headstamp. The 7mm cartridge is not headstamped, which makes its identification difficult, as it is nearly impossible to distinguish from unmarked 7mm European specimens. *Plate 11-10* illustrates the cardboard boxes for the three calibers of U.M.C. cartridges; each holds twenty-five rounds.

Several American inventors added their contributions to the evolutionary change and

---

British Pinfire Cartridge Patents

J.D. Dougal—Patent number 566 of March 3, 1859: Cartridge with a conical tube to fire front end first

R. Adams—Patent number 285 of February 13, 1860: Case with powder receives a shot cartridge with wad

T. Shedden—Patent number 389 of February 13, 1860: Paper case with base wad covered by a metal disk which holds pinfire primer

J. Rigby and W.N. Norman—Patent number 899 of April 10, 1860: Vertical or horizontal pins driven flush with case push forward and out; base wad expands into breechbolt recess on firing

W. Sear—Patent number 2533 of October 17, 1869: Case with a hollow plug threaded into base for front ignition

T. Shedden—Patent number 2954 of December 1, 1860: Paper case with a variety of bases, packed end-to-end; plug of metal, earthenware, wood, vulcanite, or other material

W.T. Eley—Patent number 916 of April 13, 1861: A means to prevent the pin being blown out when cartridge is fired

R.A. Brooman—Patent number 1738 of July 11, 1863: Pin so shaped to prevent gas escape; paper case with drawn metal base

J.H. Walsh—Patent number 1923 of August 4, 1863: Second pin on bottom aids in extraction

A. Wyley—Patent number 1785 of July 16, 1864: Fulminate placed between the ends of two rods, one of

which extends outside of case

W.W. Greener—Patent number 2349 of September 24, 1864: Primer is fitted to side of case, or at end of a horizontal tube

J. Leetch—Patent number 2907 of November 22, 1864: Pin placed to the right of center; an obturating ring of India rubber attached to end of the case acts as a gas seal

B. Thompson—Patent number 426 of February 14, 1865: Pin positioned forward in case; an opening in side of the case allows capping; outer case to obturate

J. and F.J. Jones—Patent number 2542 of October 4, 1865: Multi-facet claim describing methods for making cases of all types, including pinfire

W. Clark (J.F. Gevelot)—Patent number 592 of February 26, 1866: The hole for pin is made by punching, not drilling

W.E. Gedge (J. Audouy)—Patent number 1484 of May 18, 1867: Iron or brass case has a screw-on head to allow repriming

W.T. Eley—Patent number 591 of February 26, 1869: Metallic cup in front of the paper base, to prevent backward escape of gases

W.R. Lake (C.E. Sneider)—Patent number 3376 of December 24, 1870: Case separates on firing

J.H. Johnson (E. Cosson)—Patent number 2816 of July 11, 1876: A cup is placed in front of the fulminate

---

American Pinfire Cartridge Patents

T.L. Sturtevant—Patent number 53501 of March 27, 1866: Cap on the pin is inserted into side; base of charge chamber is conical

T.L. Sturtevant—Patent number 54038 of April 17, 1866: A shoulder on the pin serves as a valve to close the vent

G.A. Fitch—Patent number 58800 of October 16, 1866: Inside horizontal pin to the base of the shell

S.S. Rembert—Patent number 74594 of February 18, 1868: Pin extending across case explodes a cap on the opposite side

F. Wohlgemuth—Patent number 96373 of November 2, 1869: Metallic base cup screwed into or onto the tube; ignition pin is in base

W.H. Smith—Patent number 99721 of February 8, 1870: Radial opening in the base is closed by a screw

A.N.C. Gavard—Patent number 102109 of April 19, 1870: The steel tube is rolled and turned in a groove in the cut base plug

C.E. Sneider—Patent number 102984 of May 10, 1870: Pasteboard case having a flanged metallic base

D.E. Williams—Patent number 108543 of October 18, 1870: Pasteboard case having a metallic base and conical chamber

C.E. Sneider—Patent number 116640 of July 4, 1871: Separate paper cups contain the powder and shot

Plate 11-10 (left). Three sizes of pinfire cartridge boxes of pasteboard having printed paper labels, made by the Union Metallic Cartridge Company. From top: 12mm, 9mm, and 7mm calibers. *Chris C. Curtis collection; Richard McMillan photograph*

Plate 11-11 (above). Detail view of two 12mm long caliber pinfire cartridges made by Houllier and Blanchard of Paris. The cartridge on the left was cutaway to show its internal components. *Chris C. Curtis collection; Ed Prentiss photograph*

improvement of the pinfire cartridge, but none seriously attempted to enter actual production. Many of the post-Civil War American cartridge patents are listed in the chart on page 290.

Illustrated in *Plate 11-11* are pinfire cartridges made by Houllier and Blanchard of Paris; both examples are in caliber 12mm long, and have case lengths of .875 inch. These rounds, illustrated for comparison of length with the cases of their American counterparts, were made for use in revolvers, revolving carbines, or revolving rifles.

The invention of the improved pinfire cartridge had in turn created a new industry, that of

more popular and more widely accepted there, American distributors also advertised the sale of pinfire ammunition during the same period. Many differences in prices are to be noticed, as the following examples illustrate. The 1873 catalog of J.H. Johnson of Pittsburgh, Pennsylvania advertised 7mm and 9mm caliber pinfire cartridges at $3.00 per hundred, and 12mm cartridges at $3.50 for the same quantity. In his 1879 catalog, Johnson reduced the prices: 7mm caliber cartridges now went for $15.00 per thousand; 9mm for $18.00 per thousand, and 12mm for $20.00 per thousand. Two pages further into his 1879 catalog Johnson

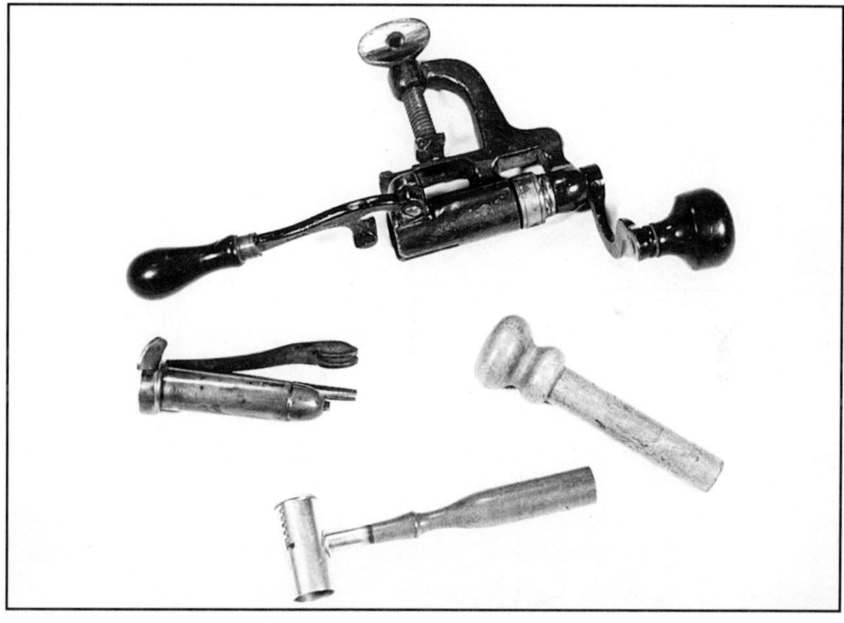

Plate 11-12. A set of reloading tools for a pinfire shotgun. From top, left to right: crimper, multi-purpose tool, wad setter, and powder measure. *Courtesy private collection; F.W. Hulbert photograph*

large-scale metallic cartridge manufacture. Scores of firms throughout the world began producing ammunition for the newly-successful breechloading arms. The charts on pages 304 through 306 illustrate some of the many headstamp variations found on pinfire cartridges that were being produced and used in all corners of the globe.

Pinfire ammunition was marketed widely throughout Continental Europe and Great Britain during the late nineteenth and early twentieth centuries. While the pinfire system generally was

offered lesser-quality pinfire cartridges for $13.50 per two thousand quantity (7mm), and $16.00 and $19.00 respectively for 9mm and 12mm caliber cartridges in the same 2000 quantity lots. The ad is made more interesting by its listing of the accepted equivalent American caliber designations opposite each European size: 7mm or .30 caliber, 9mm or .38 caliber, and 12mm or .44 caliber.

From Chicago, Illinois came the Hibbard, Spencer, Bartlett and Company catalog for 1884, which offered 7mm caliber pinfire ammunition for sale at $15.00 per thousand rounds, 9mm at $18.00 per thousand, and 12mm at $21.00 per thousand.

1897 found Sears, Roebuck & Company, also of Chicago, in their catalog selling pinfire pistol ammunition in fifty-round boxes for forty, forty-five, and fifty cents each in calibers 7mm, 9mm, and 12mm, respectively. Ammunition in the American calibers was priced slightly higher, with .32 S&W, .38 S&W, and .44 S&W Russian bringing forty-four, fifty-four, and eighty cents per fifty-round box, respectively. The same Sears catalog offered empty pinfire shotgun shells in gauges from 20 to 12, at prices increasing accordingly from

At the top of the photograph is a crimper; at center-right is a wad setter; the familiar shot and powder measure is shown at the bottom. Marked with the gauge for which it was intended, the tool at center-left was designed to perform many pinfire reloading operations; among them, the bullet-shaped main body holds the cardboard case firmly in place without altering its original size. The tweezer-like projections above the main body of the tool are for pin placement, alignment, and removal. The body is spring-loaded, and contains a slender rod projecting from the tip which properly places the percussion cap into its designated

Plate 11-13. Reloading tools made of wood, for pinfire cartridges. Each is unmarked and its purpose is unknown, but it is likely they are case holders. *Courtesy private collection; F.W. Hulbert photograph*

Plate 11-14. Reloading tools made of wood, for pinfire cartridges. Far left: shell holder; third from left: powder and shot rammer; far right: crimper. *Courtesy private collection; F.W. Hulbert photograph*

sixty-five cents to $1.20 per box of 100 primed empties. For the purpose of comparison, a twenty-round box of .45-70 caliber smokeless powder cartridges sold for eighty cents. Sears, Roebuck continued to sell pinfire ammunition for the next half-dozen years; by the end of that time the average price had increased about five cents a box.

Although on first inspection pinfire shotgun shells might appear to be fragile and disposable containers, they are indeed reloadable, and component parts were sold for that purpose. Plate 11-12 illustrates a set of shotgun shell reloading tools.

recess within the base of the cartridge.

Metallic pistol cartridges were rather more difficult to reload due to their smaller size and their method of construction. Tiny tweezers were a necessary aid for the placement of their percussion caps.

The five wooden tools illustrated in *Plate 11-13* are unmarked and unidentified, but were clearly designed for use in the reloading process. Each tool appears to be a hand-held receptacle made to house the base of the pinfire cartridge during some phase of reloading, perhaps the cementing of the paper tube onto the already capped (loaded) brass base.

A similar hand-held reloading tool also made of wood is shown at the far left in *Plate 11-14*. The main difference between this shell holder and the tools described just previously is that here the handle is made hollow to receive the cartridge case. A funnel is then placed into the opposite end, and powder and shot poured in. The tool shown third from left is simply a rammer for packing the powder and shot tightly into the shell casing. The small tool at far right is a crimper. This set of reloading tools is unmarked except for the gauge designation, "16."

Due to the limitations of space, only a few British arms, cartridges, and patents have been illustrated in this work. But many British gunmakers and sportsmen not only accepted the pinfire system, they enthusiastically embraced it. The inventive efforts of British gunmakers also extended into the field of reloading tools and methods, and several are listed below:

Lancaster—Patent number 1361 of June 16, 1858: Pinfire charging tool
Jeffries—Patent number 1900 of August 6, 1860: Pinfire charging tool
Purdey—Patent number 302 of February 5, 1861: Pinfire charging tool
Elliott—Patent number 2435 of September 3, 1862: Pinfire case extraction tool
Hawksley—Patent number 3379 of December 30, 1865: Pinfire cartridge loading tool
Erskine—Patent number 1484 of May 28, 1866: Combination pinfire-centerfire loading tool
Dixon—Patent number 2369 of August 17, 1867: Pinfire loading tool

Plate 11-15 illustrates the patent drawing from Bartram and Harwood's British patent number 3154 (of December 16, 1861) for a wad setting tool. *Plate 11-16* illustrates the actual tool made by Bartram and Harwood, having a body of brass; notice the slot cut into the lower end to accept the ignition pin of the pinfire cartridge.

Illustrated in *Plate 11-17* is the case extraction tool described in Elliott's English patent number 2435 of September 3, 1862, as being "nearly the same form and construction as that of the ordinary pocket corkscrew."

Plate 11-18 illustrates the drawing of a reloading tool from Hawksley's patent number 3379 (December 30, 1865). *Plate 11-19* illustrates another pinfire case extraction tool, this one of Hawksley's own design and manufacture.

A portion of the patent drawing from Dixon and Buttery's patent number 2369, of August 17, 1867 is illustrated in *Plate 11-20*. *Plate 11-21* illustrates a 12-gauge pinfire shotgun shell crimping tool made by Dixon; a close-up view of the "Dixon & Sons" marking on a pinfire crimping tool is shown in *Plate 11-22*.

Not all of the reloading tools from this period were small, hand-held types. A number were larger, sturdier, and intended for being either permanently or temporarily attached to a workbench or table. Such is the case of the loading apparatus described by Charles Lancaster in his British patent number 1361, of June 16, 1858. In it he included a provision whereby the plunger could be operated by hand or by a treadle. Purdey's patent number 302 of February 5, 1861 also was for a bench-mounted pinfire reloading tool. *Plate 11-23* illustrates one page from the specification drawings of William Munn's patent number 2495 of September 11, 1862. In it he stated that the reloading tool described could be attached to a bench, gun case, or an ammunition box, serving as a stand for steadying the work.

As with any type of ammunition, one of the primary concerns of those who carried and used pinfire cartridges was the always possible, if not likely, danger of unexpected detonation. With the exposed ignition pin of the pinfire cartridge poised just above the primer, individuals having live rounds about their person needed to be especially careful. A sharp blow on the pin might detonate the cartridge, although such an occurrence rarely caused hunting accidents. As the bullet or shot end of a cartridge is heavier than its base, a

text continued on page 297

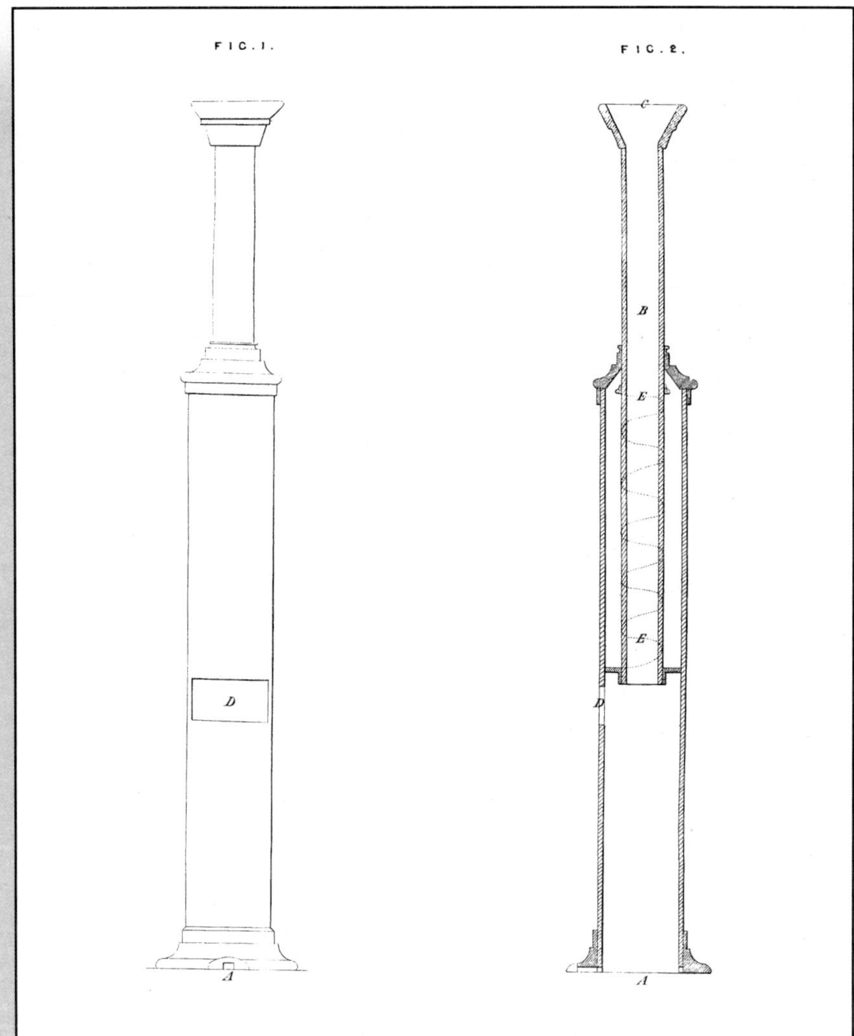

Plate 11-15. An illustration from Bartram and Harwood's English patent number 3154 of December 16, 1861, for a pinfire wad setting tool. *Chris C. Curtis collection*

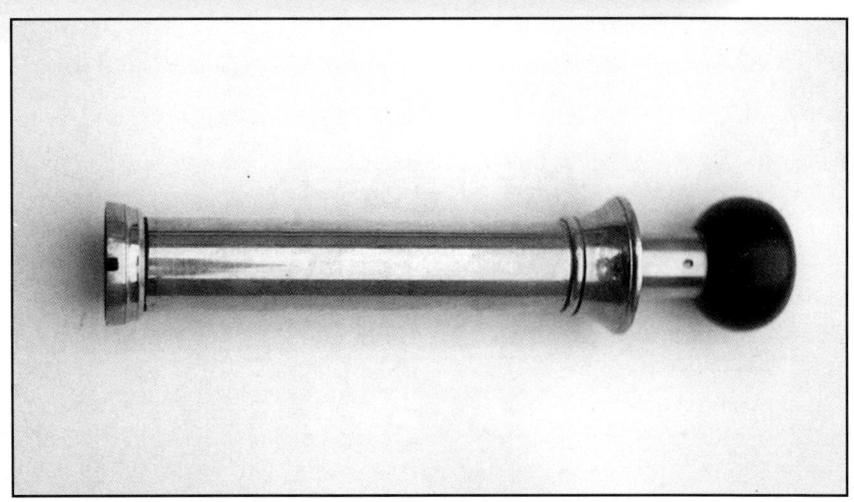

Plate 11-16. A 12 gauge pinfire cartridge wad setting tool having brass body, made in England by Bartram and Harwood. *Courtesy David Kendrew; David Kendrew photograph*

Plate 11-17 (right). A pinfire case extraction tool made by H. Elliott, and so marked, under English patent number 2435 of September 3, 1862. *Courtesy David Kendrew; David Kendrew photograph*

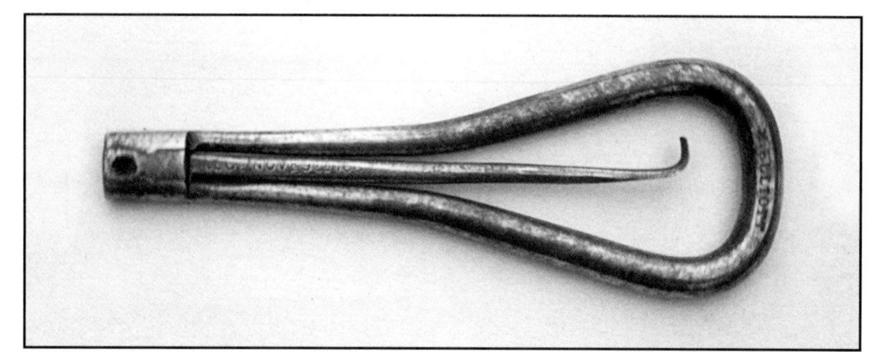

Plate 11-18 (below). An illustration from George

caption continued below

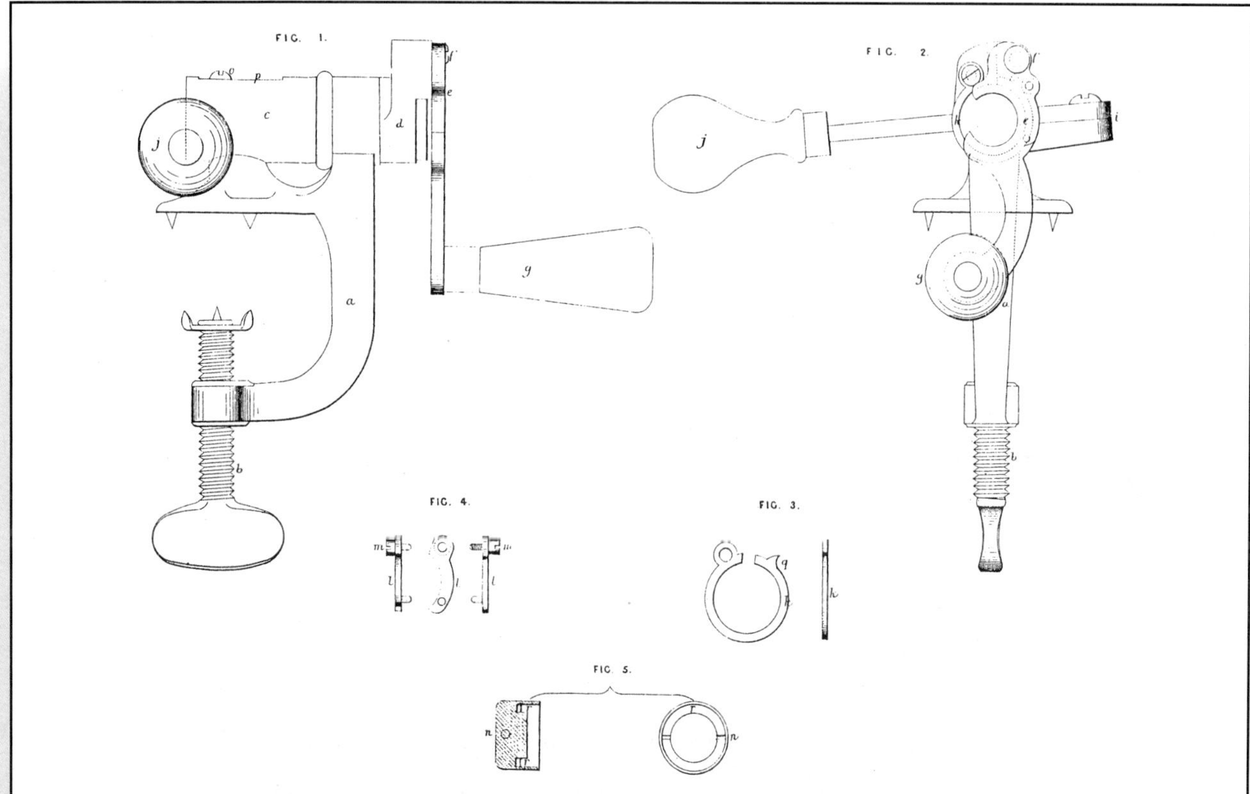

Hawksley's English patent number 3379 of December 30, 1865, for a pinfire cartridge reloading tool. *Chris C. Curtis collection*

Plate 11-19 (right). A pinfire cartridge case extraction tool made by and marked "G. & J.W. Hawksley 12." *Courtesy David Kendrew; David Kendrew photograph*

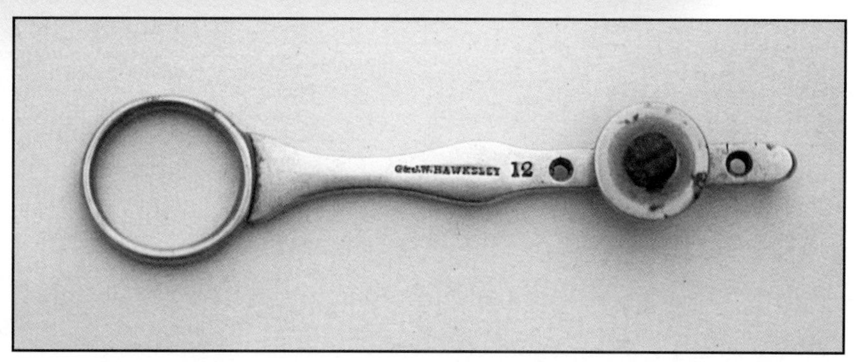

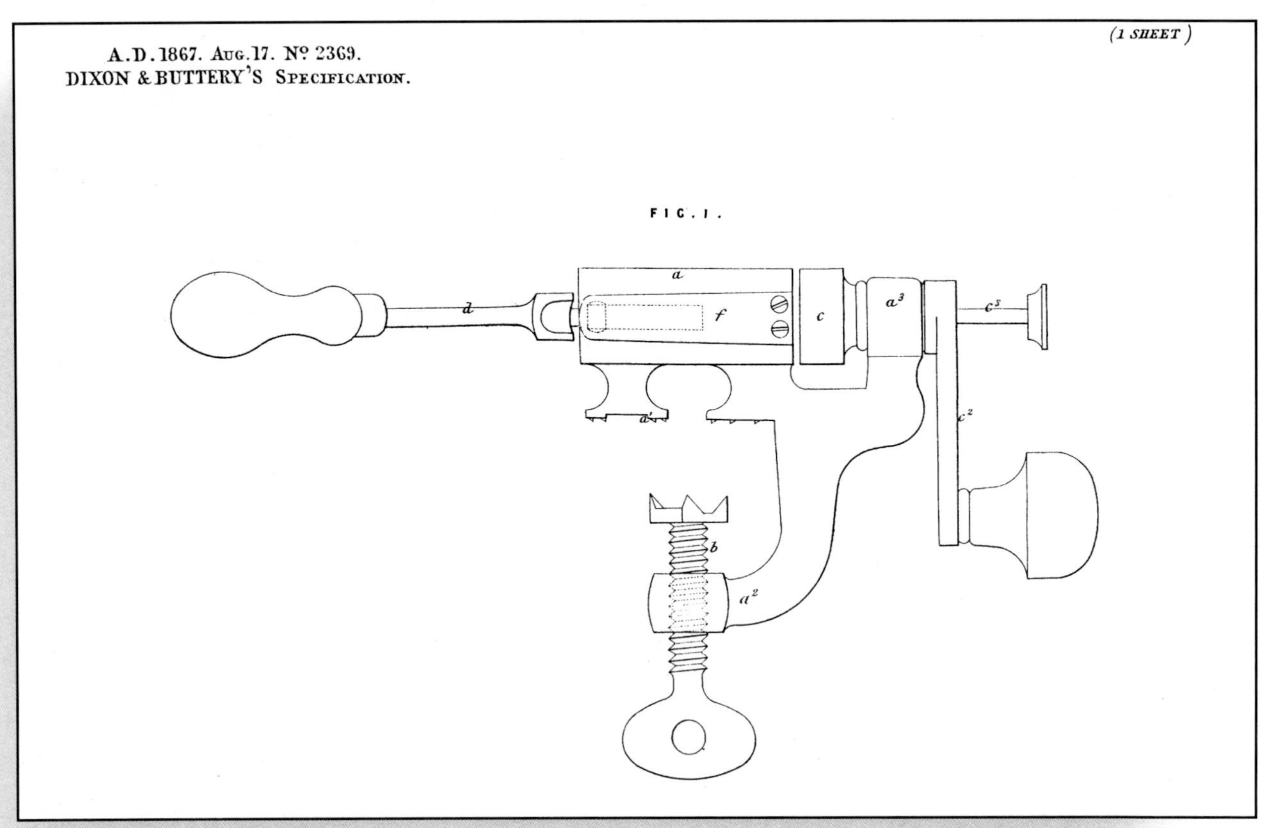

Plate 11-20 (above). An illustration from Dixon and Buttery's English patent number 2369 of August 17, 1867, for a pinfire cartridge reloading tool. *Chris C. Curtis collection*

Plate 11-22 (below). Detail view of the *"James Dixon & Sons Sheffield 12"* markings stamped onto the handle of the tool shown in *Plate 11-21*. *Courtesy David Kendrew; David Kendrew photograph*

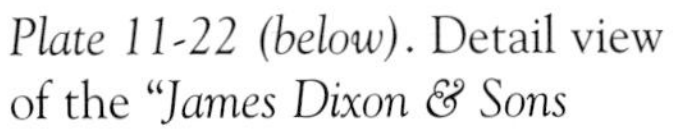

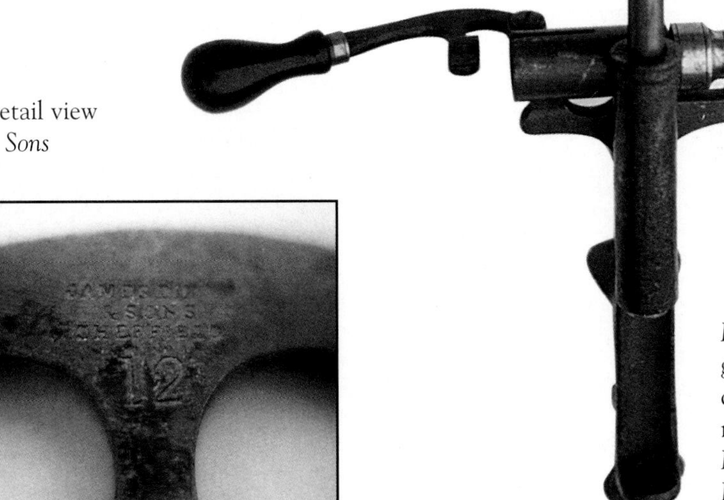

Plate 11-21 (left). A 12 gauge pinfire shotgun shell crimping tool made and marked by Dixon. *Courtesy David Kendrew; David Kendrew photograph*

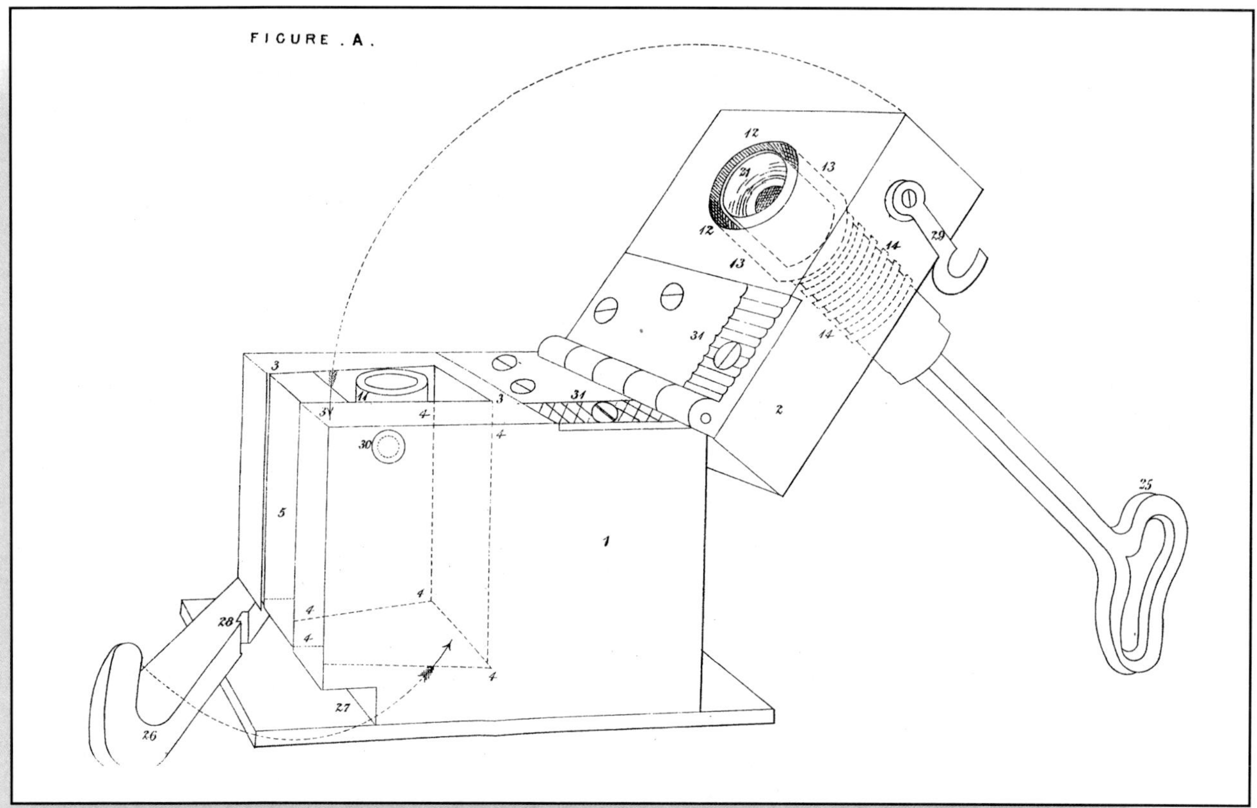

Plate 11-23. An illustration from William Munn's English patent number 2495 of September 11, 1862, for a table or workbench-mounted pinfire cartridge reloading device. *Chris C. Curtis collection*

dropped round was likely to hit bullet-first, thus virtually eliminating the possibility of the pin striking with enough force to fire the round.

Carrying loose ammunition in one's pocket might not only be dangerous, it was uncomfortable, to say the least. One practical solution was the use of a cartridge waist belt. An even more convenient way to carry a quantity of ammunition was patented in England by G.G. Bussey on May 6, 1859, patent number 1161. Bussey's cartridge holder, in which the cartridges were held in clips fixed on an endless belt, was slung over the back, out of the way but easily accessible. It is illustrated in *Plate 11-24.*

Other, smaller containers for pinfire cartridges

also were made and marketed, often in the form of a cartridge box, other times sized and shaped like the cigar and snuff boxes that were popular during the period. One example of the latter style is illustrated in *Plate 11-25*, and is marked "*Laine Brevete.*" Contained within are twenty-four separate copper tubes positioned to hold 7mm caliber pinfire cartridges so they cannot rest against one another. Whether larger, smaller, or of some different shape, these containers had a single idea in common: that of carrying loose cartridges safely in the pocket or hunting bag.

Several hundred variations of antique pinfire pistol cartridges and shotgun shells are available today to the serious student or collector. A myriad of case lengths, case materials and construction, projectile shapes, and headstamps both raised and impressed, contribute to make cartridge collecting a fascinating and rewarding pastime. While they are not as common, pinfire cartridge boxes also

Plate 11-24. A reproduction from G.G. Bussey's English patent number 1161 of May 6, 1859, for a pinfire cartridge carrier/dispenser made to be worn over the shoulder suspended from a leather strap. *Chris C. Curtis collection*

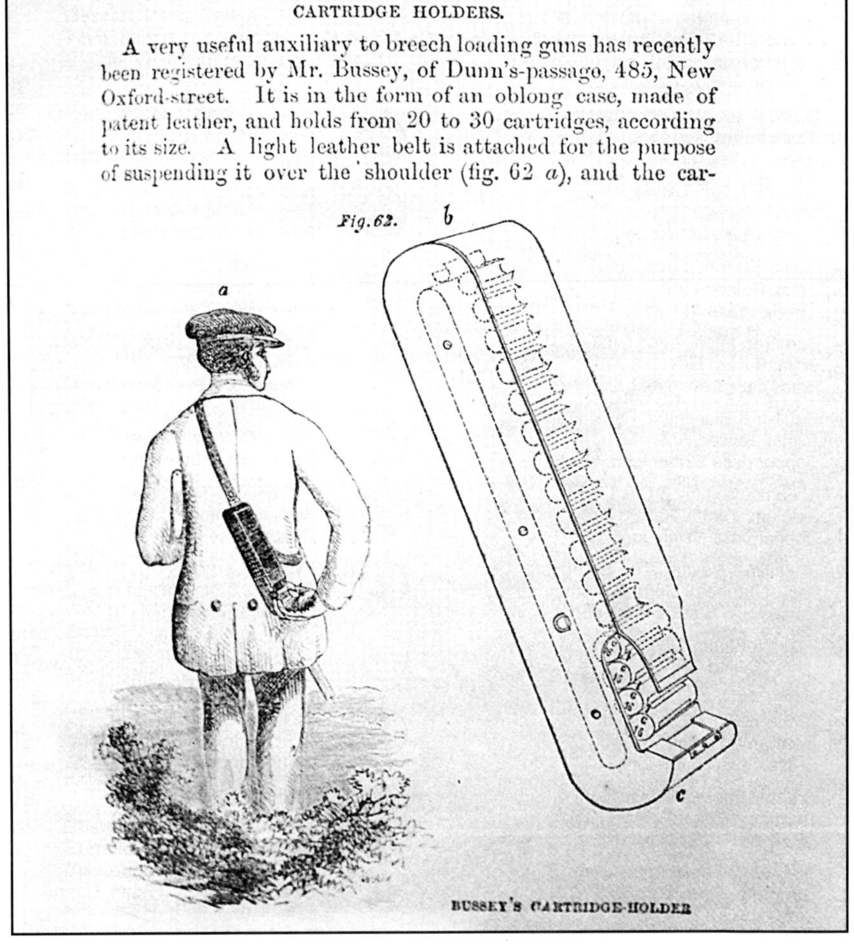

Plate 11-25. A leather-covered metal, pocket-size carrying box having inserts for twenty-four 7mm caliber pinfire cartridges. Inside lid is marked "*Laine Brevete Fabrique d'Armes 21, rue de Rivoli, 21.*" *Chris C. Curtis collection; Richard McMillan photograph*

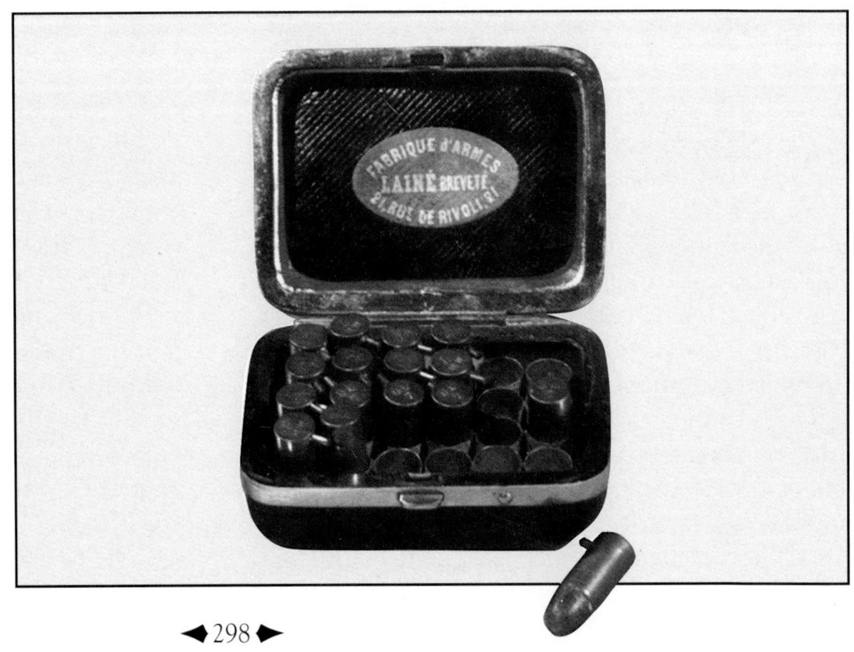

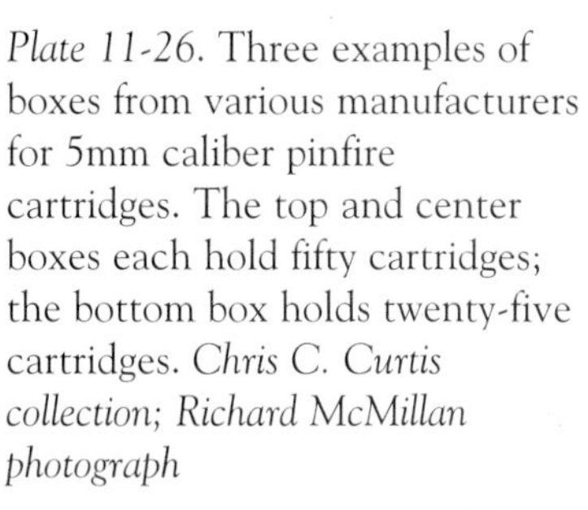

Plate 11-26. Three examples of boxes from various manufacturers for 5mm caliber pinfire cartridges. The top and center boxes each hold fifty cartridges; the bottom box holds twenty-five cartridges. *Chris C. Curtis collection; Richard McMillan photograph*

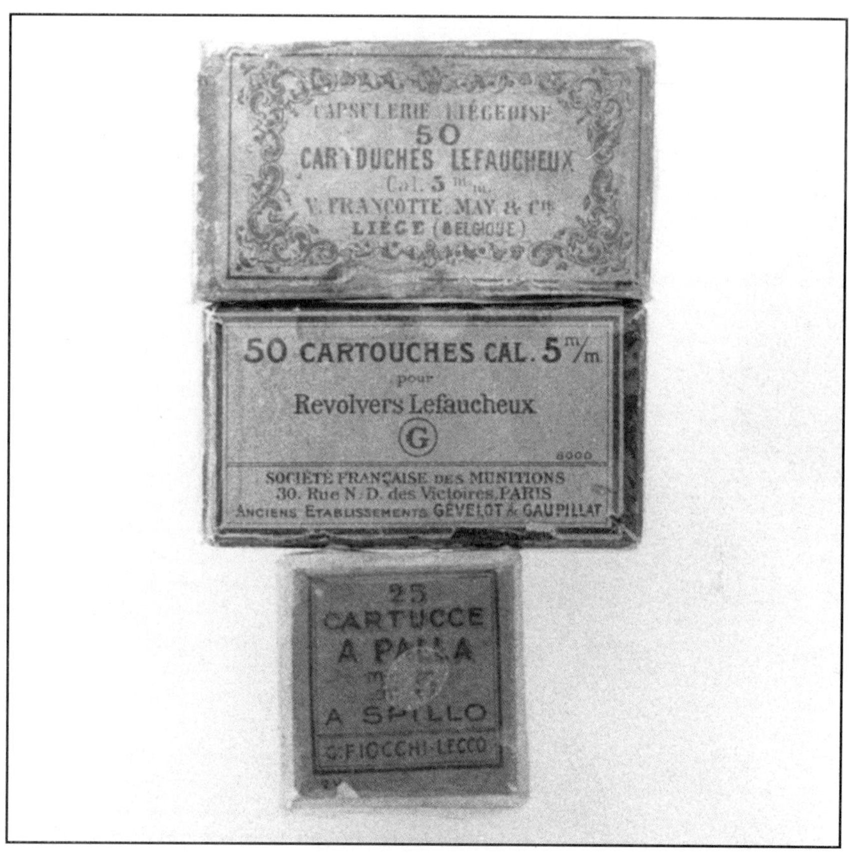

make a fascinating study. The following illustrations in this chapter are but a sample of the many variations to be found.

The manufacture of pinfire ammunition continued long after the introduction and perfection of rimfire and centerfire cartridges and their subsequent mass production. Many shooters stubbornly resisted abandoning their pinfire arms, for economical as well as sentimental reasons, as they simply could not afford to discard a perfectly good weapon merely to purchase a newer ammunition system.

And of course the manufacture of pinfire arms continued long after the pinfire system had been overshadowed by the more advanced types of firearms. During this late period pinfire arms were produced mainly for export to the world's less technologically advanced regions, such as Africa, South America, and the Far East. Fearing poten-

tial unrest or uprisals among native populations, the European officials of the colonial or local governments in those areas oftentimes forbade the possession and use of more modern arms.

Ammunition production was maintained to supply those exported pinfire arms, and the manufacture of pinfire ammunition was continued in Europe as late as 1990. Many shooters still use pinfire arms in a limited capacity, and the miniature 2mm caliber pinfire "charm pistols" currently being produced require their own tiny blank cartridges.

The pinfire cartridge, the lifespan of which now approaches the century-and-a-half mark, remains the oldest firearms ammunition still in use today.

Chapter note.

1. All cartridge patents discussed herein are French, unless otherwise noted.

Plate 11-27. Depicted is a variety of twenty-five and fifty-count boxes for 7mm caliber pinfire cartridges, by numerous English and continental European makers. *Chris C. Curtis collection; Richard McMillan photograph*

Plate 11-28. This grouping of boxes for 9mm caliber pinfire cartridges shows the great variety in label styles and manufacturers. Note that many of these labels state their cartridges are for "Lefaucheux Revolvers." *Chris C. Curtis collection; Richard McMillan photograph*

Plate 11-29. Examples of boxes for 12mm caliber pinfire cartridges made by various French and German manufacturers. Note the 12mm long cartridges at upper-center, made by *"Houllier-Blanchard, Paris." Chris C. Curtis collection; Richard McMillan photograph*

Plate 11-30. Illustrated is a tin box having an ornate printed paper label for the very rare 12mm explosive ball pinfire cartridge, an example of which is shown at the right. The copper case bears a "GJ" headstamp; the bullet is an unusual round-nose version. Details regarding the explosive device and its material are unknown. *Courtesy Eugene D. Spicer; Eugene D. Spicer photograph*

Plate 11-31. A pair of boxes for the rare 15mm caliber pinfire cartridges. Both are marked for use with the Lefaucheux revolver. *Chris C. Curtis collection; Richard McMillan photograph*

 Giulio Fiocchi, Lecco, Italy
5mm. Impressed H/S
Copper case 11mm long.

 Giulio Fiocchi, Lecco, Italy
15mm. Raised H/S
Copper case 22mm long.

 Giulio Fiocchi, Lecco, Italy
7mm. Raised H/S
Copper case 15mm long.

 Bernardo Piloni, Lecco, Italy
9mm. Raised H/S
Brass case 16mm long.

 Houllier & Blanchard, Paris, France
12mm. Raised H/S
Copper case 22mm long.

 V. Francotte May & Cie, Liége, Belgium
12mm. Raised H/S
Copper case 11mm long.

 Rheinische Westfallische Sprengstoff A.G.,
Nuremburg, Germany. 5mm. Raised H/S
Brass 11mm, paper 7mm long.

 Braun & Bloem, Dusseldorf, Germany
9mm. Raised H/S
Brass case 15mm long.

 Braun & Bloem, Dusseldorf, Germany
12mm. Raised H/S
Brass case 15mm long.

 Braun & Bloem, Dusseldorf, Germany
7mm. Raised H/S
Brass case 15mm long.

 Braun & Bloem, Dusseldorf, Germany
5mm. Raised H/S
Brass case 11mm long.

 Braun & Bloem, Dusseldorf, Germany
7mm. Impressed H/S
Brass case 14mm long.

 Gustav Genschow, Nuremburg, Germany
7mm. Raised H/S
Copper 14mm, paper 8mm long.

 Georg Eggestorff, Linden, Germany
12mm. Raised H/S
Copper case 15mm long.

 Gevelot, Paris, France
7mm. Impressed H/S
Brass case 14mm long.

 Eley Brothers, London, England
5mm. Raised H/S
Copper or brass case 11mm long.

 Eley Brothers, London, England
7mm. Raised H/S
Brass case 13mm long.

 Eley Brothers, London, England
15mm. Impressed H/S
Brass case 31mm long.

 Eley Brothers, London, England
9mm. Raised H/S
Brass case 13mm long.

 Eley Brothers, London, England
12mm *Carbine*. Raised H/S
Brass case 15mm long.

 V. Francotte May & Cie., Liége, Belgium
15mm. Raised H/S
Copper case 20mm long.

 Kynoch Cartridge Co., Birmingham, England
5mm. Raised H/S
Copper 11mm, white paper 7mm long.

 Sellier & Bellot, Prague, Czechoslovakia
7mm. Impressed H/S
Copper case 14mm long.

 Sellier & Bellot, Prague, Czechoslovakia
9mm. Impressed H/S
Copper case 14mm long.

Sellier & Bellot, Prague, Czechoslovakia
12mm. Raised H/S
Brass 16mm, green paper 10mm long.

Sellier & Bellot, Prague, Czechoslovakia
12mm. Impressed H/S
Copper case 14mm long.

Sellier & Bellot, Prague, Czechoslovakia
9mm. Impressed H/S
Copper case 14mm long.

Sellier & Bellot, Prague, Czechoslovakia
12mm. Raised H/S
Brass case 16mm long.

Rheinische Westfallische Sprengstoff A.G.,
Nuremburg, Germany. 5mm.
Raised H/S. Copper case 11mm long.

Charles Fusnot, Brussels, Belgium
12mm. Raised H/S
Copper case 15mm long.

Gevelot, Paris, France
7mm. Impressed H/S
Copper case 14mm long.

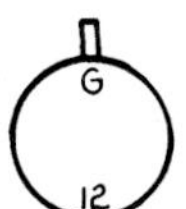

Gevelot, Paris, France
12mm. Impressed H/S
Brass case 16mm long.

Gevelot, Paris, France
9mm. Impressed H/S
Copper case 15mm long.

Gevelot, Paris, France
12mm *explosive* bullet. Raised H/S
Copper case 17mm long.

Union Metallic Cartridge Co.,
Bridgeport, Conn., USA
9mm. Impressed H/S
Brass case 15mm long.

Keller & Co., Hirtenberg, Austria
9mm. Raised H/S
Brass 14mm, paper 10mm long.

Giulio Fiocchi, Lecco, Italy
28 gauge. Impressed H/S
Brass 6mm, red paper 59mm long.

Giulio Fiocchi, Lecco, Italy
14 gauge. Impressed H/S
Brass 6mm, red paper 58mm long.

Capsulerie Liégoise Dpt,
Cartoucherie Liége, Liége, Belgium
28 gauge. Impressed H/S
Brass 7mm, tan paper 58mm long.

Gustav Genschow & Co., Durlach, Germany
14mm. Impressed H/S
Brass 10 mm, red paper 53mm long.

Capsulerie Liégeoise Dpt,
Cartoucherie Liége, Liége, Belgium
20 gauge. Impressed H/S
Brass 8mm, green paper 57mm long.

Kynoch & Co., Birmingham, England
16 gauge. Impressed H/S
All brass case 66mm long.

Eley-Kynoch, London, England
12 gauge. Impressed H/S
Brass 9mm, buff paper 51mm long.

Ste Francaise des Munitions, Anciens
Etablissements Gevelot & Gaupillat
24 gauge. Impressed H/S
Brass 7mm, blue paper 57mm long.

Rheinische Westfallische Sprengstoff A.G.,
Nuremburg, Germany. 9mm. Raised H/S
Copper case 14mm long.

Hirtenberger Patronen-Zundhutchen-u
Metallwaffenfabrik, Hirtenberg, Austria
7mm. Raised H/S. Brass case 14mm long.

The Arms and Ammunition Mfg. Co.,
London, England. 7mm. Impressed H/S
Brass case 14mm long.

Cartoucherie Francaise, Paris, France
9mm. Raised H/S
Copper case 14mm long.

Sellier & Bellot, Prague, Czechoslovakia
11 mm. Raised H/S
Brass 6mm, green paper 39mm long.

Keller & Co., Hirtenberg, Austria
7mm. Impressed H/S
Brass 14mm, orange paper 12mm long.

Eley Brothers, London, England
14 gauge. Raised H/S
Brass 8mm, salmon paper 57mm long.

Eley Brothers, London, England
10 gauge. Impressed H/S
Brass 12mm, green paper 54mm long.

Eley Brothers, London, England
12 gauge. Impressed H/S
Brass 7mm, brown paper 57mm long.

Eley Brothers, London, England
8 gauge. Raised H/S
Brass 11mm, green paper 71mm long.

Eley Brothers, London, England
10 gauge. Raised H/S
Brass 9mm, tan paper 65mm long.

Eley Brothers, London, England
12 gauge. Impressed H/S
Brass 8mm, dark brown paper 56mm long.

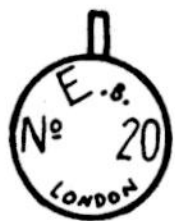
Eley Brothers, London, England
20 gauge. Impressed H/S
Brass 7mm, lt. brown paper 55mm long.

Capsulerie Liége Cartoucherie Liége,
Liége, Belgium. 14mm. Impressed H/S
Brass 7mm, tan paper 55mm long.

Gevelot, Paris, France
8 gauge. Impressed H/S
Brass 10mm, green paper 90mm long.

Gevelot, Paris, France
12 gauge. Impressed H/S (T raised)
Brass 4mm, orange/brown paper 60mm long.

Gevelot, Paris, France
12 gauge. Impressed H/S
Brass 5mm, green paper 59mm long.

Gevelot, Paris, France
4 gauge. Raised H/S
Brass 8mm, green paper 76mm long.

Ste Fse des Munitions, Anciens
Etablissements Gevelot & Gaupillat
14 gauge. Impressed H/S
Brass 7mm, blue paper 58mm long.

Cartoucherie Russo-Belge, Liége, Belgium
16 gauge. Impressed H/S
Brass 6mm, lt. green paper 59mm long.

Rheinische Westfallische Sprengstoff A.G.,
Nuremburg, Germany
24 gauge. Impressed H/S
Brass 6mm, mint green paper 57mm long.

Von Lengerke & Detmold, N.Y., USA
16 gauge. Impressed H/S
Brass 11mm, dark blue paper 53mm long.

Manufacture General des Munitions
Bourge-les-Valence, France
16 gauge. Impressed H/S
Brass 8mm, dark blue paper 57mm long.

Braun & Bloem, Dusseldorf, Germany
24 gauge. Impressed H/S
Brass 5mm, green paper 58mm long.

Braun & Bloem, Dusseldorf, Germany
12 gauge. Impressed H/S
Brass 6mm, lt. green paper 58mm long.

Sellier & Bellot, Prague, Czechoslovakia
20 gauge. Impressed H/S
Brass 5mm, lime green paper 59mm long.

BIBLIOGRAPHY

Primary Sources:

The Armouries, H.M. Tower of London, London, England.
French Patent Office, Paris, France.
H.M. Patent Office, London, England.
Illustrated London News, 1851.
Museé d'Armes de Liége, Liége, Belgium.
Museé d'Armes de St. Etienne, St. Etienne, France.
Museum of the Confederacy, Richmond, VA.
Museum of London, London Wall, London, England.
National Archives and Records Service, Washington, DC.
  a. "Correspondence on the Purchase of Arms",
     Proceedings of the Commission of Ordnance and
     Ordnance Stores.
  b. Correspondence Received by the Ordnance
     Department, 1858.
  c. Ordnance Extracts, Executive Document No. 99, 40th
     Congress, 2nd Session.
  d. Record Groups 156-21, 100, 103, 124, 125, 1001.
Natural History Museum of Los Angeles, Los Angeles, CA.
Oviedo Arsenal, Oviedo, Spain.
Springfield City Directory, City Library, Springfield, MA.
Swiss Institute of Arms and Armour, Grandson, Switzerland.
United States Patent and Trademark Office, Washington, DC.

Secondary Sources:

Albaugh, William A. III, *Confederate Faces*. Solana Beach,
  CA: 1970.
Baker, D.J. and I.M. Crudgington, *The British Shotgun, Volume
  I 1850-1870*. London, England: 1979.
Bartlett, W.A. and D.B. Gallatin, *Digest of Cartridges for Small
  Arms Patented in the United States, England, and France*.
  Washington, DC: 1878.
Blair, Claude, *Pistols of the World*. New York, NY: 1968.
Blanch, H.J., *A Century of Guns*. London, England: 1909.
Boothroyd, Geoffrey, *The Handgun*. New York, NY: 1970.
Caranta, Raymond and Jean Jordanoglou, *Pistolets et Revolvers
  d'Autrefois*. Paris, France: 1974.
Carey, A. Merwyn, *American Firearms Makers*. New York, NY:
  1953.
—, *English, Irish, and Scottish Firearms Makers*. New York, NY:
  1954.
Dunlap, Jack, *Pepperbox Firearms*. Palo Alto, CA: 1964.
Dyer, Frederick H., *A Compendium of the War of the Rebellion,
  Volume II*. 1978.
Edwards, William B., *Civil War Guns*. Harrisburg, PA: 1962.
Encyclopedia Britannica, 1956 Edition.
Ezell, Edward C., *Handguns of the World*. Harrisburg, PA:
  1981.
Frost, H. Gordon, *Blades and Barrels: Six Centuries of
  Combination Weapons*. El Paso, TX: 1972.
Gaier, Claude, *Four Centuries of Liége Gunmaking*. Liége,
  Belgium: 1976.
Gardner, Col. Robert, *Small Arms Makers*. New York, NY:
  1963.
George, J.M., *English Pistols and Revolvers*. London, England:
  1961.
Greener, W.W., *The Gun and Its Development*. London,
  England: 1881.
Heer, Eugéne, *Der Neue Støckel, Internationales Lexikon der
  Büchsenmacher, Feuerwaffenfabrikanten und Armbrustmacher
  von 1400-1900* (3 vols.). Herausgeber, Journal-Verlag
  Schwend GmbH Schwäbisch Hall: 1978.
Hesseltine and Wolf, *The Blue and the Grey on the Nile*. 1961.
History of the 11th New Jersey Volunteers. 1898.

James, Edsall, *The Revolver Rifles*. Union City, TN: 1974.
L'Armurerie Belge, *Federation des Constructeurs Belgique*. Liége,
  Belgium: 1938.
Lautissier, Gérard and Michel Renonciat, *Casimir Lefaucheux
  Arquebusier 1802-1852*. Cedex, France: 1999.
Le Genie Industriel, *Visites dans les Etablissements Industriels*.
  Paris, France: 1865.
Lockhoven, H.B., *Kleine Waffenbibliotek, Serie A, 25-26*.
  Rodenkirken, Germany: 1968-1970.
Lord, Francis A., *Civil War Collector's Encyclopedia*. Secaucus,
  NJ: 1963.
—, *They Fought for the Union*. Harrisburg, PA: 1960.
Manchester, William, *The Arms of Krupp 1587-1968*. Boston,
  MA and Toronto, Ontario: 1968.
McAulay, John D., *Civil War Pistols*. Lincoln, RI: 1992.
Medlin, Eugene and Jean Huon, *Military Handguns of France*.
  Latham, NY: 1993.
*Military History of the Kansas Regiments; Military History of the
  2nd Kansas Cavalry*, courtesy John P. Beckendorf.
Möller, T., *Gamle Danske Militaer Vaben*.
Müller, Rolf H., *Geschichte und Technik der Europaischen
  Militarrevolver, Volumes I and II*.
Nielson, O., *Den Nørske Haers Handskytevapen*. Haermuseet,
  Oslo, Norway: 1956.
Reilly, Robert M., *United States Military Small Arms 1816-
  1865*. Baton Rouge, LA: 1970.
Salvatici, Luciano, *Pistole Militari Italiane*.
Schalkhaußer, Erwin (ed.), *Handfeuerwaffen, Kataloge des
  Bayerischen Nationalmuseums*. Deutcher Kunstverlag: 1988.
Sellers, Frank, *Sharps Firearms*. North Hollywood, CA: 1978.
Serven, James E., *The Collecting of Guns*. New York, NY: 1964.
Smith, W.H.B., *Small Arms of the World*. Harrisburg, PA: 1943.
Suydam, Charles R., *U.S. Cartridges and Their Handguns*.
  North Hollywood, CA: 1977.
Todd, Frederick P., *American Military Equipage 1851-1872,
  Volume II: State Forces*. 1983.
Venner, Dominique, *Les Armes á Feu Françaises*. Paris, France:
  1979.
—, *C'es Messieurs Lefaucheux*.
Vuillemin, Henri, *Les Revolvers Militaires Français*. Paris,
  France: 1990.
—, *Le Premier Lefaucheux*. Paris, France.
Winant, Lewis, *Early Percussion Firearms*. New York, NY: 1959.
—, *Firearms Curiosa*. New York, NY: 1955.
Wirnsberger, Gerhard, *The Standard Directory of Proof Marks*.
  Paramus, NJ: 1975.

Annuals and Periodicals:

The American Rifleman, Jan. 1966, Dec. 1968, May 1977, Nov.
  1977.
Arms Gazette, Jan. 1978.
Deutsches Waffen-Journal, Feb. 1997.
Gun Digest, Ninth Edition, 1955.
The Gun Report, Oct. 1956, Jul. 1958, Jul. 1967, Apr. 1968,
  Jan. 1974, Sep. 1980, Jul. 1991.

Arms Catalogs:

Arms of the World 1911 (ALFA). Digest Books, Inc.,
  Northfield, IL: 1972 (reprint).
Francis Bannerman & Sons. New York, NY: 1902, 1905, 1907.
Dixie Gun Works, No. 124. Union City, TN.
Charles Godfrey. New York, NY: 1900, 1902.
L. Ancion Marx. Liége, Belgium: 1900, 1901, 1909.
Sears, Roebuck & Company. Chicago, Illinois: 1897, 1902.